Physical Characteristics of the Schipperke

W9-AKT-262

(from the American Kennel Club breed standard)

Topline: Level or sloping slightly from the withers to the croup.

Proportion: Square in profile.

Hindquarters: The hindquarters appear slightly lighter than the forequarters, but are well muscled, and in balance with the front. The hocks are well let down and the stifles are well bent.

Coat Texture: Abundant, straight and slightly harsh to the touch. The softer undercoat is dense and short on the body and is very dense around the neck, making the ruff stand out.

Size: The suggested height at the highest point of the withers is 11–13 inches for males and 10–12 inches for bitches.

Color: The outercoat must be black.

DEC   2005

Schipperke

◇

By Dr. Robert Pollet

Contents

KENNEL CLUB BOOKS® SCHIPPERKE
ISBN: 1-59378-281-0

Copyright © 2005 • Kennel Club Books, LLC
308 Main Street, Allenhurst, NJ 07711 USA
Cover Design Patented: US 6,435,559 B2 • Printed in South Korea

Photography by:

Mary Bloom, Booth Photography, Paulette Braun, Callea Photo, Carolina Biological Supply, Wayne Cott, Isabelle Français, Carol Ann Johnson, Bill Jonas, Kemp Photography, C. and H. G. Knebel, Dr. Dennis Kunkel, May-He-Co/California, Tam C. Nguyen, Antonio Philippe, Phototake, Charles Pikulinsky, Dr. Robert Pollet, Jean Claude Revy, Alice Roche, Greg Smith, Luis Sosa, Karen Taylor, Michael Trafford, Alice van Kempen, Bette Wynn and Mike and Sue Young.

Illustrations by Renée Low and Patricia Peters.

The publisher wishes to thank all of the owners of the dogs that are featured in this book.

The Schipperke, a Flemish name pronounced *skip-er-kay*, is a Belgian breed, as can be seen from the emblem of the Belgian specialty club, bearing the colors of the nation's flag.

Schipperkesclub

Belgian Queen Marie-Henriette, wife of King Leopold II, helped her favorite breed become fashionable around 1885. This lady in a *belle époque* dress was at the height of fashion with her clan of Schipperkes.

HISTORY OF THE

SCHIPPERKE

As with many breeds, the origin of the Schipperke, nicknamed the "Schip" or affectionately called "the little black devil," is mysterious, buried in the shadows of history. Nevertheless, much reliable historical information is available, although some statements pertaining to the breed's name and ancestry are still debatable. Other stories, such as the tale about the docking of the tail, for the greater part, belong to the folklore surrounding the breed.

BREED NAME CONTROVERSY

First of all, let us explain the meaning of the word "Schipperke" (pronounced *skip-er-kay*). This breed name has always been controversial. The name itself is Flemish, which refers to the local dialects as well as the official language of northern Belgium or "Belgian Flanders," the area that comprises the northern provinces of Belgium. The term "Flemish" often leads to the belief that it is a separate language, but this is not the case. In fact, the standard language of northern Belgium is Dutch and identical to that of the

INSET: Engraving from *Chasse et Pêche* by A. Clarys of Schipperke Exter Albert, born in 1895 and bred by F. Reusens, who was known as the "Father of the Schipperke."

Pick, referred to as one of the best Schipperkes seen in England at the time, defeated all of the best dogs from Belgium. He was a great winner in the 1890s.

Netherlands. In place of Flemish (for northern Belgium) and Dutch (for the Netherlands), the term "Netherlandish" is also generally used. Because of the confusion between Dutch and Flemish, the Schipperke has even been designated in some books and articles as a Dutch breed, though this is completely erroneous.

The meaning of the Dutch term *schip* is "ship." *Schipper* can be translated as a "skipper," "bargeman" or "boatman." Thus, *Schipperke* would mean "little captain" or "little boatman," because the affix "-ke" makes it a diminutive. Nevertheless, many authorities claim that Schipperke does not mean "little barge dog." In their opinion, more acceptable is the meaning "little shepherd." This is supported by the fact that in the dialect of the towns of Leuven (Louvain) and Brussels, *schipper* meant *scheper*, which translates as "shepherd." This interpretation has always been defended by Mr. Felix Verbanck of Ghent, a promoter and perhaps the foremost expert on the Schipperke. Thus, the most credible etymology of the breed name is that it comes from the Flemish dialect word for "little shepherd."

During the 1930s, when the breed was little known in the UK, Mrs. E. B. Holmes had the leading British Schipperke kennel. Here are five of her champions.

ANCESTRY

While the ancestry of the Schipperke is not entirely known, some authors believe that the breed belongs to the family of spitz breeds. This is a group of breeds whose similar physical character-istics include pointed muzzles, ears that are erect and rather small, vulpine heads and curled, usually bushy, tails. The smallest of the spitz breeds is the Pomeranian, which is akin to the Miniature or Toy German Spitz recognized in Europe.

The possibility that the Schipperke could be a descendant of the Pomeranian has, in fact, been considered but refuted by most breed authorities. The Pomeranian and the Schipperke do resemble each other. Perhaps the most striking point of resemblance is the tail of the Schipperke, which, if not docked, is usually curled over the back. A strong argument against the theory

Willy Anthoon's celebrated sculpture of a Schipperke captures the beauty and symmetry of the breed.

that the Pomeranian served to create the Schipperke is the fact that the Schipperke already existed and was known in Belgium before the introduction of the Pomeranian. Also, according to most breed experts, the character-istics of these breeds are entirely different. Although the Schip is an unlikely descendant of the Pomeranian, some past crossbreeding with Pomeranians cannot be denied, especially when we see Schipperkes with undocked tails curled over their backs.

Nevertheless, it has to be explained why in Belgium the Schipperke was also called "Spits" or "Spitske." Once again the reason is linguistically explained. The Dutch word *spits* simply means "pointed" or "tapering." Thus, the name "Spits" hinted at the erect ears, "tapering to a point," and also at the sharp or pointed muzzle. As an additional

Famous sculpture by Willy Anthoon of Belgian Ch. Marius des Lutins Noirs (1932).

The famous breeder F. Verbanck, of the de Royghem kennel, with two of his prized Schipperkes.

argument, it is known that the small spitz breeds in Belgium were called "Keesje" (little Keeshond) in Flemish and "Loulou" in French.

For the sake of completeness, let us explain why Schipperkes to this day are affectionately called "little black devils." Most experts accept that the very first reference to the breed is found in a chronicle of the 15th century. Wenceslas, a monk from Brussels, upon first encountering "a small, black, tailless dog," believed that he was seeing the devil in canine form. The breed has retained the nickname since that time, although fanciers use it to affectionately describe the Schipperke's mischievous personality.

THE LEUVENAAR

According to Mr. Charles Huge, a black, middle-sized, lupine (wolf-like) dog, commonly called the Leuvenaar (meaning "inhabitant of Louvain") had always existed in the province of Brabant. This dog weighed between 10 and 12 kg (about 22 to 26.5 pounds) and is now extinct. It was rather populous and was used by the farmers for guarding flocks, herding and many other tasks. Since the common people of this region, while occupied by the French army, were forbidden to own large dogs, it is perfectly logical that they would have embraced this rather small shepherd dog. The Leuvenaar dogs were used for various tasks: the smaller specimens were selected as rat-catchers and watchdogs for property and poultry, and the larger dogs for herding and guarding livestock. The smaller dogs are the ancestors of the early Schipperkes and the larger dogs are the ancestors of the early

NOT A TERRIER

In years past, some breed historians believed that the Schipperke derived from the Pomeranian (also called the German Zwergspitz) and a small terrier-type dog. Although the Schipperke does indeed possess excellent ratting abilities, the influence of a terrier ancestor, this theory currently no longer holds much weight.

TOP: Bernice, on the left, is a daughter of Ch. Lady Fantine, on the right. Lady Fantine won her championship in 1930.
BOTTOM, LEFT: Ch. Rosey Rapture won 24 Challenge Certificates (UK awards) in the 1920s and was a top-winning bitch.
BOTTOM, RIGHT: Ch. What a Game was bred by Mrs. Hirst in 1929 and became a consistent winner.

Belgian shepherd breeds. This development reveals that the Schipperke is a miniature version of the ancient black Belgian Sheepdog, called the Groenendael in its native land.

This theory connecting the Schipperke to the ancient Leuvenaar, of course, agrees with the theory that the breed name means "little shepherd." That the Schipperke in former days was called "Spits" or "Spitske," which refers to the pointed muzzle and/or ears, does not convince us that the breed descends from the spitz family of dogs. The breed has had many names over the years, including "Moorke," which means "little black animal."

TALES ABOUT TAILLESS SCHIPPERKES AND "SUNDAY COLLARS"

Volumes of myths and legends continue to surround the history of the Schipperke, and fanciers today still embrace and pass along these

> ### PURE-BRED PURPOSE
> Given the vast range of the world's 400 or so pure breeds of dog, it's fair to say that domestic dogs are the most versatile animal in the kingdom. From the tiny 1-pound lap dog to the 200-pound guard dog, dogs have adapted to every need and whim of their human masters. Humans have selectively bred dogs to alter physical attributes like size, color, leg length, mass and skull diameter in order to suit our own needs and fancies. Dogs serve humans not only as companions and guardians but also as hunters, exterminators, shepherds, rescuers, messengers, warriors, babysitters and more!

colorful tales about our beloved "little black devil."

One of the famous legends concerns the Schipperke's docked tail. The story goes that a shoemaker was so angry when a dog belonging to another member of his guild trespassed on his property that he chopped off the dog's tail entirely. When the other shoemakers observed the dog, they found that he was better-looking as a tailless little animal, so they established the custom of tail docking.

A second variation of the docked tail legend claims that a shoemaker who lost a Sunday competition was so disappointed that in revenge he cut off the tail of the winning dog. According to a

Othello and Letta, owned by Mr. L. Rive of Utrecht, the Netherlands, at the end of the 19th century.

third version, it was a boatman on the Belgian canals who removed the tail in order to avoid the Schipperke's knocking over items on board.

According to the documented history of the Belgian guilds, which were associations of craftsmen, the members of the Saint Crispin guild, the guild of the shoemakers of Brussels, organized competitive exhibitions of Schipperkes at the marketplace on designated Sundays. All of the dogs wore handsome brass collars crafted by their owners, whose skill in making collars of hammered or carved brass was so highly developed that these "Sunday collars" were true works of art. The collars were always kept spotless, polished and gleaming. Moreover, they were secured with a fastener, cleverly designed not to damage the ruff. The collars of worked brass were so lovely and so ingenious that they were actually much more important in the Sunday competitions than the beauty of the Schipperkes themselves.

HISTORICAL DATES AND IMPORTANT EVENTS

Returning to the known history of the Schipperke, we can state that these little wholly black shepherd dogs originated in Flanders, namely in the Duchy of Brabant, now the provinces of Antwerp and Brabant, more specifically the

The first French champion Schipperke earned the title in 1925.

towns of Leuven (Louvain to the French) and Brussels. The Schipperke is a very old breed and has been known for hundreds of years, at least since the monk Wenceslas's description in the 15th century.

It is generally accepted that the first specialty show organized for any breed was the competitive exhibition for Schipperkes in 1690, held in the marketplace in Brussels. This gathering was the first of the aforementioned so-called Sunday competitions held by the guild of Belgian shoemakers.

From this time on, the tailless Schipperkes, which were then called "Spits" or "Spitske," were admired by everyone, and Schipperkes with undocked tails became very rare. The Schipperke gained wide popularity in the early 19th century and became the best-known housedog.

The very first dog show in the world took place in Belgium on May 28, 1847 in Tervueren—not on June 30, 1859 in Newcastle, England, as has been published in most dog books. At this first show, only hunting dogs were entered. On July 21, 1880, the year of the 50th anniversary of Belgian independence, the second Belgian dog show was organized in Brussels, where 967 dogs were entered. Not even one Schipperke was entered, although a special class was offered for a breed described as "short-coated terriers, all black, with erect ears, without a tail, a Flemish breed, Schipperkes."

On February 18, 1882, the Societé St.-Hubert was established; this was the organization that governed all canine affairs in Belgium. On September 26, 1885, this society had already

Ch. Maroufke du Bois du Tot, an FCI winner from 1978.

been granted the title of "Societé Royale." In 1882, the year of its foundation, the society organized a show in the town of Spa, where 550 dogs were entered, for the first time including Schipperkes.

In 1883, the first volume of the Belgian Stud Book appeared, entitled *Livre des Origines Saint-Hubert* (LOSH), in which the Schipperke, considered as a pure breed, was registered. The Belgian shepherd breeds, on the contrary, were not allowed registration until 1901. In the first volume of the Stud Book, Schipperkes were registered under the heading "Short-coated terriers, with erect ears, tailless, a Flemish breed, Schipperkes."

At the Brussels show in 1885, the Belgian Queen Marie-Henriette, wife of Leopold II, was so attracted to the little black Schipperkes that she wished to own one. She acquired the winning Schipperke, called "Blak." This made the breed tremendously fashionable and popular. Before this time, the Schipperke had been the companion of the lower classes.

Strangely enough, a few years later, the popularity of the breed gradually declined and the breed nearly became extinct. One reason was the large number of exports to Britain and the US. The fall in popularity was also attributed to the fact that the dogs were not uniform in type and, as a consequence, led to an increasing divergence of opinion among show judges. As a matter of fact, the general appearance of the dogs varied according to locality. Three varieties were described: the Louvain, the Brussels and the Antwerp types.

Toward the end of the 1880s, a group of Schipperke fanciers got together to save this breed, which was threatened by the possibility of extinction. They also wanted to obtain more uniformity in type; thus, they made a list of the desired breed characteristics. This list was based on the Antwerp type of Schipperke and would later become the breed standard.

On February 12 and 19, 1888, meetings were organized by Mr. Louis Van der Snickt. Fanciers and people who could give information about the breed were present. On March 4, 1888, the Schipperke Club was formed. The same year, on June 19, the official breed standard was adopted. Two very important points of the standard were the "absent" tail and the color, which was "self-colored black" only.

The show in Brussels on August 11 and 12, 1888 was a great success, drawing 77 Schipperke entries, a number which has only rarely been surpassed in Belgium since that date. In the years following the foundation of the Schipperke Club, the breed's popularity increased

The famous International Ch. Skip du Parc de l'Hay exhibits an excellent head and expression.

At the Belgian club's specialty show in 1988, a record 117 entries were exhibited. Here are two of the winners: the Best of Breed was Ch. Athilia van de Noord-Oost-Hoek (left), and the Best Veteran was Gabar Vrouwvliet (right), handled by the author.

greatly. The most active breeder in the early years was Mr. F. Reusens, owner of the first regular kennel, which was named Exter. He has been called the "Father of the Schipperke." His first Schipperke was "Spits" (LOSH 1605), born in 1885 and registered in 1888. His

A beautiful champion Belgian Tervuren, Vallivue Bon Chance, owned and bred by Sue and Mike Young.

most important acquisition was "Franz," whelped in 1889 but registered with the mention of "unknown origin." Franz was considered to be the perfect Schipperke and is credited with being the foundation of the breed.

In 1930, the King of Belgium granted the title of "Royal" to the Schipperke Club, which was the original breed club. On May 29, 1988, the year of the 100th anniversary of the Belgian Royal Schipperke Club, 99 Schipperkes were entered at the International All-Breed Show in Brussels, which was organized by the Societé Royale St.-Hubert. The same year, on July 10, a record number of 117 Schipperkes were benched for the club's specialty show. These two shows had the largest numbers of Schipperkes ever exhibited in Belgium.

At present, the popularity of the Schipperke in Belgium is rather constant. Over a recent ten-year period, an average of 27 litters per year was registered in the

Belgian Stud Book, with the average size of a litter being three puppies.

BELGIAN SHEPHERDS AND SCHIPPERKES

It is generally accepted that the Belgian shepherds and the Schipperke have a common ancestor called the Leuvenaar. The Belgian shepherds, highly regarded the world over for their versatility, are rather similar in temperament to the Schipperke but are medium-sized and divided into four breeds that differ only in coat type and color. In Belgium and most parts of the world, these are considered varieties of one breed, the Belgian Shepherd Dog, while the American Kennel Club recognizes three of the varieties as separate breeds. The two long-haired varieties are the Groenen-dael (known as the Belgian

Three of the four Belgian shepherd breeds, from left to right: the Belgian Malinois, Belgian Sheepdog and Belgian Tervuren.

Sheepdog in the US), which is black, and the Terveuren (known as the Belgian Tervuren in the US), which is red-fawn. The short-coated variety is the red-fawn Malinois (known as the Belgian Malinois in the US) and the rough-haired variety is the reddish-fawn Laekenois (not recognized by the AKC).

It is interesting to note that most Belgian shepherd owners who consider acquiring a second dog for their homes choose the Schipperke—that other Belgian (but small!) breed. Apparently, fanciers of Belgian shepherds and Schipperkes are joined in a kind of canine alliance or family-type relationship. In France, the Belgian shepherd and the Schipperke clubs even jointly publish their monthly magazine.

THE SCHIPPERKE IN GREAT BRITAIN AND IRELAND

After the Belgian Queen Marie-Henriette acquired a Schipperke in 1885, the demand for the breed increased everywhere and the "little black devil" suddenly became very popular in England. The first recorded importation into England was in 1887, and the formation of the English Schipperke Club followed in 1890. The breed has had its ups and downs, and problems with breeding have occurred. In 1896, the question of tail docking gave rise to disputes, which eventually subsided when it could be proven that the docking was done in a humane manner.

After both World Wars, the breed declined in popularity in the UK. In the 1920s and 1930s, the outline of the Schipperke changed because breeders tried to produce a dog with a more terrier-like coat, without the thick ruff around the neck and the culottes on the backs of the thighs. After 1920, it was decided in England, contrary to the Belgian standard, to allow other solid colors besides black, such as brown, blond and cream. These colors became permissible in other Anglo-Saxon countries also.

In recent years, although the number of registrations with The Kennel Club of England is not particularly high, the breed's popularity is on the rise again. In England, the Schipperke was, and still remains, a very well-known and much-appreciated small, but superb, watchdog. In Ireland, which has become active in the breed as well, the future of the Schipperke looks hopeful.

A modern Schipperke photographed in the Netherlands, where the breed is quite popular. Notice that this Schipperke has an undocked tail, a sight that is becoming more common in Europe today.

Ch. Dante's I Gotta Line on You, known as "Chloe" to her friends, is pictured at 12 years of age. Owner, Amy Gossman.

SCHIPPERKES IN THE US
BY BETTE WYNN

Schipperkes probably existed in the US during the time of the Revolutionary War, arriving with the Belgian settlers. However, first written documentation appears in 1891 in *The American Book of the Dog,* which features an illustration of Spalding of Midnight and Darkness, two Schipperkes owned by Walter J. Comstock of Providence, Rhode Island. Comstock imported these dogs in 1888.

The American Kennel Club (AKC) Stud Books record the first registration in 1904 and the first champion (Teddy R) in 1910.

Yperland kennels of Belgian, born Victor Verhelle, produced the first Best in Show (BIS) winner, Yperland Jet Black Skipper, and remained active through the war years. The first parent club was founded in 1905, but it dissolved during World War I.

It wasn't until Isabel Ormiston of Kelso kennels began importing and breeding in the early 1920s that Schipperkes began to gain momentum in the States. The real history of the breed in America begins with Kelso. Her Ch. Maroufke of Kelso was well known as a top producer and a top winner in the show ring. Dogs of her breeding and Kelso dogs acquired by other breeders dominated the show ring for the next several decades. Her contribution to the breed can still be found in today's winning dogs. The reputation and merit of the Kelso Schips are unequaled and a huge debt of gratitude is owed to Miss Ormiston, who died in 1954.

In 1929, the Schipperke Club of America (SCA) was founded, thanks to the dedication of these early breeders. In the years following the club's formation, the breed steadily gained popularity. Today SCA entries at the national specialty can number over 200 entries, and the annual AKC registrations are around 1,000 or more, making the US the top producing country of Schipperkes in the world.

The 1930s produced the first dual titleholder, Ch. Michael Son of Ti, CDX, owned by Howard Claussen. Ti had two UD legs before his untimely death at age four years. Notable kennels that made an impact on the breed were: Burkes, Jet-O, Algene, Noirmont, Franswold, Cledlo, Marless and Walrose. Walrose had the distinction of winning Best Brace in Show at Westminster in 1949.

Of particular importance during the late 1960s and early 1970s was the outstanding show record of Ch. Klinahof's Marouf A Draco. Draco, owned by J. D. Jones, bred by Klinahof kennels, and handled by Houston Clark, was the top winning Schipperke of all time with 12 Best in Show victories. This record was to stand for many years. He also produced 40 champion offspring.

Many influential kennels that would leave a lasting influence on the breed emerged during the

Ch. Shalako's E.L. Fudge, bred and owned by Bette Wynn and Nancie Mages.

1950s through the 1970s. They include: Toni, Skipalong, Donrho, Honey Lane, Del-Dorel, Von Kay, Dream On, De Sang Bleu, De Valle Vue, San Dil, Lo-Lane, Starbrook, Jetstar, Landmark, A.R.E.S., Lynden, Elf-Mir, Kleingual, Belique, Cae, Green Lakes, Valkyra, Glen Kay, Ree-Daw, Barcarole, Spindrift, Braderie, Chestara, Knotty Knoll and Colehaven.

Both Skipalong and Jetstar produced many top winning and producing dogs that can be found in today's pedigrees, following Miss Ormiston in their overall contribution to the breed.

Ch. Skipalong Bon Fyr, bred by Skip-along kennels, is the top producing bitch of

Resting on his laurels—momentarily—here's "Thumper," owned by Sherwood and Dianne Harris. Formally this handsome Schip is Ch. Sheradin When Spirits Talk.

Ch. Dante's Fire When Ready, bred by J. and A. Gossman and owned by M. Jameson and P. Allison.

"Pat-a-caking" like the top winner he is, here's Ch. Eatchurheartout de Sang Bleu, owned by breeder Maureen Garrity. JoJo is a Best in Show and Best in Specialty Show winner.

all time with 19 champion get. Among her most famous offspring were Ch. Skipalong Gadget and Ch. Skipalong Gidget. Skipalong also held the record for Best in Show dogs. Those dogs were: Ch. Skipalong's Billy Bon Howdy Do, Ch. Skipalong's El-Bimbo Jet, Ch. Skipalong Malagold Luvalot and Ch. Skipalong Oh Baby Face.

Of notable interest during the current period is that Draco's Best in Show record was broken by Ch. Eatchurheartout de Sang Bleu in the early 1980s. "JoJo," bred and owned by Maureen Garrity, won 13 Bests in Show and was the top Schip for five consecutive years (from 1981 through 1985). His son, Ch. Dream On One in a Million, bred and owned by Marcia Bailey, defeated JoJo's record with 15 Bests in Show. These two dogs were handled by Nancie Mages,

and "Chance's" record (set in 1989) still holds today.

Schipperkes continued to flourish with new breeders such as Nanhall, De Lamer, Dotsu, Coda, Blumoon, Chatelet, Sheradin, DiDeb, Birken Wald, Mentha, Osage, Trilogy, Sidekick, Starship, Dante and Shalako. All produced Best in Show-winning Schipperkes, which indeed shows that the judges are beginning to recognize and reward the breed for its excellence.

In 2004, Shalako kennels tied the record of the Skipalong BIS dogs, producing Ch. Shalako's E.L. Fudge (also winner of a national specialty), Ch. Shalako's Simply Simon, CD, Ch. Shalako's Bartered

at BarSu and Ch. Shalako's Rockn' Whisper.

Kleingaul kennels bred Ch. Kleingauls Windjammer, another BIS dog shown in the 1990s. "Jammer" also won the SCA national specialty three times during his campaign, retiring the Schipperke Club of America challenge trophy.

Dante kennels has also won the national specialty multiple times with different dogs. Those dogs were Ch. Dante's I Gotta Line on You (bitch), Ch. Dante's Dancin' in the Dark (bitch) and Ch. Dante Fire When Ready.

Raffinee and Chatelet produced Ch. Raffinee Spirit of Chatelet, who currently holds the record for top producing male with 65 champions to his credit. Not far behind him is Ch. Sheradin When Spirits Talk, who currently has 46 champions, and is also himself a Best in Show winner.

To the credit of today's breeders, many current consistent winners are being campaigned as Veterans, proving the quality is long lasting and the breed is in good hands.

THE SCHIPPERKE IN CONTINENTAL EUROPE

In most countries on the Continent, the Schipperke is a remarkably well-known breed, although, according to the number of registrations, it is not considered one of the top breeds. The Schipperke is

popular in France and the Netherlands and, to a lesser degree, in Germany and Italy. It is a beloved breed in the Scandinavian countries, where fanciers' interest in the breed is steadily growing. In Belgium, the breed's country of origin, where the human population is about ten million, an average of 80 to 85 Schipperkes are born every year and the popularity of the breed remains relatively consistent.

In France, the Schipperke is numerically stronger than in Belgium. The French specialty club

Am. and Can. Ch. Shalako's Bartered at Bar Su is a Best in Show winner owned by Betty Wynn, Donna Kendy and Ann Grosser.

was formed in 1928. All over the world, the quality of French breeding programs is considered to be at least equal to that of Belgium. In France, a very close collaboration between the Belgian Shepherd Club and the Schipperke Club started in 1974 and is evident in the joint publication of their club magazine. This cooperation has been an important impetus for the increased popularity of the breed.

In the Netherlands, in the period following World War II, the Schipperke enjoyed only modest popularity. However, the 1970s saw a real revival of interest in the

Ch. Shalako's Simply Simon CD, owned by Bette Wynn, Ann Grosser and Donna Kenly, is a Best in Show winner.

breed. Dutch Schipperke fanciers can also be very proud of the fact that it was in the Netherlands, in 1875, that a Schipperke appeared at a dog show for the very first time in the world.

In Germany, the number of registrations is very low; specifically, an average of 15 Schipperkes each year. It is the German club for the "small dog breeder" (*Verband Deutscher Kleinhundezüchter*) that is responsible for the breed. In Germany and Austria, the Schipperke was already a part of the canine scene at the end of the 19th century, shortly after the foundation of the specialty clubs in Belgium and England. From 1971 on, dogs were imported into Germany from Belgium, the United States, Canada, France and the Netherlands. In recent years, owing to heated discussions on hereditary disorders in dogs, interest has been renewed in robust problem-free breeds such as the Schipperke.

In many other European countries as well, the Schipperke is bred and is regularly exhibited at national and international shows. This is the case in Italy and certainly in the Scandinavian countries. In Denmark, the first Schipperkes were imported from Belgium in 1903. From the 1960s on, further importations came from Sweden, the Netherlands and the United States. In Sweden, Schipperkes have been bred since

Schipperkes being judged in the Netherlands, where the competition is quite keen.

1917, but the specialty club was not founded until 1975. In Finland and Norway, where the breeding of Schipperkes began with imports from Sweden, the breed is firmly established.

ELSEWHERE AROUND THE WORLD

The Schipperke is a known and appreciated breed not only in Europe and North America but also on other continents. Schipperkes are seen in many countries throughout the world and attract attention wherever they appear.

In South Africa, dedicated breeders and fanciers have made the Schipperke flourish. Breeding started in 1927 and activity increased greatly after World War II. The specialty club was founded in 1959. The kennel of Mrs. S. M.

Moore is considered to be the biggest Schipperke kennel in the world. In many countries, even in Belgium, Schipperkes have been imported from South Africa.

In Australia, the breeding of Schipperkes began with imports from England. The Schipperke Club was formed in 1988 and the breed is firmly established as a pet dog as well as a show dog. In New Zealand, breeding began in 1968 with imports from Australia and, in the 1970s, from England. Schipperkes have a presence in many other countries, including several countries in South America. Schipperkes still continue to make themselves known and recognized throughout many parts of the world as excellent pets and alert companions in the service of their families.

SCHIPPERKE

While over 150 breeds of dog are recognized by the American Kennel Club, there are well over 330 different breeds recognized in the world today. Each breed has its own personality and characteristics. Owners recognize that the Schipperke is, in fact, a smaller version of a shepherd dog, but with other special traits as well. While it has more or less the physical appearance of a shepherd dog, the Schipperke is blessed with a stronger and sturdier construction in proportion to its size. As to his character and temperament, he certainly does not consider himself a small dog, and he is less emotional and more fearless than most of the shepherd dog breeds.

A Schipperke can be described as a lively, very busy little dog. He is quick, agile and intelligent, interested in everything, very watchful and very trainable. Perhaps the greatest quality of the Schipperke is that in one and the same dog we can find the personality and stamina of a large dog as well as the affectionate and family-loving nature of a small dog...including all of the advantages of his smaller size: his ability to fit into any size home, the ease with which he travels and the relative low cost of his food and supplies.

PHYSICAL TRAITS
In many books, the physical appearance and the expression of the Schipperke have been described as "vulpine," which means "fox-like." However, in our opinion, this description is incorrect because the Schipperke's anatomy, head and expression are actually "lupine," which means "wolf-like."

Very typical are the small erect ears; the pointed, but not weak, muzzle; and, above all, the unique silhouette of the entire body. The Leuvenaar, the ancestor of both the Schipperke and the Belgian shepherds, was a real working dog. From this common ancestry, the smallest dogs, which became the Schipperkes, were selected as rat-catchers and watchdogs. However, an increasing interest in dog shows made breeders pay more attention to appearance, and their breeding results were most successful.

Nowadays, everybody has to admit that the Schipperke is a highly charming little dog who never fails to attract attention. His eye-catching appeal comes from his very distinctive coat, which creates his unique silhouette. His nice stand-out ruff (thick coat around the neck) and typical culottes or breeches (longer hair on the backs of the thighs) are very natural and not the result of expert grooming or scissors.

When comparing the appearance of the Schipperke with toy or companion-dog breeds, we can easily see that its anatomical

The desirable Schipperke head should possess small erect ears and a pointed muzzle.

features are completely normal and without the slightest physical anomalies or signs of "dwarfism." As a matter of fact, its quickness and physical abilities in general are impressive, as well as its alertness and tirelessness.

CHARACTER OF THE BREED

The personality of the Schipperke is his most remarkable trait. He possesses typical emotional and behavioral characteristics, which cannot be found in other shepherd or companion breeds. Very distinctive above all are his curiosity and his inquisitive nature, meaning his need to see, inspect or investigate everything at close range.

In 1882, the character of the Schipperke was described in the Belgian canine magazine *Chasse et Pêche* in the following terms: "The Schipperke is a little, all

The Schipperke attracts attention wherever he goes. This is a natural, unexaggerated dog with apparent working ability.

black devil, but minus the cloven
hoof and the tail. A very demon
for rats, mice, moles and every
vermin. An indefatigable
watchdog, he rests neither day nor
night. Always on foot, nothing
escapes him that goes on within
or without his dwelling. He runs
from cellar to garret, inspecting
all the corners and holes, and as
soon as he observes anything
amiss, he warns his master by his
piercing barks. He knows the
ways of the house thoroughly,
mixes himself into everything,
giving himself airs as if he is the
boss himself. He is a prodigy of
fidelity and attachment and with
children he is gentleness personi-
fied. Let the stranger beware if, on
purpose or by accident, he lays a
hand on an object or somebody
from his house. The Schipperke
has teeth and can use them if
necessary. A good stable dog and
a great friend of horses, he is an
excellent horseman. His
happiness is to ride the broad-
backed tow-horse. Besides a good
watchdog, a good rider and a
pleasant, always well-disposi-
tioned companion, he is
moreover an excellent terrier and
hunting dog."

Today we could still describe
the Schipperke in the same terms.
He is watchful indeed, faithful
and a first-class busybody. This
all-purpose watchdog and vermin
exterminator has a character that
we can define as attentive, self-
confident, cheerful, lively,

courageous, tenacious and indefatigable. He is one of the hardiest of all small dogs. He feels equally at home living in a city apartment or exploring the countryside.

Some notable traits of the Schipperke can now be explored more closely.

HOW EMOTIONAL IS THE SCHIPPERKE?

Schipperkes are not easily disturbed or impressed. They are, on the contrary, very self-confident and can be very dominant and fearless. Unfortunately, they have no idea of the limitations of their size. This can be dangerous when they are too impetuous about guarding their property or when facing bigger dogs.

IS HE INTELLIGENT AND EASY TO TRAIN?

The Schipperke is a little shepherd dog and possesses the intelligence of the larger shepherd breeds. That means that he learns quickly and is easy to train. However, his independent nature and his strong desire to explore his surroundings can make him disobedient; for instance, when he has run away and won't come when you call him.

IS HE SUSPICIOUS AND A SUITABLE WATCHDOG?

The Schipperke is a good watchdog over his family, his home, his property and his possessions. He guards the house and its inhabitants as if he's a

If properly introduced and socialized, Schipperkes can get along well with cats. This young pup seems curious about his new feline friend while the adult is rather nonchalant.

much bigger dog! A Schipperke will become excited by and will bark at any external stimulus, such as the postman's footsteps, the ring of the doorbell or any kind of sound. He will always be suspicious of anyone trespassing in his domain.

Schipperkes enjoy one-on-one time with their owners. This Schipperke has taken a break from his walk to "pat-a-cake" his owner for a little affection.

IS HE SOCIABLE?

Dogs seek, need and enjoy companionship and should be part of the family. Schipperkes

This Schip puppy is getting to know a white German Shepherd chum.

certainly love their families; however, we've mentioned that they can be very suspicious of strangers. It can also happen that they have a special liking for and will attach themselves to one member of the family, most often their mistress. Unfortunately for dogs, the family members are frequently away during the day. Most dogs, though, enjoy regular contact with other dogs and, for that reason, many dog owners consider getting a second dog. It is very interesting to note that, in many families, the Schipperke is the little friend and companion of the Belgian shepherds, his larger canine relatives.

WHAT IS HIS NEED FOR PHYSICAL AND MENTAL ACTIVITY?

Schipperkes are curious, constantly busy and on the move. Young puppies also are full of energy and curiosity, which should be directed into good behavior. Puppies need physical exercise and plenty of rest, too, but particularly regular mental stimulation. Therefore, you have to pay much attention to your Schipperke from puppyhood to old age. Talk to your dog frequently, as you would with a child. It is amazing how much he will understand. Train your Schipperke in basic obedience for a short period of time each day; while this will keep him busy for a little while and teach him the necessary good manners, it will not be enough to avoid his becoming bored.

HOW CAN AN OWNER AVOID HIS SCHIPPERKE'S BECOMING BORED?
Schipperkes are very good in finding "work" for themselves; this pastime can be quite unpleasant or irritating for their owners. Fortunately, Schipperkes are small dogs and most of their naughty tricks are not so bad and can be easily forgiven. However, it's much better to prevent bad habits than to just overlook them. To avoid boredom, which is the cause of most of the behavioral problems in dogs, you should not restrict your Schipperke's opportunities to investigate or have social contact. Play with your Schipperke—he will love it! You can play fetch with him by throwing a ball or another toy. He

HEART-HEALTHY
In this modern age of ever-improving cardio-care, no doctor or scientist can dispute the advantages of owning a dog to lower a person's risk of heart disease. Studies have proven that petting a dog, walking a dog and grooming a dog all show positive results toward lowering your blood pressure. The simple routine of exercising your dog—going outside with the dog and walking, jogging or playing catch—is heart-healthy in and of itself. If you are normally less active than your physician thinks you should be, adopting a dog may be a smart option to improve your own quality of life as well as that of another creature.

will probably rush after it and joyfully pick it up, because most dogs have a natural desire to retrieve. Walking your dog at least once a day for at least half an hour is ideal for fulfilling his need for physical activity. Fortunately,

Meeting a fellow herder, this Schip puppy may learn some of the shepherding basics from a Border Collie.

a small dog has the advantage that he can run off his excess energy in a small yard, provided that it is safely fenced, or even a big living room.

WHAT DOES "PAT-A-CAKER" MEAN?
Schips often have a very special and beguiling trait of sitting up while waving their front paws; this is an endearing and often very effective way of begging. This special trait of pawing the air is affectionately nicknamed playing "pat-a-cake." A Schip-perke paws not only when standing on his hind legs but also when you are holding him and he wants your attention.

WHAT ARE THE NEGATIVE ASPECTS OF THE SCHIPPERKE'S CHARACTER?
The Schipperke is an energetic, marvelous little dog, but owners

should not be blind to the drawbacks of his character. While the Schipperke is a devoted watchdog, his excitability, independence and fearlessness can sometimes interfere with the task at hand. Also, although you might find that your Schipperke is a very active and busy little dog, others may perceive him as hyperactive and irritating. Another potential problem is that, because of his independent and explorative nature, you may only make slow progress with his obedience training. Moreover, a Schip's overprotective behavior could perhaps evolve into real aggression.

Your Schipperke, of course, will not always act the way you want him to act. The reactions of Schips can be extremely fast and difficult to control. Schipperkes can get excessively excited by certain external stimuli, which most often leads to habitual barking, and the breed's bark is loud, sharp and penetrating. Unnecessary and incessant barking can be a source of much annoyance to owners of Schipperkes and their neighbors. Many people are very intolerant of barking. Fortunately, most problems with dogs can be easily solved, the barking problem included. What can you do, for instance, when the doorbell rings and your Schip barks? If you go to the door and it is a friend, your Schip may quiet down after having identified the visitor. If not, you can tell your dog "it is a friend," "that will do," "it's OK" or some similar command. If it doesn't help and he continues barking, scold him and give the down command. Alternatively, he can be put into his crate or designated area and eventually he will quiet down.

With Schipperkes, a problem can also arise when they prefer one or more family members to others, to whom they do not respond. In our society, the "one-woman dog" is more common than the "one-man dog." Perhaps this is because in households where just one parent works, there are more stay-at-home moms than dads or because the dogs view women as gentler than men. Regardless, the situation can

> **DELTA SOCIETY**
>
> The human-animal bond propels the work of the Delta Society, striving to improve the lives of people and animals. The Pet Partners Program proves that the lives of people and dogs are inextricably linked. The Pet Partners Program, a national registry, trains and screens volunteers for pet therapy in hospices, nursing homes, schools and rehabilitation centers. Dog-and-handler teams of Pet Partners volunteer in all 50 states, with nearly 7,000 teams making visits annually. About 900,000 patients, residents and students receive assistance each year. If you and your dog are interested in becoming Pet Partners, contact the Delta Society at their website: www.deltasociety.org.

escalate when, for instance, the dog no longer accepts the husband and becomes aggressive toward him. This problem can also be solved with neutering or spaying, although the best way to have a well-mannered adult dog is to give him firm basic training while he is a puppy.

FURTHER CONSIDERATIONS FOR PET OWNERS

The Schipperke is a devoted and loyal family dog, and he really loves children. Schipperkes are often called "the best housedogs," and many breed lovers believe that they fully deserve this honorable title. Nevertheless,

Schipperkes make great pets for adults and children. Of course, children must learn to treat their new pets gently and respectfully.

some special traits of his character must not be ignored.

Schipperkes have strong and independent personalities and always want to be exploring and "following their noses." As a consequence, they may agree to lie down at your side or settle on your lap, but only for a short while. They will only do this until something new happens or appears. If you like a dog with an excess of personality, the Schipperke may be the breed for you; on the other hand, if you like a quiet, predictable dog, you

would do better to consider another breed.

When you train your Schipperke to walk with you or to "heel," which means to walk next to you on your left side, he can suddenly decide to explore the surroundings or to chase a fast-moving object or animal. It's obvious that curiosity forms part of his genes and that a Schipperke is extremely alert, active and enterprising. Nevertheless, the problem of a dog that runs away or that won't come when called is relatively easy to solve through proper training. The easier and safer route is to always take precautions like keeping your Schip on lead for walks or in securely enclosed areas for free exercise. Even a well-trained dog can be oblivious of his owner's calls when "on the hunt," and that's a risk you do not want to take.

PROFILE OF THE SCHIPPERKE
As a conclusion to this description of the breed's characteristics, we can give the following general portrait or profile of the Schip:

- A Belgian breed and the smallest shepherd dog in the world in fact, the breed name means "little shepherd." Character for the most part is like that of his "big brothers," the Belgian shepherd breeds.
- In appearance, a shepherd in miniature, but robust and

compact in structure; square body; abundant and dense, wholly black coat with outstanding ruff and long "breeches" on the backs of thighs; small eyes and ears; unique silhouette, not resembling any other breed; tail closely docked.

- Average weight: 12.8 pounds; dogs 14.3 pounds and bitches 11.2 pounds.
- Taken from a sampling of 50 dogs, the average height at withers: 12.75 inches; dogs 13.2 inches and bitches 12.3 inches. The AKC standard specifies 11–13 inches for males and 10–12 inches for females.
- Very self-assured and tenacious character, despite his size; no "Napoleon complex" whatsoever.
- Fast, tireless and energetic athlete, lively, active and agile:

The "little shepherd of Belgium" is a working dog in miniature, possessing a dense black coat and a self-assured character.

a piece of pure dynamite!

- A fearless watchdog, not easily frightened by larger dogs.
- An instinctive and talented ratter; hunts and destroys vermin.
- Companion of horses, sometimes nicknamed "Pat-a-cakes with Horses."
- A long-lived pure-bred; lifespan 13 to 16 years, a long commitment for the owner!
- An adaptable, undemanding housedog, well suited for both city and country living and well suited for cold climates.
- A tireless companion for children with great endurance; able to run and jump for hours and to cover distances of up to around 12 miles; when living in the city, completely happy with much less exercise.
- An easy keeper who needs minimal grooming.
- An independent thinker, curious about everything, extremely inquisitive, always looking for action.
- "His own dog"—possibly snappish when annoyed; sometimes headstrong or a bit stubborn, but will do almost anything for his master.
- Attention seeker—wants personal attention and affection from his owner and family.
- A dog who wants to be near you and does not like to be

Schips are attention seekers and enjoy the company of other dogs as well as the humans they love.

isolated or to live in a crate or a kennel. However, a crate is a necessity, for instance, for safe car travel. When he gets used to it, he will enjoy the privacy of a crate. Because a Schipperke is so curious and likely to run away, he needs a securely fenced yard or area so that he cannot climb over or dig beneath the fence and escape.

- "The best housedog," expecting to be treated like any other member of the family, admirably adapting himself to the house rules, loyal to his family, fond of children, but not everyone's friend and suspicious of strangers. Even friends and neighbors may be viewed with strong mistrust.
- An active companion who likes physical activity, e.g., playing, exploring and traveling.
- An excellent and faithful little guard dog, barking to "sound the alarm" at the slightest sign of danger.
- Intelligence abounds—learns new skills quickly and intuitively, can easily be trained, excels in obedience training, agility, flyball, etc.
- A clown who provides his family with years of joy, laughter and amusement.

Traditionally, Schipperkes have been known as favored companions of horses, as this side-saddling Schip illustrates.

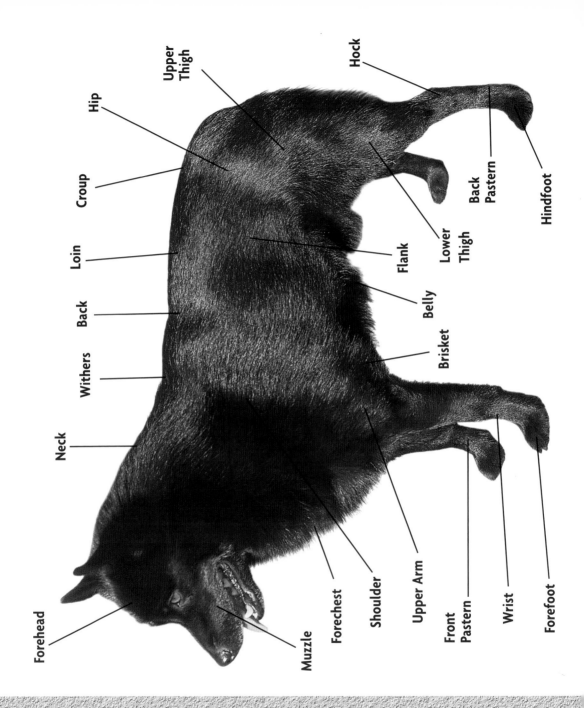

Upper Thigh

Hock

Hip

Croup

Loin

Back

Withers

Neck

Forehead

Flank

Lower Thigh

Back Pastern

Hindfoot

Belly

Brisket

Muzzle

Forechest

Shoulder

Upper Arm

Front Pastern

Wrist

Forefoot

PHYSICAL STRUCTURE OF THE SCHIPPERKE

SCHIPPERKE

Each owner of a Schipperke asks himself the question one day: "What does the perfect Schipperke look like?" or "Is my dog good enough to show and win Best of Breed?" To find the answer, it should be enough to read the breed standard, the written description of the ideal character- istics of the breed, and make that determination. However, for the novice who has not yet acquired sufficient knowledge of canine anatomy and typical canine terminology, the standard is not an adequate guide. Here we will discuss important points of major breed standards from around the world, thus imparting an overall description of the breed.

A breed standard is used by the governing kennel club to describe the ideal or "model" dog of each recognized breed. Show dogs are judged against this standard, which describes the ideal physical and temperamental characteristics of the perfect specimen of a given breed. For the Schipperke, there are three main breed standards, which fortunately are very similar. We have the

American Kennel Club (AKC) standard, which is used in the US; the Fédération Cynologique Internationale (FCI) standard, which is used in continental Europe and other FCI member countries; and England's Kennel Club standard, which is used in the United Kingdom and other non-US English-speaking countries such as Australia and South Africa.

It is clear that the Schipperke is a Belgian breed and that the original standard was drawn up in Belgium, the country of origin of the breed. The description of the breed characteristics of the Schipperke as proposed by Belgium is in fact the official standard of the FCI, approved by and used in the FCI member countries.

Many of those interested in the Schipperke are inclined to think that this small dog is, in reality, a reduced shepherd dog, more specifically a Belgian shepherd in miniature. This is only partially true. We know that an ancient shepherd dog known as the Leuvenaar is the common

**The Schipperke
should be square
when viewed
from the side,
possessing a
unique
silhouette,
unmistakable
from that of any
other breed.**

ancestor of the Schipperke and the
Belgian shepherd breeds, respectively the Leuvenaar's smaller and
bigger descendants. Yet the
morphology (form and structure)
and the type (general outline or
appearance) of these breeds are
quite different.

When comparing the
Schipperke to a Belgian shepherd,
not taking into consideration the
size of the two breeds, the distinguishing features of the

Schipperke are the following:
• Robust or blocky, thus stronger
  and more compact conformation, especially the broader rib
  cage, which is termed "cobby";
• The stronger head, which
  essentially means that the skull
  is broader and the muzzle is
  shorter than the length of the
  skull;
• The angulation (the angles
  formed at the joints by the
  meeting of the bones), which is

a little more pronounced but still completely normal and without the slightest exaggeration, which means that the legs are placed well under the body when the dog is standing.

There is no doubt that the Schipperke, just like the Belgian shepherd breeds, should be square when viewed from the side. This means that he is not longer than tall and that the body, from the front of the chest to the back of the buttocks, must fit into a square, not an oblong.

The general appearance of the Schipperke is considered very distinctive and not resembling any other breed, because of the coat with the outstanding ruff (long hair around the neck) and the culottes (longish hair at the rear of the upper thighs). The longer hair on the ridge of the neck and on the withers (the top of the shoulders), which is called the mane, gives the impression of a rising topline from rear to front. All of these distinguishing features of the coat give the Schipperke his unique silhouette.

Comparing the three major Schipperke standards, one significant difference is the UK's color allowance. The FCI and American standards are very strict as to the color; only wholly or solid black is admitted. According to England's Kennel Club standard, however, other whole colors are permissible.

As to the color of the coat, it is possible, though only temporarily, for a normal black coat to turn a little rusty red on some places of the body due to seasonal or hormonal changes or even a change of diet. In the AKC standard, the possibility of a transitory reddish cast is mentioned, as well as graying due to age. Further, according to the FCI standard, a gray undercoat is allowed if completely covered by the black outer coat.

In the FCI standard, the fine skeleton of the legs, in both the hindquarters and forequarters, has always been emphasized, but we realize that this is an anatomical characteristic that is not really compatible with a "cobby" (strong and compact) appearance.

The teeth in the FCI standard have always been described as

Although the Schipperke is traditionally black, other whole colors (like this cream-colored dog) exist and are permissible in the UK.

"perfectly adapted," which means, as mentioned in the American standard, that a scissors as well as a pincer (level) bite are acceptable.

In the new FCI standard, the shape of the head is not defined as fox-like (vulpine) but as wolf-like (lupine), and the ears are described as "very" small.

As to the size of the Schipperke, it is rather surprising that the height at the withers (distance from the withers to the ground) is not specified in either the FCI standard or England's Kennel Club standard. In the American standard, however, we read that the "suggested" height is 11–13 in (28–33 cm) for males and 10–12 in (25.4–30.5 cm) for bitches.

Very often the question arises among Schip fanciers as to how big, in fact, a Schipperke should be. Recently, we measured the heights at the withers of 50 FCI show Schipperkes, 25 males and 25 bitches. The average height for dogs was 13.2 in (33.6 cm) and for

bitches 12.3 in (31.2 cm).

According to the directives of the FCI, made clear in the so-called "FCI-Model Standard" (guidelines for what all standards should contain), three important body proportions or indices should be mentioned in every breed standard.

The first of these indices is the so-called "body index" or the proportion of the length of body to the height at withers. The length of the body is the distance from the forechest or the point of shoulder to the point of buttock. In the Schipperke, the body index ideally should be 1, meaning that the two measurements should be the same. When we measured the body lengths of 50 FCI show Schipperkes, we found that the length of body on average was 103% of the height at the withers, a result which is very reassuring. In fact, these measurements proved that in an important percentage of Schipperkes the body length really was equal to the height at the withers. The results also showed that it is realistic and certainly not idealistic to require a square body structure in the Schipperke.

The second index that should be mentioned in an FCI standard is the "depth of chest index" or the proportion of the depth of chest to the height at withers. The depth of the chest is the distance from the withers to the brisket or

Occasionally a long, silky, wavy coat is seen on a Schipperke—such a coat would disqualify the dog from the show ring.

Correct "body index;" square proportion.

Incorrect body; back short and topline rising over croup.

Correct muzzle; fine but not weak.

Muzzle too short.

average weights of 6.5 kg for males and 5.1 kg for bitches, the overall average being 5.8 kg. This translates to 14.3 lbs for males, 11.2 lbs for females and 12.8 lbs average. The AKC standard specifies height, but not weight; the FCI standard now specifies a weight range from 3 to 9 kg, with the average weight to be targeted between 4 and 7 kg.

As to the tail, the three standards differ a little in wording. The AKC standard states "docked, no tail visibly discernible," while the British standard mentions "customarily docked," although it gives a description of the natural tail as well. The main difference is in the FCI standard, which allows tails to be docked or natural.

Most Schipperkes are born with tails. De-tailing is a better term than docking, because no vertebrae at all may be visible or palpable, so as to obtain the well-rounded rear. Docking should be performed when the puppies are two to four days old by a thoroughly experienced breeder or preferably a competent veterinarian. In more and more countries now, docking is banned. When natural, the tail in the new FCI standard is described as "long, reaching at least to hock, at rest preferably hanging sabre-like, when moving raised to level of back, preferably not higher."

Summarizing from the three major standards, the desired

lower chest. The average value of this index that we obtained after having measured the 50 show Schipperkes was 0.475. This means that the depth of chest in Schipperkes is 47.5% of the height at the withers, a result that certainly is in agreement with the standard, which stipulates "chest deep."

The third important proportion is the ratio of the length of muzzle to the length of head. It is generally accepted that, in the Schipperke, the muzzle is moderate in length or shorter than the skull. According to our measurements of the 50 show Schipperkes, the length of the muzzle to the whole head is, on average, 0.4 or 40%, a result and a requirement that is now specified in the FCI standard for the Schipperke.

We also weighed the 50 show Schipperkes and we found

characteristics of the Schipperke can be presented as follows: a small, completely black, little shepherd dog, with closely docked tail (which can also be kept natural); the head not too elongated; fairly broad skull; muzzle shorter than skull, gently tapering to nose; dark, small eyes; very small, triangular, stiff, upstanding ears; strong neck; compact, robust and square body; chest deep and broad; withers very pronounced, firm back and loins, croup short and horizontal; when viewed in silhouette, topline appearing to slope gently down from the withers; normal angulations front and rear; legs rather finely boned and well under the body; coat of straight hair, slightly harsh to the touch, never silky, standing out around the neck (the ruff); hair long on the neck, the withers (the mane), the throat, the forechest (the jabot or apron) and behind the shoulders (the cape); hair also long, the points of which turned inward, on the rear of the thighs (the culottes or breeches); dense undercoat; movement smooth and firm; an excellent little watchdog, supple, indefatigable and unbelievably inquisitive.

It is important, for the preservation of the breed and its international esteem, that there be a unified type all over the world. Unfortunately, this is not really the case. The ideal Schipperke

BETTER THAN THE AVERAGE DOG

Even though you may never show your dog, you should still read the breed standard. The breed standard tells you more than just physical specifications such as how tall your dog should be; it also describes how he should act, how he should move and what unique qualities make him the breed that he is. You are not investing money in a pure-bred dog so that you can own a dog that "sort of looks like" the breed you're purchasing. You want a typical, handsome representative of the breed, one that all of your friends and family and people you meet out in public will recognize as the breed you've so carefully selected and researched. If the parents of your prospective puppy bear little or no resemblance to the dog described in the breed standard, you should keep searching!

doesn't exist. Constant efforts from breeders are necessary to improve or even maintain the quality. The main characteristics that should be preserved or improved by breeders all over the world are the robust and square structure, the finely boned legs, the small eyes and the very small ears, the abundant, wholly black coat and the unique silhouette of the body. Equally as important are the Schipperke's keen alertness and devotion to his master and family.

SCHIPPERKE

SELECTING A PUPPY

Nothing is more exciting than choosing a Schipperke puppy. When you and your family have decided that the Schipperke is a

truly suitable breed for you, whether you live in a city apartment, a suburban neighborhood or the country, you can find a recommended breeder and make a careful choice. A Schip is a faithful little watchdog with a size that makes him a suitable pet for the city owner, but he also has the spirit and the independent, enterprising personality that make him at home in any living environment.

However, before visiting a responsible breeder, you have to know what you intend to do with your new companion. Will you show or compete with your dog, or do you just want a pet? Your dog should fit into your daily routine now and, because the lifespan of a Schipperke is longer than that of most other breeds, you should plan for the dog to be a part of your life for many years to come.

You have to be prepared to introduce a dog into your family. The responsibilities you will have and the consequences of keeping a dog, even a small one, should be considered before you choose and visit a breeder. Don't forget that the small size of the Schipperke is a great advantage, but is also a very misleading characteristic. Experts and owners of the breed like to say indeed that the Schipperke is known as the "biggest small dog" or, still better, the "smallest big dog." This means that he behaves like a big dog and wants to be treated like a big dog. He is a small, confident dog, possessing all the features of any other dog. He will constantly and totally depend on you. He will claim your attention, your time and your love!

You have to realize the following before adding a Schip to your family:

• All family members should be enthusiastic about acquiring a puppy.
• Schips are playful with children, but your children should regard the dog, under your supervision, as a playmate, not as a plaything, and they should be capable of respecting the dog and handling him properly.
• Your Schipperke will require a diet that, in terms of quantity, is less than that of a big dog and will therefore be less expensive. However, small breeds require, per pound of body weight, more food than big dogs. Much more importantly, the diet, as for any other dog breed, should be well balanced. This means that all of the required nutrients should be present in the right proportions, without danger of overfeeding the Schip's little body or providing too much or too little of any nutrients.

• Taking care of your dog, feeding him, walking him, educating him, grooming him and looking after him for a lifetime will be a time-consuming commitment.
• Food, veterinary bills, etc., will be sizable financial considerations for the dog's life.

GETTING ACQUAINTED
When visiting a litter, ask the breeder for suggestions on how best to interact with the puppies. If possible, get right into the middle of the pack and sit down with them. Observe which pups climb into your lap and which ones shy away. Toss a toy for them to chase and bring back to you. It's easy to fall in love with the puppy who picks you, but keep your future objectives in mind before you make your final decision.

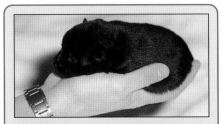

FINDING A QUALIFIED BREEDER

Before you begin your puppy search, ask for references from your veterinarian and perhaps other breeders to refer you to someone they believe is reputable. Responsible breeders usually raise only one or two breeds of dog. Avoid any breeder who has several different breeds or has several litters at the same time. Dedicated breeders are usually involved with a breed or other dog club. Many participate in some sport or activity related to their breed. Just as you want to be assured of the breeder's qualifications, the breeder wants to be assured that you will make a worthy owner. Expect the breeder to interview you, asking questions about your goals for the pup, your experience with dogs and what kind of home you will provide.

• When you go away for a weekend or on vacation, you have to take your dog with you or somebody has to look after him; nevertheless, when you take him with you, his small size will be a great advantage. Moreover, a Schip is an eager

traveler and can easily get used to being put in a crate or travel carrier.

When all of these responsibilities do not seem to be a problem, you can take the next step in choosing a reputable breeder, but do not act impulsively. Do not let your choice of breeder be determined by his proximity to your home, and do not buy the first puppy that licks your nose.

Advice on where to look or what to look for can be given by your vet, other Schip owners or a local dog club. The best, however, is to contact committee members of the national breed club, the Schipperke Club of America (www.schipperkeclub-usa.org), who will be glad to give you contact information for breeders and advice about your puppy purchase. You can ensure even further that these breeders are reputable by talking to former and current owners of their dogs.

A caring, responsible breeder follows an honorable code of ethics. This is true of the Schipperke Club of America's member breeders. When viewing a litter, he will give you good advice and assistance. You should help him by stating, as precisely as possible, the sort of puppy you want. Male or female? Do you plan on simply having a family pet? Do you want a dog for showing or advanced training, such as obedience competition?

A good breeder consistently produces typical, sound dogs and also provides reliable after-sale support for the dog's entire life. In any case, a reputable breeder should be the only place you go to look for and purchase a puppy.

A responsible breeder will show you the mother and also the father, if he is available. Their appearance and behavior will give you some idea of your puppy's mature appearance and temperament. The breeder will also explain to you how a pedigree is interpreted and inform you about the "bloodlines" (the ancestors) and the merits of the parents and grandparents. Do not underestimate the importance of the character and anatomical structure of the parents and also the grandparents if you wish your puppy to grow up to be a high-quality adult dog. However, you need to be lucky, too. You have to realize that you would be fortunate to make your dog a champion if he comes from "champion lines," but a champion coming from parents of inferior quality would be a miracle!

Equally as important is the parents' health. The breeder should have had the necessary tests done on the parents before breeding and will be happy to show you such documentation. Parents should have certification from the Orthopedic Foundation for Animals (OFA) and the Canine Eye Registration Foundation (CERF), and have been tested clear of epilepsy and MPS IIIB, a nervous-system disorder that is fatal. Schipperke breeders support the efforts of CHIC (Canine Health Information Center), a database for Schips who have three tests completed: eyes through CERF and thyroid and patellas through OFA.

Watch the behavior of the puppies together in the litter. Do not choose a shy or retiring puppy. Try to select an outgoing, confident and alert puppy that is willing to play and that comes

SIGNS OF A HEALTHY PUPPY

Healthy puppies are robust little fellows who are alert and active, sporting shiny coats and supple skin. They should not appear lethargic, bloated or pot-bellied, nor should they have flaky skin or runny or crusted eyes or noses. Their stools should be firm and well formed, with no evidence of blood or mucus.

PEDIGREE VS. REGISTRATION CERTIFICATE

Too often new owners are confused between these two important documents. Your puppy's pedigree, essentially a family tree, is a written record of a dog's genealogy of three generations or more. The pedigree will show you the names as well as performance titles of all dogs in your pup's background. Your breeder must provide you with a registration application, with his part properly filled out. You must complete the application and send it to the AKC with the proper fee. Every puppy must come from a litter that has been AKC-registered by the breeder, born in the US and from a sire and dam that are also registered with the AKC.

The seller must provide you with complete records to identify the puppy. The AKC requires that the seller provide the buyer with the following: breed; sex, color and markings; date of birth; litter number (when available); names and registration numbers of the parents; breeder's name; and date sold or delivered.

hit a metal pan with a spoon. You should not buy any puppy of the litter, even one that seems to behave normally, if most of them show fear or cannot be approached. Ideally, when entering the room where the litter is kept, the pups should all approach you, jump up on you and compete for attention. An extroverted character will be an advantage for training as well as for showing. Remember, however, that pups sleep as much as 18 hours a day and that your visit may by chance coincide with their after-dinner nap.

It is rather difficult, if you want to buy a show-quality Schipperke, to give advice on the anatomical structure or conformation. An experienced breeder should be able to guide you in your choice, as early as when the pups are seven or eight weeks old. However, very few people are experts—and even experts can make mistakes.

A good Schipperke puppy should have a firm, already compact and square body. The back or topline should be horizontal, with no dip and no weakness; the legs both front and rear should be straight and parallel to each other, not bowed and not placed too close together; and the ears should be as small as possible and firmly upright. Choose a puppy that, rather than hopping, is already able to trot

running toward you. The puppy should seem bright and look healthy. Ears and eyes should not have discharge, the coat should be clean and the skin free of scales and parasites. A puppy should not be fearful about normal noises. He should not hide, but rather show interest when you drop a metal object like a key or easily, with a parallel movement of the fore- and hindquarters while the topline remains firm and level.

Coat color is important. In the American and FCI breed standards, only all black is allowed. It is rare to find another color, but Schips can be seen in colors such as yellow and chocolate, or, more rarely, white and gray. If you want a show dog, choose a black coat! White markings should be avoided, even when confined to the toes or the forechest, because this is a disqualifying fault. It is possible, however, that a puppy will have a thick gray or brown undercoat that does not look pure-toned, but that will turn black when the adult coat appears.

Decide which sex you prefer. There are some specific differences. Males are physically more impressive because as a rule they carry more coat. They are more dominant and pugnacious and sometimes aggressive toward other males. They mark their territory in a demonstrative manner.

Bitches are more "feminine" and less powerfully built. Normally, if unspayed, they come into season every 6 months for 21 days. At the beginning, the "heat" is marked with a clear mucus-like discharge from the vagina. However, very often the licking behavior of the bitch is noticed

SELECTING FROM THE LITTER

Before you visit a litter of puppies, promise yourself that you won't fall for the first pretty face you see! Decide on your goals for your puppy—show prospect, obedience competitor, family companion—and then look for a puppy who displays the appropriate qualities. In most litters, there is an Alpha pup (the bossy puppy), and occasionally a shy fellow who is less confident, with the rest of the litter falling somewhere in the middle. "Middle-of-the-roaders" are safe bets for most families and novice competitors.

first. After about seven days, the discharge is bloodstained and can be copious. In the third week, the discharge eases up. During the period that your bitch is in season, you will have to keep her away from male dogs in order to prevent unwanted matings.

Females are generally more friendly, a little more affectionate and also more submissive. Moreover, some people find that a female is easier to house-train than a male.

Nevertheless, all of these sex-

With one Schip pup cuter than the next, it's impossible (and unwise) to make a choice based on looks alone.

related differences should not be overemphasized. In fact, both sexes are equally trainable and loyally dedicated to their owners. Many people disagree as to the differences between males and females in aggressive and affectionate behavior. We know from experience that males tend to be more aggressive, but that they can be very affectionate, too. The individual personality of the pup is what should be considered.

As to the size of the two sexes, contrary to other breeds, the rule does not apply to Schipperkes that bitches should be smaller than males. A female is often bigger than a male because a rather broad range of weights and, consequently, sizes is seen in the breed.

In conclusion, your preference as to the sex of your dog is strictly personal. Generally speaking, males and females are much the same in disposition, and both make excellent pets.

The best age to bring a pup home is between seven and eight weeks, certainly not older than

nine weeks. The reason is that during the socialization period (8 to 12 weeks) the pups should meet and be handled by a wide variety of people, be exposed to many new experiences and have contact with other dogs and other animals without becoming stressed.

You should ask the breeder whether or not the pups have been wormed and vaccinated. If you see a pot-bellied pup, this is a possible sign of worms. The breeder should send you home with documentation on the pup's health, vaccination and worming history thus far. The breeder should also show you the parents' registration documents, certificates of performance (such as breed shows, breed surveys, temperament tests, obedience or other trials, etc.) and health certificates.

When you have made your purchase, a responsible and caring breeder will also give you a diet sheet and possibly some food for the pup's first meals in his new home. You will also get the relevant paperwork: pedigree, registration papers, sales agreement, insurance information and health guarantee. You can keep in touch with the breeder for many years to come, but don't trouble him with insignificant problems.

A COMMITTED NEW OWNER

By now you should understand what makes the Schipperke a

most unique and special dog, one that may fit nicely into your family and lifestyle. If you have researched breeders, you should be able to recognize a knowledgeable and responsible Schipperke breeder who cares not only about his pups but also about what kind of owner you will be. If you have completed the final step in your new journey, you have found a litter, or possibly two, of quality Schipperke pups.

A visit with the puppies and their breeder should be an education in itself. Breed research, breeder selection and puppy visitation are very important aspects of finding the puppy of your dreams. Beyond that, these things also lay the foundation for a successful future with your pup. Puppy personalities within each litter vary, from

This good-natured Schip dam supervises the careful introduction of a human baby to her own "babies."

the shy and easygoing puppy to the one who is dominant and assertive, with most pups falling somewhere in between. By spending time with the puppies, you will be able to recognize certain behaviors and what these behaviors indicate about each pup's temperament. Which type of pup will complement your family dynamics is best determined by observing the puppies in action within their "pack." Your breeder's expertise and recommendations are also valuable. Although you may fall in love with a bold and brassy male, the breeder may suggest that another pup would be best for you. The breeder's experience in rearing Schipperke pups and matching their temperaments with appropriate humans offers the best assurance that your pup will meet your needs and expectations. The type of puppy that you select is just as important as your decision that the Schipperke is the breed for you.

THE WORRIES OF MANGE

Sometimes called "puppy mange," demodectic mange is passed to the puppy through the mother's milk. The microscopic mites that cause the condition take up residence in the puppy's hair follicles and sebaceous glands. Stress can cause the mites to multiply, causing bare patches on the face, neck and front legs. If neglected, it can lead to secondary bacterial infections, but if diagnosed and treated early, demodectic mange can be localized and controlled. Most pups recover without complications.

MOODY MOM

When selecting a puppy, be certain to meet the dam of the litter. The temperament of the dam is often predictive of the temperament of her puppies. However, dams occasionally are very protective of their young, some to the point of being testy or aggressive with visitors, whom they may view as a danger to their babies. Such attitudes are more common when the pups are very young and still nursing and should not be mistaken for actual aggressive temperament. If possible, visit the dam away from her pups to make friends with her and gain a better understanding of her true personality.

The decision to live with a Schipperke is a serious commitment and not one to be taken lightly. This puppy is a living sentient being that will be dependent on you for basic survival for his entire life. Beyond the basics of survival—food, water, shelter and protection—he needs much, much more. The new pup needs love, nurturing and a proper canine education to mold him into a responsible, well-behaved canine citizen. Your Schipperke's health and good manners will need consistent monitoring and regular "tune-ups," so your job as a responsible dog owner will be ongoing throughout every stage of his life. If you are not prepared to accept these responsibilities and commit to them for the next decade, likely longer, then you are not prepared to own a dog of any breed.

Although the responsibilities of owning a dog may at times tax your patience, the joy of living with your Schip far outweighs the workload, and a well-mannered adult dog is worth your time and effort. Before your very eyes, your new charge will grow up to be your most loyal friend, devoted to you unconditionally.

YOUR SCHIPPERKE SHOPPING LIST

Just as expectant parents prepare a nursery for their baby, so should you ready your home for the arrival of your Schipperke pup. If you have the necessary puppy supplies purchased and in place before he comes home, it will ease the puppy's transition from the warmth and familiarity of his mom and littermates to the brand-new environment of his new home and human family. You will be too busy to stock up and prepare your house after your pup comes home, that's for sure! Imagine how a pup must feel upon being transported to a strange new place. It's up to you to comfort him and to let your little pup know that he is going to be happy with you.

FOOD AND WATER BOWLS

Your puppy will need separate bowls for his food and water. Stainless steel pans are generally preferred over plastic bowls since they sterilize better and pups are less inclined to chew on the metal. Heavy-duty ceramic bowls are popular, but consider how often you will have to pick up those heavy bowls. Buy adult-sized pans, as your puppy will grow into them quickly.

THE DOG CRATE

If you think that crates are tools of punishment and confinement for when a dog has misbehaved, think again. Most breeders and almost all trainers recommend a crate as the preferred house-

COST OF OWNERSHIP

The purchase price of your puppy is merely the first expense in the typical dog budget. Quality dog food, veterinary care (sickness and health maintenance), dog supplies and grooming costs will add up to big bucks every year. Can you adequately afford to support a canine addition to the family?

training aid as well as for all-around puppy training and safety. Because dogs are natural den creatures that prefer cave-like environments, the benefits of crate use are many. The crate provides the puppy with his very own "safe house," a cozy place to sleep, take a break or seek comfort with a favorite toy; a travel aid to house your dog when on the road, at motels or at the vet's office; a training aid to help teach your puppy proper toileting habits; and a place of solitude when non-dog people happen to drop by and don't want a lively puppy—or even a well-behaved adult dog—saying hello or begging for attention.

Crates come in several types, although the wire crate and the fiberglass airline-type crate are the most popular. Both are safe and your puppy will adjust to either one, so the choice is up to you. The wire crates offer better visibility for the pup as well as

Naturally patient and trusting, Schipperke bitches make attentive mothers for their litters.

The three most common crate types: mesh on the left, wire on the right and fiberglass on top.

sized crate. A tiny crate may be fine for a very young Schipperke pup, but it will not do him much good for long! The Schipperke's compact size is a convenience in this respect, as he will not need a very large crate. Regardless, it is best to get one that will accommodate your dog both as a pup and at full size. A medium-sized crate will be necessary for a full-grown Schipperke, who stands between 10 and 13 inches high at the shoulder. Consider this measurement when choosing a crate with room to allow your adult Schip to stand, sit, lie down and turn around comfortably.

BEDDING AND CRATE PADS

Your puppy will enjoy some type of soft bedding in his "room" (the crate), something he can snuggle into to feel cozy and secure. Old

better ventilation. Many of the wire crates easily collapse into suitcase-size carriers. The fiberglass crates, similar to those used by the airlines for animal transport, are sturdier and more den-like. However, the fiberglass crates do not fold down and are less ventilated than the wire crates, which can be problematic in hot weather. Some of the newer crates are made of heavy plastic mesh; they are very lightweight and fold up into slim-line suitcases. However, a mesh crate might not be suitable for a pup with manic chewing habits.

Don't bother with a puppy-

CRATE EXPECTATIONS

To make the crate more inviting to your puppy, you can offer his first meal or two inside the crate, always keeping the crate door open so that he does not feel confined. Keep a favorite toy or two in the crate for him to play with while inside. You can also cover the crate at night with a lightweight sheet to make it more den-like and remove the stimuli of household activity. Never put him into his crate as punishment or as you are scolding him, since he will then associate his crate with negative situations and avoid going there.

towels or blankets are good choices for a young pup, since he may (and probably will) have a toileting accident or two in the crate or decide to chew on the bedding material. Once he is fully trained and out of the early chewing stage, you can replace the puppy bedding with a permanent crate pad if you prefer. Crate pads and other dog beds run the gamut from inexpensive to high-end doggie-designer styles, but don't splurge on the good stuff until you are sure that your puppy is reliable and won't tear it up or make a mess on it.

PUPPY TOYS
Just as infants and older children require objects to stimulate their minds and bodies, puppies need toys to entertain their curious brains, wiggly paws and achy teeth. A fun array of safe doggie toys will help satisfy your puppy's chewing instincts and distract him from gnawing on the leg of your antique chair or your new leather sofa. Most puppy toys are cute and look as if they would be a lot of fun, but not all are necessarily safe or good for your puppy, so use caution when you go puppy-toy shopping.

Schipperke puppies are fairly aggressive chewers. Like many other dogs, they love to chew. The best "chewcifiers" are sturdy nylon and hard rubber bones, which are safe to gnaw on and

TOYS 'R SAFE
The vast array of tantalizing puppy toys is staggering. Stroll through any pet shop or pet-supply outlet and you will see that the choices can be overwhelming. However, not all dog toys are safe or sensible. Most very young puppies enjoy soft woolly toys that they can snuggle with and carry around. (You know they have outgrown them when they shred them up!) Avoid toys that have buttons, tabs or other enhancements that can be chewed off and swallowed. Soft toys that squeak are fun, but make sure your puppy does not disembowel the toy and remove (and swallow) the squeaker. Toys that rattle or make noise can excite a puppy, but they present the same danger as the squeaky kind and so require supervision. Hard rubber toys that bounce can also entertain a pup, but make sure that the toy is too big for your pup to swallow.

TEETHING TIME

All puppies chew. It's normal canine behavior. Chewing just plain feels good to a puppy, especially during the three- to five-month teething period when the adult teeth are breaking through the gums. Rather than attempting to eliminate such a strong natural chewing instinct, you will be more successful if you redirect it and teach your puppy what he may or may not chew. Correct inappropriate chewing with a sharp "No!" and offer him a chew toy, praising him when he takes it. Don't become discouraged. Chewing usually decreases after the adult teeth have come in.

narians often tell of surgical nightmares involving bits of splintered bone, because in addition to the danger of choking, the sharp pieces can damage the intestinal tract.

Similarly, rawhide chews, while a favorite of most dogs and puppies, can be equally dangerous. Pieces of rawhide are easily swallowed after they get soft and gummy from chewing, and dogs have been known to choke on pieces of ingested rawhide. Rawhide chews should be offered only when you can supervise your Schipperke.

Soft woolly toys are special puppy favorites. They come in a wide variety of cute shapes and sizes; some look like little stuffed animals. Puppies love to shake them up and toss them about, or simply carry them around. Be careful of fuzzy toys that have button eyes or noses that your pup could chew off and swallow, and make sure that he does not disembowel a squeaky toy to remove the squeaker! Braided rope toys are similar in that they are fun to chew and toss around, but they shred easily and the strings are easy to swallow. The strings are not digestible and, if the puppy doesn't pass them in his stool, he could end up at the vet's office. As with rawhides, your puppy should be closely monitored with rope toys.

come in sizes appropriate for all age groups and breeds. Be especially careful of natural bones, which can splinter or develop dangerous sharp edges; pups can easily swallow or choke on those bone splinters. Veteri-

If you believe that your pup has ingested a piece of one of his toys, check his stools for the next couple of days to see if he passes the item when he defecates. At the same time, also watch for signs of intestinal distress. A call to your veterinarian might be in order to get his advice and be on the safe side.

An all-time favorite toy for puppies (young and old!) is the empty gallon milk jug. Hard plastic juice containers—46 ounces or more—are also excellent. Such containers make lots of noise when they are batted about, and puppies go crazy with delight as they play with them. However, they don't

A very young Schipperke gets his first introduction to a collar and lead. Purchase a collar that can expand with the puppy's growth and check it regularly for proper fit.

often last very long, so be sure to remove and replace them when they get chewed up on the ends.

A word of caution about homemade toys: be careful with your choices of non-traditional play objects. Never use old shoes or socks, since a puppy cannot distinguish between the old ones on which he's allowed to chew and the new ones in your closet that are strictly off limits. That principle applies to anything that resembles something that you don't want your puppy to chew.

COLLARS

A lightweight nylon collar is the best choice for a very young pup. Quick-clip collars are easy to put on and remove, and they can be adjusted as the puppy grows. Introduce him to his collar as soon as he comes home to get him accustomed to wearing it. He'll get used to it quickly and won't mind a bit. Make sure that it is snug enough that it won't slip off, yet loose enough to be comfortable for the pup. You should be able to slip two fingers between the collar and his neck. Check the collar often, as puppies grow in spurts, and his collar can become too tight almost overnight. Choke collars are not suitable for small dogs like the Schipperke at any age, not to mention that a choke collar would damage the hair of the Schip's abundant neck ruff. Some owners use harnesses rather than collars when walking their Schips, feeling that the harnesses are more comfortable for their dogs.

LEASHES

A 6-foot nylon lead is an excellent choice for a young puppy. It is lightweight and not as tempting to chew as a leather lead. You can switch to a 6-foot leather lead after your pup has grown and is used to walking politely on a lead. For initial puppy walks and house-training purposes, you should invest in a shorter lead so that you have more control over the puppy. At first, you don't want him wandering too far away from you, and when taking him out for toileting you will want to keep him in the specific area chosen for his potty spot.

Once the puppy is heel-trained with a traditional leash, you can consider purchasing a retractable lead. A retractable lead is excellent for walking adult dogs that are already leash-wise. This type of lead allows the dog to roam farther away from you and explore a wider area when out walking, and also retracts when you need to keep him close.

HOME SAFETY FOR YOUR PUPPY

The importance of puppy-proofing cannot be overstated. In addition to making your house comfortable for your Schipperke's arrival, you also must make sure that your house is safe for your puppy before you bring him home. There are countless hazards in the owner's personal living environment that a pup can sniff, chew, swallow or destroy. Many are obvious; others are not. Do a thorough advance house check to remove or rearrange those things that could hurt your puppy, keeping any potentially dangerous items out of areas to which he will have access.

Electrical cords are especially dangerous, since puppies view them as irresistible chew toys. Unplug and remove all exposed cords or fasten them beneath a baseboard where the puppy cannot reach them. Veterinarians and firefighters can tell you horror stories about electrical burns and house fires that resulted from puppy-chewed electrical cords. Consider this a most serious precaution for your puppy and the rest of your family.

Scout your home for tiny objects that might be seen at a pup's eye level. Keep medication bottles and cleaning supplies well out of reach, and do the same with waste baskets and other trash containers. It goes without saying that you should not use rodent poison or other toxic chemicals in any puppy area and that you must keep such containers safely locked up. You will be amazed at how many

places a curious puppy can discover!

Once your house has cleared inspection, check your yard. A sturdy fence, well embedded into the ground, will give your dog a safe place to play and potty. Schipperkes are small but athletic dogs, so a 5- to 6-foot-high fence will be needed to contain an agile youngster or adult. Check the fence periodically for necessary repairs. If there is a weak link or space to squeeze through, you can be sure a determined Schipperke will discover it. A bored Schip out in the yard with nothing to do may turn his attention to seeing what's on the other side of the fence—he needs stimulation *and* companionship. Further, his

Your Schipperke puppy should be supervised whenever he's playing outdoors. Be sure that you have Schip-proofed your yard before the puppy arrives home.

A Schipperke is quite the investigator. He will stick his nose—literally—into whatever captures his interest.

available immediately and your puppy should visit the vet within a day or so of coming home.

It's important to make sure that your puppy's first visit to the vet is a pleasant and positive one.

curious nature and high energy can make him an escape artist, and some Schips can be diggers.

The garage and shed can be hazardous places for a pup, as things like fertilizers, chemicals and tools are usually kept there. It's best to keep these areas off-limits to the pup. Antifreeze is especially dangerous to dogs, as they find the taste appealing and it takes only a few licks from the driveway to kill a dog, puppy or adult, small breed or large.

VISITING THE VETERINARIAN
A good veterinarian is your Schipperke puppy's best health-insurance policy. If you do not already have a vet, ask friends and experienced dog people in your area for recommendations so that you can select a vet before you bring your Schipperke puppy home. Also arrange for your puppy's first veterinary examina-tion beforehand, since many vets do not have appointments

THE GRASS IS GREENER
Must dog owners decide between their beloved canine pals and their perfectly manicured emerald-green lawns? Just as dog urine is no tonic for growing grass, lawn chemicals are extremely dangerous to your dog. Fertilizers, pesticides and herbicides pose real threats to canines and humans alike. Dogs should be kept off treated grounds for at least 24 hours following treatment. Consider some organic options for your lawn care, such as using a homemade compost or a natural fertilizer instead of a commercial chemical. Some dog-conscious lawnkeepers avoid fertilizers entirely, keeping up their lawns by watering, aerating, mowing and seeding frequently.

As always, dogs complicate the equation. Canines love grass. They roll in it, eat it and love to bury their noses in it—and then do their business in it! Grass can mean hours of feel-good, smell-good fun! In addition to the dangers of lawn-care chemicals, there's also the threat of burs, thorns and pebbles in the grass, not to mention the very common grass allergy. Many dogs develop an incurably itchy skin condition from grass, especially in the late summer when the world is in full bloom.

A Dog-Safe Home

The dog-safety police are taking you and your Schipperke on a house tour. Let's go room by room and see how safe your own home is for your new pup. The following items are doggie dangers, so either they must be removed or the dog should be monitored or not allowed access to these areas.

Living Room

- house plants (some varieties are poisonous)
- fireplace or wood-burning stove
- paint on the walls (lead-based paint is toxic)
- lead drapery weights (toxic lead)
- lamps and electrical cords
- carpet cleaners or deodorizers

Outdoors

- swimming pool
- pesticides
- toxic plants
- lawn fertilizers

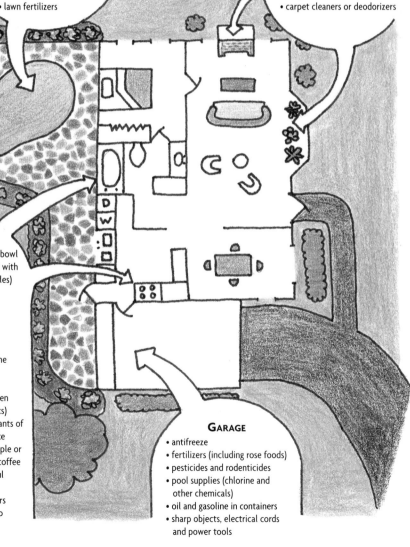

Bathroom

- blue water in the toilet bowl
- medicine cabinet (filled with potentially deadly bottles)
- soap bars, bleach, drain cleaners, etc.
- tampons

Kitchen

- household cleaners in the kitchen cabinets
- glass jars and canisters
- sharp objects (like kitchen knives, scissors and forks)
- garbage can (with remnants of good-smelling things like onions, potato skins, apple or pear cores, peach pits, coffee beans and other harmful tidbits)
- food left out on counters (some foods are toxic to dogs)

Garage

- antifreeze
- fertilizers (including rose foods)
- pesticides and rodenticides
- pool supplies (chlorine and other chemicals)
- oil and gasoline in containers
- sharp objects, electrical cords and power tools

Many plants and shrubs can be toxic to dogs; at the very least, chewing on sharp branches could injure a dog.

MEETING THE FAMILY

Your Schipperke's homecoming is an exciting time for all members of the family, and it's only natural that everyone will be eager to meet him, pet him and play with him. However, for the puppy's sake, it's best to make these initial family meetings as uneventful as possible so that the pup is not overwhelmed with too much too soon. Remember, he has just left his dam and his littermates and is away from the breeder's home for the first time. Despite his fuzzy wagging tail, he is still apprehensive and wondering where he is and who all these strange humans are. It's best to let him explore on his own and meet the family members as he feels

The vet should take great care to befriend the pup and handle him gently to make their first meeting a positive experience. The vet will give the pup a thorough physical examination and set up a schedule for vaccinations and other necessary wellness visits. Be sure to show your vet any health and inoculation records, which you should have received from your breeder. Your vet is a great source of canine health information, so be sure to ask questions and take notes. Creating a health journal for your puppy will make a handy reference for his wellness and any future health problems that may arise.

KEEP OUT OF REACH

Most dogs don't browse around your medicine cabinet, but accidents do happen! The drug acetaminophen, the active ingredient in Tylenol®, can be deadly to dogs and cats if ingested in large quantities. Acetaminophen toxicity, caused by the dog's swallowing 15 to 20 tablets, can be manifested in abdominal pains within a day or two of ingestion, as well as liver damage. If you suspect your dog has swiped a bottle of Tylenol®, get the dog to the vet immediately so that the vet can induce vomiting and cleanse the dog's stomach.

comfortable. Let him investigate all the new smells, sights and sounds at his own pace. Children should be especially careful to not get overly excited, use loud voices or hug the pup too tightly. Be calm, gentle and affectionate, and be ready to comfort him if he appears frightened or uneasy.

Be sure to show your puppy his new crate during this first day home. Toss a treat or two inside the crate; if he associates the crate with food, he will associate the crate with good things. If he is comfortable with the crate, you can offer him his first meal inside it. Leave the door ajar so he can wander in and out as he chooses.

FIRST NIGHT IN HIS NEW HOME

So much has happened in your Schipperke puppy's first day away from the breeder. He's had his first

The curious and agile Schipperke puppy can find mischief in most anything. Be certain that you have made your home safe for your puppy, or he may hurt himself or damage your possessions.

car ride to his new home. He's met his new human family and perhaps the other family pets. He has explored his new house and yard, at least those places where he is to be allowed during his first weeks at home. He may have visited his new veterinarian. He has eaten his first meal or two away from his dam and litter-mates. Surely that's enough to tire out an eight-week-old Schipperke pup...or so you hope!

It's bedtime. During the day, the pup investigated his crate, which is his new den and sleeping space, so it is not entirely strange to him. Line the crate with a soft towel or blanket that he can snuggle into and gently place him into the crate for the night. Some breeders send home a piece of bedding from where the pup slept with his littermates, and those familiar scents are a great comfort for the puppy on his first night without his siblings.

PUPPY PARASITES

Parasites are nasty little critters that live in or on your dog or puppy. Most puppies are born with ascarid roundworms, which are acquired from dormant ascarids residing in the dam. Other parasites can be acquired through contact with infected fecal matter. Take a stool sample to your vet for testing. He will prescribe a safe wormer to treat any parasites found in your puppy's stool. Always have a fecal test performed at your puppy's annual veterinary exam.

He will probably whine or cry. The puppy is objecting to the confinement and the fact that he is alone for the first time. This can be a stressful time for you as well as for the pup. It's important that you remain strong and don't let the puppy out of his crate to comfort him. He will fall asleep eventually. If you release him, the puppy will learn that crying means "out" and will continue that habit. You are laying the groundwork for future habits. Some breeders find that soft music can soothe a crying pup and help him get to sleep.

SOCIALIZING YOUR PUPPY

The first 20 weeks of your Schipperke puppy's life are the

Attention and gentle handling when your puppy first comes home helps him bond with his new family pack.

most important of his entire lifetime. A properly socialized puppy will grow up to be a confident and stable adult who will be a pleasure to live with and a welcome addition to the neighborhood.

The importance of socialization cannot be overemphasized. Research on canine behavior has proven that puppies who are not exposed to new sights, sounds, people and animals during their first 20 weeks of life will grow up to be timid and fearful, even aggressive, and unable to flourish outside of their familiar home environment.

Socializing your puppy is not difficult and, in fact, will be a fun time for you both. Lead training goes hand in hand with socialization, so your puppy will be learning how to walk on a lead at the same time that he's meeting the neighborhood. Because the Schipperke is such a terrific breed, your puppy will enjoy being "the new kid on the block." Take him for short walks to the park and to other dog-friendly places where he will encounter new people, especially children. Puppies automatically recognize children as "little people" and are drawn to play with them. Just make sure that you supervise these meetings and that the children do not get too rough or encourage him to play too hard. An overzealous pup can often nip

Once your Schipperke puppy is properly vaccinated, he can begin to make the acquaintance of other dogs or visitors. This black-and-white quartet gets along famously.

too hard, frightening the child and in turn making the puppy overly excited. A bad experience in puppyhood can impact a dog for life, so a pup that has a negative experience with a child may grow up to be shy or even aggressive around children.

Take your puppy along on your daily errands. Puppies are natural "people magnets," and most people who see your pup will want to pet him. All of these encounters will help to mold him into a confident adult dog. Likewise, you will soon feel like a confident, responsible dog owner, rightly proud of your handsome Schipperke.

Be especially careful of your puppy's encounters and experi-ences during the eight-to-ten-week-old period, which is also called the "fear period." This is a serious imprinting period, and all contact during this time should be gentle and positive. A frightening or negative event could leave a permanent impression that could affect his future behavior if a similar situation arises.

Also make sure that your puppy has received his first and second rounds of vaccinations before you expose him to other dogs or bring him to places that other dogs may frequent. Avoid dog parks and other strange-dog areas until your vet assures you that your puppy is fully immunized and resistant to the diseases that can be passed between canines. Discuss socialization with your breeder, as some breeders recommend socializing the puppy even before he has received all of his inoculations, depending on how outgoing the puppy may be.

THE FAMILY FELINE

A resident cat has feline squatter's rights. The cat will treat the newcomer (your puppy) as she sees fit, regardless of what you do or say, so it's best to let the two of them work things out on their own terms. Cats have a height advantage and will generally leap to higher ground to avoid direct contact with a rambunctious pup. Some will hiss and boldly swat at a pup who passes by or tries to reach the cat. Keep the puppy under control in the presence of the cat and they will eventually become accustomed to each other.

Here's a hint: move the cat's litter box where the puppy can't get into it! It's best to do so well before the pup comes home so the cat is used to the new location.

LEADER OF THE PUPPY'S PACK

Like other canines, your puppy needs an authority figure, someone he can look up to and regard as the leader of his "pack." His first pack leader was his dam, who taught him to be polite and not chew too hard on her ears or nip at her muzzle. He learned those same lessons from his littermates. If he played too rough, they cried in pain and stopped the game, which sent an important message to the rowdy puppy.

As puppies play together, they are also struggling to determine who will be the boss. Being pack animals, dogs need someone to be in charge. If a litter of puppies remained together beyond puppyhood, one of the pups would emerge as the strongest one, the one who calls the shots.

Once your puppy leaves the pack, he will look intuitively for a new leader. If he does not recognize you as that leader, he will try to assume that position for himself. Of course, it is hard to imagine your adorable Schipperke puppy trying to be in charge when he is so small and seemingly helpless. You must remember that these are natural canine instincts. Do not cave in and allow your pup to get the upper "paw"!

Just as socialization is so important during these first 20 weeks, so too is your puppy's

DIGGING OUT
Some Schipperkes love to dig. Others wouldn't think of it. Digging is considered "self-rewarding behavior" because it's fun! Of all the digging solutions offered by the experts, most are only marginally successful and none is guaranteed to work. The best cure is prevention, which means removing the dog from the offending site when he digs as well as distracting him when you catch him digging so that he turns his attentions elsewhere. That means that you have to supervise your dog's yard time. An unsupervised digger can create havoc with your landscaping or, worse, run away!

early education. He was born without any bad habits. He does not know what is good or bad behavior. If he does things like nipping and digging, it's because he is having fun and doesn't know that humans consider these things as "bad." It's your job to teach him proper puppy manners, and this is the best time to accomplish that...before he has developed bad habits, since it is much more difficult to "unlearn" or correct unacceptable learned behavior than to teach good behavior from the start.

Make sure that all members of the family understand the importance of being consistent when training their new puppy. If you tell the puppy to stay off the sofa and your daughter allows him to cuddle on the couch to watch her favorite television show, your pup will be confused about what he is and is not allowed to do. Have a family conference before your pup comes home so that everyone understands the basic principles of puppy training and the rules you have set forth for the pup, and agrees to follow them.

The old saying that "an ounce of prevention is worth a pound of cure" is especially true when it comes to puppies. It is much easier to prevent inappropriate behavior than it is to change it. It's also easier and less stressful for the pup, since it will keep discipline to a minimum and create a more positive learning environment for him. That, in turn, will also be easier on you!

Here are a few commonsense tips to keep your belongings safe and your puppy out of trouble:

• Keep your closet doors closed and your shoes, socks and other

A very young pup will have no idea what a collar and leash are for. Rather than trying to pull him around, just let him wear the collar and drag the leash behind him (indoors!) to let him get used to his new wardrobe.

Puppies tend to be very oral, putting their teeth and mouths on everything.

apparel off the floor so your puppy can't get at them.

- Keep a secure lid on the trash container or put the trash where your puppy can't dig into it. He can't damage what he can't reach!

- Supervise your puppy at all times to make sure he is not getting into mischief. If he starts to chew the corner of the rug, you can distract him instantly by tossing a toy for him to fetch. You also will be able to whisk him outside when you notice that he is about to piddle on the carpet. If you can't see your puppy, you can't teach him or correct his behavior.

CHEWING AND NIPPING

Nipping at fingers and toes is normal puppy behavior. Chewing is also the way that puppies investigate their surroundings. However, you will have to teach your puppy that chewing anything other than his toys is not acceptable. That won't happen overnight and at times puppy teeth will test your patience. However, if you allow

nipping and chewing to continue, just think about the damage that a mature Schipperke can do with a full set of adult teeth.

Whenever your puppy nips your hand or fingers, cry out "Ouch!" in a loud voice, which should startle your puppy and stop him from nipping, even if only for a moment. Immediately distract him by offering a small treat or an appropriate toy for him to chew instead (which means having chew toys and puppy treats handy or in your pockets at all times). Praise him when he takes the toy and tell him what a good fellow he is. Praise is just as or even more important in puppy training as discipline and correction.

Puppies also tend to nip at children more often than adults, since they perceive little ones to be more vulnerable and more similar to their littermates. Teach your children appropriate responses to nipping behavior. If they are unable to handle it themselves, you may have to intervene. Puppy nips can be quite painful and a child's frightened reaction will only encourage a puppy to nip harder, which is a natural canine response. As with all other puppy situations, interaction between your Schipperke puppy and children should be supervised.

Chewing on objects, not just family members' fingers and ankles, is also normal canine behavior that can be especially tedious (for the owner, not the pup) during the

ESTABLISH A ROUTINE

Routine is very important to a puppy's learning environment. To facilitate house-training, use the same exit/entrance door for potty trips and always take the puppy to the same place in the yard. The same principle of consistency applies to all other aspects of puppy training.

Available in a spray or cream, this substance is vile-tasting, although safe for dogs, and most puppies will avoid the forbidden object after one tiny taste. You also can apply the product to your leather leash if the puppy tries to chew on his lead during leash-training sessions.

Keep a ready supply of safe chews handy to offer your Schipperke as a distraction when he starts to chew on something that's a "no-no." Remember, at this tender age, he does not yet know what is permitted or forbidden, so you have to be "on call" every minute he's awake and on the prowl.

You may lose a treasure or two during puppy's growing-up period, and the furniture could sustain a nasty nick or two. These can be trying times, so be prepared for those inevitable accidents and comfort yourself in knowing that this too shall pass.

teething period when the puppy's adult teeth are coming in. At this stage, chewing just plain feels good. Furniture legs and cabinet corners are common puppy favorites. Shoes and other personal items also taste pretty good to a pup.

The best solution is, once again, prevention. If you value something, keep it tucked away and out of reach. You can't hide your dining-room table in a closet, but you can try to deflect the chewing by applying a bitter product made just to deter dogs from chewing.

Pups will be pups...and pups will nip. While your toe may be tasty to a teething Schip, always discourage nipping and distract your pup with a chew toy.

SCHIPPERKE

Adding a Schipperke to your household means adding a new family member who will need your care each and every day. When your Schipperke pup first comes home, you will start a routine with him so that, as he grows up, your dog will have a daily schedule just as you do. The aspects of your dog's daily care will likewise become regular parts of your day, so you'll both have a new schedule. Dogs learn by consistency and thrive on routine: regular times for meals, exercise, grooming and potty trips are just as important for your dog as they are for you! Your dog's schedule will depend much on your family's daily routine, but remember that you now have a new member of the family who is part of your day every day!

FEEDING

Feeding your dog the best diet is based on various factors, including age, activity level, overall condition and size of breed. When you visit the breeder, he will share with you his advice about the proper diet for your dog based on his experience with the breed and the foods with which he has had success. Likewise, your vet will be a helpful source of advice throughout the dog's life and will aid you in planning a diet for optimal health.

FEEDING THE PUPPY

Of course, your pup's very first food will be his dam's milk. There may be special situations in which pups fail to nurse, necessitating that the breeder hand-feed them with a formula, but, for the most part, pups spend the first weeks of life nursing from their dam. The

---

NOT HUNGRY?

No dog in his right mind would turn down his dinner, would he? If you notice that your dog has lost interest in his food, there could be any number of causes. Dental problems are a common cause of appetite loss, one that is often overlooked. If your dog has a tooth-ache, a loose tooth or sore gums from infection, chances are it doesn't feel so good to chew. Think about when you've had a toothache! If your dog does not approach the food bowl with his usual enthusiasm, look inside his mouth for signs of a problem. Whatever the cause, you'll want to consult your vet so that your chow hound can get back to his happy, hungry self as soon as possible.

breeder weans the pups by gradually introducing solid foods and decreasing the milk meals. Pups may even start themselves off on the weaning process, albeit inadvertently, if they snatch bites from their mom's food bowl.

By the time the pups are ready for new homes, they are fully weaned and eating a good puppy food. As a new owner, you may be thinking, "Great! The breeder has taken care of the hard part." Not so fast.

A puppy's first year of life is the time when all or most of his growth and development takes place. This is a delicate time, and diet plays a huge role in proper skeletal and muscular formation. Improper diet and exercise habits can lead to damaging problems that will compromise the dog's health and movement for his entire life. That being said, new owners should not worry needlessly. With the myriad types of food formulated specifically for growing pups of different-sized breeds, dog-food manufacturers have taken much of the guesswork out of feeding your puppy well. Since growth-food formulas are designed to provide the nutrition that a growing puppy needs, it is unnecessary and, in fact, can prove harmful to add supplements to the diet. Research has shown that too much of certain vitamin supplements and minerals predispose a dog to skeletal problems. It's by no

SWITCHING FOODS

There are certain times in a dog's life when it becomes necessary to switch his food; for example, from puppy to adult food and then from adult to senior-dog food. Additionally, you may decide to feed your pup a different type of food from what he received from the breeder, and there may be "emergency" situations in which you can't find your dog's normal brand and have to offer something else temporarily. Anytime a change is made, for whatever reason, the switch must be done gradually. You don't want to upset the dog's stomach or end up with a picky eater who refuses to eat something new. A tried-and-true approach is, over the course of about a week, to mix a little of the new food in with the old, increasing the proportion of new to old as the days progress. At the end of the week, you'll be feeding his regular portions of the new food, and he will barely notice the change.

means a case of "if a little is good, a lot is better." At every stage of your dog's life, too much or too little in the way of nutrients can be harmful, which is why a manufactured complete food is the easiest way to know that your dog is getting what he needs.

Because of a young pup's small body and accordingly small digestive system, his daily portion will be divided up into small meals throughout the day. This can mean starting off with three or more meals a day and decreasing the number of meals as the pup matures. For the adult, it is generally thought that dividing the day's food into two meals on a morning/evening schedule is healthiest for the dog's digestion.

Regarding the feeding schedule, feeding the pup at the same times and in the same place each day is important for both housebreaking purposes and establishing the dog's everyday routine. As for the amount to feed, growing puppies generally need proportionately more food per body weight than their adult counterparts, but a pup should never be allowed to gain excess weight. Dogs of all ages should be kept in proper body condition, but extra weight can strain a pup's developing frame, causing skeletal problems.

Watch your pup's weight as he grows and, if the recommended amounts seem to be too much or too little for your pup, consult the vet about appropriate dietary changes. Keep in mind that treats, although small, can quickly add up throughout the day, contributing unnecessary calories. This is especially so for a small dog whose daily caloric requirements are relatively low. Treats are fine when used prudently; opt for dog treats specially formulated to be healthy or for nutritious snacks like small pieces of cheese or cooked chicken.

FEEDING THE ADULT DOG

For the adult (meaning physically mature) dog, feeding properly is about maintenance, not growth. Again, correct weight is a concern. Your dog should appear fit and should have an evident "waist." His ribs should not be protruding (a sign of being underweight), but they should be covered by only a slight layer of

DIET DON'TS

- Got milk? Don't give it to your dog! Dogs cannot tolerate large quantities of cows' milk, as they do not have the enzymes to digest lactose.
- You may have heard of dog owners who add raw eggs to their dogs' food for a shiny coat or to make the food more palatable, but consumption of raw eggs too often can cause a deficiency of the vitamin biotin.
- Avoid feeding table scraps, as they will upset the balance of the dog's complete food. Additionally, fatty or highly seasoned foods can cause upset canine stomachs.
- Do not offer raw meat to your dog. Raw meat can contain parasites; it also is high in fat.
- Vitamin A toxicity in dogs can be caused by too much raw liver, especially if the dog already gets enough vitamin A in his balanced diet, which should be the case.
- Bones like chicken, pork chop and other soft bones are not suitable, as they easily splinter.

fat. Under normal circumstances, an adult dog can be maintained fairly easily with a high-quality nutritionally complete adult-formula food.

Factor treats into your dog's overall daily caloric intake, and avoid offering table scraps. Not only are certain "people foods," like chocolate, nuts, raisins, grapes and onions, toxic to dogs but feeding from the table also encourages begging and overeating. Overweight dogs are more prone to health problems. Research has even shown that obesity takes years off a dog's life. With that in mind, resist the urge to overfeed and over-treat. Don't make unnecessary additions to your dog's diet, whether with tidbits or with extra vitamins and minerals.

The amount of food needed for proper maintenance will vary depending on the individual dog's activity level, but you will be able to tell whether the daily portions are keeping him in good shape. With the wide variety of good complete foods available, choosing what to feed is largely a matter of personal preference. Just as with the puppy, the adult dog should have consistency in his mealtimes and feeding place. In addition to a consistent routine, regular mealtimes also allow the owner to see how much his dog is eating. If the dog seems never to be satisfied or, likewise, becomes

uninterested in his food, the owner will know right away that something is wrong and can consult the vet.

DIETS FOR THE AGING DOG

A good rule of thumb is that once a dog has reached 75% of his expected lifespan, he has reached "senior citizen" or geriatric status. Your Schipperke will be considered a senior at about 9 years of age; based on his size, he has a projected lifespan of 13–16 years, and some have been known to live longer! (The smallest breeds generally enjoy the longest lives and the largest breeds the shortest.)

What does aging have to do with your dog's diet? No, he won't get a discount at the local diner's early-bird special. Yes, he will require some dietary changes to accommodate the changes that come along with increased age. One change is that the older dog's dietary needs become more similar to that of a puppy. Specifically, dogs can metabolize more

An adult Schipperke can be maintained fairly easily on a complete food formulated for small breeds.

protein as youngsters and seniors than in the adult-maintenance stage. Discuss with your vet whether you need to switch to a higher-protein or senior-formulated food or whether your current adult-dog food contains sufficient nutrition for the senior.

Watching the dog's weight remains essential, even more so in the senior stage. Older dogs are already more vulnerable to illness, and obesity only contributes to their susceptibility to problems. As the older dog becomes less active and thus exercises less, his regular portions may cause him to gain weight. At this point, you may consider decreasing his daily food intake or switching to a reduced-calorie food. As with other changes, you should consult your vet for advice.

TYPES OF FOOD AND READING THE LABEL

When selecting the type of food to feed your dog, it is important to check out the label for ingredients. Many dry-food products have soybean, corn or rice as the main ingredient. The main ingredient will be listed first on the label, with the rest of the ingredients following in descending order according to their proportion in the food. While these types of dry food are fine, you should also look into dry foods based on meat or fish. These are better-quality foods and thus higher priced. However, they may be just as economical in the long run, because studies have shown that it takes less of the higher-quality foods to maintain a dog.

Comparing the various types of food, dry, canned and semi-moist, dry foods contain the least amount of water and canned foods the most. Proportionately, dry foods are the most calorie- and nutrient-dense, which means that you need more of a canned food product to supply the same amount of nutrition. In households with breeds of disparate size, the canned/dry/semi-moist question can be of special importance. Larger breeds obviously eat more than smaller ones and thus in general do better on dry foods, but smaller breeds do fine on canned foods and "small bite" formulations to protect their small mouths and teeth if fed only dry foods. So if you have breeds of different sizes in your household, consider both your own preferences and what your dogs like to eat, but remember

Water is essential for adults and pups alike. During house-training, you should pay attention to when your pup eats and drinks so you will know when he needs to relieve himself.

that dietary requirements are different for the different-sized dogs. You may find success mixing the food types as well. Water is important for all dogs, but even more so for those fed dry foods, as there is not a high water content in their food.

There are strict controls that regulate the nutritional content of dog food, and a food has to meet the minimum requirements in order to be considered "complete and balanced." It is important that you choose such a food for your dog, so check the label to be sure that your chosen food meets the requirements. If not, look for a food that clearly states on the label that it is formulated to be complete and balanced for your dog's particular stage of life.

Recommendations for amounts to feed will also be indicated on the label. You should also ask your vet about proper food portions, and you will keep an eye on your dog's condition to see whether the recommended amounts are adequate. If he becomes over- or underweight, you will need to make adjustments; this also would be a good time to consult your vet.

The food label may also make feeding suggestions, such as whether moistening a dry-food product is recommended. Sometimes a splash of water will make the food easier for a small dog to handle and more palatable for the dog, and even enhance the

Bowls of clean fresh water, both indoors and out, should be available for your Schipperke.

flavor. Don't be overwhelmed by the many factors that go into feeding your dog. Manufacturers of complete and balanced foods make it easy, and once you find the right food and amounts for your Schipperke, his daily feeding will be a matter of routine.

DON'T FORGET THE WATER!

For a dog, it's always time for a drink! Regardless of what type of food he eats, there's no doubt that he needs plenty of water. Fresh cold water, in a clean bowl, should be freely available to your dog at all times. There are special circumstances, such as during puppy housebreaking, when you will want to monitor your pup's water intake so that you will be able to predict when he will need to relieve himself, but water must be available to him nonetheless. Water is essential for hydration and proper body function just as it is in humans.

You will get to know how

much your dog typically drinks in a day. Of course, in the heat or if exercising vigorously, he will be more thirsty and will drink more. However, if he begins to drink noticeably more water for no apparent reason, this could signal any of various problems, and you are advised to consult your vet.

Water is the best drink for dogs. Some owners are tempted to give milk from time to time or to moisten dry food with milk, but dogs do not have the enzymes necessary to digest the lactose in milk, which is much different from the milk that nursing puppies receive. Therefore, stick with clean fresh water to quench your dog's thirst, and always have it readily available to him.

EXERCISE

We all know the importance of exercise for humans, so it should come as no surprise that it is essential for our canine friends as well. Now, regardless of your own level of fitness, get ready to assume the role of personal trainer for your dog. It's not as hard as it sounds, and it will have health benefits for you, too.

Just as with anything else you do with your dog, you must set a routine for his exercise. It's the same as your daily morning run before work or never missing the 7 p.m. aerobics class. If you plan it and get into the habit of actually doing it, it will become just

LET THE SUN SHINE
Your dog needs daily sunshine for the same reason people do. Pets kept inside homes with curtains drawn against the sun suffer from "SAD" (Seasonal Affected Disorder) to the same degree as humans. We now know that sunlight must enter the iris and thus progress to the pineal gland to regulate the body's hormonal system. When we live and work in artificial light, both circadian rhythms and hormone balances are disturbed.

another part of your day. Think of it as making daily exercise appointments with your dog, and stick to your schedule.

As a rule, dogs in normal health should have at least a half-hour of activity each day. Dogs with health or orthopedic problems may have specific limitations, so their exercise plans are best devised with

WATER DOGS

Whether a water dog or lap dog by trade, your dog may enjoy aquatic activity. Maybe your dog is not an Olympic swimmer, but he may like to wade in shallow water or even run through hoses and sprinklers in warm weather. Some owners provide kiddie pools in the summer in which their dogs can splash around. Give swimming a try if a clean safe lake or river is nearby. Introduce him to the water slowly, with you by his side, and don't force the issue if he doesn't seem to enjoy it—not every dog will. If your dog takes to water, try to work swimming into his exercise plan, as it provides excellent low-stress exercise.

the help of a vet. For healthy dogs, there are many ways to fit 30 minutes of activity into your day. Depending on your schedule, you may plan a 15-minute walk or activity session in the morning and again in the evening, or do it all at once in a half-hour session each day. Walking is the most popular way to exercise a dog (it's good for you, too!); other suggestions include retrieving games, jogging and disc-catching or other active games with his toys. If you have a safe body of water nearby and a dog that likes to swim, swimming is an excellent form of exercise for dogs, putting no stress on his frame.

On that note, some precautions should be taken with a puppy's exercise. During his first year, when he is growing and developing, your Schipperke should not be subject to vigorous activity that stresses his body. Short walks at a comfortable pace and play sessions in the yard are good for a growing pup, and his exercise can be increased as he grows up.

For overweight dogs, dietary changes and activity will help the goal of weight loss. (Sound familiar?) While they should of course be encouraged to be active, remember not to overdo it, as the excess weight is already putting strain on his vital organs and bones. As for highly active dogs, some of them never seem to tire! They will enjoy time spent with their owners doing things together.

Regardless of your dog's condition and activity level, exercise offers benefits to all dogs and owners. Consider the fact that dogs who are kept active are more stimulated both physically and mentally, meaning that they are less likely to become bored and lapse into destructive behavior. Also consider the benefits of one-on-one time with your dog every day, continually strengthening the bond between the two of you. Furthermore, exercising together will improve health and longevity for both of you. You both need exercise, and now you and your dog have a workout partner and motivator!

GROOMING THE SCHIPPERKE

MAINTAINING THE COAT

Schipperkes are double-coated. The outer coat is of medium length on the body and longer around the neck (the ruff), behind the shoulders (the cape), on the forechest (the jabot or apron) and on the rear of the thighs, where the points of the hair turn inwards (the culottes or breeches). This creates the Schip's unique silhouette, which is an essential breed characteristic. The undercoat is shorter than the outer coat and very dense. It assists as a support for the outer coat and its density causes the nice stand-off of the ruff around the neck. Such a splendid jacket should be kept in optimal condition, which can be done by regular grooming.

Grooming the coat of your Schipperke is a simple chore. It should be a pleasant task, not only to make your dog look beautiful but also to keep the coat and the skin healthy and your house free of dog

Your breeder can advise you about the grooming tools you will need for your Schip. Purchase quality equipment that will withstand frequent use.

hair. Grooming can be done from puppyhood onwards on a bench, a desk or a grooming table. However, never leave your Schipperke puppy unattended on the grooming surface, as in his inexperience he may decide to jump off and could injure himself.

Elaborate grooming sessions are not necessary. A simple grooming routine, at least weekly, though much better daily, is adequate. Such grooming once a day is advised during the periodic shedding or molting season. These periodic shedding processes occur as a rule twice a year, but some Schips will shed once a year.

Grooming stimulates the blood circulation of your dog and guarantees a good coat condition, but it will also be beneficial for your dog's character because it is a part of standard obedience and it teaches your dog to submit to your

Your Schipperke requires only a good daily brushing to look his best. If you begin grooming during puppyhood, the procedure should be pleasant for both of you.

authority and accept your leadership. Grooming is comforting to most dogs. However, some dominant dogs may resent it. Therefore, you should introduce the grooming routine as soon as you acquire your new pup.

Grooming a Schipperke means simple combing or brushing. A metal comb with a handle can be used to remove loose hairs and to untangle any mats or knots. You have to be careful, however, to avoid damaging or irritating the skin. The tangled hairs should not be broken or pulled out. For this reason, the teeth of the comb should be sufficiently spaced, and you have to make sure that the teeth are smooth and round at the points.

The Schip's handsome double coat, which creates the breed's distinctive silhouette, is relatively easy to keep in optimal condition.

To rid the coat of dead hair, a slicker or a bristle brush can also be used instead of a comb. A brush is used by most Schipperke owners to groom their dogs. Use a soft-bristled brush on the very young puppy. An older pup or an adult dog can be brushed with a medium-hard brush that has stiffer bristles.

To remove both dead hair and dirt, you have to brush against the lay of the hair, starting at the rear and continuing to the front. Thorough brushing is necessary on the rear of the thighs, the back and around the neck and chest. However, before brushing, you can also, without hurting the dog, carefully pick out tangles of the hair with your fingers. After having brushed "against" the lay of the coat, you can finish by brushing "with" the lay of the coat. The finishing touch of your grooming session should be the "fluffing" of the ruff and the apron, which is done by brushing forward, around the neck and on the forechest, thus against the lay of the coat.

Grooming your Schipperke for the show ring is not really different than basic grooming for the home. If you intend to show your dog, you have to learn about handling your dog in the show ring and you are advised to study the standard of the breed. The sum of the qualities that distinguish one breed from another is called "type." Standards describe the ideal type, which is greatly determined by the general outline or silhouette of a dog. The silhouette of a Schipperke is an extremely important characteristic, which should be in accordance with the

Proper grooming can only be accomplished with the correct tools handled in the proper manner. The slicker brush works nicely on the adult Schipperke's coat.

description of the ideal dog set forth in the breed standard. It is evident now that by proper show grooming, which requires thorough breed knowledge, a silhouette can be made more characteristic (or more "typical"). However, we must emphasize that exhibitors as well as judges have to realize that in Belgium the Schipperke is considered a natural breed that doesn't need to be prepared for showing with excessive grooming. The so-called "coat conditioners" especially seem suspicious.

WATER SHORTAGE

No matter how well-behaved your dog is, bathing is always a project! Nothing can substitute for a good warm bath, but owners do have the option of giving their dogs "dry" baths. Pet shops sell excellent products, in both powder and spray forms, designed for spot-cleaning your dog. These dry shampoos are convenient for touch-up jobs when you don't have the time to bathe your dog in the traditional way.

Muddy feet, messy behinds and smelly coats can be spot-cleaned and deodorized with a "wet-nap"-style cleaner. On those days when your dog insists on rolling in fresh goose droppings and there's no time for a bath, a spot bath can save the day. These pre-moistened wipes are also handy for other grooming needs like wiping faces, ears and eyes and freshening tails and behinds.

Nevertheless, it cannot be denied that a Schipperke shown in the ring should be presented in a clean and well-groomed condition, but over-grooming to the point of altering the natural appearance should be avoided.

Shaping with scissors should not be done. Foreign grooming substances or cosmetics such as hairsprays and lacquers should not be used to let the coat stand out from the body. Using substances to change the natural color of the coat is pure faking.

Your Schipperke will show you how much he appreciates your attention to keeping him clean, healthy and looking his best.

BATHING

Because your Schipperke has a hard outer coat that repels dirt and is free of doggy odor, you should not bathe your dog more than is necessary. You may never even have to give a bath to a Schipperke that is properly, regularly and thoroughly brushed. A bath is only needed when your Schipperke has become soiled with dirt or foreign substances not easily removed by brushing. Remember that soap removes the natural oil from the hair and skin and may be irritating to the dog. Only a gentle soap or shampoo that is formulated especially for dogs should be used, and thorough rinsing is necessary.

There may come a time when your Schip needs a bath, so you want these times to go as smoothly as possible. If you give your dog his first bath when he is young, he will become accustomed to the process. Wrestling a dog into the tub or chasing a freshly shampooed dog who has escaped from the bath will be no fun! Most dogs don't naturally enjoy their baths, but you at least want yours to cooperate with you.

Before bathing the dog, have the items you'll need close at hand. First, decide where you will bathe the dog. You should have a tub or basin with a non-slip surface. Small dogs like your Schipperke can even be bathed in a sink. In warm weather, some like to use a portable pool in the yard, although you'll want to make sure your dog doesn't head for the nearest dirt pile following his bath! You will also need a hose or shower spray to wet the coat thoroughly, a shampoo formulated for dogs, absorbent towels and perhaps a blow dryer.

Remember to use only a gentle-formula canine shampoo, as human shampoos are too harsh for dogs' coats and will dry them out.

Before wetting the dog, give him a brush-through to remove any dead hair, dirt and mats. Make sure he is at ease in the tub and have the water at a comfortable temperature. Begin bathing by wetting the coat all the way down to the skin. Massage in the shampoo, keeping it away from his face and eyes. Rinse him thoroughly, again avoiding the eyes and ears, as you don't want to get water into the ear canals. A thorough rinsing is important, as any shampoo residue left in the coat is drying and itchy to the dog. After rinsing, wrap him in a towel to absorb the initial moisture. You can finish drying with either a towel or a blow dryer on low heat, held at a safe distance from the dog. You should keep the dog indoors and away from drafts until he is completely dry.

NAIL CLIPPING

Having their nails trimmed is not on many dogs' lists of favorite things to do. With this in mind, you will need to accustom your puppy to the procedure at a young age so that he will sit still (well, as still as he can) for his pedicures. Long nails can cause the dog's feet to spread, which is not good for him; likewise, long nails can hurt if they unintentionally scratch, not good for you!

Dogs that exercise regularly on hard pavement will wear their nails down naturally and require clipping less often than dogs that spend time only on grass or indoors.

Some dogs' nails are worn down naturally by regular walking on hard surfaces, so the frequency with which you clip depends on your individual dog. Look at his nails from time to time and clip as needed; a good way to know when it's time for a trim is if you hear your dog clicking as he walks across the floor.

There are several types of nail clippers and even electric nail-grinding tools made for dogs; first we'll discuss using the clipper. To start, have your clipper ready and some doggie treats on hand. You want your pup to view his nail-clipping sessions in a positive light, and what better way to convince him than with food? You may want to enlist the help of an assistant to comfort the pup and offer treats as you concentrate on the clipping itself. The guillotine-type clipper is thought of by many as the easiest type to use; the nail tip is inserted into the opening, and blades on the top and bottom snip it off in one clip.

Start by grasping the pup's paw; a little pressure on the foot pad causes the nail to extend, making it easier to clip. Clip off a little at a time. If you can see the "quick," which is a blood vessel that runs through each nail, you will know how much to trim, as you do not want to cut into the quick. On that note, if you do cut the quick, which will cause bleeding, you can stem the flow of blood with a styptic pencil or other clotting agent. If you mistakenly nip the quick, do not panic or fuss, as this will cause the pup to be afraid. Simply reassure the pup, stop the bleeding and move on to the next nail. Don't be discouraged; you will become a professional canine pedicurist with practice.

You may or may not be able to see the quick, so it's best to just clip off a small bit at a time. If you see a dark dot in the center of the nail, this is the quick and your cue to stop clipping. Tell the puppy he's a "good boy" and offer a piece of treat with each nail. You can also use nail-clipping time to examine the footpads, making sure that they are not dry and cracked and that nothing has become embedded in them.

The nail grinder, the other option, is many owners' first choice. Accustoming the puppy to the sound of the grinder and sensation of the buzz presents fewer challenges than the clipper, and there's no chance of cutting through the quick. You will,

> **SCOOTING HIS BOTTOM**
> Here's a doggy problem that many owners tend to neglect. If your dog is scooting his rear end around the carpet, he probably is experiencing anal-sac impaction or blockage. The anal sacs are the two grape-sized glands on either side of the dog's vent. The dog cannot empty these glands, which become filled with a foul-smelling material. The dog may attempt to lick the area to relieve the pressure. He may also rub his anus on your walls, furniture or floors.
>
> Don't neglect your dog's rear end during grooming sessions. By squeezing both sides of the anus with a soft cloth, you can express some of the material in the sacs. If the material is pasty and thick, you likely will need the assistance of a veterinarian. Vets know how to express the glands and can show you how to do it correctly without hurting the dog or spraying yourself with the unpleasant liquid.

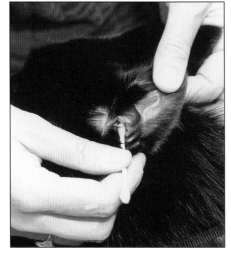

It is better to wipe your dog's ears clean with cotton balls than to probe them with a cotton swab, shown here, which could harm the inner ear.

however, need to be careful that none of the dog's coat gets caught in the grinder. Use the grinder on a low setting and always talk soothingly to your dog. He won't mind his salon visit, and he'll have nicely polished nails as well.

Ear Cleaning

While keeping your dog's ears clean unfortunately will not cause him to "hear" your commands any better, it will protect him from ear infection and ear-mite infestation. In addition, a dog's ears are vulnerable to waxy build-up and to collecting foreign matter from the outdoors. Look in your dog's ears regularly to ensure that they look pink, clean and otherwise healthy. Even if they look fine, an odor in the ears signals a problem and means it's time to call the vet.

A dog's ears should be cleaned regularly; once a week is suggested, and you can do this along with your regular brushing. Using a cotton ball or pad, and never probing into the ear canal, wipe the ear gently. You can use an ear-cleansing liquid or powder available from your vet or pet-supply store; alternatively, you might prefer to use home-made solutions with ingredients like one part white vinegar and one part hydrogen peroxide. Ask your vet about home remedies before you attempt to concoct something on your own!

Keep your dog's ears free of excess hair by plucking it as needed. If done gently, this will be painless for the dog. Look for wax, brown droppings (a sign of ear mites), redness or any other abnormalities. At the first sign of a problem, contact your vet so that he can prescribe an appropriate medication.

EYE CARE

During grooming sessions, pay extra attention to the condition of

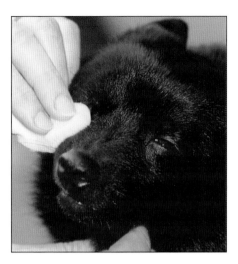

You can clean around the Schipperke's eyes with a soft cotton wipe to remove any debris that may accumulate there.

your dog's eyes. If the area around the eyes is soiled or if tear staining has occurred, there are various cleaning agents made especially for this purpose. Look at the dog's eyes to make sure no debris has entered; dogs with large eyes and those who spend time outdoors are especially prone to this.

The signs of an eye infection are obvious: mucus, redness, puffiness, scabs or other signs of irritation. If your dog's eyes become infected, the vet will likely prescribe an antibiotic ointment for treatment. If you notice signs of more serious problems, such as opacities in the eye, which usually indicate cataracts, consult the vet at once. Taking time to pay attention to your dog's eyes will alert you in the early stages of any problem so that you can get your dog treatment as soon as possible. You could save your dog's sight!

IDENTIFICATION AND TRAVEL

ID FOR YOUR DOG

You love your Schipperke and want to keep him safe. Of course, you take every precaution to prevent his escaping from the yard or becoming lost or stolen. You have a sturdy high fence and you always keep your dog on-lead when out and about in public places. If your dog is not properly identified, however, you are overlooking a major aspect of his safety. We hope to never be in a situation where our dog is missing, but we should practice prevention in the unfortunate case that this happens; identification greatly increases the chances of your dog's being returned to you.

Your Schipperke should travel in his crate whenever he accompanies you in the car rather than being left loose to roam about the vehicle.

There are several ways to identify your dog. First, the traditional dog tag should be a staple in your dog's wardrobe, attached to his everyday collar. Tags can be made of sturdy plastic and various metals and should include your contact information so that a person who finds the dog can get in touch with you right away to arrange his return. Many people today enjoy the wide range of decorative tags available, so have fun and create a tag to match your dog's personality. Of course, it is important that the tag stays on the collar, so have a secure "O" ring attachment; you also can explore the type of tag that slides right onto the collar.

In addition to the ID tag, which every dog should wear even if identified by another method, two other forms of identi-fication have become popular: microchipping and tattooing. In microchipping, a tiny scannable chip is painlessly inserted under the dog's skin. The number is registered to you so that, if your lost dog turns up at a clinic or shelter, the chip can be scanned to retrieve your contact information.

The advantage of the microchip is that it is a permanent form of ID, but there are some factors to consider. Several different companies make microchips, and not all are compatible with the others' scanning devices. It's best to find a company with a universal

microchip that can be read by scanners made by other companies as well. It won't do any good to have the dog chipped if the information cannot be retrieved. Also, not every humane society, shelter and clinic is equipped with a scanner, although more and more facilities are equipping themselves. In fact, many shelters microchip dogs that they adopt out to new homes.

Because the microchip is not visible to the eye, the dog must wear a tag that states that he is microchipped so that whoever picks him up will know to have him scanned. He of course also should have a tag with contact information in case his chip cannot be read. Humane societies and veterinary clinics offer microchipping service, which is usually very affordable.

Though less popular than

Your Schipperke must always wear his identification tag, which should be securely attached to his collar and contain your current contact information.

microchipping, tattooing is another permanent method of ID for dogs. Most vets perform this service, and there are also clinics that perform dog tattooing. This is also an afford-able procedure and one that will not cause much discomfort for the dog. It is best to put the tattoo in a visible area, such as the ear, to deter theft. It is sad to say that there are cases of dogs' being stolen and sold to research laboratories, but such laboratories will not accept tattooed dogs.

To ensure that the tattoo is effective in aiding your dog's return to you, the tattoo number must be registered with a national organiza-tion. That way, when someone finds a tattooed dog, a phone call to the registry will quickly match the dog with his owner.

HIT THE ROAD
Car travel with your Schipperke may be limited to necessity only, such as trips to the vet, or you may

PET OR STRAY?
Besides the obvious benefit of providing your contact information to whoever finds your lost dog, an ID tag makes your dog more approachable and more likely to be recovered. A strange dog wandering the neighborhood without a collar and tags will look like a stray, while the collar and tags indicate that the dog is someone's pet. Even if the ID tags become detached from the collar, the collar alone will make a person more likely to pick up the dog.

bring your dog along almost everywhere you go. This will depend much on your individual dog and how he reacts to rides in the car. You can begin desensitizing your dog to car travel as a pup so that it's something that he's used to. Still, some dogs suffer from motion sickness. Your vet may prescribe a medication for this if trips in the car pose a problem for your dog. At the very least, you will need to get him to the vet, so he will need to tolerate these trips with the least amount of hassle possible.

Start taking your pup on short trips, maybe just around the block to start. If he is fine with short trips, lengthen your rides a little at a time. Start to take him on your errands or just for drives around town. By this time it will be easy to tell whether your dog is a born traveler or would prefer staying at home when you are on the road. Fortunately for Schip owners, these little dogs usually love to travel

A trip to the country might just bring out the "little shepherd" in your Schip, although you'll want to keep a close eye on him around the barnyard animals.

and accompany their owners as often as possible.

Of course, safety is a concern for dogs in the car. First, he must travel securely, not left loose to roam about the car where he could be injured or distract the driver. A young pup can be held by a passenger initially but should soon graduate to a travel crate, which can be the same crate he uses in the home. Other options include a car harness (like a seat belt for dogs) and partitioning the back of the car with a gate made for this purpose.

Bring along what you will need for the dog. He should wear his collar and ID tags, of course, and you should bring his leash, water (and food if a long trip) and clean-up materials for potty breaks and in case of motion sickness. Always keep your dog on his leash when you make stops, and never leave him alone in the car. Many a dog has died from the heat inside a closed car; this does not take much time at all in any kind of weather. A dog left alone inside a car can also be a target for thieves.

BOARDING

Today there are many options for dog owners who need someone to care for their dogs in certain circumstances. While many think of boarding their dogs as something to do when away on vacation, many others use the services of doggie "daycare" facilities,

DOGGONE!

Wendy Ballard is the editor and publisher of the *DogGone* ™ newsletter, which comes out bi-monthly and features fun articles by dog owners who love to travel with their dogs. The newsletter includes information about fun places to go with your dogs, including popular vacation spots, dog-friendly hotels, parks, campgrounds, resorts, etc., as well as interesting activities to do with your dog, such as flyball, agility and much more. You can subscribe to the publication by contacting the publisher at PO Box 651155, Vero Beach, FL 32965-1155.

where you think your dog will be happy. It is best to do your research in advance so that you're not stuck at the last minute, forced into making a rushed decision without knowing whether the kennel that you've chosen meets your standards. You also can check with your vet's office to see whether they offer boarding for their clients or can recommend a good kennel in the area.

The kennel will need to see proof of your dog's health records and vaccinations so as not to spread illness from dog to dog. Your dog also will need proper identification. Owners usually experience some separation anxiety the first time they have to leave their dog in someone else's care, so it's reassuring to know that the kennel you choose is run by experienced, caring, true dog people.

dropping their dogs off to spend the day while they are at work. Many of these facilities offer both long-term and daily care. Many go beyond just boarding and cater to all sorts of needs, with on-site grooming, veterinary care, training classes and even "web-cams" where owners can log onto the Internet and check out what their dogs are up to. Most dogs enjoy the activity and time spent with other dogs.

Before you need to use such a service, check out the ones in your area. Make visits to see the facilities, meet the staff, discuss fees and available services and see whether this is a place

Do your research ahead of time if you need to board your dog. You want to be totally comfortable with the facility you choose.

BASIC TRAINING PRINCIPLES: PUPPY VS. ADULT

There's a big difference between training an adult dog and training a young puppy. With a young puppy, everything is new. At eight weeks of age, he will be experiencing many things, and he has nothing with which to compare these experiences. Up to this point, he has been with his dam and littermates, not one-on-one with people except in his interactions with his breeder and visitors to the litter.

When you first bring the puppy home, he is eager to please you. This means that he accepts doing things your way. During the next couple of months, he will absorb the basis of everything he needs to know for the rest of his

A puppy starts out life as a clean slate—no bad habits! It's up to you to mold his behavior and nurture a well-mannered canine citizen.

life. This early age is even referred to as the "sponge" stage. After that, for the next 18 months, it's up to you to reinforce good manners by building on the foundation that you've established. Once your puppy is reliable in basic commands and behavior and has reached the appropriate age, you may gradually introduce him to some of the interesting sports, games and activities available to pet owners and their dogs.

Raising your puppy is a family affair. Each member of the family must know what rules to set forth for the puppy and how to use the same one-word commands to mean exactly the same thing every time. Even if yours is a large family, one person will soon be considered by the pup to be the leader, the Alpha person in his pack, the "boss" who must be obeyed. Often that highly regarded person turns out to be the one who feeds the puppy. Food ranks very high on the puppy's list of important things! That's why your puppy is rewarded with small treats along with verbal praise when he responds to you correctly. As the puppy learns to do what you want him to do, the food rewards are gradually eliminated and only the praise remains. If you were to keep up with the food treats, you could have two problems on your hands—an obese dog and a beggar.

Training begins the minute your Schipperke puppy steps through the doorway of your home, so don't make the mistake of putting the puppy on the floor and telling him by your actions to "Go for it! Run wild!" Even if this is your first puppy, you must act as if you know what you're doing: be the boss. An uncertain pup may be terrified to move, while a bold one will be ready to take you at your word and start plotting to destroy the house! Before you collected your puppy, you decided where his own special

Training forms the basis of a rewarding and fulfilling relationship with your four-legged family member.

place would be, and that's where to put him when you first arrive home. Give him a house tour after he has investigated his area and had a nap and a bathroom "pit stop."

It's worth mentioning here that if you've adopted an adult dog that is completely trained to your liking, lucky you! You're off the hook! However, if that dog spent his life up to this point in a kennel, or even in a good home but without any real training, be prepared to tackle the job ahead. A dog three years of age or older with no previous training cannot be blamed for not knowing what he was never taught. While the dog is trying to understand and learn your rules, at the same time he has to unlearn many of his previously self-taught habits and general view of the world.

BASIC PRINCIPLES OF DOG TRAINING

1. Start training early. A young puppy is ready, willing and able.
2. Timing is your all-important tool. Praise at the exact time that the dog responds correctly. Pay close attention.
3. Patience is almost as important as timing!
4. Repeat! The same word has to mean the same thing every time.
5. In the beginning, praise all correct behavior verbally, along with treats and petting.

MEALTIME

Mealtime should be a peaceful time for your Schipperke. Do not put his food and water bowls in a high-traffic area in the house. For example, give him his own little corner of the kitchen where he can eat undisturbed and where he will not be underfoot. Do not allow small children or other family members to disturb the dog when he is eating.

Working with a professional trainer will speed up your progress with an adopted adult dog. You'll need patience, too. Some new rules may be close to impossible for the dog to accept. After all, he's been successful so far by doing everything his way! (Patience again.) He may agree with your instruction for a few days and then slip back into his old ways, so you must be just as consistent and understanding in your teaching as you would be with a puppy. (More patience needed yet again!) Your dog has to learn to pay attention to your voice, your family, the daily routine, new smells, new sounds and, in some cases, even a new climate.

One of the most important things to find out about a newly adopted adult dog is his reaction to children (yours and others), strangers and your friends, and how he acts upon meeting other dogs. If he was not socialized with dogs as a puppy, this could be a major problem. This does not mean that he's a "bad" dog, a vicious dog or an aggressive dog; rather, it means that he has no idea how to read another dog's body language. There's no way for him to tell whether the other dog is a friend or foe. Survival instinct takes over, telling him to attack first and ask questions later. This definitely calls for professional help and, even then, may not be a behavior that can be corrected 100% reliably (or even at all). If you have a puppy, this is why it is so very important to introduce your young puppy properly to other puppies and "dog-friendly" adult dogs.

HOUSE-TRAINING YOUR SCHIPPERKE

Dogs are tactility-oriented when it comes to house-training. In other words, they respond to the surface on which they are given approval

BE UPSTANDING!
You are the dog's leader. During training, stand up straight so your dog looks up at you, and therefore up *to* you. Say the command words distinctly, in a clear, declarative tone of voice. (No barking!) Give rewards only as the correct response takes place (remember your timing!). Praise, smiles and treats are "rewards" used to positively reinforce correct responses. Don't repeat a mistake. Just change to another exercise—you will soon find success!

around the house. You are training him to go outside, remember? Starting out by paper-training often is the only choice for a city dog.

WHEN YOUR PUPPY'S "GOT TO GO"
Your puppy's need to relieve himself is seemingly non-stop, but signs of improvement will be seen each week. From 8 to 10 weeks

When you see your Schip jump for joy over a treat, you'll understand why food rewards are so effective in training.

to eliminate. The choice is yours (the dog's version is in parentheses): The lawn (including the neighbors' lawns)? A bare patch of earth under a tree (where people like to sit and relax in the summertime)? Concrete steps or patio (all sidewalks, garages and basement floors)? The curbside (watch out for cars)? A small area of crushed stone in a corner of the yard (mine!)? The latter is the best choice if you can manage it because it will remain strictly for the dog's use and is easy to keep clean.

You can start out with paper-training indoors and switch over to an outdoor surface as the puppy matures and gains control over his need to eliminate. For the nay-sayers, don't worry—this won't mean that the dog will soil on every piece of newspaper lying old, the puppy will have to be taken outside every time he wakes up, about 10–15 minutes after every meal and after every period of play—all day long, from first thing in the morning until his bedtime! That's a total of ten or more trips per day to teach the puppy where it's okay to relieve himself. With that schedule in mind, you can see that house-training a young puppy is not a part-time job. It requires someone to be home all day.

If that seems overwhelming or impossible, do a little planning. For example, plan to pick up your

puppy at the start of a vacation period. If you can't get home in the middle of the day, plan to hire a dog-sitter or ask a neighbor to come over to take the pup outside, feed him his lunch and then take him out again about ten or so minutes after he's eaten. Also make arrangements with that or another person to be your "emergency" contact if you have to stay late on the job. Remind yourself—repeatedly—that this hectic schedule improves as the puppy gets older.

HOME WITHIN A HOME

Your Schipperke puppy needs to be confined to one secure, puppy-proof area when no one is able to watch his every move. Generally the kitchen is the place of choice

A sturdy ex-pen can be set up in the yard or taken along when traveling to temporarily provide a secure area for your Schipperke.

CANINE DEVELOPMENT SCHEDULE

It is important to understand how and at what age a puppy develops into adulthood. If you are a puppy owner, consult this Canine Development Schedule to determine the stage of development your puppy is currently experiencing. This knowledge will help you as you work with the puppy in the weeks and months ahead.

PERIOD	AGE	CHARACTERISTICS
FIRST TO THIRD	BIRTH TO SEVEN WEEKS	Puppy needs food, sleep and warmth and responds to simple and gentle touching. Needs mother for security and disciplining. Needs littermates for learning and interacting with other dogs. Pup learns to function within a pack and learns pack order of dominance. Begin socializing pup with adults and children for short periods. Pup begins to become aware of his environment.
FOURTH	EIGHT TO TWELVE WEEKS	Brain is fully developed. Pup needs socializing with outside world. Remove from mother and littermates. Needs to change from canine pack to human pack. Human dominance necessary. Fear period occurs between 8 and 12 weeks. Avoid fright and pain.
FIFTH	THIRTEEN TO SIXTEEN WEEKS	Training and formal obedience should begin. Less association with other dogs, more with people, places, situations. Period will pass easily if you remember this is pup's change-to-adolescence time. Be firm and fair. Flight instinct prominent. Permissiveness and over-disciplining can do permanent damage. Praise for good behavior.
JUVENILE	FOUR TO EIGHT MONTHS	Another fear period about 7 to 8 months of age. It passes quickly, but be cautious of fright and pain. Sexual maturity reached. Dominant traits established. Dog should understand sit, down, come and stay by now.

NOTE: THESE ARE APPROXIMATE TIME FRAMES. ALLOW FOR INDIVIDUAL DIFFERENCES IN PUPPIES.

EXTRA! EXTRA!
The headlines read: "Puppy Piddles Here!" Breeders commonly use newspapers to line their whelping pens, so puppies learn to associate newspapers with relieving themselves. Do not use newspapers to line your pup's crate, as this will signal to your puppy that it is OK to urinate in his crate. If you choose to paper-train your puppy, you will layer newspapers on a section of the floor near the door he uses to go outside. You should encourage the puppy to use the papers to relieve himself, and bring him there whenever you see him getting ready to go. Little by little, you will reduce the size of the newspaper-covered area so that the puppy will learn to relieve himself "on the other side of the door."

because the floor is washable. Likewise, it's a busy family area that will accustom the pup to a variety of noises, everything from pots and pans to the telephone, blender and dishwasher. He will also be enchanted by the smell of your cooking (and will never be critical when you burn something). An exercise pen (also called an "ex-pen," a puppy version of a playpen) within the room of choice is an excellent means of confinement for a young pup. He can see out and has a certain amount of space in which to run about, but he is safe from dangerous things like electrical cords, heating units, trash baskets or open kitchen-supply cabinets. Place the pen where the puppy will not get a blast of heat or air conditioning.

In the pen, you can put a few toys, his bed (which can be his crate if the dimensions of pen and crate are compatible) and a few layers of newspaper in one small corner, just in case. A water bowl can be hung at a convenient height on the side of the ex-pen so it won't become a splashing pool for an innovative puppy. His food dish can go on the floor, next to but not under the water bowl.

Crates are something that pet owners are at last getting used to for their dogs. Wild or domestic canines have always preferred to sleep in den-like safe spots, and that is exactly what the crate provides. How often have you seen adult dogs that choose to sleep under a table or chair even though they have full run of the house? It's the den connection.

In your "happy" voice, use the word "Crate" every time you put the pup into his den. If he's new to a crate, toss in a small biscuit for him to chase the first few times. At night, after he's been outside, he should sleep in his crate. The crate may be kept in his designated area at night or, if you want to be sure to hear those wake-up yips in the morning, put the crate in a corner of your bedroom. However, don't make any response whatsoever to whining or crying. If he's completely ignored, he'll settle down and get to sleep.

Good bedding for a young puppy is an old folded bath towel or an old blanket, something that is easily washable and disposable if necessary ("accidents" will happen!). Never put newspaper in the puppy's crate. Also, those old ideas about adding a clock to replace his mother's heartbeat, or a hot-water bottle to replace her warmth, are just that—old ideas. The clock could drive the puppy nuts, and the hot-water bottle could end up as a very soggy waterbed! An extremely good breeder would have introduced your puppy to the crate by letting two pups sleep together for a couple of nights, followed by several nights alone. How thankful you will be if you found that breeder!

Safe toys in the pup's crate or area will keep him occupied, but monitor their condition closely. Discard any toys that show signs of being chewed to bits. Squeaky parts, bits of stuffing or plastic or any other small pieces can cause intestinal blockage or possibly choking if swallowed.

PROGRESSING WITH POTTY-TRAINING

After you've taken your puppy out and he has relieved himself in the area you've selected, he can have some free time with the

SOMEBODY TO BLAME
House-training a puppy can be frustrating for the puppy and the owner alike. The puppy does not instinctively understand the difference between defecating on the pavement outside and on the ceramic tile in the kitchen. He is confused and frightened by his human's exuberant reactions to his natural urges. The owner, arguably the more intelligent of the duo, is also frustrated that he cannot convince his puppy to obey his commands and instructions.

In frustration, the owner may struggle with the temptation to discipline the puppy, scold him or even strike him on the rear end. Harsh corrections are unnecessary and inappropriate, serving to defeat your purpose in gaining your puppy's trust and respect. Don't blame your nine-week-old puppy; blame yourself for not being 100% consistent in the puppy's lessons and routine. The lesson here is simple: try harder and your puppy will succeed.

LEASH TRAINING

House-training and leash training go hand in hand, literally. When taking your puppy outside to do his business, lead him there on his leash. Unless an emergency potty run is called for, do not whisk the puppy up into your arms and take him outside. If you have a fenced yard, you have the advantage of letting the puppy loose to go out, but it's better to put the dog on the leash and take him to his designated place in the yard until he is reliably house-trained. Taking the puppy for a walk is the best way to house-train a dog. The dog will associate the walk with his time to relieve himself, and the exercise of walking stimulates the dog's bowels and bladder. Dogs that are not trained to relieve themselves on a walk may hold it until they get back home, which of course defeats half the purpose of the walk.

family as long as there is someone responsible for watching him. That doesn't mean just someone in the same room who is watching TV or busy on the computer, but one person who is doing nothing other than keeping an eye on the pup, playing with him on the floor and helping him understand his position in the pack.

This first taste of freedom will let you begin to set the house rules. If you don't want the dog on the furniture, now is the time to prevent his first attempts to jump up onto the couch. The word to use in this case is "Off," not "Down." "Down" is the word you will use to teach the down position, which is something entirely different.

Most corrections at this stage come in the form of simply distracting the puppy. Instead of telling him "No" for "Don't chew the carpet," distract the chomping puppy with a toy and he'll forget about the carpet.

As you are playing with the pup, do not forget to watch him closely and pay attention to his body language. Whenever you see him begin to circle or sniff, take the puppy outside to relieve himself. If you are paper-training, put him back into his confined area on the newspapers. In either case, praise him as he eliminates while he actually is in the act of relieving himself. Three seconds after he has finished is too late! You'll be praising him for running toward you, or picking up a toy or whatever he may be doing at that moment, and that's not what you want to be praising him for. Timing is a vital tool in all dog training. Use it.

Remove soiled newspapers immediately and replace them with clean ones. You may want to take a small piece of soiled paper and place it in the middle of the new clean papers, as the scent will attract him to that spot when it's time to go again. That scent attraction is why it's so important to clean up any messes made in the house by using a product specially made to eliminate the odor of dog urine and droppings. Regular household cleansers won't do the trick. Pet shops sell the best pet deodorizers. Invest in the largest container you can find.

Scent attraction eventually will lead your pup to his chosen spot outdoors; this is the basis of outdoor training. When you take your puppy outside to relieve himself, use a one-word command such as "Outside" or "Go-potty" (that's one word to the puppy!) as you pick him up and attach his leash. Then put him down in his area. If for any reason you can't carry him, snap the leash on quickly and lead him to his spot. Now comes the hard part—hard for you, that is. Just stand there until he urinates and defecates. Move him a few feet in one direction or another if he's just sitting there looking at you, but remember that this is neither playtime nor time for a walk—this is strictly a business trip! Then, as he circles and squats (remember your timing!), give him a quiet "Good dog" as praise. If you start to jump for joy, ecstatic over his performance, he'll do one of two things: either he will stop mid-stream, as it were, or he'll do it again for you—in the house—and expect you to be just as delighted!

Give him five minutes or so

An ex-pen for your Schipperke should have high enough sides to prevent an escape artist from climbing out.

and, if he doesn't go in that time, take him back indoors to his confined area and try again in another ten minutes, or immediately if you see him sniffing and circling. By careful observation, you'll soon work out a successful schedule.

Accidents, by the way, are just that—accidents. Clean them up quickly and thoroughly, without comment, after the puppy has been taken outside to finish his business and then put back into his area or crate. If you witness an accident in progress, say "No!" in a stern voice and get the pup outdoors immediately. No punishment is needed. You and your puppy are just learning each other's language, and sometimes it's easy to miss a puppy's message. Chalk it up to experience and watch more closely from now on.

KEEPING THE PACK ORDERLY

Discipline is a form of training that brings order to life. For example, military discipline is what allows the soldiers in an army to work as one. Discipline is a form of teaching and, in dogs, is the basis of how the successful pack operates. Each member knows his place in the pack and all respect the leader, or Alpha dog. It is essential for your puppy that you establish this type of relationship, with you as the Alpha, or leader. It is a form of social coexistence that all canines recognize and accept. Discipline, therefore, is never to be confused with punishment. When you teach your puppy how you want him to behave, and he behaves properly and you praise him for it, you are disciplining him with a form of positive reinforcement.

For a dog, rewards come in the form of praise, a smile, a cheerful tone of voice, a few friendly pats or a rub of the ears. Rewards are also small food treats. Obviously, that does not mean bits of regular dog food. Instead, treats are very small bits of special things like cheese or pieces of soft dog treats. The idea is to reward the dog with something very small that he can taste and swallow, providing instant positive reinforcement. If he has to take time to chew the treat, he will have forgotten what he did to earn it by the time he is finished!

Your puppy should never be physically punished. The displeasure shown on your face and in your voice is sufficient to signal to the pup that he has done something wrong. He wants to please everyone higher up on the social ladder, especially his leader, so a scowl and harsh voice will take care of the error. Growling out the word "Shame!" when the pup is caught in the act of doing something wrong is better than the repetitive "No." Some dogs hear "No" so often that they begin to think it's their name! By the way, do not use the dog's name when you're correcting him.

> **DON'T STRESS ME OUT**
> Your dog doesn't have to deal with paying the bills, the daily commute, PTA meetings and the like, but, believe it or not, there's a lot of stress in a dog's world. Stress can be caused by the owner's impatient demeanor and his angry or harsh corrections. If your dog cringes when you reach for his training collar, he's stressed. An older dog is sometimes stressed out when he goes to a new home. No matter what the cause, put off all training until he's over it. If he's going through a fear period—shying away from people, trembling when spoken to, avoiding eye contact or hiding under furniture—wait to resume training. Naturally you'd also postpone your lessons if the dog were sick, and the same goes for you. Show some compassion.

His name is reserved to get his attention for something pleasant about to take place.

There are punishments that have nothing to do with you. For example, your dog may think that chasing cats is one reason for his existence. You can try to stop it as much as you like but without success, because it's such fun for the dog. But one good hissing, spitting swipe of a cat's claws across the dog's nose will put an end to the game forever. Intervene only when your dog's eyeball is seriously at risk. Cat scratches can cause permanent damage to an innocent but annoying puppy.

PUPPY KINDERGARTEN

COLLAR AND LEASH
Before you begin your Schipperke puppy's education, he must be used to his collar and leash. Choose a collar for your puppy that is secure, but not heavy or bulky. He won't enjoy training if he's uncomfortable. A flat buckle collar is fine for everyday wear and for initial puppy training. Do not use a chain choke collar with your Schipperke, puppy or adult. If you need to use a training collar with an adult Schipperke, ask the advice of your breeder or a trainer. They may suggest a head collar rather than one that tightens around the neck.

A lightweight 6-foot woven cotton or nylon training leash is

> **CREATURES OF HABIT**
> Canine behaviorists and trainers aptly describe dogs as "creatures of habit," meaning that dogs respond to structure in their daily lives and welcome a routine. Do not interpret this to mean that dogs enjoy endless repetition in their training sessions. Dogs get bored just as humans do. Keep training sessions interesting and exciting. Vary the commands and the locations in which you practice. Give short breaks for play in between lessons. A bored student will never be the best performer in the class.

preferred by most trainers because it is easy to fold up in your hand and comfortable to hold because there is a certain amount of give to it. There are lessons where the dog will start off 6 feet away from you at the end of the leash. The leash used to take the puppy outside to relieve himself is shorter because you don't want him to roam away from his area. The shorter leash will also be the one to use when you walk the puppy.

If you've been wise enough to enroll in a puppy kindergarten training class, suggestions will be made as to the best collar and leash for your young puppy. I say "wise" because your puppy will be in a class with puppies in his age range (up to five months old) of all breeds and sizes. It's the perfect way for him to learn the right way (and the wrong way) to interact with other dogs as well as their people. You cannot teach your puppy how to interpret another dog's sign language. For a first-time puppy owner, these socialization classes are invaluable. For experienced dog owners, they are a real boon to further training.

ATTENTION

You've been using the dog's name since the minute you collected him from the breeder, so you should be able to get his attention by saying his name—with a big smile and in an excited tone of voice. His response will be the puppy equivalent of "Here I am! What are we going to do?" Your immediate response (if you haven't guessed by now) is "Good dog." Rewarding him at the

A little scolding may be necessary now and then, but the majority of your training must be based on positive methods.

> **TIPS FOR TRAINING AND SAFETY**
> 1. Whether on- or off-leash, practice only in a fenced area.
> 2. Remove the training collar when the training session is over.
> 3. Don't try to break up a dog fight.
> 4. "Come," "Leave it" and "Wait" are safety commands.
> 5. The dog belongs in a crate or behind a barrier when riding in the car.
> 6. Don't ignore the dog's first sign of aggression. Aggression only gets worse, so take it seriously.
> 7. Keep the faces of children and dogs separated.
> 8. Pay attention to what the dog is chewing.
> 9. Keep the vet's number near your phone.
> 10. "Okay" is a useful release command.

moment he pays attention to you teaches him the proper way to respond when he hears his name.

EXERCISES FOR A BASIC CANINE EDUCATION

THE SIT EXERCISE

There are several ways to teach the puppy to sit. The first one is to catch him whenever he is about to sit and, as his backside nears the floor, say "Sit, good dog!" That's positive reinforcement and, if your timing is sharp, he will learn that what he's doing at that second is connected to your

saying "Sit" and that you think he's clever for doing it!

Another method is to start with the puppy on his leash in front of you. Show him a treat in the palm of your right hand. Bring your hand up under his nose and, almost in slow motion, move your hand up and back so his nose goes up in the air and his head tilts back as he follows the treat in your hand. At that point, he will have to either sit or fall over, so as his back legs buckle under, say "Sit, good dog," and then give him the treat and lots of praise. You may have to begin with your hand lightly running up his chest, actually lifting his chin up until he sits. Some (usually older) dogs require gentle pressure on their hindquarters with the left hand, in which case the dog should be on your left side. Puppies generally do not appreciate this physical dominance.

Some gentle guidance may be necessary for the first few times to show your Schip what "sit" means.

READY, SIT, GO!

On your marks, get set: train! Most professional trainers agree that the sit command is the place to start your dog's formal education. Sitting is a natural posture for most dogs, and they respond to the sit exercise willingly and readily. For every lesson, begin with the sit command so that you start out with a successful exercise; likewise, you should practice the sit command at the end of every lesson as well, because you always want to end on a high note.

After a few times, you should be able to show the dog a treat in the open palm of your hand, raise your hand waist-high as you say "Sit" and have him sit. You will thereby have taught him two things at the same time. Both the verbal command and the motion of the hand are signals for the sit. Your puppy is watching you almost more than he is listening to you, so what you do is just as important as what you say.

Don't save any of these drills

only for training sessions. Use them as much as possible at odd times during a normal day. The dog should always sit before being given his food dish. He should sit to let you go through a doorway first, when the doorbell rings or when you stop to speak to someone on the street.

THE DOWN EXERCISE

Before beginning to teach the down command, you must consider how the dog feels about this exercise. To him, "down" is a submissive position. Being flat on the floor with you standing over him is not his idea of fun. It's up to you to let him know that, while it may not be fun, the reward of your approval is worth his effort.

Start with the puppy on your left side in a sit position. Hold the leash right above his collar in your left hand. Have an extra-special treat, such as a small piece of cooked chicken or hot dog, in your right hand. Place it at the end of the pup's nose and steadily move your hand down and

> **SMILE WHEN YOU ORDER ME AROUND!**
> While trainers recommend practicing with your dog every day, it's perfectly acceptable to take a "mental health day" off. It's better not to train the dog on days when you're in a sour mood. Your bad attitude or lack of interest will be sensed by your dog, and he will respond accordingly. Studies show that dogs are well tuned in to their humans' emotions. Be conscious of how you use your voice when talking to your dog. Raising your voice or shouting will only erode your dog's trust in you as his trainer and master.

forward along the ground. Hold the leash to prevent a sudden lunge for the food. As the puppy goes into the down position, say "Down" very gently.

The difficulty with this exercise is twofold: it's both the submissive aspect and the fact that most people say the word "Down" as if they were a drill sergeant in charge of recruits! So issue the command sweetly, give him the treat and have the pup maintain the down position for several seconds. If he tries to get up immediately, place your hands on his shoulders and press down gently, giving him a very quiet "Good dog." As you progress with this lesson, increase the "down time" until he will hold it until you say "Okay" (his cue for

Teaching the down command can present a challenge until your Schip learns that there is nothing to fear about assuming the down position.

release). Practice this one in the house at various times throughout the day.

By increasing the length of time during which the dog must maintain the down position, you'll find many uses for it. For example, he can lie at your feet in the vet's office or anywhere that both of you have to wait, when you are on the phone, while the family is eating and so forth. If you progress to training for competitive obedience, he'll already be all set for the exercise called the "long down."

THE STAY EXERCISE

You can teach your Schipperke to stay in the sit, down and stand positions. To teach the sit/stay, have the dog sit on your left side. Hold the leash at waist level in your left hand and let the dog know that you have a treat in your closed right hand. Step forward on your right foot as you say "Stay." Immediately turn and stand directly in front of the dog, keeping your right hand up high so he'll keep his eye on the treat hand and maintain the sit position for a count of five. Return to your original position and offer the reward.

Increase the length of the sit/stay each time until the dog can hold it for at least 30 seconds without moving. After about a week of success, move out on your right foot and take two steps

before turning to face the dog. Give the "Stay" hand signal (left palm back toward the dog's head) as you leave. He gets the treat when you return and he holds the sit/stay. Increase the distance that you walk away from him before turning until you reach the length of your training leash. But don't rush it! Go back to the beginning if he moves before he should. No matter what the lesson, never be upset by having to back up for a few days. The repetition and

The hand signal along with the verbal command reinforces what "stay" means.

TEACHER'S PET

Dogs are individuals, not robots, with many traits basic to their breed. Some, bred to work alone, are independent thinkers; others rely on you to call the shots. If you have enrolled in a training class, your instructor can offer alternative methods of training based on your individual dog's instincts and personality. You may benefit from using a different type of collar or switching to a class with different kinds of dogs.

practice are what will make your dog reliable in these commands. It won't do any good to move on to something more difficult if the command is not mastered at the easier levels. Above all, even if you do get frustrated, never let your puppy know! Always keep a positive, upbeat attitude during training, which will transmit to your dog for positive results.

The down/stay is taught in the same way once the dog is completely reliable and steady with the down command. Again, don't rush it. With the dog in the down position on your left side, step out on your right foot as you say "Stay." Return by walking around in back of the dog and into your original position. While you are training, it's okay to murmur something like "Hold on" to encourage him to stay put. When the dog will stay without moving when you are at a distance of 3 or 4 feet, begin to increase the length of time before you return. Be sure he holds the down on your return until you say "Okay." At that point, he gets his treat—just so he'll remember for next time that it's not over until it's over.

You want your Schip to reliably come to you when called. This is easier said than done, but the "Come" command could save your dog's life!

WHO'S TRAINING WHOM?

Dog training is a black-and-white exercise. The correct response to a command must be absolute, and the trainer must insist on completely accurate responses from the dog. A trainer cannot command his dog to sit and then settle for the dog's melting into the down position. Often owners are so pleased that their dogs "did something" in response to a command that they just shrug and say, "OK, down" even though they wanted the dog to sit. You want your dog to respond to the command without hesitation; he must respond at that moment and correctly every time.

THE COME EXERCISE

No command is more important to the safety of your Schipperke than "Come." It is what you should say every single time you see the puppy running toward you: "Binky, come! Good dog." During playtime, run a few feet away from the puppy and turn and tell him to "Come" as he is already running to you. You can go so far as to teach your puppy two things at once if you squat down and hold out your arms. As the pup gets close to you and you're saying "Good dog," bring your right arm in about waist high. Now he's also learning the hand signal, an excellent device should you be on the phone when you need to get him to come to you! You'll also both be one step ahead when you enter obedience classes.

When the puppy responds to your well-timed "Come," try it with the puppy on the training leash. This time, catch him off-guard, while he's sniffing a leaf or watching a bird: "Binky, come!" You may have to pause for a split second after his name to be sure

Owning two dogs means training two dogs, and each dog must be approached as an individual. These Schips have learned their lessons and enjoy a side-by-side walk with their owner.

you have his attention. If the puppy shows any sign of confusion, give the leash a mild jerk and take a couple of steps backward. Do not repeat the command. In this case, you should say "Good come" as he reaches you.

That's the number-one rule of training. Each command word is given just once. Anything more is nagging. You'll also notice that all commands are one word only. Even when they are actually two words, you say them as one.

Never call the dog to come to you—with or without his name—

"SCHOOL" MODE

When is your puppy ready for a lesson? Maybe not always when you are. Attempting training with treats just before his mealtime is asking for disaster. Notice what times of day he performs best and make that Fido's school time.

if you are angry or intend to correct him for some misbehavior. When correcting the pup, you go to him. Your dog must always connect "Come" with something pleasant and with your approval; then you can rely on his response.

Puppies, like children, have notoriously short attention spans, so don't overdo it with any of the training. Keep each lesson short. Break it up with a quick run around the yard or a ball toss, repeat the lesson and quit as soon as the pup gets it right. That way, you will always end with a "Good dog."

Life isn't perfect and neither are puppies. A time will come, often around ten months of age, when he'll become "selectively deaf" or choose to "forget" his name. He may respond by wagging his tail (and even seeming to smile at you) with a look that says "Make me!" Laugh,

The pack mentality, which is the basis of all discipline and training, is easily seen in a dog's interactions with other dogs.

> **OKAY!**
> This is the signal that tells your dog that he can quit whatever he was doing. Use "Okay" to end a session on a correct response to a command. (Never end on an incorrect response.) Lots of praise follows. People use "Okay" a lot and it has other uses for dogs, too. Your dog is barking. You say, "Okay! Come!" "Okay" signals him to stop the barking activity and "Come" allows him to come to you for a "Good dog."

throw his favorite toy and skip the lesson you had planned. Pups will be pups!

THE HEEL EXERCISE

The second most important command to teach, after the come, is the heel. When you are walking your growing puppy, you need to be in control. Besides, it looks terrible to have your dog straining at the leash, and it's not much fun either. Your eight- to ten-week-old puppy will probably follow you everywhere, but that's his natural instinct, not your control over the situation. However, any time he does follow you, you can say "Heel" and be ahead of the game, as he will learn to associate this command with the action of following you before you even begin teaching him to heel.

There is a very precise, almost military, procedure for teaching your dog to heel. As with all other obedience training, begin with the dog on your left side. He will be in a very nice sit and you will have the training leash across your chest. Hold the loop and folded leash in your right hand. Pick up the slack leash above the dog in your left hand and hold it loosely at your side. Step out on your left foot as you say "Heel." If the puppy does not move, give a gentle tug or pat your left leg to get him started. If he surges ahead of you, stop and pull him back gently until he is at your side. Tell him to sit and begin again.

Walk a few steps and stop while the puppy is correctly beside you. Tell him to sit and give mild verbal praise. (More enthusiastic praise will encourage him to think the lesson is over.) Repeat the lesson, increasing the number of steps you take only as long as the dog is heeling nicely beside you. When you end the

A properly heel-trained Schip will sit whenever his owner stops and wait for the next instruction. A proper heel begins and ends with a sit.

lesson, have him hold the sit, then give him the "Okay" to let him know that this is the end of the lesson. Praise him so that he knows he did a good job.

The cure for excessive pulling (a common problem) is to stop when the dog is no more than 2 or 3 feet ahead of you. Guide him back into position and begin again. With a really determined puller, try switching to a head collar. When used properly, this will automatically turn the pup's head toward you so you can bring him back easily to the heel position. Give

LET'S GO!

Many people use "Let's go" instead of "Heel" when teaching their dogs to behave on lead. It sounds more like fun! When beginning to teach the heel, whatever command you use, always step off on your left foot. That's the one next to the dog, who is on your left side, in case you've forgotten. Keep a loose leash. When the dog pulls ahead, stop, bring him back and begin again. Use treats to guide him around turns.

MORE PRAISE, LESS FOOD

As you progress with your puppy's lessons, and the puppy is responding well, gradually begin to wean him off the treats by alternating the treats with times when you offer only verbal praise or a few pats on the dog's side. (Pats on the head are dominant actions, so he won't think they are meant to be praise.) Every lesson should end with the puppy's performing the correct action for that session's command. When he gets it right and you withhold the treat, the praise can be as long and lavish as you like. The commands are one word only, but your verbal praise can use as many words as you want...don't skimp!

quiet, reassuring praise every time the leash goes slack and he's staying with you.

Staying and heeling can take a lot out of a dog, so provide playtime and free-running exercise to shake off the stress when the lessons are over. You don't want him to associate training with all work and no fun.

TAPERING OFF TIDBITS

Your dog has been watching you—and the hand that treats—throughout all of his lessons, and now it's time to break the treat habit. Begin by giving him treats at the end of each lesson only. Then start to give a treat after the end of only some of the lessons. At the

end of every lesson, as well as during the lessons, be consistent with the praise. Your pup now doesn't know whether he'll get a treat or not, but he should keep performing well just in case! Finally, you will stop giving treat rewards entirely. Save them for something brand-new that you want to teach him. Keep up the praise and you'll always have a "good dog."

OBEDIENCE CLASSES

The advantages of an obedience class are that your dog will have to learn amid the distractions of other people and dogs and that your mistakes will be quickly corrected by the trainer. Teaching your dog along with a qualified instructor and other handlers who may have more dog experience than you is another plus of the class environment. The instructor and other handlers can help you to find the most efficient way of teaching your dog a command or exercise. It's often easier to learn by other people's mistakes than your own. You will also learn all of the requirements for competitive obedience trials, in which you can earn titles and go on to advanced jumping and retrieving exercises, which are fun for many dogs. Obedience classes build the foundation needed for many other canine activities (in which we humans are allowed to participate, too!).

TRAINING FOR OTHER ACTIVITIES

Once your dog has basic obedience under his collar and is 12 months of age, you can enter the world of agility training. Dogs think agility is pure fun, like being turned loose in an amusement park full of obstacles. In addition to agility, Schips can participate in tracking, which is open to all "nosey" dogs (which would include all dogs). For those who like to volunteer, there is the wonderful feeling of owning a therapy dog and visiting hospices, nursing homes and veterans' homes to bring smiles, comfort and companionship to those who live there.

Around the house, your Schipperke can be taught to do some simple chores. You might teach him to carry a small basket or to fetch the morning newspaper. The kids can teach the dog all kinds of tricks, from playing hide-and-seek to balancing a biscuit on his nose. A family dog is what rounds out the family. Everything he does, including sitting in your lap and gazing lovingly at you, represents the bonus of owning a dog.

Hailing from the Skeppsklockans kennel in Sweden, this talented team of Schipperkes is dressed for an exciting outdoor excursion.

HEALTHCARE OF YOUR

SCHIPPERKE

By Lowell Ackerman, DVM, DACVD

HEALTHCARE FOR A LIFETIME
When you own a dog, you become
his healthcare advocate over his
entire lifespan, as well as being the
one to shoulder the financial
burden of such care. Accordingly,
it is worthwhile to focus on
prevention rather than treatment,
as you and your pet will both be
happier.

Of course, the best place to
have begun your program of
preventive healthcare is with the
initial purchase or adoption of your
dog. There is no way of guaran-
teeing that your new furry friend is
free of medical problems, but there
are some things you can do to
improve your odds. You certainly
should have done adequate
research into the Schipperke and
have selected your puppy carefully
rather than buying on impulse.
Health issues aside, a large number
of pet abandonment and
relinquishment cases arise from a
mismatch between pet needs and
owner expectations. This is
entirely preventable with
appropriate planning and finding a
good breeder.

Regarding healthcare issues
specifically, it is very difficult to
make blanket statements about
where to acquire a problem-free
pet, but, again, a reputable breeder
is your best bet. In an ideal
situation, you have the opportunity
to see both parents, get references
from other owners of the breeder's
pups and see genetic-testing
documentation for several generations of the litter's ancestors. At the
very least, you must thoroughly
investigate your breed of interest
and the problems inherent in that
breed, as well as the genetic testing
available to screen for those
problems. Genetic testing offers
some important benefits, but
testing is available for only a few
disorders in a relatively small
number of breeds and is not
available for some of the most
common genetic diseases, such as
hip dysplasia, cataracts, epilepsy,
cardiomyopathy, etc. This area of
research is indeed exciting and
increasingly important, and
advances will continue to be made
each year. In fact, recent research
has shown that there is an equivalent dog gene for 75% of known
human genes, so research done in
either species is likely to benefit
the other.

We've also discussed that evaluating the behavioral nature of your Schipperke and that of his immediate family members is an important part of the selection process that cannot be underestimated or overemphasized. It is sometimes difficult to evaluate temperament in puppies because certain behavioral tendencies, such as some forms of aggression, may not be immediately evident. More dogs are euthanized each year for behavioral reasons than for all medical conditions combined, so it is critical to take temperament issues seriously. Start with a well-balanced, friendly companion and put the time and effort into proper socialization, and you will both be rewarded with a lifelong valued relationship.

Assuming that you have started off with a pup from healthy, sound stock, you then become responsible for helping your veterinarian keep your pet healthy. Some crucial things happen before you even bring your puppy home. Parasite control typically begins at two weeks of age, and vaccinations typically begin at six to eight weeks of age. A pre-pubertal evaluation is typically scheduled for about six months of age. At this time, a dental evaluation is done (since the adult teeth are now in), heartworm prevention is started and neutering or spaying is most commonly done.

It is critical to commence regular dental care at home if you

> **YOUR DOG NEEDS TO VISIT THE VET IF:**
> - He has ingested a toxin such as antifreeze or a toxic plant; in these cases, administer first aid and call the vet right away
> - His teeth are discolored, loose or missing or he has sores or other signs of infection or abnormality in the mouth
> - He has been vomiting, has had diarrhea or has been constipated for over 24 hours; call immediately if you notice blood
> - He has refused food for over 24 hours
> - His eating habits, water intake or toilet habits have noticeably changed; if you have noticed weight gain or weight loss
> - He shows symptoms of bloat, which requires *immediate* attention
> - He is salivating excessively
> - He has a lump in his throat
> - He has lumps or bumps anywhere on the body
> - He is very lethargic
> - He appears to be in pain or otherwise has trouble chewing or swallowing
> - His skin loses elasticity
>
> Of course, there will be other instances in which a visit to the vet is necessary; these are just some of the signs that could be indicative of serious problems that need to be caught as early as possible.

have not already done so. It may not sound very important, but most dogs have active periodontal

DOGGIE DENTAL DON'TS

A veterinary dental exam is necessary if you notice one or any combination of the following in your dog:

- Broken, loose or missing teeth
- Loss of appetite (which could be due to mouth pain or illness caused by infection)
- Gum abnormalities, including redness, swelling and bleeding
- Drooling, with or without blood
- Yellowing of the teeth or gumline, indicating tartar
- Bad breath

Most dogs are considered adults at a year of age, although some larger breeds still have some filling out to do up to about two or so years old. Even individual dogs within each breed have different healthcare requirements, so work with your veterinarian to determine what will be needed and what your role should be. This doctor-client relationship is important because as vaccination guidelines change there may not be an annual "vaccine visit" scheduled. You must make sure that you see your veterinarian at least annually, even if no vaccines are due, because this is the best opportunity to coordinate health-care activities and to make sure that no medical issues creep by unaddressed.

When your Schipperke reaches three-quarters of his anticipated lifespan, he is considered a "senior" and likely requires some special care. In general, if you've been taking great care of your canine companion throughout his formative and adult years, the transition to senior status should be a smooth one. Age is not a disease, and as long as everything is functioning as it should, there is no reason why most of late adulthood should not be rewarding for both you and your pet. This is especially true if you have tended to the details, such as regular veterinary visits, proper dental care, excellent nutrition and

disease by four years of age if they don't have their teeth cleaned regularly at home, not just at their veterinary exams. Dental problems lead to more than just bad "doggie breath." Gum disease can have very serious medical consequences. If you start brushing your dog's teeth and using antiseptic rinses from a young age, your dog will be accustomed to it and will not resist. The results will be healthy dentition, which your pet will need to enjoy a long, healthy life.

management of bone and joint issues.

At this stage in your Schipperke's life, your veterinarian will want to schedule visits twice yearly, instead of once, to run some laboratory screenings, electrocardiograms and the like, and to change the diet to something more digestible. Catching problems early is the best way to manage them effectively. Treating the early stages of heart disease is so much easier than trying to intervene when there is more significant damage to the heart muscle. Similarly, managing the beginning of kidney problems is fairly routine if there is no significant kidney damage. Other problems, like cognitive dysfunction (similar to senility and Alzheimer's disease), cancer, diabetes and arthritis, are more common in older dogs, but all can be treated to help the dog live as many happy, comfortable years as possible. Just as in people, medical management is more effective (and less expensive) when you catch things early.

SELECTING A VETERINARIAN
There is probably no more important decision that you will make regarding your pet's healthcare than the selection of his doctor. Your pet's veterinarian will be a pediatrician, family-practice physician and gerontologist, depending on the dog's life stage, and will be the individual who

makes recommendations regarding issues such as when specialists need to be consulted, when diagnostic testing and/or therapeutic intervention is needed and when you will need to seek outside emergency and critical-care services. Your vet will act as your advocate and liaison throughout these processes.

Everyone has his own idea about what to look for in a vet, an individual who will play a big role in his dog's (and, of course, his own) life for many years to come.

TAKING YOUR DOG'S TEMPERATURE
It is important to know how to take your dog's temperature at times when you think he may be ill. It's not the most enjoyable task, but it can be done without too much difficulty. It's easier with a helper, preferably someone with whom the dog is friendly, so that one of you can hold the dog while the other inserts the thermometer.

Before inserting the thermometer, coat the end with petroleum jelly. Insert the thermometer slowly and gently into the dog's rectum about one inch. Wait for the reading, about two minutes. Be sure to remove the thermometer carefully and clean it thoroughly after each use.

A dog's normal body temperature is between 100.5 and 102.5 degrees F. Immediate veterinary attention is required if the dog's temperature is below 99 or above 104 degrees F.

For some, it is the compassionate caregiver with whom they hope to develop a professional relationship to span the lifetime of their dogs and even their future pets. For others, they are seeking a clinician with keen diagnostic and therapeutic insight who can deliver state-of-the-art healthcare. Still others need a veterinary facility that is open evenings and weekends, is in close proximity or provides mobile veterinary services to accommodate their schedules; these people may not much mind that their dogs might see different veterinarians on each visit. Just as we have different reasons for selecting our own healthcare professionals (e.g., covered by insurance plan, expert in field, convenient location, etc.), we should not expect that there is a one-size-fits-all recommendation for selecting a veterinarian and veterinary practice. The best advice is to be honest in your assessment of what you expect from a veterinary practice and to conscientiously research the options in your area. You will quickly appreciate that not all veterinary practices are the same, and you will be happiest with one that truly meets your needs.

There is another point to be considered in the selection of veterinary services. Not that long ago, a single veterinarian would attempt to manage all medical and surgical issues as they arose. That

PET INSURANCE

Pet insurance policies are very cost-effective (and very inexpensive by human health insurance standards), but make sure that you buy the policy long before you intend to use it (preferably starting in puppyhood, because coverage will exclude pre-existing conditions) and that you are actually buying an indemnity insurance plan from an insurance company that is regulated by your state or province. Many insurance policy look-alikes are actually discount clubs that are redeemable only at specific locations and for specific services. An indemnity plan covers your pet at almost all veterinary, specialty and emergency practices and is an excellent way to manage your pet's ongoing healthcare needs.

was often problematic, because veterinarians are trained in many species and many diseases, and it was just impossible for general veterinary practitioners to be experts in every species, every field and every ailment. However, just as in the human healthcare fields, specialization has allowed general practitioners to concentrate on primary healthcare delivery, especially wellness and the prevention of infectious diseases, and to utilize a network of specialists to assist in the management of conditions that require specific expertise and experience. Thus there are now many types of veterinary specialists, including dermatologists, cardiologists, ophthalmologists, surgeons, internists, oncologists, neurologists, behaviorists, criticalists and others to help primary-care veterinarians deal with complicated medical challenges. In most cases, specialists see cases referred by primary-care veterinarians, make diagnoses and set up management plans. From there, the animals' ongoing care is returned to their primary-care veterinarians. This important team approach to your pet's medical-care needs has provided opportunities for advanced care and an unparalleled level of quality to be delivered.

With all of the opportunities for your Schipperke to receive high-quality veterinary medical care, there is another topic that needs to be addressed at the same time—cost. It's been said that you can have excellent healthcare or inexpensive healthcare, but never both; this is as true in veterinary medicine as it is in human medicine. While veterinary costs are a fraction of what the same services cost in the human health-care arena, it is still difficult to deal with unanticipated medical costs, especially since they can easily creep into hundreds or even thousands of dollars if specialists or emergency services become involved. However, there are ways of managing these risks. The easiest is to buy pet health insurance and

realize that its foremost purpose is not to cover routine healthcare visits but rather to serve as an umbrella for those rainy days when your pet needs medical care and you don't want to worry about whether or not you can afford that care.

VACCINATIONS AND INFECTIOUS DISEASES

There has never been an easier time to prevent a variety of infectious diseases in your dog, but the advances we've made in veterinary medicine come with a price—choice. Now while it may seem that this choice is a good thing (and it is), it has never been more difficult for the pet owner (or the vet) to make an informed decision about the best way to protect pets through vaccination.

Years ago, it was just accepted that puppies got a starter series of vaccinations and then annual "boosters" throughout their lives to keep them protected. As more and

What else is lurking in the grass with your Schip? Insects? Parasites? Allergens? Be sure to check his skin and coat after time outdoors.

HIT ME WITH A HOT SPOT

What is a hot spot? Technically known as pyotraumatic dermatitis, a hot spot is an infection on the dog's coat, usually by the rear end, under the tail or on a leg, which the dog inflicts upon himself. The dog licks and bites the itchy spot until it becomes inflamed and infected. The hot spot can range in size from the circumference of a grape to the circumference of an apple. Provided that the hot spot is not related to a deeper bacterial infection, it can be treated topically by clipping the area, cleaning the sore and giving prednisone. For bacterial infections, antibiotics are required. In some cases, an Elizabethan collar is required to keep the dog from further irritating the hot spot. The itching can intensify and the pain becomes worse. Medicated shampoos and cool compresses, drying agents and topical steroids may be prescribed by your vet as well.

Hot spots can be caused by fleas, an allergy, an ear infection, anal sac problems, mange or a foreign irritant. Likewise, they can be linked to psychoses. The underlying problem must be addressed in addition to the hot spot itself.

"multivalent" vaccines that crammed a lot of protection into a single syringe. The manufacturers' recommendations were to give the vaccines annually, and this was a simple enough protocol to follow. However, as veterinary medicine has become more sophisticated and we have started looking more at healthcare quandaries rather than convenience, it became necessary to reevaluate the situation and deal with some tough questions. It is important to realize that whether or not to use a particular vaccine depends on the risk of contracting the disease against which it protects, the severity of the disease if it is contracted, the duration of immunity provided by the vaccine, the safety of the product and the needs of the individual animal. In a very general sense, rabies, distemper, hepatitis and parvovirus are considered core vaccine needs, while parainfluenza, *Bordetella bronchiseptica*, leptospirosis, coronavirus and borreliosis (Lyme disease) are considered non-core needs and best reserved for animals that demonstrate reasonable risk of contracting the diseases.

THE GREAT VACCINATION DEBATE

What kinds of questions need to be addressed? When the vet injects multiple organisms at the same time, might some of the components interfere with one another in the development of

more vaccines became available, consumers wanted the convenience of having all of that protection in a single injection. The result was immunologic protection? We don't have the comprehensive answer for that question, but it does appear that the immune system better handles agents when given individually. Unfortunately, most manufacturers still bundle their vaccine components because that is what most pet owners want, so getting vaccines with single components can sometimes be difficult.

Another question has to do with how often vaccines should be given. Again, this seems to be different for each vaccine component. There seems to be a general consensus that a puppy (or a dog with an unknown vaccination history) should get a series of vaccinations to initially stimulate his immunity and then a booster at one year of age, but even the veterinary associations and colleges have trouble reaching agreement about what he should get after that. Rabies vaccination schedules are not debated, because vaccine schedules for this contagious and devastating disease are determined by government agencies. Regarding the rest, some recommend that we continue to give the vaccines annually because this method has worked well as a disease preventive for decades and delivers predictable protection. Others recommend that some of the vaccines need to be given only every second or third year, as this can be done without affecting

levels of protection. This is probably true for some vaccine components (such as hepatitis), but there have been no large studies to demonstrate what the optimal interval should be and whether the same principles hold true for all breeds.

It may be best to just measure titers, which are protective blood levels of various vaccine components, on an annual basis, but that too is not without controversy. Scientists have not precisely determined the minimum titer of specific vaccine components that will be guaranteed to provide a pet with protection. Pets with very high titers will clearly be protected and those with very low titers will need repeat vaccinations, but there is also a large "gray zone" of pets that probably have intermediate protection and may or may not need repeat vaccination, depending on their risk of coming into contact with the disease.

Your Schipperke relies on you for proper care and good health. When properly maintained, the Schip will retain his lively exuberance well into his double-digit years.

These questions leave primary-care vets in a very uncomfortable position, one that is not easy to resolve. Do they recommend annual vaccination in a manner that has demonstrated successful protection for decades, do they recommend skipping vaccines some years and hope that the protection lasts or do they measure blood tests (titers) and hope that the results are convincing enough to clearly indicate whether repeat vaccination is warranted?

These aren't the only vaccination questions impacting pets, owners and veterinarians. Other controversies focus on whether vaccines should be dosed according to body weight (currently they are administered in uniform doses, regardless of the animal's size), whether there are breed-specific issues important in determining vaccination programs (for instance, we know that some breeds have a harder time mounting an appropriate immune response to parvovirus vaccine and might benefit from a different dose or injection interval) and which type of vaccine—live-virus or inactivated—offers more advantages with fewer disadvantages. Clearly, there are many more questions than there are answers. The important thing, as a pet owner, is to be aware of the issues and be able to work with your veterinarian to make decisions that are right for your pet. Be an

informed consumer and you will appreciate the deliberation required in tailoring a vaccination program to best meet the needs of your pet. Expect also that this is an ongoing, ever-changing topic of debate; thus, the decisions you make this year won't necessarily be the same as the ones you make next year.

NEUTERING/SPAYING

Sterilization procedures (neutering for males/spaying for females) are meant to accomplish several purposes. While the underlying premise is to address the risk of pet overpopulation, there are also some medical and behavioral benefits to the surgeries as well. For females, spaying prior to the first estrus (heat cycle) leads to a marked reduction in the risk of mammary cancer. There also will be no manifestations of "heat" to attract male dogs and no bleeding in the house. For males, there is prevention of testicular cancer and a reduction in the risk of prostate problems. In both sexes, there may be some limited reduction in aggressive behaviors toward other dogs, and some diminishing of urine marking, roaming and mounting.

While neutering and spaying do indeed prevent animals from contributing to pet overpopulation, even no-cost and low-cost neutering options have not eliminated the problem. Perhaps

COMMON INFECTIOUS DISEASES

Let's discuss some of the diseases that create the need for vaccination in the first place. Following are the major canine infectious diseases and a simple explanation of each.

Rabies: A devastating viral disease that can be fatal in dogs and people. In fact, vaccination of dogs and cats is an important public-health measure to create a resistant animal buffer population to protect people from contracting the disease. Vaccination schedules are determined on a government level and are not optional for pet owners; rabies vaccination is required by law in all 50 states.

Parvovirus: A severe, potentially life-threatening disease that is easily transmitted between dogs. There are four strains of the virus, but it is believed that there is significant "cross-protection" between strains that may be included in individual vaccines.

Distemper: A potentially severe and life-threatening disease with a relatively high risk of exposure, especially in certain regions. In very high-risk distemper environments, young pups may be vaccinated with human measles vaccine, a related virus that offers cross-protection when administered at four to ten weeks of age.

Hepatitis: Caused by canine adenovirus type 1 (CAV-1), but since vaccination with the causative virus has a higher rate of adverse effects, cross-protection is derived from the use of adenovirus type 2 (CAV-2), a cause of respiratory disease and one of the potential causes of canine cough. Vaccination with CAV-2 provides long-term immunity against hepatitis, but relatively less protection against respiratory infection.

Canine cough: Also called tracheobronchitis, actually a fairly complicated result of viral and bacterial offenders; therefore, even with vaccination, protection is incomplete. Wherever dogs congregate, canine cough will likely be spread among them. Intranasal vaccination with *Bordetella* and parainfluenza is the best safeguard, but the duration of immunity does not appear to be very long, typically a year at most. These are non-core vaccines, but vaccination is sometimes mandated by boarding kennels, obedience classes, dog shows and other places where dogs congregate to try to minimize spread of infection.

Leptospirosis: A potentially fatal disease that is more common in some geographic regions. It is capable of being spread to humans. The disease varies with the individual "serovar," or strain, of *Leptospira* involved. Since there does not appear to be much cross-protection between serovars, protection is only as good as the likelihood that the serovar in the vaccine is the same as the one in the pet's local environment. Problems with *Leptospira* vaccines are that protection does not last very long, side effects are not uncommon and a large percentage of dogs (perhaps 30%) may not respond to vaccination.

Borrelia burgdorferi: The cause of Lyme disease, the risk of which varies with the geographic area in which the pet lives and travels. Lyme disease is spread by deer ticks in the eastern US and western black-legged ticks in the western part of the country, and the risk of exposure is high in some regions. Lameness, fever and inappetence are most commonly seen in affected dogs. The extent of protection from the vaccine has not been conclusively demonstrated.

Coronavirus: This disease has a high risk of exposure, especially in areas where dogs congregate, but it typically causes only mild to moderate digestive upset (diarrhea, vomiting, etc.). Vaccines are available, but the duration of protection is believed to be relatively short and the effectiveness of the vaccine in preventing infection is considered low.

There are many other vaccinations available, including those for *Giardia* and canine adenovirus-1. While there may be some specific indications for their use, and local risk factors to be considered, they are not widely recommended for most dogs.

one of the main reasons for this is that individuals that intentionally breed their dogs and those that allow their animals to run at large are the main causes of unwanted offspring. Also, animals in shelters are often there because they were abandoned or relinquished, not because they came from unplanned matings. Neutering/spaying is important, but it should be considered in the context of the real causes of animals' ending up in shelters and eventually being euthanized.

One of the important considerations regarding neutering is that it is a surgical procedure. This sometimes gets lost in discussions of low-cost procedures and commoditization of the process. In females, spaying is specifically referred to as an ovariohysterectomy. In this procedure, a midline incision is made in the abdomen and the entire uterus and both ovaries are surgically removed. While this is a major invasive surgical procedure, it usually has few complications, because it is typically performed on healthy young animals. However, it is major surgery, as any woman who has had a hysterectomy will attest.

In males, neutering has traditionally referred to castration, which involves the surgical removal of both testicles. While still a significant piece of surgery, there is not the abdominal exposure that is required in the female surgery. In addition, there is now a chemical sterilization option, in which a solution is injected into each testicle, leading to atrophy of the sperm-producing cells. This can typically be done under sedation rather than full anesthesia. This is a relatively new approach, and there are no long-term clinical studies yet available.

Neutering/spaying is typically done around six months of age at most veterinary hospitals, although techniques have been pioneered to perform the procedures in animals as young as eight weeks of age. In general, the surgeries on the very young animals are done for the specific reason of sterilizing them before they go to their new homes. This is done in some shelter hospitals for assurance that the animals will definitely not produce any pups. Otherwise, these organizations need to rely on owners to comply with their wishes to have the animals "altered" at a later date, something that does not always happen.

There are some exciting immunocontraceptive "vaccines" currently under development, and there may be a time when contraception in pets will not require surgical procedures. We anxiously await these developments.

HEREDITARY PROBLEMS
The Schipperke has always been a healthy and hardy breed. He requires no special care and has a

very low incidence of medical problems. He is likely, when properly cared for, to go through life never needing the services of a veterinarian other than for routine vaccinations.

It is probable that your dog will never suffer from any hereditary defects. The breed is not confronted with anatomical defects, except occasionally patellar luxation. Nevertheless, be advised that the breeding committees of Schipperke clubs all over the world, which are dedicated to the welfare of the breed, always remain vigilant in order to avoid breed-specific problems or hereditary disorders. These problems or disorders can, as has been seen in many other breeds, become very rapidly widespread and common when no genetic tests for breeding animals are done.

In many breeds, certain anatomical characteristics, which in the standards are described as typical, specific and obligatory, are so extreme that the dogs suffer from many unpleasant defects, such as breathing problems, eye irritations, skin infections, etc. Most of the anatomical defects in dogs, which greatly impair their physical and mental health and well-being, are found more frequently in toy dogs than in other breeds.

While the Schip is small, he is not a toy dog. We think that this classification also implies that, while the Schipperke certainly is a

small dog, he is without any signs of "dwarfism" often found in small companion breeds. This means that he truly is a reduced but well-proportioned, harmonious and more strongly built form of his bigger ancestors, without anatomical disproportions but with normal bodily proportions and the same mental development. Basically, the Schipperke is a utilitarian breed. In his country of origin, the Schipperke is considered a shepherd dog.

No single anatomical part of the Schipperke, despite his small size, can be considered harmful for his health or well-being. His muzzle is not too short or pushed in; his skull is not too broad, too narrow or too domed; his skin is not too loose or too wrinkled; his body is not overloaded; his joints are not too straight or overly angulated, etc.

However, in dogs many disorders are not directly related to the physical traits of a breed, but are inherited and seen in certain bloodlines. Fortunately, we can assert that, although in the Schipperke some hereditary diseases do indeed occur, breeders are working hard to eliminate these problems through genetic testing and breeding only healthy dogs.

MPS IIIB
This serious disease has relatively recently been discovered in the Schipperke. Mucopolysacchari-

dosis type IIIB (MPS IIIB) is an inherited "storage disease" that causes problems in the nervous system that lead to the deterioration of musculature and muscle control in affected dogs. Intensive study on this disease is currently underway, but there is no cure or even treatment; MPS IIIB is fatal.

This is an inherited autosomal recessive trait, affecting males and females alike. Fortunately, a DNA test to identify the gene is available, and reputable breeders should test all potential breeding dogs and can even test puppies that are at risk. Breeders can work to eliminate the disease from the Schipperke by never breeding from affected dogs. Even breeding carriers is risky, as some of the pups will be affected by the mutant gene. If either or both parents are identified as carriers, the entire litter will have to be tested. The only completely safe instance is a litter bred from two non-affected/non-carrier dogs.

Symptoms appear in young adults, first manifested in general difficulty in getting around. Muscle control worsens as the disease progresses to where dogs cannot maneuver up or down stairs, may have tremors and eventually cannot stand up or even eat. The end result, sadly, is death. As there is no treatment available, an owner can only make his dog's life as comfortable as possible.

As a potential Schipperke owner, you must discuss this disease with your breeder before buying a puppy. It is essential that you see documentation proving that the parents have tested free of the gene for this disorder. Reputable breeders will be happy to show you the test results. Do not consider a puppy from a breeder who does not test for MPS IIIB or who claims not to know about the disease.

COUGHING

A chronic cough seems to be not uncommon in the Schipperke breed. It should not be confused with kennel cough, an infectious canine tracheobronchitis that is caused by several viruses and also a bacterium. The cause of the chronic cough is not very clear, but it certainly is connected with an imperfectly formed trachea or windpipe.

Many Schip owners have noticed that coughing can be provoked when the dog, with a collar around his neck, is pulling on the lead. The cure here, of course, is to teach your dog to walk well beside you instead of pulling ahead. This is part of basic training, but rather hard to accomplish with a Schip! Furthermore, it is advisable not to use a choke collar, but instead a harness, which fits around the chest and back. A harness can be used for training or just for walking your Schipperke.

PATELLAR LUXATION

Patellar (pertaining to the patella or kneecap) luxation (dislocation of a bone or joint) or patellar dysplasia (malformed kneecap) is a congenital malformation that is very common in small breeds. When the patella slips away, the dog is no longer able to stretch his hindleg, which he then can only keep in a bent position. When the owners of Schips recognize this problem, they can usually manipulate the patella into place again. The dislocation of the patella can be intermittent or recurrent.

The defect can be best characterized by a dog that appears normal and then suddenly carries his hind limb. When the anterior cruciate ligament in the knee joint ruptures and the dislocation of the patella is not temporary, but permanent, this can lead to limping or persistent lameness, in which case surgery is the only effective treatment.

This defect is hereditary. The exact mode of inheritance is not clearly defined, but it is likely to be polygenic (controlled by a group of genes). Dogs affected by patellar luxation should not be approved as suitable for breeding.

LEGG-CALVE-PERTHES DISEASE

This disease, also known as Legg-Perthes disease, is relatively common in small breeds. The disease is similar to hip dysplasia (HD), an inherited disorder charac-

FOOD ALLERGY

Severe itching, leading to bald patches and open sores on the feet, face, ears, armpits and groin, could be caused by a food allergy. Studies indicate that up to 10% of dogs suffer from food allergies. Dogs who suffer from chronic ear problems may actually have a food allergy. Unfortunately, there are no tests available to determine whether your dog definitely suffers from a food allergy. The dog will be miserable and you will be frustrated and stressed.

Take the problem into your own hands and kitchen. Select a type of meat that your dog is not getting from his existing diet, perhaps white fish, lamb or venison, and prepare a home-cooked food. The food should consist of two parts carbohydrate (rice, pasta or potatoes) and one part protein (the chosen meat). It's better not to start with soy as the protein source unless all of the meats cause a reaction.

Monitor your dog's intake carefully. He must eat only your prepared meals. All family members (and visiting friends) must be informed of the plan. After four or five weeks on the new diet, you will reintroduce a portion of his original diet to determine whether this food is the cause of his allergic reactions. Once the dog reacts to the change in diet, resume the new diet. Make dietary modifications every two weeks and keep careful records of any reactions the dog has to the diet.

terized by a "malformed hip joint." Sometimes there is confusion between these two diseases, because both affect the hip joint; however, HD is mostly bilateral and is found more commonly in large breeds.

Legg-Perthes disease is mostly unilateral and is characterized by necrosis (death) of the femoral or thigh bone head, which becomes flattened or malformed. It seems to be caused by an inadequate supply of blood to this area. The necrosis process is only seen during adolescence, from 3 to 13 months, but it is halted mostly by the age of 7 months, leaving a misshapen femoral head, which can be corrected by surgery. The disease causes gait abnormalities and even lameness.

The genetics of the disease are not at all clear. Some cases may be brought on by trauma, but the disease is generally thought to be hereditary and studies about its inheritance are underway. Nonetheless, as a precaution, owners are advised to discourage their Schips from dancing on their hind legs before they are fully developed.

EPILEPSY
Epilepsy, often an inherited disease in which a dog suffers spasmodic fits or seizures, has been reported in a number of breeds, including the Schipperke. Breeders are mainly concerned

THREADWORMS
Though less common than ascarids, hookworms and other nematodes, threadworms concern dog owners in the southwestern US and Gulf Coast area where the climate is hot and humid. Living in the small intestine of the dog, this worm measures a mere 2 millimeters and is round in shape. Like that of the whipworm, the threadworm's life cycle is very complex, and the eggs and larvae are passed through the feces. The cause of a deadly disease in humans, worms of the genus *Strongyloides* readily infect people; the handling of feces is the most common means of transmission. Threadworms are most often seen in young puppies; bloody diarrhea and pneumonia are symptoms. Sick puppies must be isolated and treated immediately; vets recommend a follow-up treatment one month later.

with idiopathic or functional epilepsy, a form of the disease in which the seizures cannot be attributed to external factors or influences.

A typical epileptic seizure is characterized by total loss of muscle control, starting with sudden trembling and falling down, while the dog holds his trembling legs as stiff as possible. Most seizures last one to three minutes. The dog has to be kept quiet when the seizure is over. When a seizure fails to abate after five minutes, you should wrap the dog in a blanket and transport him to a veterinarian. The vet of course should be contacted when any seizures occur.

The mode of inheritance of true idiopathic epilepsy is complex. Treatment with oral anti-epileptic drugs is possible. However, seizures can be so frequent that coma and death may occur.

The incidence of epileptic seizures in dogs is not really high, but probably higher than in humans. Canine epilepsy really is a serious problem, but many breeders are reluctant to discuss it. In some countries, research projects have been started to examine the inheritance and to survey how widespread the problem is.

ANURY OR BRACHYURY
Anury means "total taillessness" or an "inherited absence of caudal vertebrae." Brachyury is the inherited condition resulting in an abnormally short, stump or stub tail. At the present time it is sometimes still maintained that Schipperkes as a rule are born "naturally docked"—either totally tailless or with a short, stump tail. The truth is that Schipperkes may be born totally tailless, but this happens only very rarely, and only a small percentage of the puppies are born with a stump or stub tail. The great majority are born with full-length tails.

It has been reported that anury or brachyury can be linked with other defects, mostly those affecting the spinal column or the hindquarters. Breeding with Schipperkes that are born naturally docked and therefore carry the gene for anury or brachyury is strongly advised against, as this would eventually destroy the breed.

PROBLEMS IN OLD AGE
Your Schipperke will most likely live to a good old age, because the average lifespan of the breed is approximately 13 to 16 years. His high energy and activity level will only diminish from around the age of 12 years on.

Eventually, you will see your beloved companion fighting a battle with old age. He will turn gray around the muzzle. Owing to arthritis, a common joint problem in older dogs, stiffness will set in. Running, jumping and stair climbing will be difficult for him. He will be more susceptible to injury and more intolerant of pain.

Cataracts are very common in older dogs, including Schipperkes, and may develop from the age of ten years on. A cataract can be defined as a cloudiness or opacity of the crystalline lens of the eye, which can progress to complete blindness. Fortunately, old dogs with impaired vision or hearing can cope with it very easily in familiar surroundings.

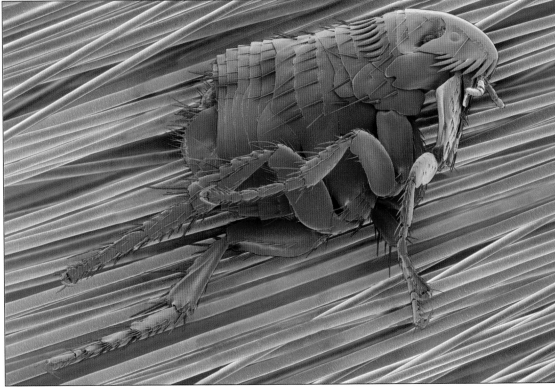

A scanning electron micrograph of a dog flea, *Ctenocephalides canis,* on dog hair.

EXTERNAL PARASITES

FLEAS

Fleas have been around for millions of years and, while we have better tools now for controlling them than at any time in the past, there still is little chance that they will end up on an endangered species list. Actually, they are very well adapted to living on our pets, and they continue to adapt as we make advances.

The female flea can consume 15 times her weight in blood during active reproduction and can lay as many as 40 eggs a day. These eggs are very resistant to the effects of insecticides. They hatch into larvae, which then mature and spin cocoons. The immature fleas reside in this pupal stage until the time is right for feeding. This pupal stage is also very resistant to the effects of insecticides, and pupae can last in the environment without feeding for many months. Newly emergent fleas are attracted to animals by the warmth of the animals' bodies, movement and exhaled carbon dioxide. However, when they first emerge from their cocoons, they orient towards light; thus when an animal passes between a flea and the light source, casting a shadow, the flea pounces and starts to feed. If the animal turns out to be a dog or cat, the reproductive cycle continues. If the flea lands on another type of animal, including a person, the flea will bite but will then look for a more appropriate host. An emerging adult flea can survive without feeding for up to 12 months but, once it tastes blood, it can survive off its host for only three to four days.

It was once thought that fleas spend most of their lives in the environment, but we now know that fleas won't willingly jump off a dog unless leaping to another dog or when physically removed by brushing, bathing or other manipulation. Flea eggs, on the other hand, are shiny and smooth, and they roll off the animal and into the environment. The eggs, larvae and pupae then exist in the environment, but once the adult finds a susceptible animal, it's home sweet home until the flea is forced to seek refuge elsewhere.

Since adult fleas live on the animal and immature forms survive in the environment, a successful treatment plan must address all stages of the flea life cycle. There are now several safe and effective flea-control products that can be applied on a monthly

> ## FLEA PREVENTION FOR YOUR DOG
> - Discuss with your veterinarian the safest product to protect your dog, likely in the form of a monthly tablet or a liquid preparation placed on the back of the dog's neck.
> - For dogs suffering from flea-bite dermatitis, a shampoo or topical insecticide treatment is required.
> - Your lawn and property should be sprayed with an insecticide designed to kill fleas and ticks that lurk outdoors.
> - Using a flea comb, check the dog's coat regularly for any signs of parasites.
> - Practice good housekeeping. Vacuum floors, carpets and furniture regularly, especially in the areas that the dog frequents, and wash the dog's bedding weekly.
> - Follow up house-cleaning with carpet shampoos and sprays to rid the house of fleas at all stages of development. Insect growth regulators are the safest option.

basis. These include fipronil, imidacloprid, selamectin and permethrin (found in several formulations). Most of these products have significant flea-killing rates within 24 hours. However, none of them will control the immature forms in the environment. To accomplish this, there are a variety of insect growth regulators that can be

THE FLEA'S LIFE CYCLE

What came first, the flea or the egg? This age-old mystery is more difficult to comprehend than the actual cycle of the flea. Fleas usually live only about four months. A female can lay 2,000 eggs in her lifetime.

PHOTO BY CAROLINA BIOLOGICAL SUPPLY CO.

Egg

After ten days of rolling around your carpet or under your furniture, the eggs hatch into larvae, which feed on various and sundry debris. In days or months, depending on the climate, the larvae spin cocoons and develop into the pupal or nymph stage, which quickly develop into fleas.

Larva

PHOTO BY CAROLINA BIOLOGICAL SUPPLY CO.

Pupa

These immature fleas must locate a host within 10 to 14 days or they will die. Only about 1% of the flea population exist as adult fleas, while the other 99% exist as eggs, larvae or pupae.

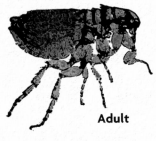

Adult

KILL FLEAS THE NATURAL WAY

If you choose not to go the route of conventional medication, there are some natural ways to ward off fleas:

- Dust your dog with a natural flea powder, composed of such herbal goodies as rosemary, wormwood, pennyroyal, citronella, rue, tobacco powder and eucalyptus.
- Apply diatomaceous earth, the fossilized remains of single-cell algae, to your carpets, furniture and pet's bedding. Even though it's not good for dogs, it's even worse for fleas, which will dry up swiftly and die.
- Brush your dog frequently, give him adequate exercise and let him fast occasionally. All of these activities strengthen the dog's system and make him more resistant to disease and parasites.
- Bathe your dog with a capful of pennyroyal or eucalyptus oil.
- Feed a natural diet, free of additives and preservatives. Add some fresh garlic and brewer's yeast to the dog's morning portion, as these items have flea-repelling properties.

sprayed into the environment (e.g., pyriproxyfen, methoprene, fenoxycarb) as well as insect development inhibitors such as lufenuron that can be administered. These compounds have no effect on adult fleas, but they stop immature forms from developing into adults. In years gone by, we relied heavily on toxic insecticides (such as organophosphates, organochlorines and carbamates) to manage the flea problem, but today's options are not only much safer to use on our pets but also safer for the environment.

TICKS

Ticks are members of the spider class (arachnids) and are blood-sucking parasites capable of transmitting a variety of diseases, including Lyme disease, ehrlichiosis, babesiosis and Rocky Mountain spotted fever. It's easy to see ticks on your own skin, but it is more of a challenge when your furry companion is affected. Whenever you happen to be planning a stroll in a tick-infested area (especially forests, grassy or wooded areas or parks) be prepared to do a thorough inspection of your dog afterward to search for ticks. Ticks can be tricky, so make sure you spend time looking in the ears, between the toes and everywhere else where a tick might hide. Ticks need to be attached for 24–72 hours before they transmit most of the diseases that they carry, so you do have a window of opportunity for some preventive intervention.

A TICKING BOMB

There is nothing good about a tick's harpooning his nose into your dog's skin. Among the diseases caused by ticks are Rocky Mountain spotted fever, canine ehrlichiosis, canine babesiosis, canine hepatozoonosis and Lyme disease. If a dog is allergic to the saliva of a female wood tick, he can develop tick paralysis.

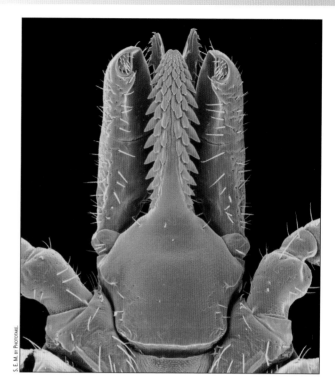

S. E. M. BY PHOTOTAKE.

A scanning electron micrograph of the head of a female deer tick, *Ixodes dammini*, a parasitic tick that carries Lyme disease.

Female ticks live to eat and breed. They can lay between 4,000 and 5,000 eggs and they die soon after. Males, on the other hand, live only to mate with the females and continue the process as long as they are able. Most ticks live on multiple hosts before parasitizing dogs. The immature forms typically reside on grass and shrubs, waiting for suscep-tible animals to walk by. The larvae and nymph stages typically feed on wildlife.

If only a few ticks are present on a dog, they can be plucked out, but it is important to remove the entire head and mouthparts,

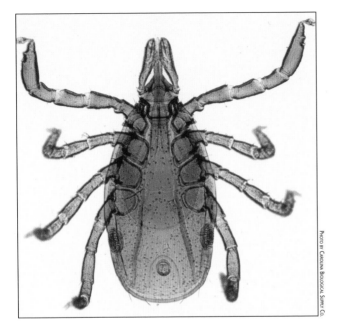

Deer tick,
Ixodes dammini.

PHOTO BY CAROLINA BIOLOGICAL SUPPLY CO.

disposed of in a container of alcohol or household bleach.

Some of the newer flea products, specifically those with fipronil, selamectin and permethrin, have effect against some, but not all, species of tick. Flea collars containing appropriate pesticides (e.g., propoxur, chlorfenvinphos) can aid in tick control. In most areas, such collars should be placed on animals in March, at the beginning of the tick season, and changed regularly. Leaving the collar on when the pesticide level is waning invites the development of resistance. Amitraz collars are also good for tick control, and the active ingredient does not interfere with other flea-control products. The ingredient helps prevent the attachment of ticks to the skin and will cause those ticks already on the skin to detach themselves.

which may be deeply embedded in the skin. This is best accomplished with forceps designed especially for this purpose; fingers can be used but should be protected with rubber gloves, plastic wrap or at least a paper towel. The tick should be grasped as closely as possible to the animal's skin and should be pulled upward with steady, even pressure. Do not squeeze, crush or puncture the body of the tick or you risk exposure to any disease carried by that tick. Once the ticks have been removed, the sites of attachment should be disinfected. Your hands should then be washed with soap and water to further minimize risk of contagion. The tick should be

TICK CONTROL
Removal of underbrush and leaf litter and the thinning of trees in areas where tick control is desired are recommended. These actions remove the cover and food sources for small animals that serve as hosts for ticks. With continued mowing of grasses in these areas, the probability of ticks' surviving is further reduced. A variety of insecticide ingredients (e.g., resmethrin, carbaryl, permethrin, chlorpyrifos, dioxathion and allethrin) are registered for tick control around the home.

MITES

Mites are tiny arachnid parasites that parasitize the skin of dogs. Skin diseases caused by mites are referred to as "mange," and there are many different forms seen in dogs. These forms are very different from one another, each one warranting an individual description.

Sarcoptic mange, or scabies, is one of the itchiest conditions that affects dogs. The microscopic *Sarcoptes* mites burrow into the superficial layers of the skin and can drive dogs crazy with itchiness. They are also communicable to people, although they can't complete their reproductive cycle on people. In addition to being tiny, the mites also are often difficult to find when trying to make a diagnosis. Skin scrapings from multiple areas are examined microscopically but, even then, sometimes the mites cannot be found.

Fortunately, scabies is relatively easy to treat, and there are a variety of products that will successfully kill the mites. Since the mites can't live in the environment for very long without feeding, a complete cure is usually possible within four to eight weeks.

Cheyletiellosis is caused by a relatively large mite, which sometimes can be seen even without a microscope. Often referred to as "walking dandruff," this also causes itching, but not usually as profound as with scabies.

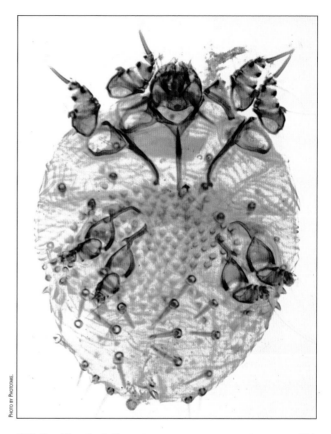

PHOTO BY PHOTOTAKE.

Sarcoptes scabiei, commonly known as the "itch mite."

While *Cheyletiella* mites can survive somewhat longer in the environment than scabies mites, they too are relatively easy to treat, being responsive to not only the medications used to treat scabies but also often to flea-control products.

Otodectes cynotis is the canine ear mite and is one of the more common causes of mange, especially in young dogs in shelters or pet stores. That's because the mites are typically present in large numbers and are quickly spread to

Micrograph of a dog louse, *Heterodoxus spiniger*. Female lice attach their eggs to the hairs of the dog. As the eggs hatch, the larval lice bite and feed on the blood. Lice can also feed on dead skin and hair. This feeding activity can cause hair loss and skin problems.

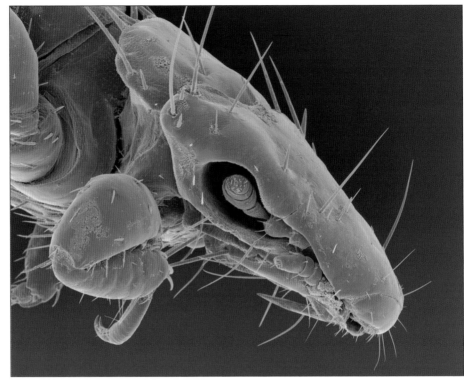

S. E. M. by Dr. Dennis Kunkel, University of Hawaii.

nearby animals. The mites rarely do much harm but can be difficult to eradicate if the treatment regimen is not comprehensive. While many try to treat the condition with ear drops only, this is the most common cause of treatment failure. Ear drops cause the mites to simply move out of the ears and as far away as possible (usually to the base of the tail) until the insecticide levels in the ears drop to an acceptable level—then it's back to business as usual! The successful treatment of ear mites requires treating all animals in the household with a systemic insecticide, such as selamectin, or a

combination of miticidal ear drops combined with whole-body flea-control preparations.

Demodicosis, sometimes referred to as red mange, can be one of the most difficult forms of mange to treat. Part of the problem has to do with the fact that the mites live in the hair follicles and they are relatively well shielded from topical and systemic products. The main issue, however, is that demodectic mange typically results only when there is some underlying process interfering with the dog's immune system.

Since *Demodex* mites are

normal residents of the skin of mammals, including humans, there is usually a mite population explosion only when the immune system fails to keep the number of mites in check. In young animals, the immune deficit may be transient or may reflect an actual inherited immune problem. In older animals, demodicosis is usually seen only when there is another disease hampering the immune system, such as diabetes, cancer, thyroid problems or the use of immune-suppressing drugs. Accordingly, treatment involves not only trying to kill the mange mites but also discerning what is interfering with immune function and correcting it if possible.

Chiggers represent several different species of mite that don't parasitize dogs specifically, but do latch on to passersby and can cause irritation. The problem is most prevalent in wooded areas in the late summer and fall. Treatment is not difficult, as the mites do not complete their life cycle on dogs and are susceptible to a variety of miticidal products.

MOSQUITOES

Mosquitoes have long been known to transmit a variety of diseases to people, as well as just being biting pests during warm weather. They also pose a real risk to pets. Not only

do they carry deadly heartworms but recently there also has been much concern over their involvement with West Nile virus. While we can avoid heartworm with the use of preventive medications, there are no such preventives for West Nile virus. The only method of prevention in endemic areas is active mosquito control. Fortunately, most dogs that have been exposed to the virus only developed flu-like symptoms and, to date, there have not been the large number of reported deaths in canines as seen in some other species.

Illustration of *Demodex folliculoram.*

ILLUSTRATION BY PHOTOTAKE

MOSQUITO REPELLENT

Low concentrations of DEET (less than 10%), found in many human mosquito repellents, have been safely used in dogs but, in these concentrations, probably give only about two hours of protection. DEET may be safe in these small concentrations, but since it is not licensed for use on dogs, there is no research proving its safety for dogs. Products containing permethrin give the longest-lasting protection, perhaps two to four weeks. As DEET is not licensed for use on dogs, and both DEET and permethrin can be quite toxic to cats, appropriate care should be exercised. Other products, such as those containing oil of citronella, also have some mosquito-repellent activity, but typically have a relatively short duration of action.

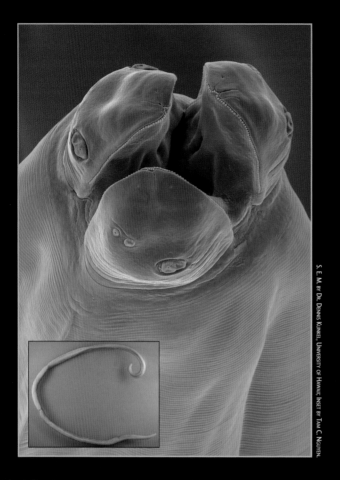

S. E. M. BY DR. DENNIS KUNKEL, UNIVERSITY OF HAWAII; INSET BY TAM C. NGUYEN.

ASCARID DANGERS

The most commonly encountered worms in dogs are roundworms known as ascarids. *Toxascaris leonine* and *Toxocara canis* are the two species that infect dogs. Subsisting in the dog's stomach and intestines, adult roundworms can grow to 7 in. in length and adult females can lay in excess of 200,000 eggs in a single day.

In humans, visceral larval migrans affects people who have ingested eggs of *Toxocara canis*, which frequently contaminates children's sandboxes, beaches and park grounds. The roundworms reside in the human's stomach and intestines, as they would in a dog's, but do not mature. Instead, they find their way to the liver, lungs and skin, or even to the heart or kidneys in severe cases. Deworming puppies is critical in preventing the infection in humans, and young children should never handle nursing pups who have not been dewormed.

The ascarid roundworm *Toxocara canis*, showing the mouth with three lips. INSET: Photomicrograph of the roundworm *Ascaris lumbricoides*.

INTERNAL PARASITES: WORMS

ASCARIDS

Ascarids are intestinal roundworms that rarely cause severe disease in dogs. Nonetheless, they are of major public health significance because they can be transferred to people. Sadly, it is children who are most commonly affected by the parasite, probably from inadvertently ingesting ascarid-contaminated soil. In fact, many yards and children's sandboxes contain appreciable numbers of ascarid eggs. So, while ascarids don't bite dogs or latch onto their intestines to suck blood, they do cause some nasty medical conditions in children and are best eradicated from our furry friends. Because pups can start passing ascarid eggs by three weeks of age, most parasite-control programs begin at two weeks of age and are repeated every two weeks until pups are eight weeks old. It is important to

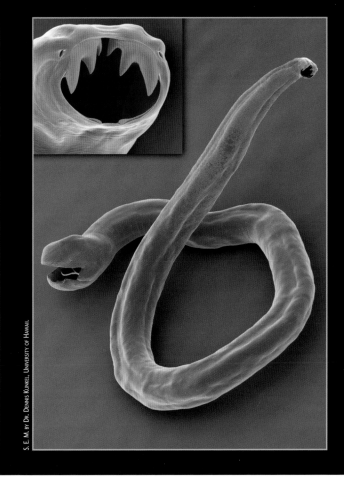

S. E. M. BY DR. DENNIS KUNKEL, UNIVERSITY OF HAWAII.

realize that bitches can pass ascarids to their pups even if they test negative prior to whelping. Accordingly, bitches are best treated at the same time as the pups.

HOOKWORMS

Unlike ascarids, hookworms do latch onto a dog's intestinal tract and can cause significant loss of blood and protein. Similar to ascarids, hookworms can be transmitted to humans, where they cause a condition known as cutaneous larval migrans. Dogs can become infected either by consuming the infective larvae or by the larvae's penetrating the skin directly. People most often get infected when they are lying on the ground (such as on a beach) and the larvae penetrate the skin. Yes, the larvae can penetrate through a beach blanket. Hookworms are typically susceptible to the same medications used to treat ascarids.

The hookworm *Ancylostoma caninum* infests the intestines of dogs. INSET: Note the row of hooks at the posterior end, used to anchor the worm to the intestinal wall.

WHIPWORMS

Whipworms latch onto the lower aspects of the dog's colon and can cause cramping and diarrhea. Eggs do not start to appear in the dog's feces until about three months after the dog was infected. This worm has a peculiar life cycle, which makes it more difficult to control than ascarids or hookworms. The good thing is that whipworms rarely are transferred to people.

Some of the medications used to treat ascarids and hookworms are also effective against whipworms, but, in general, a separate treatment protocol is needed. Since most of the medications are effective against the adults but not the eggs or larvae, treatment is typically repeated in three weeks, and then often in three months as well. Unfortunately, since dogs don't develop resistance to whipworms, it is difficult to prevent them from getting reinfected if they visit soil contaminated with whipworm eggs.

WORM-CONTROL GUIDELINES

- Practice sanitary habits with your dog and home.
- Clean up after your dog and don't let him sniff or eat other dogs' droppings.
- Control insects and fleas in the dog's environment. Fleas, lice, cockroaches, beetles, mice and rats can act as hosts for various worms.
- Prevent dogs from eating uncooked meat, raw poultry and dead animals.
- Keep dogs and children from playing in sand and soil.
- Kennel dogs on cement or gravel; avoid dirt runs.
- Administer heartworm preventives regularly.
- Have your vet examine your dog's stools at your annual visits.
- Select a boarding kennel carefully so as to avoid contamination from other dogs or an unsanitary environment.
- Prevent dogs from roaming. Obey local leash laws.

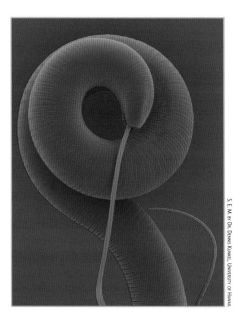

Adult whipworm, *Trichuris* sp., an intestinal parasite.

S. E. M. BY DR. DENNIS KUNKEL, UNIVERSITY OF HAWAII.

TAPEWORMS

There are many different species of tapeworm that affect dogs, but *Dipylidium caninum* is probably the most common and is spread by fleas. Flea larvae feed on organic debris and tapeworm eggs in the environment and, when a dog chews at himself and manages to ingest fleas, he might get a dose of tapeworm at the same time. The tapeworm then develops further in the intestine of the dog.

The tapeworm itself, which is a parasitic flatworm that latches onto the intestinal wall, is composed of numerous segments. When the segments break off into the intestine (as proglottids), they may accumulate around the rectum, like grains of rice. While this tapeworm is disgusting in its behavior, it is not directly communicable to humans (although humans can also get infected by swallowing fleas).

A much more dangerous flatworm is *Echinococcus multiloc-ularis*, which is typically found in foxes, coyotes and wolves. The eggs are passed in the feces and infect rodents, and, when dogs eat the rodents, the dogs can be infected by thousands of adult tapeworms. While the parasites don't cause many problems in dogs, this is considered the most lethal worm infection that people can get. Take appropriate precautions if you live in an area in which these tapeworms are found. Do not use mulch that may contain feces of dogs, cats or wildlife, and

discourage your pets from hunting wildlife. Treat these tapeworm infections aggressively in pets, because if humans get infected, approximately half die.

HEARTWORMS

Heartworm disease is caused by the parasite *Dirofilaria immitis* and is seen in dogs around the world. A member of the roundworm group, it is spread between dogs by the bite of an infected mosquito. The mosquito injects infective larvae into the dog's skin with its bite, and these larvae develop under the skin for a period of time before making their way to the heart. There they develop into adults, which grow and create blockages of the heart, lungs and major blood vessels there. They also start producing offspring (microfilariae)

A dog tapeworm proglottid (body segment).

The dog tapeworm *Taenia pisiformis*.

S. E. M. BY DR. DENNIS KUNKEL, UNIVERSITY OF HAWAII.

A Look at Internal Parasites

Ascarid *Rhabditis*

Hookworm *Ancylostoma caninum*

Tapeworm *Dipylidium caninum*

Heartworm *Dirofilaria immitis*

and these microfilariae circulate in the bloodstream, waiting to hitch a ride when the next mosquito bites. Once in the mosquito, the microfilariae develop into infective larvae and the entire process is repeated.

When dogs get infected with heartworm, over time they tend to develop symptoms associated with heart disease, such as coughing, exercise intolerance and potentially many other manifestations. Diagnosis is confirmed by either seeing the microfilariae themselves in blood samples or using immunologic tests (antigen testing) to identify the presence of adult heartworms. Since antigen tests measure the presence of adult heartworms and microfilarial tests measure offspring produced by adults, neither are positive until six to seven months after the initial infection. However, the beginning of damage can occur by fifth-stage larvae as early as three months after infection. Thus it is possible for dogs to be harboring problem-causing larvae for up to three months before either type of test would identify an infection.

The good news is that there are great protocols available for preventing heartworm in dogs. Testing is critical in the process, and it is important to understand the benefits as well as the limitations of such testing. All dogs six months of age or older that have not been on continuous heartworm-preventive medication should be

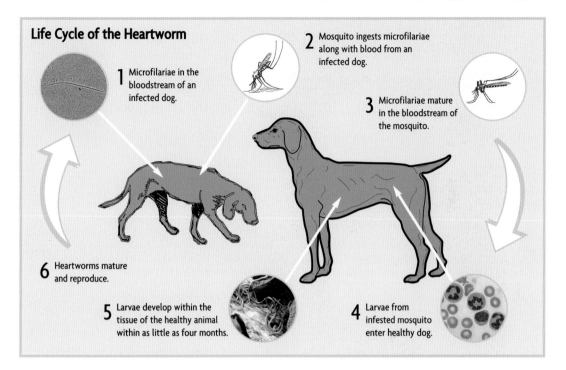

Life Cycle of the Heartworm

1 Microfilariae in the bloodstream of an infected dog.

2 Mosquito ingests microfilariae along with blood from an infected dog.

3 Microfilariae mature in the bloodstream of the mosquito.

6 Heartworms mature and reproduce.

5 Larvae develop within the tissue of the healthy animal within as little as four months.

4 Larvae from infested mosquito enter healthy dog.

screened with microfilarial or antigen tests. For dogs receiving preventive medication, periodic antigen testing helps assess the effectiveness of the preventives. The American Heartworm Society guidelines suggest that annual retesting may not be necessary when owners have absolutely provided continuous heartworm prevention. Retesting on a two- to three-year interval may be sufficient in these cases. However, your veterinarian will likely have specific guidelines under which heartworm preventives will be prescribed, and many prefer to err on the side of safety and retest annually.

It is indeed fortunate that heartworm is relatively easy to prevent, because treatments can be as life-threatening as the disease itself. Treatment requires a two-step process that kills the adult heartworms first and then the microfilariae. Prevention is obviously preferable; this involves a once-monthly oral or topical treatment. The most common oral preventives include ivermectin (not suitable for some breeds), moxidectin and milbemycin oxime; the once-a-month topical drug selamectin provides heartworm protection in addition to flea, some types of tick and other parasite controls.

THE **ABC**s OF
Emergency Care

Abrasions
Clean wound with running water or 3% hydrogen peroxide. Pat dry with gauze and spray with antibiotic. Do not cover.

Animal Bites
Clean area with soap and saline solution or water. Apply pressure to any bleeding area. Apply antibiotic ointment. Identify animal and contact the vet.

Antifreeze Poisoning
Induce vomiting and take dog to the vet.

Bee Sting
Remove stinger and apply soothing lotion or cold compress; give antihistamine in proper dosage.

Bleeding
Apply pressure directly to wound with gauze or towel for five to ten minutes. If wound does not stop bleeding, wrap wound with gauze and adhesive tape.

Bloat/Gastric Torsion
Immediately take the dog to the vet or emergency clinic; phone from car. No time to waste.

Burns
Chemical: Bathe dog with water and pet shampoo. Rinse in saline solution. Apply antibiotic ointment.

Acid: Rinse with water. Apply one part baking soda, two parts water to affected area.

Alkali: Rinse with water. Apply one part vinegar, four parts water to affected area.

Electrical: Apply antibiotic ointment. Seek veterinary assistance immediately.

Choking
If the dog is on the verge of collapsing, wedge a solid object, such as the handle of screwdriver, between molars on one side of mouth to keep mouth open. Pull tongue out. Use long-nosed pliers or fingers to remove foreign object. Do not push the object down the dog's throat. For small or medium dogs, hold dog upside down by hind legs and shake firmly to dislodge foreign object.

Chlorine Ingestion
With clean water, rinse the mouth and eyes. Give dog water to drink; contact the vet.

Constipation
Feed dog 2 tablespoons bran flakes with each meal. Encourage drinking water. Mix 1/4 teaspoon mineral oil in dog's food.

Diarrhea
Withhold food for 12 to 24 hours. Feed dog anti-diarrheal with eyedropper. When feeding resumes, feed one part boiled hamburger, one part plain cooked rice, 1/4 to 3/4 cup four times daily.

Dog Bite
Snip away hair around puncture wound; clean with 3% hydrogen peroxide; apply tincture of iodine. If wound appears deep, take the dog to the vet.

Frostbite
Wrap the dog in a heavy blanket. Warm affected area with a warm bath for ten minutes. Red color to skin will return with circulation; if tissues are pale after 20 minutes, contact the vet.

Use a portable, durable container large enough to contain all items.

Heat Stroke
Partially submerge the dog in cold water; if no response within ten minutes, contact the vet.

Hot Spots
Mix 2 packets Domeboro® with 2 cups water. Saturate cloth with mixture and apply to hot spots for 15 to 30 minutes. Apply antibiotic ointment. Repeat every six to eight hours.

Poisonous Plants
Wash affected area with soap and water. Cleanse with alcohol. For foxtail/grass, apply antibiotic ointment. Contact the vet if plant is ingested.

Rat Poison Ingestion
Induce vomiting. Keep dog calm, maintain dog's normal body temperature (use blanket or heating pad). Get to the vet for antidote.

Shock
Keep the dog calm and warm; call for veterinary assistance.

Snake Bite
If possible, bandage the area and apply pressure. If the area is not conducive to bandaging, use ice to control bleeding. Get immediate help from the vet.

Tick Removal
Apply flea and tick spray directly on tick. Wait one minute. Using tweezers or wearing plastic gloves, apply constant pull while grasping tick's body. Apply antibiotic ointment.

Vomiting
Restrict dog's water intake; offer a few ice cubes. Withhold food for next meal. Contact vet if vomiting persists longer than 24 hours.

DOG OWNER'S FIRST-AID KIT
- ❑ Gauze bandages/swabs
- ❑ Adhesive and non-adhesive bandages
- ❑ Antibiotic powder
- ❑ Antiseptic wash
- ❑ Hydrogen peroxide 3%
- ❑ Antibiotic ointment
- ❑ Lubricating jelly
- ❑ Rectal thermometer
- ❑ Nylon muzzle
- ❑ Scissors and forceps
- ❑ Eyedropper
- ❑ Syringe
- ❑ Anti-bacterial/fungal solution
- ❑ Saline solution
- ❑ Antihistamine
- ❑ Cotton balls
- ❑ Nail clippers
- ❑ Screwdriver/pen knife
- ❑ Flashlight
- ❑ Emergency phone numbers

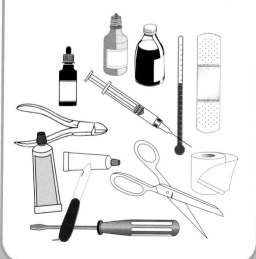

Number-One Killer Disease in Dogs: CANCER

In every age, there is a word associated with a disease or plague that causes humans to shudder. In the 21st century, that word is "cancer." Just as cancer is the leading cause of death in humans, it claims nearly half the lives of dogs that die from a natural disease as well as half the dogs that die over the age of ten years.

Described as a genetic disease, cancer becomes a greater risk as the dog ages. Vets and dog owners have become increasingly aware of the threat of cancer to dogs. Statistics reveal that one dog in every five will develop cancer, the most common of which is skin cancer. Many cancers, including prostate, ovarian and breast cancer, can be avoided by spaying and neutering our dogs by the age of six months.

Early detection of cancer can save or extend a dog's life, so it is absolutely vital for owners to have their dogs examined by a qualified vet or oncologist immediately upon detection of any abnormality. Certain dietary guidelines have also proven to reduce the onset and spread of cancer. Foods based on fish rather than beef, due to the presence of Omega-3 fatty acids, are recommended. Other amino acids such as glutamine have significant benefits for canines, particularly those breeds that show a greater susceptibility to cancer.

Cancer management and treatments promise hope for future generations of canines. Since the disease is genetic, breeders should never breed a dog whose parents, grandparents and any related siblings have developed cancer. It is difficult to know whether to exclude an otherwise healthy dog from a breeding program, as the disease does not manifest itself until the dog's senior years.

RECOGNIZE CANCER WARNING SIGNS

Since early detection can possibly rescue your dog from becoming a cancer statistic, it is essential for owners to recognize the possible signs and seek the assistance of a qualified professional.

- Abnormal bumps or lumps that continue to grow
- Bleeding or discharge from any body cavity
- Persistent stiffness or lameness
- Recurrent sores or sores that do not heal
- Inappetence
- Breathing difficulties
- Weight loss
- Bad breath or odors
- General malaise and fatigue
- Eating and swallowing problems
- Difficulty urinating and defecating

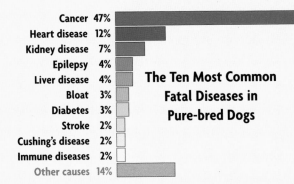

Cancer	47%
Heart disease	12%
Kidney disease	7%
Epilepsy	4%
Liver disease	4%
Bloat	3%
Diabetes	3%
Stroke	2%
Cushing's disease	2%
Immune diseases	2%
Other causes	14%

The Ten Most Common Fatal Diseases in Pure-bred Dogs

CANINE COGNITIVE DYSFUNCTION

"OLD-DOG" SYNDROME

There are many ways for you to evaluate old-dog syndrome. Veterinarians have defined canine cognitive dysfunction as the gradual deterioration of cognitive abilities, indicated by changes in the dog's behavior. When a dog changes his routine response, and maladies have been eliminated as the cause of these behavioral changes, then canine cognitive dysfunction is the usual diagnosis.

More than half the dogs over eight years old suffer from some form of this syndrome. The older the dog, the more chance he has of suffering from it. In humans, doctors often dismiss the canine cognitive dysfunction behavioral changes as part of "winding down."

There are four major signs of canine cognitive dysfunction: frequent potty accidents inside the home, sleeping much more or much less than normal, acting confused and failing to respond to social stimuli.

SYMPTOMS

FREQUENT POTTY ACCIDENTS
- Urinates in the house.
- Defecates in the house.
- Doesn't signal that he wants to go out.

FAILURE TO RESPOND TO SOCIAL STIMULI
- Comes to people less frequently, whether called or not.
- Doesn't tolerate petting for more than a short time.
- Doesn't come to the door when you return home.

CONFUSION
- Goes outside and just stands there.
- Appears confused with a faraway look in his eyes.
- Hides more often.
- Doesn't recognize friends.
- Doesn't come when called.
- Walks around listlessly and without a destination.

SLEEP PATTERNS
- Awakens more slowly.
- Sleeps more than normal during the day.
- Sleeps less during the night.

SHOWING YOUR

SCHIPPERKE

Is dog showing in your blood? Are you excited by the idea of gaiting your handsome Schipperke around the ring to the thunderous applause of an enthusiastic audience? Are you certain that your beloved Schipperke is flawless? You are not alone! Every loving owner thinks that his dog has no faults, or too few to mention. No matter how many times an owner reads the breed standard, he cannot find any faults in his aristocratic companion dog. If this sounds like you, and if you are considering entering your Schipperke in a dog show, here are some basic questions to ask yourself:

- Did you purchase a "show-quality" puppy from the breeder?
- Is your puppy at least six months of age?
- Does the puppy exhibit correct show type for his breed?
- Does your puppy have any disqualifying faults?
- Is your Schipperke registered with the American Kennel Club?

- How much time do you have to devote to training, grooming, conditioning and exhibiting your dog?
- Do you understand the rules and regulations of a dog show?
- Do you have time to learn how to show your dog properly?
- Do you have the financial resources to invest in showing your dog?
- Will you show the dog yourself or hire a professional handler?
- Do you have a vehicle that can accommodate your weekend trips to the dog shows?

Success in the show ring requires more than a pretty face, a waggy tail and a pocketful of liver. Even though dog shows can be exciting and enjoyable, the sport of conformation makes great demands on the exhibitors and the dogs. Winning exhibitors live for their dogs, devoting time and money to their dogs' presentation, conditioning and training. Very few novices, even those with good dogs, will find themselves in the winners' circle, though it does happen. Don't be disheartened, though. Every exhibitor began as a novice and worked his way up to the group ring. It's the "working your way up" part that you must keep in mind.

Assuming that you have purchased a puppy of the correct type and quality for showing, let's begin to examine the world of showing and what's required to get started. Although the entry fee into a dog show is nominal, there are lots of other hidden costs involved with "finishing" your Schipperke, that is, making him a champion. Things like equipment, travel, training and conditioning all cost money. A more serious campaign will include fees for a professional handler, boarding, cross-country travel and advertising. Top-winning show dogs can represent a very considerable investment—over $100,000 has been spent in campaigning some dogs. (The investment can be less, of course, for owners who don't use professional handlers.)

Many owners, on the other hand, enter their "average" Schipperkes in dog shows for the fun and enjoyment of it. Dog showing makes an absorbing hobby, with many rewards for dogs and owners alike. If you're having fun, meeting other people who share your interests and enjoying the overall experience, you likely will catch the "bug." Once the dog-show bug bites, its effects can last a lifetime; it's

certainly much better than a deer tick! Soon you will be envisioning yourself in the center ring at the Westminster Kennel Club Dog Show in New York City, competing for the prestigious Best in Show cup. This magical dog show is televised annually from Madison Square Garden, and the victorious dog becomes a celebrity overnight.

AKC CONFORMATION SHOWING

Interested in dog showing? Visiting a dog show as a spectator is a great place to start. Pick up the show catalog to find out what time your breed is being shown, who is judging the breed and in which ring the classes will be held. To start, Schipperkes compete against other Schipperkes, and the winner is

Ch. Dante's Over the Top is a Best in Show and Best in Specialty Show winner, owned by Amy Gossman.

GROUP SECOND

TULLAHOMA KENNEL CLUB MARCH 2005 ©KempPhoto.com

selected as Best of Breed by the judge. This is the procedure for each breed. At a group show, all of the Best of Breed winners go on to compete for Group One in their respective groups. For example, all Best of Breed winners in a given group compete against each other; this is done for all seven groups. Finally, all seven group winners go head to head in the ring for the Best in Show award.

What most spectators don't understand is the basic idea of conformation. A dog show is often referred to as a "conforma-tion" show. This means that the judge should decide how each dog stacks up (conforms) to the breed standard for his given breed: how well does this Schipperke conform to the ideal representative detailed in the standard? Ideally, this is what happens. In reality, however, this ideal often gets slighted as the judge compares Schipperke #1 to Schipperke #2. Again, the ideal is that each dog is judged based on his merits in comparison to his breed standard, not in comparison to the other dogs in the ring. It is easier for judges to compare dogs of the same breed to decide which they think is the better specimen; in the Group and Best in Show ring, however, it is very difficult

Ch. Shalako's the Rose, still in full bloom at ten years of age, was a top-ranked bitch owned by Bette Wynn and Nancie Mages. She is the dam of multiple BIS winners.

to compare one breed to another, like apples to oranges. Thus the dog's conformation to the breed standard—not to mention advertising dollars and good handling—is essential to success in conformation shows. The dog described in the standard (the standard for each AKC breed is written and approved by the breed's national parent club and then submitted to the AKC for approval) is the perfect dog of that breed, and breeders keep their eye on the standard when they choose which dogs to breed, hoping to get closer and closer to the ideal with each litter.

An outdoor specialty show for Schipperkes held in the breed's native country, Belgium. The author photographed this handsome line-up of competitors.

FIVE CLASSES AT SHOWS

At most AKC all-breed shows, there are five regular classes offered: Puppy, Novice, Bred-by-Exhibitor, American-bred and Open. The Puppy Class is usually divided as 6 to 9 months of age and 9 to 12 months of age. When deciding in which class to enter your dog, whether male or female, you must carefully check the show schedule to make sure that you have selected the right class. Depending on the age of the dog, previous first-place wins and the sex of the dog, you must make the best choice. It is possible to enter a one-year-old dog who has not won sufficient first places in any of the non-Puppy Classes, though the competition is more intense the further you progress from the Puppy Class.

Another good first step for the novice is to join a dog club. You will be astonished by the many and different kinds of dog clubs in the country, with about 5,000 clubs holding events every year. Most clubs require that prospective new members present two letters of recommendation from existing members. Perhaps you've made some friends visiting a show held by a particular club and you would like to join that club. Dog clubs may specialize in a single breed, like a local or regional Schipperke club, or in a specific pursuit, such as obedience, tracking or herding tests. There are all-breed clubs for all dog enthusiasts; they sponsor special training days, seminars on topics like grooming or handling or lectures on breeding or canine genetics. There are also clubs that specialize in certain types of dogs, like companion dogs, hunting dogs, toy breeds, etc.

A parent club is the national organization, sanctioned by the AKC, which promotes and safeguards its breed in the country. The Schipperke Club of America was formed in 1929 and can be contacted on the Internet at www.schipperkeclub-usa.org. The parent club holds an annual national specialty show, usually in a different city each year, in which many of the country's top dogs, handlers and breeders gather to compete. At a specialty show, only members of a single breed are invited to participate. There are also group specialties, in which all members of a group are invited. For more information about dog clubs in your area, contact the AKC at www.akc.org on the Internet or write them at their Raleigh, NC address.

Ch. Hafrikaantje Vrouwvliet, a handsome FCI champion.

OTHER TYPES OF COMPETITION

In addition to conformation shows, the AKC holds a variety of other competitive events. Obedience trials, agility trials and tracking trials are open to all breeds, while hunting tests, field trials, lure coursing, herding tests and trials, earthdog tests and coonhound events are limited to specific breeds or groups of breeds. The Junior Showmanship program is offered to aspiring young handlers and their dogs, and the Canine Good Citizen® Program is an all-around good-behavior test open to all dogs, pure-bred and mixed.

OBEDIENCE TRIALS

Mrs. Helen Whitehouse Walker, a Standard Poodle fancier, can be credited with introducing obedience trials to the United States. In the 1930s, she designed a series of exercises based on those of the Associated Sheep, Police, Army Dog Society of Great Britain. These exercises were intended to evaluate the working relationship between dog and owner. Since those early days of the sport in the US, obedience trials have grown more and more popular, and now more than 2,000 trials each year attract over 100,000 dogs and their owners. Any dog registered with the AKC, regardless of neutering or other disqualifications that would preclude entry in conformation competition, can participate in obedience trials.

There are three levels of difficulty in obedience competition. The first (and easiest) level is the Novice, in which dogs can earn the Companion Dog (CD) title. The intermediate level is the Open level, in which the Companion Dog Excellent (CDX) title is awarded. The advanced level is the Utility level, in which dogs compete for the Utility Dog (UD) title. Classes at each level are further divided into "A" and "B," with "A" for beginners and "B" for those with more experience. In order to win a title at a given level, a dog must earn three "legs." A "leg" is accomplished when a dog scores 170 or higher (200 is a perfect score). The scoring system gets a little trickier when you understand that a dog must score more than 50% of the points available for each exercise in order to actually earn the points. Available points for each exercise range between 20 and 40.

Once he's earned the UD title, a dog can go on to win the prestigious title of Utility Dog Excellent (UDX) by winning "legs" in ten shows. Additionally, Utility Dogs who win "legs" in Open B and Utility B earn points toward the lofty title of Obedience Trial Champion (OTCh.). Established in 1977 by the AKC, this title requires a dog to earn 100 points

> **FOR MORE INFORMATION...**
>
> For reliable up-to-date information about registration, dog shows and other canine competitions, contact one of the national registries by mail or via the Internet.
>
> American Kennel Club
> 5580 Centerview Dr., Raleigh, NC 27606-3390
> www.akc.org
>
> United Kennel Club
> 100 E. Kilgore Road, Kalamazoo, MI 49002
> www.ukcdogs.com
>
> Canadian Kennel Club
> 89 Skyway Ave., Suite 100, Etobicoke, Ontario
> M9W 6R4 Canada
> www.ckc.ca

as well as three first places in a combination of Open B and Utility B classes under three different judges. The "brass ring" of obedience competition is the AKC's National Obedience Invitational. This is an exclusive competition for only the cream of the obedience crop. In order to qualify for the invitational, a dog must be ranked in either the top 25 all-breeds in obedience or in the top three for his breed in obedience. The title at stake here is that of National Obedience Champion (NOC).

AGILITY TRIALS

Agility trials became sanctioned by the AKC in August 1994, when the first licensed agility trials were held. Since that time, agility certainly has grown in popularity by leaps and bounds, literally! The AKC allows all registered breeds (including Miscellaneous Class breeds) to participate, providing the dog is 12 months of age or older. Agility is designed so that the handler demonstrates how well the dog can work at his side. The handler directs his dog through, over, under and around an obstacle course that includes jumps, tires, the dog walk, weave poles, pipe tunnels, collapsed tunnels and more. While working his way through the course, the dog must keep one eye and ear on his handler and the rest of his body on the course. The handler runs along with the dog, giving verbal and hand signals to guide the dog through the course.

Ch. Shalako's Rockn' Whisper, bred by Bette Wynn and Jen Garrett, is the winner of Best in Show and Best in Specialty Show awards.

The first organization to promote agility trials in the US was the United States Dog Agility Association, Inc. (USDAA). Established in 1986, the USDAA sparked the formation of many member clubs around the country. To participate in USDAA trials, dogs must be at least 18 months of age.

The USDAA and AKC both offer titles to winning dogs, although the exercises and requirements of the two organizations differ. Agility Dog (AD), Advanced Agility Dog (AAD) and Master Agility Dog (MAD) are the titles offered by the USDAA, while the AKC offers Novice Agility (NA), Open Agility (OA), Agility Excellent (AX) and Master Agility Excellent (MX). Beyond these four AKC titles, dogs can win additional titles in "jumper" classes: Jumper with Weave Novice (NAJ), Open (OAJ) and Excellent (MXJ). The ultimate title in AKC agility is MACH, Master Agility Champion. Dogs can continue to add number designations to the MACH title, indicating how many times the dog has met the title's requirements (MACH1, MACH2 and so on).

Agility trials are a great way to keep your dog active, and they will keep you running, too! You should join a local agility club to learn more about the sport. These clubs offer sessions in which you can introduce your dog to the various obstacles as well as training classes to prepare him for competition. In no time, your dog will be climbing A-frames, crossing the dog walk and flying over hurdles, all with you right beside him. Your heart will leap every time your dog jumps through the hoop—and you'll be having just as much (if not more) fun!

TRACKING

Tracking tests are exciting ways to test your Schipperke's instinctive scenting ability on a competitive level. All dogs have a nose, and all breeds are welcome in tracking tests. The first AKC-licensed tracking test took place in 1937 as part of the Utility level at an obedience trial, and thus competitive tracking was officially begun. The first title, Tracking Dog (TD), was offered in 1947, ten years after the first official tracking test. It was not until 1980 that the AKC added the title Tracking Dog Excellent (TDX), which was followed by the title Versatile Surface Tracking (VST) in 1995. Champion Tracker (CT) is awarded to a dog who has earned all three of those titles.

The TD level is the first and most basic level in tracking, progressing in difficulty to the TDX and then the VST. A dog must follow a track laid by a human 30 to 120 minutes prior in order to earn the TD title. The track is about 500 yards long and contains up to 5 directional changes. At the next level, the TDX, the dog must follow a 3- to 5-hour-old track over a course that is up to 1,000 yards long and has up to 7 directional changes. In the most difficult level, the VST, the track is up to 5 hours old and located in an urban setting.

CANINE GOOD CITIZEN® PROGRAM

Have you ever considered getting your dog "certified"? The AKC's Canine Good Citizen® Program affords your dog just that opportunity. Your dog shows that he is a well-behaved canine citizen, using the basic training and good manners you have taught him, by taking a series of ten tests that illustrate that he can behave properly at home, in a public place and around other dogs. The tests are administered by participating dog clubs, colleges, 4-H clubs, Scouts and other community groups and are open to all pure-bred and mixed-breed dogs. Upon passing the ten tests, the suffix CGC is then applied to your dog's name.

The ten tests are: 1. Accepting a friendly stranger; 2. Sitting politely for petting; 3. Appearance and grooming; 4. Walking on a lead; 5. Walking through a group of people; 6. Sit, down and stay on command; 7. Coming when called; 8. Meeting another dog; 9. Calm reaction to distractions; 10. Separation from owner.

INDEX

My Schipperke

PUT YOUR PUPPY'S FIRST PICTURE HERE

Dog's Name _____

Date _____ Photographer _____

Measurement and Evaluation in the Schools

LOUIS J. KARMEL

University of Kentucky

The Macmillan Company · Collier-Macmillan Limited, *London*

This book is dedicated with love to my little women

ELIZABETH ANNE
CATHERINE LEE
MARY PATRICIA

Preface

This book is written primarily for teachers. It may also be used in introductory measurement courses for guidance and psychology students. The essence of this book is to communicate measurement and evaluation concepts to the beginning student in simple and direct language. Measurement concepts that one needs to know in actual school practice are stressed. In attempting to do this, accuracy and scholarship have not been neglected, but have been translated into readily understandable terms.

The organizational plan is intended to increase, not to discourage, student interest. Historical and scientific information is integrated throughout the book in relevant sections. The first two chapters deal with questions uppermost in the minds of contemporary students. For example, Why do we give tests? What about cultural bias? What is the relationship between IQ scores and innate ability? What do tests mean for disadvantaged students? Do our tests indicate that Negroes are equal to or inferior to white students? In the discussion of these and other questions historical and contemporary research and thinking are presented. An attempt is made to give candid answers.

The rationale of presenting issues before actual exposure to the details of measurement is based on the premise that involvement through visceral and intellectual stimulation increases motivation and breaks down some of the hostility many students have toward testing. Thus, the first two chapters attempt to capitalize on general testing interest and to present and clarify erroneous testing information propagated by test zealots and critics.

After the first two chapters the reader is gradually introduced, in nontechnical language, to technical aspects of testing and to practical applications of measurement. Standardized testing is not relegated to a secondary position; a full and detailed explanation of concepts that the nontesting expert needs to know is presented. Many measurement textbooks that are geared primarily for teachers spend proportionately little time on this area and devote themselves mainly to teacher-made tests. The need for teachers and other school personnel to understand standardized testing cannot be overemphasized. Many statements critical of testing could be eliminated if the test consumer used tests more appropriately. Teachers, especially in the elementary grades, deal with standardized testing and need to know the significance of these tests.

In a recent investigation of the role of the teacher in testing, Dr. David A. Goslin,[1] a staff sociologist at the Russell Sage Foundation, found that the average teacher is poorly prepared to use standardized test information. He found that this was especially true among elementary school teachers, who were most often responsible for the administration, interpretation, and use of standardized tests. Dr. Goslin emphasized the classroom teachers' involvement with, and responsibility for, standardized testing and their lack of adequate training for this task. This book attempts to meet this need.

Although standardized tests are discussed at length, the classroom test is not neglected. Both the good and bad points of teacher-made tests are discussed in the context of the school setting. That is, realistic suggestions for the construction of various types of teacher-made tests are presented.

In the area of statistics the author has attempted to present this material based on his years of experience in the public schools and in teaching teachers at the university level. Teachers as a group do not understand mathematical concepts as easily as they do verbal terms. Therefore, the statistics section has been written for the nonmathematical teacher. Only statistics that the teacher needs to know for classroom use and for an understanding of standardized tests are presented. Formulas and involved statistical manipulations have been kept to a minimum.

A full chapter is devoted to college entrance examinations because of the contemporary importance of admission to college and obtaining a college degree. An attempt is made to convey the basic features of the two national college testing programs. In addition, research findings concerning how college entrance tests relate to college success, the place of entrance tests in admission procedures, and the value of preparation for the tests are reviewed.

In keeping with the theme of involvement, additional readings are cited in the particular section to which they pertain rather than at the end of each chapter. The reference style conforms to the American Psychological Association's format. That is, the name and date are given in the context of the discussion, for example, Jones (1968). The sources can be found by consulting the reference list at the end of each chapter. References are arranged in alphabetical order.

In summary, this book attempts to convey basic measurement and evaluation concepts in understandable language. Case studies and "living" language are used.

I want to thank my wife, Marylin Odom Karmel, a former school teacher herself, for helping in this endeavor. Her professional advice, knowledge of the public schools, and knowledge of teachers and their problems were extremely useful in gearing the text to school usage. Her ability to say things

[1] David A. Goslin, *Teacher and Testing*. New York: Russell Sage Foundation, 1967.

clearly and avoid the professorial syndrome of verbosity has been of considerable value.

I would also like to acknowledge my everlasting gratitude to Dr. Luther R. Taff of the University of North Carolina (Chapel Hill), who provided me with the opportunity for growth both personally and professionally. And last but not least I would like to thank my students, whose questions, ideas, and approaches are reflected in this book.

L.J.K.

Lexington, Kentucky

Contents

**PART THREE: Individual Tests of
                      Intelligence and Personality**

PART FOUR: Group Standardized Testing

PART FIVE: Teacher-Made Tests and Grades

PART SIX: A School Testing and Evaluation Program

Figures

Tables

PART ONE

Reasons for Testing and Contemporary Issues

The Reasons
We Give Tests

"I am beginning to think our children are tested to death," states an irate parent. Another parent asks why the school gives tests when, "We all know they aren't very good." The critics of testing add to the concern by such statements as, "Tests are culturally biased," "Tests penalize the creative child," or, "Tests invade the privacy of the individual." Other thoughtful voices raise the issue of teacher-made tests and their relevancy for measuring student learning.

These questions are of legitimate concern and need to be answered in an objective and meaningful manner. This chapter will attempt to provide a general basis for the answers to these and other questions; Chapter 2 will deal with specific issues and problems.

It is very difficult to generalize about testing in the school situation without taking into consideration certain variables such as the philosophy and objectives of a particular school, its resources, and its geographic location. A school should administer many different types of tests because no one test can measure all the varied facets of a child's ability, interests, and personality. In the process of educational and personal development changes occur which must be considered in any meaningful picture of a human being. Even in one single area, such as intelligence, more than one test is needed over a period of years to obtain a measure of ability.

Basically, schools use tests as educational tools to promote individualized instruction. Individualized instruction is the major reason for testing. It implies that the school's basic duty to the child is to know him as an individual. Inherent in this is a recognition of the dignity and worth of the individual and his unique qualities. The basic premise for giving tests is the assumption that individuals differ and that education must be geared to these differences so that each person may develop his or her own unique potential.

If we accept this assumption of individual differences then we must also make certain other assumptions. We must realize, for example, that some children are ready to read at four whereas others are not ready until they are six or eight. Some children find school a "snap," and others find it a "drag." Certain children find mathematics easy, and others are lost. The child who finds math difficult may excel in English, whereas his mathematically superior peer may find English his most difficult subject. Some children may be academically superior in all subjects; others may be slow to learn in all areas. Some children may reveal a great deal of promise but obtain poor grades in school. Other children may have personal problems that interfere with academic success.

We will now turn our attention to the nature of tests, how they help in identifying some of the children previously mentioned, and how they can be used to individualize instruction. Before we begin our discussion of the reasons for testing we must first know the meaning of the term *test*.

Webster's *New Collegiate Dictionary* defines the word *test* as "any critical examination or trial . . . means of trial . . . subjection to conditions that show the real character of a person or thing in a certain particular," and "that with which anything is compared for proof of genuineness." According to Webster the use of *test* in education means, "Any series of questions or exercises or other means of measuring the skill, knowledge, intelligence, capacities or aptitudes of an individual or group."

Generally when we use the word *test* we mean to appraise something or someone. That is, to test is to evaluate or measure something or someone against given criteria in order to obtain data that reveals relationships between our subject and our frame of reference. For example, in our space program the vehicles and men are subject to simulated conditions of space before the actual launching. They are being *tested* to ascertain their future performance in outer space. In a school setting the child is *tested* in order to discover the degree of learning that has taken or may take place. Mary failed her spelling test. Johnny got 100 on his history test. Billy's test scores reveal a high potential for school success. Ruth's test scores show average potential for success in secretarial tasks. Mary and Johnny's past learnings are being measured; Billy and Ruth's future chances of success are being evaluated, that is, tested.

Teacher-Made Tests

In the classroom the teacher may approach testing in many different ways. She may, for example, ask her students to write "in your own words the meaning of the Fifth Amendment of the United States Constitution." Or she may say, "Discuss the implications of the Magna Charta on the United States political system." Such questions are generally referred to as essay tests.

In addition to or instead of the essay examination the classroom teacher may use the objective test. The word *objective* encompasses many different types of tests. *Objective*, as used in testing, means that the scoring is not influenced by the opinion, knowledge, or skill of the person scoring the test; or whether or not the person taking the test and the person scoring the test "communicate." Thus, any test which has predetermined correct answers may be called objective. For example, in the two previously mentioned essay questions the correct answer is subject to interpretation by the teacher. The scoring is, therefore, subjective. On the other hand, the objective test leaves little, if any, latitude for interpretation of answers because there is only one correct answer.

The true-false question and the completion and multiple-choice item are examples of the objective test. The following are items illustrative of these tests.

> *True-False.* The scoring of an essay test is subjective. T____ F____
> *Multiple Choice.* In *objective testing,* the term *objective* refers to the method of
>
> 1. identifying learning outcomes.
> 2. selecting test content.
> 3. presenting the problem.
> 4. scoring the answers.
>
> *Completion.* According to the author of your text, schools use tests as educational tools to promote ____ ____.

Why Do Teachers Use Tests?

The teacher's primary role in the classroom is to teach; whether he succeeds may be ascertained by the intellectual growth and development of his pupils. In order to gauge this progress the teacher must institute evaluative techniques. These techniques include essay and objective tests and informal procedures, such as day-to-day classroom observations and teacher judgment based on professional experience and intuition. All of these procedures aid the teacher in evaluating pupil progress. Our attention, however, will be focused on the reasons for using formal evaluative instruments called tests.

Certification of Pupil Achievement

Many educators are dissatisfied with our present system of grading. It is true that poorly constructed tests may make our present system even worse. It is also true, however, that students must be evaluated in some manner, whether it be by marks, letters of recommendation, or comments on academic levels of proficiency. The test if properly conceived and executed can be of assistance in the verification of pupil progress. The teacher, for example, needs to know if pupils have learned enough in first grade to warrant promotion to second grade. The teacher needs to know about pupil achievements in order to certify these accomplishments to other educational institutions and the world of work.

Measuring Outcomes of Instruction

Tests aid in determining the learning outcomes of classroom instruction. The teacher-made test is a reflection of what the individual teacher considers important. If a teacher-made test stresses concepts or understanding over factual recall, this is indicative of the teacher's basic educational objectives. The teacher can then evaluate the success or failure of classroom learning in relation to the test results. An analysis of student responses to the test can be helpful to the teacher in adjusting the level and direction of classroom instruction.

Incentive

Well-constructed tests which reflect classroom instruction can increase student learning by helping to develop study habits and directing intellectual energy toward the desired educational objectives. Test results can reveal areas of strength and weakness of individual students and act as motivating devices for future study. Of course, poorly constructed tests that are used as disciplinary instruments may have the opposite effect and discourage student incentive.

Teacher-made tests are an important aspect of classroom instruction and can increase or decrease academic progress, depending on their quality and relevance. A detailed discussion of various types of teacher-made tests and specific suggestions concerning their construction will be found in later chapters.

Standardized Tests

Most people have had some experience with a standardized test, in school, or the armed services or when applying for employment. In educational and psychological measurement, *standardization* means a fixed or uniform procedure in the administration and scoring of tests. A standardized test may be administered to a group or individual, but always under the same conditions. The allotted time is always the same and the answers to the questions are always scored in the same manner.

Standardized tests are the direct result of the early efforts of persons concerned with testing who sought a uniform method of measuring children's abilities and educational progress. The evaluation of academic achievement in the United States before 1860 was mainly by oral examination. Teachers or visiting examiners would present oral questions to the student. There was no method of objective evaluation of the replies nor did each student of the same grade receive the same questions. Only one student at a time was tested. The oral examination was time-consuming and revealed little indication of differences among students in areas of specific achievement, because each student was presented with a different task. There was no uniformity in questions or in the evaluation of responses.

The oral examination was gradually replaced in the last half of the nineteenth century by the written examination. The colleges began using the written test as a basis for admission. These tests were similar to our present essay test. All students were presented with the same questions and asked to respond in written discourse. This procedure had the advantage over the oral method of uniformity of tasks and completion time. However, the scoring or grading of the student's responses was still highly subjective. The scorer's standards, bias, mood, and other factors, such as neatness and clarity of handwriting, could play a part in the final evaluation.

Although these early essay tests were not standardized, they were the first attempts at standard procedures in educational testing. At the same time that educators were working on uniform school examinations, modern experimental psychology was developing. Wilhelm Wundt in 1879 established the first[1] formal psychology laboratory in Leipzig, Germany. Most of his work was devoted to the senses, especially vision. The quantitative relationship between a stimulus and the ensuing experience was of particular concern to the early experimental psychologist and remains today of great importance to educational and psychological measurement. The actual studies dealing with such sensory processes as the relationship between light or sound waves and the experienced intensity of the sensation are not of particular interest to educational and psychological measurement. However, the experimental procedures that the

---

[1] It should be noted that experimental psychology did not begin with Wundt at Leipzig. He established the *first modern formal* psychology laboratory, but many of his areas of study had been pioneered by others. Plato, Aristotle, St. Augustine, and others left their mark on the history of psychology. It was Descartes who in the seventeenth century introduced the concept of reflex action. E. H. Weber's experiments in physiology in the middle of the nineteenth century under experimental controls and quantification of this data constituted the beginnings of laboratory psychology. Also in the midnineteenth century, G. T. Fechner amplified Weber's findings in a book on psychophysics (1860). Psychophysical methods invented by Fechner laid the groundwork for psychology's first laboratory procedures.

early psychologists developed—and indeed, the discovery, that there was a difference in the perception of identical phenomena by different people— are important. Their experimental methods provided a legacy of careful attention to experimental methods, statistical techniques, and precision in the standardization of testing instruments.

The authors and publishers of standardized tests attempt to evaluate their instruments by many of the same rigorous scientific techniques that were used by experimental psychology.

Another way of thinking about a standardized test is to equate it with a recipe in cooking. If you are planning to make a crepe suzette or a chocolate cake, you will need instructions that have proved successful. If you follow these instructions *exactly*, your efforts should be rewarding. You should be able to reproduce the flavor and texture of the original recipe. The elaborate kitchens of many of the leading flour companies have a laboratory atmosphere. The exact ingredients, procedures for mixing, and conditions of baking are repeated over and over again to assure you, the consumer, of an accurate recipe. In the same way, a standardized test is subjected to rigorous experimentation on different groups of people. The conditions of testing and the reading of directions and the scoring are always the same. The person who is being tested with the X Test of Mental Abilities in Lexington, Kentucky, will receive exactly the same directions, questions, and time to complete the examination as the person who is being tested with the same standardized test in New York City or London, England. Scoring of the test will be the same no matter where the test is administered. The correct answers are fixed and no deviation from this format because of geography, culture, or subjective opinions of the test administrator is permitted.

If there are changes in the standardized directions then the test ceases to be standardized and its value is severely impaired or completely obviated. This is similar to the changing of a recipe. If you put in three cups of sugar rather than one, the chocolate cake may be more to your liking than the original recipe, but it is no longer the same cake. This is also true of the standardized test. You may change the directions, time, or scoring and thereby make the test more appropriate for your group of students. What you will have then is a classroom test, maybe an excellent one, but not a standardized test that will allow you to compare your students with other children of similar age or grade throughout the country.

The chief value of the standardized test is to provide teachers and students with an objective educational yardstick that can measure abilities or achievement free of subjective error. Let us look at some common evaluation problems found in the classroom.

Mary is a ten-year-old in the fifth grade at Jones Elementary School. She is very neat in her appearance and work. Her teachers have always found her to be a "doll" and more than willing to help with projects in the classroom. Mary's grades have always been excellent. Last fall Mary and her classmates were given a battery of standardized tests. Mary's teacher was surprised to find that Mary was only of average ability and achievement according to the test results.

Peter, who is also ten years old and in the same class as Mary, is quite a different person. Peter has done poorly in school, barely passing each year. His appearance and written work are very sloppy. When his teacher asks him to help with projects he is quite reluctant and sullen in responding. Peter's teacher was also surprised at Peter's test scores. The standardized tests revealed that Peter was of superior ability and above average in achievement.

Mary and Peter present us with the classical cases of possible teacher bias. Mary is a "model" child and the teacher likes her. Peter is sullen and difficult to teach; furthermore, he is untidy in appearance and work. Is it possible that the teacher's personal feelings have entered into the evaluation of their classroom work?

Mary and Peter's teacher, being human, cannot help being subjective in the grading of her students. The standardized test assists her by presenting data free of subjectivity. Mary and Peter may now be viewed from another frame of reference. The teacher can weigh her subjective feelings with the objective evidence and make appropriate teaching decisions.

It should be noted in our example that no definitive suggestions were made as to the new course of action open to Mary and Peter's teacher. It is still up to her to make the final educational decisions. No claim is made or intended for the infallibility of the standardized test over teacher evaluation. The standardized test is only an educational tool to be used along with other educational techniques. It provides another aid in helping the teacher and student make sound educational decisions.

Let us return for a moment to our example of cooking. In our discussion of recipes and their scientific standardization we must not lose sight of two factors. One is that the application of experimental procedures is as new in cooking as it is in educational and psychological measurement. Old recipes that our grandmothers used were as subjective as oral examinations in school. For example, if you read old cookbooks you might find this direction in a recipe: "Add enough flour to make a stiff dough." How much skill in cooking did our grandmothers need to interpret "enough" and "stiff dough"? This is not to state that our grandmothers could not bake or that their results were not as good or better than those of our present cooks. The basic point is that grandmother had intuitively or subjectively to interpret recipes, whereas present-day cooks may follow exact directions of procedure and measurement of ingredients.

Many of grandmother's teachers were able to match the quality and reliability of many of our present standardized tests. But, as in cooking, one doubts that they were able to produce their results consistently without subjective error.

The second factor to be noted is that, of course, a standardized test is not as reliable as a recipe produced in one of our modern experimental kitchens. The human variables involved make this impossible. However, standardized tests generally appraise human behavior and capacity in a more accurate manner than subjective devices, such as teacher's evaluation.

In essence, then, the standardized test is a scientific instrument that has been exposed to rigorous experimental controls. Its main features are uniformity of administration and scoring. It consists of questions that are factual in the sense that there is an agreed correct answer. Each test is subjected to careful investigation by a preliminary administration, and questions that have been found to be poor are eliminated. The actual construction and criteria that must be met in producing a standardized test will be discussed in ensuing chapters.

The reader should remember that standardized tests *are not free of error.* They are not substitutes for teacher evaluation. The teacher's own tests, as well as ratings on class projects and daily classroom performances, are as important as they ever were. Nevertheless, they add to her educational arsenal of teaching devices and enhance her effectiveness as a teacher.

Why Do Schools Use Standardized Tests?

The reader has now been exposed to the differences between teacher-made and standardized tests. A general overview of the reasons for testing has been presented. Let us now explore some of the specific reasons for standardized test usage in the school.

Grouping

The school may use the information provided by standardized tests to group pupils within a particular classroom or to form classroom groups. Thus, tests can help the teacher handle individual differences in students by indicating which children have the same or similar level of skill in a particular subject. Students in education and psychology are constantly exposed to the concept of individual differences. The arrangement of students within the classroom or the assigning of students to certain classroom groups according to ability and skill is in line with our awareness of individual differences.

In the classroom the teacher observes and experiences individual differences among her students. Teachers are often frustrated by their inability to give proper instruction to the bright child and the slow student at the same time. If the teacher is able to use an objective instrument, such as an intelligence test, along with subjective criteria, he can group children within a class according to their individual ability and gear his teaching accordingly.

If a school's philosophy is in agreement with homogenous grouping of classes, then standardized tests can help in arranging classroom groups. For example, the knowledge gained from a mathematics aptitude test may assist the junior or senior high school staff in placing some students in algebra and others in general mathematics.

Let us, for illustrative purposes, look at two students, Robert and Mike, who are to begin ninth grade next fall. Robert and Mike have taken a battery of standardized tests which will be used along with other data in their classroom assignment at Glen High School. Glen High School groups its pupils into three categories—slow, average, and advanced—for instruction in English, foreign languages, mathematics, and science. Robert's tests revealed high general ability, high achievement in English, high aptitude for foreign languages, but only average achievement and ability in science and mathematics. Mike's scores showed average general ability, poor English achievement with little chance of success in foreign languages, and poor skills and ability in mathematics and science.

Robert is advised to enroll in the "advanced" foreign language class (choice of specific language is his own decision), the "advanced" English class, the "average" algebra class, and the "average" science class.

Mike is advised to wait until the tenth grade before beginning his language studies. The school also advises the "slow" English class along with general mathematics and the "slow" science course.

The school's recommendations for classroom placement are based on a variety of factors; these include school record, teacher recommendations, and results of standardized testing. Tests add the objective dimension to the important decision of where to place pupils.

The reader should note two important facts. (1) Children should *never* be assigned to classroom groups or within a class solely on the basis of tests. The test adds an objective dimension to intelligent planning. It should *not* be used in lieu of teacher opinion but only as another measure. The combination of teacher opinion and standardized test results gives us the best basis for intelligent decisions. Either one used alone decreases the probability of sound educational planning. (2) It should also be stated that even if the class has been grouped according to ability, there will still be a wide range of talent within the class. For example, students placed in the "average" algebra class will probably present abilities and achievements ranging from barely average to very high average. The barely average pupil will probably have difficulty in mastering the material, whereas the very high average student may find some of it very boring. Yet both are in the average group. To think that because of grouping we have completely eliminated the problem of varying abilities is to misunderstand the process. Grouping does cut down the spread of talent; it does not, however, eliminate it.

Special Study and Remedial Instruction

It is, many times, very difficult for a teacher to distinguish between general low intellectual ability and a specialized problem in a particular skill, such as reading. If a teacher finds that a student is doing poorly in mathematics, he may think the student is not capable of the work. If, however, he has objective evidence that the child is capable, then he may concentrate on the subject matter and the specific difficulty within it. If, on the other hand, the evidence reveals limited ability, instruction may proceed according to the child's ability and the teacher may not expect as much as he would from a more gifted youngster. If the teacher suspects a reading deficiency he may want to utilize a reading test to ascertain the degree of deficiency. Materials and instruction may then be provided at the child's reading level. The utilization of tests that measure both achievement and ability assist in selecting from within the classroom those students who have a remediable deficit.

Evaluating Capability and Accomplishment

Some students who seem to lack intellectual ability because of poor grades may actually be of superior intelligence, but because of certain family problems and/or emotional conflicts may not be achieving up to their capacities. Tests can assist in providing an objective measure of capability without being indebted to classroom achievement or subjective appraisal.

Some examples of the use of tests in evaluating discrepancies between potential and achievement are found in every school system. As a school psychologist in the public schools, the author had occasion many times to work with pupils who had been "discovered" through the use of standardized tests. Donald S. was one such youngster. Donald S. was a fifteen-year-old ninth-grade boy who was failing English and algebra and barely passing in his other subjects. The teachers and guidance counselor suggested placing Donald in the slow-learner's English class and substituting general mathematics for algebra.

Upon reviewing Donald's test record it was found that Donald was in the top 1 per cent of his age group in intelligence. That is, Donald's intelligence test scores revealed he had more ability than 99 per cent of children his age as measured by the test.

Tests in this case provided another measure of Donald's ability. Armed with the objective evaluations of Donald, the school staff was able to institute appropriate measures. The author worked with Donald and his teachers for over a year. In the counseling sessions certain family problems were revealed and seemed to be the cause of Donald's underachievement. Progress with Donald was slow but by his senior year he was in advanced classes. The last the author heard from Donald he was a sophomore in college and doing well. If standardized tests had not been used at Donald's school, it is doubtful that Donald's problems would have been uncovered. He would have been placed in a slow-learner's group, with the probability of college quite remote. More importantly, Donald may have never realized his own potential.

Academic Reality

Tests can assist the counselor or teacher in helping to present to the student a realistic picture of his strengths and weaknesses. Mary wants to be a registered nurse. Mary's grades are average. Her test scores indicate weakness in science and mathematics. Her general school ability, as measured by standardized tests, is slightly below average. Is it realistic for Mary to pursue a career in nursing? Clerical speed and accuracy tests show that Mary is talented in office skills. Should Mary pursue a career in secretarial or office work? Charles is an eighth-grade boy who is deciding which courses to take in ninth grade. He wants to take algebra, German, and biology. His guidance counselor notes that his general school ability as measured by standardized tests is in the superior range. Algebra and language aptitude and science achievement tests reveal excellent potential. Charles' school grades, however, are only average. The counselor may feel that Charles has the ability but has not yet mastered study habits; therefore, he may advise waiting until the tenth grade to take biology. In any case standardized tests have helped provide information on which sound and realistic decisions may be made.

Educational and Vocational Goals

"Shall I go to college?" "Should I be a secretary?" "Should I go into a printing trade or auto mechanics?" These are only a few of the questions asked by youngsters. Standardized aptitude and interest tests provide meaningful information to help answer these questions.

The boy or girl who is not sure whether or not to go to college can be greatly assisted by a scholastic aptitude test.[2] The College Board Examination (SAT) is an example of a scholastic aptitude test. This test, as well as the American College Testing Program (ACT), assists students in deciding whether or not to go to college and in the choice of the college most appropriate to their abilities and needs. At the same time the college may itself select students who will profit most from the kind of education it provides.

Even with the best methods and skills in classroom evaluation, a limited and often distorted view of a student's ability and achievement results when the class standing and comparison is restricted to one school. Schools vary throughout the United States in their standards and range of student's abilities. It is difficult to determine how a student stands in any subject or ability unless one knows the group to which he is being compared.

It is important to remember that Joan may be at the top of her class at Park High School, but if she were to attend Horace High School she might be only an average student. A standardized scholastic aptitude test enables the student and college to view academic ability nationally rather than at the local level only.

In the area of work standardized aptitude and interest tests help students select vocations that are in line with their abilities and interests. James has

[2] A test designed to measure a person's potential ability to succeed in school.

decided not to go to college. He feels his abilities and interests lie in a mechanical occupation. His aptitude tests show good eye-hand coordination and finger dexterity. His scholastic aptitude test scores are about average. The interest inventory reveals interest in mechanics and science. His interests and plans correspond to the objective test data. James is, therefore, probably pursuing appropriate goals.

Transfer Students

Many schools, of course, may assign transfer students on the basis of previous school achievement, grade, and age. This is, however, a difficult procedure in some instances. Schools differ as has been previously mentioned and a child of ten in fifth grade at X school should not necessarily be placed in fifth grade in Y school. Standardized tests may aid the school in placing the new student in the grade and group appropriate to his needs and level of achievement. It also should be stated that some schools are remiss in keeping sound records and/or forwarding them in time for placement. Thus a school may find it necessary to make an evaluation of a new student for placement with little or no record of his former achievement.

Discovering Educationally and Socially Maladjusted Children

In every school there are some students who present severe problems of educational or social adjustment. Among some of these types are the withdrawn, the unhappy, the mentally retarded, and others who are not adjusting to the pattern of the school. The standardized test renders assistance to teachers and counselors in their attempts at understanding and helping these children. The following case is only one among many different possible uses of tests in this area.

Albert is a seven-year-old boy in the second grade. His teachers report that he is an isolate without any school friends. During recess he is usually found sitting alone on a swing or on the school steps. His academic progress is poor. Albert never creates any classroom problems. He usually sits in the back of the room with a stoical expression on his face. No matter what the teacher does, Albert reveals little emotion. Albert's teacher is not sure she will be able to promote him to third grade. Is Albert mentally ill? Is he "just passing through a stage?" Is he mentally retarded? Or is he an eccentric individualist?

The school psychologist is asked to evaluate Albert and make appropriate recommendations. A good portion of the school psychologist's evaluation will rest on the basis of special personality and intelligence testing. The test results will produce answers to the school's questions about Albert. They may then institute appropriate actions which will help Albert realize his maximum potential for academic and personal actualization.

Research Uses

"The individual child is our primary concern." This statement has been voiced by almost all American educators no matter what their particular philosophical orientation. This concern is reflected in measurement devices and goals. Our discussion thus far has been directed at this objective. That is, the direct measurement of factors that will help the school individualize instruction and provide educational guidance for each individual pupil.

The use of measurement instruments to assess the educational environment for future curricular changes does not immediately affect individual students. Research into all areas of the curriculum is designed to understand and develop new approaches to serve each individual student in a more effective manner. Often these investigations have little immediate significance but can serve as a piece or pieces of the educational puzzle that need to be fitted together in order to serve our students better. Let us briefly review some examples of educational research that utilize standardized testing.

McKee and Brzeinski (1966) undertook a six-year longitudinal study in which they found that with a well-designed program children could learn to read at the age of five in kindergarten. They also discovered that by the time they were in the fifth grade the children who were exposed to the same program in reading in the first grade excelled those who were given an early exposure in kindergarten but placed in regular classes in first grade. The children who began reading in kindergarten and continued in this type of program until fifth grade revealed their greatest achievement in reading, vocabulary, language, and social studies. Trends in higher achievement in arithmetic and science were also noted, although the consistency was not as great. No significant effects on spelling were evident.

The implications from this study for educational development and change are self-evident. Standardized testing was of paramount importance in that it served as objective criteria to ascertain achievement differences in groups. Instruments such as reading readiness tests, scholastic aptitude tests, and special achievement tests in reading, vocabulary, social studies, and other areas of instruction provided an objective appraisal of student ability and progress.

Taba (1966) investigated the effects of an elementary school social studies curriculum which attempted to develop abstract reasoning. It was found that students in this program excelled in the ability to discriminate, to make inferences from data, and to apply principles to new situations. At the same time these students performed adequately on standardized achievement tests which measured conventional curricular objectives.

Another research area of indirect immediacy for contemporary pupils but of direct importance for future students is the investigation of testing in professional education. Many of the graduate students of today will be the teachers and professors of tomorrow. Obviously selection is important if we are to present future generations with the best possible educational instruction.

McGuire (1968) reviews the literature in this area covering aptitude, achievement, attitude, interest, and personality tests as well as research into new types of tests and follow-up studies. His conclusions are a challenge to future investigators: "As of this date it appears that at the level of professional education much effort has gone into the development and fragmented study of predictors of success without comparable attention either to the construction and validation of reliable criterion measures or to the investigation of environmental influences on success. The challenge is clear!" (p. 58).

The utilization of standardized tests in the area of school curricula should proceed with the utmost caution. In evaluating curriculum and/or curricular experiments the school should keep in mind the objectives of the school and that of the tests. For example, if a program in modern mathematics is instituted a test of modern mathematics should be used to evaluate progress— not a test used to measure competence in traditional mathematics.

If tests are used with intelligent application to educational objectives they can serve as valuable guide posts in measuring educational outcomes. It should also be noted that in any curriculum, modern or traditional, there are common basic skills that are necessary.

Some other areas of research that utilize standardized testing are: evaluation of school children in terms of psychological and educational development and growth; the psychological growth and educational development of retarded and gifted youngsters; and, of course, continual evaluation and testing of the instruments used to assess the skills, abilities, and other topics presented in this chapter.

In essence, then, standardized testing is a valuable tool in research endeavors that attempt to provide answers to educational questions. Testing by its very nature is wedded to research and an on-going appraisal of what is and what may be.

Areas Where Standardized Tests Should Not Be Used

The reader should be aware that the "red light" areas of testing which will be discussed are not agreed upon by all authorities. It is safe to state, however, that most would at least consider them "yellow light" spheres which are to be cautiously considered.

Assigning Grades

Teachers should never use standardized test results as evaluative consideration in assigning grades. Standardized test content is general and not specifically related to the local school curriculum.

Evaluating the School

It is true that standardized tests may help in assessing schools and classes in terms of aptitude and background characteristics, for they may function as a beacon to focus on strengths and weaknesses of specific schools and classes. This is a dangerous procedure, however, for there is a strong tendency of central administrations to use the results in a judgmental or punitive manner. This may promote the "teaching for tests" syndrome, which is undesirable. It is undesirable because the local school system loses its autonomy in developing its own educational objectives. The development of curricula is then turned over to testing people. Teaching for tests also tends to be superficial, emphasizing "correct answers" rather than understandings. As previously stated, schools in particular geographic areas with particular students have particular needs and need to develop their own particular curricula. National standards cannot and should not be educational yard-sticks for all school systems. This is not to say that there are not underlying common denominators in the basic skills, or that national standards are meaningless. They do provide us with a common frame of reference that is necessary in guiding individual students in educational and vocational goals, particularly when they will be competing with students from a broad geo-graphical area. They do, however, lose much of their significance when we use them to judge the local school rather than to aid in individual guidance.

To illustrate, let us look at two very different schools. School A is situated in an urban setting with the majority of students from a disadvantaged back-ground. The educational objectives of this school are to enrich the im-poverished lives of its students and to teach basic methods of living in a twentieth-century urban complex. In addition, this school also teaches the classical academic subjects and skills. To assess its educational worth by the use of a nationally standardized achievement test is to measure only one aspect of its total program. Certainly the standardized test is applicable as individual guidance for the students of School A. For example, those students who desire to go on to college must know their chances of success based on national standards rather than on the local norms, where competition may not be as difficult.

Let us now turn our attention to School B, which is the exact opposite of School A. It is situated in an upper-middle-class suburban community. The majority of the students are above average in intelligence and achievement. To judge the worth of the whole school on the basis of nationally standardized tests would be to inflate unrealistically the school's accomplishments. One would expect School B to be above the national standards, given its setting and student body. This school must develop its own internal methods of judging its particular curriculum. Of course, it must be stated that for individual guidance the national test helps the individual student gain a realistic picture of how he compares to other students throughout the country. He may be only average at School B but above average on a national scale. This would have special meaning in planning educational and vocational objectives. It would not, however, give the central administration meaningful data to assess its whole school system or curriculum.

Teacher Evaluation

School administrators should never use the results of standardized tests to evaluate the competence of individual teachers. This procedure is wrong on several counts. First, it does not take into account the fact that class achievement is, in part, the result of previous educational history. It is not educationally valid or fair to judge a teacher who has taught a class for a semester or year as solely responsible for the student's academic performance. Secondly, innate intelligence and family cultural experiences contribute greatly to educational achievement. Thirdly, as has been mentioned previously, an achievement test measures only a small portion of the objectives of most schools. Fourthly, it is likely to cause teachers to teach for tests rather than pursue the local educational and curriculum goals. Teachers, being human, will tend to neglect areas of the curriculum that are not conducive to measurement—such areas as, for example, citizenship, discussion, and verbal ability. Skills and learning that are easily testable and found in many standardized achievement tests often become the focal point of teaching.

Evaluating teachers on the basis of test results not only blunts the horizons of teaching effectiveness, but demoralizes teachers. Teachers react to evaluative pressure in many ways. Some teach for the tests by securing old tests and concentrating on areas that are covered. Others "prepare" their students by drilling them on the exact questions or similar questions that are to be presented. Still others are so pressured that they give the exact questions and answers that are to be asked and require students to memorize them. Though these procedures cannot be condoned, they are certainly understandable when the administration places the burden of teacher evaluation on class test scores.

Finally, it should be mentioned that not only is this kind of evaluation wrong for teachers and their students, but it leads to poor testing practice. The value of the test is lessened, if not destroyed, by excessive evaluative emphasis. The basic purpose of testing is to render educational assistance to the student, the teacher, and the school.

In summary, it can be stated that tests are useful educational instruments in helping children develop and realize their own individual potential. Standardized tests should be used as objective evidence to supplement the teacher's subjective judgments. They are only one of many educational tools in helping children. They are not substitutes for teacher evaluation. The teacher's own tests, ratings on class projects, and a child's daily classroom performance are as important as they ever were. Standardized tests used properly can be of immense assistance to the teacher and to his pupils.

References

McGuire, C. H. Testing in professional education. *Review of Educational Research : Educational and Psychological Testing,* 1968, **38**, 49–60.

McKee, P., and Brzeinski, J. E. *The effectiveness of teaching reading in kindergarten.* U.S. Department of Health, Education, and Welfare, Office of Education, Cooperative Research Project No. 5–0371. Denver: Denver Public Schools and Colorado State Department of Education, 1966.

Taba, H. *Teaching strategies and cognitive functioning in elementary school children.* U.S. Department of Health, Education, and Welfare, Office of Education, Cooperative Research Project No. 2404. San Francisco: San Francisco State College, February, 1966.

CHAPTER 2

Contemporary Issues
and Problems

Major Criticisms

The critics of testing have voiced their positions loud and long. Psychologists, educators, sociologists, and scholars from other disciplines as well as lay people have been critical of testing. Many of the criticisms have been characterized by half-truths, personal bias, and misunderstanding of testing principles and objectives. The criticisms fall roughly into four categories—those that deal with the effect of testing on the individual, the effect of testing on institutions, the effect of testing on society in general, and test items per se. Let us look at some of these criticisms and see what the charges are.

Testing and the Individual

There are several charges against testing that deal with the effect of testing on the individual. The first of these charges that we shall consider is that tests damage an individual's self-esteem.

Damaged Self-esteem

The critics of testing feel that testing may predetermine an individual's social status and harm his image of himself. They state that testing places people in intellectual slots. In addition, they think it may injure his educational motivation. The child, for example, may feel, "I am not very smart. Why should I try harder? What's the use?"

The critics who are concerned with damage to a person's self-esteem through testing usually are referring to intelligence tests. These instruments are popularly called IQ tests.

The student of testing should be aware of the fact that there *is no device or measurement instrument, at this time, that can measure with absolute certainty permanent general ability to learn.* Today's intelligence tests measure many aspects of human behavior, including the influence of an individual's cultural background, school achievement, and motivation to learn and do one's best while taking a test. To state that the results of an intelligence test is a measure of innate intelligence is to do a disservice to the individual and to measurement in general. Later in this chapter a full discussion of what IQ is and what it is not will be presented. The important point to remember, for now, is that *psychologists do not know whether intelligence tests do, or do not, measure innate intelligence or capacity to learn, but they do know that an individual's past experiences are reflected in his score.*

If the results of intelligence tests are not thought of as permanent or immutable, then the criticism that they assign individuals to fixed intellectual or social slots is not appropriate. What is relevant is the use and interpretation of the results. If intelligence tests are used to stamp children into intellectual and social molds, then it is not the fault of the test but of the user. Psychologists, educators, and test publishers continually alert and warn test users against the erroneous assumption of test infallibility. On the other hand, it is true that some people use tests as if they were divinely inspired and free from human error. The critic, bearing this in mind, may concede the point that competent psychologists or counselors may effectively use tests; however, he will then state that most test users are not psychologists, counselors, or individuals trained to understand the limitations of tests. Therefore, such a critic will state, because most people do not know how to interpret tests properly, no one, or at the very most only psychologists, should use them. This critic's position, simply stated, is that the improper use of tests does more harm than good and therefore all intelligence tests should be abandoned.

The answer to this last criticism is obvious and can be answered by quoting an old folk saying, "Don't throw out the baby with the bath water." In essence, the criticism of damage to self-esteem and social cataloguing is not a basic criticism of the test per se but of the utilization and interpretation of tests. What is needed, therefore, is more education in the proper methods of test administration and interpretation. The improper interpretation of test results may harm an individual's self-esteem. It is also true that most things improperly used may be harmful to an individual. For example, milk is an excellent food and recommended as an essential part of most children's diets. Yet we know that some children and adults may drink too much and have severe gastrointestinal problems as a result. No one seriously proposes banning milk because some people have allergies to it or do not consume it in proper quantities.

The student of measurement should not take a position that precludes the possibility of harm to a child because of testing, but he should be aware that testing is only one phase of the educational process and that if it is used properly it may be of great value to most children.

Limited Evaluation

The criticism of limited evaluation of tests recognizes that a human being is a complex organism consisting of many different aspects of talent, personality, and motivation. The charge is that the use of one type of test, usually the kind dealing with verbal and quantitative skills, taps only a small portion of the abilities of most individuals. The implication is that this is the only measure used by schools and colleges in sorting students and that therefore much talent is lost to the society.

Modern educators are quite aware of the fact that many students have talents that are neither verbal nor quantitative, and contemporary education thus envisions more than "reading and 'rithmetic."

The answer to this test criticism again lies in the intelligent utilization of tests. A good evaluative program uses many measures in the evaluation of an individual. In the area of college admissions, for example, the college that has an admission or scholarship award policy based only on verbal and quantitative test scores is using testing improperly. The publishers of these tests have stated repeatedly that scores on these tests should not represent the sole consideration for admission or scholarship awards.

The proper procedure is the utilization of many different kinds of measures. In a complete evaluation of an applicant the college admission officer would want to know a candidate's past test scores in educational areas other than the linguistic and mathematical. He would want to know about the candidate's school record in terms of grades, courses, extracurricular activities, and teacher ratings before making his final decision. In this way the verbal-quantitative test is only one measure among many criteria in the selecting process. This principle applies, of course, at all levels of educational evaluation.

Abridgement of Human Choice

The third criticism of tests dealing with the effect on the individual is of a philosophical nature, and reflects our general fear that machines may rule man. *Tests reduce people to numbers,* state the critics of testing. They go on to warn that the use of tests may reduce human choice and action. This is a serious charge. Human freedom of choice is essential to our form of government and underlies most, if not all, of our educational philosophies. Any procedure or instrument that would take this precious right away is a danger to our society. Do tests constitute such a danger? Are they in fact a menace to human freedom of choice?

Let us look at the situation as objectively as possible. If we do this we must admit that tests could possibly pose such a menace if used improperly. Of course, most things if used improperly could endanger freedom. The United States government, for example, has data on each of us that could be used by the wrong people in a punitive and dictatorial manner. Yet this data is necessary to run the government and provide services to the whole society. There is no doubt that this data could provide the means to abridge freedom, as could some offices of government. Tests are no different, used improperly, without proper respect for the individual and knowledge of the inherent limitations of tests, grievous wrongs, such as the limitation of freedom of choice, could occur.

To some the use of mental tests implies that human behavior is as measurable as the dimensions of a table top. Given this frame of reference, the task of the test author would be relatively simple. Tests could be developed around finite goals and the factors that contribute to these objectives could be isolated and then measured. When factor X was mixed with factor Y the outcome would always be XY. Human behavior could be predicted, measured, and controlled with the same certainty and facility that one finds inherent in chemical solutions and reactions.

If the preceding were true, that is, if human behavior were as measurable as a table top, then the danger of eliminating human choice would be great indeed. These things are, of course, not true. Our testing instruments are far from perfect. Psychologists cannot isolate all the variables that contribute and give direction to human actions.

Under these circumstances the problem of testers playing God or of impersonal evaluation becomes quite remote. Of course it must be recognized that the improper education of test users could contribute to the improper use of measurement instruments. If the tester does not know the limitations of his instrument and is afflicted with megalomania, he may indeed act out the role of a deity and assign youngsters to given educational slots on the basis of test results.

Again, the answer to this criticism is the proper education of the test user and consumer.

Psychologists and educators are painfully aware of the limitations of tests. They know and appreciate the fact that a great proportion of decision making must be made in the maze of uncertainties, desired outcomes, and methods of achieving these outcomes. They also know that mistakes will be made.

Testing and Institutions

"The professional testers are controlling educational curricula and the destinies of our children," state the critics. This criticism of testing has created an almost paranoid quality and anxiety to the critical vendettas hurled at testing. Is there any reality to the charge? The answer is not easy. This writer has observed a subtle form of undue test influence in his duties as a counselor and psychologist in the public schools. He has seen teachers teaching for tests, principals bragging about their school's test record, a state where the Department of Education requires certain prescribed tests from K–12. Is it true, therefore, that testing people control educational goals and the destinies of individuals?

Today the answer is no, but if proper measures, such as the education of those who use these instruments, are not instituted the answer in the future may be yes. American education at the present time is too decentralized and loosely organized to control the lives of its students. In some European countries, of course, this is not true and testing (usually of the subjective essay type) is of paramount importance in the lives and destinies of students.

In the United States tests usually follow rather than lead in curricular change. Though tests may affect a phase of a student's educational experience it can be stated with some certainty that they do not determine his destiny.

Let us explore the basic problem of control and what it means in measurement terms. The teacher and/or principal who provides an atmosphere or situation of competiveness on tests is laying the groundwork for future control. For example, Mr. Jones, principal of Northern High School, gives his teachers a testing pep talk:

> Mr. Jones: Ladies and gentlemen, last year Northern's test scores in mathematics and social studies were, on the average, the lowest in the county. We must be doing something wrong in these fields. Our kids are as smart as those in the other schools and I know our faculty takes a back seat to none.
>
> Well, I think I've got the answer to help our kids make a better showing. I've asked our director of guidance to secure some old mathematics and social studies tests which are similar to the ones we give our kids in the spring. I want you to study them and gear your teaching accordingly. I know the other schools must be doing the same thing and I feel sure if we do we may even beat them. O.K., let's give it our best and show the other schools what kind of teachers and students Northern has.

The preceding illustration is a realistic possibility, although most principals would probably be more subtle in their exhortations. The teachers of Northern are now caught up in the teaching for the test syndrome. If they do not gear their teaching for the prescribed tests and their students do poorly, they open themselves to the possible loss of their position; at the very minimum they may assure the wrath and displeasure of the administration.

This kind of situation does a major disservice to measurement, education, and local control over curriculum. An accurate picture of individual and group performance is compromised by concentrating on the format and content of these tests. A true picture of the educational level of the students is at best tentative. Educational goals and objectives are reduced to recognition, memorization, and ability to respond to a test rather than true learning, which incorporates not only memorization of data but integration of this data into the student's thinking and behavior.

Of even more serious concern is the relinquishing of local and regional curriculum control. The task of devising the curriculum is handed over to a national testing center. This center, no matter how sincere and dedicated, is in no position to formulate educational objectives for all schools throughout the United States. Not only do individuals differ, but so do regions and schools. The curriculum at an upper-middle-class suburban school may not be appropriate for an urban school in a disadvantaged area.

In addition to individual differences our educational system has traditionally been based on local control by the citizens of the school district. Schools in a democracy are intended to reflect the needs and desires of the community. If the school bases its standards on the content of national tests, this tradition is seriously compromised.

Educators and psychologists are very much aware of the fallacy of using tests to measure the worth of a school. They know that conditions and objectives differ from school to school. They are also painfully aware of the limitations and fallibility of standardized tests. No responsible educator or psychologist advocates the use of tests alone to judge teachers or schools. The problem again lies not with testing, but with the improper use of tests.

In essence, then, educational personnel using tests must be aware of the limitations of measurement and proceed with the utmost caution in deriving inferences from test scores. This does not mean, of course, that national tests are of no value. Certainly, there are basic skills and data that students at given grade levels should know no matter where they reside. If test scores are evaluated within the educational objectives of the school and are interpreted in the light of the local school setting, they will add to the total evaluation. *The important point to remember is that tests are only one general method of evaluation and must be considered in the light of the student population and the school curriculum.*

Thus, we may state that the criticism of test control of education and people is generally not true today. In some isolated cases, however, it is true that uninformed teachers and principals allow tests to exert an undue influence within their schools. The solution to this situation, as in others, is more measurement education for test consumers. At the same time, all of us—psychologists, teachers, principals, and test publishers—must maintain a constant vigil against the encroachment of tests dictating educational policy.

Testing and Society

Another area of criticism attacks the entire testing movement and often has as its goal the abandonment of *all* testing. Let us examine these general charges in detail.

CULTURAL BIAS

The criticism of measurement, especially intelligence testing, that holds that tests are culturally biased is fraught with emotional overtones and half-truths. The heat engendered in this critical sphere has recently been increased by the civil rights movement. The critics state that testing is geared to middle-class values and is, therefore, unfair to children of less fortunate environments. They cite the lack of enriching developmental experiences of disadvantaged children compared with their more fortunate middle- and upper-class peers. To these critics our present tests are culturally biased. The tests, according to them, not only reflect middle-class concepts but use middle-class language, and assume all students have been exposed to middle-class experiences.

The late Dr. Loretan (1966), former Deputy Superintendent of Schools for New York City, was instrumental in eliminating the use of IQ tests in the New York City schools. His basic reason for dropping IQ tests was the problem of cultural bias. He states, "the vocabulary and concepts in most of the group IQ tests are foreign to many children in our large and varied country (and certainly to many children in New York City). We have not been able to extract cultural biases from our tests, and yet we use these tests with children who are culturally different" (p. 6).

Rosenberg (1966) in an address at the 1966 District of Columbia Psychological Association meetings applauded the New York City school system's decision to eliminate intelligence testing. He stated,

> I feel that there has been some recent heartening news from such areas as New York City, where, as you all know, intelligence testing was essentially thrown out of the school system. This may sound like an extreme measure, but if the abuses in the New York School System were anywhere as bad as the abuses that occur in the Baltimore City School System, then I say, "Better throw out the baby with the bath" and start again, if there is the slightest chance we may produce something better. To continue to damage children by inaccurate decisions based on our inadequate procedures is to contribute to what might well be called the scientific racism of the 1960's.

Rosenberg goes on to state that Drs. Wechsler and Anastasi (both well-known and highly respected psychologists) are correct in their assessment that "intelligence tests are correct, what is wrong is in society." However, he feels that they do not go far enough. He feels that the labeling of "deprived-area children with low IQ's condemns them to a status where they will be offered much less in our school systems." Rosenberg states further, "it seems to me that our assumption must be that in the poverty area the intelligence of children is actually distributed normally as it is at higher socioeconomic levels."

Anastasi (1966), questions the logic of eliminating items that differentiate groups of people. She asks,

> ... where shall we stop? We could with equal justification proceed to rule out items showing socioeconomic differences, sex differences, differences among ethnic minority groups and educational differences. Any items in which college graduates excel elementary school graduates could, for example, be discarded on this basis. Nor should we retain items that differentiate among broader groups, such as national cultures, or between preliterate and more advanced cultures. If we do all this, I shall like to ask only two questions in conclusion. First, what will be left? Second, in terms of any criterion we may wish to predict, what will be the validity of this minute residue [pp. 456–57]?

Lorge (1966) states that test makers may have attempted to eliminate bias from intelligence tests by using different processes in appraising different groups. He feels these efforts have not removed bias from measurement. It is his position that "ignorance of difference is a costly way to produce unbiased tests of intelligence" (p. 470).

Rosenberg and others who have voiced their criticism of the cultural bias of tests are correct in one sense. That is that *all* of our present tests *are culturally biased.* If they were not they would have little value in our school system.

The problem that besets this area of debate is twofold: (1) the absence of a common frame of reference in definitions of terms and (2) the inability of the critics to face reality. Rather than do this they cloud the issue with the illusion of what one would like things to be.

Let us look at the first problem, definition of terms. The labeling of group tests of school ability as intelligence tests is a grave error. This gives the impression to many people that what is being measured is innate intelligence, when in fact what is measured is *chance of success in school.* Psychologists have recognized for some time now that the term *intelligence test* may be a misnomer. Today we say that intelligence tests are tests of scholastic aptitude. Nothing concerning innate intelligence is stated or implied in this label.

The second major problem is unwillingness of the critic to face reality. Statements such as Rosenberg's that the children in poverty areas have the same normally distributed intelligence as those in higher socioeconomic levels seems to this writer an unscientific supposition.

It could be stated that a disadvantaged environment tends to inhibit the growth of normal intellectual functioning and this blockage begins from the time of birth. The constitutional theorist may, on the other hand, state with equal fervor that there is a tendency in nature to "breed true to type." That is, people who for one reason or another are unsuccessful tend to choose mates of similar backgrounds, thus perpetuating their own type, whereas those who rise above the poverty syndrome marry people with similar strivings or those that are already in a more privileged environment. Later in this chapter we will deal in detail with the question of the

Testing Program for Two High Schools

Hess High School	Washington High School
Ninth grade: 1. school ability test 2. interest test 3. general school and vocational aptitude test battery 4. achievement tests in mathematics, social studies, and English Tenth grade: 1. school ability test 2. general personality test 3. achievement tests in mathematics, social studies, and English 4. music and art aptitude tests Eleventh grade: 1. school ability test 2. achievement tests in mathematics, social studies, and English 3. national college aptitude test	Ninth grade: 1. school ability test 2. culture-fair test* 3. interest test 4. general school and vocational aptitude test battery 5. achievement tests in mathematics, social studies, and English 6. reading test Tenth grade: 1. vocational aptitude tests in specialized areas such as mechanical aptitude, manual dexterity, and stenographic aptitude 2. reading test 3. attitude questionnaire Eleventh grade: 1. school ability test 2. culture-fair test

* Culture-fair test is an instrument which attempts to measure experiences that are equally familiar or unfamiliar to *all* groups of people.

relationship between intelligence and such variables as genetics, environment, and ethnic background.

This writer would not make a definitive statement concerning the distribution of intelligence in a disadvantaged area because of the many factors that impinge on this type of evaluation. It is easy, however, to state quite definitively that there is no data to support Rosenberg's claim of a normal distribution of intelligence; on the contrary, the clinical evidence and "intuition" of many authorities would lead one to the opposite position.

The important point to remember is that it is easy for our subjective predilections to interfere with our objectivity. In the long run this interference can hurt the very cause and people we want to help.

What is cultural bias in tests? First of all, the language used is reflective of the culture. Secondly, the required test tasks are reflective of the skills and objectives of our schools, which in turn *should* be reflective of the skills

Hess High School	*Washington High School*
4. general school and vocational aptitude test battery	3. general school and vocational aptitude test battery
Twelfth grade: 1. school ability test	4. reading test
2. achievement tests in mathematics, social studies, and English	5. national college aptitude test
	6. achievement tests in mathematics, social studies, and English
3. national college aptitude test	Twelfth grade: 1. General Aptitude Test Battery (produced by Bureau of Employment Security, U.S. Department of Labor)
4. national scholarship test	
5. advanced interest test	2. national college aptitude test
	3. national scholarship test
	4. attitude questionnaire
	5. advanced interest test

and objectives of our general society. If they were not they would give little useful data to the school. The school needs to know the chances of a student's success in a school system that is, in fact, oriented to middle-class values. If the schools were oriented to another system, then our tests would not be culturally biased, but they would be inappropriate.

The basic purpose of scholastic aptitude tests is not to obtain an innate measure of intelligence, but to measure a student's academic potential for achievement in our school system. Thus the answer to the charge of cultural bias is, "Yes, tests are culturally biased, but how valuable would they be if they were not?"

The reader should not infer from this statement that our present tests cannot be improved, nor should he infer that this writer is unaware of or unsympathetic with the problems of disadvantaged children. Our present tests need a great deal of improvement, but this improvement lies in better test construction and use rather than in test elimination. Cultural handicaps will not be removed by changing our tests; only changing the conditions within our society that promote these deprivations will do that.

Too Much Testing

Some critics complain that children are being "tested to death." In answering this charge it is very difficult to define how much is too much; it should be remembered that tests are not always correct in their assessment of ability. The more information we have on a student, the better we are able to assist him and the less is the chance of error. The important question is what information is needed to help children develop themselves to their fullest potential.

Let us look at two four-year high schools in two different settings and review their standardized testing programs. The preceeding outline (pp. 28 and 29) presents these schools and their testing programs. Hess is a suburban high school located in an upper-middle-class area, whereas Washington is a city high school situated in an underprivileged setting.

(Before reading further, read and review the two testing programs cited with the following questions in mind:

1. Is there too much testing at Hess, at Washington, or at both?
2. If there is too much testing, what tests would you eliminate and why?

If you feel that your knowledge is insufficient to enable you to judge, remember that most critics of testing are no more prepared than you, and a great many do not have as good a background as yours. Discuss your feelings and thoughts with your classmates and see what they have to say. After you have done this the following discussion of the issues and problems of "testing too much" should be more meaningful.)

Let us start our discussion and analysis of Hess and Washington schools with one of the basic premises of measurement: What information is needed? Hess administers seventeen tests and test batteries over a period of four years, whereas Washington administers twenty tests and test batteries over the same period. Is either of them, or are both, testing too much? It is obviously impossible to add the number of tests and declare the school with the most the winner of the "too many tests" trophy. The appropriate and most valid method of appraising a school's testing program is to start with the school and its educational goals and objectives. Note that the present analysis will deal only with the question of the quantity and necessity of tests, not with the "ideal" program. For a more complete and detailed discussion of testing programs see Chapter 17. The answer to our question is that Hess High School is testing too much. There is no need to give a school ability test every year. This is especially true in an advantaged area. A school ability test given in ninth and eleventh grades would be more than enough. The majority of children at Hess will be going to college and will take one of the national college aptitude tests, another form of school ability test, in the eleventh and twelfth grades. Clearly Hess is in error in administering so many school ability tests.

There is also no need to administer achievement tests every year, especially in Hess' environment. The teachers and administration may want some general assessment of how their students compare nationally. This is valid and could be accomplished by testing twice, either in the ninth and eleventh grades or in the tenth and twelfth grades. Local tests constructed by the faculty would more adequately reflect the progress of Hess' students.

The inclusion of art and music aptitude tests in the general testing program is generally not warranted in any school's standardized testing program. Again, this is especially true at Hess. High school students from middle-class homes usually do not need these tests. They generally know their artistic interests and propensities by the time they are in the tenth grade. If a student needs or wants objective verification, then these tests may be administered individually.

The use of personality tests in a general testing program is open to serious question. They can have an important function but should be used only when individual cases indicate they are needed. The exception, of course, is for research purposes.

A general review of Hess' testing program reveals that there is too much duplication and that some of the tests that are being given throughout the school could be given on an individual basis.

Now let us look at Washington. Although one might challenge the value of one or two of the tests in Washington's program, on the whole it would be valid to state that the tests administered are necessary and meaningful. Therefore, Washington does not give too many tests.

In the ninth grade a general estimate of scholastic aptitude is gained by the administration of different types of ability tests. Note that three of the six tests are school ability related instruments. The administration of these instruments is especially important in an underprivileged setting. In a different area, three school ability tests in the same year would be too many. At Washington this is not the case. The school ability test helps gauge these students in comparison to other ninth graders throughout the United States. Although most research evidence does not indicate that the culture-fair test is generally a better indicator of ability to learn for disadvantaged groups than the regular school ability test, it may be of help for certain individual children. Even if it only helps a few children the expenditure of time and money will have been a small price to pay. The general school and vocational aptitude tests are a measure of ability in various vocational tasks, such as clerical skill and mechanical comprehension; in addition, they constitute another less culturally oriented measure of school ability.

One might question the administration of reading tests in the ninth, tenth, and eleventh grades; however, in an underprivileged setting reading skills are seriously impaired and the school must endeavor to bring them up to at least an average level. The ninth-grade student who cannot read above the fifth-grade level may expect serious trouble. The administration of reading tests each year would then be a reflection of the added emphasis Washington gives to reading.

In summary, it can be stated that our most important concern in judging whether a school tests too much is not quantity, but the appropriateness of the tests for a particular school in a particular geographic area with a particular student body and their own particular educational goals and objectives. In the preceding example we saw that the school that gave the most tests was not testing too much, whereas the school that gave less tests was indeed subjecting its student body to more tests than necessary.

Test Items and Specific Tests

The critics who challenge the validity of test items and of specific tests often pick one or two items from a test, show that they are poor, and then attempt to discredit the entire test and all tests of that type on the basis of these poor items.

MULTIPLE-CHOICE TESTS

The preceding technique has been the means for attacking the multiple-choice test. The critics state that multiple-choice tests favor the superficially intelligent and penalize the student who has depth, subtlety, creativity, and critical powers of discrimination. This statement has been voiced in many ways and at many different times. One of the most vocal and literate of these critics is Dr. Banesh Hoffmann. Our attention in this section will be mainly devoted to Hoffmann's criticisms because he is the most articulate of the test critics.

Dr. Hoffmann's contention that "ambiguous" questions penalize students, especially the "deep" thinkers, was investigated by Black (1963). Before discussing Black's findings let us look at an example of a question that Dr. Hoffmann considers ambiguous.

This question, according to Hoffmann (1962, p. 86), is from the Iowa Tests of Educational Development, Test 3, Part II, p. 9.

The student is asked to find the word that is spelled incorrectly. If there are none, he is to mark the last number.

1. cartons
2. altogether
3. possibilities
4. intensionally
5. none wrong

The correct answer is *intensionally*. Dr. Hoffmann, in citing this item, illustrates its deficits by quoting from a letter of a National Merit Scholarship winner. The correspondent stated that he chose *none wrong* because *intensionally* is a word that is used in logic and semantics and was spelled correctly.

The preceding example is an illustration of pedantry. Let us look at all facets of the question and then you may decide if the question does indeed penalize the deep student. First, we must admit that one constructing a spelling test should himself be able to spell; further, he should check on the word he intends to be misspelled. Hoffmann's observation that the question is poor is, therefore, granted. His further contention that this question penalizes the "deep" student or that test authors hide tests behind statistics and that therefore multiple-choice tests are not valuable is *not* conceded.

The student of measurement should know that the test is intended for the seventh through the twelfth grades. It is extremely unlikely that the vast majority of students, no matter what their intellectual level of functioning, would be familiar with the rather obscure word *intensionally* as used in logic.[1] Further, when one examines the words in the test item, the grade range is evident. The words *cartons, altogether*, and *possibilities* are obviously at a lower level of vocabulary and educational development than the word *intensionally*. Therefore, the exceptionally "deep" student might ascertain that the test author or printers made a mistake and mark *intensionally* as incorrect because they probably meant to misspell the word *intentionally*.

Let us go further, for purposes of discussion, and grant that the "deep" student missed this question because of his greater knowledge. Would he in fact be penalized? Black (1963), in seeking the answer to this question, examined items of the Scholastic Aptitude Test (SAT) to find ambiguous questions. In addition, he discussed the problem with personnel of Educational Testing Service. Nine items out of fifty-five were considered ambiguous by Black and an official of the Educational Testing Service.[2]

The next question that Black was concerned with was how many "wrong" answers he had given to the questions that offered more than one correct response. He found that he had missed only three of the "ambiguous" questions. "What this meant in terms of my SAT score was that I had been penalized 24 points on a test scaled from 200 to 800. Put another way, I had just become two percentile points brighter. The difference was certainly not enough to keep me out or get me admitted to most colleges" (pp. 115–116).

The issue in multiple-choice testing is not whether these tests have reached perfection, nor is the issue whether there are poor and ambiguous questions. Multiple-choice tests are not perfect, or anywhere near perfect. There are items that do penalize "deep" students. Ferris (1962), in replying to a criticism of Dr. Hoffmann's concerning a physics question that he had

[1] *Webster's New Collegiate Dictionary* (1961) defines intension as follows: "n. 1. *Now Rare*. Tension. 2. Intensity. 3. Intensification. 4. Energetic use or exercise, as of the mind; determination. 5. Intensiveness. 6. *Logic*. All or any of the attributes, qualities, or characteristics comprised in a concept or implied by a term; thus, the *intension* of 'triangle' implies that of 'plane figure';—opposed to *extension*" (p. 438).

[2] Publishers of the College Boards and one of the major test publishers in the United States.

constructed for Educational Testing Service, agreed that the question was ambiguous and "a good student might be disturbed by its 'ambiguity.'"

The important question is whether multiple-choice tests such as the College Board Examination discriminate between different levels of ability. If in doing so the "deep" and "creative" student is penalized, then obviously Hoffmann and other critics are correct. Choosing a dozen or more questions from tests over a period of years and showing their ambiguity or inaccurate content does not prove the case against multiple-choice testing. It only reveals that some questions were poor. It does not reveal the good questions, nor does it prove that "creative" and "deep" youngsters obtain lower test scores.

The author knows of no scientific studies or investigations by anyone in the field of testing that support the critic's contention that multiple-choice tests penalize the creative student. There are many studies, however, that demonstrate a considerable relationship, though far from perfect, between high test scores and success in college.

Until demonstrated by scientific investigation that multiple-choice tests do significantly penalize certain students, we must proceed on the premise that these tests assist in guiding young people. Of course we must continue to evaluate and re-evaluate our tests. Bearing in mind the possibility of test error, we must also consider other factors in guidance, such as school records and teacher recommendations. (See Chapter 11 for a more detailed discussion of college admissions testing.)

Problem Areas

In addition to the major criticisms previously discussed there are several issues relating to testing which present problems to many people. Often these problems are compounded by a lack of communication and a misunderstanding of the factors involved.

Intelligence and Intelligence Tests

A major problem area in testing and one which antagonizes certain groups is concerned with intelligence, intelligence testing, and IQ. Many of the problems are created by a lack of understanding of what these terms mean, and what they do not mean. Let us examine these concepts and terms more closely.

INTELLIGENCE

It is very difficult to define the word *intelligence*. Many psychologists and educators have defined intelligence as a concept that is synonymous with learning ability. Others have narrowed their definition to a self-evident fact, namely, intelligence is what intelligence tests measure.

The student of measurement should keep in mind that the term *intelligence,* as used in psychology, *has no absolute meaning.* It is frequently defined to meet the needs and orientation of the person defining it. Binet, the pioneer of intelligence tests, described intelligence as a unitary characteristic. That is, the human organism's ability to adapt and critically perceive his environment. Terman (1916), who pioneered Binet's test in the United States, defined intelligence as "an individual's ability to carry on abstract thinking" (p. 42). Wechsler (1960), states that "intelligence is the aggregate or global capacity of the individual to act purposefully, to think rationally, and to deal effectively with his environment" (p. 7).

It is evident from these different concepts of intelligence that there is no general agreement among theorists concerning the essence of intelligence, and the preceding concepts by no means exhaust the thinking on the subject. The interested reader can find further discussion of intelligence by referring to the works of Spearman (1927), Thorndike (1927), and Thurstone (1941).

IQ: What It Means and What It Does Not Mean

There is a difference between intelligence as conceptualized by the theorists and the measurement of intelligence. It is evident that the measurement of intelligence is related to the ability of a person to perform or function in a given test setting. Thus, within this frame of reference the only intelligence we know about is the specific performance of an individual on a specific test. Intelligence as an inherited quality is an abstraction when related to a specific measurement instrument. It can only be surmised from behavioral responses to a test based on what someone considers "intelligence."

The student of measurement, if he understands the tentative basis of the term *intelligence,* will be in a better position to evaluate meaningfully the literature concerning the relationship between intelligence and such variables as heredity, environment, race, and culture.

The most simple definition of IQ is, of course, intelligence quotient. The Dictionary of Psychology (Warren, 1934) states that IQ is "the ratio of an individual's intelligence, as determined by some mental measure, to normal or average intelligence for his age" (p. 141).

For some people IQ has been a magic term that is all-encompassing and definitively accurate. Since the inception of the first IQ test many teachers and parents have unreservedly labeled children as bright or dull on the basis of their IQ. The danger of this assumption is enormous. Good (1966) states, "The term IQ has been so grossly abused and it is so inappropriate to the shifting values yielded by various tests that we probably should abandon it altogether" (p. 179). As our definition stated, IQ is the ratio of the individual's intelligence as determined by a test. That is, intelligence is defined as that "something" which is measured by a mental test. This definition does not allow for differing types of intelligence, nor are psychologists certain of what they mean by this kind of intelligence. Hebb (1958), a noted psychologist, states that Binet "learned how to measure something without any very clear idea as to what it was he was measuring." Today, more than sixty years later, we measure it a bit more satisfactorily, and now it can be measured with a great variety of techniques, but we are still somewhat uncertain about what "it" is.

In addition to our uncertainty of what intelligence is, there are many variables inherent in the construction and administration of tests that limit further our equating IQ with innate intelligence. That is, errors in test construction, sampling of population, scoring, and physical and psychological conditions of the test setting. Factors such as previous schooling and cultural environment also play their part in the IQ test score.

The IQ (based on the 1960 Stanford-Binet) fixes the mean (average) at 100 with a distribution of sixteen points on either side; that is, the range of average or normal intelligence is roughly defined as falling between 84 and 116. Because this distribution is considered within the normal range, the IQ can be interpreted to indicate a child's relative position in a group. Children, for example, with scores on an IQ test above 116 would be considered above average, whereas children with scores below 84 would be considered below average, with specific numerical classifications defining more precisely their degree of deviation from the average. The IQ, then, is a method of reporting a test score related to other test scores in a given group in the same way, though more precisely, that one grade in a classroom is related to other grades.

The accuracy of the reported IQ is directly related to the worth of the test per se and its purposes and format as well as environmental and cultural factors. The group intelligence test that reports a test score in the form of IQ is evaluating, to some degree, different aspects of "intelligence" than an individual intelligence test. The boy, for example, who reads poorly will have this deficit in achievement reflected in his group IQ score. On the other hand, the same child taking an individual intelligence test will not be penalized because little, if any, reading is required. The two IQ's may then mean two different things, although they are both expressed in the same symbolic structure.

Neither the individual nor group intelligence test is completely accurate. The IQ symbol representing the results of these instruments should be viewed in the same light. That is, a reported IQ is only a relative indication of how an individual compares to others taking the same test. IQ must be considered along with other evaluative criteria such as other types of tests, classroom performance, and the observations of the teacher. A more definitive examination of test score interpretations will be presented in subsequent chapters. The important thing to remember, at this point, is that *intelligence tests are only one measure of ability, and IQ is only a symbol of this ability.*

Heredity Versus Environment

The relative influence of heredity and environment on an individual's behavior has been a constant source of controversy for many years. Views have ranged from those of the constitutionalists, who feel that all a person is and does is determined genetically, to those of the environmentalists, who feel that development is determined solely by a person's experiences. Some people, have, of course, taken the middle ground, that an individual is the result of a combination of hereditary and environmental influences. The development of the intelligence test intensified the debate. In the years since the development of individual and group tests of intelligence enormous amounts of data have been compiled which have made possible comparisons among, for example, different racial, socioeconomic, and cultural groups. Basic to all of these comparisons is the search for clues that would provide the reason for differences among these groups. Are group differences the result of heredity, environment, or a combination of these factors?

In spite of the countless studies over the last forty years the answer to this question is as difficult and as elusive as it has always been. The debate and investigations continue today, though to some it may seem useless and rather academic. It must be stated, however, that the relative influences of heredity and environment are of fundamental importance to psychologists and educators. It is obvious that if a person's potential for achievement was determined solely by inherited abilities, our educational system would have a different philosophy than it would in an environmentally oriented structure.

HEREDITY

Let us first look at the evidence for the genetic position. Conrad and Jones (1940) demonstrated a substantial correlation between the intelligence test scores of parents and those of their children. That is, parents with high IQ's tend to have children with high IQ's, whereas parents with low IQ's tend to have children with low IQ's. Some investigators of genetic factors in human differences have studied genetically related children, others have studied unrelated children from similar socioeconomic backgrounds. Identical twins have been excellent sources for study because of their presumed similar genetic characteristics. Critics have pointed out, however, that twins are exposed to the same environment and, that, therefore, environmental factors may be the dominant variables. Consequently, comparisons have been made between identical twins who lived together and those raised separately. Investigations have also been made of siblings raised together and those reared apart. Burt (1958), in supporting genetic influences on the intelligence of identical twins and others, presented the following correlations.[3]

---

[3] Correlation in measurement means the degree of relationship of two variables. A correlation coefficient (r) has as its possible limits $+1.00$ and -1.00; for example, a coefficient of $+0.90$ is very high, whereas a $+0.20$ coefficient is very low. For a more detailed explanation and discussion of correlation see Chapter 5.

	r
Identical twins reared together	0.925
Identical twins reared apart	0.876
Siblings reared together	0.538
Siblings reared apart	0.517
Unrelated children reared together	0.269

Other investigations have studied brilliant or feebleminded persons to determine if such characteristics run in families. The results of most of these studies reveal that these traits do tend to run in certain families.

Some investigators have attempted to remove children from "poor" environments to "good" environments and then measure the change, if any. Much of this research has been characterised by inadequate scientific control and statistical procedures and results have lacked any clear trend.

ENVIRONMENT

Let us now look at environment, which for the purposes of this discussion will be divided into two categories, physical and psychological.

Physical. In the physical area some of the factors which relate to the future development of the individual are (1) prenatal environment and conditions of birth, (2) dietary conditions of pregnant women, (3) disease during pregnancy, and (4) nutritional climate and physical health of the child.

In the prenatal period of development several environmental agents influencing later intellectual growth are known. Among these the most notable is German measles, which if contracted by the mother during the early stage of pregnancy will often attack the fetus and cause mental retardation.

Certain factors operating at the time of birth have been shown to have a relationship to mental impairment. Some of these factors are anoxia (oxygen deficiency), mechanical injuries, anesthesia, prematurity, and abrupt births.

Mental development may be impaired in early childhood by physical trauma to the brain, poisons, certain viruses and bacilli, and very high fever. Gross protein starvation has also been noted in some cases of mental retardation.

Psychological. A number of studies have shown that chronic psychosocial factors, such as mother-child separation, maternal neglect, and personality problems of the mother, influence the mental development of the child. Another factor that has been widely studied is the effect of a restricted environment upon mental development.

A study that compared children living in an isolated mountain environment with children living in a valley community was conducted over thirty-seven years ago by Sherman and Key (1932). The mountain children lived in an isolated valley in the Blue Ridge mountains; the village children lived at the foot of the mountains in a less isolated environment. Both groups were from disadvantaged settings but the schools for the mountain children were less adequate. Both groups scored, on the average, lower than the national average on a group test of intelligence, and the mountain children's scores were lower than those of the valley children. Decreases in scores were apparent in the older children of both groups; however, the decreases were much less for the valley children than for the mountain group.

Newman's (1940) intensive studies of identical twins who were reared in different environments reveal that when one of the twins has been exposed to a more favorable cultural and educational climate there is a strong tendency for intelligence test scores of the twin with the advantaged environment to be significantly higher.

Newman does not claim, however, on the basis of his findings that environment is more important than heredity. He holds only that when educational and cultural opportunites are unusually good or poor for either of the twins there will be definite effects on intelligence test scores (p. 189).

CONCLUSION

Our discussion thus far has revealed the difficulties involved in formulating a definitive stand at either extreme of the heredity and environmental continuum. Let us review some of the inferences, implications, and opinions of a few investigators.

Erlenmeyer-Kimling and Jarvik (1963),[4] in a review of all the twin data of the last fifty years, demonstrate the remarkable consistency in the genetic influences on intelligence as measured by an IQ test. The data also indicate that environment plays an important role in mental development.

Jensen (1968) states,

> That individual differences in mental abilities are largely hereditary in origin is well established. We still do not know all the causal links in the chain from genes to mental test scores, but this is another matter and not a necessary condition for establishing the heritability of a trait.
>
> The polemics of the heredity-environment question have largely revolved around certain unfortunate misconceptions. One misconception is the idea that heredity-environment is a dichotomy— that a given trait is the result of *either* heredity or environment. Actually, the concept of heritability refers to the genetically determined proportion of variance in individual differences in a trait. Heritability is a continuous variable, taking values between 0 and 1 [p. 5].

Jensen goes on to state that in order to improve education we should be

---

[4] The reader who is interested in exploring the area of twin studies further is also referred to the extensive work of Vandenberg (1966).

aware of the child as both a biological and social being. It is his feeling that if we do not recognize the biological basis of educability we will "restrict our eventual understanding and possible control of the major sources of diversity in human capacities and potentialities" (p. 39).

Caspari (1968), a biologist concerned with the issue of heredity and environment, feels that there is strong evidence for a genetic influence on intelligence. He feels evidence for this view is provided, in part, by genetic conditions which can lower intelligence (for example, phenylketonuria and galactosemia). He states, "There seems to exist a large number of genes influencing this character (intelligence), since almost all chromosomal aberrations found in man are accompanied by mental deficiency" (p. 51).

He goes on to discuss the ratio between heredity and environment and concludes that one cannot state which is most important unless we study a specific cultural environment. The more important question to Caspari is the interaction of heredity and environment in the production of intelligence. He concludes by stating,

> The challenge to education appears to me to reside in the problem of how to create educational methods and environments which will be optimally adjusted to the needs of unique individuals. The main contribution which a geneticist can make to educational research is to stress the fundamental biological fact that every human being is a unique individual and that his genetic individuality will be expressed in the way in which he reacts to environmental and educational experiences [p. 54].

The viewpoint of Anastasi (1958) that heredity and environment are mutually interdependent seems to be the prevailing one of many psychologists and educators in the last twenty years. Stone and Church (1957) in their concluding chapter on childhood and adolescence state this position in reference to the problem of heredity versus environment. They feel the problem is "obsolete."

> We hope that our discussion throughout this book has made it clear how obsolete such problems have become today. On the biological level, we know that the organism has to exist in a field, that it has no traits except as these are nourished on the environment in which it is embedded, that its hereditary endowment defines the framework of what it can become, and that within these limits the environment acts to shape it. On the psychological level, we have come to realize that all human behavior is both hereditary and learned, that we must take account of the cultural environment as well as the physical one and that the problem is one of defining the ways in which a growing person with his own characteristics incorporates a body of values, attitudes, beliefs, knowledge, and practices, making them his

own and at the same time being transformed by them. Now we are inclined to realize that each individual incorporates and views his culture in his own idiosyncratic way, but that he would be a very different person growing up in another culture [p. 402].

This writer has noted in the last few years a stirring among psychologists to investigate again the relationship of heredity and environment in the future development of intelligence and other behavioral characteristics. Although the literature does not now reveal this renewed interest to a great degree, it seems certain that a return to the intensive investigations of the 1930's and early 1940's will in the years to come be quite evident. The impact on the American society of the civil rights struggle and the increasing awareness of poverty has already induced psychologists and others to study the relationship of race (heredity) and culture (environment) on intellectual performance. More will be said on this topic in the next section.

Let us conclude by stating that it is generally believed today that heredity provides the structure within which mental growth takes place. The environment, on the other hand, is influential in determining the form and growth of certain abilities which might be developed. For example, Mozart and Einstein probably would have been outstanding in a primitive culture, but they would not have been outstanding in music and mathematics if these disciplines did not exist. On the other hand, it is very difficult to conceive of an environment that could create an Einstein or a Mozart without the genetically determined raw material which these men possessed.

Test Score Differences Between Races and Social Classes

The question of differences in test scores for different racial and socio-economic groups is, of course, closely related to our previous discussion of heredity and environment. If heredity determines intelligences or is at least a predisposing agent, are there significant differences between races and socioeconomic groups? If environment is the key to intellectual ability, then cultural and educational opportunity should be the determining agent in test scores. Let us look at the past fifty years of research to see if any conclusions can be drawn.

Jensen (1968) asks if an "official decision" has been made to create an impression that the issue of racial variations has been scientifically tested with conclusive results. A publication of the U.S. Office of Education (1966) states, "It is a demonstrable fact that the talent pool in any one ethnic group is substantially the same as that in any other ethnic group." Or take the Department of Labor (1965) report on the Negro family, which concludes that, "Intelligence potential is distributed among Negro infants in the same proportion and pattern as among Icelanders or Chinese, or any other."

This writer has never seen anything in the literature that supports, with scientific certitude, the statements of the U.S. Office of Education and the Department of Labor. Jensen (1968) in reviewing these statements states,

"Such statements entirely lack a factual basis and uncritical acceptance of them may unwittingly harm many Negro children born and unborn" (p. 23). The discussion that follows will be an attempt to look at some of the data— not to "make" a case for one side or the other.

RESEARCH FINDINGS

After the first intelligence tests were developed, studies were made comparing children and adults of different groups. The basic concern was to find differences, if any, in various groups of individuals. Comparisons were made between different age groups; racial, social, and national groups; urban and rural groups; and income levels. The findings indicated appreciable group differences. Children living in rural areas and in the Southern or southwestern United States, as well as Indian and Negro children, exhibited generally lower scores than children living in Northern urban areas.

In the area of social and economic levels many studies reveal, on the average, that children belonging to upper socioeconomic levels do better in intelligence tests than children from the lower strata (Tyler, 1956; Fifer, 1966; Davis, 1951). This seems to be true in England and Russia, as well as in the United States (Johnson, 1948). These studies, however, do not clarify the reasons for differences. Some studies inject the additional variable of motivational differences. These investigations point to the possibility that middle-class children try harder on tests than their lower-class peers (Eells, 1951). The interpretation of these investigations has generated conflict and confusion among scientists and lay people alike.

The first large-scale studies of group differences were the result of massive testing in World War I. The Army, at the beginning of the war, asked the American Psychological Association to help construct a method for classifying soldiers according to their mental ability. Robert Yerkes headed a committee which developed a group test of intelligence called the Army Alpha Test. The development of this test drew heavily upon Arthur Otis' work. (Otis, a former student of Terman's, had been experimenting with a group test of mental ability.) In addition, the committee devised a test for illiterates called the Army Beta Test. Almost 2 million soldiers were examined using these instruments (Chauncey and Dobbin, 1966).

The Army Alpha was a test of ability which examined the person's knowledge, simple reasoning, arithmetic, and ability to follow directions. The Army Beta was a nonverbal test. Directions were in pantomime and removed the effect of differences in language ability from the score. The Beta was administered to all men who fell below a given score on the Alpha. This group was composed of men who were handicapped by a foreign-language background or illiteracy as well as those who performed poorly on the Alpha for any other reason.

The Alpha and the Beta have gone through many revisions since World War I and are still in use today. Since their development they have served as models for most group intelligence tests.

The results from testing nearly 2 million men using both the Alpha and Beta revealed racial and regional differences. Native-born whites achieved significantly higher average scores than Negroes. Northern Negroes achieved significantly higher average scores than Southern Negroes (Yerkes, 1921). Myrdal (1944) noted that Negroes (on the Army Alpha test) from Pennsylvania, New York, Illinois, and Ohio averaged higher scores than whites from Mississippi, Arkansas, Kentucky, and Georgia.

Klineberg (1935), Klineberg (1944), and Montagu (1945) in their analysis of Yerkes' data focus their attention on the superiority of Northern Negroes over white groups from certain Southern states.

Garrett (1945) has stated that these comparisons have been made to demonstrate that education and economic opportunity are of more importance than race. He further states that all psychologists would agree that these data clearly indicate the importance of education; however, he feels it is doubtful that any definitive conclusion concerning race differences can be made on the basis of these results alone.

Garrett (1945) reported that Negroes from Ohio, Pennsylvania, Illinois, and New York scored below white soldiers of these states in the same proportion as they scored below the whites in the whole country. Garrett concludes from this that given a better education the Negro does improve his score but not his relative position to the white. He notes that white Southerners, even though they had educational deficits, did approximately as well as Northern Negroes. Thus he infers that if Southern whites had the same advantages as Northern Negroes, they would do better on the test.

Studies since World War I have shown some indications that improvement in educational opportunities can result in an increase in IQ scores. Lee (1951) found that Southern-born Negro children who moved to a Northern city and entered school as first graders improved their average IQ scores from 86.5 to 93.3 by the end of the sixth grade.

Klineberg's (1935) investigation of Negro children in New York City revealed that Negro children who spent a longer time in New York City tended to have higher IQ scores than Negro children of more recent residence.

Kardiner and Ovesey (1951) attempt to explain lower Negro intellectual performance on the basis of psychiatric findings. They see a loss of efficiency in Negro intellectual functioning because of a focusing of attention on factors unrelated to performance. That is, there is a great temptation to adjust to symbols rather than strive for the real objective. This approach may lessen frustration, according to the authors, but it also may convey the impression of less intellectual ability.

Fifer (1966) and his associates attempted to devise tests which would be "as free as possible" of cultural bias and to present these tests in a testing situation under optional conditions. Four ethnic groups were studied— Chinese, Jews, Negroes, and Puerto Ricans. Each group was divided into middle- and lower-class designations. Examiners for each group were of the same ethnic group as the one being tested. The children were tested in four areas—verbal ability, reasoning, numerical ability, and ability to deal with spatial concepts. The data showed test performance differences between middle-class and lower-class groups regardless of ethnic origin. These differences varied from group to group. Of the middle-class groups, the Jewish middle class had the highest average scores, whereas the Puerto Rican middle class had the lowest average scores. The investigators felt their study revealed "strong evidence of differential patterns of mental abilities among four . . . ethnic groups" (p. 489).

A special note on a very important study on the *Equality of Educational Opportunity* (United States Department of Health, Education, and Welfare, 1966) merits attention in our discussion of race and test score differences. This study was undertaken in accordance with Section 402 of the Civil Rights Act of 1964 which directed the United States Commissioner of Education to

> conduct a survey and make a report to the President and the Congress, within two years of the enactment of this title, concerning the lack of availability of equal educational opportunities for individuals by reason of race, color, religion, or national origin in public educational institutions at all levels in the United States, its territories and possessions, and the District of Columbia [p. iii].

The survey focused on six racial and ethnic groups—Negroes, whites, American Indians, Oriental Americans, Puerto Ricans (living in the continental United States), and Mexican Americans. The study was conducted in the fall of 1965 and involved 4,000 public schools and 645,000 pupils.

The test results revealed that, with the notable exception of Oriental Americans, the average minority student scored much lower on the battery of standardized achievement tests in every area than the average white pupil. In addition, it was found that this lower achievement for minority groups is progressively greater as the educational level increases.

In the first grade the Negro group's median (average) score in the "nonverbal" test was lower than that of any other group, whereas the Oriental American's score was higher than that of any of the six groups. In the "verbal" area the Puerto Rican group was lowest followed closely by the Negro group; the white pupils obtained the highest scores.

In the twelfth grade the Negro group obtained lower scores than any of the six groups in the following tests:

1. Nonverbal.
2. Verbal.
3. Reading.
4. Mathematics.
5. General information.
6. Average of the five tests.

Although the white group obtained the highest average scores, followed closely by Oriental Americans (United States Department of Health, Education and Welfare, 1966, p. 20), it was also found that students in the South, both white and Negro, revealed lower test scores than their counterparts in the North. [The interested reader, in addition to referring to the preceding source, may also want to read an excellent review of the survey by Borgatta and Bohrnstedt (1968).]

Martin Jenkins, an early Negro investigator of racial differences, studied gifted children of both races in the 1930's. He found that a considerable number of Negro children were within the range of the highest 1 per cent of white children, that is, an IQ of 130 or above. He further reported that sixteen published investigations presented data showing Negro children with IQ's above 130, and twelve of these were above 140.

Jenkins (1964), in discussing gifted Negroes states,

> I am not attempting here to show that approximately as many Negro children as white are to be found at the highest levels of psychometric intelligence. There appears little doubt that the number of very bright Negro children is relatively smaller than the number of bright white children in the total American population. Nevertheless, it is apparent that children of very superior psychometric intelligence may be found in many Negro populations, and that the upper limit of the range attained by the extreme deviates is higher than is generally believed [p. 88].

Spuhler and Lindzey (1967) conclude that both sides of the controversy agree in one important area, that the existing research suggests the average IQ of the American Negro is 85 or 86 whereas that of the typical American white is 100.

The studies that have been cited are only a very small sampling of the hundreds of investigations that have been concerned with racial and socioeconomic differences. The interested student who desires to explore this subject further will find an excellent resource in Shuey's (1966) exhaustive treatment of the multitude of studies on Negro and white test differences since World War I. Although Shuey has a "point of view" it does not distract from her excellent scholarship and ability to present both sides of the controversy.

In the next two sections of this chapter an attempt will be made to integrate all the previously mentioned data with the educational objective of assisting all children within our school system. Let us conclude this section with some general statements by knowledgeable authorities and organizations.

Shuey (1966) states,

> The remarkable consistency in test results, whether they pertain to school or preschool children, to children between ages 6 to 9 or 10 to 12, to children in Grades 1 to 3 or 4 to 7, to high school or college

students, to enlisted men or officers in training in the Armed Forces—
in World War I, World War II, or the Post-Korean period—to
veterans of the Armed Forces, to homeless men or transients, to
gifted or mentally deficient, to delinquent or criminal; the fact that
differences between colored and white are present not only in the
rural and urban south, but in the Border and Northern states; the
fact that the colored preschool, school, and high school pupils living
in Northern cities tested as far below the Southern urban white
children as they did below the whites in the Northern cities; the fact
that relatively small average differences were found between the IQ's
of Northern-born and Southern-born Negro children in Northern
cities; the fact that Negro school children and high school pupils
have achieved average IQ's slightly lower in the past twenty years
than between 1921 and 1944; the tendency toward greater variability
among whites; the tendency for racial hybrids to score higher than
those groups described as, or inferred to be, unmixed Negro; the
evidence that the mean overlap is between 7 and 13 percent; the
evidence that the tested differences appear to be greater for logical
analysis, abstract reasoning, and perceptual-motor tasks than for
practical and concrete problems; the evidence that the tested differences may be a little less on verbal than on nonverbal tasks; the
indication that the colored elementary or high school pupil has not
been adversely affected in his tested performance by the presence of
a white examiner; an indication that Negroes may have a greater
sense of personal worth than whites, at least at the elementary, high
school, and college levels; the unproved and probably erroneous
assumption that Negroes have been less well motivated on tests than
whites; the fact that differences were reported in practically all of
the studies in which the cultural environment of the whites appeared
to be similar in richness and complexity to that of the Negroes;
the fact that in many comparisons including those in which the
colored have appeared to best advantage, Negro subjects have been
either more representative of their racial group or more highly
selected than the comparable whites; all taken together, inevitably
point to the presence of native differences between Negroes and whites
as determined by intelligence tests [pp. 520–21].

Jensen (1969) is in general agreement with Shuey. He argues that the
failure of our educational efforts to compensate for disadvantaged environments is directly related to the false premise that IQ differences are the
result of environmental conditions and the cultural bias of tests. It is his
contention that genetic factors are more important in determining IQ.
Jensen feels that environmental deprivation can keep a child from performing
up to the level of his genetic potential, but the best programs cannot elevate
the child above that potential.

On the other side of the argument, it is of interest to note that in September 1961, at the American Psychological Association's convention, the Society for the Psychological Study of Social Issues stated the following:

> The evidence of a quarter of a century of research on this problem can readily be summarized. There are differences in intelligence when one compares a random sample of whites and Negroes. What is equally clear is that no evidence exists that leads to the conclusion that such differences are innate. Quite to the contrary, the evidence points overwhelmingly to the fact that when one compares Negroes and whites of comparable cultural and educational background, differences in intelligence diminish markedly. The more comparable the background of white and Negro groups, the less the difference in intelligence. There is no direct evidence that supports the view that there is an innate difference between members of different racial groups.

Garrett (1962) in reviewing the preceding, declares that Negro-white differences in mental tests are so regular that he feels they suggest a genetic basis.

Cronbach (1960) states,

> Racial comparisons have frequently been misinterpreted because liberal writers want to prove that there are no innate differences in ability, and certain conservatives want to prove that nonwhite groups will not profit from improved educational opportunity [p. 204].

Cronbach's view is amplified further by Spuhler and Lindzey (1967), who after citing numerous studies and summaries of studies state, "It seems clear, however, that with all this investigation the position of most modern observers is at least as much influenced by prior belief as by present findings" (p. 391).

In reviewing all the literature, one thing is quite clear, the vast majority of studies reveal very significant differences between test scores of different racial, ethnic, and socioeconomic groups. This writer's own position on the conflictual studies and interpretations is in agreement with Spuhler and Lindzey (1967), "What we can say with confidence is that racial groups differ in intelligence as measured by existing instruments. The extent to which these differences are to be attributed to biological factors (race) rather than to experiential (particularly cultural) factors remains largely unknown" (pp. 391–92).

Educational Reality and the Disadvantaged

In order to assist an individual in his choice of and preparation for education and meaningful work we must know his past achievements, present capabilities, and future potential. One method of evaluating these is by testing. Are these tests useful in guiding the disadvantaged? First, let us focus our attention on the achievement test, the area of testing that is the least controversial when dealing with the disadvantaged. Lennon (1964) states,

> It is axiomatic that the school and the teacher must know the present status of each child, and the progress he is making, with respect to certain concrete goals of instruction. . . . Whatever advantages or limitations a child brings to his school learning tasks, the school and the teacher still must be concerned with how successfully he is attaining the goals of instruction; and this is one of the contributions that the standardized achievement test makes, whether in the case of the culturally disadvantaged or the more fortunate pupil.

The school needs to know the present status and progress of both its advantaged and disadvantaged children.[5] Thus we may answer part of our question; *yes*, achievement tests are useful in guiding disadvantaged children. The teacher, of course, is in an excellent position to know whether the achievement test is appropriate for her particular students and should share this information with the school administration.

Proper test administration is very important, especially with disadvantaged children. Many articles and books have been written about the alienation of culturally disadvantaged youngsters. The test situation, unless properly handled, could reinforce this alienation. The test administrator must be especially careful to convey to children his concern and interest. Explanations concerning the purposes of testing should always be made clear before the examination begins. Disadvantaged children need to know that testing is not another obstacle or method of "getting them."

In testing these children the gravest question is, "Are IQ tests fair for the disadvantaged?" In order to address ourselves to the question of fairness or unfairness of IQ tests for the disadvantaged, we must first briefly review why IQ tests are given. In general terms, IQ tests are given in order to determine what an individual is capable of doing. What are Bill's chances for success in school? Will he need special attention? If so, what kind of instruction? Is he mentally retarded or gifted? If an IQ test can help to show that Bill needs special attention and that attention is then given, Bill has obviously received immense help.

Present performance may be gauged by school grades, teacher opinion, and standardized achievement tests. Future potential cannot be ascertained in the same way, because the teacher's judgment is already reflected in grade evaluation and opinion. Another evaluative technique must be used to make

---

[5] The following discussion of reality and the disadvantaged is based in part upon a previous publication of the author. See Karmel (1967).

sure that Bill is not being judged by factors which may be unrelated to his academic potential, such as teacher bias or poor academic background.

Thus, in using a test of future potential, along with the teacher's opinion and data from objective achievement tests, we have a situation similar to the checks and balances in our government. The teacher's opinion and evaluation is checked and weighed against what a child may accomplish on standardized achievement tests, in which his performance is compared to children all over the country, not just those in his classroom.

If IQ tests and other data help the school to understand each individual (as an overwhelming number of studies show), then certain inferences must be made. These inferences are drawn from an interpretation of the test results. *If the test data do not discriminate between individuals, the teacher or guidance counselor cannot make inferences, nor can he help the individual student.*

In attempting to facilitate learning the school is concerned with what a pupil can and will do. A pupil's race or socioeconomic status is not important in educational planning. What is important is the individual's present status and future potential, that is, what he has attained and what he may become.

We are living in a middle-class-oriented society and the school is a reflection of this society. In judging a student the school is not evaluating him in terms of his ability to "get along"; it is appraising his ability to function and grow in an educational setting.

In discussing this problem in a previous publication (Karmel 1967), the author has stated the following:

> If IQ tests are uniformly unfair to Negroes and other groups, then so are our schools and perhaps more importantly our educational aspirations for our children are in need of radical replacement. We seem to be in a quandary concerning the basic rule of education. On the one hand we demand higher and higher standards of excellence from our students and on the other hand there are those who say that we are unfair to have standards, and it is of as much value for a child to know the codes of the city street. Does recognition of a child's cultural deprivation and different mores mean one should accept, condone, and perpetuate them?
>
> The value we place on educational achievement may be contested by some, but most educators and lay people, both Negro and white, would agree on the efficacy of educational advancement as a key to the enrichment of the individual and his society. The methods in achieving this goal may differ, but in learning one must have the "stuff" to learn with no matter what the learning technique. Thus, the question of the fairness of the IQ test is directly related to the educational mores of our society for in the last analysis the IQ test is measuring the potential of Johnny to succeed in a school system oriented to society. If it was not aimed in this direction it would have little value [pp. 11–12].

In essence, then, the variables of genetics, environment, race, socioeconomic status, and cultural bias are academic questions when we are considering the practical educational reality of how well a pupil will do and how the school can best serve the individual student with his own unique potential to learn. The student of measurement should not infer from this that these variables are unimportant. On the contrary, they are extremely important when considered in their proper context. If our goal is to predict the chances for an individual pupil to succeed in our present school system, then we must have tests that reflect this system. The reasons that an individual may or may not be able to learn is an issue beyond that of testing. Testing is not geared, nor should it be, to treatment. It may be used to facilitate treatment by providing data which the school may use to render individual educational planning and guidance. To illustrate this point let us look at Smith Junior High School.

Smith Junior High School is located in a predominantly disadvantaged neighborhood. Mr. Lowell, the principal, is concerned about the appropriateness of group IQ tests for his students. This concern is shared by many of his teachers. Many feel that IQ tests are unfair because of their cultural bias. These concerns prompt Mr. Lowell to call in Mr. Fields, a testing consultant, to help guide the school in its educational planning. The faculty meeting is open for discussion and the science teacher poses the first question:

> Science Teacher: Is it fair to say that one of our students is dumb because he gets a low IQ or test score? I feel it isn't because the tests are made up for middle-class kids and our kids don't have the same exposures.
>
> Mr. Fields: I agree it is not fair to say your kids are dumb. It is fair to say, however, that the chances of success in school are not too good for your kids who obtain low scores on IQ tests.
>
> Science Teacher: What do you mean by not too good?
>
> Mr. Fields: Studies have shown that there is a high relationship between IQ scores and school success. That is, children who score at the average level or above have a better chance of staying in school and graduating and they are able to do the work required.
>
> Social Studies Teacher: I agree with the studies but it still doesn't seem fair to label these youngsters.
>
> Mr. Fields: I agree, these youngsters should *not* be labeled. The purpose of testing is to aid not hinder educational growth.
>
> Mr. Lowell: Are you saying that IQ tests are not indicative of innate intelligence?
>
> Mr. Fields: No, I am not saying that they are not indicative of innate intelligence, nor am I saying that they are able to identify innate intelligence. We truthfully do not know. What we do know is that they are very helpful in predicting school success. This is why

we prefer to call them scholastic aptitude tests rather than intelligence tests.

Math Teacher: Well, that may all be true but I know they are used to label and since they are not perfect or near perfect how can you defend them?

Mr. Fields: I cannot defend their exclusive use but in conjunction with teacher evaluations they enhance educational prediction.

Mr. Lowell: What about using a culture-free test?

Mr. Fields: There are no such tests. Yes, some tests are labeled culture-free or culture-fair, but research does not bear out the promise of their titles. They too in some measure reflect the culture.

Librarian: If we could have a test that was free of cultural bias would you recommend its use?

Mr. Fields: It would depend on several factors. First, what would its predictive utility be? Secondly, how would you use it? That is, if it predicted school success as well or better than our present instruments without penalizing youngsters because of cultural background, then of course I would use it. If it didn't predict school success but could be used as an aid in detecting youngsters with ability who could be educationally salvaged by intensive teaching, then I would still use it.

Even though your children come from disadvantaged homes you will still find some who do well on tests and you can advise these children accordingly. On the other hand, without these tests a child in your school may think he is doing quite well and not know of his standing with youngsters from different areas of the county.

Let us leave Smith Junior High School and direct our attention to individual cases. John, a six-year-old Negro child, is evaluated by an IQ test. The test reveals that he is on the borderline between dull normal and mentally retarded. This is a situation where the knowledge of cultural bias would be important. There is no doubt that John's test results should be received with more skepticism and caution than if he were white. The school should weigh other factors and not rely solely on this score. If, however, John were twelve years old and tested at the same level, the results in terms of educability and reality would be less suspect. This is not to say that there might not still be error, but the chance of making up for the cultural deprivation would be less.

The student of measurement should remember that the interpretation of IQ scores, as is true of the scores of other tests, must be made on the basis of many factors, including culture, but in the final analysis the scores should be interpreted in accordance with the objectives of testing. Whether the child is advantaged or disadvantaged he competes and lives in a society geared to middle-class objectives and values.

American education must face the problem of how best to educate the disadvantaged. Alleviation of this problem, however, will not be found in eradication of the instrument that gauges its existence. The IQ test is only an instrument to gauge what is, not what should be. Thus, the answer to cultural and socioeconomic deprivation lies in rectifying and treating the etiological agents that create the disadvantaged community, not in doing away with an instrument that helps us know of its presence. To do away with IQ tests because they measure social problems is as logical as throwing out medical procedures that indicate cancer because a treatment today is not available.

A Practical Approach to the Use of Standardized Tests

The reader has now been exposed to what an IQ is and what it is not; what "intelligence" is and what intelligence tests are; discussion of the part heredity and environment play in human behavior; test score differences in Negro and white children and adults; and interpretations of test scores for the disadvantaged. The question before us is how to translate these facts, findings, interpretations, and points of view into sound educational policy.

Sound educational decisions emanate from sound educational policy. Educational policy must be based on the best available information gleaned from experimental investigations and empirical observations. Although the issues, conflicting data, and different interpretations seem confusing, there are areas of agreement that can be used as a basis for sound educational policy. They are the following:

1. Tests are not infallible but used along with other methods of evaluation, such as teacher judgments, they are very useful in helping individuals realize their own unique potential.

2. Educators must understand the limitations as well as the advantages of tests.

3. Tests should never be used as an excuse to avoid human judgment or contact.

4. The number of tests used is determined by the amount of information needed.

5. Hereditary differences do not alleviate the fact that most investigators recognize the importance of environment in shaping the child's intellectual ability.

6. Tests should always be used in conjunction with educational objectives. Interpretation of test scores are only meaningful when applied to educational and individual goals.

References

Anastasi, A. Some implications of cultural factors for test construction. In A. Anastasi (Ed.), *Testing problems in perspective: Twenty-fifth anniversary volume of topical readings from the invitational conference on testing problems.* Washington, D.C.: American Council on Education, 1966.

Anastasi, A. *Differential psychology.* (3rd ed.) New York: Macmillan, 1958.

Black, H. *They shall not pass.* New York: William Morrow, 1963.

Borgatta, E. and Bohrnstedt, G. Review of Equality of educational opportunity. *American Educational Research Journal,* 1968, **5**, 260–65.

Burt, C. The inheritance of mental ability. *The American Psychologist,* 1958, **13**, 1–15.

Caspari, E. Genetic endowment and environment in the determination of human behavior: biological viewpoint. *American Educational Research Journal,* 1968, **5**, 43–55.

Chauncey, H., and Dobbin, J. E. Testing has a history. In C. I. Chase and H. G. Ludlow (Eds.), *Readings in educational and psychological measurement.* Boston: Houghton Mifflin, 1966. Pp. 7–8.

Conrad, H. S., and Jones, H. E. A second study of familial resemblance in intelligence. *Original studies and experiments, thirty-ninth Yearbook of the National Society for the Study of Education, Part II.* Chicago: University of Chicago Press, 1940. Pp. 97–141.

Cronbach, L. J. *Essentials of psychological testing.* (2nd ed.) New York: Harper & Row, 1960.

Davis, A. Socioeconomic influences upon children's learning. *Understanding the Child,* 1951, **20**, 10–16.

Department of Labor. *The Negro family—the case for national action.* Office of Policy Planning and Research, Department of Labor, March, 1965.

Eells, K., Davis, A., Havighurst, R. J., Herrick, E., and Tyler, R. *Intelligence and cultural differences.* Chicago: University of Chicago Press, 1951.

Erlenmeyer-Kimling, L. and Jarvik, L. Genetics and intelligence: A review. *Science,* 1963, **142**, 1477–79.

Ferris, F. L., Jr. Testing in the new curriculum: Numerology, "tyranny", or common sense. *The School Review,* 1962, **70**, 112–131.

Fifer, G. Social class and cultural group differences in diverse mental abilities. In A. Anastasi (Ed.), *Testing problems in perspective: Twenty-fifth anniversary volume of topical readings from the invitational conference on testing problems.* Washington, D.C.: American Council on Education, 1966.

Garrett, H. E. A note on the intelligence scores of Negroes and whites in 1918. *Journal of Abnormal and Social Psychology,* 1945, **40**, 344–46.

Garrett, H. E. The SPSSI and racial differences. *American Psychologist,* 1962, **17**, 260–63.

Good, W. R. Misconceptions about intelligence testing. In C. I. Chase and H. G. Ludlow (Eds.), *Readings in educational and psychological measurement.* Boston: Houghton Mifflin, 1966.

Hebb, D. O. *A textbook of psychology.* Philadelphia: W. B. Saunders, 1958.

Hoffmann, B. *The tyranny of testing.* New York: The Crowell-Collier Press, 1962.

Jenkins, M. D. The upper limit of ability among American Negroes. In J. L. French (Ed.), *Educating the gifted: A book of readings.* (2nd ed.) New York: Holt, 1964.

Jensen, A. Social class, race, and genetics: implications for education. *American Educational Research Journal,* 1968, **5,** 1–42.

Jensen, A. How much can we boost IQ and scholastic achievement? *Harvard Educational Review,* 1969, **39,** 1–123.

Johnson, D. M. Application of the standard-score IQ to the social statistics. *Journal of Social Psychology,* 1948, **27,** 217–27.

Kardiner, A., and Ovesey, L. *The mark of oppression: A psychological study of the American Negro.* New York: Norton, 1951.

Karmel, L. J. Do IQ tests discriminate against Negroes in their preparation for the world of work? *New York Personnel and Guidance Bulletin,* 1967, **19** (3), 10–13.

Klineberg, O. *Negro intelligence and selective migration.* New York: Columbia University Press, 1935.

Klineberg, O. (Ed.) *Characteristics of the American Negro.* New York: Harper and Row, 1944.

Lee, E. S. Negro intelligence and selective migration: a Philadelphia test of the Klineberg hypothesis. *American Sociology Review,* 1951, **16,** 227–33.

Lennon, R. T. Testing and the culturally disadvantaged child. Paper read at series on *Problems in Education of the Culturally Disadvantaged,* Boston, Feb., 1964. (Copies may be secured from the Test Department of Harcourt, Brace & World, Inc.; 757 Third Ave.; New York, N.Y.)

Loretan, J. O. Alternatives to intelligence testing. *Curriculum and Materials: Board of Education of The City of New York,* 1966, **20** (3), 6–9.

Lorge, I. Difference or bias in tests of intelligence. In A. Anastasi (Ed.), *Testing problems in perspective: Twenty-fifth anniversary volume of topical readings from the invitational conference on testing problems.* Washington, D.C.: American Council on Education, 1966. Pp. 465–71.

Montagu, M. F. A. Intelligence of northern Negroes and southern whites in the first world war. *American Journal of Psychology,* 1945, **58,** 161–88.

Myrdal, G. *An American dilemma.* New York: Harper & Row, 1944.

Newman, H. M. *Multiple human births.* Garden City, N.Y.: Doubleday, 1940.

Rosenberg, L. A. Scientific racism and the American psychologist. Paper presented at the meeting of the District of Columbia Psychological Association, Washington, D.C., October, 1966.

Sherman, M., and Key, C. B. The intelligence of isolated mountain children. *Child Development,* 1932, **3,** 279–90.

Shuey, A. M. *The testing of Negro intelligence.* (2nd ed.) New York: Social Science Press, 1966.

Spearman, C. E. *The abilities of man: Their nature and measurement.* New York: Macmillan, 1927.

Spuhler, J. N., and Lindzey, G. Racial differences in behavior. In J. Hirsch (Ed.), *Behavior-genetic analysis.* New York: McGraw-Hill, 1967. Pp. 366–414.

Stone, L. S. and Church, J. *Childhood and adolescence: A psychology of the growing person.* New York: Random House, 1957.

Terman, L. M. *Measurement of intelligence.* Boston: Houghton Mifflin, 1916.

Thorndike, E. L. et al. *The measurement of intelligence.* New York: Columbia Teacher's College, 1927.

Thurstone, L. L., and Thurstone, T. G. Factorial studies of intelligence. *Psychometrics Monographs,* 1941, No. 2.

Tyler, L. *The psychology of human differences.* (2nd ed.) New York: Appleton-Century-Crofts, 1956.

United States Office of Education. *American Education,* October, 1966.

United States Department of Health, Education, and Welfare. *Equality of educational opportunity: Summary report.* Catalog No. FS5.238:38000. Washington, D.C.: United States Government Office, 1966.

Vandenberg, S. Contribution of twin research to psychology. *Psychological Bulletin,* 1966, **66,** 327–52.

Warren, H. C. (Ed.) *Dictionary of psychology.* Boston: Houghton Mifflin, 1934.

Webster's new collegiate dictionary. (6th ed.) Springfield, Mass.: G. & C. Merriam, 1961.

Wechsler, D. *The measurement of adult intelligence.* (4th ed.) Baltimore: Williams and Wilkins, 1960.

Yerkes, R. M. (Ed.) Psychological examining in the United States Army. *National Academy of Science Memoirs,* 1921, **15.**

PART TWO

Testing the Test

CHAPTER

3

Test Ethics, Standards, and Procedures

The major criticisms and controversies of testing have been presented. One of the most obvious conclusions from a review of test criticism is that many times the attack should not be directed at the test per se, but at the use of tests. In this chapter an attempt will be made to give the student some guidelines for proper test usage.

Before entering the important area of test standards and procedures let us turn our attention to the principal characteristics of tests. In Chapter 1 we defined and briefly discussed what a test is in general terms. It was stated that to test is to evaluate and compare one person or variable with a given criterion or criteria. Using this definition, can we state that a psychological test evaluates intelligence or personality, or does it measure both? What do you think? What are the basic ingredients of a psychological test?

The basic purpose underlying the construction and use of psychological tests is to sample some aspect of an individual's behavior. This is true whether the behavior is mental ability or personality characteristics, whether the objective is to evaluate reading progress or interest patterns, whether the purpose is to measure attitudes or possible brain damage, whether the purpose is to measure creativity or musical talent. The list of possible behavioral samples is lengthy. The point to remember is that a psychological test is not defined by content as much as it is by function.

The psychological test is an instrument that attempts to measure an aspect of behavior in an objective and standardized manner. (See section on standardization, Chapter 1.) The primary intent is to sample human behavior without introducing human subjectivity. This goal, of course, has never been fully reached on any psychological test, because perfect standardization and objectivity have not yet been attained. On the other hand, a reasonable amount of success in this area is evident with the majority of tests.

Teacher-made tests are not generally considered psychological tests because they usually do not fulfill the requirements of objectivity and standardization. Our discussion of ethics, standards, and procedures in this chapter will be focused on psychological tests.

Some History

The development of an official body of standards for testing is relatively new. It was not until 1954 that an official statement on test procedures was published.[1] This statement represented a consensus of data that was considered most beneficial to a test consumer. In the period before 1954 test standards and quality varied according to the ethics, standards, and knowledge of individual test authors and publishers. In order to understand more fully the importance of standards in testing let us briefly review the major periods and issues.

The first use of the term *mental test* in the psychological literature was in an article by Cattell (1890). The article discussed the use of tests of muscular strength, speed of movement, reaction time, sensory discrimination, and other measures used to determine intellectual levels of college students. Other investigators, such as Ebbinghaus (1897), devised tests of arithmetic computation, memory span, and sentence completion to measure school children's intelligence. Many more investigations could be cited, but the important point is that these early efforts were to lead to the development of the Binet intelligence scales.

In 1905 Binet, along with Simon, developed the first intelligence test similar to our present tests. The 1905 scale was a tentative instrument without an objective method for deriving a total score. The second Scale (1908) introduced the term *mental age*, which compared children to normal children of the same age. (For example, a mental age of five years means a child passed all the items normal five-year-olds would pass.) In Chapter 7 we will deal with Binet's first efforts in more detail.

The work of Binet was reviewed with earnest enthusiasm in the United States and his tests were translated from French into several English versions, the most noteworthy of which was the Stanford-Binet.

[1] The first official declaration on testing standards was called *Technical Recommendations for Psychological Tests and Diagnostic Techniques*, written and published by the American Psychological Association in 1954.

The Stanford-Binet Intelligence Test was developed at Stanford University by L. M. Terman (1916). It was in this test that the term *IQ* was first used.

The genesis of modern testing may be considered to be from 1900 to 1916. This is the period during which Binet and his co-workers were developing the first scales. It was during this time that Terman (1916) and others such as Kuhlmann (1912) were translating and revising the Binet Scale.

The next fourteen years, 1916–1930, may be viewed as the "fad" period in test development. The Binet tests and revisions were individual tests in that they could be administered to only one person at a time. This period saw the emergence of group testing.[2] The development of group testing, as you will recall from our discussion in Chapter 2, was brought about by the entry of the United States into World War I. The need for swift intellectual classification of over a million recruits led to the development of the Army Alpha and Beta tests. After the war these tests were released for civilian use and served as the models for other group intelligence tests.

During this period large-scale testing programs were instituted with optimistic naïveté. Standardized tests were developed for most of the content areas of the school curriculum. The examination of college applicants for admission became routine. Instruments for evaluating many different school skills were developed and used extensively. In short, the American public became test conscious. Not only was the public aware of testing, especially IQ tests, but it and many professional educators tended to deify tests. Tests were the instruments from the promised land. This attitude of blind acceptance of testing, of course, led to many serious abuses. The fact that measurement was in its infancy was often forgotten in the rush to "be with it."

Americans are noted for their tendency to jump on the bandwagon of something new, and testing was no exception. However, educators, psychologists, and others after a time became more critical of tests and of the uses made of them. Thus, Anastasi (1968) states that, "When the tests failed to meet unwarranted expectations, skepticism and hostility toward all testing often resulted. Thus the testing boom of the twenties, based upon the indiscriminate use of tests, may have done as much to retard as to advance the progress of psychological testing" (p. 12).

This mounting criticism of testing had the beneficial effect of forcing the test producers and consumers to reconsider their methods. This period of reappraisal and broadened prospective extended from about 1930 to 1946. The exacting standards of test construction and usage which we know today owe much to this period of test development.

The successful use of tests and test batteries[3] during World War II gave rise to a measurement renaissance after the war ended. From about 1946 to 1961 may be considered the period in which testing experienced a rebirth— not so much in the construction of new tests, but in the widespread use of

---

[2] A group test may be administered to one or more individuals at a time.

[3] A group of several tests that are comparable, the results of which are used individually, in various combinations, and/or totally.

tests and test batteries. Large-scale testing programs in local school systems were launched and those administered by the College Entrance Examination Board were expanded. During this time a new college entrance examination, called the American College Testing Program, was founded.[4]

This renaissance of measurement also saw the birth of test standards. It was in this period that the American Psychological Association (1954) and the American Educational Research Association and the National Council on Measurements Used in Education, Committee on Test Standards (1955) first published recommendations for the construction and use of tests.

In the early 1960's, as had been the case in the 1930's, a negative reaction to testing became evident. This time, however, the bulk of test criticism was voiced by lay critics. Most of these critics had little knowledge of testing and did little research to back up their attacks. (See Chapter 2.)

The period from 1962 to the present may be characterized as the "illegitimate criticism" era of test history. This may be contrasted to the "legitimate criticism" period of the 1930's and early 1940's. Whereas the first period was initiated, directed, and pursued by professionals who were earnestly attempting to rectify past errors in order to produce better tests, the present critical period sees nonprofessionals attacking tests in a sensational and nonscholarly manner.[5] A destructive rather than a constructive approach is evident.

In the light of test history and the recent barrage of critical attacks on measurement the importance of standards cannot be overemphasized. As a student of measurement it is particularly important for you to be aware of the code of test ethics and standards we are about to discuss.

Ethics

The history of psychological measurement has witnessed rigorous adherence to the scientific method, personal dedication, and creativity. On the other hand, there has been needless duplication, intrusion of profit motivation, and improper scientific attitude and procedure. To combat the misuses of psychological tests, professional organizations concerned with measurement have developed ethics and standards. In 1963 the American Psychological Association published an article entitled "Ethical Standards of Psychologists." Testing is a major area of concern in this document which codifies the professional ethics of the association. The proper use of psychological tests is also featured in "Ethical Standards" (American Personnel and Guidance

---

[4] A federation of state programs founded in 1959. Objectives are similar to the College Board program. (See Chapter 11.)

[5] A notable exception is *Testing, Testing, Testing* (American Association of School Administrators, Council of Chief State School Officers, and National Association of Secondary-School Principals, 1962), a brief booklet which attempts to take a critical look at testing in a coherent and productive manner.

Association, 1961), which is the code of professional ethics of the American Personnel and Guidance Association.

In addition to these ethics statements, three professional organizations (American Psychological Association, American Educational Research Association, National Council on Measurement in Education, 1966) concerned with measurement have joined together and produced the "bible" for test standards. It is called *Standards for Educational and Psychological Tests and Manuals*. Let us briefly review some of the main points pertaining to ethics and standards as formulated by the professional organizations.

Distribution and Sale

One of the most important points in the ethical use of psychological tests is that the sale and distribution be confined to qualified users. The qualifications of the purchaser should be commensurate with the type of test being sold. For example, the school counselor may be qualified to administer, score, and interpret tests of educational ability, achievement, and interest, but he may not have the training to admininster an individual test of intelligence such as the Stanford-Binet or a personality device such as the Rorschach. The code of ethics of both the psychological and guidance associations are quite clear on this point. The American Personnel and Guidance Association (1961) states: "Different tests demand different levels of competence for administration, scoring, and interpretation. It is therefore the responsibility of the member to recognize the limits of his competence and to perform only those functions which fall within his preparation and competence" (p. 208).

The American Psychological Association (1963) states that, "Psychological tests are offered for commercial publication only to publishers who present and represent their tests in a professional way and distribute them only to qualified users. . . . The catalog and manual indicate the training or professional qualifications required for sound interpretation of the test" (p. 59).

Test Interpretation

One of the basic concerns of both professional workers using tests and the general public is test interpretation. Principle 14 of "Ethical Standards of Psychologists" states, "Test scores, like test materials, are released only to persons who are qualified to interpret and use them properly" (American Psychological Association, 1963, p. 59). The preceding principle stresses three basic points, (1) close supervision by qualified psychologists or counselors; (2) communication of test results to appropriate individuals in such a manner as to guard against misinterpretation (in most cases verbal *interpretations* of test results are given rather than numerical scores); (3) use of adequate interpretive devices in relating test results directly to parents and/or students.

Many of the abuses and misuses of tests have resulted from the use of tests by persons with little or no training. Test results should only be released to qualified personnel, and adequate facilities for further counseling should be available if the results are particularly disturbing to the individual. For example, John Smith, a senior at Exodus High School, is in the upper quarter of the class. His college entrance examination scores are very low and he is understandably very depressed and despondent over the results. At this point further counseling is certainly indicated. The counselor or psychologist could probe for the possible personal reasons for the low scores and he might discuss possible measurement factors that could account for the discrepancy.

If John Smith does not receive appropriate counseling he may decide against going to college and his self-concept could be appreciably lowered. In some cases extreme disappointment could lead to attempts at suicide. Thus even the most seemingly innocuous test results must be handled by qualified personnel who are trained to counsel as well as interpret test results.

Test Security

Test security is one of the most important ethical concerns of psychologists and educators. Control of the distribution and sales of tests is needed not only to prevent unqualified persons from using tests but to prevent public familiarity with test items which could interfere with test validity. Principle 13 of "Ethical Standards of Psychologists" (American Psychological Association, 1963) states,

> Psychological tests and similar assessment devices, the value of which depends in part on the naivete of the subject, are not reproduced or described in popular publications in ways that might invalidate the techniques. Access to such tests is limited to persons with professional interests who will safeguard their use.
>
> a. Sample items made up to resemble those of tests being discussed may be reproduced in popular articles and elsewhere, but scorable tests and actual test items are not reproduced except in professional publications.
>
> b. The psychologist is responsible for the control of psychological tests and other devices used for instruction when their value might be damaged by revealing to the general public their specific contents or underlying principles [p. 59].

It is readily apparent that if a high school senior obtained a copy of a college admissions examination, or the answers to many of the questions, the test would no longer be a measure of college aptitude for him. One of the consequences of such a situation might be admission to a college where the candidate has little chance of success.

Many times tests are invalidated by persons acting in good faith. Almost every teacher and counselor has witnessed examples of this. For example, during a school district's eighth-grade testing, the author witnessed a counselor instructing children in algebra before administering an algebra aptitude test. "Boys and girls," he said, "last year the eighth-grade had a lot of trouble with this kind of problem and I think if you understand how to do it your scores will be higher." (Walking to the board the counselor wrote a simple equation.) "Now when $X = 3$ and $Y = 3$. . . ." He proceeded to explain how that type of problem was worked.

The example problem the counselor used was not an exact duplicate of the test item, but the only difference was the numbers used. The counselor "meant well" and felt that he was "helping the kids." But was he? He was in fact hurting them. The purpose of the test was to select children for ninth-grade algebra and general math. Those students not ready for algebra who did well on the test would be in for some academic shocks. The validity of the test to predict behaviour in ninth-grade algebra had been compromised, by how much it is impossible to tell.

Invasion of Privacy

Another important ethical problem to the testing profession as well as the lay public is "invasion of privacy." This problem is especially relevent to personality tests. Some individuals, without knowing they are doing so, may reveal personal characteristics. The psychologist who uses these tests has an important responsibility to the individual being tested. *No person should be tested under false pretenses.* It is very important that the examinee know how the test results will be used. The code of ethics is very clear on this issue.

> The psychologist who asks that an individual reveal personal information in the course of interviewing, testing, or evaluation, or who allows such information to be divulged to him, does so only after making certain that the person is aware of the purpose of the interview, testing or evaluation and of the ways in which the information may be used [American Psychological Association, 1963, p. 57].

In the area of confidentiality the code is also quite explicit. "Information obtained in clinical or consulting relationships, or evaluative data concerning children, students, employees, and others are discussed only for professional purposes and only with persons clearly concerned with the case" (p. 57).

Standards

Earlier in this chapter it was stated that until 1954, there was no official guide representing a consensus concerning test standards. Though this is true, it should be noted there were informal test standards before that date. These standards could be found in textbooks and other publications. Test publishers and authors interested in quality have generally adhered to these. It is also true, however, that less dedicated or knowledgeable authors and publishers produced tests that fell short of these informal standards. In order to lessen the occurrence of inadequate tests, professional associations concerned with testing produced official statements of measurement standards. The discussion of testing standards that follows will be generally based on *Standards for Educational and Psychological Tests and Manuals* (American Psychological Association et al., 1966).[6] Our attention will be particularly focused on areas of concern to the user of tests.

Advertising

Test publishers should present their tests in an accurate and complete manner. Beware of extravagant claims in promotional materials. For example, an advertising brochure for an achievement test may state that, "This instrument measures the modern day educational objectives of American History." This, of course, is very difficult, because curricular objectives differ from school to school and from teacher to teacher. The statement suggests that the test is suitable for all classes in American History. It may indeed be an excellent test but the potential user cannot be sure, without detailed inspection, that the test is in line with the curricular objectives of his school.

Test Age

There is no specified period that a test and manual may be used without revision. It is recommended (American Psychological Association et al., 1966), however, that a publisher should withdraw a test from use if the manual is fifteen years old or more. Society and educational objectives change with time. For example, a test to predict algebra aptitude might be completely outdated by the "new math."

The relevant questions concerning test age are: What is the relationship of the test to current educational practices and to the contemporary society? How recent is the date of publication and/or revision? Is there new data with the new revision? Are there dates given for the collection of the new data and new norms?

Test Manual

The test, the manual, and all other accompanying material should be geared to helping test users evaluate test results. It is very important that

[6] A copy of *Standards for Educational and Psychological Tests and Manuals* may be obtained by sending $1.00 to the American Psychological Association, 1200 Seventeenth Street, N.W., Washington, D.C. 20036.

the users of tests know what the results mean. One method of facilitating this is making sure that all material dealing with the interpretation of the test is clear and correct. This means that it should have meaning to a school teacher as well as to a measurement specialist. This is extremely important. If the user is not able to read the manual with understanding, he will not be able to interpret the test scores adequately.

The manual should stress the vulnerability of the test and discuss factors other than the test score that need to be considered in interpreting the results. The test manual should assist the test user by stating precisely the basic purposes and uses for which the test is intended.

It is very important that the test manual indicate to the prospective purchaser and test seller the qualifications required to administer and interpret it. If a test may be used for different purposes, the manual should state the amount of training needed for each use.

Be careful of statements in manuals that do not have a statistical basis. If, for example, you read that such and such a score indicates "psychotic tendencies," look for statements that tell you what proportion of people obtaining that score have later been identified as psychotic.

It is essential that every test manual contain the *validity*[7] of the test for each interpretation to be made. It is incorrect to say "validity of the test"; one can, however, speak of the validity of particular interpretations. For example, the manual for an English test of mechanics of expression may state that the test is appropriate for high school juniors and seniors planning to go on to college. However, is it able to discriminate among those students in honors classes who are planning to matriculate at highly selective colleges?

It is essential that every test manual contain the *reliability*[8] of the test. The manual should report the evidence of reliability and the method used in obtaining it. The yardstick for reliability should apply to every score or combination of scores. For example, a test yields a verbal and nonverbal score; reliability for both scores should be reported.

Test manuals should contain directions for administration that you can understand and practice. Be sure that the directions are clear enough that your students will understand the tasks that are required. The scoring procedures should also be presented in detail and with clarity so as to eliminate scoring errors.

Norms[9] should be presented in every test manual. They should refer to

---

[7] Validity is a term used to designate the extent to which a test measures what it is supposed to measure. For example, is a reading test measuring reading ability or knowledge of science? (See Chapter 4 for a more thorough discussion of the various types of validity.)

[8] Reliability is a term that refers to the accuracy of measurement by a test, that is, the test consistency in measuring whatever it does measure. (See Chapter 4 for a more detailed discussion.)

[9] A norm is a way of describing, by statistical methods, the test performances of specific groups of students of various ages and/or grades.

specific populations so that the children being tested may be compared to these reference groups.

Testing and Scoring Procedures

The most obvious and primary consideration when discussing testing procedures is the need for rigorous adherence to standardized testing conditions as outlined in the test manual. It is unfortunate but true that many teachers and sometimes even counselors violate this basic rule. Almost all test manuals are quite explicit about the need to read the directions verbatim and follow the time limits with precision. (For an excellent discussion of this and other group testing procedures see Thorndike, 1949.)

It is impossible in a book such as this to outline all the various techniques in test administration and scoring of all psychological tests. For example, certain tests such as the Stanford-Binet and the Rorschach require specialized training, including special courses, texts, and intensive supervision. The primary purpose of the following discussion is to assist school teachers and counselors who will be called upon to administer and score group standardized tests.

Administering the Test

THE TEST ADMINISTRATOR

The administration of a group test is not a complicated procedure. Any teacher and most secretarial personnel can be trained to perform this function through an in-service program. (See Karmel, 1965.) The relative simplicity of administering group tests leads many teachers and school administrators to the erroneous conclusion that little advance preparation is necessary. This, of course, is not true. No matter who administers the tests and no matter how many years of testing experience he may have had, the examiner needs to know the peculiarities of the specific tests he is to administer. An in-service program attended by all faculty members during the first month of the school year should promote good test administration.

The first session should include a general orientation that encompasses the reason that tests are given; what they mean; and their specific implications for pupil growth and educational development. The time period for this phase of the session should be no longer than forty minutes, with at least fifteen minutes devoted to questions and discussion. After approximately forty minutes an informal coffee break to continue the discussion is a good idea.

A second session for faculty who are to administer and proctor[10] the tests

---

[10] A proctor is an assistant to the test administrator who helps by passing out test materials, keeping order, and answering student questions.

should also be planned. This session should be scheduled within two to five days of the school testing dates. The main purpose of this session is to familiarize the test administrators and proctors thoroughly with the specific tests to be used. Stress should be placed on directions for the administration of the test, especially standardizing procedures. The importance of the following test procedures should be emphasized:

1. *Test directions should always be followed without any deviation.*

This means that the test administrator does not change the directions even slightly. If the directions are poor this should be considered when choosing the test. Test administrators should understand the importance of reading directions *verbatim*. No matter how good your memory may be, never rely on it when administering a test.

2. *Student questions should be answered within the context of the test directions.*

This may mean repeating or paraphrasing test directions, or it may mean going over practice examples to clarify any confusion. Students must understand the directions before testing begins. For example, look in on the administration of an arithmetic test. Miss Hart is reading the directions.

Miss Hart: In this part of the test you will have an opportunity to show your ability to work with numbers. Look at your test booklet and you will see three sample problems. Problem number one asks you to add 15, 17, and 10. Note that on the right-hand side of the problem there are four possible answers. Choose the one that you think is right. (*Pause.*) Circle the letter of the right answer." (*Pause.*)

Student: Can we circle the number?

Miss Hart: Choose the answer that you think is right and circle the letter (*with emphasis*) of the right answer.

Student: What if none of the answers are right?

Miss Hart: Look at sample problem two and you will see next to one of the letters the words *none of these*. Remember you are to *circle* the letter next to the answer you think is right.

Miss Hart: Has everyone finished sample problem number one? (*She looks around to see if they have.*) Good, now go on to sample problems two and three.

Student: I don't understand problem number three.

Miss Hart: You don't understand problem three?

Student: Well, what I mean is how could you get 25 when—Ok, I see my mistake; never mind, I understand.

Miss Hart: Does everyone understand the sample problems? Are there any questions before we start? (*She looks around the room not only for raised hands but for possible problems by the expression of the students. Seeing that there are no questions Miss Hart continues her reading of the directions.*) Remember to choose the answer you think is right and circle the letter next to it. Do not spend too much time on any one problem. Any questions? (*Miss Hart looks around once again.*) All right, begin.

During the testing session Miss Hart and her proctors maintain a constant vigil, always available to help any student with a problem. Miss Hart knows that once a test begins questions are not to be encouraged. She knows, of course, that neither she nor her proctors may assist a student on specific items or provide clues as to the correctness of a pupil's response.

Let us return to Miss Hart and the test setting. A student has just raised his hand and Miss Hart has silently gestured for him to come to her desk.

Student: I don't understand the meaning of this question.
Miss Hart: You don't understand the meaning of the question?
Student: No, I don't.
Miss Hart: You don't?
Student: Well, what I mean is I don't remember how to do this part of it. Can you just tell me what (*student points to a section of a test problem*) I should do here?

The reader should note that up to this point Miss Hart has been non-directive, that is, she has reflected the student's questions. To do more would obviously have entailed answering the test question or giving important cues which would have the same result. Now, however, Miss Hart must be directive and make it quite clear to the student that he will have to work out his own problems:

Miss Hart: Jim, I am very sorry. (*Miss Hart smiles warmly.*) I can't answer your question. If you are stuck on that question go on to the next item. Just do the best you can.

3. *Time limits must be strictly observed.*

"Don't ever trust one clock," said an experienced teacher-tester when I administered my first tests in the schools. They never told me that in graduate school nor do I recall reading it in any measurement text but let me pass on her advice. It really does make sense. Your watch may stop running but more likely you may be holding it and inadvertently change the time (I have seen that happen). Or if you rely on the school clock the electricity could be temporarily shut off and there you are in the middle of an examination not knowing "the time of day." The following are two basic rules that should be of help: (a) if a test has sections with short time limits, five minutes or less, each examiner should have a stop watch to ensure accurate timing; (b) most tests will only require an ordinary watch with a second hand. When using a watch write down the time you begin and the time testing is to stop. (Remember to use a second time piece such as the school clock to insure reliability.)

> 4. *The examiner and his assistants should check, infrequently, on the progress of the examinees.*

The word *infrequent* is used because there is often too much circulating around the room by proctors. In a great many cases this does not serve the interest of the students and tends to make them more anxious. On the other hand, some "circulating" is necessary. The best procedure, of course, to assure student compliance with the test format is to be sure all students understand what is expected of them and how they are to respond to the test items before testing begins.

A few minutes after testing has begun the examiner and proctors should silently move around the room to check that students are working on the correct pages and that they are marking their responses in the appropriate place. After the proctors have completed their "rounds," they should return to strategically located posts where they may be available to help individual students. They should not circulate again until a new test or subtest is begun.

A final note of caution is in order. Remember it is not the duty of the examiner, nor is it necessarily beneficial to the examinee, to encourage or prompt students during the test. An exception to this rule is in the examination of young children, where it may be necessary to encourage children in the first six grades to keep working or to check their work after they have finished.

The in-service training program should be a yearly occurrence. In most schools major testing occurs in the fall. If tests are also given in the spring, it is not necessary to repeat both sessions. However, a refresher review is desirable, followed by concentration on the tests to be given in the spring. Only those faculty members who will be administering the tests need be involved. The spring session should be no longer than one class period, or approximately forty-five minutes.

PHYSICAL SETTING

Thorndike and Hagen (1969) list four desirable conditions for testing. They state that the subject should be "(1) physically comfortable and emotionally relaxed, (2) free from interruptions and distractions, (3) conveniently able to manipulate their test materials, and (4) sufficiently separated to minimize tendencies to copy from one another" (p. 542).

Anastasi (1968) suggests a room free from distraction, with adequate lighting and ventilation. Although all these recommendations seem appropriate, they really do not seem to affect test scores. For example, the author worked one summer in a test center at a major university where construction was going on and the temperature was over 95 degrees. After completing the test (a graduate admissions examination) a designated committee of these students approached the test director to complain about the hideous conditions of testing. Their complaint was so obviously justified that the director agreed to allow them to take the same examination in another setting on the following day. The new setting was in an air-conditioned building free of noise or other distractions. A comparison of test scores indicated few significant changes. In fact, two students scored several points lower on the second administration.

Super, Braasch, and Shay (1947) presented a number of distractions to graduate-student groups during the administration of a vocational and scholastic aptitude test. The experimental group was subjected to trumpets blaring in the next room, sudden opening of the door by "irate" students who would then argue noisily outside the door; and a timer that went off five minutes early. The experimenter then told the annoyed students to go on for five minutes more. Guess what happened? There were no significant differences in test scores between the experimental group with all of the distractions and the control groups that completed the tests under "ideal" conditions.

It is the feeling of this writer that psychological conditions are more important than the physical setting. Nevertheless, *one should strive for optimal testing conditions.* The following are nine conditions that, although not always possible to achieve, are desirable.

1. Maintain adequate lighting and ventilation (as good as those in the classroom setting).
2. Try to use the classroom for testing, especially with young children.
3. Post signs on the doors indicating that testing is in progress.
4. Make arrangements with the administration to suspend the class bells, fire drills, or public announcements.
5. See to it that everyone has had a chance to use the bathroom. (This is especially important with young children.)
6. See that each examinee has two usable pencils, and that there are extras for those who will need more.
7. Have desks or tables that facilitate the manipulation of test materials.
8. Try to separate the children so that they are not tempted to look at a neighbor's paper.
9. Have at least one proctor for every twenty-five students.

PSYCHOLOGICAL SETTING

The psychological climate is of primary importance; much of it is dependent on the physical conditions and the test administrator's ability to establish rapport. The psychological setting varies with the attitude of the examiner. For example, is the examiner a threatening or supporting figure? Is he the kind of person students rebel against or want to please, or are they indifferent to him?

The various methods for achieving rapport will differ somewhat according to the type of test and the ages and grades of the students. Preschool and primary school children (nursery through third grade) especially need to be treated in a warm and friendly manner. The examiner should be relaxed and "cheerful" so that the children are not threatened by the test. Children at this level should enter testing with feelings similar to those they feel when a new game is initiated. On the other hand, the older school child should be treated more realistically. That is, he should be told once again (a pretest orientation has already exposed him to the reasons for testing) to do his best and that the examination is to help him. It is always helpful to state that "hardly anyone ever finishes or is able to answer all the questions correctly."

The importance of the psychological setting has been demonstrated in numerous research studies. (See Sarason, 1950; Sacks, 1952; Wickes, 1956; Sarason and others, 1960.) These studies have revealed that testing must be interpreted in the light of the test situation and that good relations with the examiner produce better test results. For example, Wickes (1956) found that the examiner's behavior had a significant effect upon test scores It has also been shown that it is beneficial to know the children before testing them. Sarason and his associates (1960) theorize that some children perceive the "objective" examiner as a rejecting figure because of their own dependence needs.

The preceding factors make it very difficult to suggest concrete guidelines for producing the right psychological test atmosphere for all children and for all test situations. There are some general rules, however, that would be appropriate for most testing situations and most students.

1. A pretest orientation for the students should be scheduled. This meeting should include the purposes and reasons for testing. All students who will be tested should attend.

2. The test administrator should maintain a relaxed and empathetic manner throughout testing. Directions should be read in a warm (not sugary) and clear voice.

3. The examiner should convey his objectivity to the examinees without coldness or aloofness.

4. The test administrator and his proctors should refrain from any autocratic or authoritarian manner. At the same time the students must understand that testing personnel are in charge and certain procedures must be carried out in order to safeguard test validity.

5. Every effort should be made to provide the best physical conditions for testing.

Scoring Procedures

The primary consideration of teachers and counselors in test scoring is economy of time. Few things make school personnel more hostile to testing than the laborious hand scoring of tests. Teachers and counselors should not have to be concerned with this clerical task.[11] Their time can be spent more profitably in other educational endeavors; moreover, there are more accurate and reliable methods of scoring. Almost every section of the country has access to commercial test-scoring services, which are located at university test centers or private agencies. If the school cannot afford such services there are many other methods available. Let us briefly review some of these.

SCORING STENCIL

The scoring stencil is a cardboard answer sheet with the correct answers punched out. It is applicable to tests with a multiple-choice or true-false item format. The stencil is placed over the answer sheet and the number of black pencil marks that are visible is equal to the number of correct answers obtained. That is, the placement of the stencil over the student's answer sheet immediately reveals the number of right answers. Some sample items from a test that uses a scoring stencil[12] may be seen in Figure 1. This test is concerned with "word meaning"; students are requested to read the beginning part of each sentence and decide which word is best. They are then instructed to fill in the circle which has the same number as the one they have chosen.

THE SELF-SCORING ANSWER SHEET

The self-scoring answer sheet is another method of scoring found in some tests. An example of this type may be seen in Figure 2. In this example from the Kuder Preference Record a pin-punch answer pad is used. The student is given a metal pin which he uses to punch holes in circles on the answer sheet. The inside of the answer booklet contains printed sets of circles. The student's score is computed by tallying the number of holes punched in the circles.

A variation of the same principle is found in the self-scoring carbon pad. This form requests the student to mark his responses on the outside of an answer booklet with a pencil. The booklet is self-contained and cannot be opened without tearing. Squares or circles underneath the correct answers record the responses through the carbon backing onto the answer sheet. Scoring is accomplished by counting the number of marks in the squares or circles.

---

[11] This is not always true, of course, when primary teachers might want to check for difficulties in certain tasks and gear their future teaching accordingly.

[12] Items may also be answered on a separate answer sheet for machine scoring.

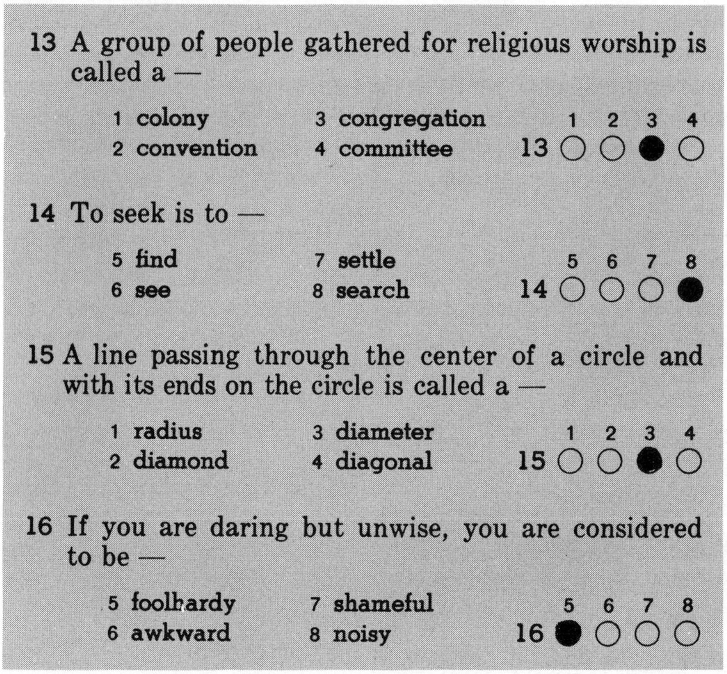

13 A group of people gathered for religious worship is called a —

    1 colony   3 congregation   1 2 3 4
    2 convention   4 committee   13 ○ ○ ● ○

14 To seek is to —

    5 find   7 settle   5 6 7 8
    6 see   8 search   14 ○ ○ ○ ●

15 A line passing through the center of a circle and with its ends on the circle is called a —

    1 radius   3 diameter   1 2 3 4
    2 diamond   4 diagonal   15 ○ ○ ● ○

16 If you are daring but unwise, you are considered to be —

    5 foolhardy   7 shameful   5 6 7 8
    6 awkward   8 noisy   16 ● ○ ○ ○

Figure 1. Sample questions from Test I, Word Meaning, of the Stanford Achievement Test, Intermediate II, Form W. (Reproduced from the *Stanford Achievement Test, Intermediate II, Form W*, © 1964 by Harcourt, Brace & World, Inc. All rights reserved. Reprinted by permission.)

MACHINE SCORING

The scoring of a large number of answer sheets by machine is faster and requires less manpower than scoring by hand. There are many machine-scoring plans from which to choose. Figure 3 illustrates an IBM-type answer sheet that has been used widely in the last twenty years. The IBM answer sheet may be scored by hand or by the 805 International Test Scoring Machine. Special electrographic pencils are needed for this answer sheet. Figure 4 reveals the newer MRC answer sheet, also used in machine scoring. The MRC answer sheet is scored on electronic test equipment at Measurement Research Center, Iowa City, Iowa. Ordinary soft-lead pencils are used with this answer sheet.

The school district should make its choice of scoring method on the basis of individual needs and financial capacity. The following are some of the major plans.

Package Plan. A school district contracts with a test publisher for tests, answer sheets, scoring and distribution (statistical analysis) of scores. This plan, though very convenient, sometimes leads schools to purchase tests

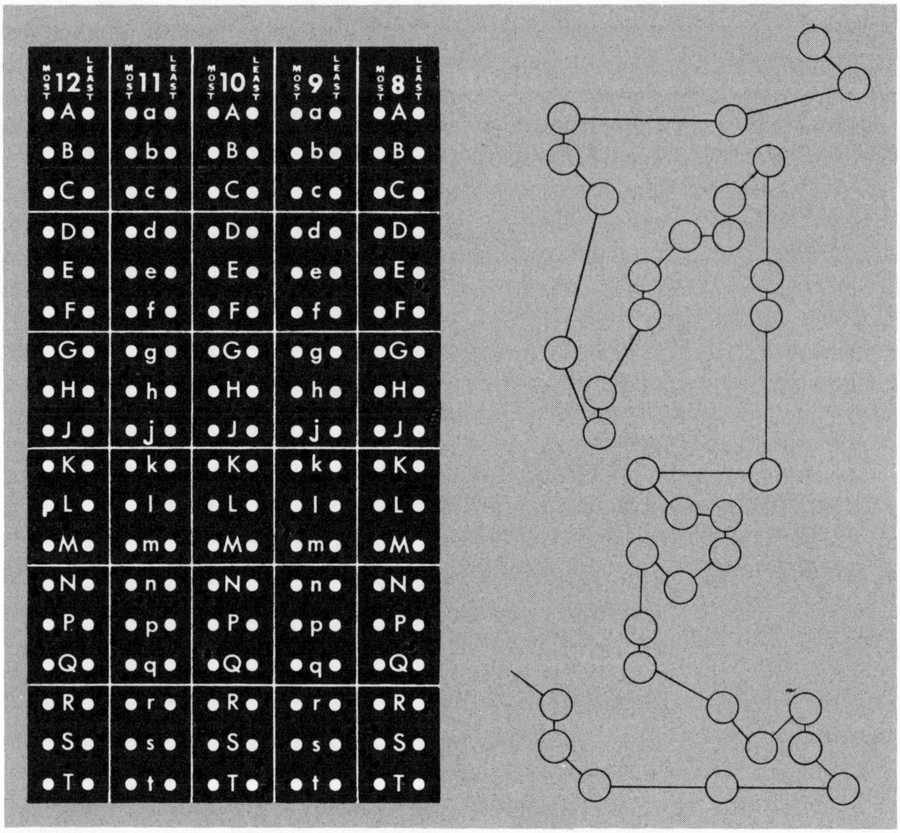

Figure 2. Front and inside views of a portion of the Pin-Punch Answer Pad of the Kuder Preference Record—Vocational Form CH. (From *Answer Pad for the Kuder Preference Record* by G. Frederic Kuder. Copyright © 1948 by G. Frederic Kuder. Reprinted by permission of the publisher, Science Research Associates, Inc., Chicago, Illinois.)

they normally would not use. Important test factors, such as the suitability of the test for the local system, are often overlooked because of the administrative ease of the plan.

Test-Scoring Plan. The test-scoring plan leaves the school district a great deal more freedom to choose tests. A school makes arrangements for test scoring with a test publisher, university testing bureau, or a company such as Testscor whose primary business is scoring tests. It is also possible to make arrangements with most of these companies to obtain a statistical distribution of your school's results.

Test-Scoring Equipment. Test-scoring equipment involves renting or purchasing machines to score tests at the local school district. Smaller school districts often join together to share the cost and use of the machines. This

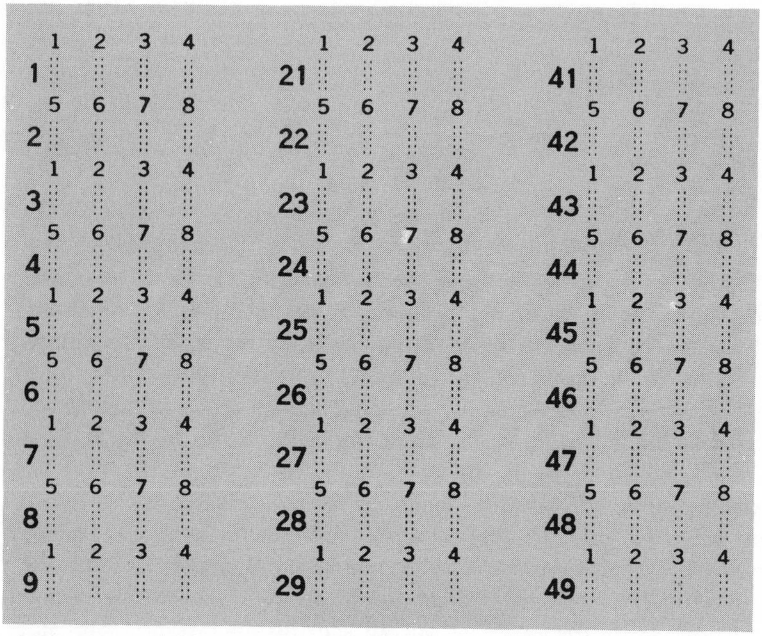

Figure 3. A section of an IBM answer sheet used with the Stanford Achievement Test Battery. (From the *Stanford Achievement Test Battery Advanced*, ©️ 1964 by Harcourt, Brace & World, Inc. All rights reserved. Reprinted by permission.)

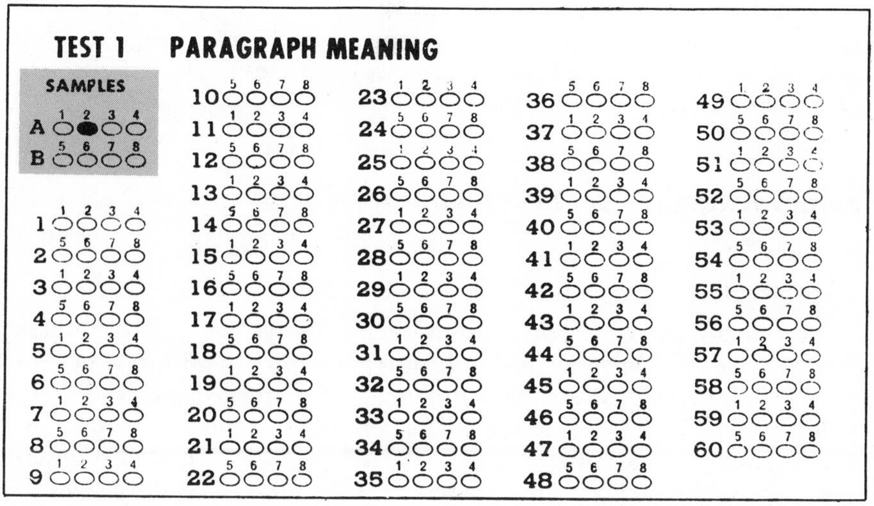

Figure 4. A section of a MRC answer sheet used with the Stanford Achievement Test Battery. (From the *Stanford Achievement Test Battery Advanced*, ©️ 1964 by Harcourt, Brace & World, Inc. All rights reserved. Reprinted by permission.)

plan is the most inexpensive if the machines are kept busy. There are several problems, however, with this plan. First of all one must train personnel in the use of the machine, and secondly the problem of machine breakdown can cause delays and expense. In addition, one must add to the cost of the machine itself the expense of special help in the form of machine operators and clerical assistants.

SCORING ERRORS

No matter what type of scoring method is utilized one must constantly be alert to the possibility of error. This means that the original machine scoring should always be rechecked by randomly selecting and rescoring by hand approximately every twenty-fifth paper. The reader should note that "every twenty-fifth paper" is an arbitrary choice; every tenth or thirty-fifth paper will also do. Each hand-scoring operation should always be independently checked. This means every hand-scored answer sheet must be scored at two different times to assure accuracy. Ideally this involves two different scorers; however, this is sometimes very difficult to manage. If two different scorers cannot be arranged then the next best thing is to rescore the papers on a different day. Rescoring does not mean a simple checking of counting and addition. It means carrying out all scoring operations from placing the key over the student's responses to deriving his score.

Personnel assigned to scoring tests should be well trained for the specific operations needed in the tests to be used. They should be cautioned to be especially careful in adding part scores (that is, adding different sub sections) to make a total score and going from raw[13] to converted scores[14] Remember the old saying that "a chain is only as strong as its weakest link"; this is also true in testing. The most sophisticated research, test design, and other important test construction factors are rendered meaningless if the scorer makes a simple mistake in addition.

Factors Affecting Test Performance

Motivation

In testing ability the *a priori* assumption is always made that the person being examined is "doing his best." If the conditions of uniformity of testing are to be maintained, every person should be motivated and expected to "do his best." The importance of motivation to the examinee's test behavior has been demonstrated in a number of studies. Incentive studies offering rewards for submission to authority figures have failed to produce significant

---

[13] Raw score is the number of correct answers.
[14] Converted score is the symbolic representation of the raw score translated into percentiles, stanines, grade equivalents.

score increases on ability tests compared to scores earned in a regular test setting. (For example, see Benton, 1936.) On the other hand, when the student is concerned over his test score, increases of scores may be seen. (See Hurlock, 1925; Gustad, 1951; Eells, 1951; and Flanagan, 1955 for interesting investigations and discussions of the problem.)

The emotional climate of the test setting and personality problems of students being examined may influence the motivation of some students. Gordon and Durea (1948), for example, administered the Stanford-Binet to eighth-grade students and retested these same children two weeks later in an atmosphere designed to lower self-esteem and produce discouragement. The second tests revealed significantly lower scores than another group of eighth-grade children who were retested under normal conditions. Goldman (1961) states that

> . . . clients who see the forthcoming test as potentially useful to them but not threatening are likely to exert optimal amounts of effort. *Lack of effort* may come from various sources: In some cases it may represent lack of interest in the test and lack of any expectation that it has something of value to offer. In other cases, lack of effort may represent just the opposite perception, that the tests are terribly important and even threatening. In such a case lack of effort may play a defensive role, permitting the individual to say afterward, "I didn't really try, because I wasn't interested in the results of this test, and they won't affect my plans in any way" [p. 115].

McClelland (1966), after investigating experimentally the role of motivation in achievement and test scores, reports that regardless of the innate ability of a person he is not going to obtain a high intelligence test score if he has little or no motivation to learn. Regarding intelligence test scores he states,

> There are two places where motivation enters into an intelligence test score: one in the accumulation of knowledge that the subject shows on the intelligence test or achievement test, and the other in the attention he gives at the time he takes the test. We know that people who have high achievement motivation will actually do better in the testing situation. So there is an intertwining here of achievement motivation and the intelligence measure [p. 537].

Many studies have revealed that achievement motivation is related to social values and child training. These in turn relate to ethnic group, religion, social class, and other factors. (See McClelland, Atkinson, Clark, Lowell, 1953; McClelland, 1955; Rosen, 1956; Winterbottom, 1958.) These studies focus on the importance of a child's background in determining the proportion of abilities he will use in a test situation.

An analysis of many of the investigations indicates that a family environment which stresses early responsibility and independence of children as well as the social values of competition and hard work leads to achievement orientation and motivation.

Atkinson (1957), in his investigation of "risk-taking behavior," found that an individual who feels there is little chance for advancement may reveal correspondingly low levels of motivation. The implications from these findings, if valid, are especially relevant in testing the culturally disadvantaged. That is, there is a strong possibility that disadvantaged groups may do poorly on tests in part because they lack the incentive to capitalize on those talents that they do have.

The student of measurement should pay close attention to the role of motivation in testing. Special caution is especially indicated in interpreting the test scores of emotionally and culturally disadvantaged youngsters.[15] On the other hand, it is also obvious that most American school children are not disadvantaged and are generally sophisticated about tests and motivated to do well in academic and test situations. These children are easily motivated and their cooperation in testing situations is not difficult to obtain. Therefore, if the classroom teacher follows the instructions of the test manual and is psychologically supportive of her pupils, it is fairly safe for her to assume that most of her students will be doing their best. The teacher who is in a disadvantaged setting will, of course, want to stress the positive importance of testing and to provide optimal motivational conditions. She will also want to consider motivational factors in her analysis of the test results.

Anxiety

Test anxiety and free-floating anxiety[16] are closely related to test-taking motivation. The highly motivated student, for example, may be so anxious to do well that his very desire may interfere with a good score. The person who is tense makes errors he would not normally commit. The student of measurement knows from his own personal experiences and observations that there is a great deal of anxiety and tension during testing.

DeLong (1955) studied the behavioral reactions of elementary students in a normal classroom setting and during the administration of tests. He reported that during testing the children reacted in an anxious and disturbed fashion.

The relationship of anxiety to test performance is not all one-sided. There are some studies that reveal that a degree of anxiety or tension enhances test performance. Review the following research and compare it with your own thinking on this subject.

---

[15] In addition to emotional and cultural factors that may interfere with optimal test performance in a school setting, special motivational problems are encountered in testing prisoners or juvenile delinquents and mentally ill patients in institutional settings. See Sears (1943); Rosenzweig (1949); Sarason (1954).

[16] Free-floating anxiety is a state of general uneasiness or dread for which there is no objective reason.

A great many investigations into the problem of anxiety and test performance have been made by S. B. Sarason and his colleagues (Mandler and Sarason, 1952; Sarason and Mandler, 1952; Sarason, Mandler and Craighill, 1952; Sarason and Gordon, 1953; Sarason, Davidson, Lighthall, and Waite, 1958; Waite, Sarason, Lighthall and Davidson, 1958; Sarason, Davidson, Lighthall, Waite and Ruebush, 1960). They developed a questionnaire to ascertain test anxiety. This instrument[17] contained such questions as:

> While taking a group intelligence test to what extent do you perspire?
> Do you worry a lot before taking a test?
> If you know that you are going to take a group intelligence test, how do you feel *beforehand*?
> While you are taking a test, do you usually think you are not doing well?

Sarason, Davidson, Lighthall, and Waite (1958) in one study of 600 children in second to fifth grade found that test anxiety increased with grade advancement. They also found that children with the greatest anxiety tended to perform at a lower level. In an earlier study (Mandler and Sarason, 1952) similar findings were reported; however, it was noted that the lessened performance caused by high anxiety tended to be overcome with time. This study and a later investigation (Waite, Sarason, Lighthall, and Davidson, 1958) led Sarason and his associates to conclude that test anxiety tended to impair test performance. They also found that social class was a factor in test anxiety. Upper- and middle-class subjects had less test anxiety than those below. They interpreted this to mean that at higher social levels there is less family pressure on intellectual achievement. Sarason and others (1960) found that with elementary school children anxiety was more pronounced in verbal than in nonverbal tests and was greater on new and different types of tests.

Sinick (1956) feels that "a high level of anxiety, whether existent or induced in *S*s, generally brings about impaired performance, but occasionally causes improvement" (p. 317). Grooms and Endler (1960) feel that for some individuals anxiety is an inhibitory factor that lowers performance.

After years of studying the problem of test anxiety Sarason and his associates (1960) state, "The most consistent finding in our studies is the negative correlation between anxiety and intelligence test scores: the higher the test score on anxiety, the lower the IQ" (p. 270). They further state that the reason is only partly because lower ability is the source of the anxiety. The vast majority of subjects who made up the negative correlation were within the average range of intelligence (90–110) and should not have academic problems. They feel that "in the case of the intellectually average but anxious child, the estimate of potential based on conventional tests may contain

---

[17] It should be noted that there was more than one form of the basic questionnaire, for example, one form for children and one for older students.

more error than in the case of most other intellectually average children" (p. 270).

Goslin (1963) makes a very practical point when he says that the place of anxiety on test performance is difficult to ascertain because often no one is in a position to point to the child whose level of test anxiety is high. Those who have taught will readily see the truth of this statement. It is also interesting to note that Sarason's data seem to reinforce Goslin's statement. The problem is further complicated because people react differently to anxiety. There are certain highly anxious persons who demonstrate an exceptional mental alertness whereas others become intellectually frozen.

What does all this mean to you the potential test user? It means that caution must be used. It is impossible to know each individual being tested and to know whether a little tension would be appropriate. The following "do's" and "don'ts" are practically oriented to school, teacher, and child and are based on research findings and personal experiences.

Do's	*Don'ts*
1. Do read the test manual's directions verbatim.	1. Don't offer incentives of any kind.
2. Do prepare students for testing either individually or in groups. This orientation should include the purposes of testing along with the uses that will be made of the results.	2. Don't orient students about testing on the day you plan to administer the tests.
3. Do be alert to the influence of anxiety on test scores in individual interpretations.	3. Don't generalize and use anxiety as the only reason for low test scores.

A final word of caution has to do with your attitude while administering the test. Assume a matter-of-fact attitude.

Practice and Coaching

It has been known for many years (See, for example, Casey, Davidson, and Harter, 1928) that IQ scores may be significantly increased if a child is coached on specific items he has missed and then given the same examination again. Contemporary research (Dyer, 1953; Dempster, 1954; Longstaff, 1954; Vernon, 1954; Wiseman, 1954; French, 1955; Lipton, 1956; French and Dear, 1959) reveals that coaching and practice may be of value to persons who have not had experience with a certain type of test or who have not had recent exposure to certain subject matter of a particular examination. The effects of coaching and practice must be broken down into various situations in order to have practical import for the test user. The following are questions and answers based on the extensive research findings of over forty years.

1. Is coaching and practice helpful in raising a person's test score?
Answer: Yes, with certain qualifications.

2. What qualifications?
Answer: Qualifications dependent on specific individuals and specific tests.

3. What about tests used to assign students to certain schools and grades?
Answer: British psychologists have conducted many studies in this area because of their concern over assignment of children to different types of secondary schools. They found that improvement of scores is dependent upon ability, the kind of tests and the type and amount of coaching given.

The investigations revealed that subjects with poor educational backgrounds are more apt to benefit from intensive coaching than those who have had excellent educational preparation. (See Wiseman and Wrigley, 1953.)

4. That's interesting, but I am especially interested in college entrance tests. Can you study for them?
Answer: The College Entrance Examination Board, noting the concern of parents in the United States over their children's test performance, has over the years conducted a series of studies to determine the effects of coaching on its Scholastic Aptitude Test (Dyer, 1953; French, 1955; College Entrance Examination Board, Trustees, 1959; French and Dear, 1959). These studies reveal slight increases in scores but none that are significant.

5. What do I advise my students?
Answer: Advise students individually. If a student has not had mathematics recently or has not been exposed to testing, a review of the former and some practice tests may be of help. For most students, however, the following statement by the College Entrance Examination Board is appropriate:[18]

The trustees of the College Entrance Examination Board have noted with concern the increasing tendency of secondary school students to seek the assistance of special tutors or of special drill at school in the hope of improving thereby scores earned on College Board examinations. The Board has now completed four studies designed to evaluate the effect of special tutoring or "coaching" upon the Scholastic Aptitude Test, the basic test offered. Three other studies have been conducted independently by public high schools. These studies being completed, we now feel able to make the following statement:

[18] *College Board Score Reports: A Guide for Counselors and Admissions Officers.* Copyright, 1966, by the College Entrance Examination Board. Used by permission of the College Entrance Examination Board.

The evidence collected leads us to conclude that intensive drill for the SAT, either on its verbal or its mathematical part, is at best likely to yield insignificant increases in scores. The magnitudes of the increases which have been found vary slightly from study to study, but they are always small and appear to be independent of the particular method of coaching used and of the level of ability of the students being coached. The results of the coaching studies which have thus far been completed indicate that average increases of less than 10 points on a 600 point scale can be expected. It is not reasonable to believe that admissions decisions can be affected by such small changes in scores. This is especially true since the tests are merely supplementary to the school record and other evidence taken into account by admissions officers.

The conclusion stated here has been reached slowly and with care, although the atmosphere in which the problem has been studied has not been entirely calm. In recent years newspapers and even radio advertisements advancing the claims of the drillmasters have increased in number and boldness. Parents, already disturbed by exaggerated notions of the difficulties of students in gaining admission to college, have demanded that the schools divert teaching energy and time to a kind of drill that is obnoxious to educators of every philosophy.

With parental concern so great, each completed study yielding negative findings with regard to the usefulness of coaching has led only to speculation that under some other set of circumstances some other set of students might make important score increases as a result of coaching for the test. The time has come to say that we do not believe it.

Tutors often show apparent good results mainly because students and scores *do* change with the passage of time. Our studies have simply shown that the scores of students who are left alone change in the same directions and to nearly the same degree as do scores of students who are tutored. The public, though, is disconcerted to see any change in a measure of "aptitude" which is regarded as un-changeable. As the College Board uses the term, aptitude is not some-thing fixed and impervious to influence by the way the child lives and is taught. Rather, this particular Scholastic Aptitude Test is a measure of abilities that seem to grow slowly and stubbornly, profoundly in-fluenced by conditions at home and at school over the years, but not responding to hasty attempts to relive a young lifetime.

In addition to changes due to growth, other changes occur because the test, while dependable, shares a characteristic common to all tests in that it cannot be made to give exactly the same score for each student each time the test is taken. Changes due to this lack of complete dependability are uncontrollable. Thus, with scores being affected by both the imperfect nature of the testing process and the student's growth, about one student in four will find that his scores actually decrease from one year to the next, while most other students will have small to moderate increases. About one student in fifteen[19] will find that his scores increase by 100 points or more between junior and senior years in high school, *and this is true whether he is coached or not*. It is not surprising then that tutors are often able to point to particular students who have made large increases in their scores.

It is possible to predict the size and number of fluctuations in scores that will occur within large groups, but fluctuations of individual scores cannot be predicted. Yet it is upon individuals that interest properly focuses, so that unexpected changes are easily, though erroneously, attributed to coaching, to the school, or to some other visible agency.

We have said nothing about the tests of achievement in specific school subjects. These have not been studied in the same way as has the aptitude test. We do know that these tests do a modest but useful job of measuring learning of the material tested. We suspect that the question of coaching for these tests is a matter of choosing a method of teaching the subject. We cannot believe that drill on sample test questions is the most productive method available.

Finally, we worry very little when parents of comfortable means decide that at worst tutoring can do no harm and therefore use their money for coaching toward College Board examinations. We are very concerned when parents purchase coaching they cannot afford or, failing to do so, feel that an unfair advantage has gone to those who have had a few weeks or months of tutoring. But we are concerned most, and have been moved to make this statement, because we see the educational process unwillingly corrupted in some schools to gain ends which we believe to be not only unworthy but, ironically, unattainable.

6. Can you practice for intelligence tests?

Answer : A great many investigations reveal that, on the average, scores will increase upon retesting if the same examination is used. (See Crane and Heim, 1950; and Heim and Wallace, 1950.) If *parallel forms*[20] are used elevations in test scores are less pronounced. The author's experience suggests that, on the whole, most children and adults tend to obtain the same general scores no matter how much testing or practice they have had.

[19] College Entrance Examination Board in a personal communication to the author states that fifteen has been extended up to twenty. That is, "About one student in *twenty* will find that his scores. . . ."

[20] Parallel forms are tests measuring the same subject matter at the same level of difficulty, using different questions.

Other Factors

Brief statements on the following variables will be made not because they are unimportant, but because they are mentioned in different sections of the text and need not be elaborated upon at this time.

RESPONSE SETS

Response sets are a tendency to choose a certain direction in responding to test items. For example, some people tend to answer no to all personal problems. Another type of response set is found in individuals who tend to guess freely, or who are afraid to guess (Goldman, 1961).

Teachers, counselors, and psychologists should not be particularly concerned with this factor, because it is the primary responsibility of the test constructor. The test user should note, however, the tendency of some tests to produce response sets and weigh this factor before purchasing a given test. (For a detailed discussion of this factor, see Cronbach, 1950, 1960; Goldman, 1961.)

CHEATING

The problem of cheating is as old as mankind. It is obvious that if a person knows the answers in advance, looks at another person's paper, starts before the signal to begin or finishes after time is called, his score will not be a reflection of his own ability and therefore will be an invalid evaluation.

One form of cheating is making oneself look "good" on interest and personality inventories. It has been found that most of these tests lend themselves to making false responses (Cross, 1950; Garry, 1953; Gehman, 1957; Noll, 1951).

The best way to avoid cheating is to be sure that you have a good test orientation. This will help convince students that an honest score is in their own interest. Another method of avoiding cheating is to be sure that the examiner has enough assistance to observe the students being tested.

References

American Educational Research Association and National Council on Measurements Used in Education, Committee on Test Standards. *Technical recommendations for achievement tests.* Washington, D.C.: National Education Association, 1955.

American Personnel and Guidance Association. Ethical standards. *Personnel and Guidance Journal*, 1961 (Oct.), 206–09.

American Psychological Association. *Technical recommendations for psychological tests and diagnostic techniques.* Washington, D.C.: American Psychological Association, 1954.

American Psychological Association. Ethical standards of psychologists. *American Psychologist*, 1963, **18**, 56–60.

American Psychological Association, American Educational Research Association, and National Council on Measurement in Education. *Standards for educational and psychological tests and manuals.* Washington, D.C.: American Psychological Association, 1966.

Anastasi, A. *Psychological testing* (3rd ed.) New York: Macmillan, 1968.

Atkinson, J. W. Motivational determinants of risk-taking behavior. *Psychological Review*, 1957, **64**, 359–72.

Benton, A. L. Influence of incentives upon intelligence test scores of school children. *Journal of Genetic Psychology*, 1936, **49**, 494–96.

Casey, M. L., Davidson, H. P., and Harter, D. I. Three studies on the effect of training in similar and identical material upon Stanford-Binet test scores. *Twenty-seventh Yearbook, National Social Studies on Education. Part 1*, 1928, 431–39.

Cattell, J. M. K. Mental tests and measurements. *Mind*, 1890, **15**, 373–80.

College Entrance Examination Board, Trustees. A statement by the college board trustees on test "coaching." *College Board News*, 1959, **5**, 2–3.

Crane, V. R., and Heim, A. W. The effects of repeated retesting: III. Further experiments and general conclusions. *Quarterly Journal of Experimental Psychology*, 1950, **2**, 182–97.

Cronbach, L. J. Further evidence on response sets and test design. *Educational and Psychological Measurement*, 1950, **10**, 3–31.

Cronbach, L. J. *Essentials of psychological testing.* (2nd ed.) New York: Harper & Row, 1960.

Cross, O. H. A study of faking on the Kuder Preference Record. *Educational and Psychological Measurement*, 1950, **10**, 271–77.

DeLong, A. R. Emotional effects of elementary school testing. *Understanding the Child*, 1955, **24**, 103–07.

Dempster, J. J. B. Symposium on the effects of coaching and practice in intelligence tests: III. Southampton investigation and procedure. *British Journal of Educational Psychology*, 1954, **24**, 1–4.

Dyer, H. S. Does coaching help? *College Board Review*, 1953, **19**, 331–35.

Ebbinghaus, H. Über eine neue Methode zur Prüfung geistiger Fähigkeiten und ihre Anwendung bei Schulkindern. *Z Psychology*, 1897, **13**, 401–59.

Eells, K. et al. *Intelligence and cultural differences.* Chicago: University of Chicago Press, 1951.

Flanagan, J. C. The development of an index of examinee motivation. *Educational and Psychological Measurement*, 1955, **15**, 144–51.

French, J. W. An answer to test coaching: Public school experiment with SAT. *College Board Review*, 1955, **27**, 5–7.

French, J. W., and Dear, R. E. Effect of coaching on an aptitude test. *Educational and Psychological Measurement*, 1959, **19**, 319–30.

Garry, R. Individual differences in ability to fake vocational interests. *Journal of Applied Psychology*, 1953, **37**, 33–37.

Gehman, W. S. A study of ability to fake scores on the Strong Vocational Interest Blank for Men. *Educational and Psychological Measurement*, 1957, **17**, 65–70.

Goldman, L. *Using tests in counseling.* New York: Appleton-Century-Crofts, Inc., 1961.

Gordon, E. M., and Sarason, S. B. The relationship between "test anxiety" and "other anxieties." *Journal of Personnel*, 1955, **23**, 317–23.

Gordon, L. V., and Durea, M. A. The effect of discouragement on the revised Stanford-Binet scale. *Journal of Genetic Psychology*, 1948, **73**, 201–07.

Goslin, D. A. *The search for ability : Standardized testing in social perspective*. New York: Russell Sage Foundation, 1963.

Grooms, R. R. and Endler, N. S. The effect of anxiety on academic achievement. *Journal of Educational Psychology*, 1960, **51**, 299–304.

Gustad, J. W. Test information and learning in the counseling process. *Educational and Psychological Measurement*, 1951, **11**, 788–95.

Heim, A. W. and Wallace, J. G. The effects of repeatedly retesting the same group on the same intelligence test: II. High grade mental defectives. *Quarterly Journal of Experimental Psychology*, 1950, **2**, 19–32.

Hurlock, E. B. An evaluation of certain incentives used in school work. *Journal of Educational Psychology*, 1925, **16**, 145–59.

Karmel, L. J. "Secretarial-Psychologist"—A new member of the psychological team? *Journal of School Psychology*, 1965, **4**, (3), 64–67.

Karmel, L. J. *Testing in our schools*. New York: Macmillan, 1966.

Kuhlmann, F. A. A revision of the Binet-Simon system for measuring the intelligence of children. *Journal of Psycho-Asthenics, Monogram Supplement*, 1912, **1**, 1–41.

Lipton, R. L. A study of the effect of exercise in a simple mechanical activity on mechanical aptitude as is measured by the subtests of the MacQuarrie Test for Mechanical Ability. *Psychology Newsletter*, NYU, 1956, **7**, 39–42.

Longstaff, H. P. Practice effects on the Minnesota Vocational Test for Clerical Workers. *Journal of Applied Psychology*, 1954, **38**, 18–20.

Mandler, G., and Sarason, S. B. A study of anxiety and learning. *Journal of Abnormal and Social Psychology*, 1952, **47**, 166–73.

McClelland, D. C. The measurement of human motivation: An experimental approach. In A. Anastasi (Ed.) *Testing problems in perspective*. Washington, D.C.: American Council on Education, 1966. Pp. 528–38.

McClelland, D. C. (Ed.) *Studies in motivation*. New York: Appleton-Century-Crofts, 1955.

McClelland, D. C., Atkinson, J. W., Clark, R. A., and Lowell, E. A. *The achievement motive*. New York: Appleton-Century-Crofts, 1953.

Noll, V. H. Simulation by college students of a prescribed pattern on a personality scale. *Educational and Psychological Measurement*, 1951, **11**, 478–88.

Rosen, B. C. The achievement syndrome. *American Sociological Review*, 1956, **21**, 203–11.

Rosenzweig, S. *Psychodiagnosis : An introduction to the integration of tests in dynamic clinical practice*. New York: Grune and Stratton, 1949.

Sacks, E. L. Intelligence scores as a function of experimentally established social relationships between child and examiner. *Journal of Abnormal and Social Psychology*, 1952, **47**, 354–58.

Sarason, S. B. *The clinical interaction, with special reference to the Rorschach*. New York: Harper & Row, 1954.

Sarason, S. B. The test-situation and the problem of prediction. *Journal of Clinical Psychology*, 1950, **6**, 387–92.

Sarason, S. B., Davidson, K., Lighthall, F., and Waite, R. A test anxiety scale for children. *Child Development*, 1958, **29**, 105–13.

Sarason, S. B., Davidson, K. S., Lighthall, F. F., Waite, R. R., and Ruebush, B. K. *Anxiety in elementary school children.* New York: Wiley, 1960.

Sarason, S. B., and Gordon, E. M. The test anxiety questionnaire: Scoring norms. *Journal of Abnormal and Social Psychology*, 1953, **48,** 447–48.

Sarason, S. B., and Mandler, G. Some correlates of test anxiety. *Journal of Abnormal and Social Psychology*, 1952, **47,** 810–17.

Sarason, S. B., Mandler, G., and Craighill, P. G. The effect of differential instructions on anxiety and learning. *Journal of Abnormal and Social Psychology*, 1952, **47,** 561–65.

Sears, R. Motivational factors in aptitude testing. *American Journal of Orthopsychiatry*, 1943, **13,** 468–93.

Sinick, D. Encouragement, anxiety, and test performance. *Journal of Applied Psychology*, 1956, **40,** 315–18.

Super, D. E., Braasch, W. F., Jr., and Shay, J. B. The effect of distractions on test results. *Journal of Educational Psychology*, 1947, **38,** 373–77.

Terman, L. M. *The measurement of intelligence.* Boston: Houghton Mifflin, 1916.

Thorndike, R. L. *Personnel selection: Test and measurement techniques.* New York: Wiley, 1949.

Thorndike, R. L., and Hagen, E. *Measurement and evaluation in psychology and education* (3rd ed.) New York: Wiley, 1969.

Vernon, P. E. Symposium on the effects of coaching and practice in intelligence tests: V. Conclusions. *British Journal of Educational Psychology*, 1954, **24,** 57–63.

Waite, R. R., Sarason, S. B., Lighthall, F. F., and Davidson, K. S. A study of anxiety and learning in children. *Journal of Abnormal and Social Psychology*, 1958, **57,** 267–70.

Wickes, T. A., Jr. Examiner influence in a testing situation. *Journal of Consulting Psychology*, 1956, **20,** 23–26.

Winterbottom, M. R. The relation of need for achievement to learning experiences in independence and mastery. In J. W. Atkinson (Ed.), *Motives in fantasy, action and society.* Princeton, N.J.: Van Nostrand, 1958.

Wiseman, S. Symposium on the effects of coaching and practice in intelligence tests: IV. The Manchester experiment. *British Journal of Educational Psychology*, 1954, **24,** 5–8.

Wiseman, S., and Wrigley, J. The comparative effects of coaching and practice on the results of verbal intelligence tests. *British Journal of Psychology*, 1953, **44,** 83–94.

CHAPTER

4

Validity and Reliability

Teachers, counselors, and others using tests often say, "Okay, I am convinced testing is a good idea and a necessary part of our evaluation program. But how do I know if the test is any good? I am not a testing specialist!" These questions are pertinent and extremely important. This chapter will be devoted to answering these and other questions relevant to test selection.

How to Evaluate a Test

There are general considerations in test evaluation that are always important. The foremost of these is whether the test measures what it is supposed to measure. Next in importance is whether the test measures consistently and accurately. In addition to these factors one is always concerned about the "practical" aspects of the test. Is it convenient to use? Is it economical and easy to administer and interpret? What about the time factor?

Three criteria for evaluating a test have already been mentioned. They are validity, reliability, and practicality. Let us now turn our attention to these specific test selection factors.

Validity

The most important variable in judging the adequacy of a measurement instrument is its validity. Here the question is "What does the test measure?" The test author's basic purpose in constructing the test, for example, may have been to measure reading comprehension. The test buyer's concern is that the test does, in fact, measure reading comprehension. If it does, to what degree? If it does to a large extent, it is considered valid. To the degree that the test measures something else—for example, spelling—its validity as a measure of reading comprehension is impaired.

A test constructed with the aim of predicting success in high school algebra is valid to the degree that those who achieve the highest scores on it also achieve the highest grades in algebra. A test designed to measure artistic aptitude is valid to the extent that it can distinguish between those who will succeed and those who will fail in artistic endeavors.

The student of measurement should remember that validity is a matter of degree. A test is almost never completely valid, nor is it usually entirely invalid. The primary question, then, in selecting a test is how valid is it? Will it serve your needs? If it does, to what degree?

Tests are used for different evaluative needs, and for each need a different method of investigation is necessary to establish validity. Different kinds of tests are used for various measurement purposes. It should be noted, however, that the purposes of many tests overlap. For example, an intelligence test's major purpose may be to measure mental ability, but it also may be used for determining personality aberrations and brain damage. Therefore, it is necessary to gather different validity data within one test as well as securing validity information on different types of tests. In our example three different uses of an intelligence test were cited. Thus, validity data would be needed in each of the three because of their differing goals. It is important to remember that the *nature of the data to be secured is dependent on the objective or objectives of testing rather than on the kind of test* (American Psychological Association and others, 1966).

The three basic types of validity we will discuss are those agreed upon by a joint committee of the American Psychological Association, American Educational Research Association, and the National Council on Measurement in Education (1966). They are (1) *content validity*, (2) *criterion-related validity*, and (3) *construct validity*. National committees[1] and numerous measurement textbooks,[2] in the past, have given different labels to essentially the same

---

[1] American Psychological Association (1954); Committee on Test Standards of the American Educational Research Association and others (1955). They suggested four types of validity information which they called *content validity, concurrent validity, predictive validity,* and *construct validity.*

[2] Cronbach (1960) and others followed the national committee's format, whereas others such as Thorndike and Hagen (1961) and Noll (1965) applied different labels. Thorndike and Hagen (p. 161), for example, used the terms "(1) represent, (2) predict, and (3) signify." Noll (p. 79), on the other hand, called the three types "curricular,

forms of validity. It is hoped that there will now be some standardization in terminology with the new pronouncements by this joint committee.

Content Validity[3]

This area of validity is especially important to teachers. The teacher who gives an examination which covers the materials and objectives of instruction within her classroom has probably given a test that has content validity. How does the teacher know that her test has content validity? Before an answer can be forthcoming certain questions must be asked. Consider for illustrative purposes a test in American history. What are the facts, skills, and concepts that have been stressed in the classroom? What are the curricular objectives? How does the content of the test match these? Does the test require knowledge and insight beyond the scope of the course and the stated instructional objectives? To answer these questions one must match test content against course content. If the instructional goals of the course are represented in the test, we may say the test is valid. It sounds easy, but is it? The analysis of the test and the course is largely a "logical" and subjective judgment. In order to make our assessment as "rational" as possible we must have an itemized list of course objectives to compare to an itemized list of test content.

It is important to remember that *content validity* is especially vital for achievement measures as well as for tests of adjustment based on observations. A standardized achievement test is judged as having content validity when its content represents the curricular goals of those using the test. Whether the test is a national standardized instrument or a local classroom test we can say it has content validity only after we have asked ourselves: Do the tasks of this test typify the educational objectives we feel are important in this area of learning? Are they the educational objectives that we have stressed in our classroom and school system? If the relationship is good, we may say the test is valid.

Test authors and publishers who produce tests for national use strive to determine the generally accepted educational aims of instruction in the area in which a test is to be constructed. The pronouncement on *Standards*[4] by the American Psychological Association and others (1966) states that the test manual should prove the claim that the content of the test is representative of the assumed educational goals, tasks, and processes. They further state,

> In the case of an educational achievement test, the content of the test may be regarded as a definition of (or a sampling from a population

empirical or statistical, and logical." It should be noted that both Thorndike and Hagen, and Noll also use the committee's labels in their discussion of each type of validity. For example, Noll's "curricular" validity and Thorndike and Hagen's "representing" validity are the same as content validity.

[3] The following discussions of validity are based in large part on *Standards for Educational and Psychological Tests and Manuals* (American Psychological Association et al., 1966).

[4] *Standards* in the ensuing pages is used to signify *Standards for Educational and Psychological Tests and Manuals*.

of) one or more educational objectives. The aptitudes, skills, and knowledges required of the student for successful test performance must be precisely the types of aptitudes, skills, and knowledges that the school wishes to develop in the students and to evaluate in terms of test scores [p. 13].

Test authors and publishers use many sources of information to establish the content of their instruments. Among these are (1) contemporary and widely accepted textbooks in the area to be tested; (2) experts in the subject field; (3) course outlines from city, county, and state school offices; (4) qualified teachers who actually teach the subject to be tested; (5) educational specialists who train, prepare, and supervise teachers in the subject field under consideration.

The test author, in constructing his test items, will draw from all the available and relevant sources of information that relate to the subject matter of his test. At the national level he is aware of variations in local school systems. He attempts, therefore, to produce a test that can be widely used. Note that the test producer *attempts* to accomplish these things. He is never completely successful because educators differ, as do school systems. This is why it was stated earlier that validity is a matter of degree. The prospective test buyer, then, evaluates the content validity in terms of how close the test items match his particular educational and instructional objectives.

What to Look for in the Test Manual

The following guidelines should be of assistance in evaluating content validity. Not all test manuals will include all these guidelines, but the better tests and manuals will include a majority of them.

1. Description of the subject matter covered and the extent of the sampling. For example, a manual of a test of English usage might describe the types of items used and the range of subject matter as well as illustrating to what degree responses to test items indicate accomplishments in such areas as spelling, grammar, punctuation and so on.

2. A short resume of the credentials of specialists who have been consulted to evaluate the appropriateness of questions and scoring procedures, and a short description of how they arrived at their judgments.

3. If the test items have been selected by a group of experts, the manual should reveal the degree of agreement among them.

4. Statements in the manual that relate to sources of information should be dated. Courses of study and methods of instruction change and what was a very good reflection of these yesterday may be a poor shadow today.

Criterion-Related Validity

Criterion-related validity is shown by comparing scores on a test with an outside criterion or criteria, such as teachers' grades or job success. The major emphasis of this form of validity is prediction. It is very useful in the selection and classification of individuals for admission to college or graduate training, the hiring of employees, and the assignment of soldiers to various military specialties. This form of validity is established by the use of an expectancy table or, in most cases, a correlation[5] between the test score and a criterion measure. The criterion is considered to be a specific measure of the area to be tested. For example, how well do College Board Scholastic Aptitude Test scores relate to freshman grades in college. A high positive correlation would demonstrate *criterion-related validity*. Let us look at some of the methods used in establishing criterion-related validity.

EXPECTANCY TABLE

The expectancy table is not used as much today as it has been. It is a simple device that can be used to communicate criterion-related validity to test users with little statistical knowledge. The expectancy table is a grid (see Figure 5) containing a number of cells with test scores along the side; at the top are final course grades, supervisor's rating, or any other criterion of success that is desired. For each person a tally is placed which shows, vertically, his test score and, horizontally, his rank on the criterion. After the completion of the tallying, the tallies in each cell are added and recorded in the cell. The figures in each row of cells are added and the sum is placed at the right of each row; the numbers, then, in each column are added and the sum is recorded at the bottom of each column.

Table 1 presents the data from Figure 5. The sum of each cell has been converted to a percentage basis by totaling the number of tallies in its row. Thus, of the twenty-two cases with scores between 60 and 69 on the Sentences test, 23 per cent (five) earned a grade of A, 63 per cent (fourteen) earned a B, and 14 per cent (three) earned a C. Not one of the cases in this group received a grade lower than C. From this data one might state that future students in rhetoric who attain scores of 60 to 69 on the DAT Sentence Test will probably be better than average students, because only 14 per cent earned grades lower than A or B. Similar interpretations may be made for other scores and individuals (Wesman, 1949).

The chief limitation of the expectancy table is that it reveals the predictive value of only one predictor at a time. A great many decisions in college admissions and guidance are made on the basis of more than one predictor. The double-entry expectancy is useful when decisions are made on the basis of two predictors.

---

[5] A statistical measure of relationship between two or more variables. (See Chapter 5 for a thorough discussion of correlation.)

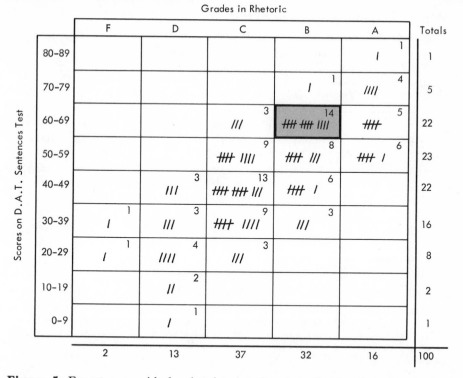

Grades in Rhetoric

	F	D	C	B	A	Totals
80–89					1 *I*	1
70–79				1 *I*	4 *IIII*	5
60–69			3 *III*	14 *HHT HHT IIII*	5 *HHT*	22
50–59			9 *HHT IIII*	8 *HHT III*	6 *HHT I*	23
40–49		3 *III*	13 *HHT HHT III*	6 *HHT I*		22
30–39	1 *I*	3 *III*	9 *HHT IIII*	3 *III*		16
20–29	1 *I*	4 *IIII*	3 *III*			8
10–19		2 *II*				2
0–9		1 *I*				1
	2	13	37	32	16	100

Scores on D.A.T. Sentences Test

Figure 5. Expectancy grid showing how students' grades in rhetoric and previously earned scores on the DAT Sentences Test are tallied in appropriate cells. (From A. C. Wesman, Expectancy tables: A way of interpreting test validity. *Test Service Bulletin*, No. 38. New York: The Psychological Corporation, 1949.)

Table 2 shows the use of a double-entry expectancy table with 294 junior high school boys and girls. The Academic Promise Tests (APT) were administered at the beginning of a course in science. After the completion of the course, the grades received were: 31 A's, 65 B's, 123 C's, 40 D's, and 35 E's. Raw scores (number right) on the APT numerical section and APT language usage section were used in constructing the table. The numbers in the cells reveal how many pupils in each of the two-test category groups received each of the five grades. For example, the number 5 at the top of the upper right-hand cell signifies that five pupils whose APT numerical score was 40 or higher and whose APT language usage score was also 40 or more received A's in their science course (Wesman, 1966).

The advantages of the double-entry expectancy table are similar to those of the single-entry table. Double-entry tables are easy to prepare and understand and require little statistical knowledge. The basic advantage of the double-entry table is that it allows simultaneous display of relationships between two predictors and a criterion.

Table 1 Expectancy Table Prepared from the Grid in Figure 5*

Total Number	Number Receiving Each Grade					Test Scores	Per Cent Receiving Each Grade					Total Per Cent
	F	D	C	B	A		F	D	C	B	A	
1					1	80–89					100	100
5				1	4	70–79				20	80	100
22			3	14	5	60–69			14	63	23	100
23			9	8	6	50–59			39	35	26	100
22		3	13	6		40–49		14	59	27		100
16	1	3	9	3		30–39	6	19	56	19		100
8	1	4	3			20–29	13	50	37			100
2		2				10–19		100				100
1		1				0– 9		100				100
100	2	13	37	32	16							

* The left-hand table summarizes the frequencies as they appear in the original grid. The right-hand table shows these frequencies converted into per cents. (From A. G. Wesman, *Expectancy tables—a way of interpreting test validity*. Test Service Bulletin, No. 38. New York: The Psychological Corporation, 1949.)

Other kinds of expectancy tables may also be constructed to answer such questions as, "How do we choose the best job applicants?" or, "What are the chances that an office worker will obtain an average rating or higher?" (For a more detailed analysis and application see Wesman, 1949, 1966; Anastasi, 1968, pp. 124–127.)

The expectancy table is especially useful in interpreting test predictions to teachers and school administrators. There are limitations, however. The primary drawback is the small number of cases used, which allows less confidence than measures using large numbers of cases. It should be remembered that the average score of a class is a more reliable figure than any individual score.

CORRELATION PROCEDURES

In the area of criterion-related validity an attempt, by empirical means, is made to correlate test scores with another criterion measure, such as school marks or another test, administered at approximately the same time (in the past referred to as concurrent validity). Correlation techniques are also used in measuring the relationship of test scores and a measure of performance or success obtained in the future. Examples of this would be correlating test scores with future success in school or employment. The question of what technique to employ is dependent on test usage; that is, it is the aim of the test to predict future behavior or assess present status.

Table 2 Relationship Between APT-N and APT-LU Scores and Grades in Science of 294 Seventh-Grade Students*

Numerical Score	Language Usage Score — 19 and Below	20–29	30–39	40 and Above	Row Total
40 and Above	A B C D E	A B C 2 D E	A 6 B 6 C 1 D E	A 5 B 2 C 1 D E	A 11 B 8 C 4 D E
30–39	A 1 B C 2 D E 1	A 1 B 7 C 8 D E	A 4 B 12 C 12 D E	A 5 B 10 C 3 D E	A 11 B 29 C 25 D E 1
20–29	A 2 B 3 C 9 D 8 E 3	A 3 B 7 C 25 D 6 E 7	A B 6 C 17 D 1 E	A 1 B 8 C 2 D E	A 6 B 24 C 53 D 15 E 10
19 and Below	A 1 B 2 C 22 D 19 E 19	A 1 B 2 C 18 D 6 E 4	A 1 B C 1 D E 1	A B C D E	A 3 B 4 C 41 D 25 E 24
Column Total (by Grade)	A 4 B 5 C 33 D 27 E 23	A 5 B 16 C 53 D 12 E 11	A 11 B 24 C 31 D 1 E 1	A 11 B 20 C 6 D E	*Grand Total* A 31 B 65 C 123 D 40 E 35

* (From A. G. Wesman, *Double-entry expectancy tables*. Test Service Bulletin, No. 56. New York: The Psychological Corporation, 1966.)

The use of correlation procedures involves the application of statistical methods. Let us, then, turn our attention briefly to what correlation means in statistical terms. Our concern in establishing criterion-related validity is the relationship between a test score and an external criterion. We must have some kind of statistical gauge to ascertain the extent of this relationship. A statistic called a *correlation coefficient* expresses the degree of relationship of our test score and outside criterion.

The correlation coefficient can have values ranging from $+1.0$ through zero to -1.0. The value $+1.0$ indicates that the agreement between two different variables, such as test scores and teacher grades, is positive. Put another way, we can say that the person who had the highest test score also had the highest grade, whereas the person with the lowest test score had the lowest grade. The order continues in exact relationship through the whole set of scores and grades. The value -1.0 indicates a perfect but negative relationship. In this situation the scores go in exactly the opposite direction from the grades. Thus, the person with the highest test score would have the lowest grade, second highest test score would have the second lowest grade, and so forth. If there is no systematic linear relationship between the test scores and grades, the correlation coefficient is zero. (See Chapter 5 for a more detailed statistical explanation.)

THE CRITERION

Thus far our attention has been directed to what criterion validity is and the various methods to establish it. It has been stated that in order to possess this form of validity one matches test scores with a criterion measure. Some may ask, "How do we know if the criterion measure is any good? What would we gain if we had a positive correlation between test scores and a poor criterion?" These are relevant questions. One of the most difficult problems that face the educator and test maker is deciding on a satisfactory criterion. This is especially true in fields that have many variables which impinge on success or failure. How does one establish, for example, a suitable criterion basis for effective teaching? Does one use supervisory ratings? If so, what about their quality? The chance of variance from supervisor to supervisor is great. The atmosphere of the school and the level of ability and interest of the students might affect the teacher's attitude and instruction. In the area of vocational selection the same problems exist in defining successful performance. Conditions of work and managerial evaluations differ. It is obvious that ratings are not always consistent and that there are many factors that affect performance.

There are other criterion measures that may also be used. A college English proficiency examination given to entering freshmen may be validated in terms of its ability to predict future test scores on a comprehensive English examination given a year later. The criterion measure here is the comprehensive English examination. The most common criterion is a measure of success such as grades in training or educational programs. Selection tests for physicians, for example, may be validated against grades earned in medical school. This procedure is open to question because of several problems. First of all, grades tend to be unreliable; but even if they were not, their validity as a basis for the criterion variable would not be very high. Teachers more than anyone else know that grades have drawbacks even in terms of success in the actual training program.

We must face the fact that no criterion measure is ever perfect. The ultimate criterion is a constellation of many factors that only, possibly, may be seen after a man has finished his productive work life. What is professional success and by whose measure do we gauge it? The reader can supply the other obvious philosophical questions and problems. The more important thing to remember is the imperfectness of criterion measures and their relative validity. Magnusson (1967) states, "The only way to make the criterion data more valid is to refine the analysis of the variable we wish to measure and as far as possible relate the criterion measurement to what we consider to be the genuine criterion" (p. 127).

Validity Coefficients

The most common method of reporting test validity is by the use of a validity coefficient, which reveals the correlation between the test and criterion. This estimation of validity by a correlation coefficient is called the *coefficient of validity*. It demonstrates the relationship between test and criterion data. The *coefficient of validity* provides an overall index of the validity of the test. It is also more consistent and less prone to sampling error than the expectancy table percentages because it utilizes all the cases in the group.

There are no test manuals at the present time that report validity coefficients near or at $+1.0$. All fall short of perfect prediction. We would, of course, like to have higher coefficients; however, any positive correlation signifies that predictions from the test will be better than guesses.

The most important thing to remember when evaluating a validity coefficient is the extent to which it may allow for the improvement of prediction and judgment. If the validity coefficient is zero, knowledge of a test score does not allow us to predict a student's score on the criterion with any accuracy at all. As the correlation between test scores and the criterion measure increases, so does our ability to predict. Thus a person who scores in the top quarter on the test will probably be in the top quarter on the criterion measure. It should be noted, however, that some of our predictions will be in error because some of those obtaining test scores in the top quarter will be in the second quarter on the criterion measure while a smaller number will be in the third quarter, and we may even find a few in the lowest quarter. The larger the validity coefficient, the less chance of predictive error.

STANDARD ERROR OF ESTIMATE

The *standard error of estimate*[6] is a statistical technique used to account for the number of individuals for whom statistically calculated predictions are

---

[6] The reader who is interested in pursuing this area in more depth can find a detailed discussion in Anastasi (1968, pp. 130–31); Nunnally (1967, pp. 117–18); Magnusson (1967, pp. 138–41); Games and Klare (1967, pp. 403–05).

wrong, and the magnitude by which the estimates are in error. If, for example, validity is perfect, then the standard error of estimate is zero; if, on the other hand, validity is zero, the standard error of estimate is maximal. Thus, the standard error of estimate decreases as validity increases. Statements concerning "improvement over chance" refer to the extent to which the standard error of estimate is reduced.

The teacher or counselor who is deciding on the selection of a test should always note with caution statements by test authors or publishers that their test is valid. It is important always to ask yourself, "Valid for what?" The sheer magnitude of a validity coefficient does not assure validity for every situation or need. What you want to know is what the test measures and what you want measured.

What to Look for in the Test Manual

The following guidelines are presented for your assistance in reviewing a test manual. The fact that not all of them may be mentioned in a test manual should not surprise you. The better tests, however, will discuss the majority of the following either in the test manual or in a technical supplement.[7]

1. There should be an accurate description of all criteria measures. Attention should be drawn to the aspects of performance not reflected in the criterion.

2. Validity of the test for each criterion about which a prediction is to be made should be given.

3. Many test-criterion correlations should be reported.

4. Time periods in the test administration and collection of criterion data should be stated.

5. The criterion score should be determined independently of test scores.

6. Tests that report validity for grade predictions should clearly state the way performance is measured. (Is it in line with your procedures?)

7. There should be measures of central tendency and variability for the validation sample. (See Chapter 5 for a discussion of these concepts.)

8. The manual should describe variables such as sex, age, socioeconomic status, and level of education when these factors are related to what is being tested. For educational tests, reference should be made to the nature of the community and selection policy, if any, of the school.

[7] For a complete listing and discussion of the recommendations see *Standards* (American Psychological Association et al., 1966, pp. 16–23).

Construct Validity

This type of validity is ascertained by investigating what traits a test measures, that is, what the test score tells us about a person. Does it relate to some abstract construct that will give us insight into the person? Some examples of such constructs are neuroticism, anxiety, and intelligence. Construct validation requires a step-by-step accumulation of data from a great many different sources. It requires a combination of logical and empirical methods of examination. Basically, when studies of construct validity are made, they are instituted to check on the actual theory that is indigenous to the test. Thus, the investigator asks, "From this theory what hypotheses may be made concerning the behavior of individuals with high and low scores?" Data is then secured in order to test these hypotheses. Inferences, based on the evidence, are then made concerning the theory's adequacy to account for the collected data. If the investigator finds that the theory is inadequate to render an explanation for the data, he will (supposedly) change the test interpretation, restate or revise the theory, or completely refute the theory. New evidence, of course, would be needed to show construct validity for a revised interpretation (American Psychological Association et al., 1966).

Cronbach and Meehl (1966) discuss, at great length, the complexities of *construct validity* and recommend its investigation "whenever no criterion or universe of content is accepted as entirely adequate to define the quality to be measured" (p. 70). They go on to state that the determination of psychological constructs that account for test performance is a good practice for almost any test.

Construct validity because of its broad range of meanings and use can create some misunderstandings. Cronbach and Meehl (1966) in their discussion of construct validity state,

> A construct is some postulated attribute of people, assumed to be reflected in test performance. In test validation the attribute about which we make statements in interpreting a test is a construct. We expect a person at any time to possess or not possess a qualitative attribute (amnesia) or structure, or to possess some degree of a quantitative attribute (cheerfulness). A construct has certain associated meanings carried in statements of this general character: Persons who possess this attribute will in situation X, act in manner Y (with a stated probability). The logic of construct validation is invoked whether loose, used in ramified theory or a few simple propositions, used in absolute propositions or probability statements [p. 71].

The knowledge that the investigator has concerning *content* and *criterion-related* validity would be used in analysing *construct* validity. For example, criterion-related validity in a college admissions test may be established by correlating test scores with college grades, but the selection of grades as the criterion may have come about through a consideration of what constructs are most likely to provide a base for devising a good selection test. Furthermore, a validity coefficient revealing a relationship between the test and grades (or any other criterion) gives us no meaningful information about the reason or reasons for the extent of the correlation. In order to be meaningful it must be grounded in the context of some theoretical proposition. Thus *construct validity* is commonly investigated when we wish to increase our knowledge of the qualities that the test is measuring.

Construct validation is useful and important at times for every kind of psychological test. For example, the degree to which a certain intelligence test is free of cultural bias would be a task for construct validation. The following are some techniques and procedures used to determine *construct validity*. (For a more complete account see Cronbach and Meehl, 1966; Anastasi, 1966, 1968; American Psychological Association, 1966.)

1. *Correlations with other tests.* The newly constructed test is correlated with established tests that are already accepted measures of the quality or trait being examined. The Stanford-Binet, for example, has served as a criterion for validation of group intelligence tests for many years. (It is also used in *criterion-related validity*.) The construct to be measured is intelligence. The assumption is that the Stanford-Binet measures intelligence; therefore, a high correlation between the new test and the Binet means the new test also measures intelligence.

2. *Factor analysis.* This statistical procedure is of particular importance to construct validity. Basically, factor analysis is a technique used for analyzing the interrelationships of psychological data. Its major purpose is to simplify behavioral description by the reduction of the number of categories from a starting multiplicity of measurement (test) variables to a few traits. After these traits have been identified, they may be used to describe the factorial composition of a test. Thus a test may be identified in terms of the major factors determining its scores as well as the weight of each factor (Anastasi, 1968).

3. *Experimentally induced effects.* In order to discover how a test would respond to changes in external conditions experimentally induced variables are presented. A test, for example, of anxiety could be administered to an individual under conditions of stress. The anxiety test scores could then be correlated with physiological and other gauges of anxiety during and after testing.

WHAT TO LOOK FOR IN THE TEST MANUAL

The following guidelines, as in the cases of content and criterion-related validity, are based on the *Standards for Educational and Psychological Tests and Manuals* (American Psychological Association et al., 1966).[8]

---

[8] For a complete account and discussion see pp. 23–24 of the *Standards*.

1. If the test is to measure a theoretical variable such as creativity or anxiety, the proposed interpretation should be stated clearly and completely. That is, a definition of the construct to be measured should be given. Thus one might say "creativity" is that ability or trait that leads to original contributions.

2. The manual should signify the degree to which the proposed interpretation has been proved.

3. Evidence concerning the effect of speed on test scores and on their relationship with other variables should be stated.

A Last Word on Validity

The reader should bear in mind that the three aspects of validity—*content, criterion-related,* and *construct* validity—are only conceptually independent. It is very rare that only one of them is important in a specific situation. In most cases a comprehensive and thorough study of a test would involve data on all types of validity.

Remember that statements in the test manual concerning validity should be specific and focused on the types of validity for the kinds of interpretations to be made. *No test is valid for all purposes, situations, or individuals.* The intended use of the test is the determining factor in the kind of evidence that is needed. Let us briefly examine each utilizing the basic kind of validity evidence needed as well as its overlap with other types of validity.

1. *Content validity.* Content validity is of primary importance in achievement tests. A test publisher consults with a group of subject-matter experts who help devise and arrange test items they feel cover the topics pertinent to the area represented by the test (content validity). Criterion-related validity is also necessary to check against a later criterion of performance. An achievement test may be used for a selection program. A theoretical analysis of what is being measured by the achievement test requires a consideration of *construct* validity. Is, for example, a score on a mathematics test reflective of mathematical ability, understanding, or memorization of data?

2. *Criterion-related validity.* Criterion-related validity is of primary importance in intelligence or scholastic aptitude tests to reveal the ability to predict school or college success. The kind of aptitudes measured is evaluated, many times, by the *content* of the test items and correlations with other tests.

3. *Construct validity.* Construct validity is of primary importance in personality tests, especially where projective techniques[9] are used. If a diagnosis is to be made, other criteria such as psychiatric opinion (*criterion-related* validity) are used at the time of testing or afterward.

[9] See Chapter 12 for a discussion of projective techniques used in personality testing.

It is obvious from our discussion that *validity* is a broad term encompassing many different factors. Our first question—"What does the test measure?"— is the one whose answer the classroom teacher, test author, and publisher needs to know. After this question has been answered, our next inquiry concerns the accuracy of the test. Let us, then, turn our attention to reliability.

Reliability

The second question we ask about a test is, "What is its reliability?" Our question is not concerned with what the test measures, but how consistently it measures whatever it does measure. What is the stability of the test score? If we measure the same person again, how consistent will the test scores be?

The reliability of a test refers to that quality of a test which demonstrates test score consistency and stability. Thus, when Mrs. Gold's eighth grade takes the Jones Test of School Ability on two different occasions, are their scores approximately the same or have they changed? If they are approximately the same, we may say the test is reliable. Henry received a score of 60 the first time he took the test and a score of 62 the second time. His scores are *consistent*. On the second administration of the same test his class, on the average, received approximately the same scores as they did on the first administration. The test seems to be reliable in that there was consistency in the results obtained when testing was repeated on the same students. A lack of consistency would have been evident if the students in Mrs. Gold's class had not obtained similar scores or held the same relative test score positions. The determination of reliability on standardized tests, of course, involves many more classes and individuals, but the principle remains the same.

Reliability is a general term referring to many different types of evidence. Each kind of evidence suggests the consistency to be expected among similar observations. Specific types of errors or inconsistencies are explained by different kinds of evidence. There is no single measure of test reliability that is always preferable. The choice is dependent upon the intended utilization of the test scores. Although there are various methods of estimating the reliability of psychological and educational tests, the most commonly used are based upon two measurements of the same subjects. The two measurements may be obtained by three different techniques:

1. *Retesting* subjects with the same test.
2. *Alternate form* of the original test, that is, correlation of original test scores with scores on another independent test (different form) with an item content similar to the original test.
3. "*Split-half*," or "*odd-even*," correlation, which involves a division of the test into two parts, one part being the odd-numbered

questions and the other being the even-numbered questions. The correlation between scores on the odd-numbered and the even-numbered items yields a reliability coefficient for the entire test.

It is apparent from our brief discussion so far that different methods of obtaining reliability take into consideration different sources of error. There are various factors that contribute to "unreliability" or inconsistency. They include (a) differences in the condition of the individual being tested—for example, mood, physical state, and so on; (b) differences in the test content or test situation; (c) variations in test administration, such as noise or differences in the administrative skill of the tester; (d) mistakes and differences in scoring and recording scores as well as variations in the process of observation (American Psychological Association et. al., 1966).

Up to this point we have discussed what reliability is and some of the general considerations in estimating its presence. Let us now return to the three specific techniques mentioned earlier: (1) retesting, (2) alternate forms, and (3) "odd-even."

Retesting

Testing individuals with the same test they have taken earlier is known as retesting. If a physician, for example, wanted to check on the accuracy of his nurse's ability to measure his patients' weight and height, he might ask her to measure each patient twice using the same procedures. An even better technique would be to have someone else do the second measuring, so that the nurse's recall of the first measurements would not influence the second ratings. The physician of course might also want to know the exact weight and height of a patient each day and how the measures vary. These two instances provide us with two separate but related investigations, measures of (1) individual variance and of (2) variation caused by the procedure of measurement.

The reliability of measurement in height and weight assessments is less complex than it is in standardized testing. However, the same principle is involved. Let us take as an example a test of English and the procedures for finding reliability under the retesting technique. The English test is administered to a class and is immediately readministered. Measurement here is contaminated because children are able to remember questions and do not spend as much time with the second test. The children who were not able to finish the first time will certainly be in a better position to complete the test the second time.

It is important not only to determine the degree of variation of individual response from one occasion to the next, but also to know the extent of sampling variance involved in deciding on a given set of items. That is, there is no reason to think that one set of fifty English usage items is superior or inferior to another equivalent set of fifty. Suppose that one set of questions deals with a unit recently covered by some of the children being examined. These items would be especially easy for them. The test might then over-estimate their level of English usage. It would do so consistently on both testings because the items would remain the same. A given set of test items is not equally valid or reliable. The point to remember, then, is that although the retesting method of determining reliability provides data regarding a particular set of items used, it is possible to obtain a very different reliability estimate if another set of items is used.

Retesting with an identical test may account for errors in answer differences to a test at a specific moment and variation in individuals from time to time. It cannot rule out, however, the variation arising out of the specific set of items chosen.[10]

Standards (American Psychological Association et al., 1966) is quite clear on this point.

> Aside from practical limitations, retesting is not a theoretically desirable method of determining a reliability coefficient if, as usual, the items that constitute the test are only one of many sets (actual or hypothetical) that might equally well have been used to measure the particular ability or trait [p. 25].

Alternate Forms

The alternate forms measurement of reliability attempts to establish reliability by correlating scores, obtained by the same individuals, on two different forms of the same test. These alternate or equivalent forms are constructed with the same basic purposes in mind. They contain items of similar difficulty and cover the same areas of knowledge or skills even though they use different questions. Individuals may be tested with one form initially and then retested with the other form. The resulting correlation between the scores on the two forms is the reliability coefficient. This type of coefficient represents two aspects of test reliability—time stability and response consistency to different samples of items.

Thus, alternate or equivalent test forms are variations on the same test theme. They are individually constructed tests created to meet the same specifications. Each form should contain the same number of items covering the same kind of content and arranged in the same format. All aspects of the test—including the degree of content difficulty, instructions, time limits, and so forth—must be comparable. Thus, two equivalent intelligence tests should contain items and questions of the same difficulty and should cover the same kinds of areas, for example, numerical ability, abstract reasoning, and vocabulary.

---

[10] Though the retest technique is not appropriate for most psychological tests, there are some motor and personality tests that are not greatly influenced by repetition and are amenable to the retest method (Lindeman, 1967).

Once we have established the equivalence of our alternate forms we may administer them either "back-to-back" (that is, with the second form immediately following the completion of the first, if we are not concerned with time stability) or separated by a time interval, if time is a consideration.

Alternate form reliability, like any other technique, is not free of problems. There is the problem of practice effect, as in retest reliability. Although the use of equivalent forms will reduce the effect of practice, it will not eliminate it. Another limitation is the *real* difference between the forms; the concern here is with the degree of difference between test items.

Given the limitations of the alternate form technique it is still the most appropriate method for most educational tests. It is, therefore, recommended that the teacher or counselor give it the greatest amount of weight in investigating the reliability of a test.

One final note of practicality is in order. The administration of a second form of a test is expensive and time-consuming; therefore, many test authors and publishers have resorted to other devices. Sometimes they are satisfactory, but more often they are poor compromises.

"Odd-Even" and "Split-Half" Reliability

If it is not practical to do testing on two different occasions or if it is desired only to sample the content consistency without taking into account individual response variation from one time to another, the "odd-even" or "split-half" technique may be used. A test of 100 items may be divided into two sets of fifty items each. One set contains all the even-numbered items, whereas the other set contains all the odd-numbered items. The relationship between scores on the even and odd sets is an "odd-even," or "split-half," correlation. The correlation coefficient for the whole test of 100 items may then be estimated by the Spearman-Brown formula. This formula thus makes it possible to obtain an estimate of reliability from one administration of one test.

The correlation obtained by comparing the odd-even test items is actually the correlation between two tests each of which is one half the length of the original test. At this juncture a correction is made by using the Spearman-Brown formula. On our 100-item test, a coefficient of 0.70 was obtained from the odd-even method. The formula is as follows:

$$\text{Reliability of entire test} = \frac{2 \text{ (reliability of } \frac{1}{2} \text{ test)}}{1 + \text{(reliability of } \frac{1}{2} \text{ test)}}$$

The actual process using our obtained coefficient of 0.70 derived from our correlating the fifty odd items with the fifty even items is:

$$\text{Reliability of entire test} = \frac{2 \,(0.70)}{1 + (0.70)} = \frac{1.40}{1.70} = 0.82$$

The correlation coefficient of 0.82, then, presents us with an estimate of reliability of an entire test where the half tests provided us with a correlation of 0.70.

The ease and convenience of the "split-half" method has led some test authors and publishers to use it when more appropriate techniques, such as the alternate form method, are indicated. Some cautions in the use of the "split-half" technique are indicated. First of all, the variation of an individual from day to day is not recorded in this type of estimated reliability. Secondly, it should not be used with a speed test, which is an examination made up of relatively easy items that most individuals, if given enough time, will answer correctly. The objective in many speed tests is to see how many items can be responded to correctly in the indicated time. In computing "odd-even" scores on a speed test, the two scores tend to be similar and the reliability coefficient may be close to +1, or perfect. For illustrative purposes, let us say a 100-item test depends entirely on speed, so that individual differences in score rest completely upon number of items tried, rather than upon errors. If Robert has a score of 84, he will have forty-two correct odd items and forty-two correct even items; if Jim obtains a score of 64, he will have thirty-two odd and thirty-two even correct. Thus with the exception of accidental errors on a few questions, the correlation would be perfect (+1.00).

Most of our tests are not speed tests—and though they may be timed, the results will generally not be as severely affected when the "split-half" technique is used with them. The important thing to remember is that the "split-half" procedure is based upon the consistency in the number of errors made by the individual. If individual differences in test scores are significantly affected by speed, a single-trial reliability coefficient is not an appropriate measure (Anastasi, 1968).

Before leaving this area of reliability, one other method of estimating internal consistency should be noted. It is the formula developed by Kuder and Richardson (1937). It does not require the division of the test into halves and rescoring and calculating a correlation coefficient. This formula is based on the assumption that every item in a test measures the same general factors as do the others. This procedure leads to a reliability coefficient that may be interpreted in the same manner as the "odd-even" coefficient. This formula has drawbacks similar to those of the Spearman-Brown formula, mentioned in our previous discussion, in that (1) it is not appropriate for speed tests and (2) it does not measure individual variance from one time to another.[11]

---

[11] The formula most commonly used is called the Kuder-Richardson "formula 20." It is stated:

$$r_{tt} = \frac{n}{n-1} \frac{S_t - \Sigma pq}{S_t^2}$$

For a more complete discussion and statistical treatment see Cronbach, 1960; Nunnally, 1967; and Magnusson, 1967. For those with a good mathematical background, Lord and Novick (1968) is an excellent advanced treatment of tests and statistical theories.

Standard Error of Measurement

In our discussion of testing thus far we have seen some of the factors that affect the accuracy of a test score. To state, then, that no test is perfectly accurate should not surprise the reader, nor should anyone at this point think that a person's test score is determined only by his ability or knowledge. It is true, of course, that usually a person is the primary determiner of his own score, but the score is also a reflection of the inaccuracy of the test itself. A statistical technique which accounts for this test error and allows us to estimate the margin of error in the test score is the *standard error of measurement*. It is especially useful, in the interpretation of individual scores, when attempting to estimate the expected degree of variation in a student's test score. If Mary, for example, obtains an IQ of 116, how much confidence can we place in this score? Will she obtain an IQ of 128 next testing session or an IQ of 104?

It is true that the reliability coefficient gives an estimate of accuracy, but it does not assist specifically in interpreting individual scores. The numerical value of the coefficient is dependent to a great degree on the range of scores in the group being examined. That is, if a group has a small spread in the ability being measured, the coefficient will be low, whereas if the group has a large spread in a particular field, it will be higher. The standard error of measurement does not have these difficulties.

Let us look at an actual school situation where knowledge of the standard error of measurement would be used. An intelligence test has been administered to the ninth-grade classes at Stevens Junior High School. Mrs. Olson, a ninth-grade teacher, is asking the counselor about one of her students.

Mrs. Olson: How did Donald Smith do on the test?

Counselor: Let's see. His IQ score is around 110.

Mrs. Olson: What do you mean "around 110"? Is it 110 or is it not?

Counselor: The reason I say "around 110" is that no score is perfectly accurate, only an estimation. His actual obtained IQ score was 110, but the standard error of measurement is 6.

Mrs. Olson: What is the standard error of measurement?

Counselor: It is a statistic which describes reliability; that is, it tells us about the accuracy of an individual test score. In Donald's case, for example, we know his obtained IQ score was 110 and that the test has a standard error of six points.

Mrs. Olson: I know you said that before, but what about the six points?

Counselor: It isn't complicated. Donald's score is 110, the standard error is 6; therefore Donald's "true" score lies somewhere between 104 and 116. You see the six points indicate the amount of test error that must be considered in the interpretation of Donald's score.

Mrs. Olson: I see, but what is a "true" score?

Counselor: A true score is one that Donald would obtain if the test was perfectly reliable. The six points provides the limits within which we may expect to find Donald Smith's "true" IQ score. If Donald were tested over and over again in the same exact situation, 68 per cent of his scores would fall within one standard error of his "true" score, 95 per cent would fall within two standard errors, and 99 per cent would fall within three standard errors.

Mrs. Olson: Hold on, I am getting a little confused. What is this "standard error"?

Counselor: Remember the normal curve and how, for example, 68 per cent of the cases fall within −1 and +1 standard deviations from the mean?

Mrs. Olson: Yes, I do. Do you mean those percentages are based on the normal curve? [*Note: A discussion of the normal curve and standard deviation can be found in Chapter 5.*]

Counselor: Precisely. The normal curve is our basic frame of reference. In more concrete terms, then, we know that your student, Donald Smith, has obtained an actual score of 110 and that one standard error would make his true score somewhere between 104 and 116.

Mrs. Olson: Hold on. Let me see if I can figure out the rest. The standard is six points. Therefore, one standard error is from 104 to 116 because you added 6 to 110 at the upper range and subtracted 6 from 110 at the lower range.

Counselor: Right. I do the same with two standard errors by doubling the 6 on both sides and I have a range of 98 to 122.

Mrs. Olson: And three standard errors would be a tripling of the standard error of six points. Donald's "true" score then, 99 out of 100 times or three standard errors, would lie between 92 and 128.

Counselor: Exactly. Now do you see why I said around 110?

Mrs. Olson: I certainly do. Thanks for the information. I'll never again think that someone who has an IQ of 116 is much smarter than someone with an IQ of 110.

Counselor: At least you won't on this test. Remember, knowing the standard error of measurement for each test is very important before you make an interpretation of test scores.

Now that Mrs. Olson knows something about standard error of measurement she would not be shocked to find that on another testing her student may obtain an IQ of as high as 122. The standard error should make us cautious in attaching meaning to minor elevations or depressions in test scores. Remember that in actual practice we do not know an individual's "true" IQ; we know only the IQ obtained on one test.

The standard error of measurement is one of the reasons that one test score should never be thought of as a fixed number but as a score *within the band* where the true score lies. A large standard error means the band is broad; consequently, we would have less confidence in our obtained score than if the standard error were smaller. For example, what if Mrs. Olson's student obtained an IQ of 110 on a test with a standard error of ten points? The band where his "true" score might be (one standard error) would be between 100 and 120. How comfortable can the teacher or counselor feel with a band that reveals there is a good chance that the student's true IQ is average (100) or superior (120)? If we carry it out to two standard errors, the band where the true score might be found is increased from the lower limits of average (90) to the very superior range (130). If, on the other hand, the standard error is two points, the teacher can feel fairly comfortable (carried out to two standard errors) that her student's obtained IQ of 110 will fall on either side of his true IQ by four points, or from 106 to 114. This range would indicate solid average ability.

Table 3 presents the relationship between the reliability coefficient and the standard error of measurement. The standard errors of measurement for different reliability coefficients and standard deviations[12] can also be seen in Table 3. Note that as the reliability coefficient increases, the standard error decreases. It is obvious then that the higher the reliability, the smaller the error in individual test scores.

A great many test manuals report both the reliability coefficient and standard errors of measurement. If the standard error of measurement is not given, Table 3 would enable you to make an approximation.

To obtain the standard error for a test from Table 3, note the reported reliability coefficient and standard deviation as given in the test manual and match them with or near the coefficients and standard deviation (SD) in the table. Let us suppose, for example, that you find that the Brown Test of School Ability has a reliability coefficient of 0.87 and a SD of 12. The first thing you would do is find the appropriate coefficient, which is 0.85 (because it is nearest to 0.87), and then go down the row (0.85) until you are next to the SD row of 12. The number 4.6 (under the 0.85 column and directly across from the number 12 under SD) is the approximate standard error of measurement.

In closing, it should be restated that the standard error of measurement and the reliability coefficient are both methods of demonstrating test reliability. The standard error is not directly comparable from one test to another and is independent of the variance of the group on which it is computed.[13]

---

[12] *Standard deviation* is a statistical term referring to score variance, that is, it is a measure of the distribution of scores. See Chapter 5 for a more complete discussion and analysis of its characteristics.

[13] The reader who is interested in a more thorough statistical treatment of the standard error of measurement should see McCollough and Van Atta (1965); Magnusson (1967); Games and Klare (1967); Nunnally (1967); and Popham (1967). For a little less statistical and more verbal discussion of this subject see Doppelt (1956); and Cronbach (1960).

Table 3 Standard Errors of Measurement for Given Values of Reliability Coefficient and Standard Deviation*

SD	Reliability Coefficient					
	.95	.90	.85	.80	.75	.70
30	6.7	9.5	11.6	13.4	15.0	16.4
28	6.3	8.9	10.8	12.5	14.0	15.3
26	5.8	8.2	10.1	11.6	13.0	14.2
24	5.4	7.6	9.3	10.7	12.0	13.1
22	4.9	7.0	8.5	9.8	11.0	12.0
20	4.5	6.3	7.7	8.9	10.0	11.0
18	4.0	5.7	7.0	8.0	9.0	9.9
16	3.6	5.1	6.2	7.2	8.0	8.8
14	3.1	4.4	5.4	6.3	7.0	7.7
12	2.7	3.8	4.6	5.4	6.0	6.6
10	2.2	3.2	3.9	4.5	5.0	5.5
8	1.8	2.5	3.1	3.6	4.0	4.4
6	1.3	1.9	2.3	2.7	3.0	3.3
4	.9	1.3	1.5	1.8	2.0	2.2
2	.4	.6	.8	.9	1.0	1.1

* From J. E. Doppelt, *How accurate is a test score?* Test Service Bulletin, No. 50. New York: The Psychological Corporation, 1956.

This table is based on the formula $SE_M = SD \sqrt{1 - r_{tt}}$. For most purposes the result will be sufficiently accurate if the table is entered with the reliability and standard deviation values nearest those given in the test manual. Be sure the standard deviation and the reliability coefficient are for the same group of people.

If we desire to compare the reliability of different tests, our best measure is the reliability coefficient. On the other hand, if we want to interpret individual scores, the most appropriate procedure is the standard error of measurement (Anastasi, 1968).

Interpretation of Reliability

The teacher or counselor who is selecting a measurement instrument wants to know about the dependability of the scores it yields. If the instrument is inaccurate what good is it? Remember, *no test can be valid unless it is reliable.* On the other hand, *a test may be reliable and not valid* because it may measure an invalid criterion consistently and with precision. If the test does not measure whatever it does measure consistently, it cannot be valid, because, if we have erratic score fluctuations we cannot know what we are measuring. If a child's raw score is 80 one day and 50 the next, is the test measuring his "guess-ability," mood, knowledge, or what? If we know the reliability of a test in a specific situation, we also know the extent of validity in that situation. That is, the boundaries beyond which validity cannot rise. In addition we know from our previous discussion that reliability helps us to know the band of test score error and exactly how much weight we may give to an individual score. A comment in this general area from the *Standards* (American Psychological Association et al., 1966) seems appropriate before we launch into our discussion of specific factors that influence reliability.

> Reliability is a necessary but not a sufficient condition of validity. Reliability coefficients are pertinent to validity in the negative sense that unreliable scores cannot be valid. But reliable scores are by no means *ispo facto* valid, since validity depends on what interpretation is proposed. Reliability is of special importance in support of, but not in replacement of, the analysis and estimation of content, criterion-related, and construct validity [p. 29].

FACTORS AFFECTING RELIABILITY

Let us turn our attention to four specific influences on test reliability.

1. *Length of test*. In our discussion of the Spearman-Brown formula it was seen that the length of a test may affect the reliability coefficient. The chance of measurement errors decreases proportionately with the length of the test. That is, the longer the test, the greater the chance that the score is a reflection of the person being tested and that it is a more accurate estimation of his ability, achievement, or any other characteristic being measured. This is logically true because we have increased the number of samplings of the characteristic we wish to measure. If, for example, in an American history course you administer a test consisting of one essay question concerning the Civil War period, how reliable will your results be? The students who happened to know that particular area would get a perfect score, whereas those who were weak in that area would get zero. Let us suppose you increased the number of questions to five, could you then feel more comfortable in evaluating your students' knowledge of the Civil War? Undoubtedly you would say yes, but with the reservation that even more questions—say, ten or fifteen more, or 100 multiple-choice—would be an even better device. Thus, by increasing the size of our sample and thereby lengthening the test we increase the reliability of our instrument.

Of course there are practical limitations to increasing the length of a test. Factors such as time available for testing, number of good questions one is able to write, and student fatigue all limit the length of the test. If you must have short tests then a more frequent testing schedule would provide a greater sampling of what you want to measure and would consequently be more reliable. In interpreting standardized test results, be wary of subtest scores based on relatively few items. If no reliability data are given for them, the best thing is to use only the total score or scores.

2. *Range of talent.* The reliability coefficient, as we have stated before, varies with the extent of talent in a group even though the stability of measurement is not affected. A wide range of talent yields high coefficients, whereas a small range produces low coefficients. Thus, to interpret a coefficient properly a measure of the variability of the group is needed.

Table 4 illustrates this range effect or spread of scores on two forms of an arithmetic test administered to twenty students. Note that changes in rank from one form to the other are rather insignificant. These data would produce a fairly high coefficient.

Table 4 Raw Scores and Ranks of Students on Two Forms of an Arithmetic Test*

Student	Form X		Form Y	
	Score	Rank	Score	Rank
A	90	1	88	2
B	87	2	89	1
C	83	3	76	5
D	78	4	77	4
E	72	5	80	3
F	70	6	65	7
G	68	7	64	8
H	65	8	67	6
I	60	9	53	10
J	54	10	57	9
K	51	11	49	11
L	47	12	45	14
M	46	13	48	12
N	43	14	47	13
O	39	15	44	15
P	38	16	42	16
Q	32	17	39	17
R	30	18	34	20
S	29	19	37	18
T	25	20	36	19

* From A. G. Wesman, *Reliability and confidence.* Test Service Bulletin, No. 44. New York: The Psychological Corporation, 1952.

However, if we examine only the five highest students and their ranks, the importance of the changes becomes greater. Student C's change in rank from third to fifth, in the larger group, represents only a 10 per cent shift (two places out of twenty). The same shift, in the smaller group, is a 40 per cent change (two places out of five). If we use the twenty on which we calculate the reliability of the test, it is evident that going from third on form X to fifth on form Y still leaves the student in the top part of the distribution. On the other hand, if the estimation of reliability is only on the group of the top five students, this change from third to fifth means a drop from the middle to the bottom of this distribution. If we based our coefficient on these five cases it would be very low. Again, it should be noted that it is not the smaller group which brings about a lower coefficient, but the narrow range of talent. If you take five other cases such as A, E, J, O, and T—who rank from first to twentieth, a coefficient as great as that based on all twenty students would be produced (Wesman, 1952).

This example illustrates why the reliability coefficient may vary although the test items and the students' performances are unchanged. Remember that *you need to have information on the range of ability in the tested group before you may correctly interpret the reliability coefficient of the test.*

3. *Ability level of the group.* The ability level of the group is a factor similar to the one just discussed. When you interpret a student's test score, remember that the most meaningful reliability coefficient is one which rests on the reference group that is comparable to that of the student. It is, of course, impossible for a test manual to present reliability for all possible group memberships.

The appropriate comparison group is based on what we want to know. If we are testing ninth-grade boys for mechanical aptitude, we should have reliability coefficients based on the scores of ninth-grade boys. The coefficients are less meaningful when they are based on "all high school" boys taking the test. They become even less pertinent when the coefficient rests on all high school and college students taking the test. The coefficient of reliability becomes increasingly meaningful the closer we can come in comparing the group we want to know about with the original group on which the coefficient was based.

4. *Method used.* It is very important to consider the procedures used in obtaining the reliability coefficient when comparing two different tests. The size of the reliability coefficient is related to the methods used. Different procedures treat various sources of variance differently.

It cannot be said that because procedure A obtains a higher coefficient that it is better than procedure B, which yields a lower reliability coefficient. For example, the "split-half" operation usually produces the highest reliability coefficient. We know that it is not the best technique and that speed may unduly influence the value of the coefficient it produces. (See the previous section on "odd-even" and "split-half" procedures.) On the other hand, the most demanding and generally most appropriate procedure—that is, the alternate or equivalent form method—when used with a time interval between test and retest yields the lowest reliability coefficients. Do not be impressed by the sheer elevation of the coefficient. The value of the reliability coefficient should be considered, but remember that the methods used are reflected in the coefficient and warrant your attention.

Height of Reliability Coefficient

A reliability coefficient should be as high as possible. Unfortunately perfection is not now possible, so we must settle for the best we can get.

The degree of reliability should be determined by the purposes and situations for which we intend to use the measurement instrument. The school psychologist who must decide on the possibility of placing a child in a mentally retarded class or state institution needs the most reliable instruments available. The counselor attempting to ascertain parental attitudes toward educational policy is of course not as concerned with reliability, because only the average figures need to be highly accurate, not the individual parental responses.

If an instrument with low reliability is the "best" or only device and you need to use it, be careful in making evaluations. Obtain all types of data and use the test results with this information on a tentative basis. As we stated in our discussion of validity coefficients, even a poor but significant coefficient is better than nothing. The basic principle to keep in mind is that the importance of the decision is equal to the need for precision in measurement. The greater our need for confidence in the stability and consistency of the test, the more we need higher reliability (Wesman, 1952).

What to Look for in the Test Manual

The following guidelines will in most cases be familiar to you from our recent discussion of reliability. They are intended only as a quick checklist to help you in evaluating a test's reliability. They represent only some of the most important features and are based largely on the recommendations in *Standards for Educational and Psychological Tests and Manuals* (American Psychological Association et al., 1966). The reader is referred to *Standards* for a complete and detailed description.

> 1. Reliability evidence should be reported to the extent that you may judge whether scores are dependable for the recommended purposes of the test. If any important data have not been obtained, this should be mentioned.
>
> 2. Every score, subscore, or combination of scores should be judged by the standards for reliability.
>
> 3. Reports on reliability or error of measurement should be given in enough detail to permit you to judge if the data are applicable to the types of persons you desire to examine. For example, is there evidence that indicates that reliability was obtained, in a mechanical comprehension test, on girls as well as boys?
>
> 4. The reliability analysis for an intelligence or achievement test intended to be used to make differentiations within one school grade should be based on pupils only within the actual grade. It should *not* be based on many grades with a broader range of ability.

5. The test manual should state if there are significant changes in the error of measurement from score level to score level.

6. Test authors and publishers should report reliability investigations in standard statistical terms (for example, standard error of measurement, reliability coefficients, and so on). It is their job to communicate with you. Do not be awed by unconventional statistics. If the statistical usage is unusual the test author should present a complete explanation of why and what these statistics mean.

7. Reliability is very important but it is not a replacement for validity. Reliability does not demonstrate validity; it can only support it.

8. If two forms of a test are used, both of which are intended for the same subjects, averages and spread of scores as well as the co-efficient of correlation between the tests should be given.

9. Sometimes measures of internal consistency are most appropriate; however, they should not be thought of as substitutes for other measures. If alternate forms are available, they should be used and alternate form reliabilities should be reported as the preferred technique. This does not mean coefficients resting on internal analysis should be omitted. It only means that alternate forms have first preference.

10. In most cases estimates of internal consistency should be based on the "split-half" or Kuder-Richardson technique. Any deviation from this should be clearly explained in the test manual.

11. Careful attention to a review of reliability coefficients based on internal analysis, especially on time factors, is important. If speed is a factor the coefficients will be exceptionally high and tend to be insignificant.

12. The test manual should indicate to what degree test scores are likely to change after a given amount of time has elapsed. The mean and standard deviation of scores and correlation at each testing should also be reported.

Practical Concerns

Until now our attention has been focused on the technical and theoretical aspects of testing. These, of course, are of primary importance in selecting tests; however, practical considerations cannot be overlooked. Financial aspects of testing and test time are necessary concerns of the school administrator and his staff. In addition, ease of administration and scoring are important factors, because teachers generally have a minimum amount of experience and training in testing.

Economic Aspects

Money is a very important consideration when formulating educational policy. Testing must take its turn in the line of educational needs awaiting financing. Fortunately, testing is relatively inexpensive, especially when compared to other educational needs. In addition, federal and state allowances almost guarantee every school district in the United States enough funds to maintain an adequate standardized testing program.

Because funds are not unlimited, it is desirable to save when possible. One of the first places where it is possible to save is in the reuse of test booklets that have separate answer sheets. Thus, the only yearly expenses are answer sheets and occasional replacements of worn-out booklets. Test booklets with separate answer sheets, however, should not be used in the primary or lower elementary grades. The end of the fifth grade or beginning of the sixth is probably early enough to begin using separate answer sheets. However, there may be situations where the children's sociopsychological, intellectual, and motor skills are very well developed, in which case an earlier grade would be appropriate. On the other hand, in some settings junior high school would be early enough.

Administrative Aspects

Tests are generally administered by teachers or other educational personnel with limited measurement training. The ease of administering a test is facilitated by simple and clear directions. A test with a great many subtests which require exact (stopwatch) timing and new directions for each section is an exacting job. This may produce a situation for possible errors in directions and timing which could affect the final results. Validity and reliability of the test scores would then be of questionable value.

Time Aspects

Saving time in test administration should be approached with extreme caution. In our discussion of reliability it was stated that the reliability of a test is dependent on the length of the test. Thus, shortening the test time is generally accomplished at the expense of test reliability. This is particularly true of some "quickie" tests on the market that claim to produce a reliable IQ score in fifteen or twenty minutes. Some tests are efficiently constructed, but in most cases reductions in testing time means loss of reliability.

Scoring Aspects

There are many teachers who have viewed testing with horror because of tedious hours spent hand scoring. To make matters worse, many times the directions for scoring required a test specialist to interpret. Today, by the use of separate answer sheets and machine scoring, this problem has at least been reduced for those teachers who teach upper elementary grades and beyond. In addition, most contemporary test manuals go to great lengths to present scoring procedures in simple and easy to understand terms.

Tests for children in the primary grades (K-3) must of necessity involve more time in scoring because young children may find separate answer sheets confusing. By the middle elementary grades (about the middle or end of the fourth grade) there are techniques, such as answer spaces at the right side of the page which can be scored with an answer key, that lessen the scoring burden. (Review Chapter 3, section on scoring for more details.) There is every reason to choose a test that is easily scored over one that it is difficult to score if this does not sacrifice validity or reliability.

Interpretive Aspects

There is no point in an elaborate testing program if the results are not meaningful in educational planning. Test results that are hard to understand or easy to misinterpret are not only a waste of time but in some cases harmful to the children we are attempting to help.

The manual should present cogent and clear statements concerning the meanings of scores. Do not administer any test, even if it has all the positive features we have discussed, until you are sure you know what to do with the results. Tests are constructed to tell us something. If they do not do this, they are a meaningless exercise in the consumption of time.

References

American Psychological Association. *Technical recommendations for psychological tests and diagnostic techniques*. Washington, D.C.: American Psychological Association, 1954.

American Psychological Association, American Educational Research Association, and National Council on Measurement in Education. *Standards for educational and psychological tests and manuals*. Washington, D.C.: American Psychological Association, 1966.

Anastasi, A. Some current developments in the measurement and interpretation of test validity. In A. Anastasi (Ed.), *Testing problems in perspective*. Washington, D.C.: American Council on Education, 1966. Pp. 307–17.

Anastasi, A. *Psychological testing*. (3rd ed.) New York: Macmillan, 1968.

Committee on Test Standards, American Educational Research Association; National Education Association; and National Council on Measurements Used in Education. *Technical recommendations for achievement tests*. Washington, D.C.: The National Education Association, 1955.

Cronbach, L. J. *Essentials of psychological testing*. (2nd ed.) New York: Harper & Row, 1960.

Cronbach, L. J., and Meehl, P. E. Construct validity in psychological tests. In C. I. Chase and H. G. Ludlow (Eds.), *Readings in educational and psychological measurement*. Boston: Houghton Mifflin, 1966. Pp. 68–92.

Doppelt, J. E. *How accurate is a test score?* Test Service Bulletin, No. 50. New York: The Psychological Corporation, 1956.

Games, P. A., and Klare, G. R. *Elementary statistics: Data analysis for the behavioral sciences.* New York: McGraw-Hill, 1967.

Kuder, G. F., and Richardson, M. W. The theory of the estimation of test reliability. *Psychometrika*, 1937, **2**, 151–60.

Lindeman, R. H. *Educational measurement.* Glenview, Ill.: Scott, Foresman, 1967.

Lord, F. M., and Novick, M. R. *Statistical theories of mental test scores.* Reading, Mass.: Addison-Wesley, 1968.

Magnusson, D. *Test theory.* Reading, Mass.: Addison-Wesley, 1967.

McCollough, C., and Van Atta, L. *Introduction to descriptive statistics and correlation: A program for self-instruction.* New York: McGraw-Hill, 1965.

Noll, V. H. *Introduction to educational measurement.* (2nd ed.) Boston: Houghton Mifflin, 1965.

Nunnally, J. C. *Psychometric theory.* New York: McGraw-Hill, 1967.

Popham, W. J. *Educational statistics: Use and interpretation.* New York: Harper & Row, 1967.

Thorndike, R. L., and Hagen, E. *Measurement and evaluation in psychology and education.* (2nd ed.) New York: Wiley, 1961.

Wesman, A. G. *Expectancy tables—a way of interpreting test validity.* Test Service Bulletin, No. 38. New York: The Psychological Corporation, 1949.

Wesman, A. G. *Reliability and confidence.* Test Service Bulletin, No. 44. New York: The Psychological Corporation, 1952.

Wesman, A. G. *Double-entry expectancy tables.* Test Service Bulletin, No. 56. New York: The Psychological Corporation, 1966.

CHAPTER

5

Statistics, Norms,
and Standard Scores

Some Statistics

This chapter is not intended for statisticians or mathematically oriented teachers (though they may read it too). It is geared to convey in simple terminology enough statistical insights to enable the reader to understand testing better. Actually, you already know some of the terms, such as *standard deviation* and *correlation coefficient*, from our previous discussions. (If the reader has been exposed to basic statistics either in course work or in other readings he could skip Statistics and go on to Norms and Standard Scores.)

Educators and psychologists talk a great deal about individual differences. Through measurement techniques as well as other devices there is a continual search to find out how humans distribute themselves on some measured characteristic or group of characteristics. These investigations form the basis for the inferences made about individual differences.

Rationale for Statistics

At this point let us pause and examine feelings that many of you may have toward statistics. Some of you may be saying, "What good are they? I

65457

121

won't be using them anyway." If you have encountered difficulty with mathematics, you are apt to be anxious. On the other hand, those of you who have experienced little difficulty or have found mathematics fun and exciting may be eager to begin. It is necessary, however, that all of you, no matter what your mathematical ability, learn simple shorthand techniques in elementary statistics. These are the tools of the trade. You will need to know simple statistical procedures in order to give meaning to your standardized testing programs; in order to evaluate properly standardized tests of scholastic aptitude, achievement, and so on; and in order to read intelligently professional books and journals.

If you are one of those who finds numbers confusing, you may take comfort from the following:

1. It is said that Charles Darwin frankly admitted trouble with statistics.

2. Sir Francis Galton, who was instrumental in introducing statistics into psychology, at times had to ask others to help or to do some of his mathematical problems.

3. The advent of the computer enables the student to concentrate on the *use* rather than on the *mechanics* of statistics. Thus, those of you who are mathematically unsophisticated need not be greatly concerned. The important thing today is understanding when to use a certain technique or method.

4. The advanced statistics that require mathematical insight and skill need not concern the teacher and school counselor.

5. Elementary statistics requires no more than an average seventh-grade understanding of arithmetic.

Language

A number of symbols and shorthand devices have been developed in order to enable us to describe the characteristics of groups and individuals in comparison with other groups. These symbols are similar to the symbols you are now putting together in order to read this page. That is, I have translated my neurological impulses into *learned word symbols* which we call thoughts. These thoughts I have further translated into learned letter symbols which are being put together to form *learned word* or *thought symbols*. These symbols you recognize as words on paper but more importantly they communicate ideas or "thoughts" to you.

In communicating the information necessary to understand tests and test results we use a different language, the language of statistics. Thus with a single number, letter, or symbol an idea may be conveyed which would require a paragraph, or even a page, of verbal discourse.

The objective of statistics in testing is to *describe* a score, a set of scores, and the various relationships between them. A score on any measure or test has little or no meaning in and of itself. Meaning is given to a score by its relationship to other scores in a given measure. Let us consider for a moment what information you need on a score or set of scores:

1. The range of scores.
2. The distribution.
3. The frequency with which the same score was obtained.
4. The average score.

Why do we need this information? Obviously, if you give a test to your students with 100 items and no one gets more than ten correct, this is not a good test for your class. A test, classroom or standardized, *must* distinguish between those students who have mastered the subject or possess a given characteristic and those who have not mastered the material or possess the characteristic. Carried further, the test should tell us the relative degree to which the student has these skills or abilities.

Even if we have a wide range of scores on our 100-item test, but most of the students receive the same score, this test is not distinguishing between students.

All this information can be conveyed quickly and simultaneously by using numbers arranged in certain ways.

Ranking Scores

One way to see quickly the range of scores is to arrange them in order from highest to lowest. Let us for a moment assume that we are all teachers of English. One of us has recently administered a vocabulary test to ten ninth-grade students. At this time we are primarily interested in scores (not in total number of questions on the test). Table 5 presents the scores from highest to lowest. A simple inspection of the scores in Table 5 reveals that they range from 3 to 8, whereas all other scores are in order of magnitude between these extremes.

Table 5 Scores on Vocabulary Test for Ninth-Grade Students

8
7
7
6
6
6
5
5
4
3

Frequency Distribution

We can simplify our picture of these scores by putting all scores that are the same together. But to account for the number of students having the same score, we need a new column of figures which will tell us how many students received that score.

The column for scores we head X; the column that represents the number of people obtaining that score we head f. N is used to designate the number of subjects tested.

Using our small group for illustrative purposes, let us look at our English scores through shorthand. (Obviously the small number cited does not require shorthand; however, when the numbers are increased a hundredfold or more, the need becomes more apparent.) Table 6 shows that three students obtained the score of 6; two scored 5 and 7, respectively; whereas scores of 8, 4, and 3 were obtained by three different students.

Table 6 Frequency Distribution of Scores on a Vocabulary Test for Ninth-Graders

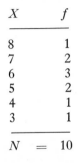

X	f
8	1
7	2
6	3
5	2
4	1
3	1
N	$=$ 10

The numbers and letters are arranged to form a *frequency distribution* of scores. *Frequency* means number of occurrences. *Distribution* means the way in which something occurs. When we put these two words together we have *frequency distribution*. Our frequency distribution shows the number of raw scores and the number of students obtaining a given score. Our shorthand system allows us to use X to represent *raw score*. Raw score means simply the number of items or questions right. The letter f represents the number or *frequency* of students obtaining a given score.

Class Interval

We can further simplify our presentation of a set of scores by grouping several together to form fewer groups. This is necessary when there is a large number of scores. For example, you have been given a set of IQ scores listed in Table 7. Scores presented in this manner do not convey much useful information. Concerning such a set of data we would generally want to know

Table 7 Scores on an IQ Test

125	133	135	137	155	127	140	133
134	129	144	136	122	151	129	121
133	142	115	136	141	120	125	138
115	127	127	133	146	110	116	134
146	121	119	126	119	117	124	121
139	128	147	118	127	128	129	132
114	116						

several things—the average IQ score, the amount of variability in this group, and the distribution of scores. In order to answer these questions we must set up a frequency distribution. This time we need to bunch up our scores in order to save time. To do this we must establish a *class interval*.

The term *class interval* may be defined as an arbitrary tool for arranging data in groups. Our data on IQ tests should be arranged so that they are easier to handle. One method of arrangement is the class interval system. Each possible score must be accounted for within the range from highest to lowest.

The first thing to be decided in constructing the class intervals for this data is the size of the class interval or group. The size of the class interval is determined by the rule that there should be not less than ten nor more than twenty class intervals. The usual grouping is fifteen. In dealing with small numbers of scores fewer class intervals are favored because of convenience. In grouping data certain minor errors are introduced into the calculations. The cruder the grouping—that is, the smaller number of groups—the greater the chance for error. In determining the size of the class interval we are guided by the need to reduce our data to the number of groups chosen.

Let us now look at our scores in Table 7; 155 is the highest and 110 is the lowest. Thus, our range is from 110 to 155. Because we have a small number of scores, we will arrange them in ten groups. Now our question is how many scores will be in each group. In determining this we obtain the range of scores; add 1 to the highest score and subtract the lowest score ($155 + 1 - 110 = 46$). We then divide 10 into 46, which is 4.6, round it off to the nearest whole number, and our class interval is 5. If we had chosen fifteen groups, our computation would have yielded 3.06 and our class interval would have been 3. You should remember that the basic purpose of grouping scores is to make a convenient representation.

In summary, the following steps were involved:

1. Highest score plus 1 minus lowest score ($155 + 1 - 110 = 46$).
2. Divide the range by number of groups desired ($46/10 = 4.6$).
3. Round off to nearest whole number ($4.6 = 5$).

Table 8 Frequency Distribution of IQ Scores with Scores Grouped by Class Intervals

Scores	Tally Marks	Frequencies (f)
155–159	1	1
150–154	1	1
145–149	111	3
140–144	1111	4
135–139	ℍℍ 1	6
130–134	ℍℍ 11	7
125–129	ℍℍ ℍℍ 11	12
120–124	ℍℍ 1	6
115–119	ℍℍ 111	8
110–114	11	2

$$\Sigma f = 50 = N$$

Table 8 shows our data grouped in class intervals of 5. In order to obtain the frequencies we have used a system of tallies. Each mark in the column marked "tally marks" represents one individual having a score in that five-point range. For instance, in the range 140–144 we see that four scores fell in this range. We do not know the exact score for any of these individuals, that is, whether a score was 140, 141, 142, 143, or 144. We have to assume that they were evenly distributed.

Graphic Representation

We may also show a set of scores by "drawing a picture" of them. Let us again refer to the data in Table 8. An inspection of the distribution shows us that the most frequent scores occur in the interval 125–129, and that the very low and very high scores are less numerous. The greatest cluster of scores is in the lower half of the range. The following are two different representations of the same data in pictorial form:

In Figures 6 and 7, the frequency of the IQ scores can be more readily viewed than in Table 8. The histogram (Figure 6) is sometimes referred to as "piling up the bodies," because each square represents an individual who obtained that score. When more than one score falls in a given class interval, it is represented by making that pile another square higher. The score intervals can be seen along the abscissa (horizontal base-line). The ordinate (vertical height) represents the frequencies. Thus, we read from the histogram that seven individuals scored in the range 130–134 and so forth.

The same data is pictured in Figure 7 in the form of a frequency polygon.

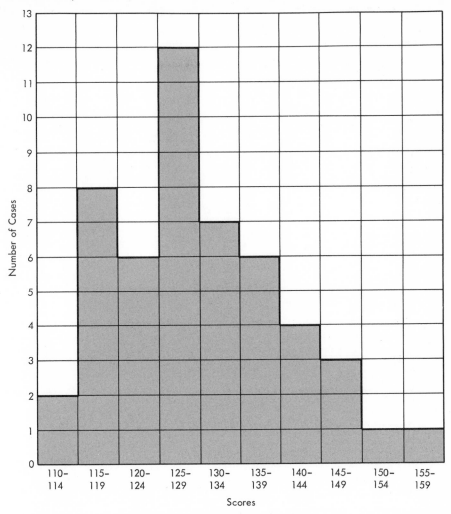

Figure 6. Histogram of fifty IQ scores.

The midpoint of each of the score intervals has been plotted. The height of the point equals the frequency in the interval. These points have been connected to show graphically the distribution of scores. The histogram and frequency polygon are generally similar devices to illustrate the same facts. There are, however, advantages and disadvantages to both. On the whole, the frequency polygon is generally preferred to the histogram because it gives a better showing of the shape of the distribution. The student who is interested in pursuing this area in more depth should consult one of the many statistics tests which offer a more definitive treatment of the subject. (See, for example, Guilford, 1965; Gourevitch, 1965; Chase, 1967.)

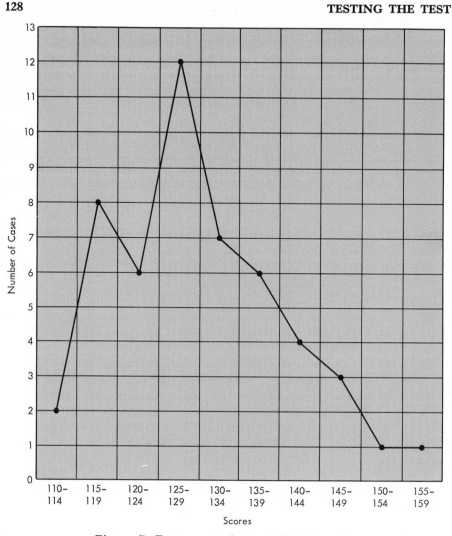

Figure 7. Frequency polygon of fifty IQ scores.

Measures of Central Tendency

We stated that one piece of information we need concerning a set of scores is the average. A measure of central tendency is just that: the average of a set of scores.

The teacher who is planning materials for her seventh-grade class needs to know something about the general abilities and achievements of her students. If, for example, she is going to order a set of reading books, she needs to know the reading skills of the typical student in order to purchase the books appropriate with their level of skills. Averages give us clues to the characteristics of a group. They do not tell us about the exceptions on either side of the average.

Chase (1967) cites three principal uses of averages:

> (1) They indicate the amount of a given condition which is typical for a defined group of individuals;
> (2) They provide a basis for comparing a condition in one group with the same condition in a second group; and
> (3) They allow us to estimate a typical condition for many individuals when we have measurements on only a portion of the total number of those individuals [p. 27].

Many people think of an "average" as the sole product of an arithmetic process, but there are different types of averages that are useful in portraying the typical of a given group. Each of these is calculated by a different procedure. These averages are the *mode*, the *median*, and the *mean*. Thus these three measures that indicate a typical condition or the average performance of a given group are what we mean by *measures of central tendency*. They are called measures of central tendency rather than averages because the word *average* is a general term. And because there are different types of statistical averages, it is a meaningless word without proper reference to the kind of average being described. For example, in describing a group's reading level at the national *median* for seventh-grade students not only are you signifying that they are typical or average in performance, but you are stating how this average was computed. You are stating precisely your statistical frame of reference. Let us look at these three measures of central tendency in terms of what they mean and how thay may be derived.

Mean ($\overline{X}$)

The mean[1] is one of the most widely used measures of central tendency; it is the arithmetic average that you have been using for years in computing your grade averages in school. For example, let us suppose that you have been asked by the Dean of Pedagogy to submit your overall undergraduate grade average for evaluation. This is a rather simple procedure for you. You sit down and count the number of A's, B's, C's, D's, and F's and their hours of credit. Let us suppose that at your college an A is equal to 4 points; B equal to 3 points; C equal to 2 points; D equal to 1 point; and F equal to zero. Let us also suppose that all your 120 hours were made up of three-hour courses. Thus you would have taken forty three-hour courses (120 ÷ 3 = 40).

---

[1] It should be noted that two other types of measures of central tendency are also used. These are the *geometric mean* and the *harmonic mean*. These are rarely used by teachers, guidance counselors, or psychologists and need not concern the beginning student.

Now let us use the frequency distribution to help compute your grade average. Remember X = raw score and f = frequency of these scores. Upon inspection of your transcript you find that you earned the following grades: (1) ten A's; (2) twenty B's; (3) five C's; (4) two D's; and (5) three F's.

Grades and Their Values in Tabular Form

X	f	fX
4	10	40
3	20	60
2	5	10
1	2	2
0	3	0
$N = 40$		112
		ΣfX

Here we have introduced some new symbols. You remember that N equals number; in this case N = number of courses. In other situations it may equal number of scores, number of persons, and so forth. Our new symbol is Σ. Σ equals summation ("adding up" or "sum up"). In your situation, then, N equals the number of courses you have taken and Σ equals the total frequency of these grades multiplied by the weighted grade. Thus, fX is frequency times grade weight or scores. A is equal to four points. You received ten A's. Ten times the weighted grade of A equals 40. Let us continue to figure out your grade average. We know that you had forty courses ($N = 40$) and the sum of these times their frequency (ΣfX) after weighting equals 112. You know that in order to find the average you must now divide the total or sum of the weighted scores by the number of courses. Your arithmetical procedure is the following:

$$
\begin{array}{r}
2.80 \\
40 \overline{\smash{\big)}\ 112.00} \\
80 \\
\hline
320 \\
320 \\
\hline
00
\end{array}
$$

Thus, your undergraduate grade average is 2.80, or a C+. Those D's and F's hurt your grade average and worked against the effect of ten A's and twenty B's. On the other hand, the A's and B's helped you in making up for the three failures and two near failures.

The following frequency distribution allows us to look at your grade average through the symbols of statistics:

Frequency Distribution of College Grades and
Steps in Calculating Grade Point Average

X	f	fX
4	10	40
3	20	60
2	5	10
1	2	2
0	3	0
N =	40	112
		ΣfX

$$\bar{X} = \frac{\Sigma fX}{N} = \frac{112}{40}, \text{ or } \bar{X} = 2.80.$$

You have just completed your grade average, or in statistical jargon, the *mean* or *arithmetic average*. The mean grade from forty different grades is therefore 2.80.

The mean uses more of the available information in a distribution than the mode and median. Less information is used in computing the others in that the mean uses all the scores. In most cases the mean provides a more sensitive index of central tendency. There are situations, however, when the use of every score can be a disadvantage. For example, you are attempting to find out the average income in your school district. There are 10,000 wage earners, most of whom earn salaries in the $8,000 to $12,000 range. There are, however, ten people whose income is $100,000 or more, and one person is reputed to earn close to $1 million a year. The arithmetic average would not, of course, be the appropriate statistic to use. The few wage earners with much greater incomes would distort the final average and would make your school district's typical income much higher than it really is.

Median (Mdn.)

In our previous illustration the case of a few high incomes was shown to distort the usefulness of the mean. The median would not be so affected because when computing it we would give equal weight to all the scores. That is, an income of $1 million would have an equal place with an income of $8,000. This is because we count frequencies up or down in calculating the median. The median is the midpoint of a set of scores. We may also say it is the score below which 50 per cent of the cases fall and above which 50 per cent of the cases fall.

Let us simplify our income data for illustrative purposes. Table 9 shows nine wage earners; one earning $100,000 a year and the rest earning under $10,000. This table illustrates the use of the median as well as how the mean can give a distorted picture of a set of numbers or scores. In this case note

Table 9 Average Incomes of Nine Wage Earners Using the Mean and Median

Wage Earner	Annual Income	Median Procedure	Mean Procedure
Jones	$100,000	(1) Counting down five cases	18,000
Smith	9,000	(2)	9 | 162,000
Leslie	8,500	(3)	9
Stern	8,300	(4)	
Foster	8,000	(5) median	72
Stevens	7,500	(4)	72
Shoemaker	7,200	(3)	
Marty	7,000	(2) Counting up five cases	0
Nelson	6,500	(1)	Mean = $18,000
$N = 9$	$162,000		Median = 8,000

how Jones' income changes the mean but has little influence on the median.

In computing the median we count up or down to exactly half of the scores or in this case the wage earners. Thus with nine salaries represented the median would be the fifth, which is $8,000. The mean income for this group is $18,000. We see that the mean is $10,000 more than the median. Both the median and the mean are "averages," but for this data the median is a more accurate representation of the typical wage of the group.

Theoretically, in a normal distribution curve the mean, median, and mode will all fall on the same point. We shall discuss this further in our discussion of the normal curve. If you have a large discrepancy between any of these three measures of central tendency for a group of data, a visual inspection is called for to determine what is distorting the figures.

Mode (Mo.)

The mode is a very crude statistic and generally not very useful. However, it is easy to find and gives a quick and rough measure of central tendency. For example, you have fifty English test scores and you want to know five minutes before a department meeting what the typical score was. You might look at the score that occurs most frequently and have a rough approximation; this most frequent score would be the mode. It is of course very possible that the mode may not indicate anything at all and be far removed from the average score. Therefore, it is recommended that you never use it except in the most pressing cases and use it then with the utmost reservations.

Measures of Variability

In describing a set of scores, in addition to central tendency it is desirable to have some data on how scores vary from the measure of central tendency. The most commonly used index of variability is called the *standard deviation*.

Standard Deviation

Generally, the term *standard deviation* is used to signify variability from the mean. Popham (1967) describes it quite well when he says, "Actually, the standard deviation is somewhat analogous to the mean. While the mean is an average of the scores in a set, the standard deviation is a sort of average of how distant the individual scores in a distribution are removed from the mean itself" (p. 16). Put another way, it is a statistic that portrays a given distribution of scores. A large standard deviation indicates a wide spread of scores whereas a small standard deviation reveals less score spread.

If we turn our attention to a particular type of distribution, which is called the "normal" curve, we may perceive standard deviation more clearly. A normal distribution is a symmetrical, bell-shaped curve, which represents a theoretical distribution of scores.

Figure 8 represents a normal curve in which you will note that most of the space is in the center with an equally decreasing amount as we go from the midline. Note that a line is drawn bisecting the curve into two equal portions. This line represents the mean (as well, of course, as the median and mode).

In a normal curve the area on both sides of the mean in which approximately 68 per cent of the scores fall is designated as plus and minus one standard deviation from the mean.

Figure 9 reveals the normal curve with the standard deviations and the percentages of cases in each deviation. The whole area of the curve represents the total universe or total number of scores in the distribution. Vertical lines have been drawn to the base line at the mean and at intervals designated as

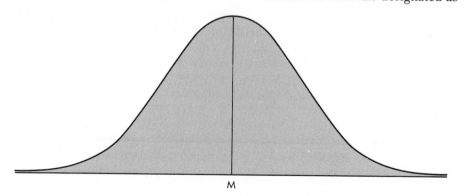

M

Figure 8. A normal curve.

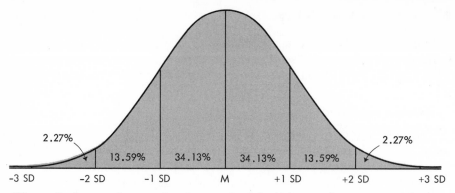

Figure 9. A normal curve showing standard deviations and percentages of cases in each.

+1 to +4 on the right and −1 to − 4 on the left. The areas between these lines contain the percentages of cases or people to be found under that section of the curve. In the theoretical normal curve there is an exact relationship (mathematical) between the standard deviation and the ratio or proportion of cases. In an IQ test with a normal distribution which has a mean of 100 and a standard deviation of 10, 34.13 per cent of the scores would fall somewhere between the mean and +1 standard deviation, or between 100 and 110 IQ points. In the same way 34.13 per cent of the scores would fall somewhere between the mean and −1 standard deviation, or between 90 and 100 IQ points.

It can thus be seen that 68.26 per cent of cases shown on a "normal curve" occur somewhere between +1 and −1 standard deviations from the mean. This means approximately two thirds of all scores in a normal distribution lie between ±1 standard deviation from the mean. Similarly, a little over 95 per cent (95.44) of scores will fall between + 2 and −2 standard deviations from the mean, and almost all the scores (99.9 per cent) will be somewhere between +3 and −3 standard deviations from the mean. Standard deviation units and percentile equivalents may be seen in Table 10.

Table 10 Standard Deviations and Percentile Equivalents*

Standard Deviation	Percentile Equivalents
+3	99
+2	98
+1	84
0 ($\overline{\text{X}}$)	50
−1	16
−2	2
−3	0.1

* Note that percentiles are rounded.

The exactness of the number of cases which will always be found in a normal curve between ±3 standard deviations from the mean enables us to use it as a gauge to compare groups and individuals. Most distributions, of course, are not "normal" and the exact relationships will not always hold. It is true, however, that many distributions are close enough to the "normal curve" that we may make certain assumptions; the standard deviation in these situations means almost the same thing as it would in the "normal curve."

If you have a student who is +1 standard deviation from the mean on a test (if, of course, the group at least approximates the "normal" distribution), you can state that he is at the 84th percentile compared to the group of people that the test producer used in determining the distribution. Put another way you can say that roughly he surpasses 84 per cent of the group to whom he is being compared (50 per cent below the mean and 34 per cent between the mean and +1 standard deviation).

In terms of scores, the standard deviation becomes greater as the scores are more widely spread. That is, the larger the standard deviation, the wider the spread of scores. Thus, we have some idea of the variability of a set of scores by the size of the standard deviation. Later in this chapter we shall discuss standard scores in relationship to the normal curve.

Correlation

In our discussion of validity and reliability (see Chapter 4) we have already encountered this area of statistics. Correlation is a measure of relationship. What is the relationship, for example, between high school grades and college success? Or what is the relationship between parental education and children's success in school? These and other questions may be answered (at least in part) by the use of a statistic called the correlation coefficient (r). We stated that a correlation of +1 signifies a perfect relationship whereas a −1 indicates the opposite. A zero correlation coefficient means there is no relationship. Before you read further go back to Chapter 4 and review correlation.

Table 11 presents two sets of scores, one set on test X and one on test Y. These scores were made by the same students, each student having one score on both test X and test Y. If we inspect Table 11 we note that the student who made the highest score on test X made the highest score on Test Y. The student who made the second highest score on test X made the second highest score on test Y, and the exact correlation continues throughout the scores. This illustrates a perfect (+1) correlation.

Figure 10 reveals the scores of Table 11 in a *scatter diagram* format. Note the class intervals that we talked about before are now used in this diagram. The scores have been grouped in class intervals of two. Each column in the diagram intersects with every row. This creates a cell at each intersection. Every cell signifies a unique combination of one of the scores of test X with one of the scores of test Y. For example, Mary has a score of

Table 11 Scores of Ten Students
on Two Tests

Students	Test X	Test Y
James	12	14
Mary	13	15
David	16	18
Joe	17	19
Kim	18	20
Cathy	20	22
Lou	21	23
Lynn	24	26
Sue	26	28
Beth	27	29

13 on test X and a score of 15 on test Y. Look at Table 11 and locate at the top the class interval containing Mary's X test score. This is in the second column from the left. Move down this column until you locate, on the left margin, the interval containing Mary's Y test score, which is in the third row from the bottom. Thus, our tally is placed in that cell which has been made by the intersection of the row and column.

Note that all the tallies fall along a straight line. This form of relationship is an indication of a linear correlation. There is a direct, and high relationship between the two sets of scores.

The teacher and counselor should remember that correlation is a measure of mutual relation. Our basic question is, "What is the relationship between two or more variables?" As you know, correlation coefficients tell us many things. Of special importance to the student of measurement is its use with reliability, validity, and prediction. It is a basic tool in estimating these very important factors.

Norms

Mrs. Stone was so proud of her son Robert because he had an IQ of 100. Mrs. Stone thought, of course, that 100 was a perfect score. She did not know that an IQ of 100 was average. As future teachers or counselors you should remember that no score is meaningful unless you know on what basis it was derived. In one test, for example, a score of 200 would really mean that the student did not answer even one question correctly. Always ask, then, for the frame of reference of the child's test scores. A number is meaningless without it. Even a simple raw score which indicates the number of items answered correctly is not meaningful unless you know how many questions were asked and what the factors are that indicate a good showing.

In order to convey meaningful information about test performance and

Scores on Test X

Scores on Test Y	11–12	13–14	15–16	17–18	19–20	21–22	23–24	25–26	27–28
29–30									I
27–28								I	
25–26							I		
23–24						I			
21–22					I				
19–20				II					
17–18			I						
15–16		I							
13–14	I								
11–12									

Figure 10. Scatter diagram from Table 11.

scores we translate the raw score into *norms*. These norms are reference points that compare raw scores with different factors. For example, a raw score of 10 on a given test may indicate a gifted child at the first-grade level whereas the same score for an eighth-grade child may indicate retardation. Thus, a raw score is given meaning only when we refer it to the appropriate norms. Some of the norms we shall discuss are age norms, grade norms, percentile norms, and standard score norms.

Age Norms

EDUCATIONAL AGE

Some standardized achievement tests use educational age as a norm. The test is administered to a representative sample (normative group) of youngsters from different schools and geographic locations and ages. Average scores are obtained for each age level. The raw score of a particular pupil can be compared to these norms and an educational age (EA) derived. If, for example, a twelve-year-old achieves an educational age score of 12, he would be considered perfectly average. If he obtained an educational age score of 10, we would interpret this as meaning he is behind his age group. These norms are most appropriate at the elementary level; however, in the area of achievement, there is serious question of their worth. Children mature at different rates and the equality of educational age norms is open to question. More importantly, there is no way of comparing educational ages, because all achievement tests are based upon unequal and different units of measurements.

MENTAL AGE

The mental age (MA) norm is provided by some test publishers for the interpretation of intelligence test scores. A child is compared with the norm of his age group. In this way we may know whether he is more "intelligent" or less "intelligent" than the average child of his age. The eight-year-old child who performs as well as the average ten-year-old is said to have a mental age of 10.

This procedure, because of its difficulties in construction as well as other factors, is being slowly phased out of testing. It is very difficult, for example, to get a representative group of children of a given age. They are many times located in different grades. The equality, as in educational age norms, of mental age units is doubtful. This is especially true as an individual goes from adolescence to adulthood and age ceases to have very much meaning. If mental age is to be used, it is most appropriate in interpreting general intelligence. We will have more to say on mental age in our discussion of IQ quotients. It should, however, be noted that Binet introduced the concept of mental age and in the latest revision of the Stanford-Binet standard scores replace age scales (Terman and Merrill, 1960).

Grade Norms

The grade norm (also called grade-placement norms) is very similar to age norms. It is obtained by finding the average scores for students at different grade levels. The same process of finding representative groups of pupils is used as in finding educational norms.

The chief advantage of grade norms over age norms is that comparisons are made among children who have had the same amount of educational exposure. The standard method of expressing grade norms is by assigning a number to each grade—for example, the number 6.0 would indicate average performance at the beginning of sixth grade; 6.5 would indicate average performance in the middle of the school year or grade. The tenths of grade placement for any testing date may be ascertained by an inspection of Table

12. Note that beneath the dates are tenths of the school year for students entering in September. For example, a student in the eighth grade during the period between February 16 and March 15 who is exactly average on a given test would have a grade equivalent of 8.6. That is, his performance is about equal to the typical student who has completed 0.6 of the eighth grade.

Table 12 Grade Placement at Time of Testing

Date of Testing	Sept. 1–Sept. 15	Sept. 16–Oct. 15	Oct. 16–Nov. 15	Nov. 16–Dec. 15	Dec. 16–Jan. 15	Jan. 16–Feb. 15	Feb. 16–Mar. 15	Mar. 16–Apr. 15	Apr. 16–May 15	May 16–June 15
Grade Placement	0.0	0.1	0.2	0.3	0.4	0.5	0.6	0.7	0.8	0.9

Reproduced from *Stanford Achievement Test Battery, Advanced, Directions for Administering.* Copyright 1964 by Harcourt, Brace & World, Inc. Reproduced by special permission of the publisher.

Table 13 presents a hypothetical distribution of raw scores and their grade equivalents which would be similar to normative data presented in a test manual. Thus, if Ray Gold, an eighth-grade student, had a raw score of 25, his grade equivalent or grade placement score would be 10.8.

Table 13 Raw Scores and Their Grade Equivalents for the X Test of Social Studies for Junior High Students

Raw Score	Grade Equivalent	Raw Score	Grade Equivalent
30	12.5	15	6.8
29	12.0	14	6.6
28	11.8	13	6.3
27	11.6	12	6.1
26	11.2	11	5.9
25	10.8	10	5.5
24	10.3	9	5.0
23	9.7	8	4.5
22	9.2	7	4.0
21	8.7	6	3.5
20	8.4	5	3.0
19	8.0	4	2.5
18	7.7	3	2.0
17	7.3	2	1.5
16	7.1	1	. . .

Most measurement authorities today question the advisability of using grade norms, especially in reporting test results to parents. This is because they seem to be so simple that misunderstandings often result from their use. At first glance one is apt to interpret from our previous example as indicating that the student is advanced enough to work at a higher grade than he is actually able to do. This assumption could be entirely untrue. Thus, Ray Gold's score indicates that he has obtained a score equal to the average score earned by children in the tenth grade. This may only mean that he has mastered most of the work at or below his grade level. The average eighth-grader, on the other hand, will of course miss more of the items.

Durost (1961b) illustrates quite well the basic point of our discussion when he states,

> A fifth-grade child who has really learned to compute accurately may do ten straight computation examples without error, while the average child who has not mastered all his number combinations or is unsure in borrowing or carrying will miss several of these problems. The higher score earned by the first child will result in his receiving a grade equivalent substantially beyond his grade placement; yet he could not work at that level successfully because he has not been exposed to the new processes and learnings normally taught in the higher grade [p. 1].

Percentile Norms

Percentiles are as easily understood as grade norms and do not suffer from the same limitations. A percentile norm rank indicates the proportion of students who fall below a given score. *It does not mean the percentage of questions answered correctly.* It means the percentage of people whose performance a student has equaled or surpassed. Thus, if 75 per cent of the students to whom Betty is being compared score lower, she is at the 75th percentile. That is, on a given test Betty has done better than 75 per cent of the students taking the test and 25 per cent have scored higher.

Tables 14 and 15 present percentile norms for the Differential Aptitude Tests. The norms in these Tables are for tenth-grade students in their first semester (fall of the year). The test manual presents similar norm tables for boys and girls from grade eight through grade twelve. Note that Table 14 presents norms for boys and Table 15 gives norms for girls. The reference, or "norm," group is especially important for accurate and meaningful test interpretations. The teacher or counselor inspecting these tables is immediately given data to assist him in knowing to whom he is comparing his students.

An inspection of Tables 14 and 15 reveals raw scores under the various tests in the battery with percentile rankings for each score. Let us suppose we want to find the percentile rankings for two students on the abstract reasoning test (Abst. Reas.). Both Susan and Wyatt have a raw score of 42. Looking at the numbers under "Abst. Reas." for boys we find that a raw score of 42 is equivalent to the 90th percentile. Wyatt's percentile norm for "Abst. Reas." is therefore at the 90th percentile level. Susan has the same raw score as Wyatt. Do you think her percentile level will therefore be the same? If Susan were a boy her percentile level would be the same. Susan is a girl, however, and we must, on this test, compare her to other tenth-grade females. Table 14 presents norms for girls similar to Susan. That is, they were tested in the tenth grade during the first semester in the fall of the year. Looking under "Abst. Reas." we find Susan's raw score of 42 equivalent to the 85th percentile. Thus, both Wyatt and Susan have the same raw scores, that is, number of correct answers, but Wyatt is at a higher percentile ranking because of normative sexual differences. When we say that Wyatt is at the 90th percentile, we are correct if we have explained beforehand the reference group, that is, if we have defined "those taking the test."

It should be noted that not every percentile is given in Tables 14 and 15. More detailed tables would reveal percentiles for each score; Tables 14 and 15, except for the extreme top and bottom, present percentiles in steps of five. Several raw scores are often equivalent to a single percentile. Though we could be more exact, this type of estimation is sufficient in most cases.

Percentiles are extensively used because they are easy to interpret and do not have the glaring shortcomings of educational age and grade norms. They have been and are being used today to report test scores on a wide variety of measurement instruments, such as intelligence, aptitude, achievement, and interest tests. Percentiles can be used with almost any group. There are, however, certain limitations in their use.

First of all, the group that is being used as a reference point presents some problems. This has been seen already in our discussion of Wyatt and Susan's test scores. The discrepancy between the raw scores and percentile equivalents on the girls and boys norms was noted. It is obvious that we need different norm groups for such factors as sex, age, and grade. The group to which you compare a pupil *in every case must be* the group to which he or she belongs. It is, for example, of no value to compare a college applicant's academic aptitude scores to the scores of the general high school population. His scores must be compared to those of other college applicants in order to get a meaningful picture.

A good illustration of the test score differences reflected in various norm groups is seen in the United States Army classification tests. The norms for these tests are based on the general population of males which includes those who have not completed elementary school to those who have obtained a college or advanced degree. No distinction, at least in the past, was made according to educational background. That is, Smith, who is a college graduate, and Jones, who did not complete high school, would be in the same normative group, with no distinctions made for different educational backgrounds. For the Army's general purposes, of course, there would be no need

Table 14 Percentile Norms for Girls for the Differential Aptitude Test, Form L, Fall (first semester), Tenth Grade

Girls — N = 2,850+

Per-centile	Verb. Reas.	Num. Abil.	VR+NA	Abst. Reas.	Clerical S and A*	Mech. Reas.	Space Rela.	LU-I: Spell.	LU-II: Gram.	Per-centile
99	46–50	38–40	82–90	46–50	88–100	55–68	53–60	96–100	55–60	99
97	45	37	79–81	45	79–87	53–54	49–52	94–95	52–54	97
95	43–44	35–36	75–78	44	74–78	51–52	46–48	92–93	49–51	95
90	40–42	33–34	71–74	43	70–73	49–50	42–45	90–91	46–48	90
85	38–39	31–32	68–70	41–42	66–69	47–48	40–41	88–89	43–45	85
80	36–37	30	65–67	40	64–65	45–46	37–39	86–87	41–42	80
75	34–35	29	62–64	39	62–63	44	35–36	84–85	39–40	75
70	32–33	28	59–61	38	60–61	43	33–34	82–83	37–38	70
65	30–31	26–27	56–58	37	59	42	31–32	80–81	36	65
60	29	25	54–55	36	57–58	41	29–30	78–79	35	60
55	27–28	24	51–53	35	56	40	28	76–77	34	55
50	26	23	48–50	34	55	39	26–27	74–75	32–33	50
45	25	22	46–47	33	53–54	37–38	24–25	72–73	31	45
40	23–24	20–21	43–45	31–32	52	36	22–23	70–71	29–30	40
35	21–22	19	40–42	29–30	51	35	21	67–69	28	35
30	19–20	18	37–39	27–28	50	34	19–20	64–66	26–27	30
25	17–18	16–17	34–36	25–26	48–49	33	18	61–63	24–25	25
20	15–16	15	31–33	21–24	46–47	32	17	58–60	22–23	20
15	13–14	13–14	28–30	16–20	43–45	30–31	15–16	54–57	19–21	15
10	11–12	11–12	24–27	13–15	38–42	28–29	13–14	50–53	17–18	10
5	9–10	9–10	19–23	8–12	32–37	25–27	12	46–49	15–16	5
3	8	7–8	15–18	6–7	27–31	21–24	11	43–45	11–14	3
1	0–7	0–6	0–14	0–5	0–26	0–20	0–10	0–42	0–10	1
Mean	26.1	23.0	49.1	31.4	55.7	38.8	27.7	72.7	32.3	Mean
SD	10.8	8.1	17.7	10.6	13.4	7.9	11.2	15.1	10.7	SD

Raw Scores

* These norms for CSA are based on the use of IBM 805 answer sheets.

Table 15 Percentile Norms for Boys for the Differential Aptitude Test, Form L, Fall (first semester), Tenth Grade

Boys

| | | | | Raw Scores | | | | | | N=2,900+ |
Per-centile	Verb. Reas.	Num. Abil.	VR+ NA	Abst. Reas.	Clerical S and A*	Mech. Reas.	Space Rela.	LU-I: Spell.	LU-II: Gram.	Per-centile
99	46–50	39–40	80–90	46–50	80–100	62–68	56–60	94–100	51–60	99
97	44–45	37–38	77–79	44–45	71–79	60–61	54–55	91–93	48–50	97
95	41–43	36	73–76	43	64–70	59	51–53	89–90	45–47	95
90	39–40	34–35	70–72	42	61–63	58	48–50	85–88	42–44	90
85	38	32–33	68–69	41	59–60	56–57	45–47	81–84	39–41	85
80	36–37	31	65–67	40	57–58	55	43–44	78–80	36–38	80
75	34–35	29–30	62–64	39	55–56	53–54	40–42	76–77	34–35	75
70	32–33	28	59–61	38	54	52	38–39	73–75	33	70
65	30–31	27	56–58	37	53	51	35–37	71–72	31–32	65
60	28–29	26	54–55	36	52	50	33–34	68–70	30	60
55	27	25	51–53	35	51	49	31–32	66–67	29	55
50	26	24	49–50	34	50	48	29–30	64–65	28	50
45	24–25	23	46–48	33	49	47	27–28	62–63	27	45
40	22–23	21–22	43–45	32	47–48	46	25–26	60–61	25–26	40
35	20–21	19–20	40–42	30–31	45–46	44–45	23–24	57–59	23–24	35
30	18–19	18	37–39	28–29	44	43	21–22	55–56	22	30
25	16–17	17	34–36	26–27	42–43	41–42	20	52–54	21	25
20	14–15	15–16	31–33	23–25	40–41	39–40	17–19	50–51	18–20	20
15	12–13	13–14	27–30	18–22	37–39	36–38	15–16	47–49	15–17	15
10	10–11	11–12	24–26	13–17	34–36	33–35	13–14	44–46	13–14	10
5	8–9	9–10	20–23	9–12	28–33	28–32	12	38–43	11–12	5
3	7	7–8	16–19	6–8	22–27	24–27	11	32–37	9–10	3
1	0–6	0–6	0–15	0–5	0–21	0–23	0–10	0–31	0–8	1
Mean	25.6	23.4	49.0	32.0	49.5	47.4	31.1	65.2	28.3	Mean
SD	10.6	8.4	17.6	10.3	12.1	9.0	12.6	15.6	10.2	SD

* These norms for CSA are based on the use of IBM 805 answer sheets.

to divide the norms according to educational level. In fact, it could be harmful. Smith might not make the officer corps because he was being compared only to college graduates. On the other hand, Jones might qualify for the corps because he was the highest in his group. Thus, normative groups must be relevant for the decisions to be made.

There must be many sets of norms for a given test. The test user may then choose those most pertinent to his situation and needs. There are practical limits, however, to the number of norm groups that can be supplied by a test publisher. Schools, therefore, need to provide their "local norms" to supplement the published percentile norms. The use of "local norms" helps the school to determine the relative standing of pupils in its own system. In some situations this comparison is often more significant than the use of national norms. Let us look, for example, at three different high schools.

Stuart High School is a secondary school located in a upper-middle- to lower-upper-class suburban community. The children who attend Stuart have been exposed to a great many cultural and educational advantages. On a standardized test of academic ability the average pupil's score at Stuart is at the 75th percentile level (in the national population the average child is, of course, at the 50th percentile level). It is obvious, therefore, that Stuart must develop its own norms in order to have more meaningful comparisons and to place children in appropriate classes.

On the other hand, Lincoln High School is a secondary school located in a large urban complex referred to as the "inner-city." The average student at Lincoln on the same test of academic aptitude scores at the 35th percentile. Thus, Lincoln needs to develop local percentile norms for the same reasons as Stuart.

Pearson High School is also located in a large metropolitan area. However, Pearson draws students from diverse socioeconomic backgrounds. The average student at Pearson scores at the 55th percentile level on the same academic aptitude test. For Pearson the national percentile norms supplied by the test publisher seem to be appropriate and a valid reference point.

Another caution in the use of percentiles involves the interpretation of differences in percentile rankings. A student, for example, who ranks at the 95th percentile may get five or six more items correct than his classmate who is ranked at the 90th percentile. The student, however, who is at the 55th percentile may get only one or two more items correct than his friend who is at the 50th percentile. (See Figure 17.)

Percentile units are *unequal*. Remember, an equal percentile difference does not necessarily represent equal raw score differences. The inequality of percentiles may be seen in Figure 11. Note alongside the "percentile equivalents" the closeness of percentiles and the distance at both extremes. See, for example, how far apart the 95th and 99th percentiles are, or the 1st and 5th percentile as compared to percentiles in the 20th to 80th percentile range.

To summarize, we may state that percentile norms are reference points which provide us with a basis for interpreting a score of an individual in relation to his status in a given group. It is important that the group is relevant to the individual and our purposes for comparison. It is also important to bear in mind that percentile units are unequal and that at the extremes of the normal curve five percentile units are not equivalent to five percentile units in the middle.

Standard Scores

In our previous discussion of raw scores the rationale for converting scores into agreed upon or standard units was presented. The use of standard scores is another method to provide comparability to the meaning of a raw score. Thus, the tester in Rich Square, North Carolina, and the tester in Tokyo, Japan, would both have a similar frame of reference. This standard frame of reference is the normal curve. A standard score is based upon the number of standard deviations a given score is from the mean. Typical standard scores can be seen in Figure 11. Before continuing, turn back to the section on standard deviation and review the concept. An understanding of the standard deviation is very helpful in attaining insight into the standard score mechanism.

In Figure 11, the first standard scores are the z-scores, which are equivalent to the standard deviations. Inspecting our normal curve in Figure 11 we can see that a standard z-score of $+1$ has between it and the mean 34 per cent of the cases. A standard score of $+1$ is then equivalent to the 84th percentile and a standard score of -1 is equivalent to the 16th percentile. This relationship is always the same with standard scores for any normal distribution. If we look further we can see that -4 and $+4$ standard scores, are equal distances below and above the mean. Thus, the standard score does not suffer from the same defect of unequal units as do the percentile equivalents.

It should be noted that z-scores may be computed for any type of distribution by equating the mean to 0.00 and the standard deviation to 1.00. The z-score equivalents in Figure 11 are correct only for a normal distribution.

The use of z-scores presents some difficulties. First of all, a standard score of zero is incorrectly interpreted by some to mean a very poor performance rather than the mean or average performance. The z-score has two other disadvantages in that half are negative value and many involve decimal fractions. To eliminate these awkward and time-consuming disadvantages different standard score systems have been developed. An inspection of Typical Standard Scores in Figure 11 reveals three other types of standard scores that do not suffer from these disadvantages.

T-scores are expressed in whole numbers with a mean of 50 and a standard

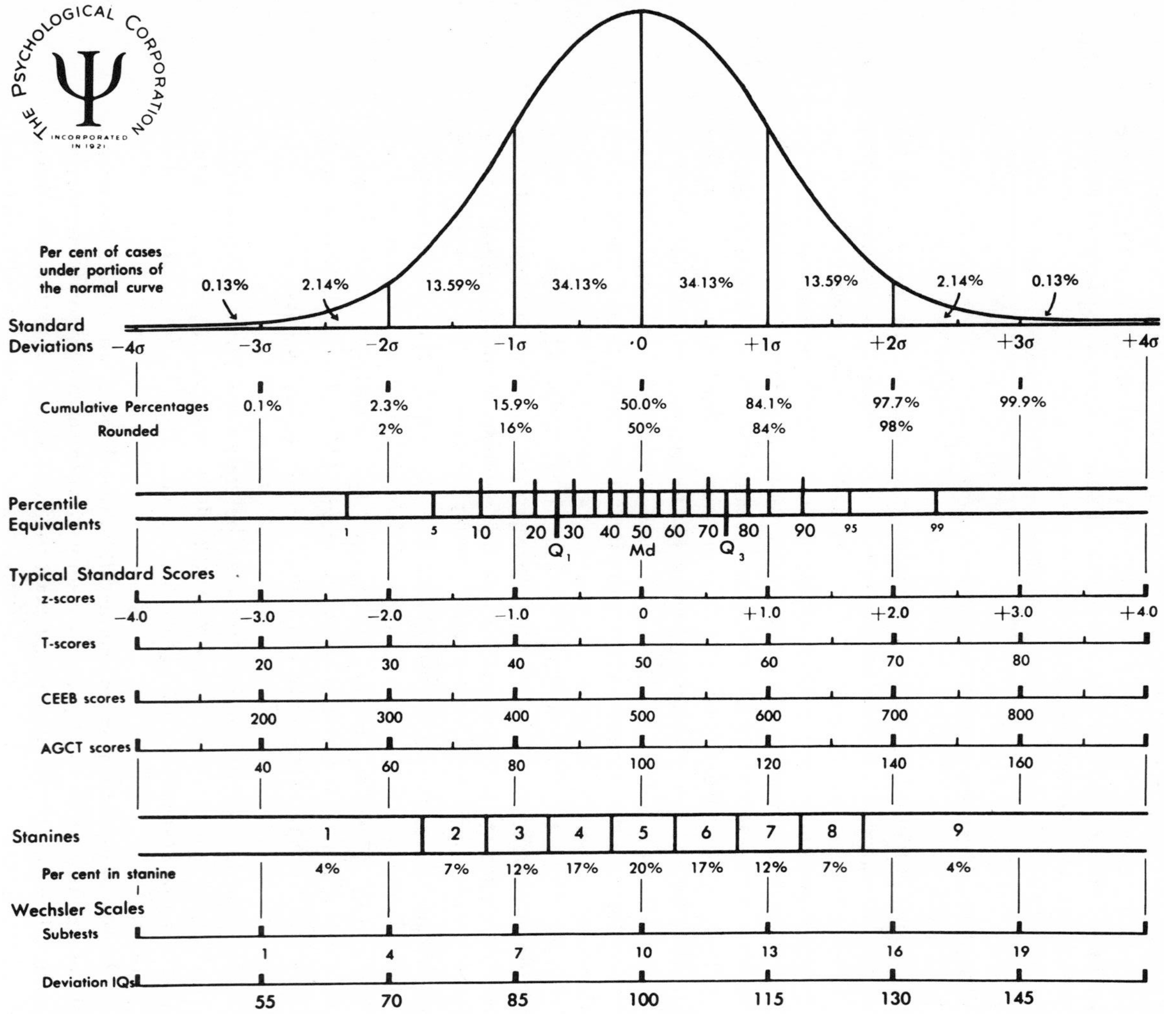

Figure 11. A normal curve showing percentiles and standard score scales. (From Test Service Bulletin, No. 48, Psychological Corporation, 1955. Reproduced by permission of The Psychological Corporation.)

deviation of 10. A T-score of 75 would be equivalent to a z-score of $+2.5$. The T-score method usually eliminates negative numbers and decimal fractions.

The CEEB (College Entrance Examination Board) has a mean of 500 and a standard deviation of 100. This eliminates both decimals and negative numbers. A high school senior, for example, who obtains a score of 600 on one of the tests would be in the 84th percentile.

The AGCT (Army General Classification Tests) scores, as can be seen in Figure 11, have a mean of 100 and a standard deviation of twenty points. This scale was developed during World War II. The United States Navy, on the other hand, expresses its test results in T-scores.

Stanines are another type of standard score; they were developed by the United States Air Force in World War II. The word *stanine* was taken from "STAndard NINE-point scale" (Durost, 1961a). Thus, a stanine scale is a nine-point scale with a mean of 5 and a standard deviation of 2. The distribution of stanines, as can be seen in Figure 11, is based upon the normal curve. Note that just below the stanines are percentages which indicate the per cent of the total found in each stanine.

The stanine score is considered by many testing authorities as the preferred method of explaining test results to students and parents and is gaining wide acceptance in our schools today. This is because stanines are easily understood and are broader in scope than other devices, yet they are precise enough for the purpose of reporting test scores. It should also be noted that in the area of research, stanines are easy to use because they are one-digit numbers. When computers are used, they are economical as well because they require only one column to signify a score on a punch card. They immediately tell the test user the standing of the pupil. For example, a student with stanines of 7, 8, or 9 is far above average in whatever measure is being sought. On the other hand, stanines of 2 or 3 indicate he is well below average. Figure 12 presents a ladder of stanines with the percentage of children reaching each rung.

Though the stanine scale is an excellent method of reporting test results it has technical limitations. Magnusson (1967) states,

> The T-scale allows finer differentiation among individuals than the stanine scale. So long as a sufficiently high reliability justifies a stricter differentiation, we will lose a certain amount of information about the individuals by giving their results as stanine scores. For a reliability of 0.91 the standard error will be $0.3s$, and for a reliability of 0.96 the standard error will be $0.2s$. For a T-scale where $s=10$, these figures indicate standard errors of 3 and 2 units respectively. The standard error is so small that the scale can be said to differentiate so accurately that one would lose valuable information if the results were to be given on a stanine scale instead of a T-scale [p. 241].

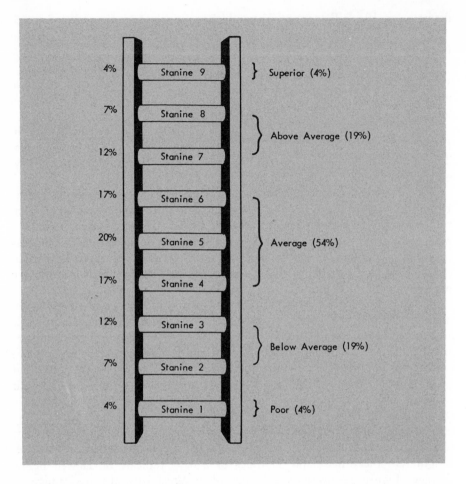

Figure 12. Stanine ladder. (Reproduced from L. J. Karmel, *Testing in Our Schools*. New York: The Macmillan Company, 1966. Copyright © 1966 by Louis J. Karmel.)

The reader who is interested in pursuing the techniques of stanine interpretation to parents and other lay persons should see Durost (1961a), Engelhart (n.d.), and Karmel (1966).

The important thing to remember about standard scores is that they are based on a normal distribution and should not be used for other data. Standard scores are meaningful only in relationship to a particular group. The standard deviation of a particular reference group and an individual's score is represented as the number of standard deviation units from the mean of the group. The main difference of the standard score over percentile rankings is that they are presented in equal steps or units.

Intelligence Quotients

A great deal of confusion, misunderstanding, and emotionalism has clouded the concept of the intelligence quotient. Basically, the intelligence quotient is no more than a formula for obtaining a type of score that was found convenient for classification of individuals. The classical formula is:

$$\text{Intelligence quotient (IQ)} = \frac{\text{Mental Age (MA)}}{\text{Chronological Age (CA)}} \times 100$$

Theoretically the intelligence quotient will be 100 for the average person. That is, if a ten-year-old child does as well on an intelligence test as average ten-year-olds in the normative group, his mental age will be 10. Translated into the formula we have the following:

$$100 \times \frac{10}{10} = 100$$

If, on the other hand, a ten-year-old does as well on an intelligence test as the average twelve-year-old, we have the following:

$$\frac{100 \times 12}{10} = 120$$

Let us look at one more example, that of a ten-year-old who has a lower mental age than his chronological years.

$$\frac{100 \times 8}{10} = 80$$

Thus our first ten-year-old is perfectly average (IQ = 100). Our second ten-year-old is above average (IQ = 120), whereas our third ten-year-old is below average (IQ = 80).

The intelligence quotient was developed originally by Wilhelm Stern for use with the Binet test of individual intelligence. (See Chapter 7.) The standard deviation of the American version of the original Binet (Stanford-Binet) is approximately 16 with a mean of 100. Many advocates of the IQ have stated that the standard deviation remains relatively uniform from age to age. That is, that an IQ of 130 indicates the same thing, relative to age group, for a four-year-old or a sixteen-year-old. Recent investigations and pronouncements from measurement specialists have not reinforced this generalization. For example, Magnusson (1967) states that "the standard deviation is not exactly the same for different ages. This means that the same intelligence quotient does not give the same relative position on distributions for different ages" (p. 242).

Another problem in the interpretation of IQ scores is the quotient variance in different tests. That is, standard deviations for various intelligence quotients varies from test to test. For example, a child or adult taking different IQ tests would obtain different intelligence quotients even though their relative positions may be the same. Engelhart (1959) presented a system to obviate this problem. His system allows for the equating of IQ's derived from different group intelligence tests. The reader should bear in mind that an IQ on X test of intelligence is not necessarily equal to an obtained IQ on Y test of intelligence. It is possible, for example, that on X test the highest obtainable IQ would be 154 whereas on the Y test the highest obtainable IQ might be 164. Again scores must be interpreted on the basis of relevant norms. The meaning of an IQ must be interpreted in the light of the test from which it was derived.

The reader should not conclude from this discussion that IQ scores derived from MA/CA are worthless. They are not and still may serve a valuable function. They give us some relative information and if the user bears in mind the standard deviation and range differences they can be useful tools.

Another word of caution is indicated. Do not confuse the previous discussion of IQ with other methods of obtaining IQ scores. The Wechsler tests of intelligence report results in an IQ format. The method used to compute IQ in these tests, however, is very different from the classical formula previously presented. The shortcomings of the IQ based on mental age have been eliminated.

Let us look back at Figure 11. At the bottom you will see the Wechsler Scales and below it the deviation IQ's. You can see that your knowledge of standard scores will be useful in understanding these scores. A person's raw score on each of the subtests is translated, using relevant norms, to a standard score. This standard score, as you can see, is based on a mean of 10 and a standard deviation of 3. The total standard scores (verbal scale, performance scale, and full scale—see Chapter 7) are then converted into IQ's. An inspection of Figure 11 shows that these IQ's are based on a mean of 100 and a standard deviation of fifteen points. Thus, roughly 68 per cent of the IQ's are between ± 1 standard deviation. Among testing people this type of estimation of IQ is known as the deviation IQ.

It should be noted that the deviation IQ does not differ from other standard score procedures. A given IQ in the distribution will always have the same relative position. A final note on this subject is of particular importance. The 1960 revision of the Stanford-Binet substituted the deviation IQ for the mental age concept. As you will recall, the formula of 100 MA/CA was originally constructed for use with the Binet. Thus, the obvious trend in testing today is to use the standard score whether we call it IQ or T-score. The *Standards for Educational and Psychological Tests and Manuals* (American Psychological Association et al., 1966) states the following:

> Standard scores should in general be used in preference to other derived scores. The system of standard scores should be consistent with the purposes for which the test is intended, and should be described in detail in the test manual. The reasons for choosing that scale in preference to other scales should also be made clear [pp. 33-34].

Practical Usage of Norms

There are two essential things to remember when trying to understand individuals by testing them. The first is the appropriateness of the test for the person and your basic purpose in testing; the second is to know how others have performed on the test. The "best" and most appropriate test that is valid and reliable will yield meaningless scores unless it is compared with other scores (Seashore and Ricks, 1950). Norms provide us with a frame of reference, for comparison.

Norms are only meaningful if they are relevant. It does little good to compare the quality of apples with that of oranges. Similarly, when Mary is compared to a normative group it should be composed of individuals of similar backgrounds. *Standards* (American Psychological Association et al., 1966), for example, cites as an essential requirement that, "Norms presented in the test manual should refer to defined and clearly described populations. These populations should be the groups to whom users of the test will ordinarily wish to compare the persons tested" (p. 35). In illustrating this essential requirement, *Standards* goes on to state,

> General aptitude tests designed for use with elementary school children might well present norms by grade-groups and by chronological age groups . . . . The manual should point out that a person who has a high degree of interest in a curriculum or occupation will generally have a much lower degree of interest when compared with persons actually engaged in that field. Thus a *high* percentile score on a scale reflecting mechanical interest, in which the examinee is compared with men-in-general, may be equivalent to a *low* percentile when the examinee is compared with auto mechanics [p. 35].

Teachers and counselors are often called upon to advise students about college and their chances for admission. Sound and meaningful advice is based on several factors, such as the student's high school grades, college admission test scores, and the academic caliber of students at the desired college. In a sense most of these are norms. That is, comparison of relevant factors of the student with relevant factors of the college. Put these together and we have meaningful comparisons. Look at Tables 16 and 17 and note the differences in median scores in each table.

Table 16 presents a general population of high school seniors, Table 17, on the other hand, is a selected group composed of high school seniors planning to go on to college.

If a student had standard scores of 18 in English, 16 in mathematics, 17 in social studies, and 19 in natural science, he would be average or above (60th percentile, 57th percentile, 51st percentile, 64th percentile) compared to the "unselected" seniors found in Table 16. If, on the other hand, we look at Table 17 we find a dramatically different picture. Comparing this

Table 16 Percentile Ranks of Unselected High School Seniors*

	Standard Score	Test 1 English	Test 2 Mathematics	Test 3 Social Studies	Test 4 Natural Sciences	Tests 1–4 Composite	Standard Score
	36						36
	35		99.9				35
	34		99.8				34
	33		99.6		99.9		33
	32		99.2	99.9	99.5	99.9	32
	31		98	99.3	98.8	99.7	31
	30	99.9	97	98	98	99.4	30
	29	99.6	96	96	96	99.1	29
	28	98.9	95	94	95	98	28
136 School	27	98	93	92	93	97	27
Systems in	26	96	91	90	90	95	26
Thirty-nine	25	93	89	86	87	92	25
States	24	91	87	83	83	89	24
9,370 Students	23	87	84	79	79	86	23
	22	82	80	74	75	82	22
	21	77	76	70	71	78	21
	20	72	72	66	68	73	20
	19	66	68	61	64	68	19
	18	60	65	56	59	63	18
	17	54	61	51	55	58	17
	16	46	57	46	49	52	16
	15	38	52	42	44	46	15
	14	32	47	38	39	41	14
	13	26	41	33	35	35	13
	12	22	36	28	30	30	12
	11	17	30	23	26	24	11
	10	13	25	19	22	18	10
	9	10	20	14	17	13	9
	8	7	16	10	13	9	8
	7	5	12	7	10	6	7
	6	4	8	4	7	4	6
	5	3	6	3	5	2	5
	4	2	5	2	4	1	4
	3	1	4	2	2		3
	2		2	1	1		2
	1						1
Median Score		16.5	14.5	16.8	16.1	15.6	

*From *Using ACT on the Campus,* © 1965 American College Testing Program, Inc. Used by permission of the American College Testing Program, Inc.

Table 17 Percentile Ranks of College-Bound High School Seniors*

	Standard Score	Test 1 English	Test 2 Mathe- matics	Test 3 Social Studies	Test 4 Natural Sciences	Tests 1–4 Com- posite	Standard Score
	36		99.9				36
	35		99.8				35
	34		99.3	99.9	99.9		34
	33		98.5	99.8	99.6		33
	32		97	99.2	98.9	99.9	32
	31	99.9	95	98	98	99.6	31
	30	99.7	93	96	96	98.8	30
	29	99.1	91	93	93	97	29
	28	98	88	89	89	95	28
882,080 Students	27	96	85	85	84	91	27
	26	92	81	80	79	87	26
	25	88	77	74	73	82	25
	24	81	72	69	67	75	24
	23	74	66	63	60	68	23
	22	67	61	57	55	61	22
	21	59	56	51	49	53	21
	20	51	51	45	44	46	20
	19	42	46	38	39	38	19
	18	34	40	33	33	31	18
	17	27	34	28	27	25	17
	16	21	28	22	22	19	16
	15	16	22	17	18	15	15
	14	13	18	13	15	11	14
	13	10	14	10	11	8	13
	12	7	10	8	9	5	12
	11	5	8	6	7	4	11
	10	4	6	4	5	2	10
	9	3	4	3	3	1	9
	8	2	3	2	2		8
	7	2	2	2	2		7
	6	1	2	1	1		6
	5		1				5
	4						4
	3						3
	2						2
	1						1
Median Score		19.9	19.8	20.8	21.1	20.5	

*From *Using ACT on the Campus,* © 1965 by American College Testing Program, Inc. Used by permission of the American College Testing Program, Inc.

same student to "college-bound" seniors, we find he is a great deal below average (34th percentile, 28th percentile, 28th percentile, 39th percentile).

Thus, in guiding a youngster or adult we must have appropriate norms. Using "unselected high school seniors" as our frame of reference, we would probably advise college or at least a junior college for our student. If we compare him to the appropriate norms, "college-bound high school seniors," our suggestions would be quite different.

One more illustration of the importance of relevant norms can be seen in Tables 18 and 19. Table 18 presents norms for high school seniors who later attended junior colleges or technical schools. Table 19, on the other hand, is made up of high school seniors who enrolled at institutions which offer bachelor's, master's, and doctor's degrees; these institutions are primarily large public and private universities (The American College Testing Program, 1965).

An inspection of Tables 18 and 19 reveals differences in median scores. Again we see that the normative or reference group is extremely important.

Guidelines. Good norms are based upon representative and random samplings of the population for which the test has been constructed. The sheer quantity of the sample does not mean the norms are appropriate. A test, for example, based on 200,000 pupils in New York City would probably be good for New York, but would not necessarily be relevant for other geographic regions. Thus, in your review of a test manual do not accept alleged national norms unless they are supported by a cogent and complete analysis of the sample of people they represent. Expect and look for specific relevant evidence to support the test author's claim for representative samplings.

School systems and other users of test data should develop their own local norms. These local norms should be revised periodically. This is especially relevant in the use of achievement tests. "Local norms are more important for many uses of tests than are published norms" (American Psychological Association et al., 1966, p. 34). Many test manuals describe the process of computing local norms. These local norms may be calculated by the same procedure used in determining national norms.

A list of some of the essential normative data that you should look for in a test manual follows:[2]

> 1. Scales used for reporting scores should be thoroughly documented and explained in the test manual in order to facilitate test interpretation.
> 2. Standard scores generally should be used for reporting raw scores.
> 3. Tables for converting grade norms to standard scores or percentile ranks should be provided.

[2] Based on *Standards* (American Psychological Association et al., 1966).

Table 18 Percentile Ranks for College Freshmen Enrolled in Junior Colleges and Technical Schools*

	Standard Score	Test 1 English	Test 2 Mathematics	Test 3 Social Studies	Test 4 Natural Sciences	Tests 1–4 Composite	Standard Score
	36						36
	35						35
	34						34
	33						33
	32		99				32
	31		98	99	99		31
	30		97	98	98		30
	29		96	96	96	99	29
	28	99	94	94	93	98	28
93 Colleges	27	98	92	91	90	96	27
27,646 Students	26	96	90	88	86	94	26
	25	93	87	84	82	91	25
	24	89	83	80	77	86	24
	23	84	79	75	72	81	23
	22	78	75	70	66	75	22
	21	72	71	65	62	69	21
	20	64	65	59	56	62	20
	19	56	59	53	50	54	19
	18	48	53	47	44	46	18
	17	40	46	41	38	39	17
	16	33	39	34	32	31	16
	15	26	33	27	27	25	15
	14	21	27	22	22	19	14
	13	17	22	17	18	14	13
	12	13	18	13	14	10	12
	11	10	14	10	10	7	11
	10	8	10	8	8	5	10
	9	6	7	5	6	3	9
	8	5	6	4	4	2	8
	7	4	5	3	3	1	7
	6	3	3	2	2	1	6
	5	2	2	1	1		5
	4	1	1	1	1		4
	3	1	1				3
	2						2
	1						1
Median Score		18.2	17.6	18.5	18.9	18.5	

*From *Using ACT on the Campus.* © 1965 by American College Testing Program, Inc. Used by permission of the American College Testing Program, Inc.

Table 19 Percentile Ranks for College Freshmen Enrolled in Doctoral-Granting Institutions*

	Standard Score	Test 1 English	Test 2 Mathematics	Test 3 Social Studies	Test 4 Natural Sciences	Tests 1–4 Composite	Standard Score
	36						36
	35						35
	34		99				34
	33		98		99		33
	32		96	99	98		32
	31		94	97	97	99	31
	30		92	94	94	98	30
	29	99	88	91	90	96	29
	28	97	84	86	85	93	28
44 Colleges	27	94	81	82	79	89	27
53,177 Students	26	90	76	75	73	83	26
	25	84	70	68	65	76	25
	24	77	65	63	59	68	24
	23	68	59	56	52	60	23
	22	59	53	50	45	51	22
	21	51	48	44	40	43	21
	20	42	42	37	35	35	20
	19	33	36	31	29	28	19
	18	25	30	26	24	21	18
	17	19	25	20	19	16	17
	16	14	20	15	15	11	16
	15	10	16	11	11	8	15
	14	7	12	8	9	5	14
	13	5	9	5	6	3	13
	12	4	7	4	5	2	12
	11	3	5	3	3	1	11
	10	2	4	2	2	1	10
	9	1	3	1	2		9
	8	1	2	1	1		8
	7	1	2	1	1		7
	6		1				6
	5		1				5
	4						4
	3						3
	2						2
	1						1
Median Score		20.9	21.3	22.0	22.8	21.8	

4. Norms should in most cases be published in the test manual at the time of distribution.

5. Standard scores or percentile ranks should reflect the distribution of scores in an appropriate reference group.

6. Normative groups should be clearly defined and described.

7. Method of sampling should be reported.

8. Achievement test norms should report number of schools as well as number of students tested.

9. Score variance because of such variables as age, sex, and education should be reported.

References

American Psychological Association, American Educational Research Association, and National Council on Measurement in Education. *Standards for educational and psychological tests and manuals.* Washington, D.C.: American Psychological Association, 1966.

Chase, C. I. *Elementary statistical procedures.* New York: McGraw-Hill, 1967.

Durost, W. N. *The characteristics, use, and computation of stanines.* Test Service Notebook, No. 23. New York: Harcourt, Brace and World, 1961. (a)

Durost, W. N. *How to tell parents about standardized test results.* Test Service Notebook, No. 26. New York: Harcourt, Brace and World, 1961. (b)

Engelhart, M. D. Obtaining comparable scores on two or more tests. *Educational and Psychological Measurement*, 1959, **19**, 55–64.

Engelhart, M. D. *Using stanines in interpreting test scores.* Test Service Notebook, No. 28. New York: Test Department, Harcourt, Brace and World (n.d.).

Gourevitch, V. *Statistical methods: A problem-solving approach.* Boston: Allyn and Bacon, 1965.

Guilford, J. P. *Fundamental statistics in psychology and education.* (4th ed.) New York: McGraw-Hill, 1965.

Karmel, L. J. *Testing in our schools.* New York: Macmillan, 1966.

Magnusson, D. *Test theory.* Reading, Mass.: Addison-Wesley, 1967.

Popham, W. J. *Educational statistics: Use and interpretation.* New York: Harper & Row, 1967.

Seashore, H. G. and Ricks, J. H. *Norms must be relevant.* Test Service Bulletin, No. 39. New York: The Psychological Corporation, 1950.

Terman, L. M., and Merrill, M. A. *Stanford-Binet Intelligence Scale: Manual for the third revision. Form L-M.* Boston: Houghton Mifflin, 1960.

CHAPTER

6

Sources of Test Information

Teachers and other school personnel need to know about tests—where to find test information, where to find critiques of tests, where to find testing books for parents, and so on. This chapter will attempt to provide this, and other information. In addition, test resource materials will be listed.

Special Resources

We shall discuss three of the most widely used resources in testing, *Standards for Educational and Psychological Tests and Manuals, The Mental Measurements Yearbooks,* and *Tests in Print.* These references are the basis for definitive test information in the field of measurement.

Standards for Educational and Psychological Tests and Manuals

Standards is a forty-page booklet published by the American Psychological Association et al. (1966) and has been frequently mentioned in this book. There is little need to elaborate its essential characteristics at this point. It is important, however, to state that *Standards* represents the collective opinions of selected psychologists and educators and as such presents the "rules of the testing road" as seen by most test experts today. Though there are no legal requirements to make one adhere to these "rules," one would hope that teachers and other school personnel would take *Standards* quite seriously. Every school should have a copy in its testing library and should make use of it when evaluating a test.

The Mental Measurements Yearbooks

The *Mental Measurement Yearbooks,* edited by Oscar K. Buros (1938, 1940, 1949, 1953, 1959, 1965), are the most valuable and important single source of information about tests. The *Yearbooks* contain detailed information and critical reviews on thousands of tests. An attempt is made to list, discuss, and criticize *every* published standardized test.

The critical reviews are written by experts in the general field of measurement and in the specific area of his or her special competency. Thus, a measurement specialist in school ability and achievement testing would review tests in that particular area only. The number of reviews for each test is based on the interest which that area of testing generates and the extensiveness of the test's utilization. Some tests of wide general interest and use, therefore, may be reviewed by two or more experts. The reviewers provide frank, detailed, and critical information about each test. The following is an example of the type of review contained in the *Yearbooks;* it is excerpted from a review by Dr. Jonathon C. McLendon, one of many reviewers of the Sequential Tests of Educational Progress (STEP). McLendon (1965) states,

> The STEP tests in social studies continue without peer, indeed almost without available counterparts, as the leading standardized series of skill tests in social studies. As previous reviewers have indicated, the STEP tests fulfill a distinctive need in social studies, a field in which tests have generally dealt mostly or only with knowledge and understanding of facts and concepts.
>
> Content validity of the STEP tests is dependent on the soundness of judgment of those three dozen persons who participated in the test construction. While this group included several outstanding teachers and other leaders in social studies education, additional evidences of content validity would be welcome. In light of the heavy emphasis that teachers place on intepretation of reading materials in social studies, content validity is weakened by the extent (37 to 51 per cent) of items that involve interpretation of visual materials. Data on item validity are not reported. Construct, concurrent, and predictive validity are evident only by implication. Correlations with SCAT scores are interesting, and useful in some ways; but more closely related criteria would serve better to guide teachers and students in interpreting and applying test results. Ideally, the reporting

of scores would facilitate recognition of levels of achievement by individuals and groups in the use of particular skills involving specified types of instructional materials or sources.

Although the STEP tests aim chiefly to measure indicated abilities, previous knowledge concerning the subject matter presented on the test doubtless aids many test takers. The seven types of skills and eight areas of understanding listed in the Manual for Interpreting Scores on the social studies tests provide no more than general and somewhat vague identifications of related behaviors; the statements of understandings appear to restate several proposed in 1957 by the Committee on Concepts and Values, National Council for the Social Studies. Hopefully the publishers of the STEP tests will be able to furnish in the foreseeable future, as promised seven years ago in their 1957 Technical Report, "empirical checks . . . . relating test scores to suitable criterion measures," which data have not yet appeared in the SCAT-STEP Supplements [p. 1224].

In addition to test reviews the *Yearbooks* provide other important and practical items of information such as the test author; test publisher; norms, for example, appropriate grade and/or age levels; prices of tests; publication and revision dates; administration time; and available forms. In addition, references are listed.

Every school or other institution using tests should have at least the last three editions of the *Yearbooks*. The first source that school testing people and testing specialists consult for testing information is the latest edition of the *Yearbooks*. A new test is usually reviewed in the first *Yearbook* that was published after the test was distributed for popular use. Some tests are continually reviewed in subsequent *Yearbooks;* others are not. Thus, for an exhaustive and detailed account one should have all the *Yearbooks;* for most school purposes, however, the last three *Yearbooks* should suffice.

Tests in Print

Another book that is useful and should be in every school is *Tests in Print* (Buros, 1961). It contains all the tests that one would find in the *Yearbooks,* test catalogues, journals, books, and other sources. The list includes over 2,000 tests that are in print as well as over 800 tests that are no longer available. This book serves primarily as a reference guide to enable you to find out where to obtain critical and detailed data on each listed test. In addition to references for further investigation it presents data on each test—for example, author, publisher, norms, forms, and any special features.

Texts and Reference Books

No single textbook can adequately cover in detail all the special areas of testing. Certain texts are written for special areas of testing or for a special audience. The following books have been selected as sources for more detailed investigations and study. It should be noted that the list is not exhaustive.

Intelligence Tests

Wechsler, D. *The measurement and appraisal of adult intelligence.* (4th ed.) Baltimore: Williams and Wilkins, 1958. Primarily centered on the author's intelligence test. Useful concepts about the nature of intelligence and IQ. Details of test construction and classification of intelligence as well as diagnostic and practical applications of IQ results.

Goodenough, F. L. *Measurement of intelligence by drawings.* (copyright renewed 1954) New York: Harcourt, Brace and World, 1926. Description of method for measuring intelligence by the use of drawings. Especially useful for primary teachers and counselors.

Terman, L. M., and Merrill, M. A. *Stanford-Binet Intelligence Scale : Manual for the third revision, Form L-M.* Boston: Houghton Mifflin, 1960. Essentially the manual for the Binet but gives the reader some knowledge of thorough test construction and a detailed idea of what IQ is.

School Tests

Ilg, F. L., and Ames, L. B. *School readiness : Behavior tests used at the Gesell Institute.* New York: Harper & Row, 1965. Combined text and manual presents Gesell Institute's view that children should be enrolled in school on the basis of development, not on chronological age or IQ. Description of tests used and how to administer and use results. One section of book is devoted to teachers, administrators, and parents.

Bauernfeind, R. H. *Building a school testing program.* Boston: Houghton Mifflin, 1963. Review of some basic test concepts plus detailed outline for testing programs from K-12.

Specialized Psychological Testing

Welsh, G. S., and Dahlstrom, W. G. *Basic readings on the MMPI in psychology and medicine.* Minneapolis: University of Minnesota Press, 1956. The editors of this book present an excellent source of technical information on the various uses of the Minnesota Multiphasic Personality Inventory (MMPI) by leading psychologists.

Burgemeister, B. B. *Psychological techniques in neurological diagnosis.* New York: Harper & Row, 1962. Presentation of psychological techniques in the diagnosis of central nervous system disorders. Reveals the tools of the psychologist in detecting these disturbances.

Levy, L. H. *Psychological interpretation.* New York: Holt, Rinehart and Winston, 1963. A book dealing with the nature of psychological interpretation and how the psychologist uses tools such as tests to derive his analysis of behavior.

Guidance Counseling

Goldman, L. *Using tests in counseling.* New York: Appleton-Century-Crofts, 1961. An excellent guide to interpretation, test selection, and research findings in measurement. Intended to help school counselors in the uses of tests in counseling.

Berdie, R. F., Layton, W. L., Swanson, E. O., and Hagenah, T. *Testing in guidance and counseling.* New York: McGraw-Hill, 1963. A text devoted to helping counselors understand pupils using tests as only one method in this task. Other factors, such as family background and physical health, are considered along with tests to give a complete picture of the student.

Vocational Testing

Super, E. E., and Crites, J. O. *Appraising vocational fitness.* New York: Harper & Row, 1962. A compilation and evaluation of useful tests for the identification of vocational aptitudes and skills. The book discusses each test in terms of its applicability, contents, administration and scoring, norms, and so forth. Individual case histories and their eventual disposition are also given.

Miscellaneous

Allen, R. M., and Jefferson, T. W. *Psychological evaluation of the cerebral palsied person: Intellectual, personality, and vocational applications.* Springfield, Ill.: Charles C. Thomas, Publisher, 1962. Significant tests for use with cerebral-palsied persons are outlined and discussed.

Albright, L. E., Glennon, J. R., and Smith, W. J. *The use of psychological tests in industry.* Cleveland: Howard Allen, Inc., Publishers, 1963. Primarily devoted to selection problems, especially useful as a reference for personnel officers.

Evaluation of pupil progress in business education. American Business Education Yearbook, Vol. 17, 1960. New York: New York University Campus Stores, 1960. Especially useful for testing students in business education.

Ismail, A. H., and Gruber, J. J. *Integrated development of motor aptitudes and intellectual performance.* Columbus, Ohio: Charles E. Merrill, 1967. An excellent source book for motor aptitude tests and their relationship to intellectual functioning.

Clark, H. H. *Application of measurement to health and physical education.* (4th ed.) Englewood Cliffs, N.J.: Prentice-Hall, 1967. Detailed description of various performance tests in physical education; paper-and-pencil tests for sports knowledge and health education. A measurement classic in the field of physical education.

The reader is again cautioned to bear in mind that the preceding list is not exhaustive and is intended only as a further guide to source material in specific areas of testing. Moreover, some of these references may no longer be pertinent when you consult them. Do not reject a new test or any test because it is not listed in this book or one of the references. Remember that authors are selective and present tests they think are valuable. In the final analysis it is your job to select tests appropriate for your needs.

Test Publishers

One of the most important sources of test information, especially about a specific test, is the publisher. (See Appendix A for a complete list of these publishers and their addresses.) The test publisher, upon request, will send a catalogue of his tests that lists pertinent data such as price, norms, time necessary to administer a given test, and number of available forms. Specific and detailed information may be obtained by requesting a "specimen set" from the publisher. The "specimen set" is generally quite inexpensive or given free of charge. It usually includes the test, answer sheet, scoring stencil, directions for administering and scoring, and manual.

The "specimen set" facilitates evaluation of the test by first-hand inspection. The manual usually contains data on how the test was constructed and standardized, as well as norms and interpretive suggestions. It is the most contemporary source of test information, but of course one must be judicious in evaluating its contents. It is asking too much to expect the test publisher to be unbiased in his reporting of the test's limitations and assets. Test publishers can be very useful as a source of information if used together with your own critical evaluations and those of testing experts, like those found in the *Yearbooks*.

Many test publishers in addition to selling tests also distribute advisory information concerning the whole field of testing. This information is usually written in an easy to understand way and is geared to the practicing school teacher and counselor or anyone else who uses tests in day-to-day practice. These advisory services are almost always objective and unbiased reports of tests and factors affecting tests in terms of construction and use. These publications that deal with commonly encountered measurement problems are available free of charge. Three of the most active of these publishers are listed:

1. The Psychological Corporation, 304 East 45th Street, New York, New York 10017. The Psychological Corporation publishes from time to time the *Test Service Bulletin*. These bulletins generally contain a three-to-five-page article on some facet of tests or testing. There are currently over twenty-two bulletins available to teachers, students, and schools. Examples of some of these bulletins are the following: No. 36, "What Is an Aptitude?"; No. 38, "Expectancy Tables—A Way of Interpreting Test Validity"; No. 39, "Norms Must Be Relevant"; No. 54, "On Telling Parents About Test Results"; No. 55, "The Identification of the Gifted"; No. 56, "Double-Entry Expectancy Tables"; No. 57, "Testing Job Applicants from Disadvantaged Groups." Some of the articles are bound together in one bulletin.

2. Educational Testing Service, Princeton, New Jersey, 08540. This publisher produces a series entitled *Evaluation and Advisory Service Series*. At present this series includes four booklets. They are: No. 1, "Locating Information on Educational Measurement: Sources and References"; No. 3, "Selecting an Achievement Test: Principles and Procedures"; No. 4, "Making the Classroom Test: A Guide for

Teachers"; No. 5, "Short-cut Statistics for Teacher-made Tests." In addition to these, several other booklets and materials are provided free of charge to students, teachers, and schools.

3. Harcourt, Brace and World, Inc., 757 Third Avenue, New York, New York 10017. This publisher produces two series of test advisory publications, *Test Service Notebook* and *Test Service Bulletin*. The notebooks are generally four pages long and focus on subjects related to test theory, administration of testing programs, results of research studies, and correct test usage. Examples of some of the currently available Notebooks are No. 11, "A Comparison of Results of Three Intelligence Tests"; No. 13, "A Glossary of 100 Measurement Terms"; No. 17, "Why Do We Test Your Children?"; No. 20, "Testing in the Secondary School"; No. 23, "The Characteristics, Use and Computation of Stanines"; No. 25, "How Is a Test Built?"; No. 27, "Fundamentals of Testing: For Parents, School Boards, and Teachers."

The *Test Service Bulletin* generally offers brief reports on effective testing programs and discussions of testing concepts. Examples of some of the currently available bulletins are No. 77, "The Intelligence Quotient"; No. 79, "Misconceptions About Intelligence Testing"; No. 91, "Finding Mathematics and Science Talent in the Junior High School"; No. 94, "Aptitude and Achievement Measures in Predicting High School Academic Success"; No. 95, "Testing: Tool for Curriculum Development"; No. 99, "Selection and Provision of Testing Materials"; No. 102, "Test Administration Guide."

Journals

The *Yearbooks* though very valuable are only published every five or six years. This means that a more contemporary source of test evaluation is needed. One such source is the professional journals that review new tests. The following journals are of particular interest to test users:

1. *Personnel and Guidance Journal.*
2. *Educational and Psychological Measurement.*
3. *Journal of Consulting Psychology.*
4. *Personnel Psychology.*
5. *Review of Educational Research.*
6. *Journal of Educational Psychology.*
7. *Measurement and Evaluation in Guidance.*
8. *Journal of Educational Measurement.*
9. *Journal of Applied Psychology.*
10. *Journal of Clinical Psychology.*
11. *Journal of Counseling Psychology.*

12. *Journal of Projective Techniques and Personality Assessment.*
13. *Journal of School Psychology.*
14. *Psychology in the Schools.*
15. *Psychological Bulletin.*
16. *Psychometrika.*
17. *American Educational Research Journal.*
18. *Journal of Experimental Education.*
19. *Contemporary Psychology.*

Psychological Abstracts and *Educational Index*

The *Psychological Abstracts* and the *Educational Index* are excellent bibliographic references in their respective fields. The *Psychological Abstracts* serve as the general guidelines for all psychological journals. Each issue contains a brief (abstract) summary of every report in the psychological journals, including the subject and important features of the report. Every year a subject and author index is given for convenience in locating material published in the previous year. The *Psychological Abstracts* also publish monthly listings of new tests. In addition, data concerning research use of tests and resultant findings are also presented.

The *Educational Index* provides a very wide listing of journal articles in the field of education. It includes lay as well as professional materials and discussions. It does not give analyses as detailed as those in the *Psychological Abstracts*. Only references are given. One could find, for example, under "achievement testing" lists of tests and articles dealing with this area or, for that matter, any other sphere of measurement relating to education.

The intelligent use of tests demands the utilization of all appropriate sources of test data. The combination of *Psychological Abstracts* and the *Educational Index*, plus the sources previously mentioned, should provide the test user with the necessary data to make intelligent choices in his evaluation and selection of measurement instruments.

References

American Psychological Association, American Educational Research Association, and National Council on Measurement in Education. *Standards for educational and psychological tests and manuals.* Washington, D.C.: American Psychological Association, Inc., 1966.

Buros, O. K. (Ed.) *The 1938 mental measurements yearbook.* New Brunswick, N.J.: Rutgers University Press, 1938.

Buros, O. K. (Ed.) *The nineteen forty mental measurements yearbook.* New Brunswick, N.J.: Rutgers University Press, 1941.

Buros, O. K. (Ed.) *The third mental measurements yearbook.* New Brunswick, N.J.: Rutgers University Press, 1949.

Buros, O. K. (Ed.) *The fourth mental measurements yearbook.* Highland Park, N.J.:
  Gryphon Press, 1953.
Buros, O. K. (Ed.) *The fifth mental measurements yearbook.* Highland Park, N.J.:
  Gryphon Press, 1959.
Buros, O. K. (Ed.) *The sixth mental measurements yearbook.* Highland Park, N.J.:
  Gryphon Press, 1965.
McLendon, J. C. Sequential tests of educational progress: Social studies. In O. K.
  Buros (Ed.), *The sixth mental measurements yearbook.* Highland Park, N.J.:
  Gryphon Press, 1965.

PART THREE

Individual Tests of Intelligence and Personality

CHAPTER

7

Individual Tests
of Intelligence

"The Greeks had a word for it, but the Romans had a word with better survival properties. Regardless of the word, what is now called intelligence has been talked about for at least 2,000 years. And as long as 2,000 years before the advent of attempts to measure intelligence, there seems to have been recognition of the fact that individuals differ in intellectual ability" (McNemar, 1966, p. 180).

The teacher and counselor will rarely administer and interpret individual tests of intelligence such as the Stanford-Binet. He may, however, use these test results in many ways to facilitate learning in his classroom. In addition, group tests of intelligence (more appropriately termed *scholastic aptitude tests*) which he will administer, and in some cases score, are based in large measure on the validity of the individual test of intelligence.

In this chapter we will discuss, in detail, two of the most widely used individual tests of intelligence, the Stanford-Binet and the Wechsler series (WPPSI, WISC, WAIS) as well as nonlanguage, culture-fair, and infant tests. In Chapter 2 we discussed the problem of defining intelligence. You will remember that intelligence is defined differently by various psychologists and that the term *intelligence* has no absolute meaning. The meaning of IQ was also discussed in general terms and later in Chapter 5 the mathematical derivation was presented. Before reading further it may be beneficial for you to review relevant sections of Chapters 2 and 5.

Stanford-Binet Intelligence Scale

History

In about 1890 the French psychologist Alfred Binet became interested in investigating reasoning and judgment. He wanted to know the ways in which "smart" and "dull" children differed. In his attempts to study these differences he used many types of measures, including size of cranium, tactile discrimination, and digit recall. These measures produced little relationship to general mental functioning.

In 1904 Dr. Binet was appointed to a commission which was to study and recommend to the educational leaders of Paris a procedure for ascertaining which children were unable to profit from a regular school setting. This commission was interested in picking out pupils who were in the mentally retarded range and placing them in a school which would provide instruction at their level of ability.

Binet was asked to produce a method to distinguish these retarded children from "normal" pupils. His first scale, published in 1905 in collaboration with Simon, drew on the knowledge gained in his earlier studies. This scale, called the 1905 scale, was designed to cover various functions which Binet considered components of intelligence. These included comprehension, reasoning, and judgment. Children between three and six years of age were called upon to give their names, copy figures, point to their right and left ear, and obey simple commands. Some of the tasks older children were asked to do were to name the months of the year, make up sentences, define abstract words, and name various coins.

In 1908 and 1911 revisions of the 1905 scale were published. Chauncey and Dobbin (1966) in discussing Binet's work made an important observation not only on Binet's procedures but on intelligence tests in general. They state,

> No test or technique measures mental ability directly. What Binet did, and what all other "intelligence test" builders after him have done, was to set up some tasks for the young intellect to attack and then to observe what happened when the intellect was put to work on them. His method was truly scientific and remarkably like the method used by physicists forty years later to detect and measure the forces released by the atom. The cloud chamber does not permit the physicist to see the atom or its electrically charged components, but it does reveal the tracks of ionizing particles and thus permits the scientist to deduce the nature of the atom from which the particles emanate [p. 5].

Lewis M. Terman, an American psychologist, began to experiment with the Binet tests in 1910. In 1916 he produced the Stanford Revision of the Binet Scale (Terman, 1916). This revision attempted to provide standards of intellectual performance for "average" American-born children from three to sixteen. Intelligence ratings were arrived at by mental age scores. Terman increased the number of tasks from Binet's original 54 to 90. The 1916 scale, for the first time, included detailed instructions for administering and scoring each subtest.

The 1916 scale was used for clinical diagnosis and research purposes during the 1920's and early 1930's. It was found that certain tests had low validity and that below the mental age of four and at the young adult levels the sampling had been inadequate. In addition, instructions and scoring lacked the precision needed for objective appraisal. In order to eliminate these faults a second revision of the Stanford scale was produced.

The second revision, published in 1937, utilized the results of past studies, personal experiences, a ten-year research and standardization project. Dr. Maud A. Merrill coauthored the 1937 revision with Terman (Terman and Merrill, 1937). This revision retained many of the characteristics of the earlier tests, such as age standards. It provided a broader sampling but remained a test of "general intelligence" rather than a test of specific kinds of abilities. Two Forms—Form L and Form M—were used. In terms of sampling and statistical techniques the 1937 scale was much more sophisticated.

The third and latest revision, Form L-M, was published in 1960. This revision combines the best features and subtests of the 1937 scale into a single form. The most radical change in the 1960 scale is in the IQ tables, which give deviation, or standard score, IQ's. This is a departure from the previous method of MA/CA × 100. (See Chapter 5.) The revised IQ is a standard score with a mean of 100 and a standard deviation of 16 (Terman and Merrill, 1960).

Characteristics

The Stanford-Binet Intelligence Scale begins with tests for the average two-year-old and progresses to levels that differentiate between average and superior adults. In order to illustrate the actual content of the test, excerpts from four different age levels are presented with brief explanations.[1]

YEAR TWO

1. Three-Hole Form Board[2]
    (Material: Form board 5 in. × 8 in. with three insets for circle, square, and triangle.)
    Procedure: The board is presented with the blocks in place.

---

[1] Lewis M. Terman and Maud A. Merrill. *Stanford-Binet Intelligence Scale: Manual for the Third Revision, Form L-M.* Copyright, © 1960, by Houghton Mifflin Company. Excerpts are reprinted with the permission of Houghton Mifflin Company.
[2] From this point on, an asterisk(*) will denote that the task is used at two or more age levels.

The Examiner[3] tells the child to watch him and he proceeds to remove the blocks placing each on the table before its appropriate recess on the side toward the child. He then says, "Now put them back into their holes."

Score: To receive credit, child must place all three blocks correctly in one of two trials.

2. Delayed Response

(Material: Three small pasteboard boxes and a small toy cat.)

Procedure: E: "Look, I am going to hide the kitty and then see if you can find it again."

Score: The child watches the E place the kitty under each box and is asked to find the kitty. If on any of the three trials the child turns over more than one box that trial is scored as a minus.

3. Identifying Parts of the Body*

Procedure: E: "Show me the dolly's hair." ("mouth," etc.—large paper doll.)

Score: The child must identify the parts on the paper doll.

4. Block Building: Tower

Procedure: Twelve 1-inch cubes are placed in erratic order before the child. The E proceeds to build a four block tower saying, "See what I'm making!" He then pushes the rest of the blocks toward the child, saying, "You make one like this."

Score: Child must build a four or more block tower in response to E's request.

5. Picture Vocabulary*

Procedure: "What's this? What do you call it?" (Eighteen 2 in. × 4 in. cards with pictures of common objects.)

Score: Recognition, e.g., plane, telephone, etc.

6. Word Combinations*

Procedure: Notation of child's spontaneous word combinations during interview.

Score: Combinations of at least two words. For example, "Mama bye bye" or "all gone" are scored plus while one-word combinations such as "bye bye" or "night-night" are scored minus.

YEAR SIX

1. Vocabulary

Procedure: "When I say a word, you tell me what it means. What is an orange?" (44 words—E stops after six consecutive words have been failed.)

Score: Importance of knowing meaning, e.g., orange—some correct answers are: "a fruit," "like a tangerine," "it's round," "a jello."

---

[3] From this point on, *Examiner* will be designated by the letter E.

2. Differences*

   Procedure: "What is the difference between a bird and a dog?"
   Score: For example, correct responses are: "a bird flies and a dog runs" or "a bird got wings and a dog got ears." Incorrect responses: "a dog chases a bird" or "a bird is white and a dog is brown" (Many more combinations for correct and incorrect responses are possible.)

3. Mutilated Pictures

   Procedure: (Five pictures with a part missing) "What is gone in this picture? or "What part is gone?"
   Score: Missing part must be named or described verbally. Credit is not received for pointing.

4. Number Concepts*

   Procedure: (Twelve 1-inch cubes) "Give me three blocks. Put them here."
   Score: Five different number combinations of blocks are requested.

5. Opposite Analogies*

   Procedure: "A table is made of wood; a window of. . . ."
   Score: Four analogies are given. Correct response, for example, for above would be "glass" or "glass and wood."

6. Maze Tracing

   Procedure: (Mazes—with start and finish points marked) "This little boy lives here, and here is the schoolhouse. The little boy wants to go to school the shortest way without getting off the sidewalk. Here is the sidewalk. Show me the shortest way. Mark it with your pencil, but don't go off the sidewalk. Start here and take the little boy to school the shortest way."
   Score: Correct if right path is chosen and if marking is more inside than outside the boundaries of the path.

YEAR ELEVEN

1. Memory for Designs*

   Procedure: "This card has two drawings on it. I am going to show them to you for ten seconds, then I will take the card away and let you draw from memory what you have seen. Be sure to look at both drawings carefully." (Card is shown for ten seconds.)
   Score: Degrees of accuracy represented in full and half credits.

2. Verbal Absurdities*

   Procedure: Statements are read and after each the question, "What is foolish about that?"
   Score: Three "foolish" statements are read and quality of insight into the absurdities is recorded and evaluated. For example, "The judge said to the prisoner, 'You are to be hanged, and I hope it will be a warning to you'."

3. Abstract Words*
   Procedure: "What is connection?"
   Score: Five words given and response evaluated on meaning, e.g., some correct responses for connection are "connect two things together," "you're kin to 'em."
4. Memory for Sentences
   Procedure: "Now listen, and be sure to say exactly what I say."
   Score: E reads aloud two statements (separately) and child is to give back statement verbatim. In order to receive credit statements must be exactly correct with no omissions or additions or change in order of words.
5. Problem Situation
   Procedure: "Listen, and see if you can understand what I read."
   Score: Statement is read and child is asked question about it.
6. Similarities*
   Procedure: "In what way are . . . , . . . , and . . . , alike?"
   Score: Three things are presented and a response that reveals understanding whether basic or superficial is scored correct.

SUPERIOR ADULT LEVEL THREE

1. Vocabulary*
   Procedure: "I want to find out how many words you know. Listen, and when I say a word, you tell me what it means. What is an orange?" (begins at six-year level)
2. Proverbs
   Procedure: "Here is a proverb, and you are supposed to tell what it means. For example, this proverb, 'Large oaks from little acorns grow,' means that great things may have small beginnings. What does this one mean?" (Three proverbs are then given.)
   Score: List of possible interpretations that are correct and incorrect are given.
3. Opposite Analogies*
   Procedure: "A rabbit is timid; a lion is . . ."
   Score: List of correct and incorrect responses. Three analogies are given.
4. Orientation
   Procedure: The person is given a card on which two problems concerning directions are given. He is not allowed to use pencil and paper.
   Score: Correct responses.
5. Reasoning*
   Procedure: Person is presented with card and reads problem while E reads it aloud. Pencil and paper are not allowed.
   Score: Time limit and possible correct answers through different mathematical methods (2) are given.

6. Repeating Thought of Passage*

Procedure: "I am going to read a short paragraph. When I am through you are to repeat as much of it as you can. You don't need to remember the exact words, but listen carefully so that you can tell me everything it says."

Score: Accurate reproduction of component ideas.

The preceding illustrations are representative of some of the tasks in the Stanford-Binet. You can see that sometimes the tasks at different age levels are completely different, whereas in other cases they are the same. (The asterisk denotes usage at more than one level.) Many of the tests at the lower age levels deal with objects and pictures, whereas at the upper levels the tests are more abstract and verbal. Such abilities as judgment, interpretation, memory, past achievement, and abstract reasoning are evaluated.

The examiner, in administering the test, begins at a level where the child with some effort is likely to succeed. Remember that the tasks at a given age level reflect the average child's ability at that age. If the child is unable to pass the tasks at the level first tried, the examiner will go back to an easier level. If the child is successful at the initial level, the examiner will continue, level by level, until he fails all tests at a specific level. Once this level has been established, the examiner credits the child with the basal age which is the highest age level at which all of the tests are passed. For example, if all tests up to and including the fifth year are passed, and one test for the sixth year is not passed, the basal age is five years. The examiner also credits the child with tasks passed at more advanced levels. Thus, if there are six tests at each year-age level, a child passing a single test obtains credit for two months of mental age. For example, Ted S. passed all tasks at the five-year level, three of six tasks at the six-year level, one of six tasks at the seven-year level, and failed all tasks at the eight-year level. Thus, the following computation to derive his mental age would be made:

1. Passed all tasks at five-year level = five years basal age.
2. Passed three of six tasks at six-year level = six months credit.
3. Passed one of six tasks at seven-year level = two months credit.
4. Failed all tasks at eight-year level = 0.

Mental age = five years, eight months.

Ted's mental age describes the level at which he is performing. This, of course, does not take into account his life age. Ted's performance in relation to children of his own age is then expressed as an IQ. An IQ has the same meaning at one age as at any other. In order to find Ted's IQ, the examiner would consult a table to convert the mental age to IQ.

Classifying Binet IQ's

The distribution of the 1937 standardization sample, as illustrated in Table 20, is still used in the 1960 revision as a frame of reference. It presents a basis for statistical classification of IQ's. As Terman and Merrill (1960) state,

> The classificatory terms used carry no implications of diagnostic significance for IQ categories. "Average or normal" has statistical meaning as designating the middle range of IQ's. So, too, IQ's 60 and below indicate "mental deficiency" with respect to average mentality on the scale and carry no necessary diagnostic implications such as are usually attached to the term "feeblemindedness." "Very superior" is applied to subjects whose IQ's fall well within the top 1.5 per cent of the group. . . . The table serves as a "frame of reference" to indicate how high or low any specific score is in relation to the general population [pp. 17 and 19].

Table 20 Distribution of the 1937 Standardization Group*

IQ	Per Cent	Classification
160–169	0.03 ⎫	
150–159	0.2 ⎬	Very superior
140–149	1.1 ⎭	
130–139	3.1 ⎫	Superior
120–129	8.2 ⎭	
110–119	18.1	High average
100–109	23.5 ⎫	Normal or average
90–99	23.0 ⎭	
80–89	14.5	Low average
70–79	5.6	Borderline defective
60–69	2.0 ⎫	
50–59	0.4 ⎪	Mentally defective
40–49	0.2 ⎬	
30–39	0.03 ⎭	

* From Lewis M. Terman and Maud A. Merrill. *Stanford-Binet Intelligence Scale: Manual for the Third Revision Form L-M.* Copyright © 1960, by Houghton Mifflin Company. Reproduced with the permission of Houghton Mifflin Company.

Wechsler Scales

History

Wechsler's first test of intelligence, the Wechsler-Bellevue Scale, was developed primarily for adults. In constructing the first scale Wechsler analyzed various standardized tests of intelligence that were already being used. He evaluated each test's claim to validity on the basis of correlations with published tests and empirical ratings of intelligence. The ratings included teacher's estimates, ratings by army officers and business executives. In addition, Wechsler attempted to rate the tests on the basis of his own and other psychologists' clinical experience. Two years were devoted to experimental work in trying out various tests on different groups with varying intellectual abilities (Wechsler, 1958).

In revising the first scale[4] Wechsler also changed the name to the Wechsler Adult Intelligence Scale (WAIS). The WAIS is a revision and complete standardization of Form I or the Wechsler-Bellevue Intelligence Scale (W-B) and provides more efficient measurement of the intelligence of adolescents and adults between the ages of sixteen and seventy-five. Wechsler (1955) states, "The extension of the *Wechsler-Bellevue Scales* and the standardization of the modified instrument are represented by the new *Wechsler Adult Intelligence Scale*" (p. 2).

The WAIS, like its predecessor the W-B, consists of eleven tests. The Verbal Scale contains six tests; the Performance Scale has five tests. All the tests in both the Verbal and Performance Scales are combined to make the Full Scale. The following are the tests in each scale:

Verbal Tests	*Performance Tests*
1. Information	7. Digit Symbol
2. Comprehension	8. Picture Completion
3. Arithmetic	9. Block Design
4. Similarities	10. Picture Arrangement
5. Digit Span	11. Object Assembly
6. Vocabulary	

The Wechsler Intelligence Scale for Children (WISC) was developed by Wechsler in 1949 before the WAIS. It was an outgrowth of the W-B Scale and overlaps with it in format and items. The main differences are the additions of easier items and independent standardization of the WISC (Wechsler, 1949). The standardization group included a sample of 100 boys and 100 girls at each age from five through fifteen years. The WISC has the same Verbal and Performance and Full Scale format. There are ten basic and two alternative tests:

Verbal Tests

1. General Information	4. Similarities
2. General Comprehension	5. Vocabulary
3. Arithmetic	6. Digit Span (alternate)

[4] The *Wechsler-Bellevue* (W-B) *Scale* is still used by some examiners. Form II of the W-B is the retest instrument for the WAIS as well as for the W-B Form I. It should be noted that the 1967 test catalog of the Psychological Corporation, publisher of the Wechsler Scales (manual), states that Form I is out of print. (Most testing people now consider the W-B as obsolete.)

Performance Tests

7. Picture Completion
8. Picture Arrangement
9. Block Design

10. Object Assembly
11. Coding or Mazes (alternate)

Digit Span and Mazes (or Coding) are considered supplementary tests, to be added if time permits or if one of the tests has been invalidated.

The latest Wechsler Scale published in 1967, is the Wechsler Preschool and Primary Scale of Intelligence (WPPSI) for children between four and six-and-a-half years of age. The WPPSI, like the WISC, consists of a series of ability tests which attempt to obtain evidence of various dimensions of the young child's intellectual competence. The WPPSI norms reflect, more than any other intelligence test, socioeconomic and racial samplings. The WPPSI contains six verbal tests (one an alternate) and five performance tests.

Verbal Tests

1. Information
2. Vocabulary
3. Similarities
4. Comprehension
5. Arithmetic
6. Sentences (alternate)

Performance Tests

7. Animal House
8. Picture Completion
9. Mazes
10. Geometric Design
11. Block Design

Eight of the eleven tests are similar to the WISC and provide the same measures as the WISC. "Sentences," "Animal House," and "Geometric Design" are new tests in the Wechsler series.

Characteristics

The Wechsler approach of grouping certain items in subtests under two basic scales (Verbal and Performance) is a radical departure from the Terman-Binet plan of grouping items according to difficulty. Binet and Terman organized their material in successive age levels whereas Wechsler organized types of tasks in the various subtests. Let us now turn our attention to the various subtests and their content. The following items are similar to those found in the WISC and WAIS. The subject is expected to give a generalized and direct answer.

Information
How many toes do you have? (WISC)
How many days in a month? (WISC)
Where does syrup come from? (WAIS)
Who wrote *Crime and Punishment*? (WAIS)

Comprehension

What should you do when your nose bleeds? (WISC)

Why should people be honest? (WISC)

Why does an airplane have a motor? (WAIS)

What does this statement mean? "A watched pot never boils." (WAIS)

Arithmetic

Seven blocks are presented in a row before the child and he is asked to count them with his finger (timed—WISC)

At 5¢ each, what will four apples cost? (timed—WISC)

A woman with $20 spends $8.50. How much does she have left? (timed—WAIS)

The price of frozen green beans is three packages for 45¢. What is the price for nine packages? (timed—WAIS)

Similarities

For subjects under eight years of age and suspected mental defectives, four "analogies" such as "Water is blue but grass is _____" are given. If two of the four items are passed the examiner continues on to the more difficult items. (WISC) For example, "In what way are a pear and apple alike?"

WAIS items similar but more difficult.

Digit Span (WAIS)

"I am going to say some numbers. Listen carefully, and when I am through, say them right after me." The examiner starts with three digits and continues until nine digits or until subject misses two trials on a series. For example, 58264 was missed, another five digits are given and if subject misses again test is stopped. If correct response is given test continues.

After completing this first series of digits subject is asked to repeat numbers backwards. For example, the examiner says "683" the subject should answer "386". Test is discontinued in same manner as previous series. WISC uses this same format for alternate test.

Vocabulary

Words such as "wagon" and "ruby" are presented to the subject on the WISC while words such as "spring" and "digress" are included in the vocabulary section of the WAIS. There are forty words on both the WISC and WAIS. After the subject has had five consecutive failures (no credit) this test is discontinued.

Picture Completion

"I am going to show you some pictures in which there is a part missing. Look at each picture and tell me what part is missing." Subject may verbalize part that is missing or point to it.

Block Design

"You see these blocks have different colors on their different sides. I am going to put them together to make something with them.

Watch me." Four blocks are arranged according to a design on the examiner's card. Subject is required to make the same design using the blocks as the model. If he is successful he is shown card number 2 which has a design that he is to copy by arranging the blocks in the same manner. Starting with designs that require four blocks and continuing (if subject does not have three consecutive failures) up to nine blocks the subject is required to accurately reproduce the model designs on the cards presented to him. Bonus credits are awarded for speed in completing tasks on more difficult designs.

Picture Arrangement

A series of comic-like pictures are presented to the subject and he is asked to put them in the correct order so they will tell a story. Bonus credits are given for speed on completing tasks.

Object Assembly

"These pieces, if put together correctly, will make a girl. Go ahead and put them together." The examiner presents subject with cut up (puzzle-like pieces) parts and asks subject to put them together. Time bonuses for speed are given.

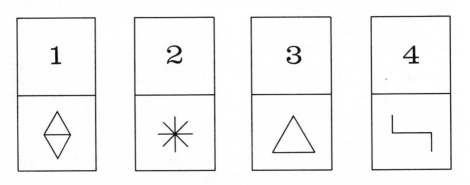

Figure 13. Example of item similar to tasks on Digit Symbol Test of the Wechsler Adult Intelligence Scale.

Digit Symbol (WAIS)

"Look at these boxes. Notice that each has a number in the upper part and a mark in the lower part. Every number has a different mark. Now look here where the upper boxes have numbers but the squares beneath have no marks. You are to put in each of these squares the mark that should go there. . . ." Each square that is correctly completed is counted as one point while reversed symbols are given half credit. See Fig. 13 for items similar to WAIS.

Coding (WISC)

Similar to digit symbol of the WAIS. Two sections, one for young children with symbols such as a ball and triangle are used, while the same format as the WAIS is used for older children.

Mazes (WISC)

Child is requested to keep pencil on paper and plot way out of maze. "This is a maze. You are to start here and find your way out here without going up any blind alley or crossing any lines."

What Wechsler Scores Mean

Raw scores on each subtest are converted into "scaled scores." These "scaled scores," or standard scores, have a mean of 10 and a standard deviation of 3. They are added together to produce three IQ's—Verbal, Performance, and Full Scale. The Verbal and Performance IQ's are added together to produce the Full Scale IQ. Wechsler was the first to introduce standard-score IQ's. He chose to place the mean at 100 and the standard deviation at 15. (The Stanford-Binet, you will recall, has a standard deviation of 16.)

Wechsler and Stanford-Binet IQ's are not equivalent. Bayley (1949) found, for example, the mean IQ of the Stanford-Binet to be ten points over that of the Wechsler IQ. In discussing the IQ differences between these two tests Cronbach (1960) states, "Since both the WISC and S-B scales were standardized on carefully selected samples, it is hard to decide which set of norms is wrong. The best we can do without much more evidence is to recognize that S-B IQ's average some 7 points higher than Wechsler IQ's during childhood and early adulthood" (pp. 195–96).

The IQ's for verbal and performance tests reveal different abilities. The performance tests taken as separate units are not reliable; however, when combined in the Performance Scale there is a very high reliability. Cronbach (1960) is quite lavish in his praise of the performance section of the Wechsler Scales. He states that the "Performance scale is probably the most dependable nonverbal measure ever developed" (p. 198).

The Wechsler Scales and the Stanford-Binet seem to measure the same ability. The concurrent validity of the Wechsler tests with the Stanford-Binet is quite high. (The reported correlations are in the 0.80's.) The Verbal Scale seems to be most closely related to the Binet test. The reliability of the Full Scale of the WAIS is 0.97 (Wechsler, 1958). The WISC reveals similar high coefficients.

Table 21 presents "Intelligence Classifications" as conceived of by Wechsler (1955), who states,

> In consonance with the theory that the only unambiguous way to define intelligence levels is by delimiting them statistically, the diagnostic equivalents . . . are offered. It is not claimed that these limits necessarily conform to universally accepted or even desired definitions. However, it is suggested that where other limits are set, their statistical basis should always be indicated [p. 20].

Table 21 Intelligence Classifications*

IQ	Classification	Per Cent Included
130 and above	Very Superior	2.2
120–129	Superior	6.7
110–119	Bright Normal	16.1
90–109	Average	50.0
80–89	Dull Normal	16.1
70–79	Borderline	6.7
69 and below	Mental Defective	2.2

* From David Wechsler. *Manual for the Wechsler Adult Intelligence Scale*. The Psychological Corporation, Copyright, © 1955.

Mental Retardation

Most states, in North America, accept the classification system illustrated in Table 22. (Some states will use 75 or even 80 as the cut-off point for mental retardation.) This classification system (IQ range only) is true for the Binet as well as the Wechsler Scales. The important thing to remember regardless of the actual IQ designation is that many authorities view the lowest 2 per cent of the population as mentally defective. Wechsler (1958), for example, states that "a definition which includes approximately the lowest 2 per cent of the population would seem to be a reasonable definition of that segment of the population which could be justifiably described as mentally defective" (p. 57).

The WISC for children over eight years of age and the WAIS for adolescents and adults (sixteen to seventy-five years of age) is an excellent instrument for ascertaining mental retardation. It should be noted, however, that accepted practice is not to rely on one test to decide if a person is retarded; a series of tests are given—including intelligence, achievement, and

Table 22 Classification of Mental Defectives According to IQ's (WAIS)*

Classification	IQ Range	Percentage Included	Probable Error
Moron	69–50	1.9	—3 to —5
Imbecile	49–30	0.32	—5 to —7
Idiot	29 and below	0.002	—7 and below

* From David Wechsler. *The Measurement and Appraisal of Adult Intelligence.* (4th ed.) The Williams & Wilkins Co. © 1958 by David Wechsler. Reproduced by permission of David Wechsler.

personality—and are considered along with past grades and opinions of school teachers.

It should be noted that sometimes a child will have emotional problems so severe that they interfere with his intellectual functioning and cause him to score in the range of mental retardation when in fact he may possess an average or even superior intelligence.

Teacher observations can also be valuable in finding these children. A sensitive teacher may notice that a child occasionally performs well, thus denoting ability, even though his usual performance is far below average.

Other Diagnostic and Clinical Features

The Wechsler Scales are more than tests that produce a psychometric IQ, important as that may be; they also assist in evaluating personality characteristics and organic brain disease. It has been found, for example, that in the majority of mental disorders impairment of functioning is greater in the performance section than in the verbal area. A fifteen-point difference or more between Performance and Verbal IQ's is considered significant (Wechsler, 1958).

ORGANIC BRAIN DAMAGE

Those who are brain-damaged consistently do better on verbal than on performance tests. They do very poorly on the Digit Symbol and Block Design tests. Memory impairment is reflected in a poor memory span (Digit Span).

SCHIZOPHRENIA[5]

The schizophrenic usually does relatively well on Information and Vocabulary and does poorly on either Similarities or Picture Completion, or

[5] Schizophrenia is a general term that refers to a related group of mental disturbances all characterized by a loss of touch with reality. The classical divisions are (1) catatonic, (2) hebephrenic, (3) simple, and (4) paranoid.

both. On the other hand, Wechsler states, "one finds some schizophrenic patients who do well on one or several of the tests which are characteristically failed by the typical schizophrenic" (p. 175).

ANXIETY TYPES

The tests most sensitive to those suffering from anxiety, whether it be pathological or of less severity, are Arithmetic, Digit Span, and Digit Symbol. It has also been noted that these people tend to have lower Performance Scores than Verbal Scores (Wechsler, 1958).

OBSESSIVE-COMPULSIVE NEUROSIS

Those suffering from obsessive-compulsive neurosis are characterized by perfectionism, rumination, and rigidity. They, for example, never outgrew "touching all the lines on the sidewalk." The quality of verbalizations is generally the most reliable sign of obsessive-compulsive trends on the Wechsler Scales. Schafer (1948) cites several examples of their verbalizations,

> "There is a good deal of dispute as to who invented the airplane but the Wright Brothers get credit for it." "If I were lost in the forest in the daytime I might follow the sun . . . or go by the moss on the north side of the trees . . . or maybe follow a stream. Do I have a compass? If I had one I'd . . ." [p. 25].

HYSTERIA

Hysteria is generally characterized by impulsiveness, egocentricity, tendency towards histrionics, and in severe cases conversion hysteria, such as paralysis of a limb with no apparent physical cause. Those with hysteria generally obtain performance scores that equal or exceed the verbal level. On the verbal section one finds relatively good scores in Comprehension and a poor showing in Information. Among the performance tests Digit Symbol is usually well performed.

GENERAL NEUROSIS

In the area of general neurosis one may see children or adults with obsessive-compulsive, hysteric, and phobic reactions. These people usually reveal themselves by doing poorly on relatively easy items in Information, Vocabulary, Digit Span, Arithmetic, Picture Completion, and Block Design while passing the more difficult items in these tests. These individuals have much higher verbal than performance scores (Schafer, 1948).

It should be remembered that none of these diagnostic signs are true in all situations. They are only rough generalizations that reveal to the skilled clinical or school psychologist some clues to the overall characteristics of the person being examined. They are, of course, used along with other tests and forms of evaluation, such as interviews and day-to-day behavioral records.

The various syndromes mentioned do not represent all the possible diagnostic categories, nor are they complete in any sense. They are intended as illustrations of the broad range and use of the Wechsler Scales that go beyond the psychometric IQ usage.

Two illustrative cases dealing with brain damage and anxiety follow to show how the Wechsler is used in actual clinical practice (Wechsler, 1958).[6]

W-BI

Vocabulary	7
Information	8
Comprehension	9
Arithmetic	7
Digits	6
Similarities	9
Verbal	39
Picture Arrangement	6
Picture Completion	1
Block Design	1
Object Assembly	2
Digit Symbol	5
Performance	15
Verbal IQ	91
Performance IQ	50
Digits forward	6
Digits backward	3

Case 0-2. White, male, adolescent, age 14. Brought to hospital because of marked change in personality. Had been normal boy until 6 months prior to admission. Illness first manifested by failure at school and increased irritability. Physical and neurological examination on admission essentially negative. Case presented to illustrate value of Scale in detecting possible organic brain conditions prior to manifestation of neurological symptoms. Psychometric organic signs are: Verbal much higher than Performance; very low scores on *both* Object Assembly and Block Design; large discrepancy between Digits forward and Digits backward. On the qualitative side, subject showed common organic manifestation of being able to reproduce designs if presented with a model of assembled blocks (200), after failing completely with the usual form of presentation.

WAIS

Information	12
Comprehension	11
Arithmetic	10
Similarities	15
Digit Span	10
Vocabulary	14
Digit Symbol	11
Picture Completion	15

Case An. 4. 16-year-old white male student who was admitted to a psychiatric out-patient clinic; revealed the typical adolescent problems: tension with his family, particularly in his relationships with his mother and sibling, difficulty in school, and struggling to find a value system, perhaps a sense of identity. His difficulties in school

[6] The following two cases are taken from David Wechsler, *The Measurement and Appraisal of Adult Intelligence.* (4th ed.) Baltimore: The Williams and Wilkins Company ©, 1958, David Wechsler. Used by permission of David Wechsler.

Block Design 11
Picture Arrangement . 14
Object Assembly 11

Verbal IQ 118
Performance IQ 116
Full IQ............. 121

forced him to leave school shortly before his admission to the out-patient clinic.

On admission patient gave a two year history of epigastric pain with an ulcer demonstrated radiologically at different stages of healing or activity. The present episode began three weeks prior to admission when an active ulcer was demonstrated by x-ray and was treated medically. He was referred to a psycho-analyst who saw him 3 times prior to admission. He was admitted in a state of acute anxiety. Diagnosis: anxiety state.

Psychometrically, this patient did not show too large inter-test variability but it is significant that the lowered scores on the Verbal part of the examination were on Arithmetic and Digit Span. The Digit Symbol was not so much out of line on the Performance part of the examination but was still one of the lower scores. In this case we seem to be dealing with an individual with chronic anxiety and a great deal of aggression directed inward. This would be better indicated by his projective technique tests. The high scores on the Similarities in contrast with the low score on Comprehension also suggests a possible schizoid trend. This case suggests a much more complicated diagnosis than the one assigned it clinically; it has been added to illustrate the presence of anxiety (along with other symptoms) revealed by the psychometric pattern.

Diagnostic Cautions

The student of measurement must be very judicious in accepting the preceding data as definitive. It is far from that and, as we have stated, diagnosis must be made in conjunction with other sources of information. Many psychologists do not feel the Wechsler scales are very authorative in clinical assessment. They would use it only as a "rough gauge" of behavioral dysfunction. Cronbach (1960) states the case quite well when he says that the "Wechsler yields a general measure of mental ability and a verbal-performance difference, and beyond that can offer hints leading to further study of the individual" (p. 202).

Evaluation of the Binet and Wechsler

The Stanford-Binet and the Wechsler Scales have few, if any, test peers. They are both standard equipment in the psychologist's battery of tests. Though he may augment them with other devices he puts his greatest faith and reliance on them. Cronbach (1960) states, for example, "Among general purpose predictors, the Wechsler and the Stanford-Binet are equally prominent, with no other serious competitor" (p. 206).

The Stanford-Binet test is essentially a standardized method of observing behavior and provides a single psychometric score which describes present general level of intellectual ability. Its psychometric vintage, mellowed by years of numerous investigations, provides data to which the examiner can turn for interpretive assistance. It excels especially at the lower age levels, and until the recent advent of the Wechsler Preschool and Primary Scale of Intelligence had no competitive peers.

The Binet deliberately concentrates on verbal and educational abilities. This is, of course, an advantage for predicting school success and a deficit (for certain kinds of predictions) for use with disadvantaged groups. The Binet does not measure all facets of "intelligence," nor does it necessarily measure inborn capacity. (This means only that we are not certain of all the ramifications of what it measures.) It is an important and excellent tool and if used properly may help in the educative process.

The Wechsler Scales seem to be, generally, as valid for prediction as the Stanford-Binet. The Wechsler covers a broader range of various abilities than the Binet. It is also more useful in clinical evaluation, especially in the diagnosis of brain and neurological disorders. The examiner need not be as highly trained in test administration, and the time to administer the tests is generally shorter. Most psychologists prefer to administer the WISC after the age of eight or nine and the WAIS to adults over sixteen years old because they feel they are more useful clinically than the Binet. On the other hand, most would not trust the WISC below eight years of age. It remains to be seen how the WPPSI establishes itself in actual practice and research investigations.

Thorndike and Hagen (1969) in reviewing the merits of the Wechsler and Binet state,

> Most psychometricians would probably agree now in preferring the WAIS as a measure for adolescents and adults, though its relation to academic success is perhaps not as clearly established as is the

> Binet's. . . . for children from 7 to 15, a decision between the two tests is not an easy one. The Binet is reported to be somewhat more difficult and time-consuming to give. The usual Binet procedure of carrying the examinee through to the point where he encounters a long series of failures is judged to be a seriously upsetting matter for some emotionally tense children. . . . The ultimate basis for choice will be the validity of the inferences that can be made from each in the situations in which they are actually used. Prediction of academic success can apparently be made about equally well from either test. It seems likely that the two tests are about equally useful for children with mental ages of 7 or above [p. 305].

Anastasi (1968) feels that the Wechsler Scales ". . . . yield an IQ with high reliability and fair evidence of validity" (p. 301). Cronbach (1960) feels that the Wechsler Scales are deficient in only one area, that is, the range is not large enough to measure very high and very low abilities with accuracy. Downie (1967) makes a related observation when he says that "Brighter subjects score higher on the Binet, and duller ones higher on the Wechsler" (p. 277).

It is obvious from our discussion that the Stanford-Binet and the Wechsler Scales are the best individual measures of intelligence presently available. They are time-consuming and expensive, however, in that only one person at a time may be examined and only highly trained individuals such as clinical or school psychologists may properly administer them. (See Merrill's "Training Students to Administer the Stanford-Binet Intelligence Scale".)

In our schools today both the Wechsler and Binet are given only when other tests and information seem unreliable or in special cases which require intensive and thorough information, as for placement of a child in a special class for retarded, emotionally disturbed, or perceptually handicapped youngsters. When used for these special purposes and administered and interpreted by a trained psychologist, they are extremely useful tools in helping provide individualized instruction. Teachers and school administrators should be certain, however, that the Binet or Wechsler results that they consider are based on the report of a trained clinical or school psychologist. (This means more than a course or two in individual testing.) This is important not only because of the highly complex nature of the tests, but also because of the clinical skills in observation needed to evaluate the psychometric scores.

Nonlanguage Tests[7]

Most intelligence tests contain, to some degree, tasks that are verbally oriented. This is not surprising because the vast majority of learning and

[7] There will be no specific distinction made between "nonlanguage" and "performance" tests in this section. Nonlanguage will suffice for both.

conceptualization takes place in a language context. Use of language in testing is not only natural but desirable, because academic progress is developed through language and tests having this orientation are thus in the best position to predict scholastic potential. Nonlanguage tests have been developed primarily to evaluate those individuals who, because of certain handicaps, cannot be properly measured with instruments containing linguistic tasks. Nonlanguage tests are especially useful with individuals who speak a foreign language or come from a culturally different environment as well as with those who have physical deficiencies in hearing and speech.

A good example of an individual nonlanguage test is Form I of the Arthur Performance Scale (Arthur, 1933, 1943). There are nine tests in the Arthur Scale.

1. *Knox Cube* is a test of immediate recall. The examiner taps four cubes in a specified series and instructs the subject to do the same. The procedure is repeated each time with the series of taps becoming greater in complexity and length.
2. *Seguin Form Board* (originally devised for use with mental defectives) consists of ten geometric figures that are to be placed in their appropriate holes in the Board. The subject is told to place them in these holes as fast as he can.
3. *Two-Figure Form Board* is a more difficult formboard than the Seguin. Cut-up pieces are to be placed into a square and cross.
4. *Casuist Form Board* is similar to the Two-Figure Form Board but more difficult because of the closer similarity of the pieces.
5. *Manikin* is a wooden figure of a man that is cut up into arms, legs, trunk, and head and is to be assembled by the subject.
   Feature Profile consists of cut-up wooden pieces to be assembled to form a face.
6. *Mare and Foal* is a picture-completion-type test which has cut-outs that are to be assembled or fitted into place.
7. *Healy Picture Completion I* is a rural scene from which ten small squares have been removed. The subject is to select the correct square from a number of pieces before him to complete each part of the picture.
8. *Porteus Mazes* is basically a simple pencil maze requiring the subject to trace with a pencil the shortest path from the entrance to the exit without lifting the pencil from the paper.
9. *Kohs Block Design* consists of designs to be reproduced using colored cubical blocks similar to children's blocks.

The Revised Form II of the Arthur Performance Scale (Arthur, 1947) is an alternate to Form I with added features such as special instructions for deaf children, revisions of the Knox Cube, Seguin Form Board, Porteus Mazes, and Healy Picture Completion. A new test called the Arthur Stencil

Design Test I was also added. This test calls for the subject to reproduce designs that are presented on cards by superimposing cut-out stencils upon a solid card.

The subject is given points for his performance on each subtest of the Arthur Scale. These points are summed and the total score is converted to a mental age equivalent. An IQ may be obtained by the classical formula of MA/CA.

Another nonlanguage test of special importance to teachers is the Goodenough Draw-A-Man Test (Goodenough, 1926). For many years teachers have used this test in primary grades as an estimation of intelligence and readiness for reading. In this test each child is provided a pencil and special sheet of paper and given the following instructions:

> On these papers I want you to make a picture of a man. Make the very best picture that you can. Take your time and work very carefully. I want to see whether the boys and girls in _____ school can do as well as those in other schools. Try very hard and see what good pictures you can make [p. 85].

Figure 14 shows drawings of kindergarten children taken from Goodenough's (1926) chapter on scoring samples. Though there is an elaborate scoring system the experienced scorer can grade "forty to fifty papers an hour, although in the beginning he may not have been able to score more than five or ten an hour" (p. 87).

The important thing to remember is that the Draw-A-Man Test is not scored on esthetic or technical qualities but on the completeness and developmental maturity of the drawing. For example, a clear indication of the neck as separate from the head and body is scored a plus, not a "mere juxtaposition." Or in scoring for the head Goodenough (1926) allows credit for "any clear method of representing the head. Features alone . . . without any outline for the head itself, are not credited for this point" (p. 91).

There are many more nonlanguage tests available for school use. A good many of these may be given in groups as well as individually. Among some of the more noteworthy are the Pintner Non-Language Test, in which all instructions may be given by pantomime, and the Nebraska Test of Learning Aptitude, which was standardized on deaf and near-deaf children (individual test).

Culture-Fair Tests

In Chapter 2 we discussed the issues surrounding the problem of cultural bias in tests. This section will not deal with the controversial aspects of cultural test bias but only with a discussion of the efforts to develop culturally fair instruments. Not too many years ago the term used was *culture-free*, however this designation was soon dropped when measurement people,

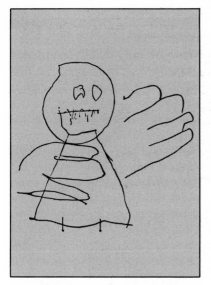

Boy, American, age 4-7, kindergarten.
Total score 10. M.A. 5-6. IQ 120.

Boy, American, age 5-10. kindergarten.
Total score 15. M.A. 6-9. IQ 116.

Girl, American, age 5-6, kindergarten.
Total score 8. M.A. 5-0. IQ 91.

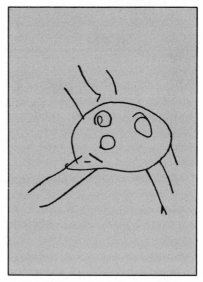

Girl, Italian, age 6-0, pre-school.
Total score 6. M.A. 4-6. IQ 75.

Figure 14. Four drawings by children showing age, score, M.A. and IQ. (From *Measurement of Intelligence by Drawings* by Florence L. Goodenough, copyright, 1926, by Harcourt, Brace & World, Inc., renewed 1954 by Florence L. Goodenough. Reproduced by permission of the publishers.)

after reviewing years of experimentation and clinical data, realized that no test is "culture-free." The aim today is not to produce an instrument free of culture but an instrument relatively fair to different cultures. For example, the American test that assumes a basic American background in football and baseball and uses items that reflect this exposure would not necessarily be fair for an English or German student and certainly would not be appropriate for an African village boy or girl.

Culture-fair tests are similar to nonlanguage tests in that they are almost always nonverbal. They must, of course, be more than nonverbal; they must also be free of cultural bias. The Army Beta (see Chapter 2) is a nonlanguage examination; however the Picture-Completion Test in it has items such as a violin, gun, and pocketknife which are cultural products.

One of the first attempts to develop a culture-free test was the Cattell Culture Free Intelligence Test. This test is based on the underlying assumption that general intelligence is a behavioral act of seeing relationships in the things with which we have to deal and that this aptitude to view relationships may be tested with simple diagrammatic or pictorial material. In addition, if the test is to be used in different cultures, the pictures or forms of objects should be universal and not confined to any cultural group. There is no evidence that, in fact, the test is useful for different cultures (Thorndike and Hagen, 1969).

Another "culture-free" test, developed in Great Britain by Raven (1938, 1947, 1962), is the Progressive Matrices. It is a nonverbal test series requiring the subject to solve problems presented in abstract figures and designs. The 1938 form consists of sixty matrices (designs) from each of which a part has been removed. The subject is required to choose the missing insert from six to eight alternatives. The 1947 form contains the two most elementary sets from the 1938 edition plus additional items. The 1962 form is a thirty-six-problem series designed for people with above average intelligence. All forms have norms obtained from an English population. The Progressive Matrices, though useful in a clinical setting, have not shown any substantial research data in terms of validity or reliability.

A great deal of research has taken place since Cattell first introduced the Culture Free Test. Since then numerous tests purporting to be culturally free or culturally fair have been constructed and tested with little positive results. (See, for example, Fowler, 1955, and Coleman and Ward, 1955.) Their predictive validity has not been as good as other "culturally biased" instruments, yet they do not eliminate this "bias." The research continues to demonstrate that lower-class children perform generally as poorly on "culture-free" instruments as on other less culturally controlled devices.

Wesman (1968) feels that the search for the culture-free or culture-fair is "sheer nonsense." He states,

> The implicit intent in the attempt to create culture-free or culture-fair tests is somehow to measure intelligence without permitting the

effects of differential exposure to learning to influence scores. This contains the tacit assumption that "native intelligence" lies buried in pure form deep in the individual, and needs only to be uncovered by ingenious mining methods. If we recognize that intelligence comprises learning experiences, it becomes clear that our attempts are not ingenious, but ingenuous [p. 269].

Infant and Preschool Tests

In spite of all our democratic conceptions, and misconceptions, about everybody being equal, there is scarcely a home in which parents and grandparents do not take a natural interest in the "smartness" of their particular baby or preschooler [Ilg and Ames, 1955, p. 189].

Gesell (1940) was one of the first to design tests based on observation of the child's perceptual, postural, and manipulative responses. His first tests were a rattle, a ring on a string, a cup and spoon, a 1-inch cube, a small sugar pellet, and a pencil and paper. The child's first reaction to the pellet occurs at about four months of age, when he sees it on a table top or other piece of furniture propped before him. This initial reaction is visual only. Three months later at seven months, he will take it awkwardly with his hands; by one year he will handle it with precision (Ilg and Ames, 1965).

Some of the questions asked by Gesell (and by psychologists today) about a child are the following: Does he sit up, stand up? If so, at what age? Does he walk and if so at what age? Does the child turn to look at a light? Does he notice a face? Can he use his hands to pick up a block, spoon, or tiny pellet? What kind of grasping motion does he use?

Gesell in 1927 began his famous longitudinal study of the normal developmental stages of the human infant. Repeated observations of 107 infants constituting a generally "normal" sample were made. The children were judged healthy with no known problems. They came from American-born parents of Northern European extraction and were considered of middle-class status in terms of socioeconomic and educational level. The infants were examined at the ages of four, six, and eight weeks and at four-week intervals until fifty-six weeks of age. Followups were made later at eighteen months, at two, three, four, five, and six years. Over a ten-year period re-examinations were made when possible. The Gesell Developmental Schedules were constructed from the data obtained (Gesell and Amatruda, 1938; Gesell 1949). (See Figure 15, which presents the materials used in testing.)

Gesell and Amatruda (1947, pp. 5–6) outlined four major areas for determining the child's level of behavioral development. They are in brief summary:

Figure 15. Gesell Developmental Schedules materials. (Reproduced by permission of The Psychological Corporation.)

    1. *Motor behavior :* Postural reactions, head balance, sitting, standing, creeping, walking, manipulation of objects and so forth.
    2. *Adaptive behavior :* Eye-hand coordination in grasping, reading, and manipulation of objects.
    3. *Language behavior :* Facial expression, gestures, postural movements, and speech. Also comprehension of other people's speech is noted.
    4. *Personal-social behavior :* Feeding, toilet training, play, smiling, and so forth.

    The Gesell Developmental Schedules are for the most part observational "tests." Approximate developmental levels in terms of months in each of the four areas are scored.
    Other infant tests such as the Cattell Infant Intelligence Scale, California First-Year Mental Scale, and the Kuhlmann-Binet are more in the classic tradition of standardized tests, although they all have items in common with the Gesell and Binet scales.
    Validity and reliability data on infant tests are generally quite low. Bayley (1949) studied the relationship of test results in the first year of life with later scores using the California First-Year Mental Scale, California Preschool

Scale and the Stanford-Binet. The results were very disconcerting. For example, scores obtained by infants tested at ten, eleven, and twelve months correlated with scores obtained at five, six, and seven years of age, at 0.20.

It is this writer's opinion that infant tests are too crude today to put much weight to their results. A much better measure is the developmental growth norms such as those developed at the Gesell Institute. If used as rough gauges of behavioral growth they may be of some help. To depend, however, on any of the infant tests is to court predictive disaster.

The Merrill-Palmer Scale (Stutsman, 1931) is one of the best-known tests designed for preschool children. The age range is from two to four. There are thirty-eight tests which yield a total of ninety-three scorable test areas. Only four call for verbal responses. Some of the tasks are "standing on one foot," "building a block tower," and "cutting with scissors."

The Minnesota Preschool Scale (Goodenough and Maurer, 1942) is another widely known preschool test. There are two forms, each containing twenty-six tests, with a format very similar to the Binet. Some of the tests are the following:

> *Test 5: Imitative Drawing.* The examiner draws a vertical stroke and then a cross. The child is to imitate each.
> *Test 8: Imitation.* A set of four cubes, on which examiner taps in a certain manner and child is requested to imitate the sequence of taps.
> *Test 14: Colors.* Child is asked to name the color of cards that are red, blue, pink, white, and brown.
> *Test 20: Paper Folding.* Examiner takes paper and folds it in three consecutive folds and then asks child to copy his actions.

The most outstanding features of the Minnesota Preschool Scale are the careful procedures that were followed in the standardization. It has been found to be especially relevant for children between the ages of three and five years.

The Wechsler Preschool and Primary Scale of Intelligence (1967), which has been reviewed earlier in this chapter, holds a great deal of promise as an instrument to relieve the paucity of good tests for preschoolers. According to Wood and Deal (1968) the tests that are presently being used most frequently for the study of infants and preschoolers are the following: Cattell Infant Intelligence Scale, California First-Year Mental Scale, Gesell Developmental Schedules, Merrill-Palmer Scale of Mental Tests, and the Stanford-Binet Intelligence Scale.

A great deal of additional research and better instruments need to be developed in this area of preschool testing. For a general overview and a more detailed analysis of infant and preschool tests the reader should consult Buros (1965).

References

Anastasi, A. *Psychological testing*. (3rd ed.) New York: Macmillan, 1968.

Arthur, G. *A point scale of performance tests*. Vol. II. *The process of standardization*. New York: Commonwealth Fund, 1933.

Arthur, G. *A point scale of performance tests*. Vol. I. (2nd ed.) Chicago: Stoelting, 1943.

Arthur, G. *A point scale of performance tests*. Revised Form II. *Manual for administering and scoring the tests*. New York: The Psychological Corporation, 1947.

Bayley, N. Consistency and variability in the growth of intelligence from birth to eighteen years. *Journal of Genetic Psychology*, 1949, **75,** 165–96.

Buros, O. K. (Ed.) *The sixth mental measurements yearbook*. Highland Park, N.J.: Gryphon Press, 1965.

Chauncey, H., and Dobbin, J. E. Testing has a history. In C. I. Chase and H. G. Ludlow (Eds.), *Readings in educational and psychological measurement*. Boston: Houghton Mifflin, 1966, Pp. 3–17.

Coleman, W., and Ward, A. Comparison of Davis-Eells and Kuhlmann-Finch scores of children from high and low socioeconomic status. *Journal of Educational Psychology*, 1955, **46,** 465–69.

Cronbach, L. J. *Essentials of psychological testing*. (2nd ed.) New York: Harper & Row, 1960.

Downie, N. M. *Fundamentals of measurement: Techniques and practices*. (2nd ed.) New York: Oxford University Press, 1967.

Fowler, W. L. *A comparative analysis of pupil performance on conventional and culture-controlled mental tests*. Unpublished doctoral dissertation, University of Michigan, 1955.

Gesell, A., and Amatruda, C. *The psychology of early growth*. New York: Macmillan, 1938.

Gesell, A., and Amatruda, C. *Developmental diagnosis: Normal and abnormal child development* (2nd ed.) New York: Hoeber, 1947.

Gesell, A. et al. *The first five years of life: a guide to the study of the preschool child*. New York: Harper & Row, 1940.

Gesell, A. et al. *Gesell Developmental Schedules*. New York: The Psychological Corporation, 1949.

Goodenough, F. L. *Measurement of intelligence by drawings*. New York: Harcourt, Brace and World, 1926.

Goodenough, F., and Maurer, K. *The mental growth of children from two to fourteen years: A study of the predictive value of the Minnesota Preschool Scales*. Minneapolis: University of Minnesota Press, 1942.

Ilg, F. L., and Ames, L. B. *Child behavior*. New York: Dell, 1955.

Ilg, F. L., and Ames, L. B. *School readiness: Behavior tests used at the Gesell institute*. New York: Harper & Row, 1965.

McNemar, Q. Lost: Our intelligence. Why? In C. I. Chase and H. G. Ludlow (Eds.), *Readings in educational and psychological measurement*. Boston: Houghton Mifflin, 1966. Pp. 180–97.

Merrill, M. A. Training students to administer the Stanford-Binet Intelligence Scale. *Testing today*. Houghton Mifflin, (three-page letter to the Editor, distributed by Houghton Mifflin, no date).

Raven, J. *Progressive matrices, Forms, 1938, 1947, 1962.* New York: The Psychological Corporation.

Schafer, R. *The clinical application of psychological tests.* New York: International Universities Press, Inc., 1948.

Stutsman, R. *Mental measurement of preschool children.* New York: World Book Co., 1931.

Terman, L. M. *The measurement of intelligence.* Boston: Houghton Mifflin, 1916.

Terman, L. M., and Merrill, M. A. *Measuring intelligence.* Boston: Houghton Mifflin, 1937.

Terman, L. M., and Merrill, M. A. *Stanford-Binet Intelligence Scale: Manual for the third revision, form L-M.* Boston: Houghton Mifflin, 1960.

Thorndike, R. L., and Hagen, E. *Measurement and evaluation in psychology and education.* (3rd ed.) New York: Wiley, 1969.

Wechsler, D. *Wechsler Intelligence Scale for Children* (manual). New York: The Psychological Corporation, 1949.

Wechsler, D. *Manual for the Wechsler Adult Intelligence Scale.* New York: The Psychological Corporation, 1955.

Wechsler, D. *The measurement and appraisal of adult intelligence.* (4th ed.) Baltimore: Williams and Wilkins, 1958.

Wechsler, D. *Manual for the Wechsler Preschool and Primary Scale of Intelligence.* New York: The Psychological Corporation, 1967.

Wesman, A. G. Intelligent testing. *American Psychologist,* 1968. **23,** 267–74.

Wood, P. L., and Deal, T. N. Testing the early educational and psychological development of children—ages 3–6. *Review of Educational Research,* 1968, **38,** 12–18.

CHAPTER
8

Projective Techniques

Projective techniques are not tests in the true sense, because there are no right or wrong answers. One cannot obtain a perfect score or fail. Certainly there are "right" answers in the sense that a group of certain kinds of responses reveal to the trained examiner personality traits which may be pathological. There are, however, no definitive raw scores that point to mental illness or the absence of disturbance.

Projective techniques are used in personality testing in order to explore the individual's world of make-believe. To accomplish this, material that is indefinite and vague is presented to the person who then is to respond in his own unique manner.

Frank (1939) introduced the term *projective techniques* long after the actual instruments had been in use. He thought of them as similar to the X-ray methods of medicine. Frank and others have delineated the projective technique from other personality instruments by focusing on the ambiguity or unstructuredness of the stimulus material, thereby allowing the subject almost complete freedom of response. With an objective personality test (see Chapter 12), on the other hand, the subject responds to a limited number of predetermined responses.

Another distinctive characteristic of projective techniques is their *indirectness;* that is, the subject being examined is not completely aware of how his responses are going to be evaluated and is therefore less inclined to fake or resist answering. For example, if someone asked you, "Do you love your mother?" How would you answer? Obviously, social and personal (at the conscious level) forces would exert a strong influence. If, on the other hand, the name *mother* was stated as one word in a group of words that you were to respond to ("first thing that comes to your mind"), you would not have time to be as defensive or control your response.

Levy (1963) does not agree completely with the distinctions between projective techniques and objective personality testing. He states,

> . . . we are forced to conclude that the identity of projective techniques as a unique class of techniques is on very shaky grounds if these are either the amount of freedom of response offered the examinee or the ambiguity of the stimulus presented to him. At best, tests might be ordered along such continua. But that such an ordering would result in a bimodal distribution, with conventionally designated projective tests making up one hump and non-projective tests the other, seems quite unlikely [p. 201].

The reader of this book need not concern himself at this point with the nuances of psychological pedantry.[1] The teacher and counselor need to know that a projective technique or device attempts to elicit free and un-guided responses through unstructured material. It is true that in a sense anything can be called a projective technique. That is, predictions may be made from a sample of behavior. The psychologist who reports his findings from intelligence testing has more to say than what the subject's IQ is. He observes the quality of performance and behavior of the person during the test and generalizes from these impressions in the same or similar manner that one does in interpreting responses on projective devices.

Projective techniques have their rationale in everyday observations. For example, did you ever notice how one person will view an accident, play, or painting in a manner unique to himself? The manner in which a person perceives things depends upon his background, and this, of course, varies with each individual. The more vague the material presented to a person, the more opportunity he has to project himself into it. Projective tests take advantage of this situation. An ink blot, a picture, or a word may suffice as a means of finding out about the person's feelings and thoughts.

The projective device originated within a clinical setting and is the favorite personality test of the clinician and to a somewhat lesser degree the school psychologist. Most projective devices have as their theoretical base the psychoanalytic system of human behavior. Psychologists, of course, with other orientations also utilize projective techniques. Projective techniques

---

[1] Ainsworth (1951) and Murstein (1961) discuss in great detail the assumptions and problems in projective techniques. The teacher who is interested in pursuing this subject further is referred to their discussions.

are not only used in ascertaining personality characteristics, but also in uncovering intelligence, creativity, attitudes, and social traits.

In our schools projective devices are only administered after other informational sources, such as classroom behavior, teacher opinion, objective tests, and interviews, have failed to provide enough information. The school psychologist is usually the only school person trained to use the projective technique, and he uses it with only a small number of students who present serious emotional and/or intellectual problems. *Projective techniques are never given to all students.* In addition, when the school psychologist does administer a projective device in almost all cases he obtains parental consent.

The number and various types of projective techniques is quite large. A review, in depth, of them all is beyond the scope of this book. We will, therefore, focus our attention on a few that you as a teacher or counselor may encounter in the schools. (For a thorough and extensive survey and evaluation of projective techniques see the Mental Measurements Yearbooks. These volumes have a separate section devoted to projective techniques.)

In the remainder of this chapter we will focus our primary attention on the Rorschach, Thematic Apperception Test, and Draw-A-Person.

Rorschach

Overview

The *Rorschach* is one of the basic diagnostic tools of most psychologists. This test is sometimes referred to as the ink-blot test. It consists of ten cards, each having a different ink blot; five are printed in black and white and five in color.

The psychologist shows one card at a time to a child (or adult), asking him to tell what the ink blot makes him think of and what it may mean to him. After the initial instructions, the psychologist does not directly help or instruct the subject except to show him the cards. After the ten cards have been given they are presented a second time. In this phase the psychologist attempts to find out what in the ink blot made the person answer as he did. For example, the psychologist may state, "What in card 1 made you think of a bat?" In this manner the psychologist gains insight as to where in the ink blot the person saw the "bat" as well as what in the person's background made him think of a bat.

Throughout the Rorschach examination, the psychologist records in detail the person's responses. After the test is completed, an analysis of the record is made. The scoring and interpretation of the Rorschach record is a long and complicated task, and the psychologist needs a great deal of training and experience to do it competently. Thus the administration and scoring of a Rorschach should not be undertaken by a teacher, counselor, or even some psychologists who have not undergone special training. The Rorschach should only be administered by trained clinical or school psychologists and only to students who are in need of it.

History

The earliest use of ink blots that we know of was recorded in a book entitled *Kleksographien*, published in Germany in 1857. The author Justinus Kerner recounts that he accidentally found out about the inherent possibilities in ink blots by noting the bizarre configurations they seemed to take on as he observed them. Kerner's most interesting finding was that it seemed almost impossible to reproduce ink blots according to a preconceived plan. He had experienced the interplay between the objective aspects of the ink blot per se and the individual perception of the observer. Kerner did not realize the significance of his observations as a method of personality diagnosis (Klopfer and Kelley, 1946).

Alfred Binet was one of the first to recognize the possible applications of the ink blots to personality diagnosis. A series of investigations made by Binet and other psychologists followed, with the focus of their attention on the content of the subject's responses to the ink blots. The ink blots were used as stimulus material for free associations (Klopfer and Kelley, 1946). It remained in this domain until Herman Rorschach, a Swiss psychiatrist, published the results of ten years of ink blot experimentation in various psychopathic hospitals in Switzerland. These findings were published in 1921 in a monograph entitled *Psychodiagnostik* (Rorschach, 1942). The chief characteristic of Rorschach's findings over that of previous investigators was the focus of attention on the manner of handling the stimulus material rather than just what was seen.

Unfortunately Dr. Rorschach died a few months after the publication of his findings. Oberholzer, Rorschach's colleague, took over and became a leader of the Rorschach technique. Oberholzer was responsible for the first publications of the technique in the United States and also trained Americans, such as David Levy, in its use. Under Levy, Samuel Beck wrote the first doctoral dissertation, in 1930, on the Rorschach technique in the United States.

Since Beck's dissertation the Rorschach has grown in influence and acceptance among American psychologists. It is now a basic tool in the evaluation of personality characteristics.

Test Administration

The relationship between the examiner and subject is extremely important. Usually other tests are given first and rapport established before the Rorschach is administered. The behavior of the subject during the administration is noted and is used in completing the diagnosis. On the other hand, Klopfer et al. (1954) state, "Although it is desirable to have 'good' rapport, it is unnecessary to assume that this is essential in order for the test report to be valid. It seems more important that the relationship, whatever it is, should be clearly perceived and understood by the examiner" (pp. 3–4).

The actual examination consists of three basic phases. Let us briefly review these in the context of an actual examination using only one of the ten cards as an example. The reader should note that in the examination each phase is continued until the completion of the ten cards and then the next phase is initiated.

Performance Phase—Card I

Examiner: I have some ink blots to show you and I want you to tell me what they make you think of, what you see, and what it might mean for you. Remember, this is not a test in the usual sense of failing or passing. You can't get a "hundred" or a "zero" as you can on a test in the classroom. People see all kinds of things in these ink blots. Now tell me what what you see and what they make you think of.[2]

Subject: It looks like a bat with large wings. It's . . . ah . . . it's flying.

Examiner: Anything else; remember, tell me what you see and what it makes you think of.[3]

Subject: Just a bat flying—nothing else. (*Subject is given the next card and responds; this procedure is followed until ten cards have been administered.*)

Inquiry Phase—Card I

Examiner: You did very well. Now we are going to go back and look at the cards again and I want you to tell me *what in the cards* made you think of what you said. In card 1 you saw a bat flying; now tell me what in the card made you think of a bat.

Subject: It just looks like a bat.

Examiner: It just looks like a bat?

Subject: Yes, it looks like a bat; it has wings, a body, and face and its shape, just looks like a bat to me. (*Procedure is followed until ten cards are completed.*)

[2] It should be noted that the language is, of course, varied according to the subject and situation, although the basic instructions remain the same.

[3] After this prompting the examiner will not say anything else throughout this phase of the examination.

Testing of the Limits—Card I

Examiner: You said you saw a bat in card one?
Subject: Yes, because of its shape.
Examiner: Any other reason?
Subject: No, just its shape.
Examiner: What about the color black?
Subject: Yes, that's right, I think black and death and bats all are the same. Like vampires—black is the color—but also the shape was important. (*This phase only used on cards in which the examiner needs more information*).

Summarizing, then, the three basic phases and their modes of operation are:

Performance. Nondirective and free association period where subject gives the first thoughts that come into his mind.

Inquiry. Some nondirective prodding to find out what made the subject respond as he did. This phase makes scoring possible and gives chance to the subject to supplement and complete his original responses.

Testing the limits. Degrees of pressure exerted to find out what in the card made the subject respond as he did. Used when two other phases have not produced rationale for responses. This phase *is not scored,* but used as clinical evidence.

Scoring

There are two widely used and different procedures for scoring the Rorschach (Beck, 1944, Klopfer and Kelley, 1946. Klopfer et al., 1954). The scoring procedure we will discuss is based on the Klopfer technique.

The examiner in scoring the Rorschach has the option of using the quantitative method and/or content analysis. Let us look at the quantitative procedure first.

First the examiner looks for the location of the response. Where in the blot did the subject see, for example, the bat. If he used the whole blot, the response is scored W. If he used a large part of the blot, it is scored D. If he only used a small unusual part of the blot, it is scored Dd. Use of the white space rather than the black ink blot is scored S.

The next concern of the scorer is the determinant for the subject's response—the characteristic of the blot that promoted the response. The primary determinants are figures in human-like action (M), animals in animal-like action (FM), abstract movement (m), shading (k), and color (c). In addition, each response is evaluated on its relevancy to the blot.

The third category is content. This area is focused on what actually is seen in the blot. Among some of the frequent content responses are human figures (H), human details (Hd), animals (A), objects from animal parts, like fur (A obj.), man-made objects (obj.), and so forth.

Each response is also analyzed to determine if it is original or popular. The definitions of original and popular response depend on the classification system used. In general terms, however, a popular response is one given by a majority of subjects, whereas an original response is one that is rarely if ever seen.

Interpretation

The interpretation of a Rorschach record is a difficult and laborious process requiring rigorous training and clinical experience. A detailed analysis here would be at best an incomplete statement. Several textbooks dealing only with the Rorschach are usual for the serious study of the technique. Therefore, the reader should note that what follows is only a simple and extremely brief summary of some of the key features of interpretation.

Quantitative Analysis. In this approach the interrelationships between various scoring classifications previously mentioned (e.g., W, FM, A, P) are noted and studied. Some of the possible interpretations, for example, are

1. A great many human responses (M) that are appropriate for the given ink blot and are sufficiently explained is a sign of high intellectual endowment.
2. When M's appear in optimal relationship with animal responses (FM), this is a sign of self-acceptance.
3. Color responses, shading, and texture give evidence of the subject's emotional life.
4. The location areas that the subject chooses may suggest his typical approach to problems and situations with which he deals in everyday life.

Content Analysis. Certain responses may be interpreted symbolically; for example, snakes and totem poles may indicate sexual feelings. The absence of human figures may indicate the subject has little empathy for people. Animal responses in young children are quite normal; however, an adult who gives a great many may be infantile. In addition, certain cards usually evoke certain responses; the absence or avoidance of these may reveal characteristics of the subject.

Synthesis. The proper interpretation of the Rorschach requires the examiner to bring to bear all the features mentioned in an analysis of the quantitative and content relationships and their frequency; of the consistency of the various hypotheses that are derived and of how well they go together with the behavorial notations and the subject's case history. This process requires not only training and skill but an intuitive approach called clinical judgment. This dependence on clinical feeling is one of the major hurdles to be overcome in the statistical validation of the Rorschach.

Evaluation

The Rorschach is a very difficult instrument on which to establish statistical validity because of its inherent reliance on the clinical experience of the person scoring and interpreting the record. The various studies and investigations do not reveal empirical validation for the scoring system of the Rorschach. The Rorschach has been found to have little predictive validity when compared to psychiatric diagnosis and other criteria. The studies that do reveal validity have been criticized on methodological grounds. Thus, it must be stated that from a statistical and experimental viewpoint the Rorschach is no better than an interview device. On the other hand, it must also be stated that a great many clinical and school psychologists view the Rorschach as a valid and reliable instrument based on their professional experiences. In addition, psychiatrists rely heavily upon the psychologists' findings, which are based largely though not completely on the Rorschach.

In the author's experience as a clinical and school psychologist the Rorschach has been found to be invaluable. Although recognizing its limitations, the author feels it is valid if administered and interpreted by a trained and experienced person. Its chief limitation to the clinical user is that it is time-consuming. The average administration, scoring, interpretation and write-up of the Rorschach takes between six and eight hours.

The Rorschach is used by the school psychologist only when other devices are inadequate and only when parental permission is obtained. In these circumstances it can be of invaluable assistance.

Thematic Apperception Test

Another projective technique in wide use is the Thematic Apperception Test (TAT). It was developed in 1935 by two psychologists, H. A. Murray and C. D. Morgan, of the Harvard Psychological Clinic (Murray, 1938, 1943). The TAT is almost as widely used as the Rorschach. Clinical and school psychologists use it as one of the basic instruments in their psychological test battery. In addition to its years of service in the diagnostic test battery, it has also served as a model for later instruments which have the same story-type format.

Test Administration

The TAT consists of a set of pictures showing human figures in different poses and actions. Some of the pictures are only for boys, others for girls, some for adults (over fourteen years of age), and others are for all individuals. There are nineteen pictures for a particular age and sex and one blank card. The psychologist, in most cases, does not administer all twenty cards but selects only those he considers particularly appropriate for a given person.

The psychologist instructs the subject to tell him a story based on the picture presented. He requests a past, present, and future for each of the stories. The exact instructions sometimes vary, but they always include the request for a past, present, and future in the subject's story. Generally, the instructions are the following:

> I am going to show you some pictures. I'd like you to tell me a story about what is going on in each picture, what has led up to it, what is happening now, and what may happen in the future. Remember that there are no right or wrong stories, only what you see. Here's the first picture—now tell me a story about what has happened and what is happening and what you think will happen.

The TAT stories are either taped or taken down verbatim by the psychologist. No time limits are given and the subject may tell a short or long story, depending on how he feels.

Scoring

The scoring of the TAT is not quite as time-consuming as the Rorschach. Many different scoring techniques have been advocated for the TAT. Shneidman (1951) presents many of the methods commonly used by recognized experts. These range from an emphasis on the content of the stories (interpersonal relations, parent-child, etc.) to a statistical-normative approach. Whatever method is used in interpretation, the examiner attempts to obtain a whole picture by analyzing all the cards administered rather than by drawing conclusions from only one card.

Let us examine one commonly used method, a content analysis of the stories. This is a clinical method whereby the examiner attempts to discover the psychodynamic causes of disturbed behavior or of the level of adjustment. The first step is to read the record for a general impression. Secondly, the examiner summarizes each story and obtains its salient features. Thirdly, each story is analyzed for possible conflict, mother-child relationships, sexual identity, hostility, aggression, defenses (for example, rationalization and projection), and so forth. After these analyses have been made, they are put together to form a general picture. Themes such as anxiety, sibling conflicts, and other disturbing features that recur on more than one card are looked for. As Lasaga (1951) states,

> If a person has extremely intense worries or conflicts, these worries or conflicts will show up again and again in a large number of the stories of the test, possibly in most of them. This means that every

> TAT certainly reflects several aspects of the whole personality of the subject being tested, but, when one or more intense conflicts exist in the subject's life at the moment the test is made, what will appear first of all in the TAT will be these conflicts [p. 145].

Let us look at the story of an eleven-year-old boy in the fifth grade. The story is in response to a TAT card which presents a boy of about the same age sitting down and looking at a violin and bow with his hands supporting his face.

> Well, this is the past. He was going with his mother to buy a violin and dropped it and tripped over it and fell flat on his face and blood came gushing out. After he had gone to the doctor, he came home and was crying because the violin was broken. Probably some day, he'll fall again, and he'll get his violin fixed. I didn't mean to say he'll fall again.

The boy who gave the preceding response was referred to this writer because of academic and social difficulties. He would not play with other children and felt inadequate with them. "I am not as good as other kids." When asked about school he stated, "I am so far behind. I am dumb."

What do you think about this boy? Read his story again. The other TAT stories as well as his Rorschach responses and other tests revealed a child who lacked social alertness and was unable to deal with social situations. More importantly, strong trends indicating possible criminal behavior as he grew older were noted. Psychotherapy was recommended.

Lasaga (1951) states that conflicts may appear at the conscious, partially conscious, or unconscious level while the subject is taking the test. Thus, Lasaga (1951) concludes that,

> When a test presents stories other than those totally objective or completely trivial, which cannot be explained literally by conflicts or facts of the patient's life; then it is to be supposed that such stories express in a symbolic or metaphoric form worries and happenings in his real life [p. 145].

Evaluation

The TAT has been used in many research investigations. Little and Shneidman (1955) in an attempt to study the clinical validity of the TAT found that even among expert interpreters a great range of validity coefficients are obtained. This study, as well as many others, fails to establish clinical validity for the TAT. It must be admitted, as with the Rorschach, that the TAT is not an objective test and that its validity and reliability in statistical terms does not warrant its use. Although statistical techniques have not supported the claims of TAT advocates, clinical day-to-day experience has shown its wide and beneficial use in clinics, hospitals, schools, and in industrial appraisal for executive employment.

Other Projective Story Techniques

Make a Picture Story (MAPS)

The MAPS test was developed by Shneidman in 1947 and has been referred to as a "younger brother" of the TAT. It is different from the TAT in that it varies the material by separating the figures and backgrounds and allows the subject to select and place his choice of figures on a blank background before he relates a story.

The materials for the MAPS consist of twenty-two background pictures (8½ by 11 in.) printed achromatically on cardboard. With two exceptions, there are no figures in any of the pictures. Some of the unstructured backgrounds are a stage and a blank card; others are semistructured, such as a forest and desertlike landscape; and others are structured, such as a medical scene and bathroom.

There are sixty-seven figures with various facial expressions and various types of dress. Among these are males and females, children, Negroes, Orientals, Mexicans, and animal figures. See Figure 16, which presents the figures used.

Shneidman (1951) illustrates a typical administration of the MAPS:

> What I am going to do is show you pictures like this, one at a time. [*Livingroom background picture was placed directly in front of the subject.*] You will have figures like this [*at this point all the figures were poured out of their envelope onto the table top*] and your task is simply to take one or more of any of these figures and put them on the background picture as they might be in real life. We might start by sorting the figures so that you can see each one. Spread them out on the table.

After all of the figures had been placed on the table by the subject, the examiner stated,

> I would like to go over the instructions . . . all you are to do is take one or more of any of these figures, put them on the background as they might be in real life, and tell a story of the situation which you have created. In telling your story, tell, if you can, who the characters are, what they are doing and thinking and feeling, and how the whole things turn out. Go ahead [p. 19].

Figure 16. Make A Picture Story materials. (From E. S. Shneidman. Reproduced by permission of The Psychological Corporation.)

The MAPS is essentially an unstandardized test investigating psychosocial areas of fantasy. A formal scoring system has been developed, but there are no statistical data that support its validity or reliability. As with the Rorschach and TAT its primary role is in clinical, rather than objective, evaluation.

The Blacky Pictures

These pictures were originally constructed to test certain psychoanalytic concepts. The Blacky Pictures (Blum, 1950) consists of ten cards that display cartoonlike drawings. These cartoon drawings center around the "adventures" of a dog called Blacky.

Blacky can be of either sex, depending on the projection and identification of the subject. The test may be used with children but was originally designed for adults. The main theme of the cartoons centers on psychosexual development. The method of administration is like that of the TAT except that the subject is asked, in addition to telling a story, to answer a set of standardized questions. School psychologists must be especially careful in administering this test because of the overt sexual connotations. As in all personality assessment, parental permission must be granted before the test is given.

The Blacky Pictures can be a useful tool with many research advantages. It is not, however, an objective or standardized instrument. Used by competent clinicians, it can be of diagnostic assistance.

Symonds Picture-Story Test

The Symonds Picture-Story is basically a projective technique designed to study the personality characteristics of adolescent boys and girls. It has the same test format as the TAT, but it uses a set of pictures constructed to study adolescent fantasy. The administration and scoring are similar to the TAT procedures. There are twenty pictures which may be given to boys or girls.

Symonds (1948) suggests that the examiner's main task in the content analysis is to record the principal psychological forces in the stories. He lists fourteen forces which should be noted in the content analysis:

> (1) Hostility and aggression, (2) love and erotism, (3) ambivalence, (4) punishment, (5) anxiety, (6) defenses against anxiety, (7) moral standards and conflicts, (8) ambition, striving toward success, (9) conflicts, (10) guilt, (11) guilt reduction, (12) depression, discouragement, despair, (13) happiness and (14) sublimation [pp. 10–12].

The Symonds test, like other clinical instruments, has little statistical validity but may be useful to the skilled examiner. A full explanation and detailed aspects of the test can be found in Symonds' *Adolescent Fantasy* (1949).

Children's Apperception Test

The Children's Apperception Test (CAT) is very similar to the TAT, but animals rather than people are employed. This substitution is based on the assumption that children can more readily identify with animals than with people (Bellak, 1954). The animals are pictured in typical activities of humans in the same manner as in books for children. The CAT is designed to stimulate fantasies centering around possible areas of conflict such as eating, sibling rivalry, aggression, toilet-training, and other developmental experiences of childhood.

The administration and scoring of the CAT, as well as its validity and reliability, are similar to the previously mentioned picture story techniques. Several studies have shown, however, no significant differences between the story responses of children exposed to human and animal figures (see Armstrong, 1954, and Furuya, 1957). It has been this writer's experience that most psychologists use the TAT for both children and adults, and only occasionally use the CAT as a replacement for the TAT.

Other Types of Projective Techniques

Word Association Test

Word association tests attempt to reveal associative connections between certain prescribed words and the free verbal responses of the subject. This technique has a long history dating back to Galton and Wundt and carried forward by the well-known psychoanalyst Dr. Carl Jung (1910). Jung used words that were common to emotional fixations. He would state a word and then record the subject's verbal reaction word and the time taken to respond. The words, reaction time, and behavioral mannerisms while responding were recorded and an analysis was then made.

Kent and Rosanoff (1910) designed a free-association test as a psychiatric screening instrument using common, "normal" words. These words tended to stimulate common associations rather than atypical responses. Frequency tables were developed that contained the number of times a response to a given word was found in 1,000 adults. If a subject replied with a different response, that is, if it was not found in the table, his response was labeled *idiosyncratic*. This test's validity was obviated somewhat when other variables in addition to mental illness, such as age, sex, culture, and education, were found to influence responses.

Sentence Completion Tests

The Rotter Incomplete Sentences Blank is a good illustration of a sentence completion test. The Rotter comes in three forms—High School, College, and Adult. All three forms have forty stems such as "The happiest day" and "I love." The High School and Adult forms differ slightly in the wording of a few items. The College form was used in the initial standardization. The subject is asked to express his true feelings in completing each stem.

The usual kind of clinical interpretations of the content of the sentences are made. In addition, numerical scores can also be obtained. The scoring method is predicated on three categories: conflict or unhealthy responses, neutral responses, and positive or healthy responses. There is no time limit.

Draw-A-Person Test

Karen Machover is responsible for the well-known Draw-A-Person projective device. It is her feeling, as well as that of many others, that a drawing of the human figure is tied up with the personality of the individual doing the drawing. Machover (1949) states,

> When an individual attempts to solve the problem of the directive to "draw a person," he is compelled to draw from some sources. External figures are too varied in their body attributes to lend themselves to a spontaneous, objective representation of a person. Some process of selection involving identification through projection and

introjection enters at some point. The individual must draw consciously, and no doubt unconsciously, upon his whole system of psychic values. The body, or the self, is the most intimate point of reference in any activity. We have, in the course of growth, come to associate various sensations, perceptions, and emotions with certain body organs. This investment in body image as it has developed out of personal experience, must somehow guide the individual who is drawing in the specific structure and content which constitutes his offering of a "person."

Consequently, the drawing of a person, in involving a projection of the body image, provides a natural vehicle for the expression of one's body needs and conflicts. Successful drawing interpretation has proceeded on the hypothesis that the figure drawn is related to the individual who is drawing with the same intimacy characterizing that individual's gait, his handwriting, or any other of his expressive movements [p. 5].

Administration of the Draw-A-Person Test (DAP) is relatively simple. The subject is given a sheet of paper (8½ by 11 in.) and a medium-soft pencil with eraser and told to "draw a person." If the subject is anxious about his drawing skill, the examiner reassures him that "this is not a test of artistic skill." After completing the first drawing, the subject is given another sheet of paper and told to draw a person of the sex opposite to the figure in his first drawing. If the first drawing was of a man, he is told "now go ahead and draw a woman." The examiner may sometimes question the subject after the completion of the drawings for "associations," asking what the person is doing or what his age is.

Interpretation of the DAP is based mainly on psychoanalytic theory (Machover, 1949). The drawing analyst looks for many things, including the size of the figure and where it is placed on the sheet. Shading, erasures, and background also lend themselves to analysis. For example, Machover states that "if the fist is clenched he may literally be expressing his belligerence" (p. 35). The types of clothing, nose (large or small), feet, neck, head, lips, and so forth, are also considered.

Research studies that have attempted to validate the DAP have yielded conflicting data. The DAP, as in the case of its projective brothers, is not easily quantified. It must almost be taken on faith. It is the type of instrument in which after years of usage one may have great confidence but have little scientific evidence with which to prove some of its claims. It has been the author's experience that it is a very valuable diagnostic tool when used by the skilled diagnostician as one of many measurement tools.

House-Tree-Person Test

The House-Tree-Person Test (HTP) was devised by J. N. Buck with certain preconceived ideas of what a house, tree, and person should mean to an individual. It is assumed by Buck that a house should evoke feelings concerning the subject's home, that a tree is symbolic of life and of an individual's capacity to enjoy his environment, that a person is seen as activating feelings about and needs in interpersonal relations (Buck, 1964).

Administration of the test is similar to that of the DAP. The subject is asked to draw a picture of a house and then the same instructions are repeated for the tree and person. After the drawings have been completed, certain questions, some of which are standardized, are asked. The scoring is both clinical and statistical and highly time-consuming. Validation studies do not substantiate Buck's basic rationale (see Fisher and Fisher, 1950).

The Bender-Gestalt Test

The Bender-Gestalt Test is not considered a projective technique in the same sense as is the TAT although similar elements are present. Cronbach (1960) sees the Bender-Gestalt as a "stylistic" test, that is, a technique which focuses on the subject's style of handling a problem, as contrasted to the TAT which examines the "whole person"—his emotions, attitudes, thinking, and so forth.

The Bender-Gestalt is based on the classical teachings of the Gestalt school of psychology. Bender (1938) chose nine of the original Wertheimer (one of the founders of the Gestalt school of psychology) patterns for her test. Figure 17 presents these nine patterns.

The Bender-Gestalt is used as a clinical instrument to evaluate intelligence, maturation, psychological disturbances, and brain damage. It is easily administered. The instructions generally are the following: "I have here nine simple designs (or figures) which you are to copy, free hand, without sketching—on this paper. Each design is on one of these cards which I will show you one at a time. There is no time limit to this test" (Pascal and Suttell, 1951, p. 11).

The rotation of the paper and reproduction of the figures are noted by the examiner. There are quantitative methods of scoring; however, most psychologists use the qualitative or clinical integration of all the responses in evaluating the subject's reproductions.

Evaluation of Projective Techniques

Our review of projective techniques has shown the wide variety of methods used to obtain a sample of conscious and unconscious behavioral characteristics. We have seen that most projective techniques have little, if any, statistical verification. It is obvious that evaluation of many, if not all, of the projective devices falls short. However, some studies do appear to present validity data, and the supporters of projective techniques feel that someday their views will be statistically established.

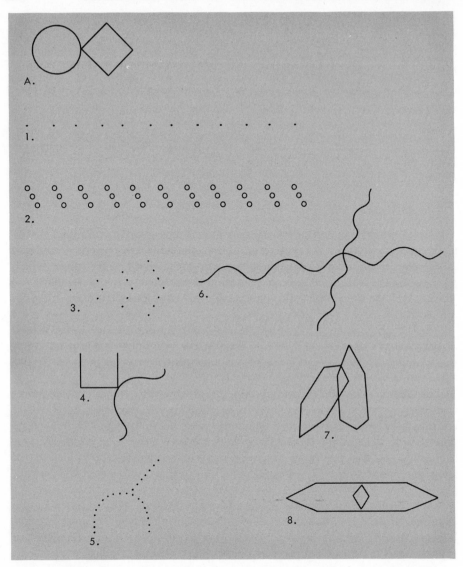

Figure 17. Designs of the Bender-Gestalt Test. (From Lauretta Bender, A Visual Motor Gestalt Test and Its Clinical Use: Research Monographs, No. 3. New York: American Orthopsychiatric Association, 1938, p. 4. Copyright, the American Orthopsychiatric Association, Inc. Reproduced by permission.)

This author believes that projective devices do not lend themselves to quantification any more than the clinical judgment of the psychiatrist or family physician can be experimentally justified. This does not prevent us from seeking help from these professionals. The positive experiences of clinical and school psychologists and their professional co-workers such as psychiatrists and social workers are testimony to the effectiveness of the projective method. Psychiatrists, by and large, do not make final disposition of a case, whether it be legal or medical, until they have seen the report of the psychologist, whose analysis and diagnosis of personality characteristics are based on projective techniques. Psychiatrists respect the analysis because they have found a high correlation between the projective findings and their own evaluations and, more importantly, between patient recovery and future behavior. Remember, the psychologist uses a battery of tests, and his opinions are based on the total picture presented by all test data, the person's history, and personal interviews.

Thus we can state that although the projective techniques generally do not meet the requirements for scientific test evaluation, from a clinician's or pragmatist's viewpoint they work. Until we have better instruments or research validation, we shall have to continue to use these devices for personality assessment.

Many schools which lack the services of a qualified full-time psychologist may have to refer a student to an outside agency. It is important to be sure of the qualifications of the person doing the testing. Certification by the state and reference statements from professional sources should be checked. School authorities should also guard against the administration of these tests without both parents' consent. In summary, projective techniques used discriminately by qualified people can be of assistance in ascertaining behavioral problems.

References

Ainsworth, M. Some problems of validation of projective techniques. *British Journal of Medical Psychology*, 1951, **24**, 151–61.

Armstrong, M. A. S. Children's responses to animal and human figures in thematic pictures. *Journal of Consulting Psychology*, 1954, **18**, 67–70.

Beck, S. J. *Rorschach's test: Vol. I, basic processes.* New York: Grune and Stratton, 1944.

Bellak, L. *The Thematic Apperception Test and the Children's Apperception Test in clinical use.* New York: Grune and Stratton, 1954.

Bender, L. *A visual motor gestalt test and its clinical use.* New York: The American Orthopsychiatric Association, 1938.

Blum, G. S. *The Blacky Pictures: A technique for the exploration of personality dynamics.* New York: The Psychological Corporation, 1950.

Buck, J. N. *H-T-P: House-Tree-Person Projective Technique.* Los Angeles: Western Psychological Services, 1964.

Cronbach, L. J. *Essentials of psychological testing.* (2nd ed.) New York: Harper & Row, 1960.

Fisher, S., and Fisher, R. A test of certain assumptions regarding figure drawing analysis. *Journal of Abnormal and Social Psychology*, 1950, **45**, 727–32.

Frank, L. Projective methods for the study of personality. *Journal of Psychology*, 1939, **8**, 389–413.

Furuya, K. Responses of school-children to human and animal pictures. *Journal of Projective Techniques,* 1957, **21,** 248–52.

Jung, C. G. The association method. *American Journal of Psychology,* 1910, **21,** 219–69.

Kent, G. H., and Rosanoff, A. J. A study of association in insanity. *American Journal of Insanity,* 1910, **67,** 317–90.

Klopfer, B., Ainsworth, M. D., Klopfer, W. G., and Holt, R. R. *Developments in the Rorschach technique.* New York: World Book Co., 1954.

Klopfer, B. and Kelley, D. M. *The Rorschach technique.* New York: World Book Co., 1946.

Lasaga, J. I. Analytic technique. In E. S. Shneidman (Ed.), *Thematic test analysis.* New York: Grune and Stratton, 1951. Pp. 144–62.

Levy, L. H. *Psychological interpretation.* New York: Holt, 1963.

Little, K. B., and Shneidman, E. S. The validity of thematic projective interpretations. *Journal of Personality,* 1955, **23,** 285–94.

Machover, K. *Personality projection in the drawing of the human figure: A method of personality investigation.* Springfield, Ill.: Charles C. Thomas, 1949.

Murray, H. A. *Explorations in personality.* New York: Oxford University Press, 1938.

Murray, H. A. *Thematic Apperception Test manual.* Cambridge, Mass.: Harvard University Press, 1943.

Murstein, B. Assumptions, adaptation level and projective techniques. *Perceptual and Motor Skills,* 1961, **12,** 107–25.

Pascal, G. R., and Suttell, B. J. *The Bender-Gestalt Test: Quantification and validity for adults.* New York: Grune and Stratton, 1951.

Rorschach, H. *Psychodiagnostics.* (translated by P. Lemkau and B. Kronenburg) New York: Grune and Stratton, 1942.

Shneidman, E. S. (Ed.) *Thematic test analysis.* New York: Grune and Stratton, 1951.

Symonds, P. M. *Manual for Symonds Picture-Story Test.* New York: Bureau of Publications, Columbia Teachers College, 1948.

Symonds, P. M. *Adolescent fantasy: An investigation of the picture-story method of personality study.* New York: Columbia University Press, 1949.

PART FOUR

Group Standardized Testing

CHAPTER 9

Scholastic and Special
Aptitude Tests

Individual tests of intelligence and personality, important as they are, represent only a small fraction of the tests being used today. Most of the testing in our schools as well as in other settings is on a group basis. These group instruments are similar to objective school examinations and differ from individual tests primarily in that they may be administered to more than one individual at a time. Later in this chapter we shall discuss the advantages and disadvantages of group tests as compared with individual tests. Let us now turn our attention to the scholastic aptitude test commonly referred to in past years as the group intelligence test. For illustration only certain tests will be named and examined; this should not be construed as an endorsement, nor should the omission of a test be interpreted as a negative evaluation. The *Mental Measurements Yearbooks* (see Chapter 6) present critical test evaluations.

Scholastic Aptitude Tests

The reason that we now use the term *scholastic aptitude test* rather than *IQ* or *general intelligence* or *group intelligence* test can be found in what these tests actually measure. Authorities differ in their interpretations of the results of these tests. Some feel that they are measures of innate intelligence, whereas others feel that they fall short of this because of their reliance on factors such as culture, educational exposure, and achievement. (See Chapter 2.) Most authorities, however, would agree that they measure with some accuracy, though not perfectly, an individual's chance of success in school, because they measure the skills required for educational progress. One of their main reasons for being is to help the school understand and plan appropriate instruction for individual students.

The issue of whether they in fact measure innate ability or intelligence is primarily of theoretical interest. The educator is concerned with educating students and meeting their needs. If the tests predict chances of success or failure in the school setting they are useful. (See Chapter 2 for a more complete discussion of this issue.) The educator can then make alterations or additions in the curriculum and tailor individual programs of study for children with special educational needs.

Investigations over a period of more than forty years have shown a positive correlation between scores on group intelligence tests and academic success. Although these studies have not shown a perfect or near perfect correlation, there is enough evidence to demonstrate their usefulness in educational planning.

Measurement experts, realizing that the group intelligence test is not necessarily a measure of innate intelligence but is a good indicator of school success, have changed the title to convey more accurately what it really measures, that is, a person's scholastic aptitude. Today most test publishers and consumers agree with this reasoning; however, because terms are not easily changed, the terms *IQ* or *general intelligence tests* can still be found.

The administration of group tests to children should not begin before the age of five or six (kindergarten or first grade). Below the age of five individual tests should be used because of the importance of assessing test behavior and the need for controlling the child's attention and motivation. (See Chapter 7.) Even with five- and six-year-old children careful attention to their test behavior and understanding of directions such as how to turn pages correctly is extremely important if valid results are to be obtained. For example, in the Handbook for the Cooperative Primary Tests (Educational Testing Service, 1967b) a pilot test is given youngsters before the scorable tests are administered, so that the children will know how to respond. Even with the pilot test, however, some children are still not sure of what they are to do.

> While experience with the Pilot Test in pretesting and norming situations has indicated that almost all children can answer almost all items on the practice test, or at least understand what they are supposed to do, the teacher may occasionally find a child who does not seem to be able to handle the tasks it presents. If, after a second trial with the Pilot Test at a later time, this still seems to be the case, the teacher is probably well advised *not* to go ahead to administer

other tests in the series to this child. Interpretations from the other tests might be more misleading than helpful [p. 7].

Group tests for the first two or three grades require no reading. The instructions are given orally and usually one or two examples are presented before the testing starts. The child marks his answer in the booklet with a soft pencil or crayon.

A good example of the scholastic aptitude test in the lower grades is the Science Research Associates, Primary Mental Abilities Test for grades two through four (Thurstone, 1963). This test attempts to measure four "mental abilities." These are defined in the Examiner's Manual (Thurstone, 1963) as follows:

> V—Verbal Meaning: The ability to understand ideas expressed in words. In the later school years this is the most important single index of a child's potential for handling academic tasks. At the lower levels it is tested by a vocabulary test in picture form; at the upper levels, by a verbal vocabulary test.
> N—Number Facility: The ability to work with numbers, to handle simple quantitative problems rapidly and accurately, and to understand and recognize quantitative differences. At the lower grade levels the N scores are determined by a pictorial test that requires no reading. Addition problems are also used. At the upper levels arithmetical reasoning problems are included.
> P—Perceptual Speed: The ability to recognize likenesses and differences between objects or symbols quickly and accurately. This ability is important in acquiring reading skills, but tends to plateau at a relatively early age. For this reason it is included only with the three batteries designed for the lower grades.
> S—Spatial Relations: The ability to visualize objects and figures rotated in space and the relations between them. The test measuring this ability appears in every level of the PMA and is important throughout the school years [p. 4].

The total time for the test is a little over one hour. The manual recommends that the test be divided in half, one part being given on one day and the second on the following day.

Each child is given a test booklet and one colored marking pencil. To illustrate the directions and tasks the child encounters, sample problems of the Verbal Meaning Test with the accompanying directions are presented in Figure 18.

Figure 19 contains a sampling of items from the other three sections of the test.

The Spatial Relations Test requires the child to find the part that completes a picture. For example, S5 is part of a square and the child must find the

Directions for Administering the Verbal Meaning Test

The examiner must have a copy of the test booklet opened to the appropriate page to use for demonstration purposes.

Since the children already have their individual PMA 2-4 test booklets, say:

Open your test booklet to the first page of pictures and fold it back like this. (*Demonstrate.*) In the first row there are pictures of a flower, a toy windmill, a leaf, and a Christmas tree. Put an X on the leaf like this.

Demonstrate on the blackboard by making an X like this

| X |

to indicate the answer chosen.

Each time you mark a picture, your mark should look like this.

Inspect each child's booklet. If a child's mark is incorrect or too light, mark the booklet for him. Then say:

Are there any questions? (*Pause to answer questions.*)

When all questions have been answered, say:

Now look at the second row of pictures. In this row there are pictures of some bread, fruit, a plant, and a pea pod. Put an X on the picture of the fruit. (*Pause.*) In the third row find the picture that finishes this story: Tommy doesn't like vegetables. He ate all of his lunch except the _____. Mark it with an X. Which picture did you mark? That's right—the carrot.

Move down to the next row of pictures. Mark the picture that finishes this story: Anne was going to her music lesson. Her mother told her not to forget to take her _____. Mark it. That's right—the violin.

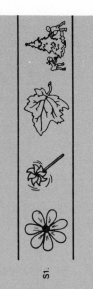

S1.

S2.

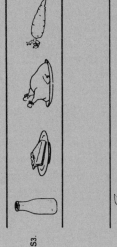

S3.

S4.

Figure 18. Sample items and directions for administering the Verbal Meaning Test. (From *Examiner's Manual PMA Primary Mental Abilities* for Grades 2-4 by L. L. Thurstone and Thelma Gwinn Thurstone. © 1963, Thelma Gwinn Thurstone. Reprinted by permission of the publisher, Science Research Associates, Inc., Chicago, Illinois.)

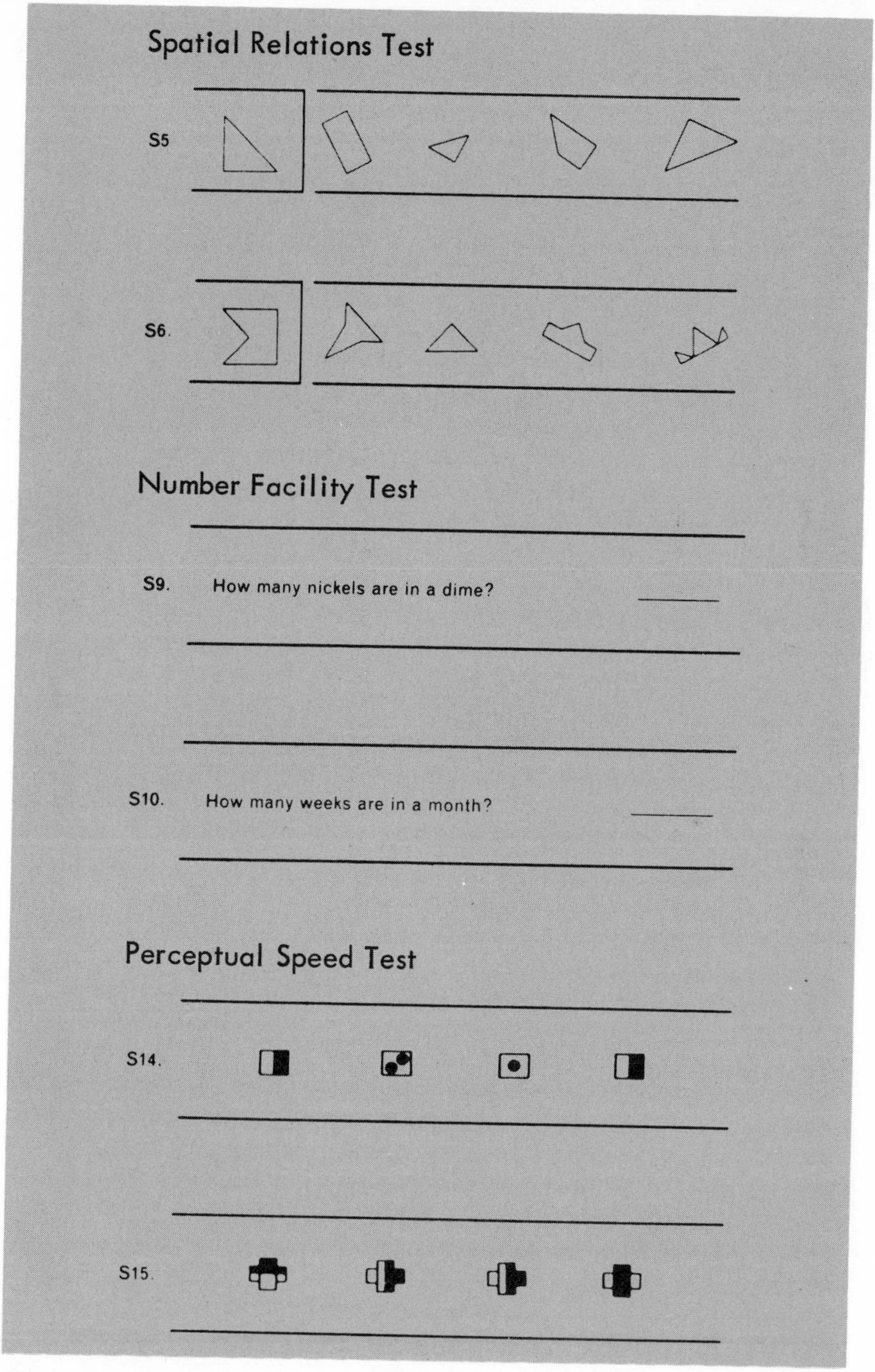

Spatial Relations Test

S5.

S6.

Number Facility Test

S9.   How many nickels are in a dime?   _____

S10.   How many weeks are in a month?   _____

Perceptual Speed Test

S14.

S15.

Figure 19. Selected sample items from the Primary Mental Abilities Test. (From *Examiner's Manual PMA Primary Mental Abilities* for Grades 2–4 by L. L. Thurstone and Thelma Gwinn Thurstone. © 1963, Thelma Gwinn Thurstone. Reprinted by permission of the publisher, Science Research Associates, Inc., Chicago, Illinois.)

223

part that completes it. The Number Facility Test requires the child to write the answer to the problem on the line. The ability to recognize similar objects or pictures is required in the Perceptual Speed Test. Here the child is asked to mark X's on the two pictures that are exactly alike.

The test is scored by counting all the correct answers in each section. Raw scores (number of correct answers) are converted to quotient equivalents and percentiles. Norms for each section are given as well as for a total score (in quotient equivalents and percentiles).

Another widely used instrument is the Kuhlmann-Finch Scholastic Aptitude Tests (Kuhlmann and Finch, 1952). This series contains tests for grades one through twelve. Over 40,000 pupils in selected schools in thirty states were included in the standardization. Total time for administration is a little over thirty minutes. The test is largely nonverbal and the publishers claim it is "fair to individuals of varying cultural backgrounds." In grades four through twelve answers may be written in test booklets or on separate answer sheets.

Figure 20 presents sample items from Test V, which is for fifth-grade students. It consists of five subtests, each of which is five minutes long. Subtest 1 requires the student to find the word that belongs in the second pair. Subtest 2 asks the student to find the picture with arms held like the first picture. A has both arms up; B has right arm up. Subtest 3 requires the student to study the first five numbers in each row to find out what number should come next. Subtest 4 presents three pictures in each row. The student looks at them and chooses the one of five possibilities that goes together with the three pictures. Subtest 5 requires the student to find the word that does not belong with the other four.

The raw score is converted to a standard IQ and mental age. The publishers offer a complete scoring service ("one-week service") providing rank order or alphabetical listing with the mental age and standard IQ.

A well-known and respected series of scholastic aptitude tests is the School and College Ability Tests (SCAT). These tests were first published in 1956. The latest revision is the SCAT Series II (Educational Testing Service, 1967c). In the general description of the tests the publishers state,

> Series II of the *School and College Ability Test* (SCAT Series II) was designed to provide estimates of basic verbal and mathematical ability. Scores will be useful in comparing a student or class with other students or classes, comparing performance on the verbal and mathematic subtests, estimating growth of these basic skills over a period of time, and in predicting success in related activities [p. 5].

The SCAT tests yield three scores: Verbal, Mathematical, and Total. Total administration time is between forty-five and fifty minutes. Actual testing time is forty minutes. There are four levels of difficulty: grades 4–6, 7–9, 10–12, and 12–14. The format of all grade levels is essentially the same, differing only in difficulty of subject matter. Each has parallel forms

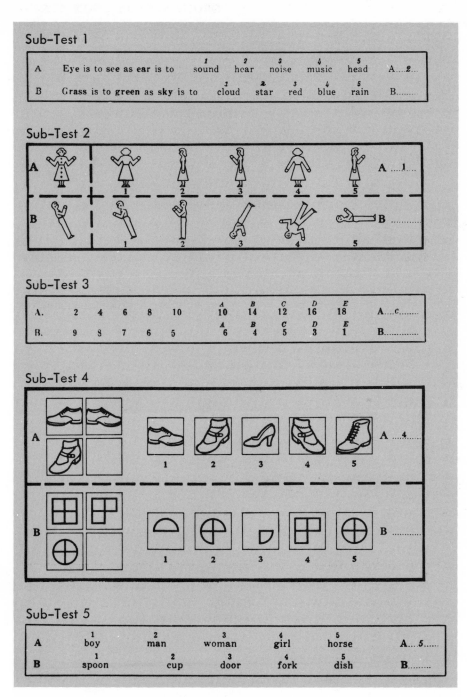

Figure 20. Sample items from the Kuhlmann-Finch Tests, Test V. (By Frederick Kuhlmann and Frank Finch. Copyright 1952 by American Guidance Service, Inc. Reproduced by permission of the publisher.)

225

comparable in content coverage and difficulty. Students record their responses on separate answer sheets. Figure 21 presents sample items from the SCAT Series II Form 4A (grades 4–6).

The SCAT yields three scores: Part I (Verbal), Part II (Mathematical), and a Total. The scores for Parts I and II are obtained by counting the number of right answers, and the total score is calculated by combining both parts. The raw scores are converted to percentile bands (for example, 86th to 96th percentile) and percentile ranks (for example, 92nd percentile). The publishers state that the verbal section of the SCAT Series II correlates 0.69 with the English grade and the mathematical section 0.58 with the mathematics grade, and the total score correlates 0.68 with the grade-point average of fifth-grade students in five selected schools (Educational Testing Service, 1967c, p. 42).

Figure 22 presents selected items from other forms of the SCAT. It should be noted that the same format and directions are employed at different grade levels; only the content of the items varies. Directions for these problems are given in Figure 21.

The following items are representative of the type of questions found in most scholastic aptitude tests. For a more complete listing of available tests and their evaluations see the *Mental Measurements Yearbooks*.

Verbal—Meaning (Vocabulary)
Underline the word that means the *same* as the first word.
   QUIET   a. Blue   b. Still   c. Tense   d. Watery

Verbal—Analogies
Hat is to head as shoe is to _____ .
   a. Arm   b. Shoulder   c. Foot   d. Log

Sentence Completion
The sun sets in the _____ and rises in the east.
   a. Summer   b. Morning   c. West   d. End

Reasoning
Study the series of letters below. What letter should come next?
   A   B   A   B   A   B   A   B
   a. B   b. D   c. A   d. E

Numbers Series
What number should come next to continue the series: 1   2   4   7   11   16?
   a. 18   b. 19   c. 20   d. 21   e. 22

Number
Add the following columns of numbers and underline R for right and W for wrong.

   (1) 16   R W   (2) 42   R   W
        38   61
        45   83
        99   176

Part I Directions

Each question begins with two words. These two words go together in a certain way. Under them, there are four other pairs of words lettered **A, B, C,** and **D.**

Find the lettered pair of words that go together in the same way as the first pair of words.

Then, find the row of boxes on your answer sheet which has the same number as the question. In this row of boxes, mark the letter of the pair of words you have chosen.

See how these examples are marked:

EXAMPLE 1   **calf : cow ::**

   A puppy : dog
   B nest : bird   *Answer*
   C horse : bull   E 1 ■ B C D
   D shell : turtle

In the first pair of words (**calf : cow**), calf goes with cow in this way— a calf is a young cow.

The only lettered pair of words that go together in the same way is **puppy : dog.** A puppy is a young dog.

Box **A** is marked because the letter in front of **puppy : dog** is **A.**

EXAMPLE 2   **minute : second ::**

   A time : clock
   B mile : travel   *Answer*
   C hour : measure   E 2 A B C ■
   D foot : inch

Part II Directions

Each of the following questions has two parts. One part is in Column A. The other part is in Column B.

You must find out if one part is greater than the other, or if the parts are equal.

Then, find the row of boxes on your answer sheet which has the same number as the question. In this row of boxes, mark:

   A if the part in Column A is greater,
   B if the part in Column B is greater,
   C if the two parts are equal.

	Column A	Column B	*Answer*
EXAMPLE 1	10	9	

The part in Column A (10) is greater than the part in Column B (9). Box A is marked because the part in Column A is greater.   1 ■ B C

	Column A	Column B
EXAMPLE 3	The value of 5 cents	The value of 1 nickel

The part in Column A is 5 cents. The part in Column B (1 nickel) is also equal to 5 cents. Box C is marked because the parts are equal.   3 A B ■

Figure 21. Directions and example questions from Part I and Part II of the School and College Ability Test. (From School and College Ability Test, Series II-Form 4A. Copyright © 1966, by Educational Testing Service. Used by permission of the publisher.)

Arithmetic Reasoning

Four $10 bills are equal to how many $5 bills?
    a. 20   b. 40   c. 10   d. 2   e. 8

Abstract Reasoning

All four-footed creatures are animals. All horses are four-footed.
Therefore: a. Creatures other than horses can walk.
            b. All horses can walk.
            c. All horses are animals.

College admissions tests are also scholastic aptitude tests. They will be presented and analyzed in Chapter 11. Tests that yield a scholastic aptitude test score but are also intended for vocational and other uses will be discussed in the following section along with professional tests.

Special Aptitude Tests

In this section we discuss vocational aptitude tests and batteries and special tests in art and music. In addition, a brief review of professional aptitude tests is presented.

The main function of the aptitude test is to measure the potential capacity of an individual. Its job is not to measure what has been learned, but what can be learned. Although aptitudes are generally thought of as being completely apart from training, it is impossible to isolate any aptitude from some kind of learning experience. Thus, aptitude tests may indirectly measure what has been learned, as well as what can be learned. Their main objective, however, is to measure the *potential to learn*, whether in school, the creative arts, or vocational pursuits.

Aptitude and interest are often thought of as being equivalent. They are not. The youngster who likes to fix things around the house, the adolescent who takes apart an automobile, the boy or girl who spends time playing the piano or painting a picture are showing interests. Whether they are revealing abilities or talents is another question. On the other hand, the individual who takes apart an automobile or practices the piano develops skills which enhance ability. Adults may indeed pursue vocations that coincide with their interests, abilities, and skills. Children, however, have not generally experienced enough different activities to judge their own particular abilities and interests adequately. Also, a child or adult may persist in an activity simply because he has developed some skill (learned ability) in that activity, although he has neither high ability or interest. One job of the school is to expose the child to new experiences and activities so that he may "try them on for size," hoping that something will fit, and he may choose a career in which his interests, skills, and abilities coincide. The objective aptitude test provides

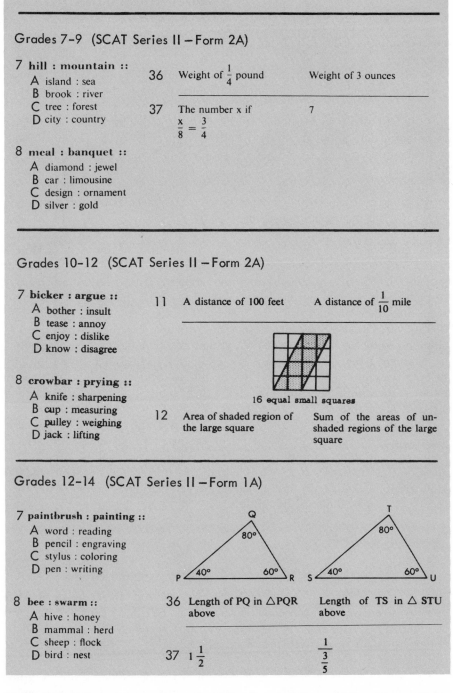

Grades 7-9 (SCAT Series II – Form 2A)

7 **hill : mountain ::**
  A island : sea
  B brook : river
  C tree : forest
  D city : country

36 Weight of $\frac{1}{4}$ pound   Weight of 3 ounces

37 The number x if   7
  $\frac{x}{8} = \frac{3}{4}$

8 **meal : banquet ::**
  A diamond : jewel
  B car : limousine
  C design : ornament
  D silver : gold

Grades 10-12 (SCAT Series II – Form 2A)

7 **bicker : argue ::**
  A bother : insult
  B tease : annoy
  C enjoy : dislike
  D know : disagree

11 A distance of 100 feet   A distance of $\frac{1}{10}$ mile

16 equal small squares

8 **crowbar : prying ::**
  A knife : sharpening
  B cup : measuring
  C pulley : weighing
  D jack : lifting

12 Area of shaded region of the large square   Sum of the areas of unshaded regions of the large square

Grades 12-14 (SCAT Series II – Form 1A)

7 **paintbrush : painting ::**
  A word : reading
  B pencil : engraving
  C stylus : coloring
  D pen : writing

36 Length of PQ in △PQR above   Length of TS in △ STU above

8 **bee : swarm ::**
  A hive : honey
  B mammal : herd
  C sheep : flock
  D bird : nest

37 $1\frac{1}{2}$ $\frac{1}{\frac{3}{5}}$

Figure 22. Selected items from the School and College Ability Tests. (From School and College Ability Test, Series II. Copyright © 1966, by Educational Testing Service. Used by permission of Educational Testing Service.)

a measure that may add a new dimension to declared interests and teacher observations in order to help guide a student to his own unique talent and potential.

In addition to helping the student discover his vocational and artistic aptitudes, the school and guidance staff need to know the answers to such questions as, "When should a child start in a reading program?" and, "Is this student ready to begin his study of algebra?" The school must have meaningful data about its student body. It especially needs to know about individual differences. Information is required to help in adjusting the levels of instruction to the needs and abilities of the pupils, who may differ widely in their range of talents. In addition, information on the strengths and weaknesses of each pupil presents a valuable background for individual vocational and personal counseling.

It is extremely important for a person's future adjustment that his educational and vocational planning be made intelligently. Many cases of educational and vocational maladjustment could have been avoided if proper guidance had been available. Many times, students at the ninth or tenth grade seem to have no real problem in making vocational decisions. Their plans seem intelligent enough from the viewpoint of the school, their family, and themselves. Others, however, are not as fortunate, and they often realize it, although some are not aware of their situation. Many adults state, "If only I had known"; the school attempts to avoid this feeling in future adults by helping the child "know" while there is time to make an intelligent decision. Other students may be unhappy about their achievement but believe their status is inevitable.

Thus it is obvious that the school needs not only to have all possible information on each individual student for program planning, but also to know each student's abilities in order to provide personal counseling. An aptitude test or battery of tests can help in this work. The counselor who has objective data about a youngster's aptitudes can help the child work toward a constructive utilization of his abilities.

Vocational Aptitude Tests

Aptitude was previously defined as the ability to learn. Thus vocational aptitude tests attempt to measure a youngster's ability to learn in certain occupations. They do not pinpoint a person's exact career; however, they do provide answers to such questions as, "Is it realistic to consider medicine as a career?" "Can Mary consider a job as a secretary?" "Would Bill be better suited to be a mechanic or an office worker?" "Should John go to college, and if so, what type of school—technical or general?"

The school needs to have information on a youngster's aptitudes to guide him intelligently into various educational programs and occupations in which he has a realistic chance of succeeding. It is important to remember, however, that aptitude tests will not make the decisions for an individual but will provide useful data in planning future objectives.

Clerical Aptitude Tests

Test instruments designed to measure clerical aptitude all have in common an emphasis upon perceptual speed. Bingham (1935) described three aspects of clerical work: doing it, checking it, and supervising it. Most clerical aptitude tests combine perceptual speed and Bingham's second phase of "checking." These tests attempt to measure abilities needed in office work—typewriting, bookkeeping, and related activities.

General intelligence, as well as specific clerical aptitude, is also needed. Super and Crites (1962) feel that the minimum IQ required for successful clerical activities is between 95 and 100. They state further that,

> When promotability is a factor to be considered in the counseling or selection of potential clerical workers, intelligence should be heavily weighted; when, on the other hand, success in a routine clerical job is in question, intelligence exceeding the minimum requirement is all that is needed, other factors then being the decisive ones [p. 160].

Detailed studies of clerical jobs reveal that speed, accuracy, motor ability, and dexterity are very important. Our discussion will be focused on tests that mainly measure speed and accuracy.[1]

The Minnesota Clerical Test[2] (The Psychological Corporation) is one of the better known and more widely used tests of clerical aptitude. It was originally constructed for adults (girls seventeen and over, and boys nineteen and above). Its suitability for younger groups was studied by many investigators. Today the range is from the seventh grade and above for both sexes.

The Minnesota Clerical Test is an instrument that attempts to measure speed and accuracy in checking 200 pairs of numbers and 200 pairs of names.

In number checking there are two columns of numbers; in name checking there are two columns consisting of pairs of names. The person checks the two members of each pair to see whether they are exactly the same. There is a very short time limit, and the results are scored for speed and accuracy. Items that are similar to the tasks on this test follow:

Number checking

7345	7354
31789	31789
85634	85634

---

[1] The reader who is interested in a more detailed discussion of clerical tests, both paper-and-pencil and psychomotor, should consult Super and Crites (1962).
[2] Originally called the Minnesota Vocational Test for Clerical Workers.

Name checking

John G. Smith	John C. Smith
The Chase Fuel Co.	The Chase Fuel Co., Inc.
Alger R. MacDonald	Alger R. MacDonald

Another well-known test of clerical aptitude is the General Clerical Test (GCT). On this test there are four separate scores—clerical, verbal, numerical, and total. These scores are derived from nine subtests. The first two tests, checking and alphabetizing, are designed to measure speed and accuracy. The verbal score is ascertained by combining spelling, reading, comprehension, vocabulary, and grammar, and the numerical score is obtained by tests of arithmetic, computation, error location, and arithmetic reasoning.

Many more tests of clerical aptitude, such as the Purdue Clerical Adaptability Test (Lawshe, Tiffin, and Moore, 1956) could be mentioned; however, our two examples serve as illustrations of the basic format of the clerical aptitude test. In our discussion of the Differential Aptitude Tests later in this chapter, we shall review one other clerical test contained in that battery.

Super and Crites' (1962) comments on the Minnesota Clerical are quite germane for most clerical tests. They state,

> When appraising clerical promise it is well to use tests of both perceptual speed and intelligence. . . . When the test is used at the junior high school level for curricular guidance purposes, grade norms are to be preferred. . . . It seems wise to use adult norms even with high school juniors and seniors. . . . In using the adult norms, emphasis should be on the occupational rather than on the general norms. . . . As a rule speed on this type of test is a good measure of accuracy. But there are occasional exceptions, and one subject will make a given score by working rapidly with errors, whereas another will make the same score by working more slowly without errors. For this reason the psychometrist or counselor should examine the responses to each test, and take the error score into account in making his interpretation [pp. 178–79].

Mechanical Aptitude Tests

In the United States the emphasis is on college training, and yet there is a large segment of our student population who, because of ability, interest, or other reasons, will not attend college. These youngsters may have mechanical ability and they should not be forgotten by their community, for society needs mechanical craftsmen as well as doctors and lawyers. The school that plans programs for these youngsters needs some basis of objective appraisal in selecting students and arranging appropriate courses of study. The mechanical aptitude test can serve this end and other vocational needs very well.

It has been discovered that some mechanical jobs require the ability to see spatial relationships and the ability to visualize actual objects from a drawing or picture, including being able to see how a whole figure can be assembled from its parts, how an object would appear when looked at from a different point of view, and how movements of one part affect movements of another. Test questions that measure this type of ability will be illustrated later in the chapter, when we discuss test batteries.

It is important to remember that different functions or abilities are sometimes placed under the heading of mechanical aptitude. Some instruments, such as mechanical information tests, depend upon past experience with mechanical objects, whereas other tests do not call upon past experience to the same degree. There is also a difference in performance on these tests between boys and girls.

Some teachers and counselors are confused by the results of mechanical aptitude tests. They assume, for example, that high scores mean a student is slated to be an engineer, whereas others interpret the same results as indicative of lower scholastic ability. These assumptions are fraught with possible errors. First of all, mechanical aptitude is only one of many abilities an engineer needs to be successful. In addition to mechanical aptitude, the aspiring engineer must have a good background in science and mathematics, as well as general scholastic ability. Secondly, the tendency for some people to think of mechanical ability as the lowest rung on the scholastic ladder is erroneous. Further, a child's doing poorly in school is no reason to assume he will do well in mechanical work. Mechanical aptitude tests, therefore, must be interpreted in connection with other tests and school achievements.

Many varieties of mechanical aptitude tests have been developed. The majority fall into two main areas: those that are administered individually and require actual manipulation of mechanical objects and those that require only paper and pencil and can be given to many children at the same time.

Individual Tests

Individual mechanical tests are made up of items that require the subject to use tools and materials and/or blocks, as well as to assemble such devices as a push button or a doorbell. Motor ability and manual dexterity are important ingredients in some of these tests.

One of the most widely used and best-known tests of dexterity is the Minnesota Rate of Manipulation Test. The age range for this test is from thirteen to fifty. The test consists of a formboard which has four rows of identical holes, with fifteen holes in each row. There are sixty identical discs, a little larger than a checker, which fit into the holes. The flat sides of the discs are painted differently from the board. The examiner places the discs in their correct positions and then turns them over and asks the subject to place them in their holes. The examination is administered in four trials. The total testing time is from six to eight minutes.

Another widely used test is the O'Connor Finger and Tweezer Dexterity

Tests. These tests are used with adolescents and adults. The Finger Dexterity Test consists of a shallow tray beside a metal plate which has 100 holes arranged in ten rows of ten holes each. Every hole is big enough to contain three metal pins, 1 inch long. The Tweezer Dexterity Test uses the opposite side of the boards and also has 100 holes, but these are just slightly larger than the pins, which allows the subject to place one in each hole. A pair of tweezers is used to pick up the pins.

In the Finger Dexterity Test the subject picks up three pins and places them in each hole, whereas in the Tweezer Test he picks up one pin at a time and attempts to place it in a hole. The score is computed on the basis of the total time required to complete the tasks.

Another test that is very popular with counseling psychologists is The Purdue Pegboard. The Purdue Pegboard is a 12- by 18-inch rectangular board with four cups which hold the test materials at one end and two rows of holes straight down the middle. The examiner first administers the test by asking the subject to put metal pins in the holes one at a time with his right hand. After completing this assignment, the subject is asked to do it again with his left hand. The examiner then asks him to do it with both hands simultaneously. The final task is to assemble the metal pin, metal washer, metal collar, and washer using the right and then the left hands and then both. Scoring is computed on the basis of the number of pins placed in thirty seconds and the number of assemblies made in sixty seconds.

Generally speaking, motor tests have been most successful in the prediction of performance on assembling and machine-operating jobs. (See Fleishman, 1953.) It should be noted, however, that jobs requiring less repetitive tasks demand more perceptual and intellectual abilities. The important thing to remember in assessing the validity of these instruments is the relationship of the test tasks to the actual job specifications.

PAPER-AND-PENCIL TESTS

Because of their convenience paper-and-pencil tests of mechanical ability are used much more widely than individual tests in schools. Among the better tests of this type is the Bennett Test of Mechanical Comprehension. This test is made up of items consisting of drawings. The items are concerned with the application of physical principles. If a student has not studied physics he will not be at a disadvantage in this examination, because knowledge of mechanical equipment is not being tested. To illustrate this a sample question from the Test of Mechanical Comprehension is shown in Figure 23.

There are sixty items in the test. Although there is no time limit, most subjects finish within twenty-five minutes. There are seven forms which vary in difficulty, normative group, and language. For example, Form AA has percentile norms for school and industrial groups, whereas Form BB is geared to a higher level, including employed technicians and engineers. Form CC (Owens-Bennett) is especially directed to engineering students, and Form WI (Bennett-Fry) is geared to women. In the area of language Form

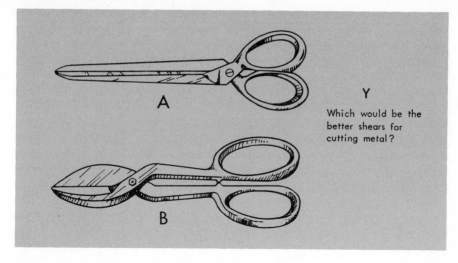

Figure 23. Sample item from Test of Mechanical Comprehension, Form BB. (Reproduced by permission. Copyright 1941, The Psychological Corporation, New York, N.Y. All rights reserved.)

AA-F is the same as Form AA, but the instructions and questions are in English and French. Form AA-S is in Spanish, using norms from Cuba. Form BB-S is also in Spanish, but the normative group is from Venezuela.

The Bennett Test is especially useful for predicting success in jobs that require the ability to understand machines. Engineers and toolmakers score very high on the Bennett.

The McQuarrie Test for Mechanical Ability is a very old test originally developed as a rough measure of mechanical and manual aptitude. It is a battery of seven subtests each designed to evaluate different factors assumed to be important in mechanical jobs. The first three—Tracing, Tapping, and Dotting—are measures of manual dexterity; the next three—Copying, Location, and Blocks—are tests of spatial perception. The last subtest, Pursuit, is a test of perceptual speed and accuracy. These differences in content have tended to make most users of the test treat each part separately in validation studies (Super and Crites, 1962).

This group test requires about a half-hour for administration. For a detailed examination of this test and other group and individual mechanical tests, see Super and Crites (1962, pp. 219–74).

Test Batteries

Test batteries have been developed to measure many things, including intelligence, general school achievement, and different vocational aptitudes. We shall confine our attention here to the batteries primarily concerned with vocational prediction.

Many studies concerning vocational prediction have been made. In one such study a group of high school students was given a vocational test battery. Two years after they completed high school, a comparison of their educational and vocational situation and their test scores was made. The study revealed that premedical students had scored very high on all the tests in the battery. Workers in mechanical and electrical trades were above average on the mechanical test and average or below on the other types of tests. This study revealed no definite evidence of success or failure based on aptitude tests in specific occupations. Many studies, however, do show certain trends that can give us some clues for vocational guidance. For example, successful workers in skilled trades do well on certain tests, whereas successful clerical workers generally have high scores on different tests.

Teachers and counselors should be very cautious in interpreting aptitude test results. It should be remembered that aptitude test results are most valid when other tests, such as group tests of intelligence, achievement scores, and the general performance record of the student in school and at home, are taken into consideration.

There are numerous vocational aptitude batteries. However, the battery that teachers are most likely to come in contact with is the Differential Aptitude Tests (DAT). There are two very good reasons for this. First, the DAT lends itself to a school setting in terms of its format and norms. It also yields a scholastic aptitude score, which makes the test useful in another area and eases the financial burden of purchasing an additional instrument. The second reason for the DAT's wide use is its careful attention to standardization procedures and the many excellent reviews of its merits by testing experts. For these reasons we will devote our attention to the DAT. The reader who is interested in reviewing other test batteries[3] should consult the *Mental Measurements Yearbooks*.

The DAT consists of eight tests and is available in two forms, L and M, with two booklets for each form. Each booklet has four tests. There is also a verbal reasoning and numerical ability combination booklet for use as a separate measure of scholastic aptitude.

The DAT was designed for use in the junior and senior high school as an aid in educational and vocational guidance. It is based on the assumption (backed by some research findings) that "intelligence" is not a single ability, but a combination of several abilities. The battery yields nine scores based on the eight tests. (Two of the eight scores combined yield an index of scholastic aptitude.) A great deal of research on the DAT has been reported, some of which may be found in the manual (Bennett, Seashore,

---

[3] Another excellent battery is the Flanagan Aptitude Classification Tests (FACT). It is not used in the schools as much as the DAT because it is geared more for industrial uses and takes longer to administer.

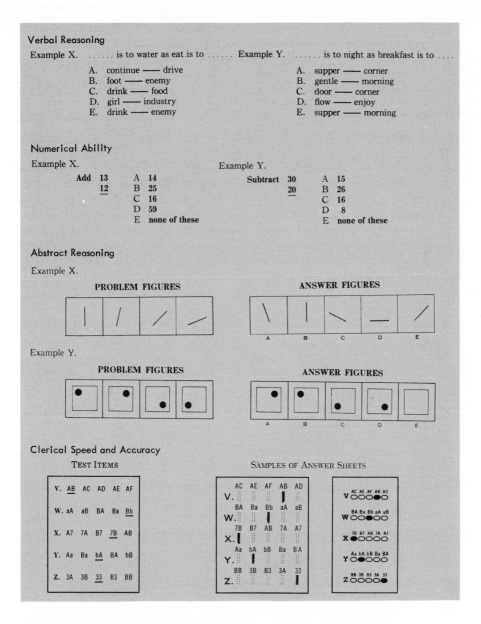

Verbal Reasoning

Example X. ...... is to water as eat.is to ......   Example Y.   ...... is to night as breakfast is to ....

A. continue —— drive	A. supper —— corner
B. foot —— enemy	B. gentle —— morning
C. drink —— food	C. door —— corner
D. girl —— industry	D. flow —— enjoy
E. drink —— enemy	E. supper —— morning

Numerical Ability

Example X.

Add 13
      12

A 14
B 25
C 16
D 59
E none of these

Example Y.

Subtract 30
         20

A 15
B 26
C 16
D 8
E none of these

Abstract Reasoning

Example X.

PROBLEM FIGURES   ANSWER FIGURES

Example Y.

PROBLEM FIGURES   ANSWER FIGURES

Clerical Speed and Accuracy

TEST ITEMS   SAMPLES OF ANSWER SHEETS

V. AB AC AD AE AF

W. aA aB BA Ba Bb

X. A7 7A B7 7B AB

Y. Aa Ba bA BA bB

Z. 3A 3B 33 B3 BB

Figure 24. Sample items from the Differential Aptitude Test Booklet 1, Form L. (Reproduced by permission. Copyright 1947, © 1961, The Psychological Corporation, New York, N.Y. All rights reserved.)

and Wesman, 1966).[4] We shall explore each of the tests to obtain some insight into their content and specific use in vocational and educational guidance.

Figure 24 presents sample items from Booklet 1 of the DAT. The Verbal Reasoning test requires the student to choose from among five pairs of words the correct combination to complete the blanks. In the Numerical Ability test five answers follow each problem. The student's task is to pick the correct answer or "none of these" if the correct answer is not given. The Abstract Reasoning test consists of "problem figures" and "answer figures." The four "problem figures" make a series. The student is required to find out which one of the "answer figures" would be the next, or the fifth, one in the series. The Clerical Speed and Accuracy test is a test to see how quickly an individual can compare letter and number combinations. Each test item contains letter and number combinations. These same combinations are on a separate answer sheet but are in a different order. In each test item one of the five is underlined. The student's job is to look at the underlined combination, find the same one on the separate answer sheet, and record his answer.

Figure 25 reveals sample items from Booklet 2 of the DAT. The Mechanical Reasoning test consists of pictures which require the student to make judgments concerning the "truth" of certain situations involving balance, weight, and other mechanically related problems. The Space Relations test is made up of patterns which can be folded into figures. Four figures are shown for each pattern. The student is asked to decide which one of the figures can be made from the pattern shown.

The Language Usage test contains two sections: the Spelling test and the Language Usage Grammar. The Spelling test presents a series of words some of which are correctly spelled and some of which are incorrectly spelled. In the grammar section the student is confronted with a series of sentences divided into four parts (A, B, C, and D). The task is to look at each sentence and decide which part is in error grammatically. If the entire sentence is free of error, the student marks "E" on his answer sheet.

The publisher of the DAT has produced a pamphlet entitled "Your Aptitudes as Measured by the Differential Aptitude Tests," an excellent description of each of the tests and what they measure. It is also a good source for understanding any aptitude test battery and is written for students, parents, teachers, and counselors. The reader is encouraged to read the following partial reproduction of this pamphlet carefully, not only for its description of the DAT but as a general guide to what many vocational (and some scholastic) aptitude batteries measure.

---

[4] A very good bibliography of over 120 references, many of which refer to research directly bearing on the validation studies of the DAT through 1964. For further references, see *Mental Measurements Yearbooks*.

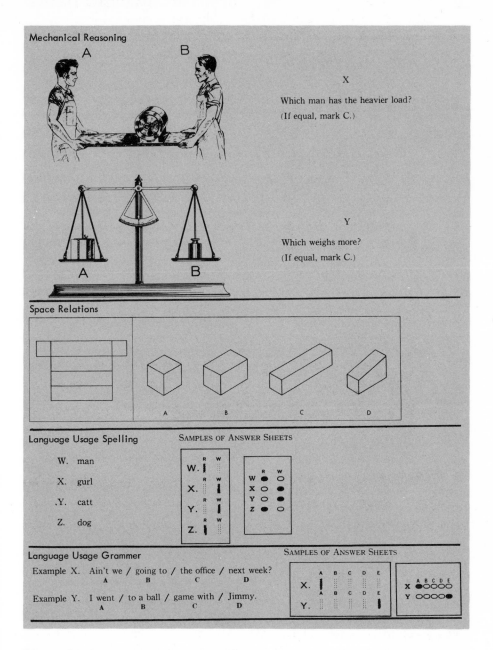

Figure 25. Sample items from the Differential Aptitude Test, Booklet 2, Form L. (Reproduced by permission. Copyright 1947, © 1961, 1962, The Psychological Corporation, New York, N.Y. All rights reserved.)

What Is Aptitude[5]

Simply—aptitude is the capacity to learn. You take aptitude tests in order to be able to make better predictions of how you can expect to develop in school and in a job.

Your DAT scores, then, are measures of your capacities to learn—to profit from various courses of study or from training required for jobs you may seek.

These tests give you a way of comparing your abilities—as of now—with those of boys and girls in your grade. The test results will help you evaluate your relative strengths and weaknesses in a variety of aptitudes which are important to your educational progress and your career choices.

Think of the DAT scores simply as useful bits of information. You will want to consider these test scores along with all sorts of other information about you that have already piled up—in your mind, in the school records, and in your family's thinking. Of course, you will want to take into consideration such facts as your school grades and other test scores; the things you like most, hobbies, and out-of-school interests; what courses are available in your school; your ambitions; your qualities of character and traits of personality such as curiosity, skill in getting along with others, and ability to stick with duties and hard tasks; job requirements; health; college entrance requirements; and so on. There are a great many things to take into account.

Aptitude tests will not pinpoint for you exactly what your career should be. These tests do *not* provide specific prescriptions or answers to such specific questions as: *Can I be a plumber? Should I plan to become a physician? Should I be a dress designer?*

But, if you and your counselors will study your DAT scores along with other information, you *can* get answers to some more general questions such as: *Is it reasonable for me to consider medicine as a career? Which would be the better job for me—mechanic or office worker? What are my particular assets and liabilities to be considered if I am thinking of becoming a secretary? Would I profit from a college education? What type of college?*

Information on your aptitudes can start you off on a meaningful study of the various educational programs and occupations you might want to consider. The freedom you have in planning your future places on you considerable responsibility for realistic thinking about yourself.

[5] Psychological Corporation, *Your Aptitudes as Measured by the Differential Aptitude Test.* Reproduced by permission. Copyright © 1961, The Psychological Corporation, New York, N.Y. All rights reserved.

VERBAL REASONING

Verbal reasoning is important in all academic and most non-academic subjects in high school. If you were to take only one test, VR would be the best all-around predictor of how well you can do in school, especially in the academic subjects. Students who score average or better should seriously consider college; those well up in the top quarter may consider the highly selective colleges.

Students above the bottom quarter on VR but without a college education may be acceptable for various supervisory and managerial jobs in business and industry. Other things being equal, for instance, the employee with more verbal reasoning ability than his fellow workers has a better chance of being selected for special training in technical work or in supervision.

Students not planning for college who have VR as the peak on their profile should consider preparing for such verbal occupations as salesman, credit manager, order taker, complaint clerk. These job names will help you think of others also in which verbal reasoning and understanding are essential.

People who do poorly on the Verbal Reasoning test should perhaps plan on going into some work that will call for less verbal ability. A person can be successful doing clerical work in an office without trying to become head of a department, or successful doing production work in a factory without expecting to become production manager.

If your scores on one or both of the Language Usage tests—Spelling and Grammar—are an inch or more below the VR on the profile chart, there is a real chance that you aren't able to use your verbal reasoning ability up to its full capacity. Talk with your counselor and teachers about what you can do to improve your writing, reading, and other language skills.

NUMERICAL ABILITY

Numerical ability is especially important in such high school subjects as mathematics, physics, and chemistry.

Students who do well on this test are also likely to do well in the arithmetic and measuring so common in business offices, factories, service shops, and stores.

Scores on this test predict, to some extent, success in nearly all high school and college courses. Numerical ability is one element of all-around ability to master academic work.

An above-average score in NA suggests planning for college or other post-high school education. A student who wants to major in such fields as mathematics, physics, chemistry, or any branch of engineering, may expect to encounter some difficulty if his NA score is not in the top third or top quarter.

Numerical ability is also useful in technical careers not requiring a college degree. A score in the second or third quarter on this test, especially if scores on Verbal Reasoning and/or the two Language Usage tests are noticeably *lower* than the NA score, suggests looking at technical training programs either in companies or in training institutes for trades and crafts.

Numerical ability is useful in such jobs as laboratory assistant, bookkeeper, statistical clerk, foreman, or shipping clerk. Many of the jobs in the skilled trades in manufacturing or construction work require considerable numerical ability.

VR + NA

Your combined score on these two tests provides a good estimate of your scholastic aptitude—your ability to complete the college preparatory courses in your school and to succeed in college.

In general, anyone with a rating in the upper quarter (75th percentile or better) should consider himself capable of performing well in college courses. Depending on your current ambitions and your choice of college, a second quarter rating on VR + NA also indicates college potential. Whether students ranking in the third quarter should enter regular liberal arts and science programs is arguable. Are you doing very well in high school? Are you prepared to work harder than your college mates? What college and what courses are you considering? Some students in the third quarter and a few in the fourth quarter who want some post-high school education will find it practical and satisfying to enter one-year or two-year junior college programs in applied arts and sciences, business training, and the like.

Besides predicting academic success, the VR + NA score gives some indication of aptitude for jobs that require more than the average level of administrative and executive responsibility.

ABSTRACT REASONING

Using diagrams, the Abstract Reasoning test measures how easily and clearly you can reason when problems are presented in terms of size or shape or position or quantity or other non-verbal, non-numerical forms. The repairman troubleshooting an unusual breakdown, the chemist, physicist or biologist seeking to understand an invisible process, the programmer planning the work of an electronic computer, the systems engineer,—all find this ability useful. Carrying out a logical procedure in your mind is important here.

Abstract Reasoning teams up with the next two tests—Space Relations and Mechanical Reasoning—in prediction of success in many kinds of mechanical, technical, and skilled industrial work.

Students standing high on Verbal Reasoning and Numerical Ability have added confirmation of their college ability if they are also above average on Abstract Reasoning. But, if VR and NA are high and AR is below average, they usually may rely on the verbal-numerical combination to see them through.

Students scoring rather low on VR but fairly high on AR have evidence of ability to reason in certain ways despite a verbal shortcoming. Vocabulary building, remedial reading, and similar exercises may help strengthen verbal reasoning power.

CLERICAL SPEED AND ACCURACY

Clerical Speed and Accuracy measures how quickly and accurately you can compare and mark written lists such as of names or numbers. This is the only one of these tests that demands fast work. It is very easy to get the right answer; speed in doing a simple task is what counts. Girls tend to score higher than boys on this test.

While CSA measures an ability that is useful in many kinds of jobs, it is not really needed or expected in most high school courses. In most school work it is more important to do your work correctly than to do it quickly. But a *very* low score sometimes indicates a source of difficulty with homework or exams.

Have you done well on others of the Differential Aptitude Tests but not very well on this one? If so, perhaps you did not work as fast as you could have worked. By practicing, you may be able to speed up quite a bit without sacrificing accuracy on tasks that you understand well.

Aptitude for CSA is important in many kinds of office jobs, such as record-keeping, addressing, pricing, order-taking, filing, coding, proofreading, and keeping track of tools or supplies. Secretaries, whose most important skills must be in stenography and office services, are better if they also can work fast and accurately on routine clerical tasks.

In most scientific research and much professional work mistakes in recording or copying can be very serious. But speed is needed, as well as accuracy. A good score on CSA is desirable, then, for a job handling data in a laboratory as well as for a job in bookkeeping or in a bank.

MECHANICAL REASONING

Students who do well on the Mechanical Reasoning test usually like to find out how things work. They often are better than average at learning how to construct, operate, or repair complicated equipment. While VR and NA are the best predictors of science and engineering grades in college and technical institutes, a high MR score is added evidence of ability in these fields.

Students who do well on this test but whose VR and NA scores suggest that a college engineering course might be very difficult, should look into opportunities in high school technical courses, apprentice training, and post-high-school technical institutes. Men in industry who become technicians, shop foremen, and repair specialists tend to be at least average in MR.

People who do poorly on this test may find the work rather hard or uninteresting in physical sciences and in those shop courses which demand thinking and planning, rather than just skill in using one's hands. Many types of work in the construction and manufacturing trades also require one to understand machinery and other uses of physical forces as well as to have manual skills.

Girls score considerably lower than boys on the MR and SR tests. Therefore a girl who does quite well on these tests, as compared with the average girl, may still be far below the average boy. A girl interested in mechanical or engineering work should ask her counselor to figure her MR and SR percentiles in comparison with boys as well as with girls.

SPACE RELATIONS

Space Relations measures your ability to visualize, to imagine the shape and surfaces of a finished object before it is built, just by looking at the drawings that would be used to guide workmen in building it. This ability makes some kinds of mathematics easier—solid geometry, for example.

To a person who does poorly on Space Relations, an architect's plans for a house or an engineer's plans for a bridge or a machine might look like nothing but several flat drawings. But how about a person who does well on this test? Such a person looking at those same plans can "see" the finished house, or bridge, or machine. He could probably "walk around" the finished structure—mentally, that is—and "see" it from various angles.

Students who do well on SR should have an advantage in work such as drafting, dress designing, architecture, mechanical engineering, die-making, building construction, and some branches of art and decoration. A good machinist, carpenter, dentist, or surgeon needs this sense of the forms and positions of things in space.

Students planning for careers not requiring college training should consider their SR score in comparison with their other aptitudes in deciding whether to look for jobs (or training courses) that deal with real objects—large or small, watches or skyscrapers—rather than with people or with finances, for example.

LANGUAGE USAGE

Language Usage is composed of two short achievement tests which measure important abilities you need to consider along with the other aptitudes assessed by the DAT.

Spelling measures how well a person can spell common English words. Among other things, it is an excellent predictor of ability to learn typing and shorthand.

Grammar measures how well a person can recognize mistakes in the grammar, punctuation, and wording of easy sentences. It is among the best predictors of ability to earn good grades generally in high school and college.

While some careers, such as writing and teaching, call for a high degree of competence in English, all careers requiring college-level education require good language skills, and so do most office and managerial jobs in business and industry.

If you do well on both of these tests and on VR, you should be able to do almost any kind of practical writing provided you have a knowledge of your topic and a desire to write about it.

On the other hand, a student fairly high in VR but low on either or both of these two language tests, probably can profit from special study or tutoring in English to bring his language skills up to the level indicated by his VR score.

The student of measurement should keep in mind the fact that *vocational aptitude batteries alone will not solve educational and vocational problems.* They will, however, provide valuable information for students and others in planning future goals when interpreted in conjunction with other evaluative criteria.

Prognostic Tests

The aptitude tests used to predict school and artistic success or failure are called *prognostic tests* by psychologists. The inquiring student may rightfully ask whether this type of special test is better than an academic aptitude test. The answer is not easy. Many testing people feel that some day the general aptitude test, such as the *Differential Aptitude Tests,* will take the place of aptitude tests designed for special fields. Today, however, prognostic tests have an important place in the school's testing program. Prognostic tests are especially useful in spotting children who may be able to perform in special academic areas. The important thing to remember is that special aptitude tests can predict failure more accurately than success, for success is in part determined by motivation, social pressures, and other factors. In general terms we may state that a person with superior intellectual endowment may or may not be successful in college, but we can be fairly certain that an individual with very low ability will be unable to succeed academically. Let us, then, look at some of these special aptitude tests.

READING READINESS TESTS

Reading readiness tests are generally used in the beginning of a child's first year in school. They help the school in gaining some indication of the child's ability to progress in reading. For example, Miss Smith, a first-grade teacher, wants to know which children are ready for reading and which children may have difficulty. She decides to use a reading readiness test to help answer this question. Upon reviewing the test scores, she finds that some children are ready to read and others are not. With this knowledge she can divide the children into groups of similar readiness and have each group work at its own level. She can use the results of the tests as a guide in starting a formal reading program and in deciding what type of prereading activities she may provide for the children.

Teachers should not feel that the scores their students receive on a reading readiness test will necessarily be an indication of the child's final level of reading achievement. A reading readiness test is used mainly to predict the ability of a child to learn from reading instruction in the first year of school and many times only in the first few months. Actually, a better source for the prediction of final reading achievement is a scholastic aptitude test. In addition, it must be remembered that each child's rate of development is different. For example, Bill may start walking at an earlier age than his brother Jim—even though Jim may start to talk earlier than Bill. In the same way some children are ready to read at five years of age, or even sooner, whereas others are not ready until they are seven or eight years old. It must be remembered also that there is an age difference of as much as eleven months among individual children placed in the same group at the first-grade level. At this age a few months makes a great deal of difference in physical and intellectual maturity, and thus affects what he is capable of learning.

There are many reading readiness tests, each having different kinds of tasks. Some require rhyming or matching sounds, and others use oral vocabulary with pictures. For example, in the latter type of problem the child is asked to identify a picture of an object that the teacher names. The teacher may say "cat" and ask the children to circle the picture of a cat from among pictures of a cat, a dog, a horse, and a bicycle. Almost all the reading readiness tests require the child to be able to match figures or simple words by sight. The test item may show a star and beside the star four figures: a star, a circle, a square, and a diamond. The child must be able to "memorize" the star and pick the star figure from among the other four figures to get the item right.

The Metropolitan Reading Readiness Test is one of the widely used readiness tests. It is made up of six tests. The first is called Word Meaning. The person doing the testing presents four pictures to the child and verbalizes a word that would identify one of the pictures. The child is then asked to point to the picture that is the same as the word. In the second test the examiner shows the child four pictures, but this time instead of calling out a word, he states a phrase or sentence. The child is then asked to point to the picture that is the same or means the same as the phrase or sentence. This test is called Sentences. The third test, Information, is similar to the first two tests, except that here the child is called upon to point out objects in terms of what they do. He may, for example, be presented with pictures of four objects including a camera and be asked to "mark the one you would take a picture with." The fourth test, called Matching, requires the child to show his ability to recognize similarities and differences in pictures of objects, numbers, and letters. The fifth test, Numbers, consists of simple arithmetic problems. In the sixth and last test, Copying, the child is asked to copy simple forms, numbers, and letters. This test attempts to find out about a youngster's physical and intellectual maturity.

Another approach in ascertaining the readiness of a child to read is to give developmental examinations. These range from the elaborate tests given at the Gesell Institute of Child Development to simple checklists of maturation. Let us briefly turn our attention to some of these.

The developmental examination tests administered at the Gesell Institute of Child Development (Ilg and Ames, 1965) fall into seven different parts:

1. *The initial interview.* Questions about age, birth date, birthday party including favorite activity and present received; siblings—names and ages; father's occupation.
2. *Pencil and paper tests.* Writing name or letters and address; numbers 1 to 20; copying six basic forms (circle, cross, square, triangle, divided rectangle, diamond in two orientations), and two three-dimensional forms (cylinder and cube in two orientations); completing Incomplete Man figure and giving his facial expression.
3. *Right and left (adaptation of Jacobson's Right and Left tests).* Naming parts and sides of body, carrying out single and double commands, responding to a series of pictures of a pair of hands in which two fingers are touching. Response is first verbal and then motor.
4. *Form tests.* Visual One (Monroe)—matching forms; Visual Three (Monroe)—memory for designs; projection into forms.
5. *Naming of animals for 60 seconds.*
6. *Concluding interview.* Reporting on what child likes to do best in general, at school indoors and outdoors and at home indoors and outdoors.
7. *Examination of teeth.* Recording of both eruption and decay or fillings [p. 35].

These separate tests give a complete picture of the child's readiness to learn. They are quite elaborate and time consuming and, of course, are not practical for everyday use in the public schools. On the other hand, the maturation checklist is a more practical school-oriented device. A good example of this approach is Banham's (1959) Maturity Level for School Entrance and Reading Readiness, a checklist for kindergarten and first grade.

There are twenty-five statements divided equally into five developmental areas. Each area begins with "The child can" and it is the examiner's job to check each statement that is representative of the child's maturational performance. Given below are the five areas and representative questions from the checklist.

BODILY COORDINATION[6]

The child can . . .
____ 1. Hop on one foot.
____ 2. Walk three yards on toes without touching heels on the floor.

EYE-HAND COORDINATION

The child can . . .
____ 3. Cut out pictures neatly, following straight lines, angles and curves.
____ 4. Draw a recognizable man of head, body, arms, and legs without copy.

SPEECH AND LANGUAGE COMPREHENSION

The child can . . .
____ 5. Pronounce compound consonants correctly in words such as basket, bottle, tree, green, please, thank, sister, brother. Baby talk is outgrown.
____ 6. Count the five fingers on each hand and add both together to make the correct total of ten.

PERSONAL INDEPENDENCE

The child can . . .
____ 7. Care for self at the toilet, requiring no assistance with paper or clothing.
____ 8. Tell own full name and address on request.

SOCIAL COOPERATION

The child can . . .
____ 9. Recite verses or sing a complete song, and will do so for the entertainment of others.
____10. Play competitive, active games with other children and keep the rules in such games as: hide and seek, hop-scotch, or cowboys and Indians.

Scoring of this checklist is based on the number of statements true for an individual child. If, for example, twenty of the twenty-five statements are true, the child is ready for first grade; fifteen to twenty true statements

[6] From "Individual Record Check List—Maturity Level for School Entrance and Reading Readiness." By Katharine M. Banham, Ph.D., Minneapolis, Minnesota: Educational Test Bureau, copyright 1959, by American Guidance Service, Inc. Reproduced by permission.

indicate readiness within three to six months. If a child scores under fifteen points, the manual recommends attendance at kindergarten or nursery school and more definitive testing (Banham, 1959).

MATHEMATICAL APTITUDE

For the appraisal of aptitude in mathematics there are many tests, among them tests of algebra and geometry. Mainly, these tests attempt to predict how well a student will do in his or her first courses in algebra and geometry. That is, they are tests used by the school to find out if a child is ready to start higher mathematics. Some children need more work in arithmetic, and many times it is best if they have a year of general mathematics before starting algebra. The results from these tests, plus the child's past academic record and teacher recommendations, help guide the school in placing the child in the course suited to his or her needs and talents.

Many of the tests of algebra aptitude contain problems of addition, subtraction, multiplication, and division. Some have problems dealing with percentages and the use of United States currency. Others have problems that require abstract reasoning and the ability to use simple arithmetical and algebraic procedures.

FOREIGN LANGUAGE APTITUDE

In recent years there has been a great deal of attention focused on foreign languages. To assist our schools in helping place students in foreign language courses, the professional test publishers have increased the number and quality of tests in this field. Basically, these foreign language aptitude tests are designed to provide an indication of a student's probable success in learning a foreign language.

Teachers and counselors may wonder what ability is actually needed to learn a foreign language. According to most authorities in this field, any person who is able to speak English in everyday life can learn a foreign language, given the time and opportunity to do so. Of course, this statement is too general to have much meaning. After all, "given the time" could mean forever. Thus the testing of foreign language aptitude assists in placing students in foreign language study who have the most chance of success. The language aptitude test measures learned capabilities that seem important to rapid success in learning a language.

The guidance counselor will use the results of the foreign language aptitude test in placing an individual in a class best suited to his abilities. Of course, as we have mentioned before, the results from one test are never used exclusively. They are used along with other test data and a child's academic record.

One of the prominent foreign language aptitude tests is the Modern Language Aptitude Test (MLAT). The MLAT can be used to measure not only modern language aptitude but also such ancient languages as Latin or Greek. There are five parts to the test. The first part is concerned with memory. The second part deals with the ability to learn speech sounds. The third part measures sound-symbol association ability and calls for knowledge of English vocabulary. The fourth part is devoted to sensitivity to grammatical structure. The fifth part deals with rote memory. In administering the test a tape recorder presents the instructions and test questions.

Tests such as the Modern Language Aptitude Test do not suggest specific languages for study but only that a person has or has not a general language aptitude.

MUSICAL APTITUDE

In the fields of music and art, the need for tests that can measure ability is self-evident. Many parents have spent much money on their child's music lessons only to find out years later that the child is tone-deaf or has little musical ability. There is no single test that can measure the desire of the child to express himself musically or his willingness to practice every day. In music, as perhaps in no other endeavor, the motivation to stick to the task and devote time to learning the skills each and every day are necessary. It does not matter how much talent a person has; if he does not have this desire to perform and the ability to stick to it, his talents will never be realized.

Most musical aptitude tests include questions aimed at discovering perceptive and interpretive abilities—that is, telling the difference in pitch and loudness. In addition, the person is tested in his esthetic judgment of a melody or harmony and a rhythmic pattern. The test most widely used by music educators and our schools is the Seashore Measures of Musical Talents. There are six parts to this test, all of which are on phonograph records, each testing a different aspect of musical ability. In the first test the person is asked to judge which of two tones is higher in pitch. In the second, he is asked to judge the louder of two sounds. In the third, time intervals are presented, and the student is asked to judge which of two is longer. In the fourth, rhythm is presented, and the individual is asked to tell if one of two rhythms is different or if they are both the same. In the fifth, the task is to judge which of two tone qualities is most pleasing. The sixth test is concerned with tonal memory; that is, the student is asked to judge whether two melodies are the same or different. In each test the judgments become increasingly harder with each item.

Many musicians and other critics have complained that the Seashore tests are not related to the musical activities of the musician. That is, the ability to tell fine differences in time and pitch are not needed by the musician. Be that as it may, the Seashore Measures of Musical Talents remains our best test of musical ability, and if used with other forms of evaluation, it can give some indication of musical talent. In the final analysis, however, you should bear in mind that the actual musical achievement and rate of progress of the person is probably the best predictor of future musical achievement.

ARTISTIC APTITUDE

In the field of aptitude in visual art, several types of tests are available. There are tests of esthetic judgment, design, and actual drawing. Critics of art tests have admitted that these tests can show differences between art students and other groups. However, they contend that this is so because of achievement rather than ability. Thus they state that we are measuring what the person has learned rather than his ability to learn or do well in the future.

One of the most widely used art aptitude tests is the Meier Art Judgment Test. This test consists of items presenting a pair of pictures of art objects. One picture is a recognized masterpiece and the other is the same picture with some slight change. The change usually affects the compositional balance of the picture as a whole. The student taking the test is asked to choose the better picture in each pair.

Other tests, such as the Horn Art Aptitude Inventory, require actual drawings. In this test, lines and dots are given from which the person must make a sketch.

As in the test of musical ability, teachers and counselors should consider such other factors as the child's interest, his achievement, and his art instructor's rating along with the test results before counseling students in definite terms. (See Super and Crites, 1962, Chapters 12 and 13, for a thorough and definitive discussion of musical and artistic aptitude tests.)

Graduate School Tests

The tests in the graduate school area are basically a combination of scholastic aptitude and achievement tests for college graduates. The Graduate Record Examination (GRE) is a very popular and widely used test for admission to graduate school. Part of the GRE is nothing more than a general intelligence or scholastic aptitude test, whereas other sections evaluate achievement in terms of specific subject-matter areas.

Another widely used test, especially in psychology and education, is the Miller Analogies Test. This test consists of analogies whose content is drawn from many different academic fields. The administration of the test is restricted to licensed centers (as is the GRE) and very rigid controls are applied to prevent leakage of content. Percentile norms are given for different groups of graduate students, including those in engineering, language and literature, physical science, social sciences, theology, business administration, psychology, and education. Students in the physical sciences and psychology, as a group, usually receive the highest scores.

In addition to these tests special examinations are given to applicants to professional schools such as schools of law, dentistry, medicine, and so forth. For a complete list of testing programs for special purposes, see Educational Testing Service (1967a).

Using the Results of Aptitude Tests

It is extremely important that the individual as well as his parents, teachers, and counselors be aware of his assets and limitations. The school counselor works with many different young people with different kinds of problems. The results of aptitude tests help him in guiding such youngsters as, for instance, the boy with average ability who hopes to be a nuclear scientist, the student whose parents view him unrealistically and aspire for him either above or below his abilities, the person who performs poorly in academic areas but is talented mechanically, the girl with superior intelligence who is not aware of her potential, the boy from a poor economic background who is willing to settle for an occupation below the one he is capable of succeeding in, and so on.

The aptitude test and/or battery can provide a basis for assisting not only in personal counseling but also in sound curricular planning. The school needs to know what courses to offer and who should take them. The data provided by aptitude test results help determine an appropriate course of action.

To illustrate, in everyday school terms, the actual use of aptitude tests, let us listen to Mr. Sanders, a high school counselor, explain the use of aptitude tests to a group of parents. He has just finished his introductory remarks concerning aptitude testing.

MR. SANDERS: Are there any questions?

PARENT: Yes, Mr. Sanders, I have a question. You said that our school gives algebra and foreign language aptitude tests to incoming freshmen to help place them in the types of courses that are suited to their abilities. Does this mean that if my son does poorly on one of these tests he cannot take these subjects?

MR. SANDERS: No, Mrs. Smith, that isn't exactly what I meant. We can only advise you and in the final analysis you and your son must make the decision. Besides, these tests do not mean that your son or daughter should never attempt algebra or a foreign language. What they do signify, however, is that the chances for success or failure, at this particular time, are greater with certain students. And it would probably be best if the child who does poorly on these tests waits at least until his sophomore year before attempting to take courses in the particular subjects. The results of these tests are not to hurt or bar students from their right of education, but only to help them make wise choices that are in line with their talents. In the long run, the child is much happier for he need not experience failure in areas where his talents are not as great.

PARENT: Do you mean to say that my child hasn't the right to try a subject, if you think he may fail?

MR. SANDERS: No, not at all. In a democratic society people have the right to fail as well as to succeed. In the school the same situation is true. The point is that the school attempts to educate everyone and different children have varied abilities. You wouldn't want to push a child into the water who couldn't swim, though it is possible he could learn while in the water—but also he might drown. In the same way we do not want to start a child in algebra if the chances are he will fail. Isn't it best to first teach the child in swimming or in algebra the essentials of these skills before expecting him to perform?

PARENT: I see your point. In other words, tests help to determine the most profitable areas of study for the child to enter at this time.

MR. SANDERS: Exactly, but a child is always given the chance to try these subjects in his second year, or even his first, if he and his parents want to go against the recommendations. Of course, we hope that the parents and child will go along with our recommendations, because the purpose of our tests is not to penalize the child but to help him.

PARENT: Mr. Sanders, may I change the subject a little?

MR. SANDERS: Certainly.

PARENT: My son's cousin is in high school and he has had aptitude tests in art and music. Why don't you give such tests?

MR. SANDERS: We do give tests of musical and artistic aptitude. However, we give this type of test when we feel it is needed. By this I mean, these tests are not given to all students. They are given only when the counselor feels a student's interests may possibly lie in these areas. Or when a child is interested in discovering his abilities and is not yet sure of what he wants to do in life.

PARENT: Is this also true for vocational tests?

MR. SANDERS: Yes and no. If you mean general vocational aptitude, yes—we do give all our students a test battery that includes tests of mechanical, clerical, and other skills needed for certain vocations. If you mean individual tests of vocational skills—no. For example, your children are given a test battery called the Differential Aptitude Tests. This test is given in the freshman year of high school and again in the junior year. This test battery gives us a general idea of the aptitudes your child may have in certain general vocational areas. In addition, it also gives us some idea of his general scholastic ability. This helps us help your child in specific vocational and collegiate planning. If this data isn't enough, then we administer an individual test in, for example, mechanical skill.

PARENT: Don't you think we are testing our kids to death?

MR. SANDERS: No, not necessarily, the more information we have on your child, the better we are able to help him. Tests are not always correct in their assessment of ability. Therefore the more tests given, the less chance of error. Again, let me stress, we give tests only to get information to help us guide your youngster. Of course, there is a point when too many tests can be a waste of time and money. But at Jones High School, we give what is necessary, we feel. As I stated, not all types of tests are given to every child. *Different tests for different reasons are given to different youngsters.*

Teachers and counselors, of course, may find that their school has different ideas from those of Mr. Sanders or they may discover that financial resources to support an ideal testing program are lacking. Today, with federal and state aid, however, most school districts can arrange to have an adequate testing program. If certain tests are needed for an individual pupil which are not available in a particular school system, it may be possible to refer the student to a public agency or a psychologist in private practice.

The important questions to keep in mind are the following:

1. What information does the school need to provide the best education for its particular students in its particular educational and geographic setting?
2. What information is needed to help each child develop his own unique potential?

Aptitude tests help provide the answers to these very important questions.

References

Banham, K. M. *Maturity level for school entrance and reading readiness: for kindergarten and first grade.* Minneapolis: American Guidance Service, Inc., 1959.

Bennett, G. K., Seashore, H. G., and Wesman, A. G. *Differential Aptitude Tests manual, forms L and M.* (4th ed.) New York: The Psychological Corporation, 1966.

Bingham, W. V. Classifying and testing for clerical jobs. *Personnel Journal,* 1935, **14,** 163–72.

Cronbach, L. J. *Essentials of psychological testing.* (2nd ed.) New York: Harper & Row, 1960.

Educational Testing Service. *An annotated list of testing programs for selection and special purposes.* (Rev.) Princeton, N.J.: Educational Testing Service, 1967.(a)

Educational Testing Service. *Handbook cooperative primary tests.* Princeton, N.J.: Educational Testing Service, 1967.(b)

Educational Testing Service. *Handbook SCAT Series II: Cooperative school and college ability tests.* Princeton, N.J.: Educational Testing Service, 1967.(c)

Fleishman, E. A. Testing for psychomotor abilities by means of apparatus tests. *Psychological Bulletin,* 1953, **50,** 241–62.

Ilg, F. L., and Ames, L. B. *School readiness.* New York: Harper & Row, 1965.

Kuhlmann, F., and Finch, F. H. *Kuhlmann-Finch scholastic aptitude tests.* Minneapolis: American Guidance Service, 1952.

Lawshe, C. H., Tiffin, J. and Moore, H. *Purdue clerical adaptability test, revised edition.* West Lafayette, Ind.: University Book Store, 1956.

Thurstone, T. G., *Examiner's manual: Primary mental abilities for grades 2–4.* Chicago: Science Research Associates, 1963.

Super, D. E., and Crites, J. O. *Appraising vocational fitness: By means of psychological tests* (Rev. ed.) New York: Harper & Row, 1962.

CHAPTER

10

Achievement Tests

In Chapter 9 we talked about aptitude tests and how they help the school in planning educational programs and guiding each individual youngster to realize his fullest potential. We stated that the primary objective of the aptitude test was to measure an individual's potential to learn or succeed, in school, at a vocation, or in an artistic endeavor. Simply stated, then, an aptitude test attempts to measure what a person can do. In this chapter we discuss tests that measure what a person has done.

The primary goal of the achievement test is to measure past learning, that is, the accumulated knowledge and skills of an individual in a particular field or fields. As we have stated, achievement and aptitude tests overlap. Can we test achievement without also testing capacity or ability? In a purely theoretical sense, we cannot. The difference between aptitude and achievement tests is one of degree or objective. Achievement tests emphasize past progress, whereas aptitude tests are primarily concerned with future potentialities. Lindeman (1967) presents the differences between aptitude and achievement tests quite well when he states,

> The primary distinction between aptitude and achievement tests is one of purpose rather than of content. Both are basically achievement tests; but one is used for prediction, whereas the other is used for assessing present knowledge and abilities. Differences in content and format between the two kinds of tests are thus due primarily to differences in the types of validity that each must have. In the case of aptitude tests, this is quite clearly predictive validity, and hence, items are selected on the basis of their prediction of future performance. In the case of standardized achievement tests, items are selected on the basis of content validity for the assessment of previously specified content and objectives [pp. 107–08].

The achievement tests used most frequently by a teacher are those he develops himself. Most teachers and principals, however, find that published standardized achievement tests and batteries can be of unique importance in many areas of the total school program.

A standardized achievement test or battery is an instrument produced by a test publisher for national use. It is developed through the efforts of professional test experts and is designed to examine educational objectives and goals. The standardized test differs from the classroom examination in its scientific development. A classroom achievement test is made up by a teacher for her own pupils and may or may not be used again. The teacher does not have the time, facilities, or training to investigate in a scientific manner the value of her tests. On the other hand, standardized achievement tests are run through rigorous scientific procedures to ensure their worth. In this chapter our attention will focus on the standardized achievement test.

Construction of Achievement Tests

The construction of an achievement test entails a careful analysis of the field to be examined. First, the reasons for the construction of the instrument must be clearly evident. Second, an exhaustive and definitive outline of the subject matter to be used is made. Third, the reasons for construction and an outline of the content are reviewed with such specialists as classroom teachers, educators, and test makers.

The fourth step is to compose test items for each part of the content outline, and then ask representative educators to comment on their importance, clarity of expression, and representativeness of subject matter. During this step some test items are modified, some are thrown out, and new items are added. The test is then administered to a sample group of children and their performance is analyzed. Let us now focus in detail on some of these steps.

Reasons and Objectives

The first step in the construction of a standardized achievement test is to state with clarity the reasons and objectives behind the instrument. Let us look at some of the stated objectives of the Cooperative Primary Tests (Educational Testing Service, 1967) as an example of this first step.

> 1. The tests will focus on skills and concepts basic to future development in reading, writing, listening, and mathematics. They will test understanding and thinking, in addition to memory or matching skills.
>
> 2. Since learning is the major goal of our schools, the tests will be clearly related to instructional processes, so that teachers can make direct use of the results with individuals and groups.
>
> 3. The tests will be designed to measure attainment of major educational objectives, regardless of particular curriculum programs and methods.
>
> 4. The tests will minimize the dependence of one skill upon another, for more definitive descriptions of pupil development. For example, no reading will be required on the Listening tests.
>
> 5. Every effort will be made to engage the interest of young children and secure valid responses and meaningful demonstrations of their ability.
>
> 6. The tests will be as convenient as possible for busy teachers to give and score [p. 6].

Content Outline

The second step involves an exhaustive and definitive outline of the subject matter to be tested. This is the outline of skills stated in the Doren Diagnostic Reading Test (Doren, 1956):

> *Unit I Letter Recognition*[1]
> A. The ability to recognize the same letter when it occurs again, to distinguish it from a letter of similar configuration.
> B. The ability to recognize as the same letter, the capital and lower case forms.
> C. The ability to recognize the same letter when presented in different type or style, whether in print or script.
> *Unit II Beginning Sounds*
> A. The ability to recognize the sound of a letter and associate that sound with its printed form.

---

[1] From M. Doren, *Doren Diagnostic Reading Test of Word Recognition Skills: Manual of Instructions with Suggestions for Remedial Activities*. Minneapolis, Minnesota: American Guidance Service, Copyright 1956. Reprinted with permission.

B. The ability to choose the correct beginning sound when supplying a word in context.

Unit III Whole Word Recognition

A. The ability to select identical words in a group of words of similar appearance.

B. The ability to make discrimination in sound and appearance in words with similar elements.

Unit IV Words within Words

A. The ability to find the two parts of a compound word, to recognize smaller known words in reading a larger compound word.

B. The ability to find small helping words within larger words which are not compound.

C. The ability to make judgments in using this form of word attack.

Unit V Speech Consonants

A. The ability to identify a new word from the auditory perception of a speech consonant.

B. The ability to recognize a word from the visual perception of a speech consonant.

Unit VI Ending Sounds

A. The ability to identify a word by its ending sound from a group of similar words by means of auditory discrimination.

B. The ability to choose the correct ending to suit context of a sentence, in words with variant endings.

C. The ability to recognize words of the same definition with dissimilar endings; that is, plurals with irregular endings.

Unit VII Blending

The ability to apply known blends in independent word attack in context.

Unit VIII Rhyming

A. The auditory ability to recognize two words that rhyme.

B. The ability to recognize, by visual perception, two words whose printed forms rhyme.

C. The ability to recognize that look-alike words do not always rhyme.

D. The ability to recognize that very unlike words may rhyme.

Unit IX Vowels

A. The ability to recognize short vowels and associate each with its letter form; to distinguish a word by its vowel sound from a group of words otherwise identical.

B. The ability to reproduce the vowel sound heard, whether in its long or short form; that is, to recognize that the same letter form has more than one sound.

C. The ability to tell from the printed word what sound a vowel should be given in words that conform to simple spelling rules.

D. The ability to recognize, by auditory perception, whether the vowel heard is long or short.

E. The ability to recognize the correct vowel sound in basic words, where spelling is in exception to the rules.

F. The ability to determine which vowel is sounded when two vowels occur together.

G. The ability to determine whether a vowel is long or short when two vowels occur together.

H. The ability to recognize that some vowel combinations create a new sound and to recognize its occurrence and exceptions.

J. The ability to recognize that in some words the printed vowel assumes the sound of a different vowel.

Unit X Sight Words
A check of the child's fund of sight words with non-phonetic spelling by means of his recognition of the same word spelled phonetically.

Unit XI Discriminate Guessing
The ability to supply missing words from a clue given by other words in context.

Sample Administration

After the standardized achievement test is constructed, it is given to a sample group of children. The results are then analyzed to find out whether the test is measuring what it is supposed to measure. For example, the authors of a social studies test have decided to construct a test that will measure the student's understanding of the currents of history that led up to the Industrial Revolution. They want to know whether they are measuring this area of knowledge or whether they are measuring reading ability, spelling, and so forth. In addition, they analyze the results to see whether children, upon retaking the test in another form, show similar scores. If they find that the test is meeting their objectives and is doing so consistently, they then consider publishing it.

This process is not merely based on inspection or intuition. After the administration of the test, usually to a thousand or more students, an analysis of each test item is made. The requirements each item must meet are (1) *easiness*, (2) *discrimination*, and (3) *distribution*. Let us briefly examine each of these.

EASINESS
Analysis of easiness is concerned with the percentage of students who answer an individual item correctly. If, for example, 100 students took an examination and thirty of them answered a specific item correctly, we would state that 30 per cent answered correctly.[2] Here is a list of sample items with percentages of students answering each item correctly.

---

[2] To find the percentage on each test item, simply tally the number of students who get a given item correct and then divide by the total number of students taking the test.

Item Number	Percentage
1	50
2	10
3	80
4	35
5	92
6	8
7	3
8	1
9	95
10	45

The preceding items reveal certain characteristics. Items 3, 5, and 9 seem to be relatively easy, whereas items 2, 6, 7, and 8 seem to be quite difficult. Items 1, 4, and 10 are between these extremes.

It is necessary to estimate percentages in an item analysis because very easy or very difficult test items tell us little about the subjects being examined. These easy items only serve to differentiate a very few students from the others. Statistically speaking, the ideal item is one that 50 per cent of the students answer correctly and 50 per cent miss. Thus it provides the greatest number of discriminations. Why? The 50 per cent are composed of different students on each item. Thus, one student may answer all items correctly and another may miss all of them. Test producers usually remove items that 80 per cent or more answer correctly or 20 per cent or less miss.

DISCRIMINATION

Discrimination analysis is used in all standardized test construction to determine the degree to which each test item measures the same thing as the total test in which it is included. First the top 25 per cent of students (total test scores) and the bottom 25 per cent are found. Then an analysis of each item is made by tallying the number of the top and bottom students who answered the item correctly. The percentage of the bottom group is then subtracted from the percentage of the top group. The resulting data indicate the extent to which a given item discriminates. The larger the difference, the better the item.

If a test item does not differentiate between the bottom and top group, it is not discriminating and is of little use. A negative difference (when the bottom group answers the item correctly more times than the top group) reveals a poor item that is probably ambiguous and is penalizing the students who know the most. Most authorities consider twenty percentage points as the minimum difference for an item that discriminates.

DISTRIBUTION

Distribution analysis is similar to easiness analysis except that all alternative answers to each item are studied. The percentage of students who mark each alternative is computed, not just the ones who obtained the correct answer; for example:

1. The sum of 40 and 40 is

	Per Cent Choosing Answer
a. 0	1
b. 80	58
c. 70	16
d. 40	25

An inspection of our example reveals several important factors. First, this is statistically a fairly good item in that a little over half (58 per cent) of the students obtained the correct answer. Second, we can see whether some of the answers are too easy and should be replaced by new answers that are better alternatives. This is obviously true of the "a" alternative, which was marked by only 1 per cent of the students.

Ambiguous items may be identified by this kind of analysis. If, for example, two alternatives, one of which is the correct answer, produce an equal or near-equal response percentage, there is a good chance that students have a good reason for choosing the incorrect alternative.

Standardization and Norms

After a careful statistical analysis of the data, the test is administered to thousands of children throughout the United States who represent a cross section of the population in terms of age, grade, geographic location, and in some cases, race and socioeconomic status. Norms are obtained from this analysis and are reported in the form of percentiles, grade equivalents, and so forth. After all this is done, a manual for administering, scoring, and interpreting the test is written. It is obvious from what has been stated to this point that a standardized achievement test is quite time-consuming and expensive to construct.

The following sections from the Directions for Administering the Stanford Achievement Test: Intermediate I Battery for Grade Four to the Middle of Grade Five (Kelley et al., 1964) present a whole, but brief, picture of what actually takes place in constructing an achievement test.

CONSTRUCTION[3]

In preparing this latest edition of *Stanford Achievement Test*, a major goal was to make sure that the content of the test would be in

---

[3] From the *Stanford Achievement Test : Intermediate I Battery*, © 1964 by Harcourt, Brace & World, Inc. All rights reserved. Reproduced by permission.

harmony with present objectives and measure what is actually being taught in today's schools. To make certain that the test content would be valid in this sense, the construction of the new edition (as of each earlier edition) was preceded by a thorough analysis of the most widely used series of elementary textbooks in the various subjects, of a wide variety of courses of study, and of the research literature pertaining to children's concepts, experiences, and vocabulary at successive ages or grades. On the basis of this analysis, the authors prepared detailed outlines of the content to be covered by all tests at all grade levels. These outlines specified the relative proportion of content to be devoted to the various skills, knowledges, and understandings within each area and served as blueprints for the tests that were ultimately to emerge. At this stage, as well as throughout the whole developmental process, reliance was placed on the judgment of subject-matter specialists in the several areas.

ITEM ANALYSIS PROGRAM

The experimental edition was administered to approximately 49,000 pupils in 19 school systems within about a month of the closing of school in spring, 1961. Because of the importance of the decisions with respect to elimination or retention of items that were to be based on results of this tryout, an effort was made to have the tryout sample a representative one with respect to such characteristics as regional distribution, size of school system, and rural vs. urban character.

Each cooperating system was asked to list the textbooks in use in each subject, at each grade level. Analysis of these lists of instructional materials indicated that the systems were widely divergent in this respect, which was, of course, desirable from the standpoint of avoiding text-related bias in the sample.

Classroom teachers administered the tests in practically all instances, in order that the administration would correspond most nearly to the typical regular administration of the tests. In addition to the experimental edition of Stanford, every pupil was given an intelligence test, the *Otis Quick-Scoring Mental Ability Test*, in order that data would be available for checking on the equivalence of ability of the groups taking the several forms (necessary for comparability of item-difficulty values); and for checking on the extent to which the item-analysis sample was a typical one with respect to general ability level. The Stanford tests were administered essentially without time limits in order that all pupils would have an opportunity to attempt all items.

The experimental administration was designed to provide item-analysis information not only for those grades in which a given battery was intended to function in its final form, but also for at least one grade below and one grade above this intended range.

This was done in order to assist in the selection of items that would discriminate among the pupils at the extremes of the ranges in the regular use of the tests, and would show an increment of growth from grade to grade.

For each of the approximately 15,000 questions in the experimental forms, a count was obtained of the number of pupils at each grade level answering the item correctly, and, in the case of multiple-choice items, the number of pupils selecting each of the incorrect responses to the item as well as the correct response. The numbers answering correctly were converted to per cents, and these per cents for successive grades for a given item were considered to constitute an "item profile," revealing the extent to which an item correlated with progress through school. These item profiles were considered one of the most important indices of item validity, and considerable weight was attached to them in the selection of items for the final forms. Results of this item tryout permitted identification of ambiguous items, of items either too easy or too difficult for the grades for which they were intended, and of items unsatisfactory in other respects. Such items were eliminated from consideration for retention in the final forms.

Each teacher participating in the administration of the experimental editions was asked for comments, criticisms, or suggestions for improving the tests. Teachers were asked to comment with respect to clarity of questions and directions, appropriateness of content, format, and typography, suitability of item types, and other aspects of the test.

The content of the final forms of the test was selected from the total body of material tried out experimentally in such a way that the final tests conform to the original specifications with respect to content, relative emphases, etc., that they are of appropriate difficulty for the grades in which they are intended to be used, and that the several forms are highly comparable in content and difficulty.

THE STANDARDIZATION PROGRAM

The first step in the standardization program was the establishment of specifications for the norm group with respect to such characteristics as geographic distribution, types of school systems to be included, numbers of pupils desired per grade, and the extent of participation within cooperating systems. The distribution according to region and size of system was established in such a way that the norm sample would duplicate these characteristics for pupils in average daily attendance in public and private schools throughout the country. It was further decided that in all participating systems *every* pupil in regular classes in at least six consecutive grades would be included in the standardization program so that there would be no question of selection within systems.

The desired representation in terms of number and kinds of systems was worked out on a state-by-state basis, and invitations were extended to school systems in the various states meeting the desired specifications. A sufficiently large number of systems were invited to avoid undue influence by any one system. A total of 264 school systems drawn from 50 states participated; over 850,000 pupils were tested as part of this program.

THE NORM SAMPLE

Public schools (integrated, segregated white, and segregated negro), private nonsectarian, and private sectarian schools were included in the sample. The geographical distribution and the distribution according to size of the systems comprising the norm group are reported in Table 6.

In addition to size and geographical representation, two additional pieces of information known to be related to achievement were obtained. These were the median family income and the median number of years of schooling completed by those over 25 years of age. Regional averages of these two factors were compared with census figures [pp. 23–24].

The reader should note that the preceding selection was but a brief summary. Test publishers produce technical manuals or supplements that contain in detail all the steps in the test's construction.

Differences Between Teacher-Made and Standardized Tests

1. The standardized test is based on curricular content and objectives common to representative schools throughout the nation. The teacher-made test is based on the content and objectives of one classroom or in some instances of a department within a school.
2. A teacher-made test may be constructed for a limited topic, whereas a standardized test encompasses large areas of content or skills.
3. Professional educators, psychologists, classroom teachers, and statisticians develop standardized tests. The teacher-made test is usually created by one or a limited number of teachers.
4. The teacher-made test can be evaluated only in terms of a single classroom or school. The standardized test provides evidence of the performances of different groups of children in different educational and geographic settings.
5. The standardized test is created, developed, and constructed by various educators and test specialists who attempt to follow

scientific procedures.[4] The teacher-made test is usually constructed by a person untrained in measurement and without much experience with scientific techniques.

The standardized test has obvious advantages over the teacher-made test; however, some of the unique attributes of the standardized test are also disadvantages. The consensus of professional experts on curricular objectives, along with a careful analysis of textbooks and courses of study, presents a good general picture, but it does not allow for individual differences in terms of local school goals and student populations. It is at best a compromise—a blending of the best thinking, a consensus, an average—not a tailor-made evaluative instrument for a given educational setting. In addition a published test is fixed at the point in time when it was developed and published and is not flexible to new situations and educational change. It cannot measure limited local needs. It can, of course, be revised, and the better tests are, as educational goals are changed and modified.

The chief value of the standardized test resides in its national scope, which enables the school district to compare its progress with that of other schools throughout the country. It enables the guidance staff to compare student progress with potentiality as indicated by aptitude tests. The norms presented in the standardized test manual make these comparisons possible.

Ebel presents three common fears or misconceptions educators have regarding standardized achievement tests. The first of these is the feeling that the goals of education are too subtle and complex to be effectively measured. Ebel (1968) in discussing this states,

> Teachers of young children know that the development of skills in the tool subjects and the establishment of solid foundations for understanding and interest in the major fields of human knowledge are concrete, specific, important objectives. But some of them may feel that tests, especially objective standardized tests, fail "to get at" the real essentials of achievement in these skill and foundation subjects. This mystical devotion to a hidden reality of achievement which is more essential than overt ability to perform has never satisfied the research worker. He wants to know the nature of this hidden reality and what evidence there is that it is important [p. 257].

The second fear is "overconcern" with possible anxiety and stress caused the child by testing. Ebel (1968) feels that it is more conducive to mental health for the child to know how he is really progressing than to shield him from the educational facts of life. "In education, as in medicine and justice,

---

[4] *Scientific* here refers to use of the scientific method and measurement procedures which attempt to gauge validity, reliability, standard error of measurement, and so forth.

an excess of present sympathy can postpone or even defeat the procedures necessary for an individual's future welfare" (p. 259).

Ebel's third point is the overemphasis on the uniqueness of the school's objectives compared to the objectives outlined in a standardized test. He suggests that what constitutes a good education in Maine is not radically different from what constitutes a good education in California. He states that a teacher should not expect a standardized test to reveal data on how well she has taught everything, "but only on the things that all teachers ought to have taught." On the other hand Ebel concludes with the very important point that: "For those achievements which are truly and rightly unique to a particular school or teacher, locally constructed tests are the best answer" (pp. 259–60).

In weighing the advantages and disadvantages of standardized achievement testing, the student of measurement should not think in black or white terms. The teacher-made test is a valuable and important gauge of day-to-day classroom progress. The standardized test allows the teacher and school to see the student's and institution's achievement in a national perspective. The use of both the teacher-made and standardized test provides a whole educational picture of the student and school.

Thus the user of standardized achievement tests can make broad comparisons between schools or classes or between areas of achievement and aptitude. In addition to the national norms furnished by the test publisher, each school with a complete testing program may develop local norms. Over a period of years the guidance counselor or principal of a specific school will be in a position to say what the scores mean for his particular school.

Types of Achievement Tests

Standardized achievement tests can be divided into three groups. The first group consists of *general achievement test batteries*, which are tests that cover many of the basic subject-matter areas of a school's program as well as study skills. In using these batteries the school does not have to administer separate tests, nor does it have to scan the market for tests in each subject field. The authors of the general batteries attempt to produce an instrument that will cover the general needs of an achievement testing program for our schools. This type of achievement test is used from elementary school through high school and even at the college level.

The second kind of achievement test covers single subject areas, such as social studies, science, or mathematics.

The third kind of achievement test is limited to specific areas within general subject-matter fields, such as ancient history, biology, and algebra.

The general achievement battery is the basic type of evaluative instrument used in the elementary schools. The single achievement test covering broad or specific subject areas is used along with the general achievement battery at the junior and senior high school level. We shall examine achievement batteries and tests covering different subject-matter areas and at different grade levels.

Achievement Test Batteries

The general achievement test battery provides the best all-around evidence concerning academic progress. Some authorities recommend that they be administered every year if the school can afford it. (See Nunnally, 1964.) We shall have more to say on this subject in our discussion of school testing programs. However, decisions on when and how often any test should be administered are dependent on the local school and its unique needs.

SCOPE AND CONTENT

Achievement test batteries differ from one another in their (1) breadth of coverage and (2) level of understanding required. General achievement batteries cover subject-matter and school skills from the primary grades through high school. Table 23, for example, illustrates the range of content and subtests employed in the various forms of the Stanford Achievement Test. Note that in the primary battery only six types of subject-matter are measured, whereas the intermediate battery attempts to evaluate ten different content areas. It is also interesting to note the progression to that point and then the reduction in the number of areas afterward, paralleling the changing emphasis in the school curriculum ladder.

Now we turn our attention to the specific content in widely used batteries and discuss what each subtest attempts to measure.

Word Meaning. Almost all achievement batteries have a subtest concerning word knowledge.[5] The batteries, however, vary in the degree to which they measure this area. Some evaluate word understanding in the context of a paragraph, whereas others measure it more directly and yield a separate word knowledge or vocabulary score. Others combine both approaches and yield paragraph-reading and vocabulary scores. Two of the most widely used methods, in the multiple-choice format, are shown in the following examples. (In the primary grades, pictures are used.)

1. *Boy* means almost the same as
   a. girl
   b. man
   c. woman
   d. child

---

[5]A notable exception is the Sequential Tests of Educational Progress (STEP), a battery widely used and respected.

Table 23 Stanford Achievement Test—Subtests For Various Grades

Subtests	Primary I (Middle of Grade 1 to Middle of Grade 2)	Primary II (Middle of Grade 2 to End of Grade 3)	Intermediate I (Grade 4 to Middle of Grade 5)	Intermediate II (Middle of Grade 5 to End of Grade 6)	Advanced (Grade 7 to the End of Grade 9)
Word Reading	X				
Paragraph Meaning	X	X	X	X	X
Vocabulary	X				
Spelling	X	X	X	X	X
Word Study Skills	X	X	X		
Arithmetic	X				
Word Meaning		X	X	X	
Science and Social Studies Concepts		X			
Language		X	X	X	X
Arithmetic Computation		X	X	X	X
Arithmetic Concepts		X	X	X	X
Arithmetic Applications			X	X	X
Social Studies			X	X	X
Science			X	X	X

2. *Boy* means the opposite of
    a. girl
    b. child
    c. man
    d. woman

Reading. This basic content area, common to all general achievement batteries, presents the student with connected passages from a story or event. The tests vary in types of questions and length of passages. Some are based on passages from fifty to 100 words, with two or three questions on each passage. Others have a small number of long passages (500 or more words), with as many as twenty test questions referring to a single passage. Figure 26 illustrates some sample questions from the Reading Test of the Cooperative Primary Tests for grades 1 and 2, each illustrating different methods of evaluating reading achievement. The children are instructed to read what is in the arrow, then mark the box that goes best with it. Question 1 attempts to evaluate comprehension by having the student identify an illustrative picture with a word stimulus. Question 2 evaluates comprehension in the same manner but uses poetry. Questions 3 and 4 attempt to evaluate the student's ability to extract meaning from a paragraph, and question 5 evaluates the student's ability to interpret the passage he has read.

An example of a test item based on a paragraph and questions measuring more complex types of reading achievement follows.[6] In the actual test there are a total of nine questions on the sample paragraph.

The electoral college is the group of officials directly *responsible* for electing the president of the United States. Each of the fifty states has its own electoral college. According to Article II, Section 1, of the Constitution, each state selects the members of its electoral college in whatever way its legislature sees fit, on the basis of one elector for each senator, and one for each representative to which the state is entitled in Congress. This means that the number of electors in each state varies according to its population, and that some states, such as heavily populated New York and California, have a greater number of electoral votes than *sparsely* settled states such as Nevada. The total number of electors from all the states *constitutes* the national electoral college.

1. Perhaps the best title for this paragraph would be
    a. "The Importance of Electoral Votes."
    b. "The National Electoral College."

[6] From *Test 7-Reading* of the *High School Placement Test.* Copyright, 1962, by the Scholastic Testing Service, Inc. Used by permission of the Scholastic Testing Service, Inc.

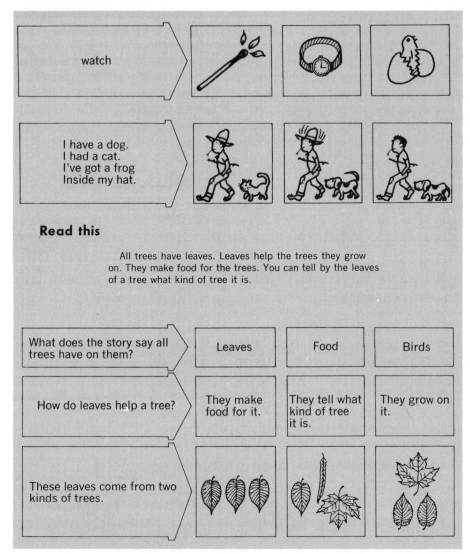

Figure 26. Sample questions from Reading, Cooperative Primary Tests, Form 12A. (From *Cooperative Primary Tests, Reading, Form 12A.* Copyright © 1965 by Educational Testing Service. All rights reserved. Reprinted by permission of Educational Testing Service.)

    c. "The Electoral College of States."
    d. "How a President Is Elected."
2. The number of electors to be chosen from each state was established by
    a. the Bill of Rights.
    b. the Twelfth Amendment.

      c. each state's Constitution.

      d. Article II, Section I, of the Constitution.

  3. All the state electoral colleges together form the

      a. Hall of the House of Representatives.

      b. National Electoral College.

      c. House of Representatives.

      d. Constitutional Convention.

Arithmetic. As with reading, all achievement batteries attempt to appraise arithmetic skills and understanding. The batteries differ in their degree of emphasis on computational skills, problem solving, concepts, and understanding.

One of the difficulties that test authors encounter in appraising arithmetic ability, especially in the area of problem solving, is the separation of reading achievement from mathematical skill. The mathematics section of the Sequential Tests of Educational Progress (STEP) attempts to overcome this obstacle. Educational Testing Service (1957), which developed the test, asked themselves: "What are the important threads of emphasis which should underlie a good mathematics program for general education from grades 4 through 14?" (p. 77). The major concepts[7] they evolved are (1) number and operation, (2) symbolism, (3) measurement and geometry, (4) function and relation, (5) proof-deductive and inferential reasoning, and (6) probability and statistics.

These concepts receive varying degrees of emphasis at different grade levels of the test. Two per cent of the elementary items, for example, contain the concept of symbolism, whereas the college-level form devotes 13 per cent of its items to this concept. Questions involving number and operation, on the other hand, account for one half of the total number of items at the lowest grade level and represent only one fifth of the total at the college level (Educational Testing Service, 1957). See Figure 27 for some representative items for grades 10, 11, and 12.

The Stanford Achievement Test battery provides different arithmetical items under different subtests. Figure 28 presents some samples from the Intermediate I Battery. The Computation Test measures skills in addition, subtraction, multiplication, and division. Some of the areas that the "Concepts" test measures are understanding of place value, roman numerals, the meaning and multiplication of fractions, rounding whole numbers, and geometric terms. The Arithmetic Applications test attempts to measure mathematical reasoning with problems that are taken from everyday life. The authors of the test state that they have attempted to keep the reading vocabulary below the problem-solving level to avoid interference with the measurement of mathematical reasoning. Computational tasks are kept to a minimum to avoid contamination of the measure (Kelley et al., 1964).

---

    [7] The student interested in a further clarification and discussion of these six major concepts is referred to the STEP Manual (Educational Testing Service, 1957).

To get some idea of the average number of passengers per car, the theater manager made the following tabulation of the number of passengers in every other car on opening night.

No. of Passengers Per Car	No. of Cars
1	100
2	300
3	400
4	200

For these 1000 cars, what was the average number of persons per car?

A 2.0   **B** 2.5   **C** 2.7   **D** 3.0

According to one plan for traveling to Mars, the round trip would take nearly three earth years, including a stay on Mars of 449 earth days. If 34,000,000 miles is taken as the distance between Mars and earth, which of the following can be used to determine the average speed of travel in miles per hour?

A $\dfrac{(3 \times 365 - 449) \times 12}{34,000,000}$

B $\dfrac{34,000,000}{(3 \times 365 - 449) \times 24}$

C $\dfrac{2 \times 34,000,000}{(3 \times 365 - 449) \times 24}$

D $\dfrac{34,000,000 \times 24}{2 \times (3 \times 365 - 449)}$

To avoid downdrafts, the top of a chimney should be 2 feet above the highest point of the roof. A side view of Bob's house, with dimensions, is shown in the figure below.

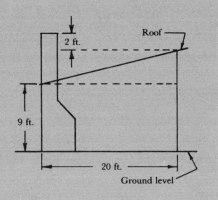

How many feet above ground level should the top of the chimney be, if the sloping roof rises 1 foot for every 4 horizontal feet?

A 11   **B** $13\frac{1}{4}$ **C** 16   **D** 19

In 1915, New York City had its record snowstorm for April. 10.2 inches of snow fell at the rate of 0.42 inches per hour. About how many hours did the snowstorm last?

A 4   **B** 24   **C** 42   **D** 125

Figure 27. Sample items from Sequential Tests of Educational Progress, Mathematics, Form 2A. (From *Cooperative Sequential Tests of Educational Progress, Mathematics, Form 2A.* © Copyright 1956, 1957. All rights reserved, Cooperative Test Division, Educational Testing Service. Reprinted by permission of Educational Testing Service.)

Language Skills. Another almost universal area in most achievement batteries is the section dealing with skills in using language. The detailed coverage of the batteries vary somewhat, but in general they include material on capitalization, spelling, punctuation, case, number and tense. Some examples of items similar to those found in the batteries follow.

> *Usage*
> 1. My little sister _____ walk yet.
>   a. doesn't
>   b. don't
>   c. neither

Test 6: Arithmetic Computation.

1		2		3	
3 2 +8 6	a 114 b 118 c 124 d 128 e NG	1 1 9 − 8 5	f 23 g 24 h 33 i 134 j NG	7 4 × 2	a 78 b 146 c 148 d 128 e NG

Test 7: Arithmetic Concepts.

20 Which is six thousand twelve?

     e 600012   g 6012   e f g h
     f 60012   h 6,12   20 ◯ ◯ ◯ ◯

21 Which of these fractions is the largest?

     a $\frac{2}{6}$ c $\frac{2}{5}$ a b c d
     b $\frac{2}{4}$ d $\frac{2}{3}$ 21 ◯ ◯ ◯ ◯

22 If the sum is 6 and one addend is 2, the other addend
is —

     e 4   g 8   e f g h
     f 6   h 12   22 ◯ ◯ ◯ ◯

Test 8: Arithmetic Applications.

Saturday Specials	
Shoes	$7.95
Sweater	$3.99
Dress	$8.98
Socks	50¢

15 The dress costs how much more than the shoes cost?
     a 3¢   b $1.00   c $1.07   d $16.93   e NG

16 How much will the socks and shoes both cost?
     f $8.45   g $8.00   h $7.45   i $8.55   j NG

17 If Susan buys the sweater and uses a ten-dollar bill to pay for it,
what should be her change?
     a $6.01   b $4.00   c $6.00   d $1.01   e NG

Figure 28. Sample items from Stanford Achievement Test, Intermediate I Battery, Form W. (From the *Stanford Achievement Test: Intermediate I Battery.* © 1964 by Harcourt, Brace & World, Inc. All rights reserved. Reproduced by permission.)

2. Did Bob and Mary play _____together?
    a. good
    b. well
    c. neither

Capitalization
Directions: Underline the words that should be capitalized:

on february 22, 1732 the father of our country, George washington was born. He was the first president of the united states. thomas jefferson was born in the same state as George washington. thomas jefferson was our third president. Do you know what states washington and jefferson were born in? john adams was our second president. George washington and thomas jefferson were born in virginia.

Punctuation
Directions: In the sentences below, certain spaces are underlined. Insert the correct punctuation marks only where you think they are needed. Remember, *not all* the underlined spaces need punctuation marks.

Mrs__ Robert Jones
2548 Lansdowne Ave__
Springfield__ Illinois
Dear Mrs__ Jones__
     I have recently seen __ your collection of paintings in the museum at Chapel Hill__ North Carolina__ Do you plan to sell any in the near future__ If so__ please advise__ since I am interested in purchasing some of them__

Spelling
     Some tests provide the teacher with a list of standardized words which are to be read to the students. The student writes the words as the teacher pronounces them. Other tests use the multiple-choice format as illustrated below:

The table was *there* very own.   Right   Wrong
Mark the word that is misspelled
     ____desk
     ____chair
     ____cup
     ____cecret
Bill enjoyed his class in
     a. psology
     b. psychology
     c. pschology

Study Skills. Educators, especially since the 1920's, have stated that one of the major purposes of schooling is to provide individuals with the tools for learning on their own after formal schooling has been completed. Consequently, most schools devote considerable time to developing study skills and techniques. Most of the achievement batteries appraise such skills by presenting such tasks as reading graphs, charts, maps, and tables and finding information in reference sources. Some tests incorporate these tasks in content areas such as mathematics and social studies.

The SRA Achievement Series labels these areas as Using Sources of Information and Reading Charts. The following are some sample questions from the SRA Achievement Series for grades 6 to 9.

USING SOURCES OF INFORMATION[8]

Directions: This is a test to see how well you can use reference materials. Some of the questions ask about which source you would use; the other questions ask about what is in a certain type of reference book. There is only one correct answer to each question. Now read the sample question below.

(1) If we wished to find something about Abraham Lincoln, which of these would be best to use?
  a. A magazine.
  b. A newspaper.
  c. A history book.
  d. A spelling book.

Another part of this test is designed to test a student's ability to use a table of contents. The student is presented with a table of contents and asked questions such as the following:

(2) The table of contents tells us that trouble with the law is discussed in
  a. Chapter I.
  b. Chapter II.
  c. Chapter III.
  d. Chapter IV.

READING CHARTS

Directions: This is a test to see how well you can read graphs, tables, and maps. First, glance at the chart in order to get an idea about its contents. Then read each question and refer back to the specific graph, table, or map to decide which ONE of the four possible answers is correct. There is only one correct answer to each question.

[8] From SRA Achievement Series 6–9 by Louis P. Thorpe, D. Welty Lefever, and Robert A. Naslund. Copyright, 1955, by Science Research Associates, Inc. Reprinted by permission of the publisher.

Figure A is a sample graph. It indicates the number of words that Bob spelled correctly on each of ten days in April.

(1) We can tell from the graph that Bob had 15 words correct on
   a. Monday, April 1.
   b. Tuesday, April 2.
   c. Wednesday, April 3.
   d. Thursday, April 4.

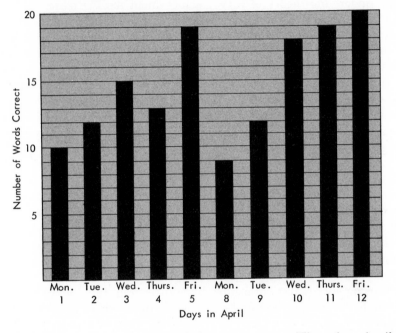

(2) How many words did Bob have correct on Thursday, April 11?
   a. 13.
   b. 18.
   c. 1.
   d. 19.

Content Areas. The areas we have been concerned with so far are common to the educational core of primary and elementary school and to some extent are relevant for high school and college. In the upper grades less emphasis is placed on core areas and more on subject or content fields. Students learn not only science, for example, but specific fields within science, such as biology and physics. We call these content areas.

In recent years content areas have played a lesser role in standardized testing. This is because many educators and testing people feel that items of information are less common to curricular objectives throughout the United States than are skills. It is, therefore, very difficult to construct content areas that are representative of most schools.

Social studies and science are the areas generally presented in achievement batteries when content areas are appraised. Social studies generally includes history, civics, and geography, and science usually contains subtests in physics, biology, and astronomy.

Survey Achievement Tests

The underlying theory of survey achievement tests is basically the same as for the subtests in general achievement batteries. A survey reading test, for example, includes most of the same kinds of items and materials found in the reading subtest of a general battery. The basic difference between a survey test and a general battery resides in the depth and extent of coverage. The survey test usually concentrates in much more detail on a single area than does the general battery. Further, general batteries do not usually include special subjects, and even when they do, it is at a superficial level as compared to the survey test. This is especially true in areas such as chemistry, biology, physics, algebra, and economics.

WHEN TO USE SURVEY TESTS

Survey achievement tests should not be used except for some special reason. The general battery, especially at the primary and elementary school level, is the usual instrument of choice. This is because the general battery and the various subtests are standardized on the same students and developed on the same underlying philosophy. Thus evaluation of student scores on different subtests is based on the same principles and normative population. When using survey tests in arithmetic and reading, for example, it is more difficult to determine the pupil's relative status in these areas because discrepancies in scores could be due to differing degrees of academic progress or to differences in educational principles and the student population used for test standardization.

In certain situations, however, the survey test is the best choice. There are four basic types of special situations that may call for the use of a survey test.

1. *To provide more definitive data on a student who does poorly on a specific subtest of a general achievement battery.* If, for example, a student does poorly on the arithmetic subtest of a general battery and the school wants more detailed information on strengths and weaknesses, they may obtain a more complete picture by administering a survey or special test for arithmetic.

2. *To measure special areas of the high school curriculum that are not covered or are only briefly presented in a general achievement battery.* For example, if a school wants an index of achievement in biology, they will have to use a survey test of biology rather than a general battery which appraises general achievement in science.

3. *To help students plan future educational courses within the school.* For example, does the student have enough mathematical background to take a second year of algebra? An algebra survey test in conjunction with other data could assist the student in making a sound decision.

4. *To help counsel students for college.* If, for example, a student is planning to enroll in a premedical course of study, it would be helpful to him to know his achievement in chemistry, biology, mathematics, and physics as compared to other students throughout the country. Survey tests in these areas could provide this kind of data.

Of course, the preceding situations are only guidelines and are subject to varying circumstances. Special situations not covered by our four basic types may arise. On the other hand, there will be situations that in theory call for the use of a survey test but do not in actual practice. Factors such as time, money, and the need for certain information must be weighed in each individual case.

A great many different kinds of survey tests are available. They range from tests in Greek and Hebrew to agriculture and driver education. We shall therefore focus our attention on reading tests, which should serve as a representative sample.

AN EXAMPLE: SURVEY READING TESTS

The survey reading test is one of the most widely used types of standardized tests. It is very similar to the reading subtests of general achievement batteries. Typically covered are (1) ability to read paragraphs and answer questions concerning their content, (2) word and sentence meaning, and (3) speed of reading.

The basic difference between the survey reading test and a reading subtest of a general battery is, as mentioned earlier, that the survey test attempts to appraise reading skills in greater detail. The survey reading test is therefore generally longer and takes more time to administer.

The major reason for administering a survey reading test is to obtain data for planning group reading activities and individual remedial and developmental reading instruction. If a general battery is administered, a survey test is still needed to secure additional detailed information about pupils who reveal reading problems on the general battery.

Let us turn our attention to an actual survey reading test. The SRA Reading Record (Buswell, 1959) is representative of many of the survey tests used in our schools. The test is intended for junior and senior high school students (grades 6 to 12). Four basic skills in reading are measured: (1) rate of reading, (2) reading comprehension, (3) everyday reading skills, and (4) reading vocabulary. A total reading score, which reveals the student's overall reading comprehension, is obtained by totaling the student's scores on the four tests. Sample items from each of the four areas follow.

RATE OF READING[9]

Directions for Test 1. The first test is a paragraph reading test. Read the material as rapidly as you can, but read it carefully. You will be asked questions about it. When the examiner says STOP, look at the number at the end of the line you were reading. Find this number on the Answer Pad and punch the circle next to it. You will have 2 minutes for Test 1. You are not expected to read all of the material in the time allowed.

A Century of Agricultural Progress[10]

    Difficult as it may seem for many of us to believe, the greatest problem of all nations has been to make this old   1
earth yield enough of food stuffs to satisfy the hunger of the many millions that inhabit it. Especially has this been   2
true during the World Wars and most keenly have people everywhere been brought to realize it. Yet until com-   3
paratively recently the genius of the race has not been directed toward improving methods of agriculture. La-   4
bor-saving devices for multiplying the man power and efficiency of the artisan and mechanic began to appear,   5
but the farmer plodded on in the primitive ways of his fathers. Each householder was almost entirely self-sus-   6
taining, producing nearly all that he and his family re- quired. He sold but little and bought less. There was no   7
need for producing more, and a virgin soil and large crops did not stimulate inventive genius along agricul-   8
tural lines. But with the building of cities, the growth of manufacturing and the great divisions of labor it   9
became imperative that the farmer should provide food, not only for his own family, but for the ever increasing   10
army of those not engaged in agriculture. To do this brought profits, and the incentive of private gain en-   11
couraged efforts toward increased productiveness and the development of new devices and better methods.   12

READING COMPREHENSION

Directions for Test 2. In this test you will be asked questions about the material you have just read. You are *not* to look back at Test 1. Decide which of the four answers to each question is right. Then punch circle (a), (b), (c), or (d) for the right answer.

You will have 5 minutes for Test 2. You are not expected to finish in the time allowed.

[9] From *SRA Reading Record* by Guy T. Buswell. Copyright 1947, Science Research Associates, Inc. Reprinted by permission of the publisher.

[10] This sample represents about one fifth of the complete reading passage.

1. The material in Test 1 is mainly about
   (a) gasoline motors   (b) planting   (c) farm machinery
   (d) Cyrus McCormick

2. The greatest problem of all nations is to produce enough
   (a) machinery   (b) food   (c) clothing   (d) horses

3. An increase in non-agricultural population compelled farm production
   (a) to increase   (b) to decrease   (c) to remain the same
   (d) to double

4. Inventive genius along agricultural lines was stimulated by
   (a) better methods   (b) speculation   (c) private gain   (d) chance discovery

EVERYDAY READING SKILLS

Directions for Test 4. In the next test, there is a telephone directory on the left-hand page, and a list of names and addresses on the right-hand page. Following each name and address are four telephone numbers. Pick out the right number for each name and punch the circle for that number. You will have 3 minutes for Test 4. You are not expected to finish in the time allowed.

Abbott Jas E 5370 Laurel......7901
Aitken Edmund 6721 61st av...9520
Alsdorf Ernest M 1912 Elm rd. 7210
Anderson Mrs Dora 441 Ridge..611
Angelo A T 106 Douglas av....0461
Arntzen C R 3946 Barrypoint..3639
Austin Henry 631 Water......5301
Baker Darwin 405 W Maple....228
Baker Duncan 117 N Parkway..5488
Baker John R 244 Summer av ...037

16. Duncan Baker, 117 N. Parkway
    (a) 5422   (b) 543-J
    (c) 5488   (d) 4478

In addition to the preceding tests, there is a test which presents a map, a table, and a graph with questions concerning them. Another test presents an advertisement and a list of articles appearing in the advertisement. Following each article are four prices. The student is to pick out the right price. Still another test in this area requests the student to answer questions based on an index to a book.

VOCABULARY

Directions for Test 8. This is a test of technical vocabulary. You are to decide which of four words or phrases means the *same as* the first word, and punch the circle for that word. You will have 3 minutes for Test 8. You are not expected to finish in the time allowed.

1. biography . . . .   (a) a graph   (b) a scientific instrument
                        (c) a textbook   (d) a life history

2. narrative . . . . . (a) tells a story   (b) an argument
                        (c) a scientific report   (d) a law

Directions for Test 9. In Test 9 there are nineteen sentences, each followed by four words. One of the four words could be used in place of the *last* word in the sentence without changing the meaning of the sentence. Decide which word could be used in place of the last word in the sentence, and punch the circle for that word. You will have 3 minutes for Test 9. You are not expected to finish in the time allowed.

3. During the recent typhoon the waves were titanic.
   (a) choppy   (b) unusual   (c) artistic   (d) gigantic

4. During the trial all of his statements were substantiated.
   (a) disproved   (b) impudent   (c) verified   (d) forgotten

Directions for Test 10. This is a test of general vocabulary. You are to decide which of four words means the *same as* the first word, and punch the circle for that word. You will have 3 minutes for Test 10. You are not expected to finish in the time allowed.

6. hinder . . . .   (a) rear   (b) risk   (c) prevent   (d) persuade

7. imperial . . . . .   (a) cruel   (b) royal   (c) governor
                          (d) colonial

Different reading tests stress different facets of reading skills and are represented in various tests in varying proportions. The test user should examine the actual test items in order to determine what skills the test is really measuring—not only with reading tests but with all achievement tests or batteries. Only the test consumer, after critically examining the test items, can gauge the validity of the achievement test for his own objectives. The same general principles that guide the use of reading survey tests are also generally relevant for other types of survey tests.

The survey test, then, is a measure of the skills and knowledge that comprise a given subject. Certain areas are represented within each test. Emphasis is sometimes directed in slightly different ways within each test. The test should be chosen that best serves the particular purposes and needs.

Diagnostic Achievement Tests

The diagnostic achievement test attempts to measure in detail academic strengths and weaknesses in a specific area, in contrast to the survey test, which attempts to measure overall progress. Many teachers will find diagnostic achievement tests to be familiar friends, because a great deal of a teacher's time is spent in diagnosing the work habits and special academic problems of her students. The diagnostic achievement test attempts to do the same thing.

The diagnostic test indicates specific aspects of a child's educational development. For example, a survey reading test shows that Priscilla, who is in sixth grade, has an overall reading level equal to children beginning the third grade. Diagnostic reading tests reveal that Priscilla tends to make reversal errors in reading, for example, substituting *was* for *saw*. Her word recognition is fairly good. Her ability to recognize short vowels and to apply known consonant blends is very poor. These findings, along with other classroom and standardized test data, help in planning concrete educational treatment.

The diagnostic achievement test is an extension of what most teachers attempt to do in their everyday practice. The diagnostic test presents exercises and problems that provide opportunities for students to reveal skills and work habits. It provides the teacher with a systematic technique for evaluating these skills and habits. We shall examine some of the unique features of the reading and arithmetic devices.

READING

There are several types of diagnostic reading tests. Some have specialized subtests yielding scores for different aspects of total reading ability. These are similar to the survey subtests such as those for rate and comprehension, and location of information. Another approach is the diagnostic oral reading test. Gray's Oral Reading Paragraphs is a good example of this technique. This test consists of a standard set of twelve short paragraphs, ranging in difficulty from first to eighth grade. The pupil is given a copy of the standardized paragraphs and directed to read them orally when the examiner gives the signal. A record is kept of the time required to read each paragraph and the errors made. If a word is wholly or partially mispronounced, the examiner notes this. Omitted words, substitutions, and repetitions are recorded. The student is allowed to continue reading until he makes seven errors in each of two paragraphs.

The recording of a student's oral reading is valuable because it enables the teacher to understand the actual process of the child's reading. It helps the teacher pinpoint specific trouble areas.

Another type of test is Doren's Diagnostic Reading Test (1956) which was mentioned earlier in this chapter. This test is administered in a clinical manner rather than in the strict standardized approach. The directions are loose and the teacher proceeds to some extent on her perceptions of the children's receptivity to the tasks. For example, the directions for time state: "Allow ample time for all the children to finish each subtest. . . . The examiner should determine how much of the test is to be given at any one time. It will depend on the age of the children and their attention span" (p. 7). There are eleven subtests, each measuring a different reading skill, as follows:

Unit 1. Letter Recognition
Unit 2. Beginning Sounds
Unit 3. Whole Word Recognition
Unit 4. Words Within Words
Unit 5. Speech Consonants
Unit 6. Ending Sounds
Unit 7. Blending
Unit 8. Rhyming
Unit 9. Vowels
Unit 10. Sight Words
Unit 11. Discriminate Guessing

Doren (1956) in her discussion of norms presents the basic approach to the interpretation of diagnostic tests:[11]

> In contrast to an achievement test, a diagnostic test is not administered with a fixed norm as its attainment goal. Individuals in need of diagnosis have been classified by previous comparison with a norm, or by teacher observation, as in need of more thorough examination. In an achievement test, the number of correct responses is the measure of the degree of success. In a diagnostic test, it is the mistakes which an individual makes that will indicate his areas of need, and an exact identification of the types of error will direct the examiner to specific remedial work.
>
> . . . If an examiner assumes that a child is normal because he attains a norm and looks no further for specific areas of possible improvement, no diagnostic purpose is served by the test. Attention must be directed to the exact nature of the wrong answers. It is misleading to a teacher to provide a norm for a diagnostic test because it can serve no useful purpose. It is of utmost importance that a teacher understands that she must observe the mistakes and do something to correct them. The teacher must study the individual test papers, and make adjustment in her program to correct the deficiencies [p. 17].

[11] Margaret Doren, *Doren Diagnostic Reading Test of Word Recognition Skills: Manual of Instructions with Suggestions for Remedial Activities.* Copyright 1956, American Guidance Service, Inc. Used by permission of the publisher.

Teacher's Diagnosis

for Pupil _____

Published by the
Public School Publishing Co.
Bloomington, Illinois

DIAGNOSTIC CHART
FOR
INDIVIDUAL DIFFICULTIES
FUNDAMENTAL PROCESSES IN ARITHMETIC
Prepared by G. T. Buswell and Lenore John

Name_____ School_____ Grade_____ Age_____ IQ_____

Date of Diagnosis: _____ Add._____; Subt._____; Mult._____; Div._____

Teacher's preliminary diagnosis_____

ADDITION: (Place a check before each habit observed in the pupil's work)

____ a1 Errors in combinations	____ a15 Disregarded column position
____ a2 Counting	____ a16 Omitted one or more digits
____ a3 Added carried number last	____ a17 Errors in reading numbers
____ a4 Forgot to add carried number	____ a18 Dropped back one or more tens
____ a5 Repeated work after partly done	____ a19 Derived unknown combination from familiar one
____ a6 Added carried number irregularly	____ a20 Disregarded one column
____ a7 Wrote number to be carried	____ a21 Error in writing answer
____ a8 Irregular procedure in column	____ a22 Skipped one or more decades
____ a9 Carried wrong number	____ a23 Carrying when there was nothing to carry
____ a10 Grouped two or more numbers	____ a24 Used scratch paper
____ a11 Splits numbers into parts	____ a25 Added in pairs, giving last sum as answer
____ a12 Used wrong fundamental operation	____ a26 Added same digit in two columns
____ a13 Lost place in column	____ a27 Wrote carried number in answer
____ a14 Depended on visualization	____ a28 Added same number twice

Habits not listed above._____

(Write observation notes on pupil's work in space opposite examples)

(1)			(5)	
5 6			$6 + 2 =$	
2 3			$3 + 4 =$	

(2)			(6)	
2 8			5 2 4 0	
9 4			1 3 3 9	

(3)			(7)	
1 2 1 3			7 8 4 6	
2 5			7 1 9 2	

(4)			(8)	
1 9 1 7			3 8	
2 9			5 7	
			8 9	
			2 7	

Figure 29. Example of Record Sheet used in the Buswell-John Diagnostic Test for Fundamental Processes in Arithmetic. (From the *Buswell-John Diagnostic Test for Fundamental Processes in Arithmetic* by G. T. Buswell and Lenore John. Reprinted by permission of the publisher, Test Division of the Bobbs-Merrill Co., Inc., of Indianapolis, Indiana.)

ARITHMETIC

A good example of the diagnostic test in arithmetic skills is the Buswell-John Diagnostic Test for Fundamental Processes in Arithmetic. The student is presented with a series of problems in addition, subtraction, multiplication, and division. The items are to be orally worked out by the student. The examiner listens while the student verbalizes what he is doing and why he is doing it. The examiner records specific types of errors on a diagnostic chart provided by the test publishers. Figure 29 presents one page of the record chart.

The manual cites various work habits and provides samples of each. Two examples similar to those listed are

Neglecting to carry

$$
\begin{array}{r}
\text{Example:} \quad 233 \\
695 \\
\hline
828
\end{array}
$$

Borrowing Error

$$
\begin{array}{r}
\text{Example:} \quad 648 \\
74 \\
\hline
674
\end{array}
$$

The manual points out that the teacher should not be satisfied with simply making a diagnosis and checking the items. She should also study the pupil's work habits, that is, how he attacks the problem and what processes he uses, and gear her teaching accordingly. This approach is basic to use of any diagnostic test. Diagnostic tests are given only to children who need special attention because of scholastic difficulties. They are clinical tools and should only be used in that manner. That is, their statistical validation is open to a great deal of error and cannot be thought of as having the same degree of validity or reliability that other instruments, such as the survey and general achievement battery tests, have. Thus, the clinical or subjective approach is indicated in using these tests as aids in learning rather than as definitive assessments of academic progress.

Major Uses in the School

Our discussion in this section will center on the primary uses of achievement tests in the school setting. It should be noted that only the major uses will be discussed in practical school terms.

Understanding the Student

To guide a youngster properly in his educational planning an understanding of his level of achievement is extremely important. The school must know his educational achievement to plan for future academic goals, possible remedial assistance, and eventually his or her vocation. In order to present the important role of achievement testing in understanding the individual pupil, let us listen in to an actual counseling situation. Mr. Smith, the junior high school counselor, is talking to Bob Fein, an eighth-grade student who is concerned about his future high school program.

MR. SMITH: Well, Bob, how can I help you today?

BOB: I'm not sure what courses I should take in high school, you know, whether I should start with algebra or not and so forth.

MR. SMITH: Well, how do you feel about it?

BOB: I don't know. My problem is this: you told me that I was above average on my aptitude tests in arithmetic and science, but yesterday you said that my achievement tests were not as good. Now, does that mean that I should not take algebra and science my first year in high school?

MR. SMITH: How have you done in your class work?

BOB: Oh, just fair.

MR. SMITH: I see. Just fair?

BOB: What I mean by "just fair" is a little under C.

MR. SMITH: Well, let's examine your whole record, both your test scores and school grades. It seems that you have above-average ability in most areas. However, your class work is below average, and the achievement tests show that you are a little below grade level in reading, arithmetic, and science. Thus it looks like you have the ability to learn, but you haven't been applying yourself.

BOB: Are you saying, Mr. Smith, that I haven't learned as much as I should have by this time?

MR. SMITH: Yes, in a sense I am saying that. What do you think?

BOB: I . . . I don't know. My parents say that I don't study enough. Could this be the reason?

MR. SMITH: It may well be. On the other hand, there could be other reasons.

BOB: I guess so, but what should I do as far as my high school program goes?

MR. SMITH: The final decision, of course, rests with you. I can point out some general guidelines that may be of help. First, there is no doubt that you have the ability to do average or above-average work in school. Second, your class record and achievement scores indicate that you are below your grade level in some important areas of education. This means that even though you have the ability to learn algebra and science, your lack of progress in these areas may prevent you from doing well in these fields in high school. I would recommend, therefore, that you put off algebra and biology until the tenth grade and concentrate on making up your learning deficiencies by taking general math and general science your first year.

BOB: My parents won't like that, especially since all my friends are starting with algebra and biology. My parents and friends will think I'm stupid, won't they?

MR. SMITH: The important thing, Bob, is that you know that you are not stupid. Besides, your future education will benefit by a firm grounding in the essentials. If you take algebra and biology and fail, how will you feel then?

BOB: Not very good.

MR. SMITH: Of course not. You see, Bob, ability and achievement are, many times, quite different. I am sure you know of guys who could make outstanding baseball players, but never perform well because they haven't learned the basic skills in playing the game. If you take a guy who might be another Babe Ruth and put him in the major leagues before he is ready he may never realize his potential. On the other hand, if you put him in the minor leagues and give him the experience to learn, he may become another Babe Ruth. In the same way, if you have the ability to do well in algebra and biology but lack the learned skills, you need some experience in the minor leagues—that is, general math and general science—before you come up to the big leagues. Then you may become a major league performer. Do you understand what I mean?

BOB: I think I do. In other words, you are saying that by trying a subject that I am not ready for, I may fail it.

MR. SMITH: Yes, not only is there a good chance of your failing, but more important, your failing or having extreme difficulty in passing may close that door of learning to you forever. That's one of the reasons we give achievement tests. We want to know how ready you are to learn new subjects based on your past learning.

BOB: Thank you, Mr. Smith, I will tell my parents what you said.

The case of Bob Fein is, of course, only one example of the many uses of achievement tests in helping to understand and guide students. This example reveals the practical importance of the use of achievement test results along with other data in educational guidance.

Identification of Children for Intensive Study

Achievement tests help spotlight those youngsters who need special attention. It is true, of course, that every child should be studied as an individual, and most of our schools attempt to do this. However, every school system has those pupils who need special assistance more than their peers. They are often difficult to distinguish from the others because they do not seek special help, nor do their teachers or parents often know of their problems.

One way of finding out who these children are is to administer an achievement battery.

The child who needs intensive study may show great differences in his performance on different subtests, or he may perform far below his grade or age level. Sometimes his performance, as in the case of Bob Fein, is far below his capabilities as shown by a group scholastic aptitude test. The school counselor or teacher, in studying a student's test performance, thinks of the following questions:

1. Is the student's achievement related to his aptitude? That is, is the child falling behind the level we expect of him?
2. Does he have a reading problem? If so, do we have an indication of the child's academic aptitude based on a nonreading test?
3. Does he have a problem in some specific school subject? If the answer is yes, further study and testing may be needed.

In order to convey the practical usage of the achievement test let us look at an actual case that I encountered when I was employed in the public schools. A fifteen-year-old boy was referred to me because of marked differences in his various test scores and a poor school record. The boy had excellent scores in some of his aptitude tests, such as mechanical reasoning, abstract reasoning, and space relations. His other aptitude scores were extremely low. His group intelligence test showed an IQ at the level of mental retardation. His achievement tests showed great differences, such as a very low score in social studies, an extremely high score in mathematics, an average score in English, and an extremely high score in science.

I decided that an individual intelligence test and a reading achievement test were needed. The results of these tests showed that the boy was in the superior range in intellectual ability and was equal to first-year college students in reading achievement. After these tests were administered the boy was referred to a school social worker for further study. During the counseling sessions with the social worker, certain facts of the boy's life were obtained. It developed that this boy's parents, who were both physicians, had been killed in an automobile accident when the boy was twelve years of age, and since that time he had been living with his uncle.

When confronted with the results of his test performances the boy admitted he had not tried to do his best on certain tests because "I didn't feel they meant anything anyway."

I now knew that circumstances outside of the boy's abilities were affecting his performance both in the classroom and on standardized tests. I asked myself certain questions: "Why does he feel certain courses are not important?" "Is there a relationship between the auto accident and the loss of his parents to his scattered performances?" These and other questions had to be answered before any progress could be made in counseling the boy. I therefore decided to administer some personality tests. (See Chapter 8 for explanation of projective and personality tests.)

The test results revealed a boy who was suffering from a "burnt child reaction." That is, the trauma of his parents' deaths had acted on him as though someone had pushed him over a cliff. The boy had probably always had personality problems and had always been near the edge of the cliff. The push or shove was the auto accident and the ensuing deaths. He now felt that his goal in life was to replace his parents by becoming a physician himself. This, of course, was understandable. However, the child lost sight of reality in thinking that he could become a doctor without passing courses not directly related to the sciences. This is why he did not work in social studies and did not attempt to do well on achievement tests outside the scientific areas.

Through the use of tests and interviews a clearer picture was obtained of this boy's problems, which were interfering with his ability to learn and perform in school. In counseling sessions he was helped to think more realistically about his goals and the means of obtaining them. This is an example of a boy whose vocational goals were in line with his aptitudes but who was unable to harness his abilities in all school subjects because of emotional problems.

Of course, the above case is rather rare in the schools, for most children do not experience the shock of losing both parents. However, it is not rare for a child to be placed in a grade or level below his abilities because of poor achievement. Quite often this inability to use his potential is due to emotional problems. A careful comparison of the child's achievement test scores with his scores on aptitude and intelligence tests can help to identify those few youngsters who need intensive study and help.

Teacher Aids in Program Planning

At the beginning of each school year the classroom teacher is usually given a general outline of subject material to be covered along with educational objectives. Decisions must be made concerning various subject fields and how much time should be given to a review of the previous year's work. In addition, the teacher is faced with the problem of planning independent work for those children capable of going beyond the regular classroom course of study. Most teachers want to form groupings within the class so that students of similar abilities and skills can work together at a common level. For example, the first-grade teacher may want eventually to group her children in reading in three or four sections. Section 1 might be the top group section 2 might be the average, and section three might include students below average in reading. Section 4, if needed, might consist of those children who are not yet ready to learn to read.

In order to carry out these educational plans and goals, the teacher needs to know her students' abilities, skills, and past learning achievements as soon as possible. One way to do this is to administer achievement tests (survey, diagnostic, or battery). The results of the tests will give the teacher an indication of the relative achievement level of her group of children—that is, whether the group is superior, average, or below average in the basic skills she will attempt to develop. The scores will provide clues to the group's strengths and weaknesses. The teacher can then adapt her plans to the group as a whole and to the individuals within the group.

Of course tests themselves are only one indication or clue for the teacher. The good teacher, in addition to using the results of tests, obtains certain impressions of her students by contact with them. *The deepest understanding of an individual child comes only through working with that child.* Test scores, however, enable the teacher to have an objective frame of reference in addition to her subjective estimation of the group and the individual child.

Planning and Evaluating Schoolwide Programs

In order to provide the best possible education, a school must always examine and re-examine its curriculum and system of instruction. The achievement battery is used as an aid in the evaluation of the curriculum. The results of the tests provide some indication of how well a school or school system is doing in relationship to other schools. For example, Roosevelt Junior High School wanted to find out how its students' test scores compared with the scores of other children throughout the country. Roosevelt therefore averaged its children's test scores and compared them to the national averages provided by the test publisher. In science and social studies Roosevelt's average student was one grade level below the national standard or average. In mathematics and English its students were above the national average. Roosevelt's teachers were thus enabled to find the weak spots in their programs of instruction.

There are, of course, certain dangers in using this method for evaluating a school's course of study. First of all, this type of evaluation does not give a complete picture. The achievement test can only evaluate the knowledge and skills it covers. Usually these skills are only a small part of the total objectives of our modern school. A danger that is always present in this kind of evaluation is the relative simplicity of giving objective tests and then stating whether or not the curriculum is up to standard. Good school systems use other methods of evaluation in addition to test results, which enables them to gain deeper insights into the whole school program.

One must also remember the problem of local goals and objectives before critically evaluating a school's instructional program. It would be unfair to say that a particular school is not adequate because the students are below the national average. A particular school may place greater emphasis upon certain subjects and delay others because of its particular situation and educational philosophy. For example, one school may stress meanings and understandings of subject matter rather than factual knowledge. If such a school uses an achievement battery that emphasizes factual content, its students may do poorly; yet this does not mean that the school is necessarily doing a poor educational job. The difficulty with national achievement tests is the problem of making the questions appropriate to most schools in the country. Because the curricula of our schools are not controlled by a single administration, this is a difficult task. Therefore, each school must use the battery in the light of its own particular goals and instructional program.

One must also take into account the geographic location of a school or school system. Schools and communities differ in their social and economic levels. Related to these differences are the ranges of abilities of students in the public schools. These factors must be taken into account when achievement is considered. These differences may be lessened by developing local norms for the school or school system. For example, students who attend schools in the north suburban areas of Chicago generally come from privileged homes. That is, they come from affluent families, who have a fairly high cultural level and who are able to provide their children with experiences that many American families cannot afford, such as visiting the many museums in Chicago, attending plays for children, and attending the children's concerts of the Chicago Symphony Orchestra. In this kind of area the average student does better than the average student in other areas of the country. If the local schools in this area applied only national averages, they would not have a complete picture of their instructional programs. But by establishing local averages they can get a picture of how well the child is doing when compared with his fellow students, who share similar backgrounds and experiences. For the same reasons, a disadvantaged area in Chicago, or elsewhere in the country, may want local averages, as well as national averages, to obtain a more complete picture. By using local averages the disadvantaged area can tell the relative progress of its students, who start out with so much less than the average national student in abilities, motivations, and experiences.

Grouping

To group or not to group, is that the question? How do you feel about this question that has concerned educators for close to sixty years? The bandwagon for and against grouping has changed directions many times in those years. Since Sputnik (about 1957) the educational bandwagon has been directed toward grouping children according to abilities and achievement. The last few years, however, have seen some attempts to redirect the wagon in the other direction. Our task here is not to affirm or negate educational grouping, but to present the uses of standardized achievement tests, in grouping, if you as educators decide on that course of action.[12]

---

[12] I am personally very much for grouping because I see it as an instructional technique in helping children learn. Even when grouping is practiced, there is still a range of abilities and achievement in the classroom. It does, however, narrow the range so that the teacher can gear her instruction to most of the children.

Most grouping of children into separate tracks or classes occurs during junior and senior high school. The achievement test is one of several measurement instrument used in this process. One needs first a scholastic aptitude test, to obtain an overall picture of school ability; second, a reading test; and third, a record of classroom progress.

The use of these various techniques presupposes, of course, that children are not grouped according to IQ, "good grades," or achievement test scores, but according to specific and particular situations based on the student's whole scholastic potential and achievement. A high IQ, for example, does not mean a student should be placed in an advanced mathematics course. His achievement in mathematics must match his potential in order for him to succeed in advanced mathematics.

Achievement tests help in grouping by presenting a standardized picture of a student's academic progress. They eliminate teacher bias in academic evaluation. They do not, however, provide the sole basis for grouping decisions.

Research

The standardized achievement test is a valuable aid in educational research. For example, Hyde Senior High School wants to know if team teaching is more successful than the standard "one teacher, one class" approach. Two groups of eleventh-grade United States history students are tested with a history achievement test in the beginning of the year. One group continues along the classical pattern while the other is exposed to team teaching. At the end of the term a parallel form of the same test is given. A comparison between the group scores is then made. If the team teaching group obtains higher achievement scores one might say that further explorations in this instructional method is indicated. On the other hand, if the one teacher, one class approach group scored as high or higher, one might have some reservations about continuing team teaching.[13]

The achievement test may also be used to evaluate teachers. Yes, some schools do use achievement batteries to evaluate their teachers. The teacher is judged by the performance of his class on the achievement tests. How do you feel about this use of achievement tests? What do you think are some possible problems?

[13] It should be noted, of course, that other variables in this kind of investigation must be considered. The two groups should be matched not only in terms of how much knowledge they have of United States history before instruction begins but also on the basis of intelligence, school grades, and historical interests. In addition, the experimental design would have to consider teacher differences in terms of effectiveness and skills. Also allowances for the "Hawthorne effect" (that is, the special attention one group receives) would have to be made. Thus, it is plain that this example is intended only as an illustration of a use of the achievement test, not as a good example of sound experimental design.

Obviously, this procedure has many shortcomings. This is because the achievement of a class is related not only to the teacher's ability but also to the group's educational history. It does not seem fair to hold a teacher solely responsible for his group's present achievement level. Secondly, as has been stated, achievement is based in part upon aptitude as well as experiences not gained in school. Thirdly, an achievement test can measure the success of only a small portion of the goals of schools today.

On the other hand, if we evaluate teachers collectively or in groups rather than as individuals, the achievement test may serve a sound function. That is, in research investigations of teacher effectiveness rather than as definitive guides for the continued employment of a teacher. The school that uses the achievement test for teacher evaluation does not truly understand the limitations of this form of testing and evaluation. If the school administration had insight into these limitations, it would not run the risk of unhappy teachers teaching "for the tests" rather than for the students.

Remember, the achievement survey, battery, or diagnostic test are only instruments to be used in assessing the whole child. They have no inherent power to provide complete answers by themselves, but when used with other evaluative instruments and the school record they provide valuable insights into the academic achievement of students. In the same way we can use them to gain insights into the school's national standing and as an evaluative tool in curriculum assessment as long as we remember they are only one part of the whole academic picture. Let us end our discussion of achievement instruments with the following summary statement concerning achievement tests, from Educational Testing Service (1961), one of the nation's largest test publishers.

> There is no single achievement test or test battery that will be "best" for all pupil populations, all curriculum objectives, all purposes, and all uses. Even tests universally recognized as "good" are not equally "good" for different school settings, situations, and circumstances.
>
> The recommended procedure for achievement test selection then consists of three phases:
>
> 1. study of our own school characteristics and testing needs;
> 2. analysis of characteristics and capabilities of available tests;
> 3. matching (a) the population of norm groups, or reliability samples, and of validity studies for each test to our own pupil population, (b) the content of each test to our own curriculum content and objectives, (c) the validity evidence, reliability data, scoring system, and interpretive material for each test to our own testing purposes and prospective uses of test scores [pp. 32–33].

References

Buswell, G. T. *Manual for the SRA Reading Record*. (2nd ed.) Chicago: Science Research Associates, Inc., 1959.

Doren, M. *Doren Diagnostic Reading Test of Word Recognition Skills: Manual of instructions with suggestions for remedial activities*. Minneapolis: American Guidance Service, 1956.

Ebel, R. L. Standardized achievement tests: Uses and limitations. In W. L. Barnette (Ed.), *Readings in psychological tests and measurements*. (Rev. ed.) Homewood, Ill.: The Dorsey Press, 1968. Pp. 256–61.

Educational Testing Service. *Sequential Tests of Educational Progress: Manual for interpreting scores—mathematics*. Princeton, N.J.: Educational Testing Service, 1957.

Educational Testing Service. *Selecting an achievement test: Principles and procedures*. (Number 3, Evaluation and advisory service series, 2nd ed.) Princeton, N.J.: Educational Testing Service, 1961.

Educational Testing Service. *Cooperative Primary Tests: Handbook*. Princeton, N.J.: Educational Testing Service, 1967.

Kelley, T. L., Madden, R., Gardner, E. F., and Rudman, H. C. *Stanford achievement test—directions for administering: Intermediate I battery for grade 4 to the middle of grade 5*. New York: Harcourt, Brace, and World, 1964.

Lindeman, R. H. *Educational measurement*. Glenview, Ill.: Scott, Foresman, 1967.

Nunnally, J. C. *Educational measurement and evaluation*. New York: McGraw-Hill, 1964.

CHAPTER

11

College Entrance
Examinations

The American college today is faced with the problem of accommodating large numbers of young people who want a college education. The history of higher education has been different from that of the public schools. Americans have prided themselves on the fact that public schools were for all children no matter what their academic potential or achievement. Colleges and universities, on the other hand, have not attempted to educate all the people; they have accepted only those with the academic abilities to profit from a higher education. Therefore, colleges have always been faced with the problem of selective admissions. As a consequence colleges have been using standardized tests and other selective criteria even before the number of college applicants became so large.

Colleges differ as to the testing instruments they use for selection. Some administer their own tests, others prefer to use the services of the College Entrance Examination Board (CEEB) or the American College Testing Program (ACT). The basic difference between the Scholastic Aptitude Test of the CEEB and the ACT lies in the grouping of items and in the scores provided. The ACT provides tests organized into sections and produces scores more nearly related to the traditional disciplines, whereas the Scholastic Aptitude Test is organized in a verbal-quantitative manner (Juola, 1961).

Most of our discussion in this chapter will be devoted to the CEEB and ACT, which represent the greatest percentage of admissions testing in the United States. Let us first briefly review some of the other tests used by colleges and administered at the local level.

College-Administered Tests

Among the most prominent tests used by colleges not participating in the CEEB and ACT programs are the following: The College Qualification Tests of the Psychological Corporation, the School and College Ability Tests of the Educational Testing Service, Ohio State University Psychological Test, Form 21 of the Ohio College Association, and the College Classification Tests of Science Research Associates. All of them are similar in terms of what they attempt to measure. The Ohio State University Psychological Test differs from the others in that there is no time limit. The School and College Ability Tests is the same instrument, at the college level, mentioned in Chapter 9. To illustrate the kinds of items generally found on most of the preceding tests, let us look at the College Qualification Tests.

The College Qualification Tests (CQT) is a multipurpose battery which serves as a basis (partial) for college admissions, placement, and counseling. It is also used in some scholarship award programs. There are three tests:

> 1. *CQT-Verbal.* This section is basically a vocabulary test with synonym-antonym questions. It attempts to measure verbal aptitude, which is an important ability needed for college success.
> 2. *CQT-Numerical.* This section attempts to measure mathematical skills in arithmetic, algebra, and geometry.
> 3. *CQT-Information.* This is a test of general information in the areas of science (physics, chemistry, biology) and social studies (history, government, economics, geography). It was constructed to measure the student's general background. This section yields two subscores, Science and Social Studies, as well as a total Information score.

The level of the test ranges from grades eleven through thirteen. The manual presents norms based on freshmen in state universities, private colleges, Southern universities, and junior colleges as well as norms for six different degree programs.

College Entrance Examination Board

One of the oldest and best known of the major selection testing programs is the College Entrance Examination Board (CEEB). The CEEB is an association of 579 colleges (as of 1966) with additional representatives from secondary schools. Chauncey[1] and Dobbin (1966) in their discussion of the history of testing state the basic reason for the creation of the CEEB.

> The College Board examination program was started at the turn of the century as the result of a proposal that colleges requiring examinations for admission would do both the high schools and the applicants a service by setting a common examination on which an applicant could earn admission to any of a number of colleges. Until the College Board was formed, a student who wanted to enter his application at three colleges had to take three different examinations at three different times and places. The principal of any high school that had many college-going graduates had an exasperating time trying to arrange for and comply with the multitude of examinations his seniors needed to take . . . not to mention preparing the students for the examinations [p. 17].

The first tests consisted of essay questions. In 1926 an objective test called the Scholastic Aptitude Test (SAT) was used for the first time. The use of the SAT increased slowly at first, but as more schools began to require it for admission and as the number of college applicants increased, the SAT became a "household name" to aspiring college students. In 1966 over 800 colleges and 250 scholarship programs required students to take the SAT as part of the admissions process. In the years since 1926 thousands of research studies have been conducted by these and other educational institutions, as well as by private investigators, to ascertain the predictive validity of the SAT (College Entrance Examination Board, 1966c).

The CEEB is a nonprofit membership association of colleges, secondary schools, and educational organizations. The CEEB program of tests consists of the Preliminary Scholastic Aptitude Test (PSAT), the Scholastic Aptitude Test (SAT), and the Achievement Tests. The CEEB will make special arrangements for administering these tests to handicapped students (College Entrance Examination Board, 1966a).

The CEEB has its tests administered at testing centers throughout the world. These centers are usually located in a high school or college. The tests are administered by local qualified personnel either at the high school or college level. There is strict adherence to standardized procedures. The administrator is even required to call Princeton or Berkeley, long distance, for certain types of irregularities.

Figure 30 shows the extensive coverage of the CEEB and the location and addresses of the two service centers.

The centers administer the test and send them back to the CEEB head-quarters in their geographic region for scoring. The results are then sent to

---

[1] President of Educational Testing Service, publishers of the CEEB tests.

Figure 30. Service centers for the CEEB. (From *Bulletin of Information: College Board Admissions Tests.* Copyright © 1966 by College Entrance Examination Board, New York. Reproduced by permission of the College Entrance Examination Board.)

the student and his secondary school as well as to the colleges to which he is applying for admission. Score reports are sent free of charge to the first three colleges of the applicant's choice. There is a nominal charge for each additional college.

Test Dates and Schedule. Although dates and number of administrations of the College Board may vary, the usual number is five times during a calendar year. These are usually on Saturday during the months of December, January, March, May, and July. The Scholastic Aptitude Test is administered first at 8:30 A.M. and concludes approximately at 12:30 P.M. The Achievement Tests and Writing Sample are begun at 1:30 P.M. and usually finish at 5:45 P.M.

The Preliminary Scholastic Aptitude Test

The Preliminary Scholastic Aptitude Test (PSAT) is basically a shorter version of the Scholastic Aptitude Test. The PSAT is given to students in their junior year of high school. The College Board investigated students' academic performance in college based on three years of high school, and found that by the time a child is a junior in high school his performance in college can be predicted by his three years of grades and an aptitude test almost as well as by his senior year grades and test scores. Because of this finding, the College Board decided to offer the PSAT to encourage earlier college guidance of a higher level. Thus the College Board recommends the PSAT for juniors. Colleges that are College Board members will consider the PSAT scores in early counseling and in giving advice to prospective students concerning their chance of acceptance and success.

The PSAT is a two-hour examination. There are two scores, verbal and mathematical. The scores are reported on a scale ranging from 20 to 80.

Some educators may wonder if the PSAT is really necessary. You may be saying to yourself, "Look here, by the time a student is in his junior year the school already has information useful for counseling him about college plans. I have also read that a pupil's performance in college preparatory courses is the most important indicator of college success or failure. And besides all of the above, what about those standardized tests you have been talking about? Isn't that enough testing? Why is the PSAT needed or helpful anyway?"

The PSAT may be helpful in several ways. For instance, the child who gets all A's at one high school may be only a C student at another school. The PSAT helps solve the problem of different standards among high schools by serving as a national yardstick that can be used to measure a student's ability as compared to other boys and girls throughout the nation. In addition, the school counselor will have information concerning the required scores needed for admission on this test by various colleges and universities. He, therefore, can help students in early planning for college in a realistic and meaningful manner.

It is not wise, however, to assume that a student's PSAT score is the only factor in predicting college success or failure. Suppose, for example, that John scores below 30 on the PSAT and is thinking of going to college. His academic record is good, and he seems to be motivated to work in school. In addition to these factors his family can offer him strong financial and moral support. If this is the case he can probably still gain admission to college, if, with the counselor or teacher's support and guidance, a college is carefully selected.

After a student has taken the PSAT, he will be given his scores and a booklet entitled "Your College Board Scores: Preliminary Scholastic Aptitude Test." This booklet contains information on the meaning and interpretation of these scores. For example, a student may compare his scores to all juniors and seniors in the country by using the tables provided.

SOME TECHNICAL DETAILS

The score range of the PSAT, as was mentioned earlier, is from 20 to 80 and is equivalent to the score scale of the SAT, which ranges from 200 to 800. The placement of a zero after the PSAT score reveals what the student's probable SAT score would have been if he had taken the SAT instead of the PSAT. The CEEB (1966d) cautions students in their matching of scores.

> . . . your PSAT scores and your SAT scores may be somewhat different from your theoretical true scores. There is, in fact, approximately 1 chance in 5 that your actual senior-year-SAT-verbal score will be 50 points or more higher than your predicted SAT-verbal score, and there is also approximately 1 chance in 5 that it will be at least 50 points lower. The same holds true for your mathematical score [p. 12].

The equivalency between the two tests lends itself to comparisons of scores between individual students and groups of students tested on different dates in different years. It should be noted, of course, that grade levels must be considered in these comparisons. This is because a junior who has obtained the same score as a senior may actually be a better student.

The PSAT, like any other test, cannot be interpreted as representing the exact college potential of every student. The standard error of measurement for both the verbal and mathematical sections is approximately three points. The reliability coefficient based on the Kuder-Richardson Formula 20 is 0.88 for both sections. (See Chapter 4 for discussion of reliability and standard error of measurement.)

The Scholastic Aptitude Test

The SAT is the oldest examination of the College Entrance Examination Board. This test measures skills basic to schoolwork. Like the PSAT it has two sections, verbal and mathematical. *It is a test of ability, not of factual knowledge.* The verbal section emphasizes ability to read with understanding and to reason with words. The reading material consists of passages from such academic fields as the humanities, social science, and science. The mathematical section measures the individual's aptitude in solving problems and stresses mathematical reasoning rather than factual recall of high school mathematics.

Verbal and mathematical talents are, of course, related to college success. Usually the scores of any individual on the SAT are closely related to his success as a student. One usually finds, therefore, that a student who has a good academic record will score high on the SAT, whereas the student who has performed poorly in school is very likely to receive a low score. Of course, there are exceptions to every rule; the SAT is far from being a perfect predictive yardstick of collegiate success.

The administration time for the SAT is three hours. All items are presented in an objective format.

Scores on the SAT, as you remember, are reported in numbers ranging from 200 to 800. About two thirds of the students taking the SAT score somewhere between 400 and 600. In terms of a general grading system, in which zero is at the bottom and 100 is a perfect score, we can state that 200 is equal to zero, and 800 is equal to 100. Therefore, an individual cannot receive a score below 200 or one above 800.

The standard error of measurement for both the verbal and mathematical sections is approximately thirty points. The reliability coefficient based on the Kuder-Richardson Formula 20 is 0.90 for the verbal section and 0.88 for the mathematical section.

Why Take the SAT?

Not all students should take the SAT. The student who does is interested in obtaining admission to a college that requires the SAT as one of the criteria for selection. It helps these schools in evaluating applicants from all over the world by providing them with a standard frame of reference to judge a variety of college applicants. It helps the student in evaluating the college by comparing his scores with the average student at the college of his choice.

Can Students Study for the SAT?

The best answer to give to the question of whether one can study for the SAT would be to say yes, if the pupil begins in the first grade of school. Though this may sound like an evasion of the question, it is a most honest and logical answer, because school skills are the direct result of practice and instruction over a long period of time. You cannot expect Johnny to study for a few weeks or even months and acquire the skills that he should have learned years before. No one believes that one can learn to play the trumpet or sing or become a major-league baseball player overnight. All these skills require years of practice and development. By the same token, one cannot learn to read well or reason logically in a few hard sessions of cramming.

Research into the problem of preparation for the SAT has shown that cramming or special course preparation does not raise the student's score enough to make it worth while. (See Chapter 3 for a thorough discussion of this problem.) Thus, the best preparation for the student is to do his school-work in earnest, read widely, and observe and think about his environment throughout his school years. The administrators of the College Board Examinations state that the student should avoid cramming and come to the test well rested. Each student who plans to take the SAT is given a booklet describing the test. In this booklet the suggestion is made that the student go over the practice questions carefully so that he will understand the directions clearly and not use precious time for this purpose when he comes to the actual testing situation.

SAMPLE QUESTIONS FROM THE SAT

The verbal and mathematical sections of the SAT are divided into six half-hour segments. As the test progresses the questions become more difficult. The following items are similar to those found in the verbal and mathematical sections of the SAT[2]:

VERBAL SECTION

Antonyms (Opposites)
Directions: Each question below consists of a word printed in capital letters, followed by five words or phrases lettered A through E. Choose the lettered word or phrase which is most nearly *opposite* in meaning to the word in capital letters.
Since some of the questions require you to distinguish fine shades of meaning, be sure to consider all the choices before deciding which one is best.
EXAGGERATION: (A) slight misunderstanding   (B) silence
(C) accurate representation   (D) truth   (E) understatement
CHRONIC: (A) slight   (B) temporary   (C) wholesome
(D) patient   (E) pleasant

[2] The following sample questions are reprinted from the 1966–1967 edition of *A Description of the College Board Scholastic Aptitude Test*, copyright © 1966 by the College Entrance Examination Board. Used by permission of the College Entrance Examination Board. This booklet, which contains many illustrative examples of the different kinds of questions that are used in the Scholastic Aptitude Test, is revised annually and is supplied without cost to high schools for distribution to students before they take the test. This booklet as well as other CEEB materials may also be obtained on request by writing either of the College Entrance Examination Board addresses: Box 592, Princeton, N.J. 08540; or Box 1025, Berkeley, Calif. 94701.

Sentence Completion

Directions: Each of the sentences below has one or more blank spaces, each blank indicating that a word has been omitted. Beneath the sentence are five lettered words or sets of words. You are to choose the one word or set of words which, when inserted in the sentence, *best* fits in with the meaning of the sentence as a whole.

High yields of food crops per acre accelerate the _____ of soil nutrients.

(A) depletion
(B) erosion
(C) cultivation
(D) fertilization
(E) conservation

From the first the islanders, despite an outward _____, did what they could to _____ the ruthless occupying powers.

(A) harmony . . . assist
(B) enmity . . . embarrass
(C) rebellion . . . foil
(D) resistance . . . destroy
(E) acquiescence . . . thwart

Analogies

Directions: In each of the following questions, a related pair of words or phrases is followed by five lettered pairs of words or phrases. Select the lettered pair which best expresses a relationship similar to that expressed in the original pair.

TRIGGER:BULLET::

(A) handle:drawer
(B) holster:gun
(C) bulb:light
(D) switch:current
(E) pulley:rope

BICYCLE:LOCOMOTION::

(A) canoe:paddle
(B) hero:worship
(C) hay:horse
(D) spectacles:vision
(E) statement:contention

GENERAL UNDERSTANDING

This type of question measures scholastic aptitude by testing the extent of information and the mastery of key concepts within a very broad domain of knowledge: the arts and sciences, current events, sports, and so forth. The emphasis is not on the ability merely to remember facts in any given field; a wide range of information is required to receive a high score on this group of questions. Moreover, many of the questions test the ability to use these facts in such a manner as to demonstrate an understanding in depth of a particular concept. Thus, it is simple enough, given the concept "evolution," to link it superficially to Darwin, but a better understanding of this concept is demonstrated by correctly completing a question such as the . . . one given below.

Before animals could evolve from a completely aquatic environment to a terrestrial one, it would have been most necessary for an adaptation to occur in the
(A) digestive system
(B) circulatory system
(C) respiratory system
(D) locomotor system
(E) nervous system

Reading Comprehension was not illustrated here because of space limitations. In this type of question, passages from published material are presented and questions follow designed to test the student's understanding of the material. Approximately half of the testing time of the verbal section is devoted to this task.

MATHEMATICAL SECTION

[Note the following directions and example; the student is presented with this data to help him in solving the problems. This eliminates, to some extent, the variable of previous course work.]
Directions: In this section solve each problem, using any available space on the page for scratchwork. Then indicate the *one* correct answer in the appropriate space on the answer sheet.

The following information is for your reference in solving some of the problems.
Circle of radius r:
Area $= \pi r^2$
Circumference $= 2\pi r$
The number of degrees of arc in a circle is 360.
The measure in degrees of a straight angle is 180.

Triangle:
The sum of the measures in degrees of the angles of a triangle is 180.
If $\angle CDA$ is a right angle, then

(1) area of $\triangle ABC = \dfrac{AB \times CD}{2}$

(2) $AC^2 = AD^2 + DC^2$

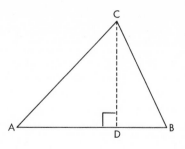

Definitions of symbols:
  $<$ is less than $\leqq$ is less than or equal to
  $>$ is greater than $\geqq$ is greater than or equal to
  $\perp$ is perpendicular to $\|$ is parallel to

Examples: What is the weight of 28 feet of uniform wire if 154 feet weigh 11 pounds?

(A) 2 lb.   (B) $\dfrac{28}{11}$ lb.   (C) $\dfrac{11}{2}$ lb.   (D) 7 lb.   (E) 14 lb.

If $16 \times 16 \times 16 = 8 \times 8 \times P$, then $P =$
(A) 4   (B) 8   (C) 32   (D) 48   (E) 64

The town of Mason is located on Eagle Lake. The town of Canton is west of Mason. Sinclair is east of Canton, but west of Mason. Dexter is east of Richmond, but west of Sinclair and Canton. Assuming they are all in the United States, which town is farthest west?
(A) Mason   (B) Dexter   (C) Canton   (D) Sinclair
(E) Richmond

If $x > 1$, which of the following increase(s) as x increases?

  I. $x - \dfrac{1}{x}$

  II. $\dfrac{1}{(x^2 - x)}$

III. $4x^3 - 2x^2$
(A) I only   (B) II only   (C) III only   (D) I and III only
(E) I, II, and III

The cost of electrical energy in a certain area is as follows

	Cents per kilowatt-hour
First 100 kilowatt-hours	3
Second 100 kilowatt-hours	2.5
Third 100 kilowatt-hours	2

How many kilowatt-hours can one obtain for $5.00?
(A) 175 kw-hr   (B) 180 kw-hr   (C) 200 kw-hr   (D) 225 kw-hr
(E) 250 kw-hr

[Directions and explanation for solving another type of mathematical problem that is included in the SAT follow.]

Directions : Each of the questions below is followed by two statements, labeled (1) and (2), in which certain data are given. In these questions you do not actually have to compute an answer, but rather you have to decide whether the data given in the statements are *sufficient* for answering the question. Using the data given in the statement *plus* your knowledge of mathematics and everyday facts (such as the number of days in July), you are to select answer

A if statement (1) ALONE is sufficient, but statement (2) alone is not sufficient to answer the question asked;

B if statement (2) ALONE is sufficient, but statement (1) alone is not sufficient to answer the question asked;

C if BOTH statements (1) and (2) TOGETHER are sufficient to answer the question asked, but NEITHER statement ALONE is sufficient;

D if EACH statement is sufficient by itself to answer the question asked;

E if statements (1) and (2) TOGETHER are NOT sufficient to answer the question asked and additional data specific to the problem are needed.

Example :

  What is the value of x?
  (1) $PQ = PR$
  (2) $y = 40$

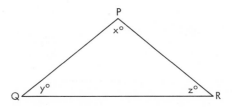

Explanation :

According to statement (1), $PQ = PR$; therefore, $\triangle PQR$ is isosceles and $y = z$. By statement (2), $y = 40$; hence $z = 40$. It is known that $x + y + z = 180$; since y and z are known, this equation can be solved for x. Thus the problem can be solved, and since statements (1) and (2) are both needed, the answer is C.

Note: In the data sufficiency questions which follow, figures are generalized illustrations and are not necessarily drawn to scale.

In a four-volume work, what is the weight of the third volume?
(1) The four-volume work weighs 8 pounds.
(2) The first three volumes together weigh 6 pounds.

If x is a whole number, is x a two-digit number?

(1) x^2 is a three-digit number.

(2) $10x$ is a three-digit number.

The preceding sample questions from the CEEB booklet have been selected from a total of thirty-three questions, each of which has a detailed explanation of the method of solution and the correct answer. In addition to these thirty-three questions and discussions of each, fifty-seven additional questions are given with time limits which approximate the actual testing situation. This booklet is an invaluable aid to students preparing for the SAT and is the best way to study for the examination.

Achievement Tests

The College Board Achievement Tests are constructed by a committee appointed by the College Board which includes both college and secondary school teachers. These people work with measurement specialists at Educational Testing Service. The development of the test follows the same procedure inherent in any proper standardized achievement test construction. (See Chapter 10.)

The College Board Achievement Tests consist of the following one-hour tests:

American History and Social Studies	Hebrew
	Latin
Biology	Mathematics, Level I
Chemistry	(Standard)
English Composition	Mathematics, Level II
European History and	(Intensive)
World Cultures	Physics
French	Russian
German	Spanish

Ten of the fourteen tests are administered at the regular testing dates; the remainder are given at less frequent intervals. In addition, seven additional tests, called Supplementary Achievement Tests are available at no cost to secondary schools. These tests are not given at the usual College Board centers. They are usually given by the local school on the first Tuesday in February of each year (College Entrance Examination Board, 1966b). These tests include the following:[3]

French Listening
   Comprehension
	Russian Listening
	   Comprehension

---

[3] New tests are being developed. These include a new two-hour test of composition and of literature as well as a new language test which will be included in the supplementary series.

German Listening	Spanish Listening
Comprehension	Comprehension
Italian Listening	Greek Achievement
Comprehension	Italian Achievement

The scores on the achievement tests are reported on the standard 200 to 800 College Board scale. Results are reported in the same manner as with the SAT.

In the following discussion of the specific achievement tests, the questions presented represent some of the sample items from the CEEB booklet (1966b) which is given to students planning to take the achievement tests. The information contained in this booklet is intended to help the student understand the types of questions that will be asked and the manner in which they will be presented.

English Composition

The English Composition test uses a multiple-choice and essay format. The intent of this test is to examine a student's ability to communicate ideas correctly and effectively, to organize ideas logically, and to use language with sensitivity to tone and meaning (College Entrance Examination Board, 1966b).

Correctness and Effectiveness of Expression. There are four different types of questions used in the area of correctness and effectiveness of expression. One kind presents sentences which may pose problems in grammar, usage, choice of words, and idiom. The student is asked to find the error in one of the underlined parts or if there is none, to choose the letter E. Several of these examples follow:[4]

Had we known of your desire to go with us, we most certainly would of
      A   B   C

invited you to join our party. No error
           D   E

No one finds difficulty to agree to the view that most apparel is bought
     A   B

for the sake of respectable appearance rather than for the protection of
       C   D

the person. No error
         E

[4] These examples and those on the following pages are from *A Description of the College Board Achievement Tests.* Copyright © 1966 By College Entrance Examination Board, New York. Used by permission of the College Entrance Examination Board.

Another type of question requires the student not only to recognize errors but also to choose the best manner of phrasing a given part of the sentence. In the following sample question the student can choose (A), which represents the original sentence, or one of the alternatives.

> For eight years he lives in New York and he still does not know how to find Yankee Stadium.
> (A) For eight years he lives in New York and
> (B) Having lived for his last eight years in New York,
> (C) Although he has lived in New York for eight years,
> (D) Despite eight years' existence in New York,
> (E) After his having lived eight years in New York,

The third type of question, which deals with correct and effective expression, is in a sentence format in which the possible source of error is not underlined and no possible optional corrections are offered. Some of the following illustrate these items:

> No sentence has more than one kind of error. Some sentences have no errors. Read each sentence carefully; then on your answer sheet blacken space
> A if the sentence contains *faulty diction,*
> B if the sentence is *wordy,*
> C if the sentence contains *clichés* or *inappropriate metaphors,*
> D if the sentence contains *faulty grammar* or *sentence structure,*
> E if the sentence contains *none* of these errors.
> One of the sources of the king's income was an entire monopoly of the whole manufacture and sale of salt.
> His mother mentioned that he will go to kindergarten next fall, but she will be very much surprised if he liked it.
> While the chemist was experimenting in his laboratory, he detected a new cleansing compound.

The fourth type of question dealing with correct and effective writing is similar to the one preceding, except the sentence is always correct. The student is asked to change the sentence according to given directions, that is, to "rewrite" it. In the following two examples the correct process and procedure are illustrated:

> *Sentence:* Coming to the city as a young man, he found a job as a newspaper reporter.
> *Directions:* Substitute He came for Coming.
> (A) and so he found
> (B) and found

(C) and there he had found
(D) and then found
(E) and had found

Your rephrased sentence will probably read: "He came to the city as a young man and found a job as a newspaper reporter." This sentence contains the correct answer: (B) and found. A sentence which used one of the alternate phrases would change the meaning or intention of the original sentence, would be a poorly written sentence, or would be less effective than another possible revision.

Sentence: Owing to her wealth, Sarah had many suitors.
Directions: Begin with Many men courted.

(A) so
(B) while
(C) although
(D) because
(E) and

Your rephrased sentence will probably read: "Many men courted Sarah because she was wealthy." This new sentence contains only choice D, which is the correct answer. None of the other choices will fit into an effective, correct sentence that retains the original meaning.

The Essay Test. The essay test requires the student to write on an assigned topic. It is evaluated for the College Board by school and college English teachers, and the resulting grade is made part of the total English Composition test score. An example of such an assignment is the following:

Directions: You will have 20 minutes to plan and write an essay on the topic given below.

"It is a common assumption that only the old are resistant to change. We forget that the teen-ager, despite his interest in rockets and rock 'n' roll, is the conservative of the human family. The teenager typically finds a pattern and follows it without deviating an inch; he avoids being different as he would avoid a contagion."

Comment upon this statement, using your associates and yourself as the basis for an opinion. Try to answer the question: To what extent is the statement correct, so far as my experience and observation will help me to decide? Use illustrations to support your opinion.

You are expected to express your thoughts carefully, naturally, and effectively. Be specific. Remember that how well you write is much more important than how much you write.

You must fit your essay on one special answer sheet. You will receive no other paper on which to write. You will find that the space provided is enough if you write neatly and legibly, and if you write on every line. Do not write too large, and do not leave wide margins.

In addition to the essay test, sometimes the English Composition test may include a poorly written passage printed with wide spaces between the lines so that the student can make appropriate corrections directly on the paper.

The Writing Sample
The student is given one hour to write on an assigned topic. Copies of the essay are forwarded to the student's secondary school and to the colleges where he is seeking admission. The essay in this sample is not graded by the College Board.

Foreign Languages
Achievement tests in this area measure competencies in Latin, Hebrew, French, German, Russian, and Spanish. Percentile ranks are presented for students having two, three, or four years of study.

The CEEB divides the questions into four main areas:[5]

Situation Questions. Situation questions attempt to measure familiarity with the language as it is used in everyday situations. They are intended to test a student's ability to read and visualize different kinds of situations and to be conversant with colloquial speech.

Usage Questions. Usage questions attempt to measure correct language patterns.

Vocabulary Questions. Vocabulary questions are presented in incomplete sentences and several words or phrases. The student's task is to choose one of the words or phrases without altering the basic meaning of the sentence.

Reading Comprehension Questions. These items are generally based on passages of from 100 to 300 words. They involve understanding the author's point of view.

In addition to English and foreign language tests, the CEEB offers, as has been previously noted, achievement tests in other academic areas. These tests cover three basic academic areas, history, mathematics, and science.

History
The history area is divided into two tests, the American History and Social Studies Test and the European History and World Cultures Test. Each test contains around 100 questions and has a time limit of one hour. Content in each test varies in difficulty and format. Some questions are presented in the standard multiple-choice form; some require students to match a statement with a given idea, event, or person in a list; and others require the student to apply knowledge to presented material such as maps and graphs or written statements. The student is required to exhibit knowledge of facts and terms and the ability to apply this information.

---

[5] For the modern language tests. The Latin test is divided into two sections, Vocabulary and Reading Comprehension.

MATHEMATICS

The mathematics area is divided into two tests, Mathematics Test, Level I and Mathematics Test, Level II. Mathematics Test, Level I (Standard) attempts to measure broad general areas of mathematics generally covered in college preparatory courses in mathematics. Half of the questions deal with algebra and plane geometry; the rest range from topics in coordinate geometry and elementary trigonometry to number theory. The wide range of topics is intended to sample achievement of students with different backgrounds; it is not expected that students will be knowledgeable about all the topics presented. Mathematics, Level II (Intensive) is geared for students with high ability in mathematics who have been exposed to accelerated or advanced courses in mathematics. This test is only recommended for students who are applying to colleges which require it or for those advanced students with high ability and intensive academic preparation during four years of college preparatory mathematics.

SCIENCE

The science area is divided into three tests, one in biology, one in chemistry, and one in physics. All three tests cover a full year of course work. Each test is timed for one hour and attempts to measure what the student knows about the subject and how well he can use this knowledge. The CEEB states (1966b) that these tests measure,

> (1) the ability to demonstrate an understanding of basic scientific concepts and principles; (2) the ability to apply these concepts and principles to familiar and unfamiliar situations; (3) the ability to handle quantitative relations in science (emphasized more in physics and chemistry than in biology); (4) the ability to interpret cause-and-effect relationships; (5) the ability to interpret experimental data; and (6) the ability to apply laboratory procedures to the problems arising in each field [p. 96].

In interpreting achievement test scores it is important to remember that what is considered a good score at one college may not be considered good at another. Colleges vary in the score they require for admission and placement.

In order to understand better what these scores mean, one must consider several factors. First of all, because all students do not take all the achievement tests, an individual may be competing with more able students on one test than on another. For example, the average score on the Advanced Mathematics Test is generally around 600, whereas the average Social Studies score is about 500.

Secondly, a student's foreign language score should be considered in relation to the number of years he has studied the language. It has been found that students taking these tests differ significantly in their scores according to the number of years of foreign language study. According to the College Board, students with three years of a language score eighty points higher than those with two years of study; those with four years of study generally score sixty points higher than those with three years of study.

American College Testing Program

One of the newer college admissions testing programs is the American College Testing Program (ACT). The ACT is a federation of state programs founded in 1959. It is an independent and nonprofit corporation. The American College Testing Program (1965) states that their main purposes are to:

> provide estimates of a student's academic and non-academic potentials which are useful in the admissions process
> provide dependable and comparable information for pre-college counseling in high schools and for on-campus educational guidance
> provide information useful in granting scholarships, loans, and other kinds of financial aid
> help students present themselves as persons with special patterns of educational potentials and needs
> help colleges place freshmen in appropriate class sections in introductory courses such as English and mathematics
> help colleges identify students who would profit from special programs such as honors, independent study, and remedial programs
> help colleges estimate whether a student should be considered for advanced placement and further examination with more intensive or advanced placement tests
> help colleges examine and improve their educational programs [p. 7].

There are over 1,500 educational institutions and agencies in fifty states and the District of Columbia in the ACT program. This includes institutions of diverse objectives and curricula such as technical schools, universities, four-year liberal arts colleges, junior colleges, and nursing schools (American College Testing Program, 1967a).

The ACT examination is administered five times a year in 2,000 test centers in the United States and Canada. The testing dates are in October, December, February, May, and August. In December and May the ACT is also given overseas.

The ACT Test Battery[6]

The ACT Test Battery is made up of four tests—English Usage Test, Mathematics Usage Test, Social Studies Reading Test, and Natural Sciences Reading Test—which attempt to measure abilities necessary for college work by appraising how the student can apply what he has already learned. There is no attempt to measure specific and detailed subject matter.

The English Usage Test attempts to measure the student's understanding of capitalization, punctuation, usage, phraseology, style, and organization. This test has eighty items and requires forty minutes to administer. Items and format are similar to the English achievement test of the CEEB.

The Mathematics Usage Test attempts to appraise a student's mathematical reasoning ability. There are forty items; administration time is fifty minutes. The emphasis in the examination is on the solution of practical quantitative problems that are presented in many college mathematics courses. Mathematical techniques used in high school courses are also covered.

The Social Studies Reading Test attempts to measure evaluative reasoning and problem-solving skills required in social studies by appraising student comprehension of reading passages culled from representative social studies materials. In addition, items that test understanding of basic concepts, knowledge of reference sources, and awareness of study skills especially needed in college social studies curricula are measured. There are fifty-two items; the test administration time is thirty-five minutes.

The Natural Sciences Reading Test has fifty-two items; the total time for administration is thirty-five minutes. This test attempts to measure critical reasoning and problem-solving skills needed in the natural sciences. The major emphasis is on the development and testing of hypotheses and the appraisal of scientific reports. A sample passage and questions follow:

TEST IV. NATURAL SCIENCES READING TEST[7]

Directions: Read the passage through once and then return as often as necessary to answer the questions.

Zeolites—a special family of crystalline minerals—have a unique molecular structure that explains their peculiar behavior. X-ray diffraction studies show that these crystals possess a porous structure, each crystal containing a precisely arrayed network of minute cavities linked by apertures. Water molecules (lost on heating) and exchangeable ions lie in these cavities and can pass through the apertures. This makes possible the unusual properties of reversible dehydration and ion exchange not found in most other crystals.

[6] Sources for the descriptions of the various ACT tests and other information concerning ACT are American College Testing Program, 1965, 1967a, and 1967b. The interested student should use this information only as a general guide or orientation. For specific, detailed and current information write to: The ACT Program, P.O. Box 168, Iowa City, Iowa 52250.

[7] From *ACT Student Registration Manual.* (1967–68 ed.) Copyright 1967 by American College Testing Program, Inc. Reproduced by permission of the American College Testing Program, Inc.

Because heat so directly affects the behavior of molecules, the regulation of temperature gives precise control over the sieving properties of a zeolite. Molecules that are no wider than the free diameter of the apertures enter the crystals more readily at lower temperatures. The "mesh" of the sieve can be altered not only by changing its temperature but also by introducing different ions into it. Ion exchange and temperature, working separately or together, can adjust the mesh of a molecular sieve to the needs of a particular separation problem.

12. Which of the following happens when zeolite crystals are heated?
    A. Ion exchange takes place.
    B. Small molecules enter the molecular sieve.
    C. The crystals lose water vapor, which may later be recaptured.
    D. The crystal decomposes permanently, with the loss of water vapor.

13. X-ray diffraction of zeolite shows
    A. numerous interstices
    B. water molecules
    C. charged atoms
    D. the position of the exchangeable ions

ACT Scores and What They Mean

ACT uses two types of scores for reporting test results, standard scores and percentile norms. ACT uses a scale from 1 (low) to 36 (high) as its standard scores. The scale is the same for each of the four tests. Raw scores are obtained by totaling the number of correct responses. These raw scores are then converted into the ACT standard scores. The standard scores are converted into percentile ranks in order to compare students with others in specified groups. In addition to the scores on these four tests, the student will receive another score. This score, called the *composite score,* is an average of the four tests and indicates the student's general ability to succeed in college. Copies of the ACT scores, reported in percentiles, are sent to the student's high school and to three colleges of his choice.

The standard score system of ACT was developed to facilitate test interpretation for teachers and counselors. It was originally constructed for the Iowa Tests of Educational Development (ITED) and modified for ACT use. The basic and major purpose is not only to help convey test scores in a meaningful manner but to be sure that test scores are interpreted with proper respect for errors of measurement inherent in the scores. The probable error of measurement itself was used as the unit of measurement in the scale and is slightly larger for the ACT-tested population than for the ITED. It, of course, varies from test to test. The American College Testing Program (1967b) states,

For the ACT population as well as for other populations, however, the scale automatically prevents test users from attaching significance to raw-score differences that are only a small fraction of the standard error of measurement, since a given scale score spans many trivial raw-score differences.

The following are a few of the important normative characteristics of this scale.

1 is the lowest possible standard score.

36 is the highest possible standard score.

16 is the approximate median (middle) score of unselected national samples of first-semester high school seniors.

20 is the approximate median score of first-semester college-bound high school seniors [p. 8].

It is important in interpreting a student's score to know with whom he is being compared. ACT lists six different norms or reference groups.

1. Unselected high school seniors includes high school seniors in general, both those who may and those who may not go on to college.

2. College-bound high school seniors.

Groups 3, 4, 5, and 6 are composed of students enrolled at different types of institutions of higher learning who took the ACT as high school seniors:

3. *Type 1* (junior colleges, technical institutes, and normal schools offering two-year programs).

4. *Type 2* (schools offering only the bachelor and/or first professional degree, for example, B.A., B.S., and M.D., bachelor of pharmacy, or B.S. in engineering).

5. *Type 3* (schools offering the master's and/or second professional degree).

6. *Type 4* (schools offering Ph.D. and equivalent degrees).

To illustrate how percentile rankings derived from different normative groups may help the student understand his scores, let us look at the case of Jack Ellis. Jack received a standard score of 20 on the ACT English test.[8] He was ranked in the 72nd percentile when compared to unselected high school seniors; when compared to college-bound students, he was in the 55th percentile; when compared to freshmen in Type 1 colleges, he was again in the 72nd percentile; when compared to freshmen in Type 2, he was in the 62nd percentile; when compared to freshmen in Type 3, he was in the 59th percentile; and when compared to Type 4 freshmen, he was in the 44th percentile.

[8] The percentile rankings for Jack's standard score of 20 are based on norms supplied by ACT in their publication *Using ACT on the Campus*, '67–68 (ACT, 1967b). See Chapter 5 for ACT percentile tables.

The preceding example shows that it is extremely important to remember with whom a student is being compared. In the unselected group there are pupils from large and small schools, some of whom are not planning to go to college, whereas others are outstanding students planning to enroll in college. Thus these students represent a wide range of abilities. The College-bound group is made up of students who took the ACT and are planning to go on to college. Note that Jack's percentile rank in this group is 55 as compared to 72 in the Unselected group. Now let us look at the four colleges. Jack's percentile ranking as compared to Type 1 students reveals the same percentile ranking as the Unselected group. This indicates that the Type 1 group probably has the same range of abilities as the Unselected group.[9] Type 2 shows a more select group, and Jack's percentile ranking falls from 72 to 62. Type 3 is slightly more select than Type 2, and Jack's ranking falls four percentile points, whereas in Type 4, the most select group, Jack is only at the 44th percentile, indicating that in this type of college he would be slightly below the average, whereas in Type 1 he was almost in the upper quarter of students.

These reference or norm groups are extremely important in selecting an appropriate college. Jack would probably be very successful, all other things being equal, at a Type 1 college and moderately successful at a Type 2 college. Enrollment in Type 3 and Type 4 colleges would entail a great deal more effort and present a greater possibility of failure.

ACT Self-reports

In the actual test setting the student is requested to report his recent grades, before his senior year, in each of the four subject areas to be tested, English, mathematics, social studies, and natural sciences. ACT (1967b) states,

> Perhaps the most reliable research finding in education is that high school grades are predictive of college grades; further, that academic aptitude tests and high school grades combined are a better predictor of college grades than either alone. This knowledge led ACT to initiate regular collection of self-reported high school grades. . . . These self-reports are considered estimates of high school academic achievement, for presumably high school grades depend on both academic aptitude and other characteristics such as persistence and study habits [pp. 4–5].

ACT Student Profile

The ACT Student Profile is an interesting and unique instrument, based on the assumption that the quality of education a college provides is partly

---

[9] Median score for *Unselected* group is 16.5 and mean score for *Type 1* group is 16.9. See Chapter 5 for ACT percentile tables.

dependent on the amount of relevant data it has about its students. The Student Profile asks for this kind of information. For example, the student indicates his vocational plans; his probable major area of study; the kind of degree he wants; the size of his hometown; the kind of housing he wants at college; and other data helpful to the college in student guidance. The ACT Student Profiles may be used in admissions, planning freshman courses, advanced placement, scholarship and loan programs, student counseling, and so on.

Although school grades and test scores indicate academic potential, other factors bearing on success in nonacademic activities must also be considered. This is supported by the research literature. For example, Holland and Richards (1965), after studying the relationship of academic and nonacademic accomplishment of over 7,000 college freshmen, state,

> Some of the practical applications of our findings seem clear. If a sponsor is interested only in finding students who will do well in the classroom in college, then high school grades and tests of academic potential are the best techniques available. On the other hand, if a sponsor wishes to find college students who will do outstanding things outside the classroom and in later life, then he should continue to make an effort to secure a better record of the student's competencies and achievements in high school. Our results support some of the items used for this purpose in typical application blanks for admission to college, scholarships, and fellowships, but they also suggest the potential usefulness of a more active effort to secure a more reliable and valid record of each student's past achievement and involvement [p. 22].

Research—A Brief Review of Recent Studies

Munday (1965) investigated the predictive validity of the ACT tests with the SAT and SCAT[10] tests for a sample of twenty-one colleges and universities. Grades in specific courses and overall grade averages were studied. It was found that predictive validity varied from school to school and from course to course. It was also found that the ACT and SAT tests possessed about the same relative degree of predictive validity. The SCAT was not found to be as good a predictor as either the ACT or the SAT.

Angoff (1965) in an investigation of talented students found the SAT to be a good instrument for identifying students of high ability.

Lins, Abell, and Hutchins (1966), in an investigation of the SAT and the ACT, found that they could not equate them. They concluded that because the predictive abilities of neither test were very high, the use of "cutoff"

[10] School and College Ability Tests.

practices by some college admissions offices were open to serious question. Boyce and Paxson (1965), on the other hand, in a study of the predictive validities of eleven tests, including the ACT and SAT, found moderate validities, ranging from 0.42 through 0.64. The grade point average of the student at the end of the first quarter was used as the criterion of success or failure.

Barth (1965) found that success on the SAT and CEEB writing sample did not require knowledge of the terminology of present school grammar. They stated, "Only a knowledge of certain questions of usage and a sensitivity to language . . . are required."

Hoyt (1968) in a study of 169 students from four colleges found a great deal of diversity in freshman classes and colleges. Wide differences in grading practices at different institutions were noted. These differences, according to Hoyt, explain the low correlation that he found between the grades and the ACT composite score. The correlation of the mean college grade point average with the ACT was only 0.34. This finding confirmed earlier studies.

The Practical Meaning of College Entrance Examinations

College admissions tests are not perfect, or even close to perfect, in forecasting how a student will perform in college. There is no one device available today to predict with 100 per cent accuracy a student's future success or failure in college. The tests that are available today, however, do present a fairly good indication of a student's chances when coupled with high school performance.

Colleges do not rely on test scores as their sole criterion for admission. The formula used by most colleges in determining admission is the high school record (academic and extracurricular), teacher and counselor recommendations, high school standardized test scores, and of course, college entrance examinations.

Scores on the CEEB and ACT can only be interpreted in the light of the individual college. A score of 500 on the verbal section of the SAT, for example, may be a satisfactory score for College X and far below what is acceptable for College Y. Soldwedel (1966), in discussing this problem, states,

> Generally you can assume that (1) low test scores may adversely affect chances of admission; (2) high scores will help but do not by themselves guarantee acceptance. The trouble with this generalization is that it does not answer the questions *How low?* and *How high?*
>
> How low is bad and how high is good will be determined by whatever the traffic will bear. You may find it difficult to get answers to the questions from admissions people. And there is good reason for

the reluctance. What colleges would like to get, in terms of student body performance on standardized tests, and what they actually take are often two different things. Certainly it must be added that there are institutions with sufficient endowment funds to hold rigidly to a test performance score. These are not in the majority, however. Colleges, faced with the necessity of reaching a certain quota of freshmen, may dip to lower test scores as applicants are sifted. On the other hand, some colleges are reluctant to divulge the minimum test scores they require because all strive for upward mobility and do not want to be saddled with the lowest score from year to year [p. 51].

Let us take the case of Jane and Bill to illustrate the place of college admissions tests in screening applicants.

Jane is an attractive senior girl at Glen High School. Her high school record shows that she is a good student. Her academic average is B+. She has been a cheerleader for three years and is presently the editor of the school newspaper. Her teachers like her and will give her excellent recommendations. On the Scholastic Aptitude Test she obtained a score of 400 on the verbal section and 350 on the mathematics section. Her achievement scores in English composition, French, and social studies are all somewhere in the 400's. Jane would like to attend an eastern girls' school, and her parents have money set aside for this.

The standards of the better girls' schools in the east are fairly high, and generally, test scores such as Jane's would not be acceptable to these schools.

The eastern school may feel that Jane has overextended herself in high school and could not live up to their standards. Thus, even though her record is excellent, she may not gain admission to this type of school. Factors such as the type of high school Jane attended would be very important. If Jane's high school is one of excellent academic reputation, she may still gain admission. The important thing to remember is that Jane could be admitted to other colleges in the country. And even with her low college entrance examination scores she may still gain admission to a highly selective school because of her other outstanding credits. Thus Jane is not "doomed" because of her college entrance examination scores.

Now let us look at a different situation. Bill is a senior at North High School. He is a rebellious boy who is not very interested in school and cares little about homework. Consequently, his grades in school have been rather poor. His grade average is C. He has done little in the way of extracurricular activities and is generally disliked by his teachers. On the College Board examinations he received the following scores: verbal—650; mathematics—700; English composition—600; French—650; chemistry—700.

These scores indicate that Bill has the ability to succeed in college. Even with these excellent scores, however, he may find some college doors closed to him because of his poor academic record. However, he will probably gain admission to some college because of his promising potential.

The reader can see from the two examples cited that test scores are not the only criteria that the college uses for admission. Certainly most students do not present such extreme cases. However, there are variations, and for this reason the person's whole record is taken into account. In Jane's case, it is possible that she has developed good study skills and has devoted a lot of time to her homework. The chances are that these habits will carry over in her college work and help her earn higher grades than her College Board scores would indicate—that is, if she has made good grades on quizzes and final examinations in high school and has not received her high grades because of her appearance and ability to get along with her teachers.

In the case of Bill we may state that in predicting success or failure in college there are certain negative signs even though his test scores are very high. Why? Because Bill has operated below his potential for so long, the chances are that he will continue to do so in college. Study habits have to be developed, and Bill has apparently not done this. In addition, he does not seem motivated to do so. He may state that this will all change in college, but the chances are that he will continue this pattern.

Of course, there are many exceptions to what has been stated. We are speaking in general and in terms of probability, not certainty. There are students like Bill who not only change their school pattern but go on to be scholars and prominent people in the arts and sciences. In general, however, this does not happen. Still, because of the chance that it may, Bill should be encouraged to go on to college, and counseling, to ascertain the reasons for his underachievement, should be planned.

The important thing for those who are going to deal with students to remember is that college admissions tests are to help students and are not intended to hurt them. Remember that the individual who enrolls in a college that is beyond his abilities may "flunk out" or quit in discouragement. If, on the other hand, he is guided into a college that is commensurate with his needs and abilities, he is more likely to complete his education.

References

American College Testing Program. *General information bulletin.* Iowa City, Iowa: American College Testing Program, 1965.

American College Testing Program. *ACT student registration manual.* (1967–68 ed.) Iowa City, Iowa: American College Testing Program, 1967.(a)

American College Testing Program. *Using ACT on the campus—'67–'68.* Iowa City, Iowa: American College Testing Program, 1967.(b)

Angoff, W. H. The College Board SAT and the superior student. *Superior Student,* 1965, **7**, 10–15.

Barth, C. A. Kinds of language knowledge required by college entrance examinations. *English Journal,* 1965, **54**, 824–29.

Boyce, R. W., and Paxson, R. C. The predictive validity of eleven tests at one state college. *Educational and Psychological Measurement,* 1965, **25** (4), 1143-1147.

Chauncey, H., and Dobbin, J. E. Testing has a history. In C. I. Chase and H. G. Ludlow (Eds.), *Readings in educational and psychological measurement.* Boston: Houghton Mifflin, 1966.

College Entrance Examination Board. *Bulletin of information—college board admissions tests, 1966–67.* Princeton, N.J.: College Entrance Examination Board, 1966.(a)

College Entrance Board Examination. *A description of the College Board achievement tests, 1966–1967.* Princeton, N.J.: College Entrance Examination Board, 1966.(b)

College Entrance Examination Board. *A description of the College Board Scholastic Aptitude Test, 1966–1967.* Princeton, N.J.: College Entrance Examination Board, 1966.(c)

College Entrance Examination Board. *Your College Board scores: Preliminary Scholastic Aptitude Test.* Princeton, N.J.: College Entrance Examination Board, 1966.(d)

Holland, J. L., and Richards, J. M. *Academic and non-academic accomplishment: Correlated or uncorrelated?* ACT Research Report No. 2. Iowa City, Iowa: American College Testing Program, 1965.

Hoyt, D. P. Description and prediction of diversity among four-year colleges. *Measurement and Evaluation in Guidance,* 1968, **1,** 16–26.

Juola, A. E. Selection, classification, and placement of students. In P. L. Dressel (Ed.), *Evaluation in higher education.* Boston: Houghton Mifflin, 1961.

Lins, L. J., Abell, A. P., and Hutchins, H. C. Relative usefulness in predicting academic success of the ACT, the SAT, and some other variables. *Journal of Experimental Education,* 1966, **35,** 1–29.

Munday, L. *Comparative predictive validities of the American College Tests and two other scholastic aptitude tests.* ACT Research Report No. 6. Iowa City, Iowa: American College Testing Program, 1965.

Soldwedel, B. J. *Preparing for college.* New York: Macmillan, 1966.

CHAPTER

12

Personality, Attitude,
and Interest Inventories

The last three chapters have focused on academic potential and performance. These are the basic ingredients of school life. They are not, however, the only elements essential to success in school or life. The child (and the adult) must also be able to harness his talents in fields that satisfy his needs. The problem of vocational choice is of paramount importance to the individual student and to the society that needs to utilize the resources of its people. This is where interest inventories may be of assistance.

In addition to helping children become aware of their interests the school is also concerned with the mental health of its pupils. A child with an emotional problem is sometimes unable to use his abilities and becomes a school failure or dropout. The school is, therefore, vitally concerned in helping its boys and girls find their interest areas and spotting those children who need psychological guidance. This chapter will be devoted to illustrating the nature, use, and reasons for personality, attitude, and interest tests in the school.

Personality Inventories

The word *personality* has different meanings to different people. To some it is another word for *popularity*; the person either has it or lacks it. To many psychologists personality is the total sum of the characteristics and behavior of a person; this includes everything from intelligence to social relations. To other psychologists personality comprises the distinguishing characteristics of a person. Obviously, *personality* is a broad and general term that lay and professional people define differently. It is impossible to define it in exact terms, for the definition is dependent upon the concepts of the individual explaining its meaning.

Educators generally view personality in terms of adjustment. They are concerned with the functioning of the child in the classroom. Is the child well adjusted enough to learn, or does he have problems that interfere with the learning process? When educators need to know the answer to this and other questions of adjustment, personality inventories may be administered in the schools.

Personality inventories are sometimes referred to as personality tests. They are not tests, but self-reports. There are no right or wrong answers to specific items. The student is asked to respond to statements and questions concerning his own feelings, emotions, family and school situation, and personal needs. The questions asked are many times specific: "Do you often feel unhappy?" "Can you make friends easily?" "Do you suffer from headaches?"

Personality inventories are objective self-reports, as contrasted with projective techniques, which are generally administered individually and require subjective interpretation of objective stimuli by the individual. Projective tests are indefinite and require the person to respond in his own unique manner. (See Chapter 8.) The personality inventory, on the other hand, is structured and is usually presented in an objective format, similar to tests of aptitude and achievement.

There are many personality inventories in use today (also referred to by some as temperament or adjustment inventories). We will briefly review some of these, but our attention will be focused on the most widely used and respected personality inventory, the Minnesota Multiphasic Personality Inventory (MMPI).

Thorndike Dimensions of Temperament

The Thorndike Dimensions of Temperament (TDOT) is an inventory which requests the student to describe himself with respect to ten dimensions of temperament. Table 24 presents these dimensions and a brief description of each. Note that this inventory does not attempt to probe for deep psychopathology; its aim is to describe a person.

The TDOT is appropriate for juniors and seniors in high school, college students, and adults of equal educational levels. The items are printed in a reusable booklet and the responses, which are marked on a separate answer sheet, may be machine- or hand-scored.

Table 24 Description of *TDOT* Dimensions

Dimension	Abbreviation	Positive End	Negative End
1. Sociable	(Soc)	Sociable Likes to be with other people, to do things in groups, to go to parties, to be in the middle of things	Solitary Likes to be by himself, to do things by himself, to read or engage in other kinds of solitary activities
2. Ascendant	(Asc)	Ascendant Likes to be in the center of the stage, to speak in public, to "sell" things or ideas, to meet important people; tends to stand up for his rights or his point of view	Withdrawing Tends to avoid personal conflict, to dislike being in the public eye, to avoid taking the initiative in relation to others, to accept being imposed upon
3. Cheerful	(Che)	Cheerful, Objective Seems to feel generally well and happy; satisfied with his relations with others, accepted by others, at peace with the world	Gloomy, Sensitive Often seems to feel moody, depressed, at odds with himself; sensitive to the criticism of others; prone to worry and anxiety
4. Placid	(Pla)	Placid Even-tempered, easygoing, not easily ruffled or annoyed	Irritable Short-tempered, annoyed or irked by a good many things, inclined to "blow his top"
5. Accepting	(Acc)	Accepting Tends to think the best of people, to accept them at face value, to expect altruism to prevail	Critical Tends to question people's motives, expecting self-interest, conscious of the need for each to look out for himself

Table 24 Description of *TDOT* Dimensions (continued)

Dimension	Abbreviation	Positive End	Negative End
6. Tough-Minded	(T-M)	Tough-Minded (Masculine) Tolerant of dirt, bugs, and profanity; enjoys sports, roughing it, and the out-of-doors; uninterested in clothes or personal appearance; rational rather than intuitive	Tender-Minded (Feminine) Sensitive to dirt, both physical and verbal; concerned with personal appearance; aesthetic interests; intuitive rather than rational
7. Reflective	(Ref)	Reflective Interested in ideas, in abstractions, in discussion and speculation, in knowing for its own sake	Practical Interested in doing and in using knowledge for practical ends, impatient with speculation and theorizing
8. Impulsive	(Imp)	Impulsive Carefree, happy-go-lucky, ready to do things at a moment's notice	Planful Careful to plan life out in advance, systematic, orderly, foresighted
9. Active	(Act)	Active Full of energy, on the go, quick to get things done, able to get a lot done	Lethargic Slow, easily tired, less productive than others; likes to move at a leisurely pace
10. Responsible	(Res)	Responsible Dependable, reliable, certain to complete tasks on time, even a little compulsive	Casual Often late with commitments, rushes to meet deadlines; has difficulty getting things done, unpredictable

From *Thorndike Dimensions of Temperament, Manual,* by Robert L. Thorndike. (Reproduced by permission. Copyright © 1966, The Psychological Corporation, New York, N.Y. All rights reserved.)

The test booklet presents twenty sets (labeled from A to T), each of which contains ten statements. The student is directed to read quickly through the statements and then go back and choose the three that are "most like you." He signifies his response by blackening the answer space marked L (like) beside the number of the item. He is then requested to go back and blacken the answer space marked D (different) beside the three statements that are

SAMPLE SET   SAMPLE OF ANSWER SHEET

1. The program you watch most regularly on television is a news broadcast.

2. You are likely to keep people waiting for you.

3. Nothing seems to work out quite right for you.

4. You often seem to be given the "dirty" job to do.

5. You would rather read a history book than a novel.

6. You are usually "on the go."

7. You tend to "blow up" in an emergency.

8. You look forward to the years ahead.

9. You usually plan things well in advance.

10. You generally find other people enjoyable.

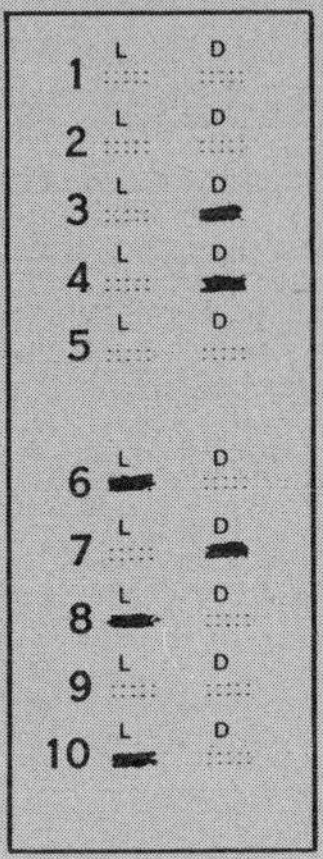

Figure 31. Sample set of items from Thorndike Dimensions of Temperament. (Reproduced by permission. Copyright © 1963, The Psychological Corporation, New York, N.Y. All rights reserved.)

"most different from you." Figure 31 illustrates the types of items that are presented. Thorndike (1966), in describing his test, states,

> Evidence tends to support the contention that the $TDOT$ portrays the individual both as he sees himself and as others see him. Though it does not pretend to delve into deep layers of inner personality dynamics, the inventory appears to be quite successful in providing a differentiated picture of the manifest personality [p. 5].

The norms for each of the ten dimensions of the TDOT are based on 4,008 students in grades eleven and twelve from twenty high schools and 1,493 freshmen from ten colleges. Separate tables are presented for each sex. In addition to examining these students, Thorndike asked each one to complete six questions relating to home and family background and educational and vocational aspirations. Variations in mean scores among certain subgroups were found to be statistically significant.

The following are brief summaries of these findings as reported by Thorndike (1966).

Sociable. The rural respondents appear less sociable than those from towns or cities. There is a suggestion of higher sociability among males majoring or planning to major in business.

Ascendant. Greater ascendance tends to go with town or city residence, with higher parental socio-economic status, with higher parental education, with plans for college education among high school pupils, and with plans for a professional career.

Cheerful, Placid, Accepting. These scales show no clear differences among the groups on any of the breakdowns.

Tough-Minded. This attribute tends to be somewhat higher in rural groups. For boys, there are substantial differences associated with vocational plan, with scores on the trait being high for those planning agricultural careers and low for those planning to enter the professions.

Reflective. This dimension has a number of correlates. Among boys it is associated with an urban environment, professional occupation of father, plans for a college education for self, intention to major in social science, and aspiration to a professional occupation. Among girls it is also associated with high parental education and aspiration for a college education for self, with a planned college major in languages or in arts, and perhaps with aspirations to a professional career.

Impulsive. This trait shows few correlates. It has some tendency to be high for girls who aspire to a college major in arts.

Active. This scale shows no clear group differences.

Responsible. This scale shows only slight differences. There is a suggestion that children of more highly educated parents report themselves to be less reliable. Girls majoring or aspiring to major in arts rate themselves low on this trait. [pp. 27–28].

Overall validity and reliability for TDOT are lower than the reported coefficients of most aptitude and achievement tests. In discussing reliability Thorndike (1966) readily concedes this and states that the "reliability of

TDOT is lower than one is accustomed to expect in tests of ability, but compares favorably with many other personality inventories" (p. 9).

The student interested in pursuing the technical aspects of this test further in terms of validity, reliability, and correlations with other measures is referred to the TDOT test manual (Thorndike, 1966).

Mooney Problem Check List

Another type of personality inventory is represented by the Mooney Problem Check List. The Mooney, along with its sibling inventories, is not a test; it goes one step further, however, in that it yields no scores. Mooney and Gordon (1950), in describing the utility of their test, state that the "usefulness of the Problem Check List approach lies in its economy for appraising the major concerns of a group and for bringing into the open the problems of each student in the group" (p. 3).

MAJOR USES

Some of the major uses of the Mooney in a school setting are the following:

Counseling
> To prepare pupils for interviewer by having them think over their own problems.
> To facilitate communication between counselor and student.
> To save time for the counselor by providing a quick overview of various problems.

Research
> To provide information useful for curriculum planning, individualized instruction and counseling needs.
> To measure the effect of certain school activities and school oriented problems and objectives.

Homeroom and Group Guidance
> To help students identify personal problems and needs.
> To provide material for discussion in group guidance and orientation programs.

The Mooney Problem Check List has four forms to be used for different age levels: junior high school (*J*), high school (*H*), college (*C*), and adults (*A*). They are all self-administering and for counseling purposes require no scoring. It should be noted, however, that for certain objectives, such as research purposes, the problems checked may be summarized by simply counting the total responses in a number of problem areas. These areas differ according to the form. The problem areas and number of items in each for the junior high school and high school and college forms are as follows (Mooney and Gordon, 1950):

Junior High School Form
210 items, 30 in each area
 I. Health and Physical Development (HPD)
 II. School (S)
 III. Home and Family (HF)
 IV. Money, Work, the Future (MWF)
 V. Boy and Girl Relations (BG)
 VI. Relations to People in General (PG)
 VII. Self-centered Concerns (SC)
College and High School Forms
 330 items, 30 in each area
 I. Health and Physical Development (HPD)
 II. Finances, Living Conditions, and Employment (FLE)
 III. Social and Recreational Activities (SRA)
 IV. Social-Psychological Relations (SPR)
 V. Personal-Psychological Relations (PPR)
 VI. Courtship, Sex, and Marriage (CSM)
 VII. Home and Family (HF)
 VIII. Morals and Religion (MR)
 IX. Adjustment to College (School) Work (ACW) (ASW)
 X. The Future: Vocational and Educational (FVE)
 XI. Curriculum and Teaching Procedure (CTP)

The usual analysis of validity and reliability are not relevant to this type of instrument. The interested student should consult the manual (Mooney and Gordon, 1950) for specific types of validity, reliability, and norms reported. In addition, a bibliography of research and use of the instrument is presented.

The following are some typical items from the junior high school form:

Directions[1] Read the list slowly and as you come to a problem which troubles you, draw a line under it.

 1. Often have headaches 61. Being teased
 2. Don't get enough sleep 62. Being talked about
 3. Have trouble with my teeth 63. Feelings too easily hurt
 4. Not as healthy as I should be 64. Too easily led by other people
 5. Not getting outdoors enough 65. Picking the wrong kind of friends

 6. Getting low grades in school 66. Getting into trouble
 7. Afraid of tests 67. Trying to stop a bad habit

[1] Sample items from the *Mooney Problem Check List—Junior High School Form.* (Reproduced by permission. Copyright 1950 by The Psychological Corporation, New York, N.Y. All rights reserved.)

8. Being a grade behind in school	68. Sometimes not being as honest as I should be
9. Don't like to study	69. Giving in to temptations
10. Not interested in books	70. Lacking self-control

In addition to the 210 items there are three questions that ask the student to write in his own words about problems troubling him and to say whether he would like to spend some of his school time talking to someone about them. The Mooney in essence, then, is not a measuring device in the usual sense. Cronbach's (1960) appraisal of it states quite cogently that the "Mooney Problem Check List is of considerable value because it draws attention to specific concerns the client is ready to talk about and wants help with. It is, in effect, a preliminary interview rather than a measuring device" (p. 487.)

Minnesota Multiphasic Personality Inventory

The Minnesota Multiphasic Personality Inventory (MMPI) was designed to provide an objective measure of some of the most important personality characteristics that relate to personal and social adjustment. It attempts to provide, in a single test, scores on all the most important aspects of personality (Hathaway and McKinley, 1951).

The MMPI is one of the most respected and widely used personality inventories in existence today. More research has been done with it and on it than any other inventory now available. The diversity of problems that have been examined with the MMPI is truly outstanding. In addition to the numerous studies of a psychological and psychiatric nature, studies relating personality characteristics to success in practice teaching, cancer, brain lesions, multiple sclerosis, low-back pain, and characteristics of and criteria for nursing students have also been done. These are only a very small fraction of the various kinds of investigations reported.

The first MMPI investigations appeared in 1940. The test materials and the first formal manual were published in 1943. The number of articles, books, dissertations, and other investigations dealing with the MMPI has been enormous.

FORMAT

The MMPI consists of 550 statements to which the subject is asked to respond in three ways: "true," "false," or "cannot say." The MMPI is given in two forms, individual (card form) and group (booklet). In the individual form the test administrator presents the subject with a box of 550 small cards with printed statements on each. Instructions are on the cover of the box and ask the subject to sort the cards into three stacks according to the three preceding categories. The group form presents these same 550 statements[2] in a printed format in the usual type of group test booklet.[3] The instructions in the test booklet request the person to "read each statement and decide whether it is *true as applied to you* or *false as applied to you*. . . . If a statement does not apply to you or if it is something that you don't know about, make no mark on the answer sheet" (Hathaway and McKinley, 1943). The subject records his answers on a separate answer sheet which may be hand- or machine-scored. The MMPI was originally designed for individuals sixteen years of age and over, although it has been used successfully with fourteen-year-old high school students (Hathaway and Monachesi, 1953, 1961). The card form is recommended for testing small groups or individuals and should be used when testing older persons, disturbed persons, hospital patients, or persons with low educational achievement or intellectual ability. The group form yields the same results, however, for high school and college and professional people (Hathaway and McKinley, 1951).

The MMPI items cover broad areas of content ranging from statements dealing with health and psychosomatic symptoms and neurological disorders to sexual, religious, political, educational, and social attitudes. Items similar to those found in the MMPI follow:

> I have been healthy during the past three years.
> I do not become fatigued easily.
> Important sexual facts should be taught to children.
> I sometimes like to swear.
> I definitely lack self-confidence.

SCORES

Clinical Scales. The MMPI provides scores on nine "clinical scales." They are as follows:

1. Hypochondriasis (Hs).	6. Paranoia (Pa).
2. Depression (D).	7. Psychasthenia (Pt).
3. Hysteria (Hy).	8. Schizophrenia (Sc).
4. Psychopathic Deviate (Pd).	9. Hypomania (Ma).
5. Masculinity-feminity (Mf).	

The preceding scales consist of statements that differentiate between the following diverse groups: patients in the general wards of the University of Minnesota Hospitals (254 patients who were in the hospital for physical disease); a normal group of individuals who were bringing relatives or friends to the University Clinic (724 cases); precollege high school graduates who

---

[2] Actually, the booklet presents 566 items, sixteen of which are duplications of the basic 550 items.

[3] A new form (Form R) allows scores to be obtained from only the first 399 items. Numbers 400–566 are designated for research.

came to the University Testing Bureau for precollege guidance (265 cases); and patients (221) in the psychopathic unit of the University Hospitals and the outpatient neuropsychiatric clinic (Hathaway and McKinley, 1956).

In addition to the basic nine scales a unique feature of the MMPI is its four "validity scales." They are not validity scales in the usual testing sense but are attempts to note carelessness, malingering, misunderstanding, and test-taking attitudes of the subject. These four scales are the following:

> 1. *The Cannot Say Score*(?). The "cannot say" score is the total number of statements that the subject responded to by not answering "true" or "false."
>
> 2. *Lie Score* (L). "True" responses to statements in the lie scale present the respondent in an unfavorable light; "false" responses present him in a favorable light. Dahlstrom and Welsh (1960), in referring to this scale, state that "these attributes are clear, unambiguous, and generally socially unfavorable. It was assumed that most people would be willing to endorse the statements of the L scale as true about themselves even though the items deal with disapproved actions and feelings." (p. 49).
>
> 3. *Validity Score* (F). The validity score is based upon a group of items rarely endorsed by the original standardization group, including the mentally ill patients. Many of the items relate to peculiar thoughts and beliefs and lack of control over impulses. It is highly unlikely that any subject would exhibit all or a majority of these behavioral patterns. The F score serves as a check on the whole record. A high F score indicates other scores are probably invalid because the subject was careless or did not understand the statements or that possible scoring errors were made.
>
> 4. *The K Score* (K). The K score is the most recent of the validity scales and was developed as a measure of test-taking attitudes which appear either as defensiveness or as a need to represent one's worst features. College students tend, as a group, to have higher K scores (psychological defensiveness and sophistication) than individuals of less sophistication and those who consciously or unconsciously desire to place themselves in a "poor light."

After scoring the MMPI, the examiner reviews the four validity scales before proceding further. If any or all of these scales are over the designated ceiling, the record is considered suspect; if they are extremely high, it is considered invalid.

In addition to the basic nine scales of the MMPI, a tenth was added, the Social Introversion (Si) scale. Welsh and Dahlstrom (1956) present studies in which a high relationship was found between the Si scale and the number of extracurricular activities participated in by high school and college students.

Over 200 new scales, in addition to those already mentioned, have been developed by independent investigators. Very few of these investigators took part in the original construction of the MMPI. These scales vary widely —for example, Academic achievement (Ac), College achievement (Ae), Aging (Ag), Alcoholism (Al), Adjustment to prison (Ap), Anxiety reaction (Ar), Success in baseball (Ba), Delinquency (De), Ego strength (Es), Low back pain (Lb), and so forth (Dahlstrom and Welsh, 1960). In addition to scale variance studies, graduate schools and professional groups have utilized the MMPI as a basis for characterization of personality and as a screening device. (See for example, Karmel, 1961.)

INTERPRETATION

Normally the interpretation of the MMPI is based on only fourteen scales (nine "clinical," plus Si and the four validity scales) and possibly several other "pet" scales of the examiner. Scores are converted to norms based on the original sample and according to sex. These norms are reported in the form of T scores (standard scores) with a mean of 50 and a SD of 10. A score of 70 or higher is generally considered as the point above which psychopathology might be inferred. The skilled examiner, however, is more interested in the total profile configuration and the relative peak scales (highest elevation) than the score per se. On the other hand, extremely high scale scores reveal in most cases blatant psychopathology.

The MMPI can be given by people not trained in psychology; however, it is dangerous for persons not skilled in its use to interpret the results. Usually, the MMPI is given only by the school psychologist and then only after parental permission has been obtained. This is not the kind of test that is given to all students; it should be given only to those who have revealed emotional problems. We will have more to say about this later in the chapter.

The qualified school psychologist in his interpretation of the MMPI will avail himself of several excellent resources as a basis for his interpretation. One of the older and staple sources is *An Atlas for the Clinical Use of the MMPI* (Hathaway and Meehl, 1951) which provides coded profiles and short case histories. A more recent aid is the *MMPI Handbook* (Dahlstrom and Welsh, 1960). It is the most comprehensive and usable source for profile interpretations. Another source that is limited to college students is Drake and Oetting's (1959) *MMPI Codebook for Counselors*.

In addition to the use of codebooks the school psychologist now has at his disposal computer interpretations. The Psychological Corporation offers an MMPI reporting service which provides a one-page report of diagnostic and interpretive statements of an individual's personality. Figure 32 presents a sample of this type of report.

Other investigators are now engaged in computer programming of the MMPI and other inventories. For example, Finney (1966, 1967) has developed a program that scores and interprets psychological tests by computer. As originally developed, it takes as input either the MMPI alone or the MMPI

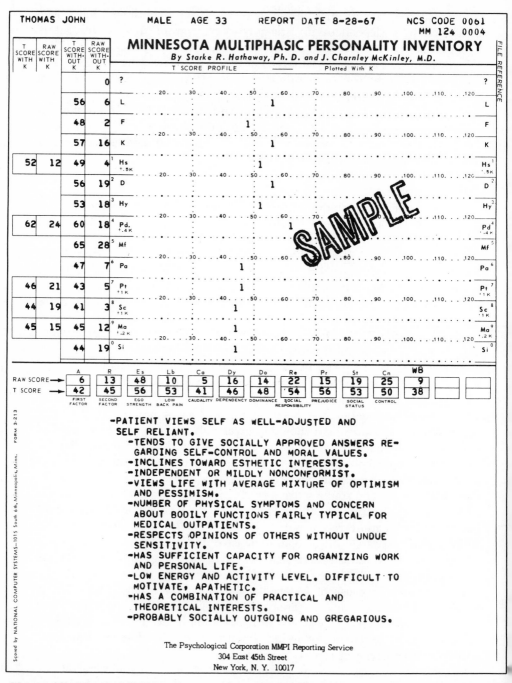

Figure 32. Sample MMPI computer report. (Reproduced by permission. Copyright 1943, 1951, © 1967 by the University of Minnesota. Published by the Psychological Corporation, New York, N.Y. All rights reserved.)

and California Psychological Inventory. A large number of scales are scored, 101 with MMPI alone or 124 with MMPI and CPI. About fifty of the scales used were developed from Finney's own research.

The report is built by selecting statements and then combining them into paragraphs. Each of the 101 scales yields one statement chosen from among eight possible ones, depending on the individual's T score on the scale. By this method, 101 statements are chosen from a repertory of 808. The statements written for the standard clinical scales of the MMPI, such as "Hy" and "D," draw on the large pool of information from research and clinical experience which has become public knowledge over the years. Reconciling statements are written to eliminate contradictions among statements (Finney, 1967).

Besides the statements based on individual scales, the report includes other statements based on configurations or combinations of scales, and statements based on computed factor scores on five dimensions: factors A (anxiety), B (boldness), C (compulsivity), D (disability), and E (enmity).

Finney and his coworker, Dr. Dwight Auvenshine, have subsequently developed several different kinds of reports written for different purposes. The Finney-Auvenshine program now writes any of seven kinds of reports:

1. Report for Industrial Personnel Counselors.
2. Report for Counselors and Caseworkers.
3. Report for Correctional Counselors.
4. Report for the Individual Himself.
5. Report for Physicians and Surgeons.
6. Short Report for Psychiatrists and Clinical Psychologists.
7. Detailed Report for Psychiatrists and Clinical Psychologists.

The report, designed to be read by an individual himself, is sent only to a qualified physician, psychiatrist, clinical psychologist, counselor, or caseworker, who may or may not decide to release it to the tested individual and who will interpret it to the individual before doing so.

Finney and Auvenshine are now extending their work to other objective psychological tests.

The School and Personality Inventories

Educators may well ask, "Why give personality inventories in the school?" This is a legitimate question. Let us first state a basic and very important premise. That is, *personality inventories are not given to all youngsters.* They are administered only to those who have displayed behavior patterns that could indicate emotional problems.

In order to clarify the role of the MMPI in the school, let us take the case of Bill. Bill was referred to the school psychologist by the school social worker because of his inability to get along in the classroom. Bill's test record showed he was in the superior range of school ability. However, his grades were very poor, F's and D's. Bill would spend much of his time drawing pictures and "goofing off." The social worker was unable to come up with a clear diagnosis, so after receiving parental permission, Bill was given the MMPI. The test results showed Bill was the type of boy who was unable to cope with his environment. It was obvious that Bill was sick and needed immediate treatment. Thus the social worker, on the basis of the MMPI and other data, referred Bill to an agency that could help him.

Some Basic Problems in the Use of Personality Inventories

One of the basic problems in administering personality inventories is the amount of reading required. A student who is slow in reading may tire of the test and respond without careful consideration of the test item. In addition to the amount of reading, difficulty with words is a problem. If the vocabulary and abstractness of the ideas are beyond the student's comprehension, he may respond to the test item in a careless manner. Some tests, like the MMPI, have scales to detect this problem, but most others do not.

Another difficulty is the reluctance of some individuals to be honest in their answers. For most personality inventories the person must be honest in his response in order to get a valid picture. Studies have shown that most personality inventories can be faked. That is, the person with some psychological insight can give whatever picture of himself he desires. However, on the MMPI this is not as likely to happen, because there are scales that indicate whether or not a person is responding truthfully.

The problem of faking means that a student's scores on a personality inventory are subject to error, and the interpretation of these scores must be done with extreme caution. For example, let us suppose that a personality inventory is given to a ninth-grade boy who has been giving his teachers a difficult time. To this boy, teachers may be a symbol of authority against which he rebels. Therefore, if the test is given by a teacher or other authority figure, there is good chance that he will not be honest in his answers. Secondly, one must remember that pupils are taught to do their best on tests in school. This being the case, many children are not going to reveal their personal problems. Besides, some children who reveal a healthy adjustment on an inventory may in actuality be defensive and unable to reveal their real problems.

Remember also that personality inventories are middle class in thinking. Items often have different meanings for different socioeconomic levels and ethnic groups.

The educator should view the use of the personality inventory as only one step in attempting to ascertain the problems that interfere with a student's academic performance. Personality inventories may provide a quick gauge of what troubles the pupil. Most school counselors do not have the training required to administer more complex instruments such as projective devices, and they can use personality inventories as screening instruments in order to make intelligent referrals to appropriate resources in the community. Of all the inventories available, the MMPI is the most reliable and valid. Its judicious use by trained school personnel can facilitate behavioral analysis and lead to the proper handling of disturbed children. (For a technical review of the limitations and assets of personality inventories, see Megargee, 1966, Chapters 5, 6, and 7.)

Attitude Inventories

The attitude inventory is basically a self-report or questionnaire designed to measure a person's bias toward some group, social institution, social concept, or proposed action. One of the most common and primitive forms of this type of appraisal is the opinion poll. In such a poll a group of questions might be presented to a community on a facet of school policy and the results tabulated to express the consensus of community opinion.

The greatest use of attitude inventories has been in research endeavors which attempt to discover attitude differences, kinds of experiences that can change attitudes, and the influence of a man's attitudes on his view of the world. Thurstone (1959), for example, developed thirty scales for measuring attitudes toward war, Negroes, Chinese, capital punishment, church, censorship, and other practices, issues, and groups of people.

Minnesota Teacher Attitude Inventory

In a more immediate area of concern to educators is the Minnesota Teacher Attitude Inventory (Cook et al., 1951), designed to assess pupil-teacher relations. It is based on ten years of experimentation and standardized on teachers from different communities, schools, and grade levels. It is used in selecting teachers and in counseling student-teacher candidates. The range is from high school seniors through adulthood.

The following items are similar to those found in this inventory:

Most students are resourceful if you leave them on their own.
A teacher should never let his students know that he is ignorant of a topic.

This inventory is especially useful for research purposes, but a great deal of caution must be exercised in any practical usage such as counseling or selection.

Survey of Study Habits and Attitudes

Another attitude inventory of special interest to educators is the Survey of Study Habits and Attitudes (Brown and Holtzman, 1966). This survey was developed to help discover why some students with high scholastic aptitude do poorly in school, whereas others with only average ability do well. The authors recommend its usage as a:

1. *Screening instrument*. Administered to twelfth grade or college students at the beginning of the school year. Used later for individual counseling and as a technique to discover students who may need immediate help.
2. *Diagnostic instrument*. Provides format for systematic recording of student's feelings and practices involving schoolwork.
3. *Teaching aid*. In elementary courses in psychology and education to help communicate effective methods of study.
4. *Research tool*. In educational or counseling processes.

The student is presented with 100 statements in the Survey of Study Habits and Attitudes (SSHA) booklet and is asked to respond, in terms of a five-point scale, to each statement by choosing one of the following:

R—*Rarely*, 0 to 15 per cent of time
S—*Sometimes*, 16 to 35 per cent of time
F—*Frequently*, 36 to 65 per cent of time
G—*Generally*, 66 to 85 per cent of time
A—*Almost always,* 86 to 100 per cent of time

The following are some sample statements from the SSHA.[4]

I believe that teachers intentionally schedule tests on the days following important athletic or social activities.

I believe that a college's football reputation is just as important as its academic standing.

With me, studying is a hit-or-miss proposition depending on the mood I'm in.

I am careless of spelling and the mechanics of English composition when answering examination questions.

I believe that one way to get good grades is by using flattery on your teachers.

I think that it might be best for me to drop out of school and get a job.

Figure 33 presents a sample of a diagnostic profile for a college freshman. The profile includes the scales and what they mean.

[4] Reproduced by permission. Copyright 1953, © 1965, The Psychological Corporation, New York, N.Y. All rights reserved.

Allport-Vernon-Lindzey Study of Values

A different type of attitude inventory from those thus far cited is the Allport-Vernon-Lindzey Study of Values (1960).[5] The Study of Values was developed to measure the relative prominence of six basic interests, motives, and other evaluative attributes. The classification, based upon Spranger's *Types of Men* (1928), is as follows:

Theoretical. The basic interest of the theoretical type of man is the discovery of truth. In pursuing this objective, he takes a "cognitive" attitude, that is, he is empirical, rational, and critical in his "intellectual" approach to life.

Economic. The economic type of man is characterized by interest in what is useful and practical. This type is very similar to the stereotype of the average American businessman. This is the kind of man who wants education to be practical and looks upon pure research or unapplied data as wasteful.

Aesthetic. The aesthetic type of man places the highest value on form and harmony; his major interest is in the artistic facets of life; each unique experience is encountered from the point of view of grace or symmetry.

Social. The social type of man's highest value is altruistic love or philanthropy.

Political. The political type man is characterized by his dominant interest in power, influence, and renown. This man does not necessarily limit or engage in political activities per se; his power needs can be channelized in all sorts of activities and vocational pursuits.

Religious. The religious type of man is mystical, concerned with the cosmos as a whole and relating himself to its embracing totality.

The actual test is designed for college students and adults (with at least some college education) and consists of items based upon familiar situations to which alternative answers may be chosen. There is no time limit. The authors suggest three basic uses for the Study of Values:

1. Counseling, vocational guidance and selection.
2. Classroom demonstration. As a teaching aid in beginning courses in psychology, education, and so on.
3. Research. For investigation of group differences, changes in values, comparison with other attitude and interest scales, resemblances between peer groups and family, and so forth.

Two sample items with directions from the Study of Values follow:

[*Part I.* If the subject agrees with alternative (a) and disagrees with (b) he places 3 in the first box and 0 in the second box or vice versa.

---

[5] The classification of the Study of Values as an attitude inventory is arbitrary. Actually, it has a great deal in common with interest and personality instruments and could also be included under either designation. It is in fact a combination of all three types.

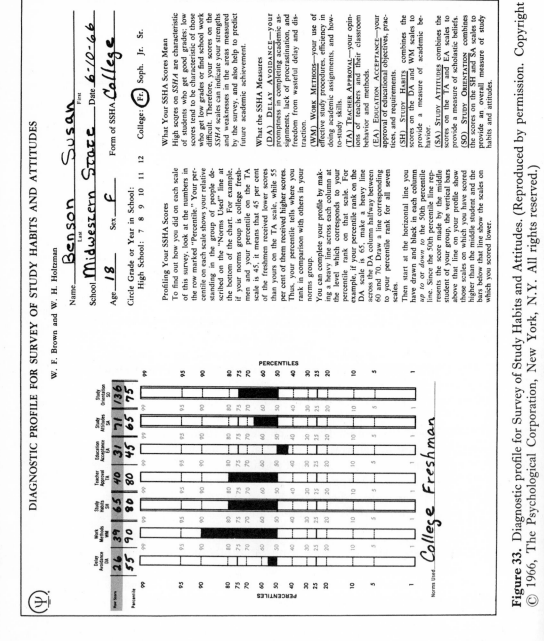

Figure 33. Diagnostic profile for Survey of Study Habits and Attitudes. (Reproduced by permission. Copyright © 1966, The Psychological Corporation, New York, N.Y. All rights reserved.)

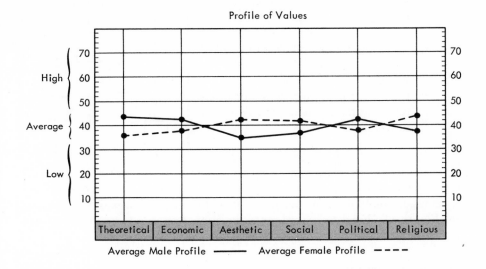

Figure 34. Average profiles of males and females on the Allport-Vernon-Lindzey Study of Values. (From *Allport-Vernon-Lindzey Study of Values.* (3rd ed.) by Gordon W. Allport, Phillip E. Vernon, and Gardner Lindzey. Copyright © 1960 by G. W. Allport, P. E. Vernon, and G. Lindzey. Reproduced by permission of Houghton Mifflin Co.)

If there is only a slight preference for one over the other, they are rated 2 and 1 respectively.]

Example[6]

When witnessing a gorgeous ceremony (ecclesiastical or academic, induction into office, etc.), are you more impressed: (a) by the color and pageantry of the occasion itself; (b) by the influence and strength of the group?

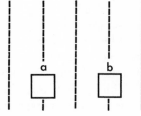

[*Part II*. The subject is asked to rate four possible attitudes or answers in order of personal preference, allocating 4 to the most attractive and 1 to the least attractive alternative.]

Example :

Do great exploits and adventures of discovery such as Columbus's, Magellan's, Byrd's and Amundsen's seem to you significant because—

a. they represent conquests by man over the difficult forces of nature

[6] From *Allport-Vernon-Lindzey Study of Values* (3rd ed.) by Gordon W. Allport, Phillip E. Vernon, and Gardner Lindzey. Copyright © 1960 by G. W. Allport, P. E. Vernon and G. Lindzey. Reproduced by permission of Houghton Mifflin Co.

b. they add to our knowledge of geography, meteorology, oceanography,
etc.

c. they weld human interests and international feelings throughout the
world

d. they contribute each in a small way
to an ultimate understanding of the
universe.

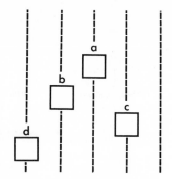

Scoring is an easy task because no key other than the simple instructions on the detachable page of the test booklet are required. Total scores on the six values are plotted on the profile presented on the last page of the booklet. (See Figure 34.) Final scores are reflective only of *relative* trends because it is impossible to obtain high or low scores in all areas.

Interest Inventories

Each person makes a variety of decisions regarding the type of activities in which he will participate. Some individuals show preferences for sports, and others spend their time in reading or pursuing such hobbies as building model airplanes. Thus each person shows a preference for some activities and little interest or even aversion to others. Measuring these tendencies to like or dislike certain activities is the main objective of the interest inventory.

Interest inventories are administered in the schools because it has been found that interests are related to academic success, job satisfaction, and eventual adjustment to and pleasure in adult life. For these reasons, it is important that every student have an understanding of his relative degree of interest in various activities. The counselor, in helping an individual student, wants the answers to such questions as, What are the interests of this pupil? How does his interest in science compare to his interest in social activities? How does his interest in a certain type of activity compare to those of other persons?

But why give interest tests when all one has to do is to ask the person his likes and dislikes? After all, no one knows John as well as John knows himself. John may state that he likes arithmetic or wants to be an engineer, but such expressions of interest are of limited value. Authorities investigating this problem suggest that "single" expressions of interest may be unreliable and lack permanence. An individual's statement that he is interested in being a fireman may be true when he is a certain age, but not necessarily true later in his life. People's interests are influenced by many factors, and their expressed interests may not represent their true desires and needs.

An adolescent from a middle-class community who is asked whether he is interested in going to college may answer affirmatively because he feels that it is the thing to do, although he really has little interest in a college education. He answers yes because the word *college* is a symbol of respect and status in his environment. Parental pressures and the desire for the prestige associated with the college graduate may have influenced his answer.

Fowler (1945), in an article dealing with the value of expressed interests of students, states,

> There are two chief arguments, both supported by ample studies, against dependence upon self-estimated interests in choosing an occupation. One of these arguments concerns the factors which interfere with making a realistic choice, factors leading students to declare occupational goals too hard to reach. . . . The second major argument . . . calls attention to the frequent disagreement between self-estimated and measured interests [p. 1].

In support of the preceding points one can add the experience of vocational counselors who deal with adults. It is not uncommon for the vocational counselor to see persons who are in occupations in which they claim to have interest but who are actually occupationally misfitted. For example, during a counseling session with a teenage boy, concerning future vocational plans, the boy stated, "I want to be in something I like—not like my father." During future counseling sessions the fact of the father's unhappiness in his job as an electrical engineer was repeated over and over. At the conclusion of the counseling sessions with the boy a conference with the father was arranged.

Mr. Snow, the boy's father, was a well-groomed man in his middle forties. He appeared to be a moderately successful man. He began the interview by asking about the progress of his son and stating, "I don't want my son to be unhappy in the profession he chooses. That's why I asked you to see him and give him tests and guidance. I've seen too many men in jobs they weren't suited for." The counselor asked him if he was happy in his work, and he replied that he was. Noticing an uneasiness in his reply, the counselor waited for him to continue. There was a long pause and then he sheepishly admitted that he wasn't really sure his answer was true. He rather reluctantly agreed to take an interest inventory.

On this particular test Mr. Snow scored high in the areas of social service and sales. His scientific and mechanical interests were considerably lower. When the results of the tests were discussed with him, he told how he had decided to become an engineer.

His father, who had been an engineer, died when Mr. Snow was in the second grade, and his mother had never remarried. Mr. Snow's mother always held up to her son the fact that his father had been a good man and would have liked his son to become an engineer. Therefore Mr. Snow never thought of any career but engineering. Because he did well in science and mathematics, it was assumed that engineering was a good vocational choice for him.

After the test results were presented to Mr. Snow, he admitted that he was unhappy in his work and missed the opportunity to work with people. After a series of counseling interviews, Mr. Snow talked to his employer and asked to be given a chance in engineering sales. His employer granted his request, and today Mr. Snow is much happier in his vocational situation. A year after the interviews he said, "I am a new man in this work. For the first time in my life, I can be happy when Monday comes and not dread going to work."

Of course, not all people who rely on self-estimates in selecting their occupations are unhappy with their choices; some are very happy. Self-estimates are, however, often poor indicators for future occupational placement. This is the reason the counselor attempts to look at more than what the individual says he wants to be or do in life.

As we have mentioned, a person's stated interests may not always mirror his true feelings. Thus professionals in this field construct their instruments to ask a variety of questions concerning the person's likes and dislikes. Questions such as whether he would rather read a book or go to the movies are asked rather than whether he would rather be a lawyer or a teacher.

In the following discussion of interest inventories we devote our major attention to the most widely used and respected instruments, the Strong Vocational Interest Blank and the Kuder interest inventories. We also briefly review a newer instrument, the Minnesota Vocational Interest Inventory, which is a departure from the classical models.

Strong Vocational Interest Blank

The Strong Vocational Interest Blank (SVIB) was first published in 1927 after several years of research; it has the longest continuous history of any widely used inventory. The inventory has been revised twice (1938 and 1966) since its initial publication.

The basic purpose of the SVIB is best described in the following introductory statements from the Manual (Campbell, 1966b),

> Men in different jobs have different interests. The *Strong Vocational Interest Blank* (SVIB) is a device to identify such differences among those occupations that college students usually enter. The SVIB accomplishes this by providing an index of the similarity between a person's interests and those of successful men (or women) in each of a wide range of occupations.
>
> The Strong Blank is designed to help guide the student and the employee into areas where they are likely to find the greatest job satisfaction. It is emphatically not a measure of general or specific abilities, including intelligence. Such traits—which are probably

> more related to a man's *performance* on a job than to his *satisfaction*
> there—should be determined by other means and considered along
> with interest measures and personal experiences in planning future
> careers [p. 1].

The SVIB is mainly middle-class in orientation in that it is most appropriate
for the professions and business and social-service occupations. It is not
usually administered to noncollege people because of the item content and
research data, which have been structured and focused on men and women
who have had some college education. The Manual (Campbell, 1966b)
recommends that "with people under 17 years of age, the test should be used
only with relatively mature boys and girls" (p. 2).

Administration of the SVIB is relatively simple. The individual is given
the booklet and an answer sheet and told to read the questions and respond
to them according to the directions. Most people take from thirty to fifty
minutes to complete the inventory; there is no time limit. There are 399
items. The SVIB may be scored by hand, although this is a laborious task,
or by four different test-scoring services.

The men's form was revised in 1966, and comparable research for a future
revision of the women's form is now underway. Let us direct our attention
to the men's form as illustrative of the basic content and format of the SVIB.

The booklet is divided into eight sections. The first section (100 items)
presents items (occupational titles) such as those in Figure 35, to which the
subject is asked to respond by indicating one of three possible responses,
"Like," "Dislike," or "Indifferent."

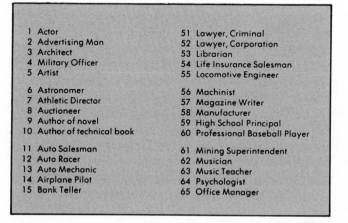

Figure 35. Example of items from men's SVIB booklet (Form T399) (Reprinted
from *Manual for Strong Vocational Interest Blanks for Men and Women* by Edward
K. Strong, Jr., revised by David P. Campbell with the permission of the publishers,
Stanford University Press. Copyright © 1959, 1966 by the Board of Trustees of the
Leland Stanford Junior University.)

The other seven sections and their contents are as follows:

Section 2 (thirty-six items). School subjects.

Section 3 (forty-eight items). Amusements and hobbies.

Section 4 (forty-eight items). Occupational activities.

Section 5 (forty-seven items). Feelings toward different kinds of people, for example, "military men," "energetic people."

Section 6 (forty items). Student is presented with ten items and requested to select the three he least prefers.

Section 7 (forty items). Student is presented with pairs of activities and asked to indicate in each case which he prefers or he may state he likes both.

Section 8 (thirty-nine items). Student is asked to respond to such statements as "am always on time with my work" or "win friends easily" by checking "Yes" (it is true of me), "?" (cannot say), or "No" (it is not true of me).

There are fifty-nine scales for the men's form; thirty-four scales for the women's form. The student's scores are presented on a specially devised profile form. Figure 36 shows the men's profile form, illustrating the scales with an actual profiled case.

High scores are those over 45 and low scores those under 25. To clarify the use of the SVIB in an actual school situation the following case from the Manual (Campbell, 1966b) is presented:[7]

This 18-year-old college student sought counseling near the end of his freshman year to determine whether "I should continue with or change my major," which was engineering. He was maintaining about a C average but complained of being bored by the courses.

In high school his favorite subjects had been mathematics and science, his principal avocation music (he was an accomplished pianist). His mother was a free-lance writer, his father an artistic person who had been variously engaged in interior decorating and window display work.

On the College Entrance Examination Board, using national norms, he ranked at the 27th percentile on the verbal test and at the 90th percentile on mathematics aptitude. On a test of mechanical comprehension, he ranked at the 60th percentile of engineering freshmen; on a test of spatial visualization, at the 93rd percentile. On an art judgment test, he scored on the 54th percentile of art students. On the Minnesota Multiphasic Personality Inventory, he had a peak of

[7] Reprinted from *Manual for Strong Vocational Interest Blanks for Men and Women* by Edward K. Strong, Jr., revised by David P. Campbell, with the permission of the publishers, Stanford University Press. Copyright © 1959, 1966 by the Board of Trustees of the Leland Stanford Junior University.

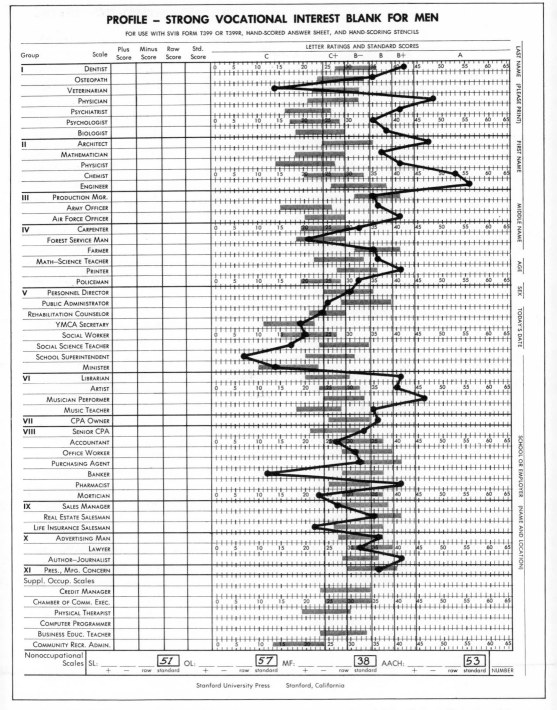

Figure 36. An example of a SVIB profile. (Reprinted from *Manual for Strong Vocational Interest Blanks for Men and Women* by Edward K. Strong, Jr., revised by David P. Campbell with the permission of the publishers, Stanford University Press. Copyright © 1959, 1966 by the Board of Trustees of the Leland Stanford Junior University.)

76 on masculinity–feminity, suggesting more "feminine" interests and attitudes than usual, especially for engineering students.

His profile on the Strong Vocational Interest Blank (Fig. 36) yielded high scores scattered through several groups. He showed very strong resemblance to engineers and chemists, architects, physicians, and musicians. In discussing the results, the counselor pointed out that though engineering seemed compatible with his interests and aptitudes, perhaps it might conflict with some of his values and personality traits. The client observed that engineering "isn't very creative" and that he found many fellow engineering students rather unexciting personalities. He inquired about physics as a possible major and was advised that his profile gave little reason to suppose it would be better for him than engineering. The counselor suggested that he consider architecture and provided him with occupational information in this field.

In his evaluation of the SVIB profile, the counselor judged that the high scores in artist, architect, and musician represented some creative–artistic element in the client's make-up and felt that the MF scores on both the SVIB and the MMPI tended to support this interpretation. The client had had excellent exposure to music and had rejected it as a career. Neither had he shown any willingness to pursue the biological sciences. The counselor felt that architecture might fulfill his creative–artistic needs while calling upon his engineering background, his superior mathematical aptitude, and his talent for spatial visualization. The client tried courses in architecture, liked them, and transferred to that department. He received his bachelor's degree in pre-architecture with a superior record despite his mediocre scholastic aptitude score. He was offered an apprenticeship with an architect of international reputation on the basis of some sample work and was thoroughly pleased with his vocational decision.

This case, of course, provides only one small illustration of how the SVIB is used to help students. The profiles are never (or at least should not be) handed to the student. In a one-to-one setting, the counselor should explain the meaning of the scores interpreted in the light of other data and should counsel accordingly. For a more definitive explanation of the SVIB in terms of content, counseling uses, and technical data, see Campbell, 1966b, and Super and Crites, 1962. In addition, the studies by Harmon (1968) and Dolliver (1968) deal with the development and possible limitations of the SVIB.

The long history of the SVIB has provided an opportunity to compare data on men tested in the 1930's with that on men tested in the 1960's. Some reports on these studies have already been published. For example, one study was a comparison between the SVIB profile of 100 bankers who took the inventory in 1934 and a similar 100 bankers (same jobs and exactly the same banks as the 1934 bankers) tested in 1964. The two profiles were very similar, which seems to indicate that bankers of the 1960's share similar patterns to those of the 1930's (Campbell, 1966a).

Campbell (1968) in a review of some of the thirty-year comparisons states four main findings:

1. Several items on the SVIB show shifts in popularity in the last thirty years.
2. A single scale may be constructed to discriminate between occupations tested in the 1930's and those tested in the 1960's.
3. Positively related to extroverted activities and negatively to blue-collar and outdoor activities.
4. General shift of the population toward more verbal activities while outdoor and skilled trades activities are less popular. Interests in other areas seem to be at about the same level.

Kuder Interest Inventories

The first Kuder Preference Record was published in 1939. It was a vocational interest inventory constructed to yield seven independent scores on the following scales: Literary, Scientific, Artistic, Persuasive, Social Service, Musical, and Computational. The second record form (Preference Record Form B) rectified many of the faults of the first; for instance, the amount of reading required for each choice was cut in half. Two scales were also added, Mechanical and Clerical.

The third form (Preference Record C) added a Verification scale. This scale was composed of responses that almost everyone selects and a score to find those who did not answer items carefully was derived. Because users of Form B requested a scale measuring interest in agricultural, naturalist, and outdoor activities, a study was begun to see if such a scale could be developed. The result was a new scale, Outdoor, which was included in Form C (Kuder, 1964).

Two more forms since Form C have been developed and published. Form E came first as a logical continuation of, although not necessarily a replacement for, Form C. Form E used simpler language and was developed with younger children in mind. The items showed little resemblance to Form C (Kuder, 1964). The latest addition is the Kuder DD Occupational Interest Survey (Kuder, 1966a). Its format is quite different from the other Kuder inventories. It has a new scoring technique and compares a person's interests with other persons in specific vocations. We shall briefly review Form C and the Occupational Survey, leaving the bulk of our attention for Form E, which has the most direct meaning for school personnel.

KUDER PREFERENCE RECORD FORM C

This inventory has been widely used in the schools for a good many years. It is usually given in the ninth or tenth grade. The inventory consists of 168 questions. Each question is made up of three choices of activity, to which the person taking the test must respond by choosing the one he likes most and the one he likes least. Figure 37 illustrates the actual set of instructions and sample problems. There is no time limit. The average time for high school students has been found to be around thirty minutes to one hour and for college students approximately forty minutes. Scoring may be done by hand if pins are used (Form CH, see Figure 37). The directions are easy to follow and students may score the inventory themselves.

There are two profile sheets available for use in interpreting the nine scales and the Verification scale. One profile sheet contains the norms for boys and girls in grades nine through twelve and the other presents norms for men and women. The examiner first checks the Verification score to see whether the inventory has been carefully completed. Next, he locates the highest score, the two highest, or in some cases even the three highest. (There are many possible combinations—even no high scores). He then consults an occupational table which lists the scales and the various possible professions and vocations under that scale. For example (Kuder, 1960),

> *Scientific*
>   *Professional:*
>   Chemist
>   County Agricultural Agent
>   Dentist
>   *Semiprofessional:*
>   Aviator
>   Weather Observer
>   *Clerical and Kindred:*
>   Physician's Assistant
>   *Protective Service:*
>   Detective

Form C may be used to help youngsters identify occupations they are interested in for further study and as a check on their choice of occupation to see whether it is consistent with the type of thing they ordinarily prefer to do.

KUDER E GENERAL INTEREST SURVEY

This instrument, according to Kuder (1964), was constructed in response to the need for an interest inventory to be used with younger students, especially at the junior high level. Language was kept to a sixth-grade level. In addition, other innovations were developed such as an improved scale for finding careless responses, lack of understanding, or faking. On the

KUDER PREFERENCE RECORD
VOCATIONAL
FORM CH

Prepared by G. Frederic Kuder, Editor, *Educational and Psychological Measurement*

Professor of Psychology, Duke University

This blank is used for obtaining a record of your preferences. It is not a test. There are no right or wrong answers. An answer is right if it is true of you.

A number of activities are listed in groups of three. Read over the three activities in each group. Decide which of the three activities you like **most**. There are two circles on the same line as this activity. Punch a hole with the pin through the left-hand circle following this activity. Then decide which activity you like **least** and punch a hole through the right-hand circle of the two circles following this activity.

In the examples below, the person answering has indicated for the first group of three activities, that he would usually like to **visit a museum most**, and **browse in a library least**. In the second group of three activities he has indicated he would ordinarily like to **collect autographs most** and **collect butterflies least**.

EXAMPLES

Put your answers to these questions in column O.

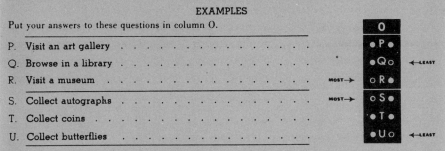

P. Visit an art gallery . . . .

Q. Browse in a library . . . . ←LEAST

R. Visit a museum . . . . MOST→

S. Collect autographs . . . . MOST→

T. Collect coins . . . .

U. Collect butterflies . . . . ←LEAST

Some of the activities involve preparation and training. In such cases, please suppose that you could first have the necessary training. Do not choose an activity merely because it is new or unusual. Choose what you would like to do if you were equally familiar with all of the activities.

In some cases you may like all three activities in a group. In other cases you may find all three activities unpleasant. Please show what your first and last choices would be, however, if you *had* to choose.

Some activities may seem trivial or foolish. Please indicate your choices, anyway, for all of the groups. Otherwise we cannot give you a complete report. Your answers will be kept strictly confidential.

Please do not spend a lot of time on one group. Put down your first reaction and go on. Do not discuss the activities with anyone. An answer is worthless unless it is your own judgment.

Figure 37. Instructions and sample problems from Kuder Preference Record Vocational (From *Kuder Preference Record Vocational Form CH* by Frederic Kuder. Copyright 1948, by G. Frederic Kuder. Reprinted by permission of the publisher, Science Research Associates, Inc., Chicago, Illinois.)

technical side longer scales were constructed because younger student's responses tend to be less reliable.

There are 168 items on this form. The instructions and format are very similar to Form C. Figure 37 also serves as an illustration of Form E's general instructions and items. It generally takes forty-five to sixty minutes to administer; however, there is no definite time limit. Hand scoring is similar to that of Form C.

The student can score and plot his own profile by following the directions on the Profile Leaflet provided. The first step is to check the Verification score. Students whose scores on this scale are under a certain number (15) may proceed to construct their profiles. Scores over the prescribed number indicate that the student's responses may not be valid.

Figure 38 presents a portion of the Leaflet for grades 6 to 8. The Profile Leaflet also contains an interpretation of the various scales. A major portion of this interpretation follows. Note that it is directed to the student to help him understand the meaning of his scores.

Interpreting Your Interest Profile[8]

You are interested in something if you enjoy doing it. Your interest profile indicates whether your interests in the ten areas measured are high, average, or low compared with those of other boys or girls at your grade level across the nation.

A score above the top dotted line in any column is a high score. It means that you have indicated a preference for activities in that area more frequently than most young people at your grade level. (The percentile on the same line as your score for an interest area tells you what percentage of students expressed preference for activities in that area less frequently than you did.) A score between the two dotted lines means that your interest in the area represented is about average. A score below the bottom dotted line is a low score. It indicates that you have not expressed preference for activities in that area as often as most young people.

Like most people, you probably have scores that are high in some areas, low in some, and average in others. Looking at *all* your scores is important, because most school subjects and jobs involve a combination of two or more interests.

The more interested you are in a school subject, a job, or anything you do, the greater your chances are for success in it. It is easier and more satisfying to put your efforts into activities you enjoy than into those you dislike. Of course, no one can do *only* what interests him.

[8] From *Profile Leaflet Grades 6–8*, Kuder E. © 1963, G. Frederic Kuder. Reprinted by permission of the publisher, Science Research Associates, Inc., Chicago, Illinois.

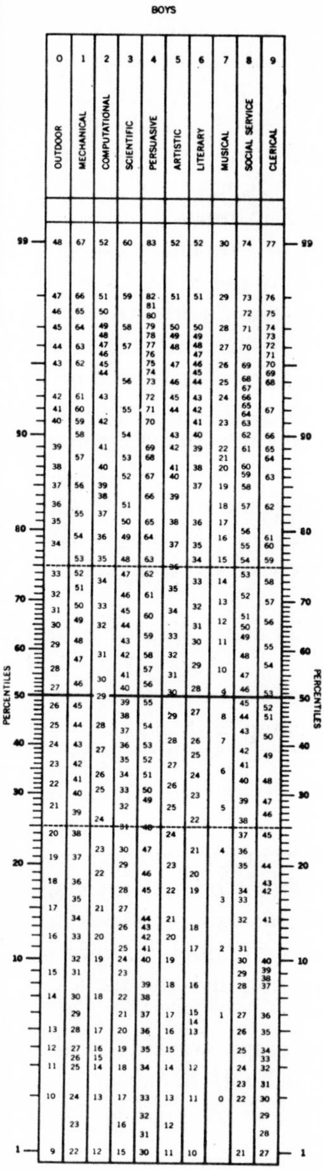

BOYS

GIRLS

HOW TO PROFILE YOUR SCORES

To get a picture, or profile, of your scores, follow the directions below carefully, using the profile form at the left if you are a boy and the one at the right if you are a girl.

1. Look at your V score on the back page of your answer pad.* If it is 15 or over, tell the teacher or counselor who has given you the *Kuder General Interest Survey*. He may want you to take it again, because a high V score usually means that something has gone wrong and there is some question concerning the value of your other scores. If your V score is *less* than 15, go on to Step 2.

2. Copy the scores for scales 0 through 9 from your answer pad in the boxes at the top of the profile chart. Be sure to put the scores in the correct boxes.

3. In each column, find the number that is the same as your score in the box at the top of that column. Draw a line through the number from one side of the column to the other. If your score is higher than the highest number in the column, draw a line across the top of the column. If your score is lower than the lowest number in the column, draw a line across the bottom.

4. With pencil, blacken the entire space between the line you have drawn in the OUTDOOR column and the bottom of the chart. Do the same for the other columns.

Now you have a profile of your interests in the ten areas listed across the top of the chart. Of what use is the profile to you?

*If you did not use a pin-punch answer pad, your counselor or teacher will give you your scores.

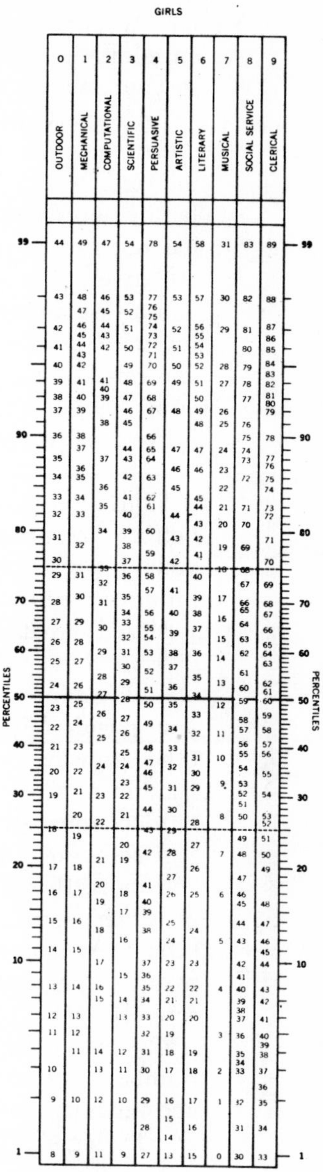

Figure 38. Profile leaflet for Kuder General Interest Survey. (From *Profile Leaflet Grades 6–8*, Kuder E. © 1963, G. Frederic Kuder. Reprinted by permission of the publisher, Science Research Associates, Inc., Chicago, Illinois.)

Studying your interests, however, will help you direct your activities mainly into channels where you are more likely to achieve satisfaction. In addition, such study may help you find some things that appeal to your interests even in chores that you dislike.

An important fact to keep in mind is that low scores sometimes mean that you haven't had enough of an opportunity to develop interests in certain areas. Imagine, for example, a young person whose family and friends are not particularly interested in music, and who has not had an opportunity to learn to play an instrument, to listen attentively to records, or to go to concerts. He may not score as high in musical interest as someone who has had more experience with music. You have to be introduced to or discover an activity before you can like it or dislike it. Participating in something you've decided you might like may in turn tend to strengthen your interest in it. As you mature and are exposed to a variety of new experiences, some of your old interests may change and some new ones may develop.

High interests are not *better* than low interests; nor is one interest better—or worse—than another. What counts is knowing what your interests are and considering them whenever you have an important educational or vocational decision to make.

Here is what the ten interest areas measured by the *Kuder General Interest Survey* mean.

Outdoor interest means preference for work or activity that keeps you outside most of the time—usually work dealing with plants and other growing things, animals, fish, and birds. Foresters, naturalists, fishermen, telephone linemen, and farmers are among those high in outdoor interest.

Mechanical interest means preference for working with machines and tools. If you like to tinker with old clocks, repair broken objects, or watch a garage mechanic at work, you might enjoy shop courses in school. Aviator, toolmaker, machinist, plumber, autombobile repairman, and engineer are among the many jobs involving high mechanical interest.

Computational interest indicates a preference for working with numbers and an interest in math courses in school. Bookkeepers, accountants, bank tellers, engineers, and many kinds of scientists are usually high in computational interest.

Scientific interest is an interest in the discovery or understanding of nature and the solution of problems, particularly with regard to the physical world. If you have a high score in this area, you probably enjoy working in the science lab, reading science articles, or doing science experiments as a hobby. Physician, chemist, engineer, laboratory technician, meteorologist, dietitian, and aviator are among the occupations involving high scientific interest.

Persuasive interest is an interest in meeting and dealing with people, in convincing others of the justice of a cause or a point of view, or in promoting projects or things to sell. Most salesmen, personnel managers, and buyers have high persuasive interest. If you have a high score in this area, you may enjoy such activities as debating, selling tickets for a school play or dance, or selling advertising space for the school paper.

Artistic interest indicates a preference for doing creative work with the hands—usually work involving design, color, and materials. If you like to paint, draw, sculpture, decorate a room, design clothes, or work on sets for school plays, you are probably high in this interest. So are artists, sculptors, dress designers, architects, hairdressers, and interior decorators.

Literary interest is an interest in reading and writing. Persons with literary interest include novelists, English teachers, poets, editors, news reporters, and librarians. If you have a high score on the literary scale, English is probably one of your favorite subjects, and you may enjoy writing for the school paper or magazine.

Musical interest usually is demonstrated by persons who enjoy going to concerts, playing an instrument, singing, or reading about music and musicians. Musicians, music teachers, and music critics are among those who have directed high musical interest into a vocation.

Social Service interest indicates a preference for activities that involve helping people. Nurses, Boy Scout or Girl Scout leaders, vocational counselors, tutors, personnel workers, social workers, hospital attendants, and ministers, rabbis, and others in religious service are among those high in this interest area.

Clerical interest means a preference for work that is clearly defined for you—work that involves specific tasks requiring precision and accuracy. If you have high clerical interest, you probably enjoy school subjects and activities that require attention to detail. Jobs such as bookkeeper, accountant, file clerk, salesclerk, statistician, teacher of commercial subjects, and traffic manager fall in this area.

The ten interest areas discussed here are not the *only* ones; nor is the classification system used the only one possible (for example, interests may be classified by specific occupations or by preferences for certain kinds of personal situations). The interest areas described, however, are the ones that will mean most to you in making decisions about school subjects and broad fields of work to explore.

Scores in related interest areas are much higher for some occupations than for others. For example, authors, editors, and reporters are at the 97th percentile in literary interest. Musicians and music teachers are at the 99th percentile in musical interest. Mechanics and repairmen, on the other hand, are at the 65th percentile in mechanical interest—their highest score; and surgeons are at the 75th percentile in scientific interest.

Some occupational groups have scores nearly as high—or higher—in apparently unrelated interest areas as in related areas. In one survey the highest percentile for lawyers and judges was 82, on the literary scale. The next was 61, on both the musical and the clerical scales. In another survey the second-highest interest for surgeons was outdoor interest, with a percentile of 68. Their next-highest interest was literary, with a percentile of 66. The main reason for results of this type is that people often have more than one strong interest. They may go into a career that makes use of their combined interests, or they may direct one or more of their strong interests into a satisfying after-work activity that provides a change of pace and broadens the range of their activities. Businessmen may find relaxation and a chance to get away from people and pressures in such activities as hunting and fishing. One retail salesman, for example, may enjoy many do-it-yourself activities involving high mechanical interest. Another may enjoy fishing or gardening or acting in a community theater. A businessman may, in his free time, play in a string quartet, paint or sculpture, or engage in some other kind of activity not clearly related to the work he performs for a living.

Knowledge of your interests can tell you only what you *enjoy* doing; *it cannot tell you how well you do these things*. What you do well depends on many things besides interest—particularly, your abilities. Your counselor can help you find out whether your abilities measure up to your interests. He can help you with your decisions about what course of study and school subjects to take. Your counselor may also be able to suggest ways in which you can explore and broaden your interests—extracurricular activities you might enjoy, books appropriate to your interests, and kinds of part-time or summer jobs you might want to consider. At various points during your school years—especially before making plans for college or a job—you may want to reexamine your interests. Your counselor can suggest other Kuder interest inventories for this purpose.

The Survey is not intended to be the basis of vocational choice. It is intended as background information to be utilized in the whole process of choosing a career. In the seventh and eighth grades the Survey can help students choose electives, high school courses, and areas of study, for example, college track or commercial track. In the ninth or tenth grade the Survey provides the opportunity for the student to re-examine his interests, plan his high school program, or, if he has decided to drop out of school, help in choosing immediate vocational pursuits.

The relationship of Form E to Form C was studied. Correlations were obtained ranging from 0.69 to 0.82 for boys, with a median of 0.76; and from 0.65 to 0.86 for girls, with a median of 0.79 (Kuder, 1964). For definitive data on validity, reliability, and other technical information see the Manual (Kuder, 1964) and Buros (1965).

Kuder DD Occupational Interest Survey (*OIS*)

This interest inventory is primarily geared for high school juniors and seniors to help them make immediate vocational or educational choices. It also may be used with college freshmen and adults in employment counseling, placement centers, and Job Corps type programs (Kuder, 1966b).

The format of the items is very similar to that of the other Kuder inventories. There are 100 sets of three activities each, and the student is asked to indicate his preference by marking one "most" and one "least" for each set. The scores are reported and plotted on a special table. See Figure 39 for a sample report. The results show the degree to which the student's preferences resemble those typical of people in various occupations and areas of study. About 80 per cent of the people in the occupations and areas of study listed (satisfied with their vocations) obtain scores of 0.45 or more on the scale for their job or area of study (Kuder, 1966b).

An important feature of the OIS is the fact that scores for it represent the correlation of a person's interest with those of people in a number of specifically defined occupations. (The person's scores for these occupations are compared directly with each other.) This is a departure from other Kuder inventories, which are based on a general reference group. (See discussion on technical aspects of inventories at the end of this chapter.) In addition, the verification score is improved and should lead to the identification of faking or misunderstanding.

A Final Word on the Kuder Inventories

A common denominator of all the instruments is the forced-choice format—the student must answer "most" or "least" to three possible activities. They all share a heritage of many years of dedicated research and analysis since the publication of the first inventory in 1939. With all the research done by Kuder and his associates as well as by independent investigators, it is of interest to note the following caution in interpreting the results of any of the Kuder instruments (or any instrument, for that matter):

> Factors other than ability may make it unfeasible for a subject to give serious consideration to an occupation or field of study in which he has high interest scores. For example, a student with a high score on the Farmer scale, for whom moving into a rural area is highly unrealistic, should not regard farming as a good possibility for him to explore. In any case the student should not feel pressured to pursue investigation of a particular field, regardless of how high his interest scores or how great his abilities in that field. The principal purpose of his scores is to point out promising possibilities for future occupations or studies, from the point of view of his own pattern of interests.

Report of Scores — Kuder Occupational Interest Survey

(FORM DD)

NAME SEAVILLE SALLY LOCATION ________ DATE OF SURVEY ________

OCCUPATIONAL SCALES WOMEN		Score
Accountant	XXX	.32
Bank Clerk	XXX	.32
Beautician	XXXX	.37
Bookkeeper	XX	.28
Bookstore Manager	XXXX	.37
Computer Programmer		
Counselor, High School	XXXXX	.40
Dean of Women	XXXXX	.42
Dental Assistant	XXXX	.39
Department Store Saleswoman	XXXX	.36
Dietitian, Administrative	XXXXXX	.45
Dietitian, Public School	XXXXX	.43
Florist	XXXX	.39
Home Demonstration Agent	XXXX	.38
Home Ec Teacher, College	XXXXX	.43
Interior Decorator	XXX	.32
Lawyer	XXXX	.36
Librarian	XXX	.30
Math Teacher, High School	XXX	.31
Nurse	XXXXX	.41
Nutritionist	XXXXXX	.46
Occupational Therapist	XXXXX	.40
Office Clerk	XXX	.30
Physical Therapist	XXXXXX	.48
Primary School Teacher	XXX	.31
Psychologist	XXXX	.38
Psychologist, Clinical	XXXX	.39
Religious Educ Director	XXXXX	.41
Sci Teacher, High School	XXXX	.39
Secretary	XXX	.32
Social Caseworker	XXXXX	.40
Social Worker, Group	XXXXX	.42
Social Worker, Medical	XXXXX	.41
Social Worker, Psychiatric	XXXX	.39
Social Worker, School	XXXXX	.41
Stenographer	XXX	.30
X-Ray Technician	XXXXX	.44

COLLEGE MAJOR SCALES WOMEN		Score
Art & Art Education	XXXX	.35
Biological Sciences	XXXXXX	.46
Bus Ed & Commerce		
Drama		
Elementary Education	XXXXX	.42
English	XXXX	.35
Foreign Languages	XXXXX	.42
General Social Sciences	XXXXXX	.45
Health Professions		
History	XXXXX	.43
Home Economics Education	XXXXXX	.47
Mathematics	XXXXX	.43
Music & Music Education	XXXXXX	.48
Nursing	XXXXXXX	.50
Physical Education		
Political Science		
Psychology	XXXXX	.43
Sociology		
Teaching Sister, Catholic		

OCCUPATIONAL SCALES MEN		Score
Acc't, Certified Public		
Architect	XXX	.32
Automobile Mechanic		
Automobile Salesman		
Banker		
Bookkeeper		
Bookstore Manager		
Bricklayer		
Building Contractor		
Buyer	XXX	.34
Carpenter		
Chemist	XXXX	.35
Clothier, Retail		
Computer Programmer		
Counselor, High School		
County Agricultural Agent		
Dentist	XXXX	.39
Electrician		
Engineer, Civil	XXX	.30
Engineer, Electrical		
Engineer, Heating/Air Cond		
Engineer, Industrial		
Engineer, Mechanical		
Engineer, Mining & Metal		
Farmer		
Florist		
Forester		
Insurance Agent	XXXX	.35
Interior Decorator		
Journalist	X	.22
Lawyer		
Librarian		
Machinist		
Mathematician	XXX	.32
Math Teacher, High School		
Meteorologist		
Minister		
Nurseryman		
Optometrist	XXXX	.38
Osteopath		
Painter, House		
Pediatrician	XXXX	.39
Personnel Manager	XXXX	.37
Pharmaceutical Salesman		
Pharmacist	XXXXX	.43
Photographer	XXXX.	.37
Physical Therapist		
Physician	XXXX	.39
Plumber		
Plumbing Contractor		
Podiatrist		
Policeman		
Postal Clerk		
Printer		
Psychiatrist	XXXX	.38
Psychologist, Clinical		
Psychologist, Counseling		
Psychologist, Industrial		
Psychology Professor	XXX	.34
Radio Station Manager		
Real Estate Agent	XXX	.33
Sales Eng, Heating/Air Cond		
Sci Teacher, High School		
School Superintendent		
Social Caseworker		
Social Worker, Group		
Social Worker, Psychiatric		
Statistician	XXX	.32
Supv/Foreman, Industrial		
Travel Agent	XXXX	.38
Truck Driver		
Television Repairman		
University Pastor		
Veterinarian	XXXX	.35
Welder		
X-Ray Technician		
YMCA Secretary		

COLLEGE MAJOR SCALES MEN		Score
Agriculture	XXX	.33
Animal Husbandry		
Architecture	XXX	.32
Art & Art Education		
Biological Sciences		
Business: Acc't & Finance	XX	.28
Business & Marketing	XXX	.33
Business Management		
Economics	XXX	.34
Elementary Education		
Engineering, Chemical	XXXX	.35
Engineering, Civil	XXX	.31
Engineering, Electrical	XXX	.33
Engineering, Mechanical	XXX	.31
English		
Foreign Languages		
Forestry		
History		
Law (Grad School)		
Mathematics		
Music & Music Ed		
Physical Education		
Physical Sciences	XXXX	.36
Political Science & Govt	XXXX	.35
Premed, Pharm & Dentistry	XXXXX	.43
Psychology		
Sociology		
U.S. Air Force Cadet		
U.S. Military Acad Cadet		

V 51

M ____ S ____

MBI ____ F ____

W ____ D ____

WBI . Mo

7-3696

Figure 39. Sample report form for Kuder Occupational Interest Survey. (From *Kuder DD Occupational Interest Survey Interpretive Leaflet*: Grades 11–12. © 1966, G. Frederic Kuder. Reprinted by permission of the publishers, Science Research Associates, Inc., Chicago, Illinois.)

The scores should help him make decisions by suggesting a variety of choices to explore; they should under no circumstances be regarded as pointing to the only possible paths open to him [Kuder, 1966a, p. 4].

Minnesota Vocational Interest Inventory

The Minnesota Vocational Interest Inventory (MVII) provides information on the interest patterns of men in *nonprofessional occupations*. It is intended as a guidance tool for counselors working with students and other individuals who are planning vocations in the semiskilled and skilled occupations (Clark and Campbell, 1965). Individual scores represent the similarity of the interests of the person taking the MVII to those of men in a variety of nonprofessional occupations.

The MVII has 158 sets of three items to which the person responds by choosing the item he would like to do most and the item he would like to do least. The actual format is the same as the Kuder Form C in terms of the triads of three items and the task of selecting one most and one least desired activity (forced-choice method). Figure 40 presents the profile sheet used in plotting the results. The shaded bands reveal the scores of the middle third of a group of skilled tradesmen.

In interpreting the results, a written explanation (on the other side of the profile sheet) is given to help the student understand the meaning of the scales and his scores on them. Scoring may be done by hand or machine. There is no time limit. Most individuals are able to complete the inventory in less than forty-five minutes (Clark and Campbell, 1965).

Practical Implications of Interest Inventories

Many studies concerning the relationship between interest and ability have been made. Most of them show a slight relationship between academic achievement in a field and interest in it. There is also some indication that those of high ability in a certain field will show some interest in it. However, this relationship is too low for us to state that an interest inventory can be used to determine ability or, on the other hand, that an ability or achievement test can reveal interest. The counselor must have both types of information for sound vocational counseling. It is important, therefore, to remember that if a student has a high score in scientific interest, it does not necessarily mean that he has the ability to become a scientist. In making a vocational choice, the interest pattern of a student must be viewed along with his past academic record and achievement and aptitude test scores.

Let us examine an actual counseling situation to see how interest inventories are used. Ralph Laine, counselor at Education High School, is thinking about one of his students. The boy, Jerry, is attempting to decide on a career. His highest interest scores are in mechanical and artistic areas. Mr. Laine,

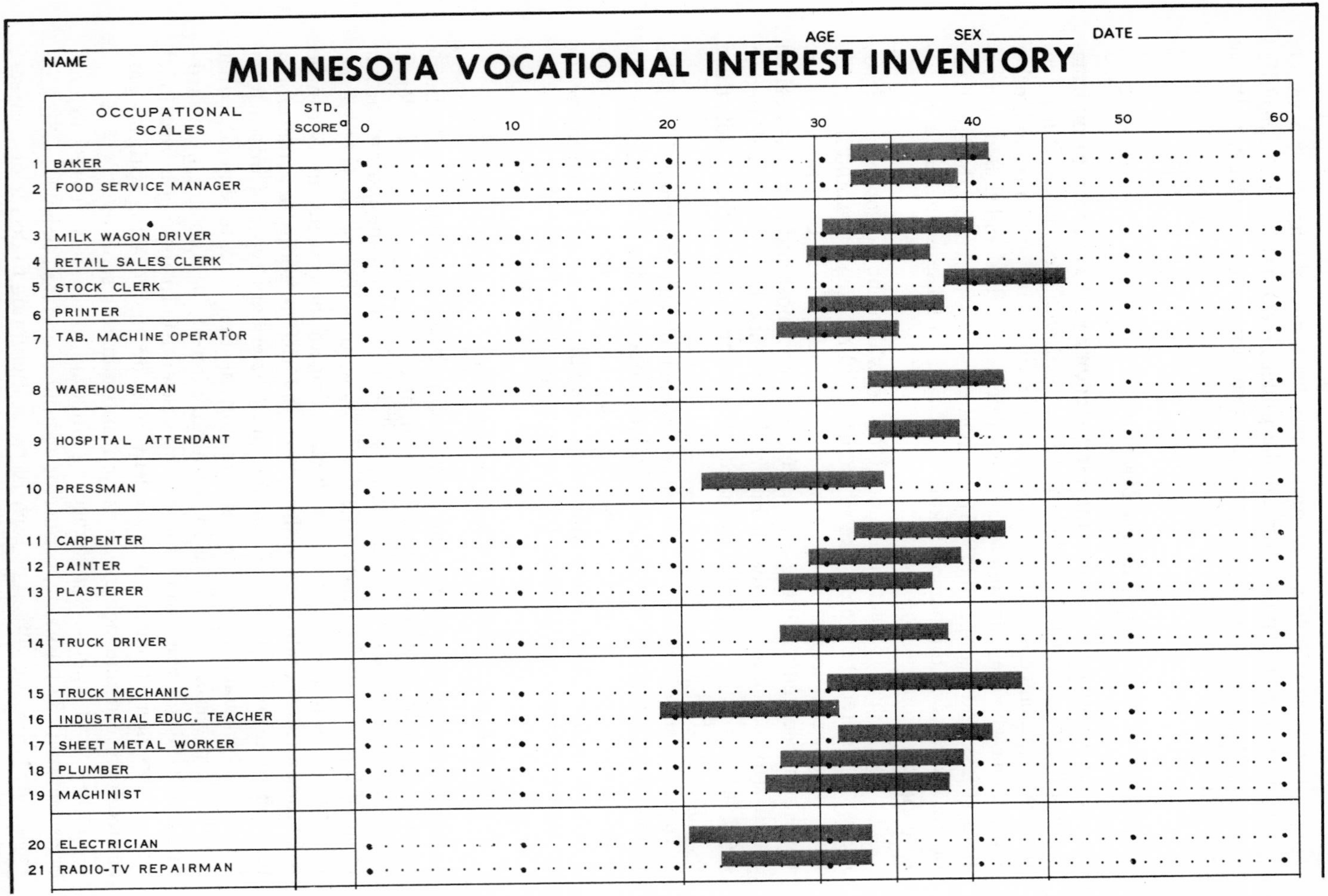

MINNESOTA VOCATIONAL INTEREST INVENTORY

NAME

AGE _____ SEX _____ DATE _____

| STD. SCORE a | 0 | 10 | 20 | 30 | 40 | 50 | 60 |

OCCUPATIONAL SCALES

1 BAKER
2 FOOD SERVICE MANAGER
3 MILK WAGON DRIVER
4 RETAIL SALES CLERK
5 STOCK CLERK
6 PRINTER
7 TAB. MACHINE OPERATOR
8 WAREHOUSEMAN
9 HOSPITAL ATTENDANT
10 PRESSMAN
11 CARPENTER
12 PAINTER
13 PLASTERER
14 TRUCK DRIVER
15 TRUCK MECHANIC
16 INDUSTRIAL EDUC. TEACHER
17 SHEET METAL WORKER
18 PLUMBER
19 MACHINIST
20 ELECTRICIAN
21 RADIO-TV REPAIRMAN

362

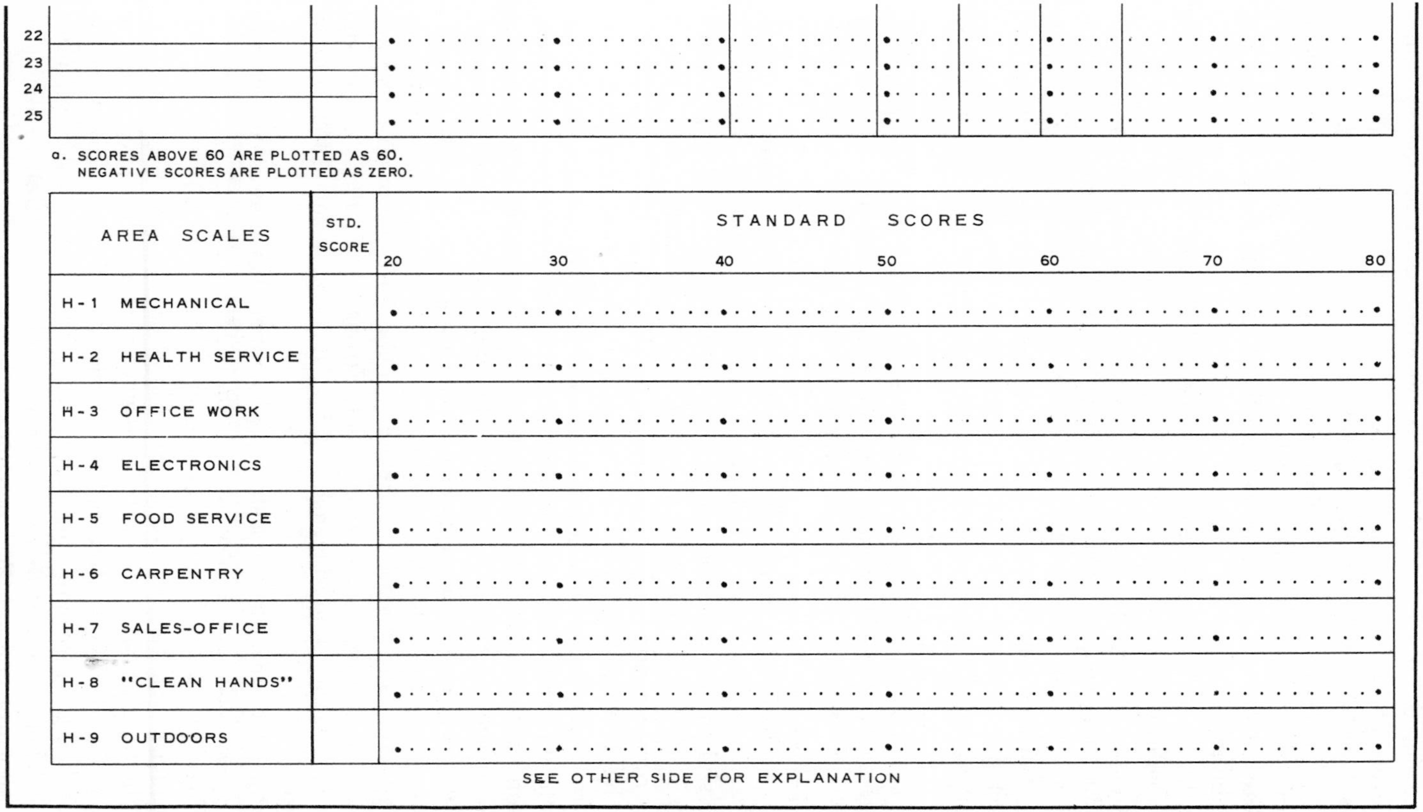

Figure 40. MVII profile sheet. (Reproduced by permission. Copyright © 1965. The Psychological Corporation, New York, N.Y. All rights reserved.)

after reviewing the results of the interest inventory, looks up Jerry's ability and achievement test scores as well as his class record. He does this because he knows that ability as well as interest are required for success in a vocation. From the class record and test data Mr. Laine can see that there is a good chance of college for Jerry. He therefore points out to Jerry occupations that utilize his interest and abilities. He discusses with Jerry, for example, the possibility of becoming an architect, an artist, or a teacher of art. In addition, he points out occupations at the semiprofessional level that do not require a college education, such as draftsman, decorator, and taxidermist. He does not, however, go into other fields that do not require even a high school education, such as upholstering or tailoring. Although the job is still far from simple, the interest test has narrowed the field, and Mr. Laine and Jerry can now concentrate on the occupations requiring mechanical and artistic activity.

In viewing the interest patterns of a student, there are certain facts in addition to those already mentioned that one must bear in mind. First, interest patterns generally reveal themselves in mature children at the age of fifteen or sixteen. However, some develop definite interests as late as age twenty-two, and others may never develop these patterns. Second, interest patterns generally seem to be established in a person before he has had a chance to have extensive occupational experience. Third, because a person has certain interests, we cannot say definitely that he will be successful in the areas of his interest. Other factors, such as ability, must also be considered. It is self-evident, therefore, that interest patterns *cannot* predict school achievement. Fourth, interest scores may predict the relative happiness or feeling of satisfaction a person may receive from certain types of work. Fifth, most people may be satisfied in many different types of schoolwork and in a number of different jobs. Sixth, if a person wants to fake his interests, he can do this easily. The Kuder has keys that sometimes reveal faking, but they are not foolproof. Of course, most people seeking vocational guidance tend to be honest in their answers, at least at the conscious level. And seventh, motivation and personality may enter the picture and distort the meaning of the interests of an individual as revealed by an inventory (Carter, 1949; Strong, 1943, 1955; Super and Crites, 1962; Darley and Hagenah, 1955; Campbell, 1966b, 1968; Kuder, 1964, 1966a).

The student of measurement should remember that interest inventories are only systemized surveys of what a person is interested in. *Don't forget the person.* Some people *do not* need to have an interest inventory to point out their vocational choices. They are sure of what they want and where they are going. Whether they are right or wrong is not the point; they have a right to make their own decisions. Interest inventories should not be given on the basis that "it's good for him" but on the basis of the needs of the individual student. (For an excellent discussion of some of the practical problems in interest measurement, see Weitz, 1968.)

TECHNICAL ASPECTS

Most of the major innovations in interest inventories have been based on empirical data. These data have at times been very complete and other times not very extensive. As Campbell (1966b) in his discussion of the SVIB states, "the available information has not been nearly so extensive as desired and decisions had to be based on common sense and educated guesses" (p. 49).

The Strong Vocational Interest Blank and the Kuder inventories have both been intensively investigated. This is not the place to review their credentials in terms of exact validity and reliability coefficients. The interested student may pursue this by referring to the latest manuals and other references previously cited in this chapter. It can be stated, however, that in general both yield scores that are acceptable in terms of reliability for teen-age individuals or older persons. These inventories reveal reliability coefficients that are fairly comparable to ability tests.

The main task in appraising the validity of interest inventories is judging the honesty of the person's responses. As Thorndike and Hagen (1969) state, "There isn't really any higher court of appeal for determining a person's likes and preferences than the individual's own statement" (p. 395). There is no doubt that a person can fake his responses, but as we have stated before if he comes of his own volition there is little reason for a conscious distortion.

In the area of concurrent validity the situation is different. The occupational-interest scales for the Strong were, for example, devised to distinguish members of occupational groups from people in general. Percentage overlaps[9] for each scale on SVIB were computed. They range from 15 to 52, with a median of 31 per cent overlap for the men's form and 16 to 42, with a median of 34 for the women's form. Thus the scales as a whole are fairly successful in separating the groups (Campbell, 1966b). Most of the Kuder (with the notable exception of Kuder's Occupational Interest Survey, 1966[10]) inventories attempt to distinguish between members of vocations and people in general.

Strong's (1955) classical investigation revealed the predictive validity of his instrument. This study showed a high degree of agreement between interest scores in 1927–30 and occupations of these people in 1949. A great deal of accumulated evidence reveals that on the whole both the Strong and Kuder have some validity as predictors of vocational choice.

The validity and reliability of the Minnesota Vocational Interest Inventory is promising but must still await further research before it can take its place next to the Strong and Kuder.

The selection of one interest inventory over another is dependent on

---

[9] The percentage of scores in one distribution that can be matched by scores in another distribution. If the distribution of the two groups are identical, the overlap is 100 per cent. A complete separation means a zero overlap.

[10] See Findley (1966) for an excellent critique of the OIS.

pupil needs, age, and occupational horizons. As a general rule, the Strong is never given before the senior year of high school, whereas the Kuder inventories may be first administered in junior high school.

If the teacher or counselor recognizes that the interest inventory is tentative and that it is not a measure of ability but only of declared interests and uses it along with other data, most students can profit from the experience of taking an interest inventory.

References

Allport, G. W., Vernon, P. E., and Lindzey, G. *Study of Values : Manual*. (3rd ed.) Boston: Houghton Mifflin, 1960.

Buros, O. K. *The sixth mental measurements yearbook*. Highland Park, N.J.: The Gryphon Press, 1965.

Brown, W. F., and Holtzman, W. H. *Survey of Study Habits and Attitudes : Manual*. New York: The Psychological Corporation, 1966.

Campbell, D. P. Stability of interests within an occupation over thirty years. *Journal of Applied Psychology*, 1966, **50,** 51–56. (a)

Campbell, D. P. *Strong Vocational Interest Blanks : Manual*. (Rev.) Stanford, Calif.: Stanford University Press, 1966.(b)

Campbell, D. P. Changing patterns of interests within the American society. *Measurement and Evaluation in Guidance*, 1968, **1,** 36–49.

Carter, H. D. *Vocational interests and job orientations : A ten year review*. Stanford, Calif.: Stanford University Press, 1949.

Clark, K. E., and Campbell, D. P. *Minnesota Vocational Interest Inventory : Manual*. New York: The Psychological Corporation, 1965.

Cook, W. W., Leeds, C., and Callis, R. *The Minnesota Teacher Attitude Inventory*. New York: The Psychological Corporation, 1951.

Cronbach, L. J. *Essentials of psychological testing*. (2nd ed.) New York: Harper & Row, 1960.

Dahlstrom, W. G., and Welsh, G. S. *An MMPI handbook : A guide to use in clinical practice and research*. Minneapolis: The University of Minnesota Press, 1960.

Darley, J. G., and Hagenah, T. *Vocational interest measurement : Theory and practice*. Minneapolis: The University of Minnesota Press, 1955.

Dolliver, R. H. Likes, dislikes, and SVIB scoring. *Measurement and Evaluation in Guidance*, 1968, **1,** 73–80.

Drake, L. E. and Oetting, E. R. *An MMPI codebook for counselors*. Minneapolis: University of Minnesota Press, 1959.

Findley, W. G. The Occupational Interest Survey. *Personnel and Guidance Journal*, 1966, **44,** 72–77.

Finney, J. C. A programmed interpretation of the MMPI and the CPI. *Archives of General Psychiatry*, 1966, **15,** 75–81.

Finney, J. C. Methodological problems in programmed composition of psychological test reports. *Behavioral Science*, 1967, **12,** 142–52.

Fowler, F. M. Interest measurement questions and answers. *School Life,* 1945 (December).

Harmon, L. W. Optimum criterion group size in interest measurement. *Measurement and Evaluation in Guidance,* 1968, **1,** 65–72.

Hathaway, S. R., and McKinley, J. C. *Booklet for the Minnesota Multiphasic Personality Inventory.* New York: The Psychological Corporation, 1943.

Hathaway, S. R., and McKinley, J. C. *Minnesota Multiphasic Personality Inventory: Manual.* (Rev. ed.) New York: The Psychological Corporation, 1951.

Hathaway, S. R., and McKinley, J. C. Construction of the schedule. In G. S. Welsh and W. G. Dahlstrom (Eds.), *Basic readings on the MMPI in psychology and medicine.* Minneapolis: University of Minnesota Press, 1956. Pp. 60–63.

Hathaway, S. R., and Meehl, P. E. *An atlas for the clinical use of the MMPI.* Minneapolis: University of Minnesota Press, 1951.

Hathaway, S. R., and Monachesi, E. D. *Analyzing and predicting juvenile delinquency with the MMPI.* Minneapolis: University of Minnesota Press, 1953.

Hathaway, S. R., and Monachesi, E. D. *An atlas of juvenile MMPI profiles.* Minneapolis: University of Minnesota Press, 1961.

Karmel, L. J. *An analysis of the personality patterns, and academic and social backgrounds of persons employed as full-time counselors in selected secondary schools in the state of North Carolina.* (Doctoral dissertation, University of North Carolina), Ann Arbor, Mich: University Microfilms, 1961. No. 62–3134.

Kuder, G. F. *Administrator's manual Kuder Preference Record Vocational—Form C.* Chicago: Science Research Associates, 1960.

Kuder, G. F. *Kuder E General Interest Survey manual.* Chicago: Science Research Associates, 1964.

Kuder, G. F. *Kuder DD Occupational Interest Survey general manual.* Chicago: Science Research Associates, 1966.(a)

Kuder, G. F. *Kuder DD Occupational Interest Survey Interpretive Leaflet Grades 11–12.* Chicago: Science Research Associates, 1966.(b)

Megargee, E. I. (Ed.) *Research in clinical assessment.* New York: Harper & Row, 1966.

Mooney, R. L., and Gordon, L. V. *The Mooney Problem Check Lists: Manual* (Rev. ed.) New York: The Psychological Corporation, 1950.

Spranger, E. (translated by P. J. W. Pigors) *Types of men.* Halle: Niemeyer Verlag, 1928.

Strong, E. K. *Vocational interests of men and women.* Stanford, Calif.: Stanford University Press, 1943.

Strong, E. K. *Vocational interests 18 years after college.* Minneapolis: University of Minnesota Press, 1955.

Super, D. E., and Crites, J. O. *Appraising vocational fitness: By means of psychological tests.* (Rev. ed.) New York: Harper & Row, 1962.

Thorndike, R. L. *Thorndike Dimensions of Temperament: Manual.* New York: The Psychological Corporation, 1966.

Thorndike, R. L., and Hagen, E. *Measurement and evaluation in psychology and education.* (3rd ed.) New York: Wiley, 1969.

Thurstone, L. L. *The measurement of values.* Chicago: University of Chicago Press, 1959.

Weitz, H. Some practical problems in interest measurement. *Measurement and Evaluation in Guidance,* 1968, **1,** 56–62.

Welsh, G. S., and Dahlstrom, W. G. (Eds.) *Basic readings on the MMPI in psychology and medicine.* Minneapolis: University of Minnesota Press, 1956.

PART FIVE

Teacher-Made Tests and Grades

CHAPTER

13

Teacher-Made Tests

Like it or not one must measure outcomes of instruction. It is true that the experts who specialize in test construction do not always do a good job and that they have the assistance of subject-matter specialists to help them. We have seen the problems of validity and reliability in the construction of standardized tests. How can one, then, expect a classroom teacher who has had one course in testing to do a good job?

It is true that no matter how much you read about classroom tests in this or other books, you will never conceive or produce a test that will really meet the ideal standards of test construction. However, you will probably do well enough for your own purposes, if you follow correct test construction methods. Reading the following material will not solve all your test problems, but it should help. Remember, just as the standardized test is a reflection of educational goals and procedures, so is the teacher-made test, but even more so because the teacher knows what the specific objectives are and what methods have been employed to reach them.

Standardized Versus Teacher-Made Tests

There should be no battle between standardized and teacher-made tests. Most schools use both types of instruments; each has its own advantages

Table 25 Advantages and Limitations of Standardized and Nonstandardized Tests of Achievement

Criterion	STANDARDIZED Advantages	Limitations
1. Validity		
a. Curricular	Careful selection by competent persons. Fit typical situations.	Inflexible. Too general in scope to meet local requirements fully, especially in unusual situations.
b. Statistical	With best tests, high.	Criteria often inappropriate or unreliable. Size of coefficients dependent upon range of ability in group tested.
2. Reliability	For best tests, fairly high—often .85 or more for comparable forms.	High reliability is no guarantee of validity. Also, reliability depends upon range of ability in group tested.
3. Usability		
a. Ease of Administration	Definite procedure, time limits, etc. Economy of time.	Manuals require careful study and are sometimes inadequate.
b. Ease of Scoring	Definite rules, keys, etc. Largely routine.	Scoring by hand may take considerable time and be monotonous. Machine scoring preferable.
c. Ease of Interpretation	Better tests have adequate norms. Useful basis of comparison. Equivalent forms.	Norms often confused with standards. Some norms defective. Norms for various types of schools and levels of ability are often lacking.
Summary	Convenience, comparability, objectivity. Equivalent forms may be available.	Inflexibility. May be only slightly applicable to a particular situation.

From Julian C. Stanley, *Measurement in Today's Schools*, 4th ed., © 1964. Reprinted by permission of Prentice-Hall, Inc., Englewood Cliffs, N.J.

and disadvantages. Obviously, teacher-made intelligence, personality, special aptitude, and interest tests are not the question here. The real question is when to use the standardized achievement test and when to use the teacher-made achievement test. A general rule of thumb is that the teacher-made test is *always* used as the instrument of choice to appraise outcomes of local classroom instruction. On the other hand, the standardized achievement test is used to provide information to the teacher, school, and student in terms of how local achievement compares to national norms. In Table 25 we find a comparison of the relative strengths and weaknesses of the standardized and the teacher-made, or "nonstandardized," tests.

Purposes of Teacher-Made Tests

"The test is the message." The teacher, in the most direct and meaningful manner, tells the student what he *really* thinks is important through his

| NONSTANDARDIZED | | | |
| Essay | | Objective | |
Advantages	Limitations	Advantages	Limitations
Useful for English advanced classes; afford language training. May encourage sound study habits.	Limited sampling. Bluffing is possible. Mix language factor in all scores. Usually not known.	Extensive sampling of subject matter. Flexible in use. Discourages bluffing. Compares favorably with standard tests.	Narrow sampling of functions tested. Negative learning possible. May encourage piecemeal study. Adequate criteria usually lacking.
	Reliability usually quite low.	Sometimes approaches that of standard tests.	No guarantee of validity
Easy to prepare. Easy to give.	Lack of uniformity.	Directions rather uniform. Economy of time.	Time, effort, and skill are required to prepare well.
	Slow, uncertain, and subjective.	Definite rules, keys, etc. Largely routine. Can be done by clerks or machine.	Monotonous.
	No norms. Meaning doubtful.	Local norms can be derived.	No norms available at beginning.
Useful for part of many tests and in a few special fields.	Limited sampling. Subjective scoring. Time consuming.	Extensive sampling. Objective scoring. Flexibility.	Preparation requires skill and time.

tests. This unfortunately often results in the student studying for a test rather than for what he can learn. Although we can discourage studying only for tests, it is doubtless impossible to eliminate it. Therefore remember that you will communicate your subject-matter emphasis through the tests you give.

Tests serve the teacher with valuable insights into his or her instructional effectiveness. The teacher can ask himself, "Are the students learning what I want them to learn?" and then find the answer in his students' test results.

In addition, tests of course provide the teacher with information on individual progress. Without this kind of data it is almost impossible to make decisions on passing and failing students, grouping, remedial help, or providing enriching experiences for the advanced pupil. Testing also aids in evaluating the class as a whole.

Tests, of course, provide part of the basis for assigning grades. If used properly they can forestall parental shock at report card time. The parent who has seen his child's test papers knows fairly well what grades his child will receive.

Reviewing tests with parents and teachers can help the child learn the material not yet incorporated into his intellectual and educational storehouse. The teacher can spot the kinds of problems that are troubling the student and work on his areas of weaknesses.

Planning Ahead

There you are, Miss Fry, your first month of teaching and you've done a pretty fair job so far. Now you have to decide how to evaluate what the students have learned because you must turn in the first report card grades next week. "Now what kind of test should I give these kids?"

Quality tests do not spring forth full blown. They are planned in detail when you detail the overall goals of the course. Questions dealing with the type of test to use, the amount of material to be tested from text and classroom discussions, and so on should be decided before you begin classroom instruction.

Defining Objectives

Defining objectives is not new to those of you who have been exposed to a "methods" course in education. You know that defining goals or objectives is a primary ingredient of the teaching process. Noll (1965) states the case very cogently when he says, "To try to teach and evaluate without defining objectives is like starting out on a journey without knowing where to go. It may be pleasant to wander around for a while, but it is doubtful that any sort of progress can be made without some direction" (p. 104).

General Objectives

Usually there are two kinds of objectives, general and specific. For example, many years ago a group of educators set forth objectives that have become known as the *seven cardinal principles* of education (United States Department of Interior, 1918). These general objectives are the following:

1. To promote good health.
2. To teach command of the fundamental processes.
3. To provide for worthy home membership.
4. To aid in the selection of a vocation.
5. To offer civic education.
6. To assure worthy use of leisure time.
7. To promote ethical character.

Another illustration of general objectives is the classical eight-year study (Aikin, 1942).

1. The development of effective methods of thinking.
2. The cultivation of useful work habits and study skills.
3. The inculcation of social attitudes.
4. The acquisition of a wide range of significant interests.
5. The development of increased appreciation of music, art, literature, and other esthetic experiences.
6. The development of social sensitivity.
7. The development of better personal-social adjustment.
8. The acquisition of important information.
9. The development of good physical health.
10. The development of a consistent philosophy of life.

Another excellent source of ideas for general educational objectives is the *Taxonomy of Educational Objectives* (Bloom, 1956, and Krathwohl, 1964). The original conception of the taxonomy was to encompass three behavioral spheres—cognitive, affective, and psychomotor. The cognitive area covers objectives related to recall or recognition of knowledge and problem solving. The affective domain deals with changes in interest, values, and attitudes and the development of appreciation and adjustment. The psychomotor area covers objectives relating to manual and motor skills. Bloom's (1956) work covered the cognitive domain, whereas Krathwohl (1964) dealt with the affective area. Work in the psychomotor domain has not yet been published. Let us first, very briefly, review Bloom and his committee's work as it relates to our concern for objectives. The committee made the following statement concerning their findings for the classroom teacher (Bloom, 1956):

> Use of the taxonomy can also help one gain a perspective on the emphasis given to certain behaviors by a particular set of educational plans. Thus, a teacher, in classifying the goals of a teaching unit, may find that they all fall within the taxonomy category of recalling or remembering knowledge. Looking at the taxonomy categories may suggest to him that, for example, he could include some goals dealing with the application of this knowledge and with the analysis of the situation in which the knowledge is used [p. 2].

The classification of cognitive educational objectives falls into six major categories:

1.00 Knowledge.
2.00 Comprehension.
3.00 Application.
4.00 Analysis.
5.00 Synthesis.
6.00 Evaluation.

These major categories are broken down in subsections, for example, some of the headings under Knowledge are as follows:

    1.00 Knowledge.
      1.10 Knowledge of specifics.
        1.11 Knowledge of terminology.
        1.12 Knowledge of specific facts.
      1.20 Knowledge of ways and means of dealing with specifics.
      1.30 Knowledge of the universals and abstractions in a field.

Under every heading there is a definition and discussion of the meaning of that heading. These are further clarified by illustrations of the kind of educational goals included in the specific category. In addition, at the end of each of the sections there is a review of the types of test items that may be used to test achievement of the various facets of each objective. It is highly recommended that the classroom teacher obtain a copy of Bloom's (1956) *Taxonomy of Educational Objectives*, an excellent resource for preparing classroom units of study and tests.

Krathwohl (1964) and his committee's work in the affective domain produced the following major categories:

    1.0 Receiving. Sensitivity to the existence of certain stimuli.
    2.0 Responding. Active attention to stimuli, for example, going along with rules and practices.
    3.0 Valuing. Consistent belief and attitude of worth held about a phenomenon.
    4.0 Organization. Organizing, interrelating, and analyzing different relevant values.
    5.0 Characterization by a value or value concept. Behavior is guided by value.

For a detailed discussion of these objectives see Krathwohl's *Taxonomy of Educational Objectives*.

Specific Objectives

In the area of specific objectives we are concerned with *specific subject matter*. This means skills, concepts, facts, principles, and so forth. A good method of setting forth your instructional objectives is to outline them.

The construction of objectives should not become laborious. Do not be overwhelmed by the process; use it to your advantage. This means construct objectives for units of study, including evaluation methods, in a manageable manner. For example, let us look at a unit on arithmetic.

General Objective
   A. To develop skill in the process of calculating two- three-, and four-digit problems in addition and subtraction.

Specific Objectives
   A. Addition.
      1. Problems requiring carrying (also called exchanging).
      2. Problems not requiring carrying.
      3. Use of decimal points.

   B. Subtraction.
      1. Problems requiring borrowing.
      2. Problems not requiring borrowing.
      3. Use of decimal points.

Let us translate our "general" and "specific objectives" in arithmetic to actual test questions:

ADDITION

1.	34 +48	67 +26	834 +287	5468 +7679
2.	65 +32	15 +61	213 +381	8065 +1924
3.	4.2 +3.3	5.33 +6.11	7.88 +1.33	88.44 +16.67

SUBTRACTION

1.	30 −19	46 −27	634 −488	7586 −5797
2.	48 −32	84 −63	975 −960	3345 −2214
3.	5.7 −4.5	6.8 −1.9	8.43 −7.99	666.3 −566.2

Figure 41 presents an actual blueprint of a test derived from instructional objectives in social studies.

Objectives:	I. The foundations of our Constitutional Government (30% of all items)	II. Principles and Development of our Constitutional Government (70% of all items)
1. Knows terms and vocabulary (10%)	1. Inalienable Rights 2. Tyranny 3. Compromise 4. Confederation (1 or 2 items)	Preamble Legislative Executive Judicial Federalism Unitary governments Elastic clause Residual powers Sovereignty Concurrent powers Check and balance system Suffrage (4 items)
2. Knows dates, events, persons and places (5%)	1. Articles of Confederation – 1781 2. Magna Charta – 1215 3. Bill of Rights – 1689 4. Petition of Right – 1628 5. Declaration of Independence – 1776 6. Setting of Constitutional Convention – Members, Agreements 7. Ordinance of 1787 (0-1 item)	Ratification of Constitution – 1788 Federalist papers – Authorship and purposes (2 items)
3. Knows generalizations, concepts and principles (35%)	1. Provisions of Magna Charta, Bill of Rights, Petition of Right 2. Principles embodied in the Declaration of Independence 3. Weaknesses of Articles of Confederation 4. Provisions of Ordinance of 1787 (6 or 7 items)	1. Restrictions on the states and national government 2. Powers belonging only to the states 3. Powers belonging only to the national government 4. Powers shared by state and national government 5. Provisions of first III Articles 6. Changes and amendments to Constitution – how made 7. Provisions of Bill of Rights (14 or 15 items)
4. Can trace development of our national form of government (20%)	1. Identifies influences and trends that contributed to the establishment of representative assemblies in the colonies 2. Explains the development of representative government in the colonies between 1607 and 1776 3. Shows how the ordinance of 1787 affected the development of our country (3 or 4 items)	1. Identifies events, forces, and ideas that lead to separation of powers in federal government 2. Identifies forces that lead to amendments to the Constitution (8 or 9 items)

Objective	Topic I	Topic II
5. Can express generalizations and concepts in own words (10%)	1. Equality of man 2. Governments derive their just powers from the consent of the governed 3. Explains why the articles of Confederation were not a complete failure (1 or 2 items)	1. Explains the meanings of the Amendments to the Constitution 2. Our Government as a democratic republic (4 items)
6. Can point out relationships, similarities, and differences (10%)	1. Relationships between national origins of the colonists and provisions of Mayflower Compact 2. Abuses set forth in declaration of Independence and whether these abuses are found in our country today (1 or 2 items)	1. Relationship between preamble of Constitution and the Articles of Confederation 2. Similarities and differences between national and local government 3. Similarities and differences between Virginia Plan and New Jersey Plan and the Constitution as it was adopted (4 items)
7. Can apply generalizations and principles to novel situations (10%)	1. Identifies advantages and disadvantages of confederate type organizations such as United Nations (1 or 2 items)	1. Points out differences to be expected between our government and a government organized on other principles 2. Identifies acts that violate the Bill of Rights and the right that is violated by each act. 3. Predicts probable outcomes if Constitution were not flexible 4. Explains the process by which Puerto Rico could be made a state 5. Identifies whether proposed laws are in conflict with the Constitution 6. Identifies errors in parliamentary procedure (4 items)

Total time for test — 50 minutes
Total number of items on test — 60 (Topic I — 18 items; Topic II — 42 items)

Figure 41. Test blueprint for a unit on How Our National Government Functions. (From Robert L. Thorndike and Elizabeth Hagen, *Measurement and Evaluation in Psychology and Education*. © 1961 by John Wiley & Sons, Inc. Used with the permission of John Wiley & Sons, Inc.)

Steps in Test Construction and Administration

So far we have talked mostly in general terms. Let us now get down to practical situations by outlining, step by step, the actual process of test construction and administration.

1. *"Get Ready" Stage.*
    a. Secure all the instructional materials bearing on the intended test, for example, books, notes, and content outline or unit objectives.
    b. List the objectives you want your test to measure.
2. *"Get Set" Stage.*
    a. Plan type of test to be used and the general format of the test.
    b. Write a preliminary draft of the items to be used.
    c. Plan the length of test. How long do you want the test to be—the whole class period, or a shorter time?
    d. Go over test items. Do this several days after you have written the preliminary draft. Take out the items that do not seem relevant and polish others.
    e. Arrange items in order. Rate your items for difficulty and place the easiest first so as not to discourage the students and to give the poorer students some motivation to continue with the test.
    f. Instructions. Be sure you know what you want the students to do and are able to communicate your wishes to them.
    g. Decide on the "Rules of the Scoring Road." Be sure you have written the correct answer before testing. This is as true for essay questions as for objective items.
3. *"Go" Stage.*
    a. Time. Whatever you decide upon, be consistent. For example, do not state, "You will have thirty minutes to complete the test" and then give the slower students an hour. It is not fair to the others who attempted to complete the assignment in the stated time. Generally allow enough time for at least 90 per cent of the students to finish.
    b. Physical Conditions. Try to maintain a quiet, disturbance-free room. Do not walk around the room, tap a pencil, talk to other teachers, and so on.
    c. Administration. Do not be hostile in tone or manner when giving directions. Your voice should be clear and instructions easily understood by all the students. Testing is difficult for all of us. Do not make it worse by using it as punishment.

Evaluation of Your Test

The reader has already been exposed in earlier discussions to what constitutes a good measuring device. In this section we will of necessity repeat some of these factors as they relate to teacher-made tests. Ebel (1965, pp. 281-307) has summarized the characteristics of a good test by noting the following ten qualities:[1]

1. *Relevance.* Is your test measuring your educational objectives and actual instruction? This is the validity aspect of the classroom test.

2. *Balance.* How close does your test come to the "ideal"? That is, do your items reflect your stated objectives?

3. *Efficiency.* How much time does your test take to administer? Is it taking too much? A compromise between available time for testing and scoring and other needs must be made.

4. *Objectivity.* There should be agreement by experts on the "right" or "best" answer to a question. Objectivity does not refer to the type test (for example, multiple-choice or completion items) but is directly concerned with the scoring of the test.

5. *Specificity.* Are you testing the subject matter presented in the classroom? That is, does the test discriminate between those students who have learned the subject matter and those who have not on a better than chance basis?

6. *Difficulty.* The difficulty of test items should be at the level of the group being tested. Generally, we can consider a test appropriate if each item in the examination is passed by half of the students.

7. *Discrimination.* A test item discriminates if more good students answer it correctly than do poor students.

8. *Reliability.* Is the test measuring whatever it does measure consistently?

9. *Fairness.* Does each student have an equal chance to demonstrate his knowledge? The test should be constructed so that each student has an equal chance to "show his stuff."

10. *Speediness.* Are scores influenced by speed of response, and if so to what degree? In testing achievement, speed should play a very minor role in determining a student's score. There should be sufficient time for *almost all* students to finish the test.

Types of Teacher-Made Tests

There are basically two types of teacher-made tests. They are essay and objective. There are, however, many forms of the objective type while the essay is generally confined to a "short answer" or "discussion" format. The following list of different types of objective teacher-made tests are cited

---

[1] Slight modifications in terms of descriptions, but not qualities—for example, *Relevance*—have been made.

to show the scope and breadth of available formats. Some of these will be discussed in the following chapters.

OBJECTIVE TESTS[2]

1. Simple recall.
   a. Basic.
   b. Problem type.
   c. Maps, charts, and so on.
2. Completion.
   a. Basic.
   b. Matching.
   c. Analogies.
   d. Maps, charts, and so on.
3. Alternative Response.
   a. Basic.
   b. Two-clause.
   c. Three alternatives.
   d. Converse.
   e. With correction.
   f. With qualifications.
   g. With diagrams.
   h. With analogies.
4. Multiple Choice.
   a. Basic.
   b. Recall.
   c. Common principle.
   d. Results.
   e. Causes.
   f. Charts, maps, and so on.
   g. Analogies.
5. Matching.
   a. Basic.
   b. Three columns.
   c. Master list.
   d. Analogies.
6. Rearrangement.
   a. Chronological.
   b. Order of importance.
   c. Order of difficulty.
   d. Length, weight, logic, and so on.

In the chapters that follow we will discuss many of the preceding types of teacher-made tests. The reader is already familiar with some from the chapter on achievement tests.

[2] Adapted from A. J. Lien *Measurement and Evaluation of Learning: A Handbook for Teachers*. Dubuque, Iowa: Wm. C. Brown Company Publishers, 1967.

Essay Versus Objective Tests

There are no definitive rules for whether the essay or the objective test is better, nor are there rules for when one type should be used in preference to the other. The teacher is in the best position to select one form over the other. The basis for the selection rests with the particular purposes and needs of the classroom setting and, more specifically, with what the teacher wants to measure and the available time for this task. Table 26 presents a summary of a few of the major characteristics of the two types of tests.

Table 26 A Comparison of Essay and Objective Tests

	Essay	*Objective*
Abilities Measured	Requires the student to express himself in his own words, using information from his own background and knowledge. Can tap high levels of reasoning such as required in inference, organization of ideas, comparison and contrast. Does *not* measure purely factual information efficiently.	Requires the student to select correct answers from given options, or to supply an answer limited to one word or phrase. Can *also* tap high levels of reasoning such as required in inference, organization of ideas, comparison and contrast. Measures knowledge of facts efficiently.
Scope	Covers only a limited field of knowledge in any one test. Essay questions take so long to answer that relatively few can be answered in a given period of time. Also, the student who is especially fluent can often avoid discussing points of which he is unsure.	Covers a broad field of knowledge in one test. Since objective questions may be answered quickly, one test may contain many questions. A broad coverage helps provide reliable measurement.
Incentive to Pupils	Encourages pupils to learn how to organize their own ideas and express them effectively.	Encourages pupils to build up a broad background of knowledge and abilities.
Ease of Preparation	Requires writing only a few questions for a test. Tasks must be clearly defined, general enough to offer some leeway, specific enough to set limits.	Requires writing many questions for a test. Wording must avoid ambiguities and "giveaways." Distractors should embody most likely misconceptions.

Table 26—Continued

| **Scoring** | Usually very time-consuming to score. | Can be scored quickly. |
| | Permits teachers to comment directly on the reasoning processes of individual pupils. However, an answer may be scored differently by different teachers or by the same teacher at different times. | Answer generally scored only right or wrong, but scoring is very accurate and consistent. |

From *Making the Classroom Test: A Guide for Teachers*, Educational Testing Service Evaluation and Advisory Service Series No. 4. © First Edition Copyright 1959 by Educational Testing Service. Second Edition 1961. Reprinted by permission of Educational Testing Service.

The student of measurement should remember that neither the essay nor the objective test alone is completely satisfactory in measuring academic progress. Each has its own advantages and disadvantages and it's your responsibility to use the right test in the right place for the right purpose.

Teachers, Tests, and Reality

An attempt has been made in this chapter to give some guidelines for constructing tests. In the following chapters detailed examples and suggestions for developing essay and objective tests will be presented. It should be noted, however, that the time available will be the common denominator in our discussions.

Remember also that no single teacher-made test should be the only basis of important educational decisions. Day-to-day classroom performance, scores on standardized tests, and academic achievement measured by a series of teacher-made tests over a period of time should be considered in the whole picture of pupil evaluation, As Nunnally (1964) states, "To reach important conclusions about students on the basis of only one teacher-made test would be as unwise as it would be for the prospector to abandon his claim because the first shovelfull was not brimming with gold" (p. 106).

References

Aikin, W. M. *The story of the eight-year study, with conclusions and recommendations.* New York: Harper & Row, 1942.

Bloom, B. S. (Ed.) *Taxonomy of educational objectives. Handbook 1: The cognitive domain.* New York: David McKay, 1956.

Ebel, R. L. *Measuring educational achievement.* Englewood Cliffs, N.J.: Prentice-Hall, 1965.

Krathwohl, D. R., Bloom, B. S., and Masia, B. B. *Taxonomy of educational objectives. Handbook 2: The affective domain.* New York: David McKay, 1964.

Lien, A. J. *Measurement and evaluation of learning: A handbook for teachers.* Dubuque, Iowa: Wm. C. Brown, 1967.

Noll, V. H. *Introduction to educational measurement.* (2nd ed.) Boston: Houghton Mifflin, 1965.

Nunnally, J. C. *Educational measurement and evaluation.* New York: McGraw-Hill, 1964.

United States Department of Interior, Bureau of Education. *Cardinal principles of education.* Bulletin No. 38, 1918.

CHAPTER

14

The Essay Test

In 1854, Horace Mann substituted a uniform written examination for the usual oral testing of students in the Boston public schools (Chauncey and Dobbin, 1966). Before Mann's "step forward" the examination of students consisted of interrogation by the teacher or a board of school officials. Since Mann's radical change the essay test has undergone a great deal of investigation and critical comment. Let us very briefly review some of the studies and comments as they relate especially to reliability. We shall keep them in mind in our later discussion of developing and scoring essay tests. Above all they should serve as cautionary lights in our use and application of the essay test in the total evaluation of our students.

Reliability

In 1912 and 1913, Starch and Elliott (1912, 1913a, 1913b) produced the first studies on the reliability of grading essay tests. These three classical investigations covered the subject matter of high school English, history, and mathematics.

In the area of English the investigators selected two English themes of supposed equal quality and asked 142 English teachers to grade them on the basis of 100 per cent. The first paper revealed grades ranging from 50 to 98, with a median of 80.2. The second paper received grades ranging between 64 and 99, with a median of 88.2 (Starch and Elliott, 1912).

Starch and Elliott (1913a), in their study of history tests, found an even larger discrepancy of grades. The range was over seventy points on the same 100 per cent basis. In their mathematics investigation they sent a plane geometry paper to 138 geometry teachers for grading, because they thought that mathematics should be more subject to grading consistency. Their results revealed a grade range between 28 and 95 (Starch and Elliott 1913b).

In a later and more sophisticated investigation Falls (1928) requested 100 English teachers to grade a paper already evaluated by a committee as excellent. The 100 teachers did not know that a committee had previously evaluated the paper or that the writer, a high school senior, was a reporter for a large city daily paper. Grades on this paper were between 60 and 98. In addition, comments placed the writer's grade level in school from fifth grade to a junior in college. Study after study has confirmed these findings.

As the years have gone by, research designs, methods, and procedures of analysis have become more sophisticated but the results have generally been the same. For example, in a more contemporary study Myers, McConville, and Coffman (1966) used 145 readers and 80,000 essays. They found average single reader reliabilities of 0.41. The average reliability rose to 0.73 when the number of readers was increased to four. This dramatic increase was achieved under controlled conditions with trained readers who read the essays as a whole and then utilized a four-point scale. This research revealed that if a teacher is going to give essay tests, then several graders should be used.

James (1927) attempted to study the reliability of grades assigned by the same instructor. He selected four compositions that were judged to be of the same quality and asked forty-three English teachers to judge them. Two were in good handwriting and two in poor. Two months later the same themes were presented to the same teachers but with the handwriting reversed— that is, the two that had been in poor handwriting were reproduced in good penmanship and vice versa. The results revealed a one letter grade difference in favor of the good handwriting.

Most of the research on essay tests has involved the reliability of graders of essay tests. A paucity of data exists concerning the actual reliability of the instrument itself. Cureton (1958) in a discussion of this problem states that in order to obtain an estimate of essay test reliability, two equivalent forms are necessary at the beginning and that they must be administered to the individuals at an optimal time interval. Each reader would have to read all of the answers to a specific question on both forms. If this situation could be created then a correlation between grades obtained on one form with those obtained on the other could be considered as an estimate of reliability.

Payne (1968) states that one method of increasing the reliability of an essay test "is to increase the number of questions and restrict the extensiveness of the answers. The more specific and more narrowly defined the questions, the less likely they are to be ambiguous to the examinee. This should result in more uniform comprehension and performance of the assigned task, and the reliability of the instrument and scoring should be increased" (pp. 80–81).

The teacher who wants to administer essay tests in spite of the research findings on reliability should heed Payne's advice but at the same time be very cautious in interpreting the scores. Some of the advice on the construction of essay tests which will be discussed later in this chapter should help, but caution should still be the watchword. It should also be noted that the research and implications for the reliability of the essay test that have been made are in reference to evaluation. The educational process, of course, involves more than evaluation. Teachers may feel that the essay test, though not necessarily reliable in the measurement sense, may be an excellent instructional device. That is, it may help the student learn to organize his thoughts and express them in writing. We will have more to say on the advantages of the essay test later in this chapter.

Validity

Achievement tests are validated on the basis of whether or not they cover the subject matter taught and the goals of the unit of study. Validity, as is the case with reliability, tends to be higher as the number of questions are increased. Essay tests necessarily contain a relatively small number of questions. Thus the sampling of the objectives outlined in the unit or course specifications will be small and therefore will tend to lower the validity of the test. It is common after taking an essay test for students to feel that some of their study time was "wasted" because so much of the course was not measured in the four, five, or six essay questions presented to them.

Another problem in the validity of essay tests is the evaluation of more than one area of learning. For example, some instructors reduce the score for poor spelling or grammar on a history paper, thereby lowering the history grade. The resultant grade does not reveal what the student knows about history alone but also what kind of speller and/or grammarian he is. This type of "history" evaluation generally does not serve the cause of history or that of spelling and grammar very well. Our old definition of validity certainly applies here—that is, whether or not the test measures what it is supposed to measure. If you are testing history, *then test history, not English*. If, on the other hand, you feel that educational objectives are best served by evaluating English usage and content, then give two grades—one for English and one for history, but be sure and follow through on the report card. If history alone is on the card, give only the history grade or add the English evaluation so that parents and other school personnel in future years will have a clear understanding of how the pupil was evaluated and in what areas.

There is another case familiar to everyone. This is the tendency of students to expound at length on essay examinations often without specifically answering the question. An adept student may raise his grade because of this facility, because of a general rather than specific knowledge of the subject matter. The tendency of graders to reward the more verbose students lowers the overall validity of the test.

Advantages and Disadvantages of the Essay Test

The essay test, despite low reliability and validity, is held in high esteem by many teachers from elementary through graduate school. Let us look at some of the common arguments given in defense of essay tests and their merit.

Thorndike and Hagen (1961) state that the distinctive advantage of the essay test lies in the requirement of asking the student "to produce, rather than merely to recognize the answer." They go on to state:

> Thus, it minimizes the possibility of getting the answer by blind guessing or by using little cues to outguess the test maker. It can, if the questions are well prepared, bring out the examinee's ability to select important facts or ideas, relate them to one another, and organize them into a coherent whole. Emphasizing this integrative type of product, it elicits, so it is claimed, better study habits in those who are preparing for it [p. 42].

Does the essay test in fact present a chance for the student to show his organizational skills? The answer is dependent on the quality of the test. If the test is well constructed it probably can. The problem, however, is that often the student is not presented with an examination geared to this goal. The student may find himself at a loss in attempting to answer a long discussion question—for example, "Discuss the antecedents of pop art." This type of essay problem does not enhance organizational ability nor does it call for the student's skill in selecting important facts or ideas. The student faced with our example problem would have to ask himself first of all, "What does the teacher want? Does she want me to start with the Egyptians or primitive period of art or does she want me to trace the development of pop art in the twentieth century?" On the other hand, if the problem was stated in the following manner, "Discuss the influence of cubism on pop art," the student would have an idea of where to start and develop his line of reasoning; he would know what the teacher wanted. Similarly, all the students would be dealing with the same problem and therefore give the teacher a better basis for comparison. Used in this manner the essay test can be useful in evaluating a student's ability to organize, select, and integrate important ideas and trends.

Another hallmark of essay tests is that they require students to answer questions in their own words and handwriting. We have already discussed some of the problems in this area in our review of reliability and validity. You will remember the James (1927) study which revealed that good penmanship usually yielded one grade higher than poor handwriting. In addition, the student who can use the English language effectively will generally do better on discussion questions. The student who may not write as well either in terms of penmanship or English usage may, in fact, actually know more about zoology or history and yet receive a lower grade. It is very difficult not to be influenced by such external factors as neatness, handwriting, sentence structure, spelling, and vocabulary. This is not to state that these factors are not important. On the contrary, they are legitimate and necessary educational objectives. If people cannot communicate their knowledge and ideas, how do we, or society in general, know that they possess either? The problem, then, is not the worth of grammar and penmanship but how to evaluate a student's knowledge and understanding of biology or history without evaluating other skills and knowledge.

A major disadvantage of the essay test, as has already been mentioned, lies in the scoring. How do you evaluate the answer given? What are the degrees of correctness? Downie (1967) in reviewing the merits and limitations of essay tests states,

> If we cannot truly assert that essay tests foster skill in writing and answer adult needs better than objective tests, why use the essay test? Probably for most classroom situations they are unnecessary except to evaluate how well a student can write a theme or essay. If we want to assess style, quality, and other aspects of writing, it is obvious that the essay test item has to be used. Even here though studies have shown that objective tests of writing ability can predict achievement in writing, the latter measured by both teachers' estimates and grades received, better than do the essay tests [p. 202].

This writer, though agreeing with the studies of the essay test's poor reliability, cannot go along with the pessimistic view of Professor Downie. Properly constructed essay tests can serve as aids in developing and fostering skills in writing. People learn by doing, not by showing potential to do. One cannot learn to play the piano because one's musical ability is potentially great. One learns to play the piano by playing the piano. One learns to organize and express oneself in written discourse by actual writing experience. In a strict measurement sense the essay test is not the best device for evaluation. In an educational sense, which includes measurement, however, the essay test may be used as a useful instructional tool in facilitating learning.

Construction of Essay Tests

Let us now proceed to the ingredients that make essay tests more useful to classroom evaluation. First of all, we can improve the essay examination by limiting it to the objectives that it measures best, for example, skills in the selection and organization of important facts and ideas. Second, we grant the deficits of the essay test, such as limited sampling, and go on from there and attempt to write the best essay questions possible. Let us now venture forth into the practical ways of writing good essay questions. The following steps are based on the *judgment* of "test experts," not on experimentally established procedures.

1. What do you want to find out about the student's achievement? If your goal is to determine the degree to which he can apply facts, then phrase your question in a manner that calls upon this process. Write down your evaluation goals and refer to them as you write the questions. Ask yourself continually, "Does this test bring out information that I want?"

2. Phrase your questions in a precise and cogent manner. Avoid cluttering your questions with excessive clauses and difficult words. Remember, use simple sentences that everyone in the classroom can read with ease and understanding.

3. Generally begin your essay questions with such words or phrases as *contrast, compare, present original example of,* and *state the reasons for.* Do not begin essay questions with such words as *what, who, list,* and *discuss* (unless you detail the concepts you want discussed very specifically and thereby explain what you mean by *discuss.* These words are either too nebulous or are prone to elicit mere recitation of facts.

4. Define and narrow the subject area of the question. For example, in an American history class one might say, "Describe the various facets of colonial life in America." It would be better, however, to say: "Explain and describe the following facets of American colonial life: (a) the people, (b) the economy, (c) everyday life, (d) intellectual pursuits." The first question was too broad and general to evoke anything but good guesses as to what the teacher wanted. The second approach presents the student with specific facets of colonial life to discuss and explain. In addition it tells the student that a relatively long time will be required to answer the question whereas the first question gave no indication of time requirements.

Another example of improving an essay question that is too general is the following:

> **Poor**   Explain why you think the United Nations has been a success or a failure.
>
> **Better** An important function of the United Nations is to help settle disputes between nations. Describe how one dispute was handled successfully, pointing out how the settlement illustrates a general strength of the United Nations. Describe also how one dispute was handled unsuccessfully, pointing out how this illustrates a general weakness of the United Nations. Your essay should be about 300–400 words in length

(2 or 3 pages in longhand). [Educational Testing Service, 1961, p. 22.]

5. Never write essay questions with the words *what do you think*, *in your opinion*, or *write all you know about*. Thorndike and Hagen (1961) state,

> ... when a teacher asks "Why do you think that the Articles of Confederation provided a poor basis for the formation of our central government?," he is not really interested in the student's opinion. He actually wants to determine whether the student knows the fundamental weaknesses of the Articles of Confederation, as stated by the teacher or text. Therefore the question would be better if written: "Why did the Articles of Confederation prove to be unworkable as a framework for our national government?" [p. 54].

If the purpose of the essay test is to obtain student attitudes (which are impossible to grade) or to measure the ability of a student to present a logical defense of his position then *you* or *in your opinion* are permissible. The teacher should, however, be careful in the case of measuring the student's ability to present a sound and rational position to grade on that premise and *not* on the position per se.

6. Construct your questions so that they may be answered at all degrees of competency. Every student should be able to respond to the question. However, the students may reveal varying levels of knowledge and understanding in their responses. Do not present questions that only the top 10 per cent can answer or questions that do not differentiate between the bottom 10 per cent and the top 10 per cent. The difficulty of the question should lie in the response, not in the vagueness or remoteness of the question.

7. Allow enough time for students to respond to the questions. Remember you are attempting to measure understanding and ability to apply facts not how fast students are able to write or organize their thoughts. If you give more than one essay question you might suggest a time allowance for each question.

8. Require all students to respond to the same questions. Do not offer alternative choices among the essay questions presented. For example, if you present six questions and ask the students to choose four to write on, you will not have a common basis upon which to evaluate different individuals within the classroom. Presenting the same questions to all the students gives a common reference point in comparing students and increases the validity of the test.

Grading Essay Tests

Grading essay tests is extremely important and is as important, if not more so, than the construction of good questions. Of course, both are needed if we are to be as fair as possible to our students. The following suggested procedures should help in this endeavor:

1. Prepare in advance the "ideal" answer and the number of credit points to be allowed for each question. The model answer will serve as the measurement criterion for each student's answer. Knowing in advance the number of points to be allowed for each question will make scoring consistent from paper to paper.

2. Grade all papers without knowledge of the author. This prevents bias from entering into grading procedures. If you know who wrote the paper your appraisal of him as an individual and student may influence your scoring either at a conscious or unconscious level. The following procedures can be used in facilitating anonymity. Although some of these procedures may seem overly elaborate or not even necessary, they are devised to help make your tests more valid and fair for all students. The important thing to remember is not the devices per se, but the underlying principle of grading papers with the least amount of bias, prejudice, or halo effect.

A. Prepare a paper with all of the students' names and an equal list of numbers. Pass the sheet among the students and ask each to select a number and place it before his name. After the last student has completed this task ask him to place the sheet of paper face down in one of your opened desk drawers. Each student will then use the number he has selected on his test, rather than his name. Thus, in grading the papers, you will not know who wrote it. After the papers are graded, you can match the numbers with the names for recording grades and returning papers.

B. Ask students to write their names on the back of their last sheet of paper.

C. If the answers are written in a test book with the name on the front, turn back the front cover. Instruct students to place name only on the front cover.

3. Grade only one question at a time for all papers. That is, start with question 1 on the first paper and grade it according to your "ideal" answer and then proceed on to the next paper and grade only question 1. Follow this procedure until you have gone through all the papers then come back and start with question 2 and so forth until all the questions have been read. This enables you to judge the responses of all your students to the same question consecutively. Otherwise you may be influenced by what the student has written on a previous question.

4. Write comments as well as awarding grades. Remember that a prime reason for giving the essay test is to facilitate learning. Written analysis or comments on the student's answer for each question will help achieve this goal probably more than a grade.

5. Average two or more graders' ratings. If two or more teachers are using the same test and have agreed upon the scoring procedure and all the factors are held constant, except for different graders, then an average of the scores for each test produces a more reliable rating. This, of course, takes time and would probably be done only in very important situations such as promotion or graduation.

A Case History

The following case history of an essay test and one teacher's approach is presented to illustrate some of the points we have covered in actual practice. After reading it evaluate what Mr. Frank did and did not do. How would you rate his approach based on our previous discussions?

An Essay Test to Measure a Special Ability in Eighth-Grade American History[1]

Mr. Frank's eighth-grade American history class had been studying the fighting that took place between the Indians and the settlers in the western states. The class had just completed several discussions on the rights of each side.

The major purpose of having these discussions was to improve the pupils' ability to find and express convincingly facts and arguments in support of their opinions.

Mr. Frank decided that he would like to give a test to measure his class's skill in this ability. At first, he considered giving an objective test. He thought he might list a number of arguments presented by both the Indians and the settlers and then ask the class to identify those which were backed up by facts. But then he decided against using this kind of test. An objective test would require the student to select sound arguments: it would not call upon him to develop and present them convincingly as he would do in actual discussion. Accordingly, Mr. Frank decided that an essay test would satisfy his purposes best.

Since the subject matter of the test was limited, it was unnecessary for Mr. Frank to prepare a written plan for the test. In a sense, the test questions themselves constituted the test plan. Here is the test he prepared. It had three questions:

1. Pretend that you are a settler and give three general reasons why you think your side is right in the war with the Indians. For each of the reasons, describe an actual happening to support your argument.

2. Pretend that you are an Indian and give three reasons why you

[1]From *Making the Classroom Test: A Guide for Teachers,* Educational Testing Service Evaluation and Advisory Service Series No. 4. © First Edition Copyright 1959, by Educational Testing Service. Second Edition 1961. Reprinted by permission of Educational Testing Service.

think your side is right in the war with the settlers. For each of the reasons, describe an actual happening to support your argument.

3. Look at the six reasons given by both sides and decide which one would be most dangerous if everyone accepted this kind of reasoning. Give two examples of how people might do bad things if they accepted this kind of reasoning.

Before scoring the papers, Mr. Frank analyzed the points which he thought would appear in an ideal response and decided how much he would count for each point. He decided not to take off credit for mistakes in spelling and English usage. But he planned to show the English teacher any paper which was especially poorly written so that the English teacher might give help in composition writing to those pupils who needed it.

After Mr. Frank corrected the papers, he found that most of the pupils had proceeded well on Questions 1 and 2 requiring reasons and examples. However, many of them had floundered on Question 3, which required them to point out the dangerous implications of one argument. Because of their difficulty with Question 3, Mr. Frank decided to organize a series of classroom debates, so that the students would get practice in extending, attacking, and defending an argument.

On an essay test of this sort, scores are not highly reliable. On a second reading, after a little time lapse, Mr. Frank would find it difficult to give every paper the same mark as on the first reading. Furthermore, several teachers grading the same papers would probably not agree very closely with one another. Therefore, Mr. Frank avoided giving an exact numerical score for each paper but instead assigned three general grades: good, average, and poor. However, he wrote many comments on the papers so that the pupils would have a better idea of the strengths and weaknesses of their arguments. He also read several papers to the class for discussion purposes, making full use of the test as an instructional device.

References

Chauncey, H. and Dobbin, J. E. Testing has a history. In C. I. Chase and H. G. Ludlow (Eds.), *Readings in educational and psychological measurement*. Boston: Houghton Mifflin, 1966. Pp. 3–18.

Cureton, E. E. Definition and estimation of test reliability. *Educational and Psychological Measurement*, 1958, **18,** 715–38.

Downie, N. M. *Fundamentals of measurement: Techniques and practices*. (2nd ed.) New York: Oxford University Press. 1967.

Falls, J. D. Research in secondary education. *Kentucky School Journal*, 1928, **6,** 42–46.

James, H. W. The effect of handwriting upon grading. *The English Journal*, 1927, **16,** 180–85.

Myers, A. E., McConville, C., and Coffman, W. E. Simplex structures in the grading of essay tests. *Educational and Psychological Measurement*, 1966, **26,** 41–54.

Payne, D. A. *The specification and measurement of learning outcomes.* Waltham, Mass.: Blaisdell Publishing Co., 1968.

Starch, D., and Elliott, E. C. Reliability of grading high school work in English. *School Review*, 1912, **20,** 442–57.

Starch, D., and Elliott, E. C. Reliability of grading work in history. *School Review*, 1913, **21,** 676–81. (a)

Starch, D., and Elliott, E. C. Reliability of grading work in mathematics. *School Review*, 1913, **21,** 254–57. (b)

Thorndike, R. L., and Hagen, E. *Measurement and evaluation in psychology and education.* (2nd ed.) New York: Wiley, 1961.

Additional Readings

In addition to the readings below, the preceding references are also excellent sources of information on test construction.

Adams, G. S. *Measurement and evaluation in education, psychology, and guidance.* New York: Holt, 1964. See Chapter 10.

Cox, R. C. Item selection techniques and the evaluation of instructional objectives. In D. A. Payne and R. F. McMorris (Eds.), *Educational and psychological measurement: Contributions to theory and practice.* Waltham, Mass.: Blaisdell Publishing Co., 1967. Pp. 157–61.

Educational Testing Service. *ETS builds a test.* Princeton, N.J.: Educational Testing Service, 1965. This is a twenty-four page booklet on how a standardized test is constructed. Much of it can be adapted for classroom use.

Engelhart, M. D. Suggestions for writing achievement test exercises. In D. A. Payne and R. F. McMorris (Eds.), *Educational and psychological measurement: Contributions to theory and practice.* Waltham, Mass.: Blaisdell, 1967. Pp. 138–47.

Foreman, E. Improving the reliability of a teacher-made test: A case study. In D. A. Payne and R. F. McMorris (Eds.), *Educational and psychological measurement: Contributions to theory and practice.* Waltham, Mass.: Blaisdell, 1967. Pp. 152–57.

Lien, A. J. *Measurement and evaluation of learning: A handbook for teachers.* Dubuque, Iowa: Wm. C. Brown Co., 1967. See Chapter 5.

Lindeman, R. H. *Educational measurement.* Glenview, Ill.: Scott, Foresman, 1967. See Chapter 4.

Mosier, C. I., Myers, M. C., and Price, H. G. Suggestions for the construction of multiple-choice test items. In C. I. Chase and H. G. Ludlow (Eds.), *Readings in educational and psychological measurement.* Boston: Houghton Mifflin, 1966, Pp. 272–81.

Noll, V. H. *Introduction to educational measurement.* (2nd ed.) Boston: Houghton Mifflin, 1965. See Chapters 5, 6, and 7.

Remmers, H. H., Gage, N. L., and Rummel, J. F. *A practical introduction to measurement and evaluation.* (2nd ed.) New York: Harper & Row, 1965. See Chapter 8.

Stanley, J. C. *Measurement in today's schools.* (4th ed.) Englewood Cliffs, N.J.: Prentice-Hall, 1964. See Chapters 6 and 7.

CHAPTER
15

The Objective Test

Horace Mann's "step forward" in 1845, when he introduced a uniform written examination was, as was stated in the previous chapter, a radical departure from the traditional oral examination. Mann's most important contribution to student evaluation was the introduction of the concept of requiring all students to answer the same questions. This idea was basic to later standardized tests. The beginning of the "second step forward" can be seen in the early history of standardized testing. This history has been reviewed earlier and it need not be mentioned again except to say that teacher-made objective tests grew with, and parallel to, the standardized testing movement. The objective test was developed in order to overcome some of the disadvantages of the essay test. We have already discussed some of the merits and limitations of both kinds of instruments. The critics of objective tests state that they measure only factual recall, emphasize memorization of obscure details, encourage too much guessing, do not deal with conceptualization, and do not present the student with the opportunity to practice writing.

Although we have dealt with the preceding criticisms in part in the previous chapters, in this chapter we will consider them in reference to what constitutes an objective test. Most importantly, however, our main attention will be focused on practical methods of improving and utilizing the objective test for classroom use and analyzing the results.

Characteristics

The objective test is so called because the scoring procedure is determined when the test item is written. That is, the correct answer, usually only one, is completely stated before testing. Thus the grader can be completely objective about the answer. We mentioned that the major drawback of essay tests lies in scoring the test. Objective tests attempt to overcome this deficiency. It should be noted that the word *objective* is in reference only to the rules for scoring. These scoring rules for objective tests are absolutely clear before testing begins. The actual content and coverage of objective tests, however, may be as subjective as the essay test. It is possible that the teacher may be wrong in what she designates as the correct answer. The important point to remember is that the teacher must be sure of what she considers to be the correct answer. In an essay test teachers sometimes have a great deal of difficulty setting up their own standards for the correct answer. The objective test item, however, must have only one correct answer, and this is decided when the item is written, not when it is graded.

The objective test is a structured examination. That is, each examinee is presented with exactly the same problem. The essay question, no matter how good it is phrased, will have different meanings to different students. The objective test, on the other hand, being completely structured, must be answered in a prescribed manner. The student is not called upon to organize his response as he is in the essay format.

The objective test requires the student to *recognize*, not *recall*, the correct answer. This is because most objective tests present given alternatives (with the exception of the completion item), one of which is the correct response. It should be noted, however, that objective items can be constructed to appraise recalling and the use of previously learned information, although in most cases the objective test does not tap this source of knowledge.

In our previous discussions of reliability, we have noted that an increase of items tends to increase the reliability of the test. The objective test lends itself to this task more readily than the essay because each item of the objective test is short and requires less response time. Thus the greater number of items in the objective test can sample more topics.

Scoring the objective test is routine, because a scoring key is established at the time the test is constructed. The score, therefore, will be the same no matter who scores it. The student who is the teacher's pet or the "bad boy," the handwriting expert or the scribbler will all obtain the same scores if they choose the same responses.

General Rules for Item Writing

The following rules should be observed when writing objective tests:

1. Observe the rules of good English usage. Gear your language to the whole group of students. Attempt to communicate to the students

in readable language that is not stilted or complex. Be sure that even the duller students can understand the items.

2. Avoid questions that do not have answers that would be agreed upon by most experts. Do not use "trick" items in which the correct answer is dependent upon obscure key words.

3. Avoid items that answer other items in the test.

4. Use your test items to tap important, not trivial, areas of knowledge.

5. Identify any authorities cited in your item.

Types of Objective Items

There are many different types of objective items. Our attention will be focused on the most prominent.

True-False Items

Do not use true-false items if at all possible. The true-false item has been very popular with teachers, probably because it is easy to construct and requires little time. Do not allow the ease of construction to lure you into the true-false trap. Good true-false items are not easy to write and even the good ones have many limitations. The following statements are representative of the major drawbacks of the true-false item:

1. The true-false item tends to be greatly influenced by guessing. If, for example, a true-false test contained 100 items, it is very probable that most students could obtain a score of around 50 by guessing. This restricts the range and meaning of the scores. What is the relationship of John's score to guessing? Can one really say that Mary is a better student than Jane, or is she a better guesser? The longer you make the test the less chance of measurement error resulting from guessing; however, guessing still has an undue influence on scores.

2. It is almost impossible to make statements either absolutely true or false. For example, read the following statements and see if either is absolutely true or false.

T F   Adolph Hitler was responsible for World War II.
T F   People only exist in relationship to other people.

Although many historians and political scientists would place the major responsibility for World War II on Hitler and Germany, they would also trace the conflict to World War I and the resulting economic sanctions. The answer, of course, would need to be qualified. The second statement might fit neatly into some philosopher's bag or be warmly embraced by the sociologist. Other philosophers and psychologists might disagree entirely with it, or agree only if certain qualifications and nuances are added. Who is right? There are few, if any, ideas in the world of today that are so absolutely certain that simple true-false statements can be applied to them.

3. True-false tests foster poor test-taking habits. Students are clever and will second-guess the teacher who employs the true-false item and discern patterns, such as "She usually gives more items that are true," or, "Did you notice her true-false tests are in patterns of fives—five true and then five false?"

Granted that the preceding examples are obvious and one-sided, could you disprove their validity? Could the perfect item that you come up with be repeated in different areas over 100 times or more?

If you must write true-false items, bear in mind the following "yellow lights":

1. Stay away from broad generalizations which obviously give the answers away. Statements that include such terms as *never*, *only*, *always*, *all*, and *every* tend to do this.

2. Avoid items that are partly true and partly false.

3. Do not write unusually long and complex statements. Statements of this kind are generally true and many students are aware of this.

Completion Items

Completion items require the student to fill in a blank that completes the sentence or answers a specific question. For example:

1. The Constitution requires that a member of the United States Senate be at least _____ years old.

2. How old does a person have to be in order to be eligible for the United States Senate? _____.

The first statement requires the student to complete the sentence, whereas the second asks the student to supply the answer. This last form is also called by some a short-answer item. For the purposes of our discussion both will be included under completion items.

The completion item is related to the essay item and serves as a bridge between the objective and essay test. On the one hand, it is objective, in the sense that a prearranged answer can be chosen before testing; on the other hand, it is related to the essay test because the student must produce the correct answer rather than recognize it. The completion item is especially useful for appraising your student's knowledge of facts, such as names and dates. Its major limitation is its major asset; that is, its use to appraise factual knowledge. It does not measure the student's ability to apply or use this kind of information. In addition it is difficult to phrase items with clarity and yet not confuse students. Also some areas of study do not lend themselves to the simple task of asking for pure facts.

The following are some suggestions for writing completion items:

1. Write completion items in your own words and be sure that you limit correct responses to your actual achievement goals.

2. Refrain from writing items that can be completed by general intellectual ability rather than knowledge of the subject.

3. Do not give away the answer by varying the blanks according to the number of letters in the word. Blanks should always be of standard length.

4. Do not mutilate a passage with too many blanks.

> *Poor :* In (1917) Puerto Ricans were made (citizens) of the (United States) and given the right to (elect) an upper house with the (President) reserving the (right) to (veto bills) and appoint the governor and certain other officials.
>
> *Better :* Puerto Ricans were made citizens of the United States and given the right to elect an upper house with the President reserving the right to veto bills and appoint the _____ and certain other officials in the year of _____.

5. The important word or words to be fitted in should be at or near the end of the blank. This allows the student the opportunity to read the problem before the blank is seen.

> *Poor :* _____ _____ was the first United States Astronaut.
>
> *Better :* The name of the first United States Astronaut is _____ _____.

6. Construct your specific questions in a direct manner rather than using incomplete sentences.

> *Poor :* Columbus discovered America in _____.
>
> *Better :* In what year did Columbus discover America? _____.

7. State the words in which the answer is to be given.

> *Poor :* Where does the Congress of the United States hold its sessions? _____.
>
> *Better :* In what city does the United States Congress hold its sessions? _____.

Matching Items

The matching item's major advantage is that it condenses a great deal of material into a limited amount of space. An example of this type item is as follows:

1. James Fenimore Cooper _____   a. Compensation

                                                b. The Deerslayer

2. Ralph Waldo Emerson   _____   c. Ethan Brand

                                                d. Ichabod

3. Nathaniel Hawthorne   _____   e. The Legend of Sleepy
                                                     Hollow

4. Edgar Allan Poe   _____   f. A Psalm of Life

                                                g. The Raven

In the blank spaces students are requested to write the letter of each of the titles on the right that corresponds to the authors on the left.

The matching item is not particularly well suited to measuring the student's ability to conceptualize. It is useful for appraising specific aspects of a subject field, such as dates, leading personalities, definition of terms, meaning of words, and association of authors with titles of books.

The following are some suggestions for writing matching items:

    1. All matching items should be presented intact. All items for each set should be on a single page. Do not split the items from one page to another. This may be confusing and time-consuming for the student.

    2. The list of answer choices should contain at least two or three more items than the number of problems, which will reduce the effect of guessing. If both lists contained an equal number of items, the student could more easily arrive at the correct response through the process of elimination.

    3. Do not mix subject fields. This means for example, that if you have dates in a response list, you should not mix names or other unrelated items with them.

    4. The instructions should clearly state the basis for matching. Students should be told specifically what they are to do. For example, if one answer is to be used more than once, be sure to explain this in the directions.

    5. Present response items in a logical order if at all possible—alphabetically, chronologically, or any other format that assists the student in quickly perceiving all the items. For example, note the alphabetical list of authors and titles in our previous example.

Remember that you are attempting to appraise the student's knowledge of the subject field not his intellectual acumen in figuring out obscure test directions. If your matching items and directions are unclear, you may penalize the student who knows the subject but is not test-wise or skillful at figuring out puzzles.

Multiple-Choice Items

The multiple-choice format is one of the most popular and effective of all the objective tests. It consists of two parts: (1) the stem, which states the problem, and (2) a list of options, one of which is to be selected as the answer. The stem may be stated as a question or as an incomplete statement. It does not matter much which form is used. Most experienced test writers prefer the incomplete statement because it allows the reader a smooth transition from reading the stem to selecting the appropriate item. On the other hand, inexperienced test writers prefer the question form because it is easier to construct and helps the writer to state the problem cogently.

In constructing an incomplete statement item, be very careful in phrasing the options. Each option should follow the stem in a smooth manner. An awkwardly phrased option may be a cue that it is not the correct answer. Examples of both forms follow:

> *Question:* What is one of the important causes of mental
> retardation?
> A. Poor schools.
> B. Smoking.
> C. Heredity.
> D. Nuclear fallout.

> *Incomplete statement:* One important cause of mental retardation is
> A. poor schools.
> B. smoking.
> C. heredity.
> D. nuclear fallout.

The multiple-choice item can be used to appraise almost any educational objective with the exception, of course, of student organization and ability to produce answers. Some of the areas it is effective in measuring are the following:

1. Information.
2. Vocabulary.
3. Isolated facts.
4. Cause-and-effect relationships.
5. Understandings.
6. Insight and critical analysis.
7. Solution of problems.
8. Interpreting data.
9. Application of principles.

Many people believe that the multiple-choice item is a superficial exercise requiring little thought and no understanding. In order to combat this myth the Educational Testing Service (1963) prepared a booklet to show in concrete terms the falseness of the charge. Note that in Figure 42 a piece of sculpture is presented and the student is required to place it in its proper

In which of the following centuries was the piece of sculpture shown above most probably produced?

(A) The fifth century B.C.
(B) The fourteenth century A.D.
(C) The sixteenth century A.D.
(D) The eighteenth century A.D.
(E) The twentieth century A.D.

Figure 42. Example of a multiple-choice item testing depth of knowledge. (From *Multiple-Choice Questions: A Close Look*. Copyright © 1963, Educational Testing Service. All rights reserved. Reprinted by permission of Educational Testing Service.)

time period. Here the student must apply learned data to the situation. It is not simply an exercise or recitation of memorized information.

The multiple-choice item is very versatile and relatively free of some of the problems that afflict other types of objective items. The multiple-choice item does not require that one option or alternative be completely correct. On the contrary, the requirement is only that one option be significantly more correct. The difficulty of a multiple-choice item will depend on the "almost right" aspect of the options.

The construction of a good multiple-choice test item is difficult. Developing plausible incorrect options taxes the ingenuity of the teacher. The end product, however, is well worth the investment of time and energy. It is, therefore, recommended that you consider using the multiple-choice item for most of your objective tests. It is hoped the following suggestions and examples will help in this endeavor:

1. The stem of a multiple-choice item should pose a clear question or problem. It should not be a series of unrelated ideas some of which are true and others false.

Poor : In the Midwest
    A. there are many mountains.
    B. tornadoes occur most frequently in the Spring.
    C. people are politically more conservative.
    D. Chicago is the largest city.

In the preceding example note that the stem consists of a vague phrase "In the Midwest." What does that mean? It does not clearly convey the problem to the student. Should the student answer (D), which the teacher intended, or (B), which is also plausible, or how about (C)?

Better : The most heavily populated city in the Midwestern region of the United States is
    A. New York.
    B. Chicago.
    C. Cleveland.
    D. Los Angeles.

Note that if the student chooses (A) or (D) he shows his lack of knowledge of the location of the Midwest, whereas a (C) response would show his knowledge of this but a lack of information of the largest Midwestern city. Most importantly, however, the stem clearly focuses on the most heavily populated city in the Midwest, and only one answer is correct.

2. The stem should include as much of the item as possible. Note the preceding examples. The *poor* example has three words, whereas the *better* example has most of its words in the stem and very few in the options. This approach facilitates economy of reading time and communication of the problem to the student.

3. Incorrect options should be logically related to the stem. If you supply obviously incorrect options, the student, by sheer logic and elimination, may obtain the correct response. Note the following examples:

Poor : Schizophrenia is a term used in psychology to characterize
   A.   racial discrimination.
   B.   a group of children.
   C.   a group of psychotic reactions.
   D.   a group of Indians.

The student who has read and listened in class at even a very minimal
level should be able to guess that (C) is the correct response. He
therefore rules out all other options. We have appraised only his
intellectual ability to rule out obviously incorrect alternatives.

Better : Schizophrenia is a term used in psychology to characterize
   a group of
   A.   neurotic reactions.
   B.   organic disturbances.
   C.   psychotic reactions.
   D.   manic-depressive reactions.

In the *better* version the student knows that all four options are
psychological terms dealing with disturbed behavior. The problem is
which alternative best characterizes schizophrenia. The knowledgeable student knows that (A) is incorrect because schizophrenia constitutes a loss of reality. He also knows that schizophrenia may have
an element of organicity (physical causes) and sometimes behavior
similar to those classified as manic-depressive. He chooses (C)
because he knows that the other responses, although related, are
separate diagnostic entities and schizophrenia includes a group of
psychotic reactions. Thus using all plausible options curtails intelligent guessing.

4. The length of the options should be consistent and not vary with
their correctness or incorrectness. If this is not done students will
become aware of the fact that the long options are correct or vice versa.
Using our previous example, let us modify the options:

Poor :   A.   neurotic reactions.
   B.   organic disturbances.
   C.   psychotic reactions which reveal various degrees of ego
         disintegration.
   D.   manic-depressive reactions.

Note that in the changed version the correct answer (C) is longer,
whereas in the original (*better* version) all four of the options are
consistent in length.

5. The stem should not contain an excessive number of words
unless your goal is to evaluate the student's ability to select basic
facts, or unless your objective is to play an intellectual variety of
hide and go seek. Note the following two examples:

Poor: On March 4, 1801, Thomas Jefferson, leader of the victorious Republican Party, walked from his capital boarding house and took the oath of office. He looked the part of a farmer and, indeed, he was one, for his biggest interest, next to his country, was his affection for his beautiful home and estate in Virginia. He was a philosopher and lover of peace and was happiest when he could think about problems in art, religion, or science. The most important event of his first administration was
A. the repeal of the Naturalization Act.
B. the purchase of the Louisiana territory.
C. the repeal of the excise tax.
D. bringing the Barbary pirates to terms.

Better: The most important event of Thomas Jefferson's first administration was
A. the repeal of the Naturalization Act.
B. the purchase of the Louisiana territory.
C. the repeal of the excise tax.
D. bringing the Barbary pirates to terms.

Note that in the *poor* example the student had to wade through irrelevant material before arriving at the problem, whereas in the *better* example the stem immediately confronted the student with his task.

6. Maintain correct English usage throughout the item.

7. Place the correct option randomly throughout the test. That is, do not place most of the options in the (A) position, (B) position, and so on. Nunnally (1964) suggests a method that is easy to do and will arrange your items in a random order:

One way to rearrange the alternatives in a random sequence is by the use of shuffled cards. If, for example, there are five alternative answers for each item, the letters *a, b, c, d,* and *e* are written respectively on five cards. These are then shuffled four or five times and dealt out. The letter on the first card determines the position of the first alternative as it appeared when the item was constructed, which, ... is usually the correct alternative. The next card dealt determines the position of the first incorrect alternative, and so on until the positions of all five alternatives are determined. When such a random procedure is used, students cannot accurately detect patterns in the ordering of alternatives [pp. 124–125].

8. Do not use such options as *none of these, both* a *and* c *above,* or *all of the above.* The only time you may use such terms is in a mathematical problem requiring mechanical computation. For example,

Poor : Mary has an IQ of 103. Her intelligence is
    A. superior.
    B. genius.
    C. average.
    D. none of the above.

The use of *none of the above* might penalize the good student who knows "too much." Instead of answering (C), he might think the teacher wants (D), because IQ is not necessarily equivalent to intelligence and therefore on the basis of a test one cannot classify Mary's intelligence. If, on the other hand, we substitute *below average* for *none of the above,* the student is forced to make a decision, and knowing that an IQ of 103 in the general classification system is considered average, he will respond appropriately and save his dissent or criticism of the item for later discussion.

9. Accentuate the positive and eliminate the negative. In a learning situation it is much better to emphasize the positive than the negative aspects of learning. There are times, however, when the only thing one can do is to have students look for an option that does not relate or follow from a given principle. Negative statements used sparingly are acceptable. The problem is, however, that you may be reinforcing learning of erroneous concepts; it is also confusing to students who are geared to looking for correct rather than incorrect responses. If you must use a negative word in the stem it should be set off from the sentence by capitalization or underlining. For example,

According to the United States Constitution, citizens do NOT have the right to
    A. free assembly.
    B. freedom of religion.
    C. make arrests.
    D. advocate sedition.

10. Develop your test according to your educational objectives and the rules of good test construction. This last suggestion is obvious but nevertheless needs to be said. Remember that the "ideal" test, following the suggestions that have been made, is meaningless if it does not measure what *you* want. This means that you must judge the skills, understandings, facts, and other factors you consider important within the structure of good test construction. A test ideal from a test maker's point of view may be poor from a teacher's perspective. The important thing to do is to combine both so as to have the best possible instrument to help you help your students in their educational progress.

Mechanical Operations

Thus far our attention has been directed to improving the quality of objective test items. This section will be devoted to the clerical or pedantic aspects of test construction. Though it may not be as glamorous or as creative, it is a necessary part of test production.

Item Writing

Professional item writers use separate 5- by 8-inch cards on which they write their items. This procedure may be of help in putting together the final product. At the bottom of the card, list the area and skills tested by the item. The intended answer key (A, B, C, or D) should be written on the back of the card.

Assembly

You now have a group of items that need to be integrated into a test format. Check the items against your course objectives and make sure you have covered all the areas you consider important. Be sure you have enough items to make your test reliable.

Editing and Arranging

Be sure that your items follow the suggestions for good item construction. Check your English usage to see that it is grammatically correct and that you have not inadvertently misspelled or omitted a word. Next, see if you can arrange for a colleague to read over your test and attempt to answer the questions. Incorporate his suggestions into your test if they seem appropriate.

After you have edited your examination arrange the questions in order of difficulty. This can be done by establishing categories representing degrees of difficulty—for example: *very hard, hard, average, easy, very easy*. The distribution of item difficulty should be similar to the normal curve distribution. That is, there should be a few *very hard* and a few *very easy* questions. The rest of the items should be of moderate difficulty. There is no point in having items that no students can answer or items that everyone answers correctly. Before you administer the test, of course, you can only estimate the difficulty of items; however, as we shall discuss later, an item analysis of the test results will establish the degrees of difficulty more accurately.

After you have ascertained the degrees of item difficulty your next step is to arrange them in the order that they will be presented to the student. First, be sure not to mix different formats—that is, all multiple-choice items should be in the same section, all matching items should be in the same section, and so forth. Second, within each type of item, arrange your problems by degree of difficulty, starting with the *very easy* and ending with the *very hard* items. It is very important to do this because some students, especially the younger ones, may be discouraged by difficult problems in the beginning and consequently either not finish or not do their best. This arrangement is also helpful to students who work slowly. These students may know the answers to the easier questions but in a timed test may never reach them. If possible, also try to have topics follow in logical and coherent blocks of questions. Do not present, for example, an item on the Constitution, then one on the Bill of Rights, then one on the Constitution, and so forth. It is much more desirable to group the Constitution questions together and then the Bill of Rights questions together. This presents whole blocks of subject matter together and allows the student to attack the problems from a common frame of reference. (If you arrange according to groups you will then, of course, place the items within groups from *easy* to *hard*.)

Directions

The detailed nature of test directions will depend on the grade and test sophistication of your students. Explicit and understandable directions are extremely important. You may present your written directions on the front page along with a place for name, date, class, and any other data you deem necessary.

The directions should be completely clear on the exact method to be used in recording the answers. In addition, the student should be told of the proposed scoring procedure and credits to be allowed for each section or item of the test.

The following is an example which may be adapted for most objective tests.

> *Directions:* This is a fifty-minute test. There are seventy-five questions. Mark only *one* answer to each question. Mark the answer you think is correct (see example below) by drawing an "X" through the letter that best corresponds to the correct answer for each problem. Do not make any marks on the test. Make all of your marks on the separate answer sheet.
>
> Do not waste time on questions that seem too difficult. It is better to go on and finish the test and then go back to the difficult questions. Remember it is better to make a careful guess than to spend too much time on any one item or to leave an answer blank. Your score will be based on the number of correct answers you mark.
>
> *Example:*
>
> | *Test Problem* | *Answer Sheet* |
>
> The first president of the United States was
>
>   A. Abraham Lincoln
>   B. George Washington
>   C. Benjamin Franklin   A   X   C   D
>   D. Thomas Jefferson

Table 27 presents an example of a teacher-made answer sheet.

Table 27 Part of a Teacher-Made Answer Sheet

| Name _____ | Class _____ |
| Date _____ | Name of Test _____ |

Directions: Mark an X through the letter that corresponds to the best answer in the following way:

Example: A xx C D

Remember, mark only one answer to each question.

Question:	Answer:	Question:	Answer:
1.	A B C D	25.	A B C D
2.	A B C D	26.	A B C D
3.	A B C D	27.	A B C D
4.	A B C D	28.	A B C D
5.	A B C D	29.	A B C D

Physical Layout

Remember, not only should your whole test, questions and language, be geared for student understanding, but also the physical layout should be arranged for your convenience in scoring. Here are some simple suggestions that will help you and your students:

1. Test material and all items pertaining to it should go on the same page. Do not, for example, have the test items that refer to a chart on a separate page but include the problem, items, and chart on the same page. Do not break up an item by having the stem and one or two options on one page and the rest on the next page.
2. Arrange to have each multiple-choice option on its own line.
3. Arrange your answer sheet (see Table 27) so that the answers are all in one column. This helps if you score by sight and is also convenient if you use a scoring key which can be placed beside the column.

Reproduction

You now have before you the edited and arranged questions, directions, and answer sheet. Now type a rough draft to see how it looks. Decide on your space requirements and other necessary mechanical problems. After you have done this, reproduce the test, using a mimeograph or any other process that is available to you. A good rule of thumb is to produce at least ten extra copies for unexpected needs. Next duplicate your answer sheets.

Scoring

Prepare your scoring key by marking the correct answers on an answer sheet. Although you could stop at this point and score the tests by comparing the key to the student's answer sheets, you should spend a little more time now to save your eyes and time in the future. A good method to accomplish this is to produce a *scoring stencil*. The scoring stencil is simply an answer sheet with the correct answer punched out; it is placed over an answer sheet, thereby making it possible to count the correct responses. There are many ways of constructing a scoring stencil. One method is to paste a correctly marked answer sheet on a piece of cardboard or a group of five or six papers pasted together, and punch out holes in the marked spaces.

In a large school system you may have an electrical scoring machine such as the IBM 805, which will save a great deal of time. In that case you will, of course, use standard IBM answer sheets similar to those used with standardized tests. You will then only have to record the correct answers on an IBM answer sheet using an IBM pencil or with some machines, a number 2 pencil. This stencil is then placed in the machine.

Item Analysis

Many teachers think that after they have developed, produced, administered, and scored a test they are through. This is not the case at all. If you stop after scoring you will be losing much valuable data about your test and student reactions. Test analysis will give you clues to the achievements of your class and will aid in future teaching objectives. It will also tell you about the weaknesses of your test and help you make improvements in future examinations.

The discussion that follows will be brief because the methods for analyzing test results were already presented in the chapter on achievement tests (Chapter 10). The same methodology of item analysis in standardized achievement tests, for the most part, can be used with your classroom tests.

You will first want to ascertain the degree of difficulty of your items. This can be done in a small classroom (less than forty students) by selecting the top ten and lowest ten students according to their test scores.[1] For each of the ten top students go through the test and mark a 1 next to each response chosen. Do the same for the lowest ten using a different mark, such as an ×. For example, note the following history item and the responses of the top and lowest ten.

	The first president of the United States was
	A. Abraham Lincoln
× × × × × × × × 1111111111	B. George Washington
×	C. Benjamin Franklin
×	D. Thomas Jefferson

[1] For the most reliable and theoretically correct method which would be needed for larger groups see Chapter 10.

An inspection of our example reveals that all the top ten students chose the correct answer and eight of the lowest ten also responded correctly. This data, although based only on a sampling of the class, would be very valuable to the teacher. On the basis of our example the teacher might decide that the easiness level is too high and that the item does not discriminate between good and poor students. For larger groups of students and for tests of 100 questions or more, mechanical methods such as scoring and punch cards would need to be used.

In analyzing data you will look for questions that no one answers correctly or that receive the same number of correct responses from "poor" students as from "good" students. The question or the options may be poorly stated.

If you are using a test primarily to rank your students for grading purposes, your questions (ideally) should be so difficult that on a five-option multiple-choice item only 60 per cent of the group obtain the right answer, on a four-option multiple-choice item 62 per cent obtain the right answer, and on each true-false item 75 per cent mark the correct response (Educational Testing Service, 1961).

A Case History

The following case history is presented as an illustration of some of the concepts, procedures, and problems in objective test construction that face the teacher. In many ways it is a synthesis of our previous discussion placed in an actual school setting.

An Objective Achievement Test on Fifth-Grade Arithmetic[2]

It was near the end of the school year and Mrs. Jackson, fifth-grade teacher, decided to give her pupils an arithmetic test covering the year's work. Her first step was to list the kinds of information she hoped to get from the test. She decided that, most of all, she wanted to get a general picture of class achievement with some indication of over-all areas of strength and weakness. Secondary purposes she listed were (1) to identify those pupils who might be especially weak in a particular arithmetic skill and (2) to measure the relative abilities of her students for purposes of report-card grading.

In trying to get an accurate picture of over-all class achievement, she decided that there were two ways in which she could classify the year's work: one was according to *the kind of computation required*, and the other was according to *the way the problem was presented*.

[2] From *Making the Classroom Test: A Guide for Teachers*, Educational Testing Service Evaluation and Advisory Service Series No. 4. © First Edition Copyright 1959 by Educational Testing Service. Second Edition 1961. Reprinted by permission of Educational Testing Service.

The kinds of computation required were

1. Multiplication
2. Division
3. Addition and Subtraction of Fractions
4. Measuring (distance, time, weight, temperature, etc.)
5. Decimals

The ways the problems were presented were

1. Simple computation, such as $21\overline{)\$1.05}$ or $1/2 + 1/3$
2. Problems requiring use of procedures learned previously, such as

    John missed 1/5 of the twenty words on a spelling test. How many words did he miss?

    or

    A group of twenty-nine children were making programs for a school assembly. They needed 435 programs. How many did each child have to make?

3. Problems requiring original thinking by pupils and use of "number sense." In these problems the pupils could not depend on previously learned procedures for a method of solution but must develop their own procedures for solution. Two problems of this type follow:

    Problem one. Explain how you, as a fifth-grade pupil, using ten blocks, could prove to a fourth-grade pupil that 1/2 is bigger than 2/5.

    Problem two. You are standing directly in front of Building A and looking off at Building B in the distance. Here is the way the two buildings look to you:

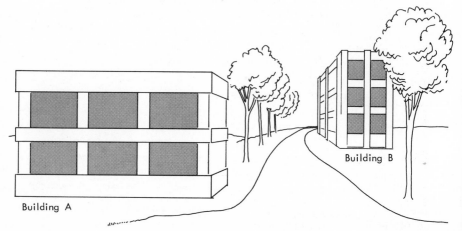

Building A

Building B

The rooms in both buildings are the same height. By looking at the windows, decide which of the following is true:

(A) Both buildings are the same height.
(B) Building A is two-thirds as high as Building B.
(C) Building A is one and one-third times as high as Building B.
(D) Building A is twice as high as Building B.
(E) You can't tell from looking at the buildings which one is higher.

(Answer: B)

Using these two ways for classifying the questions (according to the kind of computation required and according to the way the problem was presented), Mrs. Jackson was now ready to make *a written plan* for the test. She intended that this plan would provide for a test *paralleling* the emphasis given to various points in class.

Mrs. Jackson wrote out her test plan in the form of a "two-way grid." In a two-way grid each question is classified in two dimensions.

The two-way grid that Mrs. Jackson made for the arithmetic test is on page 6. Since she planned to allow an hour for the test, she thought 40 questions would be about the right number. The numbers in the boxes represent questions—these questions to be of a type described by the two dimensions of the grid.

Way Problem Presented

Kind of Computation Required	Routine Computation	Thought Problems Following Procedures Taught Previously	Thought Problems Requiring Students to Develop New Procedures
Fractions	7	4	1
Multiplication	2	3	1
Division	3	4	1
Measuring	1	5	1
Decimals	3	3	1

After Mrs. Jackson completed the two-way grid, she found it relatively easy to write most of the questions for the test. She was able to write many questions by paralleling questions from the arithmetic textbook itself. However, she found it quite challenging to write the five problems which would require students to develop new procedures.

Mrs. Jackson believed that the test covered understandings and skills in which her pupils had been well prepared. Therefore, she expected the very best students to get all or nearly all of the questions right, and she expected even the below-average students to get a majority of the questions right. She did not, however, make the mistake of deciding in advance that some minimum score—say 28 questions right (70%)—would represent a passing mark. She knew from previous experience that sometimes her questions turned out to be more difficult than they first seemed to her. She decided to wait until she could look at the scores actually made on the whole test and could scrutinize carefully any questions which proved particularly troublesome.

As it happened, most of the students did well on the test, although no one had a perfect paper. On the basis of the test, Mrs. Jackson felt that her class had achieved the objectives of the work in arithmetic. She did notice, however, that a number of students had difficulty with the problems involving decimals. Therefore she decided to spend more time working on decimals in the few weeks remaining in the school year. And then there was one student who failed all the division problems, although he did fairly well on the rest of the test. She arranged to give this student special help in division.

Most of the students had between 30 and 35 questions right. However, there were a few who scored above, and a few who fell below this middle range. Knowing which students were in the middle and which were above or below was useful to Mrs. Jackson in assigning report-card grades. Of course she also took into account each pupil's class work and his standing on other tests.

In evaluating her test, Mrs. Jackson felt it had been reasonably successful in meeting the purposes for which she had planned it. The test had given her a good picture of over-all class achievement and it had pointed up the weakness in decimals. It had not been planned to be highly diagnostic, but it had helped to identify one pupil who was especially weak in division. In addition, although the test did not rank all of her students in the exact order of their arithmetic abilities, it had given her information that was useful for grading purposes.

References

Educational Testing Service. *Making the classroom test: A guide for teachers.* Evaluation and Advisory Service Series, No. 4. (2nd ed.) Princeton, N.J.: Educational Testing Service, 1961.

Educational Testing Service. *Multiple-choice questions: A close look.* Princeton, N.J.: Educational Testing Service, 1963.

Nunnally, J. C. *Educational measurement and evaluation.* New York: McGraw-Hill, 1964.

16

Grades and Report Cards

Thus far we have primarily devoted our discussions to instruments that attempt to appraise student progress *objectively*. In this chapter our attention will be directed to the assignment of labels to test results and other evidence of pupil achievement. The best-constructed tests will be rendered useless if after reviewing the results the teacher assigns grades without a structured and coherent plan. Grading is subjective, but this subjectivity may be kept to a minimum by appropriate grading practices.

The assignment of report card grades is a difficult task. However, if a logical and rational system is followed, these tasks become less difficult. In addition, if information concerning a student's ability and progress is reported in understandable terms, fewer parents will become irate.

Philosophy

The individual teacher must think about grades in the context of learning and reality, must formulate a philosophy and approach to grades and report cards and then act accordingly. In determining this philosophy, questions dealing with the effects of grading on learning and motivation must be answered. These philosophical conclusions must then be translated into the context of the school setting and its own unique demands and realistic problems. If, for example, you decide that grading is inaccurate and unreliable and the school policy is directly in conflict with your ideals, do you completely capitulate or do you, on the other hand, go on strike and refuse to cooperate with the school administration? Or do you work within the system and attempt to modify existing practices?

This chapter is based on the last approach—that grades are with us, like it or not, and our job is to make them as accurate and effective as possible. The teacher who is against grades can in the classroom place more emphasis on the rewards of learning and less on the importance of grades. The teacher can take part in teacher committees formed to review and modify the existing grading policies. This approach incorporates individual philosophy within the reality of the school setting.

Purposes of Grades

Remmers, Gage, and Rummel (1965) list eleven common purposes of marking systems:

1. Information for parents on pupil status or progress
2. Promotion and graduation
3. Motivation of school work
4. Guidance of learning
5. Guidance of educational and vocational planning
6. Guidance of personal development
7. Honors
8. Participation in many school activities
9. Reports and recommendations to future employers
10. Data for curriculum studies
11. Reports to a school the pupil may attend later [p. 288]

In reviewing the preceding eleven points the teacher who is adamantly opposed to grades must admit that they do serve many functions. Some of these purposes, such as "motivation" and "guidance of learning," may possibly be discarded in an ideal situation where students learn "for the sake of learning," but some of the other purposes would be difficult to fulfill without grades or another type of evaluative device.

Assigning Test Grades

Students need to know how well they perform on a classroom test. They must know the areas of their subject-matter strength and weakness. This can be accomplished by going over the test, item by item, and allowing the students to ask questions. The teacher and his students can together decide whether certain competencies are lacking or whether there was a misunderstanding of the test question. The teacher may decide that a test item was poor and the student's "incorrect" response might be considered correct.

Students also need to know what their final scores mean. Not many students in our American schools will be satisfied to know only how many questions they answered correctly. They want an evaluation, "Is my score good, fair, or bad?" Let us look at some possible approaches.

Percentages

A traditional approach in assigning test grades is arbitrarily to decide that all students who answer 92 per cent of the questions correctly receive an A; those who answer 85 per cent correctly receive a B; 75 per cent correctly receive a C, and so forth. This type of assignment does a grave injustice to the objective test, because many easy items would have to be included to ensure that the average pupil obtained a score over 75 per cent. In our earlier discussion of the objective test it was stated that a test that had too many easy or too many hard questions was a poor test. Thus to follow the percentage system the teacher would have to go against one of the basic rules of objective test development. It is, therefore, strongly recommended that this type of grading not generally be used with objective tests.

The use of this grading system in essay tests, however, is not as inappropriate as it is with objective tests. The percentage assignment is only another method of conveying the teacher's evaluation of the paper. It should be mentioned, however, that a grade of 86, for example, might be confusing to the student, because in essay examinations the criteria for scoring are not always evident.

Grading on the Curve

Grading on the curve theoretically assumes a given number of grades, A through F, which are determined by the relative positions of the students in comparison to one another. For example, note the following distribution:

Grade	Percentage of Students
A	10
B	15
C	50
D	15
F	10

This form of grading, which presupposes that achievement will be normally distributed in a given classroom and that, therefore, a certain number of A's, B's, C's, D's, and F's must be given in relationship to the normal curve distribution, is a *prostitution of statistics* and a poor and unfair way to grade. The classroom does not contain enough pupils for the assumption to be made that there is a normal distribution of students. A much greater number than the usual twenty to forty pupils per class would be needed. Thus, the teacher may have a bright or dull class which is not at all representative of different levels of ability. If the teacher follows the curve in this setting, some children in the bright group would be doomed to failure and some children in the dull class would have to receive A's. Promotion and test grades would then be linked to the chance of what group a student found himself in. If an average pupil could arrange to be in the dull group, he probably would graduate in the top of his class. The use of the curve in the upper-middle-class high school and college and graduate school presents a similar problem. In these settings there tends to be a skewed curve, that is, students at the low end may be in the bright range of ability in the general population and students at the top in the very superior classification. If curving was adhered to completely in such situations, bright and superior students might have difficulty in graduating. Thus in a statistical sense the curve is an erroneous method of evaluation because the groups are too small, and in selected groups there is not a representative distribution.

Stanley (1964) in discussing the problems of "grading on the curve" cites an amusing story:

> On the first day of class a graduate professor of Latin informed the seven students taking his advanced course that he had learned of grading on the curve the previous summer and would use it in this class, resulting in certainty that one of the seven students would fail the course. As the students left at the close of class, one of them muttered to the other six, "I'm sure to be the one who fails, so I'm dropping the course right now."
>
> "But you can't do that," the others exclaimed, "because we don't know which one of us would fail then."
>
> So the six pitched in and paid the predestined failure to stay in the course and absorb the failing grade [pp. 326–27].

In addition to its statistical limitations, the curving of grades leads to undesirable attitudes. The quest for grades and the competitiveness among students is greatly increased. The typical student cannot help but hope that his friends will do poorly so as to enhance his own grade.

Still another drawback lies in the position in which it places the teacher. If she assists one student to do better on a test, she is automatically relegating another pupil at least one slot back. In some cases this may mean helping one student to pass at the expense of another's failure.

Lindvall (1961) examines the problem of the distribution of test scores, stating that the assumptions based on the normal curve:

> involve about as many subjective judgments on the part of the teacher as does any other grading procedure. The teacher must use his judgment in constructing a test he feels should produce a normal distribution of scores if given to a large group of pupils. . . . This assumption can never really be given an exact check. The form of the distribution of any set of test scores depends on the difficulty of the items included in the test as well as on the ability of the students, and it is doubtful that many teachers consistently produce tests that yield aproximately normal distributions. As a result most teachers using the normal-curve method of grading are probably using it with measures that are not distributed normally.
>
> Even under ideal conditions the normal curve method is not the objective and scientific procedure for assigning grades that some persons assume it to be [p. 256].

Our discussion of "grading on the curve" leads to only one conclusion: if this grading method is taken to mean that a set number of students must pass and a given number must fail, then this approach should never be used in classroom evaluation.

Absolute Standards

The teacher says, "I have my standards and the children must meet them if they want to pass the test. I don't care if everyone passes or everyone fails. They must meet my standards." This approach is not confined to any one discipline, but the number who actually enforce such standards is probably not very large. It is difficult to have absolute standards when dealing with children because children as well as groups differ. Not many teachers would give all F's or all A's; nor would principals or parents accept them.

The Answer?

There is no easy solution to the assignment of grades on an examination. The fairest approach seems to be an intelligent combination of some of the approaches already mentioned. Absolute standards should be tempered by the performance of the class as a whole. A given amount of material must be learned, and within this frame of reference grades will be decided on the relative merits of the entire class performance. This may sound like curving, and it is in the sense of comparing students to one another. It is not in the sense of predetermining how many people must receive certain grades.

In determining grades for a specific test, one must keep in mind the purposes of the test in relationship to the instructional objectives of the unit.

These goals will weigh heavily in the consideration of grade categories. For example, you are teaching arithmetic in fourth grade. One of your basic objectives is to teach children the multiplication tables. A passing grade in fourth-grade arithmetic means partly that a child has learned how to multiply. In this situation an absolute standard in grading is necessary. You cannot certify that a child has learned how to multiply on the basis of his class ranking in a given test or on an arbitrary percentage of the questions answered correctly. Grading must be in line with your educational objectives.

In another situation where there is more latitude in objectives, the teacher may want to allow the B, C, and D grades to be distributed according to the performances of the students. There will, of course, not be a predetermined number of grades. The A and F grades may entail the classical percentages approach, allowing these percentages to be relevant to the specific educational objectives. In an objective examination the minimum level for a passing grade should probably be kept between 40 and 45 per cent, because even poor students will be able to guess some of the answers.

Individual test grades should be a device to convey relative performance. Of course, the student's test scores throughout the semester or year should be averaged. The final results may be quite different from an assigned grade on one test.

In awarding test grades what is important is the relationship of these symbols to overall educational concerns and objectives. Combining these with the most appropriate mechanical means for assignment of grades will produce the most equitable evaluation.

Assigning Report Card Grades

The teacher has prepared the educational unit, taught the lessons, and measured the outcomes. Now final grades must be assigned. What factors should be considered? Should classwork as well as tests be counted? How should different sources of evaluation be weighed?

Keeping in mind the educational goals, the teacher must decide what evidence will indicate the accomplishment of these goals. A decision must be made concerning the relative weight to be placed on different types of data, including examinations, quizzes, papers and reports, and classroom participation.

Examinations and Quizzes

All the student's *raw scores*, not his test grades, on the objective tests and quizzes he has taken are totaled. For example, Bill Ross, a student, has obtained scores of 40 and 55 on the two objective tests. Each test had a total of 60 items. The maximum possible score that Bill could receive would be 120. His overall objective test score is 95. The same process is used for grades obtained on quizzes. Each student's scores are tallied in the same manner. These cumulative scores are graded according to the educational goals by using the techniques discussed in the previous section.

Papers and Reports

Reliability in evaluating papers and reports is quite low. However, this work represents an important aspect of the learning process and needs to be considered in the total evaluation. If papers and reports are to receive equal weight with quizzes and/or examinations, a composite grade of all papers may be simply obtained by assigning numbers to the various letter grades given for each paper or report. For example, consider the following table.

Bill Ross's Papers and Reports

	Grades	Composite Grade
Papers	A, B, B	3.3 (B)
Reports	B, C, D	2.0 (C)

$(A = 4, B = 3, C = 2, D = 1, F = 0)$

Process:

Papers	Reports
$4 + 3 + 3 = 10$	$3 + 2 + 1 = 6$

$$3 \overline{)10} \quad \begin{array}{r} 3.3 \\ \end{array}$$

```
        3.3                      2
    3 | 10                   3 | 6
        9                        6
       ‾‾                       ‾‾
       10                        0
```

Classroom Participation

Classroom work is a very important area of evaluation but one of the most difficult to quantify. Questions that need to be answered in this area are, "How well does the student work with others? What is his role in class discussions?" "How deep and pertinent are his contributions to these discussions?" "How well does he perform in class projects?" "How well does he perform in class recitations and blackboard work?"

The answers to these questions are not easy and are subject to many distortions. They are nevertheless important. Probably it is best *not* to include them in an overall grade evaluation. They should be noted, however, in the child's cumulative record, and if there is space on the report card for comments, a brief written description and analysis of these traits should be given.

Combining Data from Different Sources

Now we are at the juncture where we must translate our calculations into the form of a letter grade. One of the most feasible methods is to reduce all the scores to a common denominator or numerical scale. If, for example, all our data are to receive equal value in determining the final grade, we can use the method described in the section on papers and reports. Let us look at Bill Ross's record as an example of this method:

Average Scaled Scores

Quizzes	Objective Tests	Papers	Reports	Final Average	Grade
2.4	3.0	3.3	2.0	2.6	C+

In the preceding example the quizzes and objective test grades were assigned the same values as papers and reports, that is, A = 4, B = 3, C = 2, and so forth. These sources of evaluation were given equal weight to simplify the example. If we were to decide to weight different areas differently, the same basic process could be followed but more value would be given to the areas of most importance. For example, if the quizzes and objective tests were to be counted as worth two times as much as the other factors, their value would become 4.8 and 6.0, respectively. (We would then, of course, divide the total by 6 rather than by 4.)

Report Cards

The great majority of report cards contain both grades and a list of check items, especially in the elementary grades. The report card, no matter what its format, should keep subject-matter achievement separate from effort, neatness, citizenship, behavior, and so forth. The report card is an important tool of communication, deserving of the best efforts to provide understandable answers to parental questions such as, "How does my child compare to the other children in reading?" "Does he make friends easily?" "What about his behavior in the classroom?"

There is no one report card that can serve as a model. The local school system must devise the type that best serves its needs. The important thing to remember is that it serves as a line of communication between the teacher and parents. The meaning of the grades and symbols used should be clear.

Evaluation and Reality

All teachers are not going to follow the rules for proper measurement, and, as we have stated before, even if they do we cannot expect perfect tests or grades. What can the teacher do in light of the tenuousness of testing and grading? The answer is easy. The teacher should avoid taking tests or grades too seriously. Nunnally (1964) states this quite well:

> Teachers, students, and parents should learn to take the results from one test, and even the final grades from a whole term, with a large grain of salt. Such grades should be considered as only highly tentative indications of the student's basic abilities, his application to schoolwork, and his attitudes toward learning. Bad grades during one term may correctly spell trouble for the future; or they may equally well mean that the teacher was biased in grading the student, that the tests were poorly constructed, that the teacher has unreasonably tough standards for grading, or that the student is going through a "phase" which he will outgrow later [p. 164].

On the whole, most teachers do a pretty good job of evaluation. The dramatic exceptions cloud the picture. Think back to your own student days in elementary and high school. How many times did you think you were unfairly graded? How about evaluation in college? Probably your college grades do not seem as valid as your elementary and high school evaluations. If that is true maybe it is because the college professor does not have as much data upon which to base his evaluation—daily recitations, class projects, observations and so forth.

The important thing to remember in your evaluation is to attempt to minimize personal bias or prejudice in awarding grades. At the same time one must face reality and admit to students and parents that grades are only an attempt to evaluate performance. Do not be afraid to admit that there is not always a great deal of difference between a C and a B. However, you will usually be confident of the validity of the extremes. That is, an A is awarded on very evident criteria, as is the awarding of an F, especially when it means a student will be held back a semester or year in his school life. Try to emphasize learning and de-emphasize the importance of grades. Follow your grade evaluations with either oral or written descriptions of student progress, especially with children who are experiencing learning difficulties.

References

Lindvall, C. M. *Testing and evaluation: An introduction.* New York: Harcourt, Brace and World, 1961.

Nunnally, J. C. *Educational measurement and evaluation.* New York: McGraw-Hill, 1964.

Remmers, H. H., Gage, N. L., and Rummel, J. F. *A practical introduction to measurement and evaluation.* (2nd ed.) New York: Harper & Row, 1965.

Stanley, J. C. *Measurement in today's schools.* (4th ed.) Englewood Cliffs, N.J.: Prentice-Hall, 1964.

PART SIX

A School Testing and Evaluation Program

CHAPTER

17

Planning and Using
a Testing Program

This chapter deals with the actual mechanics of planning and using standardized tests in a comprehensive school testing program. Our discussion is focused primarily on paper-and-pencil group testing. These tests are generally administered to all pupils in a given grade at the same time. Projective techniques, apparatus-type tests, and other clinical instruments will not be discussed because they are not part of a general group testing program.

The intent, then, of this chapter is to present an outline and discussion of what constitutes a sound testing program in terms of specific and concrete suggestions. These suggestions should not be taken as the final word in testing programs. Test selection and the objectives of a testing program must meet individual needs and be developed in conjunction with the educational goals of a particular school within a particular geographic setting for particular groups of students.

There are, however, general guidelines and essential steps to be taken in the development and implementation of a testing program, as follows:

1. Determine the objectives of the testing program.
2. Select tests that meet these objectives.
3. Arrange a time schedule for administering the tests.
4. Arrange for an in-service test orientation for teachers.

5. Arrange for a pretest orientation for students.
6. Administer the tests.
7. Score the tests.
8. Record the test results.
9. *Use* the test results.

Determining the Objectives

Tests are useful only if they supply the school, the teacher, the student, and the parent with meaningful information. To administer tests because it is fashionable to do so or because the government provides funds for testing is an exercise in futility.

Although it may seem obvious to the reader that tests should be given for specified purposes and then used, this is not always the case. Many years ago, for example, this writer had occasion to be in a school system that applied for governmental funds for testing. The request was granted and the school administered a great many different tests without ever thinking of what they wanted to measure. They had received money and they were going to spend it all. The natural consequences of this "nonthink" action was a great deal of wasted time and energy. After the tests were administered and scored, no one knew what to do with them. They were finally stacked in neat piles and found their last resting place in the school basement. The government had spent money; the teachers had spent time; the students had spent energy; and the test publishers and authors were a little richer. These were the only results of testing in this school.

A Testing Committee

The first step in planning the objectives of a standardized testing program is to involve appropriate personnel. Almost all the school's staff and administration have a vital interest and responsibility in planning the testing program. Personnel at different levels willl be able to utilize some or all of the test results.

A standing testing committee is one method of involving staff participation in the development of a school-wide testing program. This committee should be composed of school personnel who have interest and needs that may be served by testing, and should represent the special interests of various groups within the school. If there is a director of testing or research, he should be appointed to give technical assistance. The guidance counselor and/or school psychologist can also serve in an advisory capacity. In addition, representatives from the school administration and instructional staff will need to participate in the committee to voice their special needs and interests. In a large system the directors of instruction and curriculum could serve as representatives.

What is important is that the committee represent the various interests within the school system.

The committee's work should not stop when a testing program has been developed. The committee needs to direct its energy toward a continual evaluation of the testing program, making changes, modifications, and additions as the need arises.

The involvement of teachers and other school personnel in the planning and directing of a testing program lessens the likelihood of misuse of tests. Misuse involves not only the filing away of unused test data but also incorrect interpretation of that data. Involving teachers in the planning of a testing program may also help keep them from feeling that outside materials and unnecessary work are being imposed on them.

Practical Aspects

The purposes of a testing program in a given school system should relate directly to that system's own educational goals and needs. First the needs of the students, the instructional program, and administrative concerns should be surveyed. Research data will evolve from this process. The school testing program should be geared to practical needs, not to what a textbook states or what a consultant thinks is in vogue. Consultants, textbooks, and testing experts have their place and can make valuable contributions. Their assistance, however, should come after the local school has decided on its own unique objectives and practical needs. Theoretical research dealing with curriculum problems or administrative issues are worthy in themselves of the school's time and energy, but the practical problems of educating children must come first.

Structure

A practical approach must be developed within a rational and cohesive system, which provides tools of assessment and defines the limits of the program. In planning a testing program, considerations for administration, scoring, and reporting results must be based on the availability not only of funds but also of personnel. Teachers often complain of delayed feedback of test results. Giving tests in the fall and not making the results available until spring is a good way to lose the support of the faculty. The importance of reporting test results to teachers as soon as possible cannot be overemphasized. It is much better to have a small program that the school can handle than an elaborate one that causes discontent.

The structure of the program should be definitively geared to specific purposes. The program should state in clear and cogent terms its purposes and range of objectives. For example, the statement "to diagnose instructional problems" is very nice, but to what does it refer? A better statement might be, "to diagnose problems in seventh-grade arithmetic." Thus, a specific purpose has been formulated and further action, such as selection of tests in arithmetic achievement, may be directly formulated.

When to Begin Planning

The testing committee needs to plan for testing well in advance of the intended dates of administration because: (1) committees should not be rushed in their important deliberations and (2) selecting, ordering, receiving, and inventorying tests is time-consuming. Lennon (1962) in addressing himself to this problem states,

> A testing program should be planned between six months and a year in advance of the time when it is actually to take place, depending somewhat on whether it is a spring or a fall program, on local budgeting practices, on the size of the system and consequent communications and training problems, and similar factors. When a major program is being contemplated, one that covers many subjects at many grade levels with a single battery, it will ordinarily be desirable to think in terms of establishing a program that will be maintained for several years. In giving thought to this type of program, it is well to have in mind such matters as the availability of alternate forms, and the possibility that revised editions of the test in question will be appearing over the period of the proposed program [p. 3].

Selecting Tests

Selecting the tests that meet the school's objectives and needs is a difficult task. There are many published standardized tests but only a small number of quality instruments that will be suitable for local needs. The testing committee needs to appraise the intended test not only in terms of suitability for local purposes but also in the technical sphere of validity, reliability, and standard error of measurement. These basic concepts are crucial factors in selecting tests. In addition, practical problems such as cost and time to administer and score the test must be considered. The committee should be aware of these criteria in their test selections. The committee member who is the director of testing or research should direct the technical evaluation. If there is no director of testing and research, then the school psychologist and/or guidance counselor should serve in this capacity. The committee will, of course, have available basic references such as test catalogs, Mental Measurements Yearbooks, Tests in Print, Psychological Abstracts, and Standards for Educational and Psychological Tests and Manuals, reviewed in Chapter 6. In the following two sections essential types of tests needed at different levels and the rationale for their use will be presented.

Suggestions for a School Testing Program

The recommendations that follow are based on a general core of test needs from kindergarten through twelfth grade. It must, however, be stated once again that the local school should develop its own testing program according to its own needs and objectives. On the other hand, the local school, no matter what its specific needs or problems, should consider certain essential areas in their measurement program. The suggestions that follow are directed to these essential elements.

Kindergarten Through Sixth Grade

The elementary school is primarily concerned with the development of basic skills and tools in the essential areas of reading, writing, and arithmetic. This may sound like an old-fashioned view, but basically the three R's are still the essential ingredients needed to build upon for future educational progress.

It should be noted again that our discussion is confined to paper-and-pencil tests. It is assumed that the teacher will use other techniques to measure such things as citizenship and social adjustment. Our concern here is the measurement of academic promise and achievement. It is also assumed that children have been given physical examinations, including eye and hearing tests.

READING READINESS TESTS (K-1)

The reading readiness test is usually the first test a child encounters in his school career. The reading readiness test has many shortcomings in terms of validity and reliability. Even more important, however, there is a great deal of confusion as to what constitutes readiness. Still, the first-grade teacher needs to know something about her pupils and their readiness to learn. The readiness test, with all its shortcomings, will provide a rough estimate upon which to begin a program of individualized reading instruction. Later, as the teacher becomes better acquainted with her students she will make appropriate changes based on new data. In the meantime, however, the reading readiness test has served a useful function.

READING TESTS

Marshall McLuhan notwithstanding, reading is still the most important learned skill in the education of an individual. The mastery of this skill enables the student to acquire other knowledge to build upon and expand his intellectual horizons. The absence of this basic skill spells academic trouble for the student. If reading is the single most important skill to be learned in the elementary school, it follows that the most important test to be given is the reading test. It should be placed at the top of the testing list of priorities.

Financial resources permitting, a reading test should be administered every year beginning in the second grade. If there are limited funds, the reading test may be administered in the beginning of the third grade to all students. Future testing would focus on students experiencing difficulties in classroom reading. It is best, however, to measure all children's reading growth each year in order to gear the instructional program to individual needs. The reason for testing reading in the beginning rather than at the end of the academic year is that children may go down or up in their reading levels over the summer. The teacher needs to know the level of student reading achievement at the beginning of the school year, not levels three to seven months old.

SCHOLASTIC APTITUDE TESTS

The scholastic aptitude test helps the teacher understand the range of possible student progress. It presents objective data to aid the teacher in understanding individual student achievement both in the classroom and on other standardized tests.

The scholastic aptitude test should not be administered earlier than the end of the second grade or beginning of the third grade. In the first grade a reading readiness test is generally preferable to the scholastic aptitude test. The assignment of an IQ or "intelligence" score (even if we call it scholastic aptitude, not everyone has received the message) at the beginning of a child's school career may do a great deal of harm. Teachers are likely to be less rigid about a child's maturational level of readiness than they are about his mental ability. Although we delay our testing of scholastic aptitude until the end of the second or third grade, we must remember that even at this point reliability is not very satisfactory.

If a scholastic aptitude test is given at the end of the second grade, we want to administer another test at the end of the fourth or beginning of the fifth grade. If only one test of this type is to be given in elementary school, the fourth or fifth grade is preferable because of the greater reliability of scholastic aptitude tests at this level. If financial resources for testing are plentiful, scholastic aptitude can, of course, be more frequently measured, depending on the needs of the particular school. Additional testing will also serve to increase the reliability of results.

ACHIEVEMENT BATTERIES

A minimal program in grades 1 through 3 would involve measuring achievement in the basic skills. These include reading, arithmetic, language, and listening. If reading skills are adequately appraised by the achievement battery, the school could eliminate the separate reading test or use a different type of test such as an oral reading instrument. If monetary conditions allow, it would be best to begin these tests in the beginning of the second grade and continue testing in the fall of each year. If a school system can afford to administer the battery only once during the elementary program, the beginning of the fourth grade is best. This would enable the school to plan their instructional program for the next three years, based on the academic achievement of the children. With these data, provisions can be made for accelerated or enriched programs as well as for remedial instruction for those children who reveal educational retardation.

At the upper grades of elementary school the achievement battery should include tests in content areas such as social studies and science. These more specialized areas should not be included until fifth or sixth grade.

SPECIALIZED TESTS

The four types of tests presented so far form the core of a good testing program. Individual needs of schools and students, however, may necessitate supplementary instruments. For example, the school in a disadvantaged setting may want to include a culture-fair test. If a community has a school psychologist and can afford individual intelligence testing, kindergarten would be an appropriate place for administration. Because the individual intelligence test is much more reliable than the group test, it provides an excellent base for programming individual instruction, if combined with a reading readiness test. However, the vast majority of school systems cannot afford this luxury.

Personality inventories and projective techniques are administered only upon referral from the teacher to the school psychologist. They should never be administered routinely.

Seventh Through Twelfth Grade

In the junior and senior high school the scope of testing enlarges along with the increase in the number of educational choices and decisions that must be made. Among the most important issues facing the student at this level are what courses to take and when; educational and vocational goals; and whether to go to college or learn a trade. These issues do not replace our previous concern with the basic skills and proficiency in content areas. The specific subject matter broadens as the educational ladder is climbed, but underneath the diversity and complexity of new courses the essentials of reading, writing, and arithmetic remain basic to educational growth and academic sophistication.

SCHOLASTIC APTITUDE TESTS

The scholastic aptitude test is of paramount importance at this level of education, because decisions concerning courses of study and plans for college must be made. The school abilities of students as measured by the scholastic aptitude test at this level is much more accurate than at lower levels. We can, therefore, consider a single measure of scholastic aptitude at this level more likely to represent the true ability of the student than a single measure obtained at the elementary level.

If only one scholastic aptitude test can be administered during the period between seventh and twelfth grade, the most appropriate time is the eighth or ninth grade. If monetary resources are adequate, a scholastic aptitude test should be administered at the beginning of the seventh grade, at the end of the eighth grade, and again at the beginning of the tenth grade. Those students who are going on to college will probably take the PSAT in the eleventh grade and/or the SAT or ACT in the twelfth grade.

SPECIAL APTITUDE TESTS

Special aptitude tests can provide important information for students who are not planning to go on to college as well as for those who are planning to major in special areas in college. As you know from our previous discussion of special aptitude tests, there are two types, (1) separate tests that measure specific aptitudes and (2) those which combine measures of different aptitudes into a single test battery, such as the Differential Aptitude Test battery (DAT).

If a battery such as the DAT is given, the school may also use it as a scholastic aptitude test. In the ideal situation, however, it would be best to use the scholastic aptitude score from a battery such as the DAT only as a check on other measures.

Special aptitude tests have the most relevance for the student and school beginning with the ninth grade. A test battery such as the DAT is highly recommended. The battery should generally be administered during the time of year in which students will not be taking other tests and early enough in the year that results will be meaningful. Generally, the middle or later part of the first month of school is a good time. The ninth and eleventh grades seem to be the most propitious levels for administering special aptitude tests, because there is then enough time for the student and school to make decisions on course and vocational plans. The same tests should be given in the eleventh grade as were given in the ninth, using a different form in order to check estimates of aptitude and note changes in performances.

ACHIEVEMENT TESTS

Although the teacher's classroom tests will be the final word in estimating grades and school achievement, the standardized achievement test can be of assistance in planning course selection and vocational goals. When achievement tests in specific content areas such as social studies, English, science, and mathematics are used to facilitate educational decisions, they should be administered in the eighth and the tenth grades.

If these tests are to be used for administrative purposes rather than guidance, the ninth and eleventh or twelfth grades are most appropriate. From data gathered at these times, the administration has a record of growth and achievement of the student body as a whole. It is of no help, however, for individual guidance to present students with these tests when it is too late to make many changes in their educational plans.

READING TESTS

Reading is as important at the secondary level as it is in the elementary school. The reading test may be used to advise students in course planning. More important, it can help spot children who need special help. Remedial action can then be instituted. The reading test should be given as early as possible in the seventh and tenth grades. This will help ensure immediate attention for those children who need improved reading skills. Seventh and tenth grades were chosen because they are the beginning grades of junior and senior high school. In another system appropriate changes would need to be made.

INTEREST INVENTORIES

Interest inventories provide important supplementary data to be used with aptitude and achievement test results. This wedding of data can assist the student in his vocational planning. A good time to administer the interest inventory is in the ninth grade so that interest patterns may be considered in planning courses of study.

PERSONALITY INVENTORIES

The administration of personality inventories to all students is not recommended, except for research purposes. Personality inventories, along with clinical techniques such as projective devices, should be administered only by a qualified clinical or school psychologist upon referral and with the full knowledge and written permission of both of the student's parents.

Scheduling of Tests

The test committee has been hard at work establishing objectives and selecting tests and appropriate grades for their administration. Now some of the school administrators take charge and help steer the committee into a discussion and plan of *when* and *how* to schedule the administration of the tests. They examine the reasons that most schools usually schedule testing for the fall or spring.

Adams (1964) suggests five basic advantages of testing in the fall:

(1) It permits the teacher to obtain a complete test record for each student. When students have been tested the preceding spring, pickup testing is necessary for new entrants. (2) The data are up-to-date. During a long vacation, many students lose in varying degrees their proficiency in certain skills; on the other hand some students have gained in reading achievement through their summer reading. Others may have gained in skill subjects through attendance at summer school or through special tutoring. (3) Fall testing places the emphasis on the analysis of student needs, rather than the evaluation of teaching.

(4) More time is available for the administration and scoring of tests and the analysis of results. End-of-year pressures can result in tests being filed away without being used. (5) Up-to-date test results can be used as a basis for grouping students for differentiated work or special corrective instruction. Moreover, scores on survey tests serve as a starting point for the use of supplementary diagnostic methods to determine specific retraining needs [p. 499].

Spring testing does not have as many advantages as fall testing. It does, however, enable teachers and the guidance staff to base the programming of the following year on objective data. It is also a good time to administer achievement tests, as the school administration is usually attempting to gauge its standing and progress at a national level. The administration may also be interested in data for research concerning the effectiveness of teaching.

The choice of the time of year for testing is also dependent on local conditions and needs. If, for example, a school system is divided into an eight-year elementary and four-year high school plan, the receiving high school will want to test eighth-graders in the early spring in order to make intelligent decisions regarding number and types of courses to offer. In addition, counselors will want to talk to students and parents concerning course selections. This is especially true when homogeneous grouping is practiced.

Scheduling tests is a complex task when the whole school is involved. In an all-school testing program at the senior high school level, classes should be discontinued during the hours of testing. The mornings are generally considered the best time for testing because the students are fresh and probably at their best. The afternoon classes can be held as usual, or all the classes can be scheduled with shortened time periods.

The following is a testing schedule for Brook High School. Classes at Brook resume at their regular times at 11:10 A.M. The tenth, eleventh, and twelfth grades are similarly scheduled.

Brook High School Testing Schedule

| | | Ninth Grade: | |
Date	Time	Test	Student
Sept. 23	8:45–11:00	DAT Form L (Booklet I)	A–M
		(Booklet II)	N–Z
Sept. 24	8:45–11:00	DAT Form L (Booklet I)	N–Z
		(Booklet II)	A–M

To save money Brook High School divided the ninth grade into half by assigning students whose last name began with the letters A through M to one group and the rest of the students to the second group. Thus only half the number of test booklets need be purchased. While one half was responding to items in Booklet I, the other half was answering questions in Booklet II. The following day the groups were reversed. Note also the time allocation. The manual allows two hours for Booklet I and one hour and fifty-five minutes for Booklet II, which takes into consideration a ten-minute break after the second test and time for distributing and collecting materials and answering questions. The time schedule has allowed fifteen extra minutes to assure that all testing will be accomplished before time is up.

Three hours should be the maximum time for testing at the high school level. At lower levels it is better to spread the testing over a period of several days so as not to tire young children excessively. Consult the test manual for methods of dividing the time properly. Be sure that all the school staff and the students know when testing is scheduled. It is a good idea to reproduce a schedule and hand it out to all teachers and students.

Tests should be administered during normal school hours. Do not give tests before a holiday or the day before a "big" game or dance. Tests should be scheduled at a time when there will be a minimum of distraction.

Test Orientation

General Orientation for Faculty

Each year before testing is to begin, teachers need a refresher course in standardized testing. This orientation should be presented no sooner than two weeks, and no later than two days before the tests are to be administered.

The director of this in-service testing program should be a member of the test committee who is especially qualified in testing, such as the school counselor or psychologist. A teacher representative from the test committee should be at the side of the director, helping him to present the materials, and as a symbol that the testing program has been a joint teacher-administrator effort. (See Chapter 3 for a discussion of an in-service testing program.) The program should cover the following essentials:

1. Why the school is administering standardized tests.
2. What these tests mean and what they do not mean.
3. A brief description of each test to be used and its purposes.
4. How tests can help the classroom teacher.
5. Good test administration, including the importance of following directions exactly.
6. Questions from the faculty.

Selection and Orientation of Test Administrators

Unless a school is exceptionally fortunate to have extra school psychologists and counselors available, the school must rely on teachers to administer the tests. This is not a real problem if teachers are properly prepared. A special in-service program for test administrators should be conducted after the general in-service program previously discussed.

The selection of test administrators in a large system can be made by the department chairman. He should be sent a brief communication stressing the importance of testing and the vital role of the test administrator. A list of selection criteria should accompany the communication. These essential criteria are as follows:

1. Reads fluently.
2. Has good pronunciation.
3. Follows directions scrupulously.
4. Thinks on his or her feet.
5. Communicates well with students.
6. Has some interest in doing the job.

The training or orientation of test administrators should encompass the following objectives:

1. Complete understanding and familiarity with the test and manual.
2. Understanding of and appreciation for standardized test procedures.

These objectives may be accomplished by having the test administrators take turns administering the tests to each other. If there are too many teachers to allow enough time for this approach, the director of the in-service program can administer two to four items of each test to the group. This will give them practice in what the test is all about. The director's method of reading the directions and speech pattern can serve as the model for test administration. A full question and answer period should follow.

In Chapter 3 we discussed proper test administration and scoring procedures. Several points are worth noting again.

1. Test administrators must follow the directions verbatim.
2. Questions should be answered within the context of the test directions.
3. Two time pieces should be used—the wall clock and a wristwatch or, in tests with short time limits, a stopwatch.
4. Test administrators should circulate around the room after testing has begun to see whether there are any problems.
5. Special care should be taken in scoring—always spot-check scores.

Pretest Orientation for Students

Students should be called together in an assemblylike program. The reasons for testing and what the results may mean for the students should be candidly presented. This general overview of testing may be conducted by one of the specialists.

A follow-up of the assembly on testing should be given in home rooms by representatives from the office of testing or the school psychologist or counselor. This should be an informal question and answer session. The importance of testing as an aid to each student should be emphasized.

In the lower grades teachers may want to use special tests that help a child learn to respond correctly to directions and formats of standardized tests. Still another approach may be movies that explain how to take a standardized test. Educational Testing Service sells and rents such a film.

Recording Test Scores

There should be a test record sheet in a counselor's notebook or a notation of the test and results in the cumulative record of the student. Another copy should be filed in the central administration office for use in case the counselor or teacher misplaces his records. The records in the central administration office should not be open for casual inspection.

In the actual recording of test data extreme care must be taken to achieve accuracy. Not only must the scores be accurate, but they must convey a meaningful picture to the casual professional glance. A good test record form should include the following data:

1. Full name of the test, including the specific form used.
2. Date administered, including the year, month, and day of testing.
3. Grade of student when test was taken.
4. Norm group used.
5. All scores that are useful and meaningful for analysis.

A Sample Testing Program

Our attention has been focused on the mechanics of developing a testing program. It may be constructive to illustrate some of our theoretical and practical suggestions in an actual school situation. The following testing program of the South Bend Community School Corporation, South Bend, Indiana, is presented as an illustration of the efforts of one school system. The reproduction of this program in no way constitutes an endorsement of the program, nor should it be construed as the "model" test program. It does present, however, the hard work of many school people and a testing committee and their resultant product. Some sections of the program have been omitted in order to save space and conform to the requirements of the topic. The complete program is printed in a booklet entitled Program of Testing (South Bend Community School Corporation, 1968).

Figure 43 shows the administrative structure, committee work, and dates.

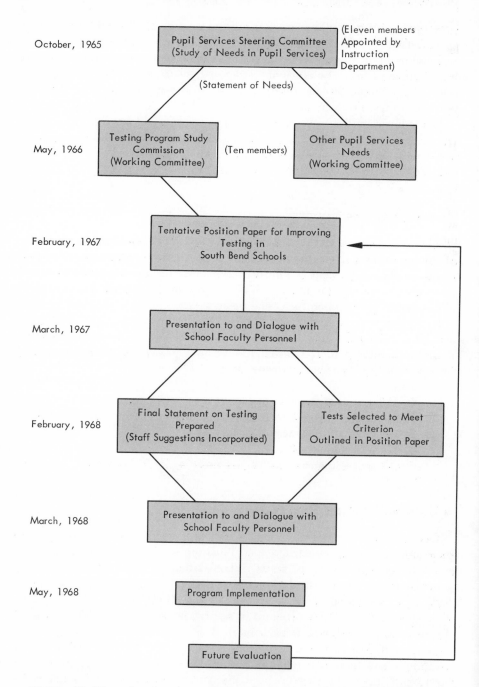

Figure 43. Chart showing the evolution of a testing program. (From *Program of Testing*. South Bend Community School Corporation. Reprinted by permission.)

Note the length of time taken. The Testing Program Study Commission[1] was composed of ten people representing the following school areas: guidance (4), school psychology (2), teaching (3), coordinator of testing (1).

In addition, other school groups were consulted and their recommendations incorporated into the final product.[2]

I. TESTING PHILOSOPHY[3]

The test information is a portion of the school's total information-gathering program for accumulating an objective record of a pupil as he progresses through school. This progress record contains family information, health information, attendance records, pupils' grades, and other pupil information assembled in one place—the cumulative record. The school faculty is prepared to use this information to improve the educational program for each student.

The faculty has certain ethical and legal responsibilities while working with test information of individuals and groups of children: (1) to use the information in ways that will help the student maximize educational experiences; (2) to exercise care in reporting test information to parents and the public to insure accuracy of interpretation and to avoid any false claims and misconceptions; (3) to understand that there may be privileged communication of test information within the school system as long as the information is related from professional to professional on a need-to-know basis.

The total testing program of the South Bend Community School Corporation is divided into three specific categories: *The Basic Testing Program, Supplemental Testing,* and *Special Testing.*

1. *Basic Testing Program*

The purpose of the basic testing program is to provide information about students whose terminal educational goals are: a college degree, college or post high school attendance, a high school diploma, or less than a high school diploma. This additional information provided

[1] The following persons constituted the Testing Program Study Commission: Mr. Gerald O. Dudley, Assistant Coordinator of Guidance, Chairman; Mrs. Patricia Carmichael, Coordinator, Resource Teachers; Mr. Frank Grubb, Counselor; Mr. Dennis Kunce, Counselor; Mr. Richard Matthews, Assistant Coordinator, Psychological Services; Mr. Alan Rensberger, Counselor; Dr. Harry Robe, Coordinator of Testing; Mrs. Evelyn Robinson, Teacher; Mr. Jack Shively, Psychologist; Mrs. Mary VanDeGenahte, Teacher.

[2] The following groups played an active part in an advisory capacity: members of the Superintendent's Faculty Committee, Elementary Instruction Council (elementary school principals), Secondary Instruction Council (secondary school principals), Curriculum Development Council (coordinators), Pupil Services Steering Committee, school counselors.

[3] Reprinted by permission of the South Bend Community School Corporation, South Bend, Indiana. (From *Program of Testing.* South Bend Community School Corporation, Spring, 1968.)

about students by their own efforts is obtained, using standardized tests, only when that information cannot be obtained in any other way or cannot be obtained as economically as through the use of tests.

The basic group testing program is more than a list of standardized tests and the dates for administering them. It includes:

. . . an orientation for staff, students, and parents of the rationale for giving the test and the use that may be made of the results.

. . . a strict adherence, by test administrators, to the testing conditions described by the test publisher in the testing manual— provision for the child or class to be given the teacher's (or tester's) undivided attention during testing period.

. . . direction for careful observation of the students during testing to detect and report any significant behavior which might affect test results but which might not be evident in the test results.

. . . provision for make-up testing of students absent during regular testing sessions, make-up testing for those whose test results or behavior seem inappropriate, as well as testing of students new to the school who do not have immediately available test results on file.

. . . immediate and accurate test scoring, using electronic data processing where possible, to insure a fast return to those using the test results.

. . . reporting the results in a manner most useful to the staff, students and parents for making pre-school, in-school, and post-school decisions.

. . . a means for correctly interpreting the results to those who will use them, the most important user being the student.

. . . a provision for permanently recording and storing *all* standardized test results for future reference.

. . . provision to safeguard individuals' rights through the procedures used in transfering test results outside the school corporation.

. . . a system for purchasing, storing, distributing, and collecting test materials economically.

. . . provisions for a continuing evaluation of the total testing program, considering the concepts stated above.

2. *Supplemental Testing*

In addition to the basic testing program, optional group testing materials and services are provided for those staff members needing additional student information that can be provided by testing. A list of approved tests available for use in supplemental testing as well as the procedures for requesting the tests are distributed to each school annually. The concepts for using supplemental testing are the same as those included above in the basic group testing program.

3. *Special Testing and Assessment*

Individualized testing and assessment is provided to fill gaps in needed test information or to provide extra information when needed. Examples of this type of testing are: individually administered tests by reading diagnosticians, resource teachers, speech and hearing diagnosticians, school counselors, and school psychologists to diagnose learning difficulties, personality disorders, behavior disorders, et cetera; tests administered to students new to the school system to help determine their appropriate level of readiness for educational placement; assessment measures used in educational research programs; admissions tests for use with college-bound students; et cetera.

II. TEST RATIONALE

Standardized tests are used to serve three basic purposes in the South Bend Schools: *The FIRST purpose is to provide a diagnosis of the readiness each child displays for engaging in future educational activities.*

The SECOND purpose is to provide periodic measure of pupil progress toward the educational objectives of the school.

The THIRD purpose is to assist in determining occupational, vocational, technical, professional goals, and programs for students including those whose abilities, achievements, motivation, background, and self-concept do not lend themselves to traditional objectives.

The tests selected for use in the basic testing program are given routinely to all pupils in a given grade to provide the information needed at that grade level, or to provide an accumulation of information needed at later grade levels for helping to make educational decisions. *The sample of learning activities measured by the tests does not include all the activities offered in the classroom but does include a significant portion of these activities to be considered valid and usable as one measure of progress or prediction of later success.*

During KINDERGARTEN the major portion of the curriculum is directed toward helping each child learn to play and work with groups of children under the direction of an adult, to enlarge his vocabulary, and to become accustomed to the school environment. Test information prior to or early in KINDERGARTEN is not a part of the basic testing program but a part of special testing administered by the psychological and health department. Test results at this level are combined with child growth information from parents to help determine whether individual children are socially and emotionally ready to participate in KINDERGARTEN. This allows some children to enter KINDERGARTEN who become five years of age after October 1 but prior to October 15 of that current school year *only* if they are socially, emotionally, and mentally ready for this experience.

It also protects other children from entering KINDERGARTEN when they are not socially, emotionally, and mentally ready for this experience.

Group testing in KINDERGARTEN comes near the end of the year and involves a test of general mental ability as well as a measure of readiness to begin reading and number work in the first grade. These measurements of reading and number work readiness supplement the information given to the first grade teacher by the KINDERGARTEN teacher in a conference for the purpose of individualizing instruction. *The results of these measurements are never used as the sole criteria for KINDERGARTEN retention or for forming first grade groups.*

During the FIRST, SECOND, and THIRD grades the major instructional consideration is given to developing and practicing the skills necessary for reading and arithmetic. Because of the constant practice and teacher observation of the development of skills of each child, the most appropriate standardized test at this time consists of diagnostic reading and arithmetic tests administered and scored by the classroom teacher at those times when such information is most useful. The usual time for this testing is when the instructional group has completed the FIRST, SECOND, or THIRD grade reading programs and may not necessarily coincide with the end of the year. There usually is a group within the classroom being tested at a time—probably an instructional group. When there are two or more instructional groups, each group is tested at the time a grade level program is completed. The skill development of each child observed by the teacher and analyzed with the use of diagnostic testing information is then systematically communicated to the next year's teacher to provide a valid basis for continuity in reading and arithmetic skills development. This test information like all other information gathered by the regular testing program is permanently recorded in the child's record.

Near the end of the THIRD grade a measure of language arts and mathematics skills development is administered to *all* children to provide a summary of primary grades skills development as well as a basis for the educational program at the beginning of the intermediate grades.

In grade FOUR, reading and arithmetic skill development is still an important part of the curriculum, but broad concepts have been introduced in the areas of science, social studies, language, and vocabulary as well as the development of sound patterns of study skills. Near the end of this grade the child's first standardized measure of educational progress is taken in each of these achievement areas. At the same time, a measure of ability is given to determine the general operating level of each student. A comparison between ability and achievement is provided at this level to draw attention to those students for whom there is a significant difference between test performance in these two areas. This comparison provides a clue to learning difficulties which might be further analyzed or corrected by special testing or individually altered educational programs. The FOURTH grade achievement test information is item-analyzed and summarized by broad concepts in each skill area. The FIFTH grade teacher receives this information about the students in her classroom at the beginning of that school year so that the strengths and weaknesses of each child may be focused upon in individualized instruction. The same pattern of achievement and ability testing is followed in GRADES SIX, EIGHT, and NINE with information in item-analyzed form being provided teachers at the beginning of the alternate school years.

A measure of tested vocational aptitudes is given in the fall of the NINTH grade to be used in helping the student plan his high school program of studies as well as provide further clues in preparing vocational objectives. This same measure, summarized by school results, provides a basis for the type of course offerings needed in the school to develop the special talents of groups of students.

Early in the SEVENTH grade and again in the NINTH grade a measure of tested interest in occupational areas is given each student to be used in further planning and refining the student's educational and occupational goals as well as provide a basis for serious study concerning suitable areas of choice for life vocations.

III. TEST RESULTS AND THEIR USE

NOTE: Test information provided on *individual students* for any reason, except as a part of college application procedures, requires signed parental permission prior to release of the information. This signed release then becomes a part of the student's cumulative record. *The usual request for a transcript is not considered a request for release of test results.* (See Figure A) *Students applying to college routinely complete the release form.*

1. Teacher use:
   a. To assist the teacher in discovering, within the classroom, the lower and upper range of abilities and achievements to serve as a guide to the materials and techniques of instruction used.
   b. To serve as a guide for grouping students in the classroom for subject or course instruction according to the group's measured proficiency in that subject or course.
   c. To reveal changing patterns of achievement over a long period for both individual students and classroom groups.
   d. To help reveal the strengths and weaknesses of individual

students within subject areas, or discover special talents individual students display which might be considered in daily instruction.

e. To aid in the identification of individual students who are in need of additional testing, specific program assignment, or other consideration.

2. Counseling and guidance use:
   a. To interpret test results to individual students in order that they may gain a realistic self-concept in relation to their tested abilities, interests, achievements, and aptitudes.
   b. To interpret test results to parents and faculty in order that they may gain a realistic concept of the child's tested abilities, interests, achievements, and aptitudes.
   c. To supply a developmental pattern of objective data for the cumulative record and subsequently for other schools and colleges.
   d. To assist in the optimum class placement of students.

3. Administration (within the building) use:
   *a. To provide a summary of information to permit judgment of the extent to which the total school is meeting its educational objectives.
   *b. To indicate strengths and weaknesses in the achievement of all students in the school in relation to over-all measures of student ability.
   c. To aid in determining the courses to be offered in the school.
   d. To serve as an aid to grouping children.
   Tests are never used as the only data to evaluate the effectiveness or ineffectiveness of teaching because of the questionable validity in using standardized tests without consideration of other factors which contribute to student growth.

4. Administration (central office) use:
   a. To help in determining the effectiveness of the curriculum in achieving the schools' over-all objectives.
   b. To screen and interpret generalized test data that may be used in public relations programs.
   c. To provide information to other agencies such as juvenile court, guidance centers, colleges and universities, etc.
   d. To aid in providing information for surveys, follow-up studies, research studies, and other school-wide studies needed periodically for school administration.
   e. To act as a clearing house for individuals and organizations that wish to evaluate or analyze data about or from students.

IV. MECHANICS OF TESTING

The Guidance Department of the South Bend Community School Corporation is responsible for the coordination of the total group testing program. The department coordinates the program in collaboration with teachers, counselors, principals, curriculum coordinators, management information services, and psychological services.

1. Orientation to Testing

Each of the elementary, junior high, and high schools has one person designated as testing liaison for the school. If a counselor is present in the school and has test and measurement training, he may be appointed to this role; otherwise another qualified person on the certified staff is appointed by the school principal as the school's testing liaison. All standardized testing within the building is coordinated through this representative.

Approximately three weeks prior to the administration of the tests in the basic testing program, the coordinator of guidance meets in workshops with the schools' testing liaison grouped by high school feeder areas to discuss the following:

1. What the test measures
2. Reason for testing
3. Preparation of the students and testing room for testing
4. Logistics of conducting the testing
5. Ways of observing and recording students' attitudes, conditions, and reactions during testing
6. Prepared samples of test results
7. Methods of using the test results
8. Recommendation that those who administer tests should take it themselves prior to testing

At least two weeks prior to giving the test each school's test liaison conducts a like workshop for the teachers who will be giving and using the tests in the building. This allows one week for any follow-up orientation necessary by the coordinator of guidance to discuss the use of the tests results, if needed, prior to testing.

Prepared information is sent to the parents along with the report card immediately preceding the actual testing date describing the testing instrument, the date and reason it is being given, and the use the parents and students might make of the results.

2. Test Administration

Standardized tests in the basic testing program are administered to students in classroom-size groups by the students' own teacher (who has been prepared in a workshop session). Tests should be scheduled for testing on Tuesday, Wednesday, or Thursday.

To aid in uniformity, tape recordings or the public address system may be used to give directions.

To aid in determining any invalidity of scores due to the testing environment or examinees' behavior observed during testing, a test administrator's observation check list (See Figure B) is provided for use during testing. Any report of results which contains probable invalidity will have a notation stated, "May be invalid."

Make-up testing shall be conducted during the regular school day within a reasonable time after the child has returned to school.

Any new pupils entering the school without test data shall be administered the minimal tests which other pupils on his grade level have taken during the year.

V. TEST SCORING AND REPORTING

All tests in grades four through twelve are machine scored directly from the answer card provided for student use. Appropriate reports are prepared from the test results for use by teachers, counselors, administrators, coordinators, directors, or other certified employees. Examples of these reports are used in the testing workshop prior to actual testing.

Notice that the test has been given is forwarded to parents along with the report card immediately following the testing date encouraging the parents to visit the school and discuss the test results in the context of all other information relevant to the progress the student displays in school.

Each student in the junior and senior high schools is encouraged to discuss the present and past test results with his councelor as one means of increasing self-understanding and facilitating decision-making.

All diagnostic tests in grades K through THREE and all supplemental testing are scored in the building under the direction of the principal or counselor. The KINDERGARTEN measures of general mental ability and reading and number readiness are hand-scored at Management Information Services. The THIRD grade measure of language arts and mathematics skills development is also hand-scored there.

Press labels are prepared for every standardized test given and returned to the school along with any other report forms so that each student's test results will be recorded in the cumulative record. This guideline does not include tests that accompany textbook series but does include the results of special testing which are recorded by hand in the cumulative record. All test data on pupils from other school systems are transferred to the cumulative record of the student concerned. It is the responsibility of the principal to see that all data from basic, supplemental, and special testing are recorded properly in the cumulative record.

In addition to permanently recording test results in the cumulative record, the test results are also maintained in raw score form on IBM cards at Management Information Services so that all or part of the information may be recalled easily at a later date.

VI. TEST SCORE INTERPRETATION

All standardized group test data K through TWELVE is available to students, parents, certified employees, and juvenile authorities on a need-to-know basis. The results are *interpreted* by the teachers, counselors, coordinators, and/or administrators using grade equivalent or stanine comparisons on both local and national norm basis. *The results are always interpreted as being an independent judgment of a student's performance which needs to be viewed in combination with teacher grades and non-academic information as well as the student's physical, social, and emotional growth.*

VII. TEST MATERIAL PURCHASING, STORING, AND DISTRIBUTION

All test materials for the basic and supplemental testing programs are purchased, stored, distributed, and collected centrally under the direction of the Guidance Department. Test scoring is accomplished in cooperation with Management Information Services.

Test materials (booklets, answer media, report forms, and instruction and interpretation manuals) are requested from testing companies during the summer months when possible so that the advantage of bulk rates may be gained for economy.

A list of supplement tests available to any principal or counselor who wishes to test individuals or groups of students with additional group tests is provided annually. Every request for supplemental testing is considered by the coordinator of guidance and appropriate elementary or secondary director and/or curriculum specialist.

1. Requests for supplement testing are made for tests other than those in the basic testing program. Delivery will be made as soon as possible.

2. The request contains the following information: school, person making request, test name, form, grade level, number of students to be tested, date of requested testing, reasons for needing supplemental testing information, use to be made of the test results, and any additional information.

Schedule of Tests—Primary School Level

Grade	Measurement	Specific tests used	Date given	Timing	Remarks
Kdgn.	Mental Ability	To be determined through study during the Spring of 1968	February	30–40 min.	Teacher-machine scored. Fall reported to 1st grade teachers.
Kdgn.	Readiness		April	1 hour	
1,2,3	Diagnostic Reading	1. Doren Diagnostic Test of Word Recognition Skills. OR	As needed	varied	Teacher scored. Used only with those children where more information is needed.
2,3		2. Stanford Diagnostic Reading Test, Level I, Form W, Grades 2.5—4.5	As needed	varied	
2,3	Diagnostic Arithmetic	1. Stanford Diagnostic Arithmetic Test, Level I, Form W, Grades 2.5—4.5 OR	As needed	varied	Use only those parts that are appropriate to the material studied.
1,2		2. California Arithmetic Test, 1957 edition, 1963 norms, lower primary level, Form W.	As needed	varied	
3	Skill development	1. Cooperative Primary Test, Form 23A.			Each test to be used with ½ of the students. Teacher-machine scored. Fall reported to 4th grade teachers.
		2. Comprehensive Tests of Basic Skills Level 1, Form A, Grades 2,3,4.	April	3 hours	

Schedule of Tests—Intermediate School Level

Grade	Measurement	Specific tests used	Date given	Timing	Remarks
4 6	Mental Ability	Cooperative School and College Ability Tests, Series II, Level 4, Form A	April, May March, April	45 min.	Machine scored. Fall reported to next years teachers.
4	Achievement	Stanford Achievement Test: Intermediate I Battery; Subtests: *Word Meaning, Paragraph Meaning, Spelling, Word Study Skills, Language*, Form W.	April, May	2 hrs. 10 min.	Machine scored.
		Cooperative Sequential Tests of Educational Progress; Subtests: *Social Studies, Science, Mathematics*; Level 4, Form A.	April, May	3 hrs. 10 min.	Fall reported to next year's teachers.
6	Achievement	Stanford Achievement Test: Intermediate II Battery; Subtests: *Word Meaning, Paragraph Meaning, Spelling, Language*; Form W.	March, April	1 hr. 50 min.	Correlated with Mental Ability Tests in the Same Grade
		Cooperative Sequential Tests of Educational Progress; Subtests: *Social Studies, Science, Mathematics*; Level 4, Form A.	March, April	3 hrs. 30 min.	Concept Analyzed and Reported.

Schedule of Tests—Junior High and High School Level[4]

Grade	Measurement	Specific tests used	Date given	Timing	Remarks
7	Interest	Kuder General Interest Survey, Form E, Grades 7–12.	Oct., Nov., Dec.	non-timed	Student self-scored and profiled.
8 / 9	Mental Ability	Cooperative School and College Ability Tests, Series II, Level 3, Form A	Jan., Feb. / Jan., Feb.	45 min.	Machine Scored. Fall reported to next year's teachers.
8 / 9	Achievement	Cooperative Sequential Tests of Educational Progress; Subtests: *Reading, Writing, Listening, Social Studies, Science, Mathematics*; Level 3, Form A.	Jan., Feb. / Jan., Feb.	7 hrs.	Machine Scored. Fall reported to next year's teachers. Correlated with mental ability tests in the same grade. Concept analyzed and reported.
9	Interest	Minnesota Vocational Interest Inventory.	Oct., Nov., Dec.	About 45 min.	Machine scored and reported in area scales.
9	Vocational Aptitude	Aptitude Test for Occupations.	Oct., Nov.	1 hr. and 47 min.	Machine Scored.

[4] The reader should note that no tests are scheduled after the ninth grade. The philosophy and objectives of the South Bend Community School Corporation do not include scheduled testing after this level. Although this author feels that testing after the ninth grade is an important and integral part of the educational process, as stated before, each school must develop its own program according to its own unique needs and philosophy.

VIII. TESTING PROGRAM EVALUATION

A test review committee meets annually to review the total testing program. The committee is guided by the concepts and testing rationale contained in the testing philosophy. The committee is appointed by the school superintendent and made up of three members from Guidance, one member from Psychological Services, one member from Research, one member from Management Information Services, three classroom teachers, with recommendations from curriculum coordinators and the Instruction Department.

Figure A

Test Release Authorization

This is to authorize the South Bend Community School Corporation to release all group test information regarding:

_____
(Pupil's Name)

to: _____
(School or Agency)

In authorizing this action, I release the South Bend Community School Corporation from all responsibility concerning the use or interpretation of these test results *provided* they are transferred only to qualified college or school authorities, employers, or juvenile authorities.

_____
Name

_____
Relationship

Test Administrator's Observation Check List

Test administration may be one of the most misunderstood and neglected parts of standardized testing. It is too often thought of only as (1) keeping students quiet; (2) policing, to prevent copying or other forms of cheating; (3) urging students to be rapid or continuous in responding to test items.

These three frequently accepted responsibilities by test administrators may rank very low on a continuum of duties.

What should you do in order to give the students the kind of service they deserve?

Figure B

TEST ADMINISTRATOR'S CHECK LIST

School _____ Grade Level _____

Teacher _____ Date _____

Name of Test _____

_____

Interruption in Test _____

Test Improperly Timed _____

Directions Given Incorrectly _____

(USE FOR IRREGULARITIES ONLY)

Student's Name	Administration								Student's Condition						Teacher's Comments
	Difficulty with practice	Did not understand directions	Lost place on answer sheet	Did not do items in sequence	Did not begin test immediately	Lingered on certain parts	Answered without reading questions	Finished unusually early	Eye glasses needed but not worn	Sick during test	Extremely nervous	Limiting physical handicap	Was not motivated	Tired and sleepy	

Use number or letter to indicate part of test.

The observations you make during testing are very important, as they help to determine whether the testing results should be considered as "typical performance" of the student. Any report of results which contains probable invalidities will have the notation, "May Be Invalid."

1. You should be familar with the testing being given so that you can have an awareness of the tasks required of the students. You can be a better observer if you can gauge, to some degree, the student's attitude and reactions to the test.
2. You should check physical setting for space, lighting, temperature, ventilation, and appropriateness of seats, desks, etc. The testing procedures should be coordinated with other school activities so that interruptions are unlikely.
3. You should try to create a pleasant non-threatening atmosphere during the test.
4. You should respond to individual questions quietly (to the individual only) in accordance with standardized procedure.
5. Keen observation of students' behavior while they are being tested is of utmost importance if the test results are to be meaningful. You should bear in mind that sound interpretation of test scores will, to a large extent, depend on how well the students' behavior was observed and recorded during the testing situation.

Figure B contains a Test Administrator's Observation Check List that may be helpful to you while you are testing. The name of the test, date, teacher's name or room number, and student's name should be recorded before the testing period.

The information to be recorded during testing is divided into four sections:

1. A section that would influence the outcome of all students being tested:
   a. Interruptions during the test (i.e., fire drill)
   b. Test improperly timed (indicate how much)
   c. Directions given incorrectly (how and which test)
2. Administration: eight columns for placing check marks
3. Student's condition: six columns for placing check marks
4. Teacher's comments: space for recording unusual behavior or condition.

Reporting Test Results to Students and Parents

Teachers and counselors are faced with the problem of how best to convey test results to students and parents. If they reveal too much, they may psychologically damage the student. If they do not reveal anything, the student and his parents do not benefit from the tests. Besides, many parents will not stand for being excluded from the "test score club." Parents have a right to know about their child's abilities and achievements and the student has a right to know meaningful information about himself. Durost (1961), in discussing the problems of telling parents about test results, presents four philosophical premises that should form the basis of school policy:

1. Parents are entitled to information related to their children's progress in school, especially as it relates to future educational or vocational plans.
2. Test information given to parents must be expressed in understandable terms.
3. Test results are best revealed in terms of a simple scale broadly based. (Some common means of interpretation, such as intelligence quotients and grade equivalents, appear to be more precise than they really are.)
4. The information should have uniform meaning to parent and educator and demonstrated relevance (validity) for the purpose in mind such as grouping, promotion, and guidance [p. 1].

Specific IQ scores should never be given to parents. Grade equivalents or placement scores are not a satisfactory means of reporting, because misunderstanding often results from their use. (See Chapter 5.) Percentiles and stanines are most appropriate for conveying test results to students and parents.

Ricks (1959) poses the question, "Are any numbers necessary?" Although he would not impose a ban on using numbers in reporting test data, he notes that some very good counselors do not present any numerical data at all. Verbal techniques such as, "You score like people who . . . " or "Your son (or daughter) scores like students who . . . " are an excellent way to communicate information about test scores.

This mode of test interpretation in an actual situation might take the following form:

Counselor (or teacher): Mary, you score like people who have a difficult time in college. On the other hand, your scores reveal a great deal of promise in commercial areas such as filing and typing. You may want to consider a secretarial school after high school graduation.

Counselor (or teacher): Your son Wally scores like students who find the ivy league schools difficult but seem to manage well in smaller private four-year colleges.

Counselor (or teacher): You score like students who do better in algebra if they take general mathematics in the ninth grade and algebra later.

In conveying test data to students and parents, the teacher or counselor should be sure to emphasize that test scores are tentative and that their real meaning lies in using them with other information such as school grades, classroom performance, and teacher evaluation. This does not mean tests should be scoffed at or relegated to an insignificant part in the educational enterprise. It does mean that the accuracy of the scores and what they *probably* signify for the individual must be candidly presented. At the same time cases that do not bear out test scores may be cited, as, for example, the following case.

Jerry M. was born in Germany during the early 1930's. His father was a professor of history in a well-known German university. One day Jerry's father took him for a walk down the main street. In front of Jerry, who was five years old, were three rather muscular men in brown shirts with swastika arm bands. Jerry, being no different from most young boys, was awed by their uniforms. He ran up to one of the soldiers and greeted him with a salute. The soldier kicked Jerry and sent him sprawling to the gutter. Jerry's father was then beaten into unconsciousness. Jerry and his father were Jews.

Not long after this incident, Jerry and his family migrated to the United States, where his father was employed as a professor in a well-known university. Jerry was enrolled in the first grade. After a few months Jerry's teacher found that he was making little progress in reading and learning English. The father was sent for and recommendations were made for individual intelligence testing. Jerry's teacher felt that he was a retarded child. The psychologist's report was in agreement with the teacher. Jerry had a reported IQ of 65. There was no doubt that Jerry should be in a special education class for educably mentally handicapped children. (The astute reader may question the reliability of the tests in that Jerry was still new to the English language. This was no problem, because the psychologist giving the test was also a German immigrant and was able to administer the test in German.)

The father was quite upset about the findings, as most parents would be, and would not accept them. He chose to send Jerry for psychiatric help. The psychiatrist's report showed that Jerry was emotionally disturbed and needed intensive psychotherapy. After five years of psychotherapy, Jerry's IQ score had risen from 65 to 90. Although this was remarkable, Jerry was still far from being a scholar. At the end of the ninth grade Jerry was only a year behind his class in most of his subjects, and his IQ score had risen to 110.

The last the writer heard of him, Jerry was studying for his Ph.D. in chemistry. Certainly, this is an extreme case and by no means the usual run of affairs. Also, let me point out that psychotherapy is not a cure for mental retardation. Jerry was never mentally retarded; however, the trauma of his life in Germany and other factors prevented him from using all of his intellectual capacity.

This case is obviously a highly unusual situation. For most children tests are fairly accurate in estimating achievement and potential to achieve. However, because we deal with people rather than numbers, the exceptions must always be kept in mind. The reader who is interested in pursuing the effects of emotional problems on intelligence and the expression of mental ability in autistic children can read the extensive writings of Dr. Bruno Bettelheim. In *The Empty Fortress* (Bettelheim, 1967), for example, the problem of determining the intelligence of autistic children is explored.

The teacher and counselor must bridge the gap that separates them from students and parents in order to realize the full effectiveness of tests. This can only be done if a concentrated effort is made to present information in relevant and understandable terms.

References

Adams, G. S. *Measurement and evaluation in education, psychology, and guidance.* New York: Holt, Rinehart and Winston, 1964.

Bettelheim, B. *The empty fortress.* New York: The Free Press, 1967.

Durost, W. N. *How to tell parents about standardized test results.* Test Service Notebook, No. 26. New York: Harcourt, Brace and World, 1961.

Lennon, R. T. *Selection and provision of testing materials.* Test Service Bulletin, No. 99. New York: Harcourt, Brace and World, 1962.

Ricks, J. H. *On telling parents about test results.* Test Service Bulletin, No. 54. New York: The Psychological Corporation, 1959.

South Bend Community School Corporation. *Program of testing.* South Bend, Ind. South Bend Community School Corporation, Spring, 1968.

APPENDIX

A

Major Publishers of
Standardized Tests[1]

American College Testing Program
(ACT)
P.O. Box 168
Iowa City, Iowa 52240
  319-338-3671

American Guidance Service, Inc.
Publishers' Building
Circle Pines, Minnesota 55014
  612-786-4343

The Bobbs-Merrill Company, Inc.
4300 West 62nd Street
Indianapolis, Indiana 46206
  317-AX1-3100

Bureau of Educational Measurements
Kansas State Teachers College
Emporia, Kansas 66801
  316-343-1200

Bureau of Educational Research &
Service
C-6 East Hall
State University of Iowa
Iowa City, Iowa 52240
  319-353-3823

C. H. Stoelting Company
424 North Homan Avenue
Chicago, Illinois 60624
  312-722-3833

California Test Bureau
  West of Mississippi (main office):
Del Monte Research Park
Monterey, California 93940
  408-373-2932
  East of Mississippi:
206 Bridge Street
New Cumberland, Pennsylvania 17070
  717-774-0430

[1] Test catalogues are sent free of charge on request.

461

Center for Psychological Service
1835 Eye Street, N.W.
Washington, D.C. 20006
    202-541-4465

Committee on Diagnostic Reading
    Tests, Inc.
Mountain Home, North Carolina 28758
    704-OXford 3-5223

Consulting Psychologists Press, Inc.
577 College Avenue
Palo Alto, California 94306
    415-326-4448

Education-Industry Service
1225 East 60th Street
Chicago, Illinois 60637

Educational and Industrial Testing
    Service
P.O. Box 7234
San Diego, California 92107
    714-488-1666

Educational Records Bureau
21 Audubon Avenue
New York, New York 10032
    212-L08-6700

Educational Testing Service
Princeton, New Jersey 08540
    609-921-9000

    Western office:
    1947 Center Street
    Berkeley, California 94704
        415-849-0950

    Midwestern office:
    990 Grove Street
    Evanston, Illinois 60201
        312-869-7700

Follett Publishing Company
1010 West Washington Boulevard
Chicago, Illinois 60607
    312-666-5858

Grune and Stratton, Inc.
381 Park Avenue South
New York, New York 10016
    212-MU6-2077

Guidance Testing Associates
6516 Shirley Avenue
Austin, Texas 78752
    512-GL2-6969

Harcourt, Brace and World, Inc.
757 Third Avenue
New York, New York 10017
    212-572-5000

Houghton Mifflin Company
110 Tremont Street
Boston, Massachusetts 02107
    617-423-5725

Institute for Personality and Ability
    Testing (IPAT)
1602 Coronado Drive
Champaign, Illinois 61820
    217-352-4739

Ohio Testing Services
    (Ohio Scholarship Tests)
Division of Guidance and Testing
State Department of Education
751 Northwest Boulevard
Columbus, Ohio 43212
    614-469-4590

Personnel Press, Inc.
20 Nassau Street
Princeton, New Jersey 08540
    609-924-7000

Personnel Research Institute
Western Reserve University
Cleveland, Ohio 44106
    216-CE1-7700

The Psychological Corporation
304 East 45th Street
New York, New York 10017
    212-679-7070

Psychological Test Specialists
Box 1441
Missoula, Montana 59801

Psychometric Affiliates
Chicago Plaza
Brookport, Illinois 62910
312-233-5133

Richardson, Bellows, Henry and
Company, Inc.
355 Lexington Avenue
New York, New York 10017
212-682-6300

Scholastic Testing Service, Inc.
480 Meyer Road
Bensenville, Illinois 60106
313-766-7150

Science Research Associates, Inc.
259 East Erie Street
Chicago, Illinois 60611
312-944-7552

Sheridan Psychological Services, Inc.
P.O. Box 837
Beverly Hills, California 90213
213-474-1744

State High School Testing Service for
Indiana
Room 109, A.E.S. Annex
Purdue University
Lafayette, Indiana 47907

Teachers College Press
Teachers College
Columbia University
New York, New York 10027
212-870-4215

University Bookstore, Purdue University
360 State Street
West Lafayette, Indiana 47906
743-1288

University of London Press Ltd.
Little Paul's House, Warwick Square
London E.C.4, England

Western Psychological Services
Box 775
Beverly Hills, California 90213
213-GR8-6730

APPENDIX

B

Glossary of Common Measurement Terms[1]

academic aptitude (*scholastic aptitude*) A combination of inherited and acquired abilities needed for schoolwork.

accomplishment quotient (*AQ*) The ratio of educational age to mental age; EA ÷ MA. (Also called *achievement quotient*.)

achievement age The average age on an achievement test. If a child obtains an achievement age of 11 years 8 months on a reading test, his score is equal to those of children of 11 years 8 months, who on the average receive a similar score.

achievement test A test that measures the amount of knowledge or skills that a child has learned in a particular subject field.

age equivalent The age for which a given score is the real or estimated average score.

age norms Values considered as average on a certain test for children of various ages.

age-grade table A table showing the number of students of various ages in each grade.

alternate-form reliability The closeness of correspondence, or correlation, between results on alternate (equivalent or parallel) forms of a test; thus, a measure of the extent to which the two forms are consistent or reliable in measuring whatever they do measure, assuming that the examinees themselves do not change in the abilities measured between the two testings.

---

[1] This glossary includes some of the common terms used in measurement. It has been reproduced, with some revisions and additions, from Test Service Notebook No. 13, with permission, published by Harcourt, Brace & World, Inc.

aptitude The ability to acquire new knowledge and proficiency with training. It is a combination of inborn capacity or ability and/or acquired skills.

aptitude test A test that measures the potential ability or capacity of a person to learn various skills and acquire new knowledge.

arithmetic mean The sum of a group of scores divided by the number of scores, which produces an average.

average A general term applied to measures of central tendency. The three most widely used averages are the *arithmetic mean*, the *median*, and the *mode*.

battery A group of several tests that are comparable, the results of which are used individually, in combination, and/or totally.

ceiling The top score or upper limit of a test.

class analysis chart A chart, usually prepared in connection with a battery of achievement tests, that shows the relative performance of members of a class on the several parts of the battery.

coefficient of correlation (*r*) A measure of the degree of relationship, or "going-togetherness," between two sets of measures for the same group of individuals. The correlation coefficient most frequently used in test development and educational research is that known as the *Pearson* (*Pearsonian*) *r*, so named for Karl Pearson, originator of the method, or as the *product-moment r*, to denote the mathematical basis of its calculation. Unless otherwise specified, "correlation" usually means the product-moment correlation coefficient, which ranges from .00, denoting complete absence of relationship, to 1.00, denoting perfect correspondence, and may be either positive or negative.

completion item A test question requiring the student to complete or fill in a word or words in a phrase or sentence from which one or more parts have been deleted.

correction for guessing A reduction in score for wrong answers, sometimes applied in scoring true-false or multiple-choice questions. Many question the validity or usefulness of this device, which is intended to discourage guessing and to yield more accurate rankings of examinees in terms of their true knowledge. Scores to which such corrections have been applied—e.g., rights minus wrongs, or rights minus some fraction of wrongs—are often spoken of as "corrected for guessing" or "corrected for chance."

correlation Relationship of "going-togetherness" between two scores of measures; tendency of one score to vary concomitantly with the other, as the tendency of students of high IQ to be above average in reading ability. The existence of a strong relationship—i.e., a high correlation—between two variables does not necessarily indicate that one has any causal influence on the other.

criterion A standard by which a test may be judged or evaluated; a set of scores, ratings, etc., that a test is designed to predict or to correlate with.

decile Any one of the nine percentile points (scores) in a distribution that divide the distribution into ten equal parts; every tenth percentile. The first decile is the 10th percentile, the ninth decile the 90th percentile, etc.

deviation IQ A comparison of a person's score to a score considered average for his age.

diagnostic test A test used to locate specific areas of a child's weakness or strength and that determines the kind of weaknesses.

difficulty value The per cent of some specified group, such as students of a given age or grade, who answer an item correctly.

discriminating power The ability of a test item to differentiate between persons possessing much of some trait and those possessing little.

distractor Any of the incorrect choices in a multiple-choice or matching item.

distribution (frequency distribution) A tabulation of scores from high to low, or low to high, showing the number of individuals that obtain each score or fall in each score interval.

educational age (EA) See *achievement age*.

equivalent form Any of two or more forms of a test that are closely parallel with respect to the nature of the content and the difficulty of the items included, and that will yield very similar average scores and measures of variability for a given group.

evaluation program Such a program involves the use of testing and nontesting instruments and techniques for the appraisal of growth adjustment and achievement of the child.

extrapolation A process of estimating values of a function beyond the range of available data.

factor In mental measurement, a hypothetical trait, ability, or component of ability, that underlies and influences performance on two or more tests, and hence causes scores on the tests to be correlated. The term "factor" strictly refers to a theoretical variable, derived by a process of *factor analysis*, from a table of intercorrelations among tests; but it is also commonly used to denote the psychological interpretation given to the variable—i.e., the mental trait assumed to be represented by the variable, as verbal ability, numerical ability, etc.

factor analysis A statistical technique for analyzing the relationship among a set of scores.

forced-choice item Generally, any multiple-choice item in which the child is required to make a choice of answers provided him.

grade equivalent A score that indicates a child's average performance in terms of grade and month. A grade equivalent of 7.2 is interpreted as the second month of the seventh grade.

grade norm The average score that a child in a certain grade receives on a test.

group test A test that can be administered to one or more individuals at the same time by one examiner.

individual test A test that can be administered to only one individual at a time.

intelligence quotient (IQ) The ratio of a child's mental age (MA) to his chronological age (CA). The formula is $IQ = MA/CA \times 100$.

interpolation In general, any process of estimating intermediate values between two known points. As applied to test norms, it refers to the procedure used in assigning interpreted values (e.g., grade or age equivalents) to scores between the successive average scores actually obtained in the standardization process. In reading norm tables, it is necessary at times to *interpolate* to obtain a norm value for a score between scores given in the table; e.g., in the table given here, an age value of 12–5 would be assigned, by interpolation, to a score of 118.

Score	Age Equivalent
120	12–6
115	12–4
110	12–2

inventory test As applied to achievement tests, a test that attempts to cover rather thoroughly some relatively small unit of specific instruction or training. The purpose of an inventory test, as the name suggests, is more in the nature of a "stock-taking" of an individual's knowledge or skill than an effort to measure in the usual sense. The term sometimes denotes a type of test used to measure achievement status prior to instruction. Many personality and interest questionnaires are designated "inventories", since they appraise an individual's status in several personal characteristics, or his level of interest in a variety of types of activities.

item A question or exercise in a test.

item analysis The process of evaluating single test items by any of several methods. It usually involves determining the difficulty value and the discriminating power of the item, and often its correlation with some criterion.

Kuder-Richardson formula(s) Formulas for estimating the reliability of a test from information about the individual items in the test, or from the mean score, standard deviation, and number of items in the test. Because the Kuder-Richardson formulas permit estimation of reliability from a single administration of a test, without the labor involved in dividing the test into halves, their use has become common in test development. The Kuder-Richardson formulas are not appropriate for estimating the reliability of speeded tests.

mean See *arithmetic mean.*

median The point at which a given group of test scores is divided into two equal parts. Half the scores fall below the median and half above it.

mental age (MA) The age for which a score on an intelligence test is average or normal. For example, if a score of 60 on an intelligence test is equal to a mental age of 7 years 9 months, then 60 is the average score that would be made by a random group of children 7 years 9 months of age.

mode The score that occurs most frequently in a distribution of scores. For example, the mode score is 55 in the following scores of children on a reading test: 10, 30, 35, 55, 55, 55, 55, 60, 67, 69, 72, 72, 78, 79, 84, 85, 88, 90, 94, 96, 98, 99.

multiple-choice item A test item in which the examinee's task is to choose the correct or best answer from several given answers, or options.

multiple-response item A special type of multiple-choice item in which two or more of the given choices may be correct.

N The symbol commonly used to represent the number of cases in a distribution, study, etc.

normal distribution curve This is a method of representing the distribution of various levels of ability and other characteristics within our society. In a normal distribution, scores are distributed symmetrically about the average, with as many cases at various equal distances above the average as below the average, and with cases concentrated near the average and decreasing in number the further one departs from the average.

norms A way of describing, by statistical methods, the test performances of specific groups of students of various ages and/or grades. Norms are used to describe average, below-average, and above-average performances. Grade, age, and percentiles are commonly used types of norms.

objective test A test in the scoring of which there is no possibility of difference of opinion among scorers as to whether responses are to be scored right or wrong.

It is contrasted with a "subjective" test—e.g., the usual essay examination to which different scorers may assign different scores, ratings, or grades.

omnibus test A test (1) in which items measuring a variety of mental operations are all combined into a single sequence rather than being grouped together by type of operation, and (2) from which only a single score is derived, rather than separate scores for each operation or function. Omnibus tests make for simplicity of administration: one set of directions and one over-all time limit usually suffice.

percentile A score in a group of scores below which falls the percentage of scores indicated by the given percentile. For example, the 25th percentile denotes the score below which 25 per cent of the scores fall. Thus the person obtaining a percentile rank of 25 is considered as equaling or surpassing 25 per cent of the group taking the same test.

percentile rank The per cent of scores in a distribution equal to or lower than the score corresponding to the given rank.

performance test In a way, every test may be considered a performance test. However, pencil-and-paper or oral tests are not usually regarded as performance tests. Generally, a performance test requires the use and manipulation of physical objects and the use of physical and manual skills not restricted to oral and written answers. The important thing is that the test response is identical with the behavior about which information is desired.

personality test A test that attempts to measure everything that constitutes a person's mental, emotional, and psychological makeup.

power test A test that attempts to measure level of performance rather than a child's speed in answering questions. There is little, if any, emphasis on time.

practice effect A term test people use in describing the influence of previous experience with a test. For example, Johnny took the same test two months ago. Will his previous experience with this test help him achieve a higher score?

profile A graphic portrait of a child's test results on several tests.

prognostic technique A test used to predict future success or failure in a specific academic subject or field.

projective test A method of testing to determine personality characteristics. The person is presented with a series of ink blots, pictures, unfinished sentences, and so on. The term *projective* is used because it is believed that a person "projects" into his answers and statements his own needs and feelings.

quartile One of three points that divide the cases in a distribution into four equal groups. The lower quartile, or 25th percentile, sets off the lowest fourth of the group, the middle quartile is the same as the 50th percentile, or median; and the third quartile, or 75th percentile, marks off the highest fourth.

random sample A sample of the people of a population made in such a way that every person of the population has equal chance of being included. This method attempts to eliminate bias.

range The extent of difference between the highest and lowest scores on a test. For example, 98 is the highest score and 10 is the lowest; therefore the range is between 10 and 98.

raw score Usually the number of right answers, or some such formula as rights minus one-half wrongs, which gives a total score.

readiness test A test that measures the degree to which a child has achieved certain skills or information needed for undertaking some new learning activity. For example, a reading readiness test indicates the degree to which a child is at a developmental stage where he may profitably begin a formal program of reading instruction.

recall item An item that requires the examinee to supply the correct answer from his own memory or recollection, as contrasted with a *recognition item,* in which he need only identify the correct answer, e.g., "Columbus discovered America in the year —?" is a recall item, whereas "Columbus discovered America in (*a*) 1425, (*b*) 1492, (*c*) 1520, (*d*) 1546" is a recognition item.

recognition item An item requiring the examinee to recognize or select the correct answer from among two or more given answers. See *recall item.*

reliability The extent to which a child would obtain the same score if the test were to be readministered. That is, is the test consistent in measuring whatever it does measure?

reliability coefficient The coefficient of correlation between two forms of a test, between scores on repeated administrations of the same test, or between halves of a test, properly corrected.

representative sample A sample that corresponds to or matches the population of which it is a sample with respect to characteristics important for the purposes under investigation—e.g., in an achievement test norm sample, proportion of pupils from each state, from various regions, from segregated and nonsegregated schools, etc.

scholastic aptitude See *academic aptitude.*

skewness The tendency of a distribution to depart from symmetry or balance around the mean.

Spearman-Brown formula A formula giving the relationship between the reliability of a test and its length. The formula permits estimation of the reliability of a test lengthened or shortened by any amount, from the known reliability of a test of specified length. Its most common application is in the estimation of reliability of an entire test from the correlation between two halves of the test (*split-half reliability*).

speed test A test that measures a child's performance by the number of questions he can answer in a certain amount of time.

split-half coefficient A coefficient of reliability obtained by correlating scores on one half of a test with scores on the other half. Generally, but not necessarily, the two halves consist of the odd-numbered and the even-numbered items.

standard deviation (*SD*) A measure of the variability or dispersion of a set of scores. The more the scores cluster around the mean, the smaller the standard deviation.

standard error (*SE*) An estimate of the magnitude of the "error of measurement" in a score—that is, the amount by which an obtained score differs from a hypothetical true score. The standard error is an amount such that in about two-thirds of the cases the obtained score would not differ by more than one standard error from the true score. The *probable error* (*PE*) of a score is a similar measure, except that in about half the cases the obtained score differs from the true score by not more than one probable error. The probable error is equal to about two thirds of the standard error. The larger the probable or the standard error of a score, the less reliable the measure.

standard score A general term referring to any of a variety of "transformed" scores, in terms of which raw scores may be expressed for reasons of convenience, comparability, ease of interpretation, etc.

The simplest type of standard score is that which expresses the deviation of an individual's raw score from the average score of his group in relation to the standard deviation of the scores of the group. Thus:

$$\text{Standard score (z)} = \frac{\text{raw score (X)} - \text{mean (M)}}{\text{standard deviation (SD)}}$$

By multiplying this ratio by a suitable constant and by adding or subtracting another constant, standard scores having any desired mean and standard deviation may be obtained. Such standard scores do not affect the relative standing of the individuals in the group nor change the shape of the original distribution.

More complicated types of standard scores may yield distributions differing in shape from the original distribution; in fact, they are sometimes used for precisely this purpose. *Normalized standard scores* and *K-scores* (as used in Stanford Achievement Test) are examples of this latter group.

standardized test A test that has definite directions for administering, scoring, and use.

stanines A nine-point scale. It divides the norm population into nine groups. The mean score from 1 to 9 is 5.

survey test A test that measures general achievement in a given subject or area, usually with the connotation that the test is intended to measure group status, rather than to yield precise measures of individuals.

test-retest coefficient A type of reliability coefficient obtained by administering the same test a second time after a short interval and correlating the two sets of scores.

true-false item A test question or exercise in which the examinee's task is to indicate whether a given statement is true or false.

true score A score entirely free of errors of measurement. True scores are hypothetical values never obtained by testing, which always involves some measurement error. A true score is sometimes defined as the average score of an infinite series of measurements with the same or exactly equivalent tests, assuming no practice effect or change in the examinee during the testings.

validity A term used to designate the extent to which a test measures what it is supposed to measure. For example, is the reading test measuring Bill's reading ability or his knowledge of science?

References for More Extensive Glossaries

English, H. B. and English, A. C. *A comprehensive dictionary of psychological and psychoanalytical terms.* New York: Longmans, Green, 1958.

Warren, H. D. (ed.) *Dictionary of psychology.* Boston: Houghton Mifflin, 1934.

APPENDIX
C

Representative Tests

This appendix includes representative tests in areas of concern to the teacher and school counselor. Tests such as projective devices which require specialized training are not listed.

This test list is by no means exhaustive. The reader *should not* construe the listing of a test to mean approval by the author, nor should he interpret the omission of one as his disapproval.

The names of tests, grade ranges, publishers, and *Mental Measurement Yearbooks* (MMY) volume and page citation or test publication dates are presented for reference research. (See Chapter 6 for a discussion of sources of information.) The reader should refer to Appendix A for the addresses of publishers.

Name of Test	Grade Range* (or age)	Publisher	MMY (or date)
INDIVIDUAL INTELLIGENCE TESTS			
Cattell Infant Intelligence Scale	3–30 mos.	Psychological Corporation	6-515
Full Range Picture Vocabulary Test	2 yrs. & up	Psychological Test Specialists	6-521
Minnesota Preschool Scale	1–6 yrs.	American Guidance Service (Educational Test Bureau)	6-528
Peabody Picture Vocabulary Test	2-18 yrs.	American Guidance Service	6-530
Pictorial Test of Intelligence	3-8 yrs.	Houghton Mifflin	6-531
Porteus Maze Test	3 yrs. & up	Psychological Corporation	6-532
Quick Test	2 yrs. & up	Psychological Test Specialists	6-534
Stanford-Binet Intelligence Scale	2 yrs. & up	Houghton Mifflin	6-536
Van Alstyne Picture Vocabulary Test	2-7 yrs.	Harcourt, Brace & World	6-537
Wechsler Adult Intelligence Scale (WAIS)	16 yrs. & up	Psychological Corporation	6-538
Wechsler Intelligence Scale for Children (WISC)	5–15 yrs.	Psychological Corporation	6-540
Wechsler Preschool and Primary Scale of Intelligence (WPPSI)	4–6 yrs.	Psychological Corporation	1967
DEVELOPMENT SCALES			
Arthur Point Scale of Performance Tests:	4 yrs. & up		4-335
Form I		Stoelting	
Form II		Psychological Corporation	
Bayley Infant Scales of of Development	Birth to 15 mos.	Psychological Corporation	1968
Gesell Developmental Schedules	4 wks-6 yrs.	Psychological Corporation	6-522
APTITUDE TEST BATTERIES			
Academic Promise Tests (APT)	6-9	Psychological Corporation	6-766
Differential Aptitude Tests (DAT)	8-13, A	Psychological Corporation	6-767

* Note that numbers indicate grade range while age is specifically designated by years or the letter A (Adult).

Name of Test	Grade Range (or age)	Publisher	MMY (or date)
Flanagan Aptitude Classification Tests (FACT)	9–12, A	Science Research Associates	6-770
General Aptitude Test Battery (GATB)	16 yrs. & up & 9–12, A	U.S. Employment Service	6-771
Multiple Aptitude Tests, 1959 Edition	7–13	California Test Bureau	6-776
SRA Primary Mental Abilities, Revised	k–12	Science Research Associates	6-780

SCHOLASTIC APTITUDE TESTS

Name of Test	Grade Range (or age)	Publisher	MMY (or date)
Academic Ability Test	12	Educational Testing Service (Cooperative Test Division)	1963
American College Testing Program Examination	12 & Jr. Coll.	American College Testing Program	6-1
California Test of Mental Maturity, 1963 Revision	4–16, A	California Test Bureau	6-444
College Entrance Examination Board Scholastic Aptitude Test (SAT)	11 & up	Educational Testing Service (for CEEB)	6-449
College Qualification Tests	12 & up	Psychological Corporation	6-450
Cooperative Primary Tests	1–3	Educational Testing Service (Cooperative Test Division)	1967
Cooperative School and College Ability Tests (SCAT) (also Series II, 1968)	4–16	Educational Testing Service (Cooperative Test Division)	6-452
Culture Fair Intelligence Test	4–13 yrs. & 10–16, A	Institute of Personality and Ability Testing	6-453
Goodenough-Harris Drawing Test	3–15 yrs.	Harcourt, Brace & World	6-460
Graduate Record Examinations (GRE)	16–17	Educational Testing Service	6-461, 6-762
Henmon-Nelson Tests of Mental Ability, Revised Edition	3–17	Houghton Mifflin	6-462
Kuhlmann-Anderson Intelligence Tests, Seventh Edition	k–12	Personnel Press, Inc.	6-466
Lorge-Thorndike Intelligence Tests (multilevel edition)	k–12	Houghton Mifflin	(6-467) 1964
Miller Analogies Test	Grad. Sch.	Psychological Corporation	6-472
Ohio State University Psychological Test, Forms 21 and 23	9–16, A	Science Research Associates	5-359

Name of Test	Grade Range (or age)	Publisher	MMY (or date)
Otis-Lennon Mental Ability Test	1–16	Harcourt, Brace & World	(6-481) 1967– 1968
Pintner General Ability Tests—Revised	k–12 & up	Harcourt, Brace & World	(5-368) 1966– 1968
Progressive Matrices	5 yrs. & up	H. K. Lewis & Co., Ltd. (U.S. distributor: Psychological Corporation)	6-490
SRA Tests of Educational Ability, 1962 Edition (TEA)	4–12	Science Research Associates	6-495
Tests of General Ability (TOGA)	k–12	Science Research Associates	6-496

SPECIAL APTITUDE TESTS

Mathematics:

Lee Test of Geometric Aptitude, 1963 Revision	Hi. Sch.	California Test Bureau	6-647
Orleans-Hanna Algebra Prognosis Test	Hi. Sch.	Harcourt, Brace & World	(4-396) 1968
Orleans-Hanna Geometry Prognosis Test	Hi. Sch.	Harcourt, Brace & World	(4-427) 1968

Foreign languages

Modern Language Aptitude Test	9–16, A	Psychological Corporation	6-357
Modern Language Aptitude Test— Elementary	3–6	Psychological Corporation	1967
Pimsleur Language Aptitude Battery	6–12	Harcourt, Brace & World	1966

Mechanical aptitude tests:

Revised Minnesota Paper Form Board Test	9–16, A	Psychological Corporation	6-1092
SRA Mechanical Aptitudes	9–12, A	Science Research Associates	4-764
Test of Mechanical Comprehension (Bennett)	9 & up	Psychological Corporation	6-1094

Motor tests:

Purdue Pegboard	9–16, A	Science Research Associates	6-1081
Stromberg Dexterity Test	A	Psychological Corporation	4-755

Clerical aptitude tests:

Minnesota Clerical Test	8–12, A	Psychological Corporation	6-1040

Name of Test	Grade Range (or age)	Publisher	MMY (or date)
Short Employment Tests	*	Psychological Corporation	6-1045
Short Tests of Clerical Ability	*	Science Research Associates	6-1046
Artistic aptitude tests:			
Horn Art Aptitude Inventory	12–16, A	Stoelting	5-242
Meier Art Tests: 1. Art Judgment 2. Aesthetic Perception	7–16, A	Bureau of Educational Research and Service, University of Iowa	6-346
Musical aptitude tests:			
Musical Aptitude Profile	4–12	Houghton Mifflin	1966
Seashore Measures of Musical Talents, Revised Edition	4–16, A	Psychological Corporation	6-353
Wing Standardized Tests of Musical Intelligence	8 yrs. & up	National Foundation for Educational Research in England and Wales, the Mere, Upton Park, Slough, Bucks, England	6-354

ELEMENTARY ACHIEVEMENT TEST BATTERIES

Iowa Tests of Basic Skills	3–9	Houghton Mifflin	6-13
Metropolitan Achievement Test	1–12	Harcourt, Brace & World	6-15
SRA Achievement Series	1–9	Science Research Associates	6-21
Sequential Tests of Educational Progress (STEP)	4–14	Educational Testing Service (Cooperative Test Division)	6-25
Stanford Achievement Test, 1964 Revision	1–9	Harcourt, Brace & World	6-26

HIGH SCHOOL ACHIEVEMENT BATTERIES

Iowa Tests of Educational Development	9–12	Science Research Associates	6-14
Metropolitan Achievement Test	1–12	Harcourt, Brace & World	6–15
Sequential Test of Educational Progress (STEP)	4–14	Education Testing Service (Cooperative Test Division)	6-25
Stanford Achievement Test: High School Battery	1–9	Harcourt, Brace & World	1965

* No specific grade or age range.

Name of Test	Grade Range (or age)	Publisher	MMY (or date)
SPECIAL ACHIEVEMENT TESTS			
Blyth Second-Year Algebra Test—Revised Edition	Hi. Sch.	Harcourt, Brace & World	(5-443) 1966
Cooperative Science Tests	6–9 7–9 Hi. Sch. Hi. Sch. Hi. Sch.	Educational Testing Service (Cooperative Test Division)	6-867a, 6-872a, 6-887a, 6-909a, 6-931a
Cummings World History Test	9–13	Harcourt, Brace & World	(5-817) 1966
Dunning-Abeles Physics Test	11–13	Harcourt, Brace & World	(5-753) 1967
MLA Cooperative Foreign Language Tests	Hi. Sch.	Educational Testing Service (Cooperative Test Division)	6-378, 6-392, 6-402, 6-416, 6-426
Modern Math Understanding Test	4–9	Science Research Associates	1966
Nelson Biology Test— Revised Edition	9–13	Harcourt, Brace & World	(5-728) 1965
READING TESTS			
Davis Reading Tests	8–13	Psychological Corp.	
Diagnostic Reading Scales	1–8	California Test Bureau	6-821
Diagnostic Reading Tests	k–13	Committee on Diagnostic Reading Tests, Inc.,	6-823
Durrell Analysis of Reading Difficulty, New Edition	1–6	Harcourt, Brace & World	5-660
Gates-McKillop Reading Diagnostic Tests	2–6	Teachers College Press	6-824
Nelson-Denny Reading Test	9–16, A	Houghton Mifflin	6-800
Stanford Diagnostic Reading Test	2–8	Harcourt, Brace & World	1967
INTEREST INVENTORIES			
Brainard Occupational Preference Inventory	8–12, A	Psychological Corporation	1968
Gordon Occupational Check List	Hi. Sch.	Harcourt, Brace & World	6-1056

Name of Test	Grade Range (or age)	Publisher	MMY (or date)
Guilford-Zimmerman Interest Inventory	10–16, A	Sheridan Psychological Services	6-1057
Holland Vocational Preference Inventory	Colleges & A	Consulting Psychologists Press	6-115
Kuder General Interest Survey	6–12	Science Research Associates	6-1061a
Kuder Occupational Interest Survey	9–16, A	Science Research Associates	(6-1062) 1964–1966
Kuder Preference Record—Personal	9–16, A	Science Research Associates	6-132
Kuder Preference Record—Vocational	9–16, A	Science Research Associates	6-1063
Minnesota Vocational Interest Inventory	Hi. Sch. & A	Psychological Corporation	1965
Strong Vocational Interest Blank (SVIB)	17 yrs. & up	Stanford University Press,	(6-1070, 6-1071) 1966, 1968

PERSONALITY AND ATTITUDE INVENTORIES

Adjustment Inventory (Bell)	9–16, A	Consulting Psychologists Press	6-59
California Psychological Inventory (CPI)	13 yrs. & up	Consulting Psychologists Press	6-71
California Test of Personality	12–16, A	California Test Bureau	6-73
Edwards Personal Preference Schedule (EPPS)	College & A	Psychological Corporation	6-87
Eysenck Personality Inventory	Hi. Sch., College, A	Educational and Industrial Testing Service	6-93
Gordon Personal Inventory	8–16, A	Harcourt, Brace & World	6-102
Gordon Personal Profile	9–16, A	Harcourt, Brace & World	6-103
Guilford-Zimmerman Temperament Survey	12–16, A	Sheridan Psychological Services	6-110
IPAT Children's Personality Questionnaire	8–12 yrs.	Institute for Personality and Ability Testing	6-122
Minnesota Multiphasic Personality Inventory (MMPI)	16 yrs. & up	Psychological Corporation	6-143
Minnesota Teacher Attitude Inventory	12–17	Psychological Corporation	6-699

Name of Test	Grade Range (or age)	Publisher	MMY (or date)
Mooney Problem Check List	7–16, A	Psychological Corporation	6-145
Personality Inventory (Bernreuter)	9–16	Consulting Psychologists Press	6-157
Sixteen Personality Factor Questionnaire	15 yrs. & up	Institute for Personality and Ability Testing	6-174
Study of Values	13 & up	Houghton Mifflin	6-182
Thorndike Dimensions of Personality	11 & up	Psychological Corporation	1963, 1966

INDEX